Clearing Services for Global Markets

Clearing forms the core part of a smooth and efficiently functioning financial market infrastructure. Traditionally, it has been provided by clearing houses, most of which today act as a 'central counterparty' (CCP) between the two sides of a trade. The rapid growth of cross-border trading has sparked discussion on the most efficient industry structure – particularly in Europe and the USA. At the heart of this discussion lies the question of whether the implementation of a single clearing house creates greater benefits than a more competitive but interlinked market structure. This is the starting point for this book, which analyses the efficiency of clearing and clearing industry structure. Along with clear-cut definitions and a concise characterisation and descriptive analysis of the clearing industry, the book determines the efficiency impact of various cross-border integration and harmonisation initiatives between CCPs. This serves to identify the most preferable future structure for the clearing industry.

Tina P. Hasenpusch works for Barclays Capital in London. Prior to her career at Barcap, she completed her PhD in Banking and Finance at the European Business School in Germany with a *summa cum laude*. Tina also worked in the Trading and Clearing Market Development department of Eurex, the world's leading derivatives exchange and clearing house. Her research focus and expertise are in the fields of securities and derivatives trading, clearing and settlement systems.

Advance praise for *Clearing Services for Global Markets*

'The book features three real-world case studies bringing clearing to life. It is a thorough and insightful exposition of clearing and a must-read for anyone interested in the subject matter.'

PAUL J. BRODY
Chief Financial Officer of Interactive Brokers Group and Timber Hill LLC, and Board Member of the Options Clearing Corporation

'Only few academic contributions have been published on clearing and no comprehensive and readable standard literature exists. I can definitely see this book filling the void in becoming a standard work on clearing.'

ORLANDO CHIESA
Senior clearing house expert

'This book's unique character and contribution result from an unprecedented number of interviews and feedback sessions with academics and industry experts. The list of these people truly reads like the "Who's Who" of the derivatives world. This book is essential for anyone with an interest in clearing issues.'

DENNIS DUTTERER
Independent clearing consultant and former President and Chief Executive Officer of the Clearing Corporation

'I don't know of anyone who has thought as deeply and written as thoroughly about the key issues related to clearing as Tina Hasenpusch. Anyone interested in the mysterious but critically important process of clearing, especially in the issues that arise as markets and clearing become more global, should read this book.'

MICHAEL GORHAM
Industry Professor and Director of the IIT Stuart Center for Financial Markets and co-author of *Electronic Exchanges: The Global Transformation from Pits to Bits*

'This is a great piece of work! It becomes the textbook for anybody interested in the process of clearing trades. It is extremely well researched and written.'

CHRISTOPHER K. HEHMEYER
President and Chief Executive Officer of PensonGHCO, founding partner of Goldenberg, Hehmeyer & Co., former Chairman of the Board of Trade Clearing Corporation and Director of the Chicago Board of Trade

'If anyone ever had doubts about how exciting clearing could be – this book will change your thinking. You will find that, despite its scope, it turns out to be a surprisingly fun read.'

Clearing Services for Global Markets

A Framework for the Future Development
of the Clearing Industry

Tina P. Hasenpusch

CAMBRIDGE
UNIVERSITY PRESS

CAMBRIDGE UNIVERSITY PRESS
Cambridge, New York, Melbourne, Madrid, Cape Town,
Singapore, São Paulo, Delhi, Tokyo, Mexico City

Cambridge University Press
The Edinburgh Building, Cambridge CB2 8RU, UK

Published in the United States of America by Cambridge University Press, New York

www.cambridge.org
Information on this title: www.cambridge.org/9781107404472

© Tina P. Hasenpusch 2009

First published 2009
First paperback edition 2011

A catalogue record for this publication is available from the British Library

Library of Congress Cataloguing in Publication Data
Hasenpusch, Tina P., 1978–
Clearing services for global markets : a framework for the future development of the clearing
industry / Tina P. Hasenpusch.
     p.   cm.
Includes bibliographical references and index.
ISBN 978-0-521-51871-0 (hardback)
1. International clearing.   I. Title.
HG3892.H37   2009
332.1′78 – dc22   2009020678

ISBN 978-0-521-51871-0 Hardback
ISBN 978-1-107-40447-2 Paperback

This book is for my beloved parents, Heike Maria and Bruno Hasenpusch
With love and gratitude

Table of contents

List of figures

List of abbreviations

a/c/e	alliance/CBOT/Eurex
ADECH	Athens Derivatives Exchange Clearing House
AEV	alternative execution venue
AEX	Amsterdam Exchange
AFEI	Association Française des Entreprises d'Investissement
AFTI	Association Française des Professionnels des Titres
AG	Aktiengesellschaft
AMEX	American Stock Exchange
API	Application Programming Interface
Arca	Archipelago
ATS	Alternative Trading Systems
BIS	Bank for International Settlements
BMIM	Business Model Impact Matrix
BoNY	Bank of New York
BOTCC	Board of Trade Clearing Corporation
BOX	Boston Options Exchange
BSE	Boston Stock Exchange
BV	Besloten Vennootschap (Dutch limited company)
BVLP	Bolsa de Valores de Lisboa e Porto
BXS	Brussels Stock Exchange
CBOE	Chicago Board Options Exchange
CBOT	Chicago Board of Trade
CC&G	Cassa di Compensazione e Garanzia
CCorp	Clearing Corporation
CCOS	Clearing Corporation for Options and Securities
CCP	central counterparty
CCP.A	CCP Austria
CEO	Chief Executive Officer
CEPS	Centre for European Policy Studies
CESAME Group	Clearing and Settlement Advisory and Monitoring Expert Group
CESR	Committee of European Securities Regulators
Cf.	confer
CFE	CBOE Futures Exchange
CFO	Chief Financial Officer
CFS	Centre for Financial Studies

CFTC	Commodity Futures Trading Commission
CH	clearing house
CM	clearing member
CM_{AG}	globally active clearing member with agency focus
CM_{AR}	regionally active clearing member with agency focus
CM_{AR-G}	regionally-to-globally active clearing member with agency focus
CM_{PG}	globally active clearing member with proprietary focus
CM_{PR}	regionally active clearing member with proprietary focus
CM_{PR-G}	regionally-to-globally active clearing member with proprietary focus
CME	Chicago Mercantile Exchange
CMXchange	Commodities Management Exchange
Co.	Company
COMEX	Commodity Exchange
CONSOB	Commissione Nazionale per le Società e la Borsa
COO	Chief Operating Officer
Corp.	Corporation
CPSS	Committee on Payment and Settlement Systems
CSCE	Coffee, Sugar and Cocoa Exchange
CSD	Central Securities Depository
CSE	Chicago Stock Exchange
DBAG	Deutsche Börse AG
DCO	Designated Clearing Organisation
DrK	Dresdner Kleinwort
DTB	Deutsche Terminbörse
DTC	Depository Trust Company
DTCC	Depository Trust and Clearing Corporation
DVP	delivery versus payment
Dwpbank	Deutsche WertpapierService Bank AG
EACH	European Association of Central Counterparty Clearing Houses
EBIT	Earnings before interest and tax
ECAG	Eurex Clearing AG
ECB	European Central Bank
ECMI	European Capital Markets Institute
ECN	Electronic Communication Network
ECSDA	European Central Securities Depositories Association
EDX	Equity Derivatives Exchange
e.g.	exempli gratia
EMCC	Emerging Markets Clearing Corporation
Endex	European Energy Derivatives Exchange
ESF	European Securities Forum
et al.	et alii
ETF	exchange traded fund
EU	European Union
EUR, €	euro
EX	exchange

FAZ	Frankfurter Allgemeine Zeitung
FCM	futures commission merchant
FED	Federal Reserve Bank
FESE	Federation of European Securities Exchanges
FIA	Futures Industry Association
Fig.	figure
FOA	Futures and Options Association
FOW	Futures and Options World
FSA	Financial Services Authority
FSAP	Financial Services and Action Plan
FUTOP	Guarantee Fund for Danish Options and Futures
FWB	Frankfurter Wertpapierbörse
GCC	Guarantee Clearing Corporation
GCL	Global Clearing Link
GCM	general clearing member
GCS	Generic Clearing System
GHCO	Goldenberg, Hehmeyer & Co.
GSCC	Government Securities Clearing Corporation
HKFE	Hong Kong Futures Exchange
ICC	Intermarket Clearing Corporation
ICCH	International Commodities Clearing House
ICE	Intercontinental Exchange
ICM	individual clearing member
ICSD	International Central Securities Depository
IDEI	Institut d'Économie Industrielle
IDEM	Italian Derivatives Exchange Market
i.e.	id est
IFM	Institute for Financial Markets
IMF	International Monetary Fund
Inc.	Incorporated
IOSCO	International Organisation of Securities Commissions
IPE	International Petroleum Exchange
IPO	initial public offering
ISE	International Securities Exchange
IT	information technology
KCBT	Kansas City Board of Trade
KDPW	Krajowy Depozyt Papierów Wartościowych (National Depository for Securities)
KELER	Hungarian Central Depository and Clearing House
LCH	London Clearing House
LCH.C Group	LCH.Clearnet Group Ltd
LCH.C Ltd	LCH.Clearnet Ltd
LCH.C SA	LCH.Clearnet SA
LEC	Linked Exchanges and Clearing
LIBA	London Investment Banking Association

LIBOR	London Interbank Offered Rate
Liffe	London International Financial Futures Exchange
LLC	Limited Liability Company
LLP	Limited Liability Partnership
LME	London Metal Exchange
LON	London
LSE	London Stock Exchange
Ltd	Limited
M&A	mergers and acquisitions
MATIF	Marché à Terme d'Instruments Financiers
MBSCC	Mortgage-Backed Services Clearing Corporation
ME	market expert
MEFF	Mercado Español de Futuros Financieros
Mgmt.	Management
MiFID	Markets in Financial Instruments Directive
MGX	Minneapolis Grain Exchange
mn.	million
MTF	Multilateral Trading Facility
N.A., n.a.	not applicable
NASD	National Association of Securities Dealers
NASDAQ	National Association of Securities Dealers Automated Quotation System
NCM	non-clearing member
NFA	National Futures Association
No.	number
NOS	Norwegian Futures and Options Clearing House
NSCC	National Securities Clearing Corporation
NYBOT	New York Board of Trade
NYCC	New York Clearing Corporation
NYMEX	New York Mercantile Exchange
NYSE	New York Stock Exchange
OCC	Options Clearing Corporation
OECD	Organisation for Economic Cooperation and Development
OFT	Office of Fair Trading
OMLX	OM London Exchange
OTC	over-the-counter
p.	page
PBOT	Philadelphia Board of Trade
PHLX	Philadelphia Stock Exchange
P&L	profit and loss
PLC, plc	Public Limited Company
pp.	pages
prop.	proprietary
RAROC	risk-adjusted return on capital
REG	regulator

Repo	repurchase agreement
SA	Société Anonyme
SBF	Société des Bourses Françaises
SCCP	Stock Clearing Corporation of Philadelphia
SEC	Securities and Exchange Commission
SEHK	Hong Kong Stock Exchange
SFOA	Swiss Futures and Options Association
SGX	Singapore Exchange
SIM	Scale Impact Matrix
SIS	SegaInterSettle
SOFFEX	Swiss Options and Financial Futures Exchange
SOM	Finnish Securities and Derivatives Exchange Clearing House
S&P	Standard & Poor's
SSF	single stock futures
STP	straight-through processing
SUERF	Société Universitaire Européenne de Recherches Financières
SWX	SWX Swiss Exchange
TCIM	Transaction Cost Impact Matrix
TIBOR	Tokyo Interbank Offered Rate
TIFFE	Tokyo International Financial Futures Exchange
UK	United Kingdom
US	United States
USA	United States of America
USD, $	US dollar
USFE	US Futures Exchange
Vol.	volume
VPN	Value Provision Network
VPS	Norwegian Central Securities Depository

Acknowledgements

All researchers and authors who undertake projects as comprehensive as this one need support from others. I have been unusually fortunate in having had a large number of generous and essential supporters who trusted in the value of this project and who made the time that I spent researching for and writing this book so rewarding. The book could have never taken shape without them; I am therefore exceedingly grateful to one and all.

Naturally, this acknowledgement could not begin without an emphatic thank you to my supervisor, Prof. Dr Dirk Schiereck, who was key to the realisation of this project, which is also my dissertation. I am deeply indebted to him for all of his encouragement, support and guidance. I also owe a special thank you to Prof. Dr Roswitha Meyer. Her participation in this endeavour was my great good fortune. Her support was a crucial source of motivation at times when the completion of this book seemed millions of miles away.

Another person who nurtured and helped this book grow is Orlando Chiesa. To him I owe a very special acknowledgement. He supported this project back when it was merely the germ of an idea. I am indebted to him for always having taken the time to answer my questions and challenge my thoughts, no matter how busy he was. He not only managed to calm my mind when it was going in zigzags, but also helped me to see the forest through the trees. For similar reasons, I am also indebted to Dennis Dutterer, who supported this project in various ways from its infancy. His backing opened many doors and paved the way for the successful completion of this book. A very special thank you is also owed to Dr Thomas Book, who was one of the very early supporters of this research project and a source of constant encouragement, backing and inspiration.

I am honoured to offer my utmost gratitude to all of the individuals who agreed to support this project by taking a substantial amount of their precious time to provide input and share their knowledge in the form of interviews and beyond. Their participation endowed me with broad and distinguished insight into the issues of clearing. Whilst it should be noted that these individuals are not associated with the final conclusions of this study and that the findings of this research do not necessarily reflect their views, I am deeply grateful to Manuela Arbuckle, Richard Berliand, Paul Bodart, Brooksley Born, Paul Brody, Richard Brown, Phil Bruce, Mary Ann Callahan, Patrick Cirier, Ed Condon, Danny Corrigan, Peter Cox, John Damgard, Bernie Dan, John Davidson, Mike Dawley, Dr Gary Alan DeWaal, Adrian Farnham, Ann Flodström, Bill Floersch, Yew-Meng Fong, Andrew Foster, Daniel Gisler, Linda Glover, Prof. Dr Michael Gorham, Fred Grede, Gabriele Gründer, George Haase, David Hardy, Richard Heckinger, Chris Hehmeyer, George Hender, Neil Henderson, Karsten Hiestermann, Stephen Hurst, Richard Jaycobs, Hugo Jenkins, Alfred Kirchmann, David Krell, John Lawton, Jon Lloyd, Wayne Luthringshausen, Steve Martin, Natalie Markman, Dr John Mathias, Jim McCormick, Mike McErlean, Jim McNulty, John McPartland, Christopher Meens, Hank Mlynarski, Otto Nägeli, Aisling O'Reilly, Tomas Ostlund, Dr Patrick Parkinson, Ananda Radhakrishnan, Kenneth Rosenzweig, Martin Peters, Prof. Dr Susan Phillips, Dr Harvey Pitt, Andreas Preuss, Kenneth Raisler, Rainer Riess, Dan Roth, Jürgen Röthig, Bernie Sapato, Sascha Scheer, Claus Schnee, Kurt Settle, Philip Simons, Mark Spanbroek, Jürg Spillmann, John Tanner, Bill Templer, Bernie Till, Evert van den Brink, Joachim Vetter, Barbara Wierzynski, Alex Wilkinson, Armin Winterhoff, James Worlledge, Alan Yarrow, Mark Young and John Yuill.

I would also like to offer a very special thank you to the following individuals, who provided various forms of support and contributed to the successful realisation of this book:[1] Walter Allwicher, Gesa Benda, Manuela Biess, Paul Bowes, Brendan Bradley, Patrick Deierling, Chip Dempsey, Juan Echeverri, Bill Ferri, Rudi Ferscha, Gabriel Frediani, Gerd Haaf, Amin Hessari, Prof. Dr Mark Holder, Claudia Kirsch, Jeff Morgan, Andrea and Martin Mosbacher, Robert Orth, John Parry, Sieglinde Scharnowske, Prof. Dr Susan Scott, Brigitte Steden, Robert Steigerwald, Uwe Velten, Jens Wagner, Dan Waldman, Gudrun Würdemann, Patrick Young and Eliane Zapp-Roussel. I am thankful to Prof. Dr Jim Moser, who was kind enough to undertake the onerous task of reading parts of the manuscript and provide valuable comments and feedback. I am also beholden to Prof. Dr Patrick van Cayseele for readily sharing his insight on the network economics of clearing.

I want to express my appreciation to Jan Kurek, who was always there to step in at the last minute to save the day when any IT-related troubles, viruses, bugs

---

[1] Note that, again, these individuals are not associated with the final conclusions of this study and that the findings of this research do not necessarily reflect their views.

or other headaches arose. Furthermore, I am grateful to Hilary Abuhove, who did a stunning job in proofreading the manuscript in an incredibly thorough and efficient manner. Her comments and feedback were most valuable and witty.

Finally, I would like to thank Chris Harrison, the Publishing Director for Social Sciences at Cambridge University Press, for his support in realising this book. It is also a great honour to extend my gratitude to the International Capital Market Association for sponsoring this publication. In this context, I would particularly like to thank Godfried De Vidts for having paved the way with his generosity and help. My appreciation also goes to Allan Malvar for a very fruitful collaboration.

Whilst the time I spent researching for and ultimately writing this book was very rewarding in many ways, it kept me busy and occupied my mind almost 24/7. Particularly during the last months prior to completion, I was completely absorbed by my writing. I am most grateful for having shared this very intense time of my life with someone who was remarkably patient, understanding and supportive at all times. Not only did he perform to perfection the dreary job of keeping me largely isolated from the clutter of daily life, but he also provided light when there was dark. The realisation of this book is indebted to his unwavering and loving support. Therefore my very special thank you goes to you, Christoph!

A thank you must also go to Juliane, my very best friend, without whom the sun would simply have shone less brightly.

This book is dedicated to my parents with all my love. Without their support, belief, trust and inspiration, this book would never have seen the light of day. I am most grateful for their encouragement and backing, which allowed me to prioritise my research over time and budget constraints. My parents taught me that: 'The future belongs to those who believe in the beauty of their dreams.'[2] This book is as much their dream come true as it is mine. My mother especially gave me encouragement when I most needed it and reminded me of the light at the end of the tunnel when I myself could no longer see it. It was her inspiration and foresight that brought this book to life. Mom and Dad, thank you so much – this is to you with all my heart!

Last but not least, it should be noted that I take responsibility for all errors and omissions.

---

[2] Eleanor Roosevelt.

Forewords

Whereas clearing is often unglamorously referred to as the plumbing of securities and derivatives markets, it is in fact the core part of a smoothly and efficiently functioning financial market infrastructure. Clearing services have traditionally been provided by clearing houses – most of which today act as a 'central counterparty' (CCP) between the two sides of a trade. In this role the clearing house becomes the buyer to every seller and the seller to every buyer in a trade. CCP clearing forms an integral part of the clearing process in most developed markets. The rapid growth of cross-border trading, which spans many clearing houses and increases cross-border interdependence, has sparked discussions on the most efficient industry structure – particularly in Europe. Public and private stakeholders of clearing have continuously debated this topic, but have failed to reach a consensus to date. At the heart of this discussion lies the question of whether the implementation of a single clearing house creates greater benefits than a more competitive but interlinked market structure. A lack of in-depth research in this field has meanwhile hindered a fruitful debate, resulting in a recurring and largely interest-driven repetition of platitudes.

This is the starting point for Ms Hasenpusch's study, whereupon she analyses the efficiency of clearing and clearing industry structure. Commencing with clear-cut definitions together with a concise characterisation and descriptive analysis of the current state of the clearing industry, the study determines the efficiency impact of various cross-border integration and harmonisation initiatives between CCPs. This serves to identify the most preferable future clearing industry structure. Whilst the study primarily focuses on analysing the European exchange-traded derivatives clearing industry, a final step applies the research results to European exchange-traded cash equities clearing as well as to the European clearing industry with respect to its global positioning. This study is unrivalled in its breadth and depth of analysis – to my knowledge, there exists no comparable analysis of clearing costs and clearing industry structure. The study's unique character and contribution are the result of close collaboration with a large number of stakeholders. In 79 interviews and more than 20 feedback sessions conducted over the course of the research, European and American clearing experts shared their knowledge, enabling Ms Hasenpusch to integrate theoretical findings with insights and case studies from the real world. The findings provide an objective body of knowledge that forms the basis for substantiated recommendations for the future development of the clearing industry.

With this study, Ms Hasenpusch delivers a significant contribution to the new field of clearing-related research. The analysis contains many intriguing results and is written in a way that will engage the reader from start to finish. I trust that it will serve to increase substantially the understanding of this exciting element of financial market infrastructure and receive a duly broad audience.

Professor Dr Dirk Schiereck

An efficient and well-functioning post-trade environment is an essential prerequisite for the continued successful development of the global capital market. While not endorsing its findings, the International Capital Market Association is pleased to support independent research of this type which explains the current issues facing the market clearly, making a thoughtful and impartial contribution to the ongoing industry debate over the future of clearing.

The International Capital Market Association (ICMA)

1 Introduction

Very definitely there is a whole host of topics related to clearing. I believe that clearing is a topic that has always been regarded as sort of an operational thing. The exchanges' matching engines have had the glamour. But I think in the long run the value added of clearing exceed the value-added of matching![1]

Clearing is often regarded as less glamorous than the creative and headline-grabbing business of trading,[2] but it constitutes the core of modern financial market infrastructure.[3] Clearing services not only benefit individual market participants, but markets as a whole by increasing their efficiency. Actually: 'this dimension of financial markets is fundamental for the proper functioning of the whole. It is, in fact, the very essence of the markets, because it constitutes the basic process of exchange between buyers and sellers.'[4]

When buyers and sellers execute a trade, they enter into a specific legal obligation, i.e. to buy or sell securities[5] or, in the case of derivatives,[6] another underlying. The life cycle of a trade consists of trading, clearing and settlement. Clearing and settlement are commonly referred to as post-trade services. Commonly mentioned in the same breath, the two terms are often confused or thought to be synonymous. Whilst settlement refers to the fulfilment of the legal obligation,[7] clearing is the process that occurs in between execution and

---

[1] Interview with James G. McCormick.   [2] Cf. Berliand (2006), p. 27.
[3] Cf. Dale (1998c), p. 230.   [4] European Commission (ed.) (2006a), pp. 2–3.
[5] Securities comprise cash equities, such as stocks, and fixed income products. Cf. Deutsche Börse Group (ed.) (2005a), p. 7.
[6] Derivatives (including futures and options) are financial instruments that derive their value from some other item, i.e. the so-called 'underlying'. An underlying can be a security, group of securities, an index, interest rates, currencies, commodities, etc. A 'future' is the obligation to buy or sell the respective underlying at a certain time in the future for a certain price. In the case of the buyer, an 'option' is the right, but not the obligation, to take or make delivery of the respective underlying. For the seller, an option is the obligation to take or make delivery of the underlying.
[7] Settlement is often performed by a so-called Central Securities Depository (CSD) or International Central Securities Depository (ICSD), which holds the security and performs the transfer of the title from the seller to the buyer. Refer to Chapter 2 for other possible settlement institutions. Another comingling

settlement, i.e. during the respective time lag. In the context of trading securities, this time lag is usually minimal, but it can be substantial in derivatives trading. During this lag, trades need to be processed, managed, monitored and ultimately prepared for settlement.[8] Clearing is usually carried out by a so-called clearing house, which can either be a department of an exchange or a separate (independent) legal entity carrying out the designated function of clearing. Most clearing houses today act as a central counterparty (CCP). In this role, the clearing house is legally involved in every trade by becoming the buyer to every seller and the seller to every buyer, thus replacing the original counterparties.

The importance of post-trade services – and of clearing in particular – is rooted in the fact that financial market transactions commonly do not involve goods that are physically exchanged. The traded instruments often do not even exist physically. This level of abstraction, as well as the immobilisation and dematerialisation of traditional paper-form securities, has transformed the modern post-trade infrastructure.[9]

1.1 Problem definition

> There are important economic gains to be had from improving the efficiency of cross-frontier clearing . . . What has proved more elusive is finding the best way of achieving this.[10]

There is general consensus that smoothly running and efficient post-trade services are a necessary precondition for the efficient functioning of financial markets. These services are also considered indispensable for economic growth and financial markets integration.[11] 'From a market perspective, their importance derives from the fact that clearing and settlement costs can be viewed as a subset of transaction costs. These are the costs faced by an investor when carrying out a trade. Expensive and inefficient clearing and settlement limit the development of efficient markets.'[12]

---

of terms often occurs with reference to the process and function of settlement and safekeeping (custody). Closely associated with securities settlement are custody services. The final phase of a securities transaction, once settlement has occurred, consists in the custody service. Custody refers to the safekeeping of assets and the administration of these securities on behalf of intermediaries and investors. For the purpose of this study, the term 'settlement' refers to the integrated services provided by CSDs and ICSDs.

[8] For a detailed definition of clearing, see Chapter 2.   [9] Cf. Huang (2006), p. 10.
[10] McCreevy (2006a), p. 2.   [11] Cf. European Commission (ed.) (2006a), pp. 2–3.
[12] Tumpel-Gugerell (2006).

In light of rapidly growing cross-border trading volumes, the sophistication of information technology, financial market deregulation, and the ongoing integration and harmonisation of the financial market infrastructure, building a sound, efficient and integrated post-trade infrastructure has become both a focus area for market participants[13] and a goal for official policy[14] – particularly in the United States (US) and Europe.[15]

Despite this shared goal, there is currently no consensus on how actually to measure the efficiency of post-trade services.[16] Additionally, although it is generally believed that integration and harmonisation of the post-trade industry serves to increase its efficiency, there is no unequivocal structural preference among public and private stakeholders. At the centre of this debate is the question of whether a monopolistic single entity within a defined economic area is better suited to realise an efficient and integrated clearing infrastructure than are several competing, differently organised, but possibly interlinked entities. This persistent lack of consensus on the most preferable (in terms of efficiency) future structure of the post-trade industry has sparked special concern as well as a broad dispute among public and private stakeholders of post-trade services in the US and Europe.

In the US, this debate has been raging for several decades. While Congress put an end to further discussions about the securities and options post-trade industry by encouraging the establishment of centralised clearing and settlement arrangements in the late 1980s and early 1990s, there is no such policy mandate for the futures clearing industry.[17] Market participants (such as exchanges, clearing houses, banks/brokers and investors) have thus maintained recurring consultations and discussions on the most preferable structure of the US futures clearing industry – but have so far failed to reach consensus. Notably, since the announcement of the merger of the two Chicago futures exchanges on 17 October 2006 – the Chicago Mercantile Exchange (CME) and the Chicago Board of Trade (CBOT) – the debate has regained traction in the American public and private sectors.

In Europe, other issues have driven the quest for the optimal structure for the post-trade industry. The launch of the European Monetary Union, particularly the introduction of the euro, has put European market integration at

---

[13] See, e.g. JPMorgan (ed.) (2005), p. 1; and Merrill Lynch (ed.) (2006), p. 6.
[14] Cf. Corporation of London (ed.) (2005), p. 10.
[15] References to Europe in the context of this study refer to the European Union.
[16] Cf. European Commission (ed.) (2006e), p. 1.
[17] For details on the American clearing industry, refer to section 2.5.2.

the top of the financial agenda.[18] An efficient post-trade industry is considered a prerequisite for advancing the integrative process as well as for reaping the full benefits of an integrated European financial market.[19] The development of clearing and settlement arrangements is therefore considered to be of great strategic importance for the European economy.[20] While the first efforts to improve the efficiency of European post-trade arrangements date back to the 1970s,[21] the debate on industry structure and its efficiency gained significant momentum between 2004 and 2006, when the European Commission (the Commission) launched its consultative and policy-oriented communication on measures to improve the efficiency of clearing and settlement. The communication included a proposal to prepare a framework directive on clearing and settlement aimed at increasing the efficiency of the European post-trade industry.[22] The Commission ultimately dropped the proposal in 2006 in favour of an industry-led approach:

One thing I am absolutely sure about is: whatever we do, we should work with the grain of the market. The role of the Commission is not to pick winners nor dictate a particular outcome. Nor determine the final architecture. Many have argued that a pan-European clearing and settlement system operated as a utility would be the best solution for capital markets in the EU. They may be right. Again, it is not our role to impose a particular model on the market. The Commission's role is to ensure the markets work efficiently, that unnecessary barriers are done away with and that EU Treaty provisions, particularly competition policy, are applied to the full.[23]

The Commission's initiative culminated in the development of a Code of Conduct (the Code), sponsored by Internal Market and Services Commissioner Charlie McCreevy. It was signed and prepared by the three main European industry associations and their members in November 2006.[24] The initial scope of the Code applies exclusively to the post-trade processes of cash equities. The decision to focus on cash equities was spurred by various factors: the soaring cross-border trading volumes in cash equities have shifted investors'

---

[18]   Cf. European Central Bank (ed.) (2001a), p. 15; Bank of New York (ed.) (2004), p. 1; and Chabert/Chanel-Reynaud (2005), p. 1.

[19]   Cf. European Commission (ed.) (2006a), p. 2.

[20]   Cf. Werner (2003), p. 17; Group of Thirty (ed.) (2003), p. 1; and Köppl/Monnet (2007), p. 3017.

[21]   Cf. European Commission (ed.) (2006a), p. 3.

[22]   For details of the European Commission's strategy with regard to clearing and settlement, refer to European Commission (ed.) (28.04.2004); and European Commission (ed.) (2006a), pp. 32–9.

[23]   McCreevy (2006a), p. 3.

[24]   The three main industry associations are the Federation of European Securities Exchanges (FESE), the European Association of Central Counterparty Clearing Houses (EACH) and the European Central Securities Depositories Association (ECSDA).

focus to driving down the related costs;[25] studies comparing European and American cross-border securities settlement costs intensified the call to overhaul the European securities clearing and settlement system;[26] and discussions about European stock exchange consolidation also served to put cash equities post-trading arrangements into the limelight.[27]

While the measures detailed in the Code address the areas of transparency of prices and services, access and interoperability, and the unbundling of services and accounting separation, they do not codify a particular industry structure.[28] The Code provides a framework for the future development of European cash equities clearing, but European clearing houses must still find a way to implement the Code. The solution to creating a more efficient European post-trade industry remains elusive because it involves highly complex structural issues.[29] It is therefore hardly surprising that disagreement vis-à-vis the optimal structure of the industry continues to prevail. European market participants, such as exchanges, clearing houses, banks and investors, have thus been conducting ongoing consultations with the European Commission as well as public discussions on the most preferable future structure of the clearing industry – but stakeholders have not yet reached a consensus.

The debate on the efficiency and structure of the European post-trade industry – particularly concerning derivatives clearing – has regained significant traction since the Commission invited comments on its endeavour to extend gradually the scope of the Code to include post-trade arrangements of fixed income and derivatives instruments in October 2007.[30]

Finally, the efforts to establish a consensus on the most preferable future structure of the post-trade industry have been complicated by the comingling of the post-trade services terms 'clearing' and 'settlement'. As outlined above, the two terms are frequently – and mistakenly – used interchangeably in the public discussions accompanying the efforts to create a smoothly functioning post-trade infrastructure; academic and non-academic publications commit the same fallacy. While this partly results from the lack of generally accepted, clear-cut definitions, few people – even within the financial industry – understand the complex mechanics of post-trade services and their

---

[25] Cf. Goldberg *et al.* (2002), p. 3; and European Parliamentary Financial Services Forum (ed.) (2006), p. 1.

[26] Cf. Werner (2003), p. 17.   [27] Cf. AFEI *et al.* (eds.) (2006), p. 1.

[28] Cf. FESE/EACH/ECSDA (eds.) (2006); and European Commission (ed.) (02.11.2006). Refer to http://ec.europa.eu/internal_market/financial-markets/clearing/communication_en.htm for details on the European Commission's communication, the Code of Conduct, and other documents.

[29] Cf. Lannoo/Levin (2003), p. 2.   [30] Cf. European Commission (ed.) (2007), p. 3.

different providers in detail.[31] However, even among experts, negligent use of the terminology is widespread.

1.2 Literature and research gap

Since the launch of the European Monetary Union, an increasing number of academic and non-academic publications researching the issues of industry structure and efficiency of European post-trading arrangements have emerged. Nonetheless, an important – but commonly overlooked – research gap persists: the majority of these studies analyse cross-border settlement and safekeeping arrangements between (International) Central Securities Depositories, but neglect CCP clearing issues. The common comingling of the terms 'clearing' and 'settlement' only serves to obscure this major shortcoming, especially in the eyes of non-experts. When studies claim to analyse post-trading arrangements, they imply a comprehensive analysis of both clearing and settlement issues; yet most publications have exclusively concentrated on post-trade services provided by CSDs/ICSDs.[32] The often negligent or imprecise use of terminology in this context threatens to erode steadily the discussion on the most preferable structure of the European post-trading industry due to the spurious implication that findings on CSD/ICSD issues cover all relevant clearing issues.

The Code was explicitly designed to increase the efficiency of cash equities clearing *and* settlement arrangements in Europe, thus giving direction to the development of CSDs/ICSDs *and* CCPs. It should be noted, however, that due to the aforementioned gap in research, there were no studies on the industry structure and efficiency of European CCP arrangements to consult for the Code's establishment. The European Commission has acknowledged the gap: 'In fact, we are not aware of any empirical studies of European CCP activities.'[33]

As the limited contributions on the industry structure and efficiency of European CCP arrangements are essentially by-products of CSD/ICSD-related studies, a brief overview of relevant literature is provided in the following. This serves to clarify which studies concentrate on settlement and safekeeping arrangements between CSDs/ICSDs, but leave aside CCP

---

[31] Cf. Group of Thirty (ed.) (2003), p. 2.
[32] Cf. EACH (ed.) (2004a), p. 1; and EACH (ed.) (2004b), p. 1.
[33] European Commission (ed.) (2006c), pp. 8–9.

clearing issues, as opposed to contributions which take CCP arrangements into account.

Hart/Russo/Schönenberger (2002) chart the evolution of CCP services in Europe and the United States. Scott (2003) performs a comprehensive analysis of the key issues surrounding strategic developments in the clearing and settlement industry. A report published by London Economics (ed.) (2005) provides a description of the securities trading, clearing and settlement infra-structures of the cash equities and bonds markets in the 25 Member States of the European Union (EU) as of March 2005. These contributions are among the few covering CCP-related issues.

A significantly larger number of studies have been devoted to the organisa-tion of the European post-trade industry, with a particular focus on CSD/ICSD arrangements: Malkamäki/Topi (1999) analyse the major trends and driv-ing forces of change in securities settlement systems. Various publications investigate the state and process of the ongoing integration of the Euro-pean securities post-trade infrastructure; these studies identify sources of inefficiency in the current CSD/ICSD cross-border arrangements and mea-sures to counteract them; see, e.g. Russo/Terol (2000), Giovannini Group (ed.) (2001), Giovannini Group (ed.) (2003), Hirata de Carvalho (2004) and Baums/Cahn (2006). Schmiedel/Schönenberger (2005) and the Euro-pean Commission (ed.) (2006c) include CCP arrangements in their respec-tive analyses. Schulze/Baur (2006) underscore the importance of integrating and harmonising the European post-trade industry with their finding that an 18 per cent reduction in securities clearing and settlement costs could increase the gross domestic product by around 0.6 per cent in the EU.

Milne (2005) reviews the role of standard setting as it affects competition in securities settlement, in the light of the establishment of pan-European and global arrangements for securities settlement. Löber (2006) presents and evaluates the existing EU legislative framework for post-trade arrangements and describes current EU initiatives to increase efficiency, with a specific focus on legal CSD/ICSD-related aspects. Huang (2006) examines legal and regulatory issues pertaining to CCPs and explains why the application of CCP clearing could have ramifications for Europe and beyond. The author also briefly explores the case for a Single CCP at both the European and global levels, concluding that:

In an ideal world, a single robust and efficient CCP with effective risk management, operating within the EU or even across the globe, would be able to maximise the effect of transaction offsetting and better risk management with more efficient collateral management for the markets. In practice, the approach of maintaining a level of competition in financial services may seem more likely, in the EU in particular.[34]

Several contributions to the field analyse and discuss alternative models for European securities settlement. Giddy/Saunders/Walter (1996), Giordano (2002), Niels/Barnes/van Dijk (2003), Chabert/Chanel-Reynaud (2005) and Chabert/El Idrissi (2005) research frictions in the settlement of European cross-border transactions and discuss alternative scenarios for a more integrated approach to European settlement arrangements. Milne (2002) examines how competitive forces can be harnessed to further the integration and consolidation of European post-trading arrangements, especially with respect to securities settlement. A number of studies present theoretical models designed to provide conclusions on the future structure of European settlement and safekeeping arrangements. Kauko (2002), Werner (2003), Tapking/Yang (2004), Holthausen/Tapking (2004), Rochet (2005), Kauko (2005), Van Cayseele (2005) and Köppl/Monnet (2007) all provide alternative models. Kröpfl (2003), Van Cauwenberge (2003), Serifsoy/Weiß (2005), Van Cayseele/Voor de Mededinging (2005) and Knieps (2006) contribute to the debate on the structure and organisation of European CSDs/ICSDs. Milne (2007) provides a detailed review and discussion of many of these and other papers.

Increasingly, empirical studies are investigating the existence of economies of scale in European settlement and depository systems; see Schmiedel/Malkamäki/Tarkka (2002), Van Cayseele/Wuyts (2005) and Van Cayseele/Wuyts (2006). Besides these studies, others (many of which were produced or commissioned by interested stakeholders) aim at identifying and examining the costs of European securities post-trading activities:[35] Lannoo/Levin (2001), Giovannini Group (ed.) (2001), London Stock Exchange/Oxera (eds.) (2002), AFTI/Eurogroup (eds.) (2002), Deutsche Börse Group (ed.) (2002) and Euroclear (ed.) (2003) focus on CSD/ICSD-related costs, while Morgan Stanley/Mercer Oliver Wyman (eds.) (2003), NERA Economic Consulting (ed.) (2004) and Deutsche Börse Group (ed.) (2005a) also take into account CCP-related costs. Regarding these studies, the European Commission finds: 'While useful, none of the results have been universally accepted as providing an accurate description of the prices or costs incurred by investors in acquiring post-trade services in Europe.'[36] Oxera (ed.) (2007), which was thus assigned

---

[34] Huang (2006), pp. 232–3.

[35] For a comparison and overview of the different cost studies, refer to Scott (2003), pp. 13–16; Schmiedel/Schönenberger (2005), pp. 28–30; and European Commission (ed.) (2006b).

[36] European Commission (ed.) (2006e), p. 1. Also see European Commission (ed.) (07.11.2006), p. 1.

by the European Commission to close the research gap, developed a methodology to monitor changes over time in prices, costs and volumes of securities trading and post-trading activities (covering services provided by CSDs/ICSDs and CCPs).[37] Despite Oxera's important contribution, two important research gaps continue to persist: no research to date has been provided on derivatives clearing costs. Furthermore, no comprehensive analysis of both direct and indirect clearing-related costs has been undertaken.[38] Because measuring and isolating indirect costs is a difficult and highly complex task, Oxera's study does not incorporate indirect costs.

To summarise, the existing research on the industrial organisation of the post-trade industry reveals a major shortcoming: although clearing services provided by CCPs play a crucial role for financial markets integration,[39] there is no comprehensive analysis of the industry structure and efficiency of European CCP arrangements. So far, contributions have focused on CSD/ICSD-related research. Regarding the existing literature on CSDs/ICSDs, Milne (2007) finds that '[d]espite the economic importance of this industry it remains under-researched';[40] the same is even more true for the area of CCP clearing. The scant research on the organisation of CCPs has thus far only been an offshoot of CSD/ICSD-related research. Furthermore, all of these CCP studies concentrate on securities clearing, and exclude aspects relevant for derivatives clearing.

Understanding the industrial organisation of clearing therefore requires a great deal of new work. 'We need thorough descriptive analysis of the industry . . . so that the profession fully understands the processes and services involved. We need new theoretical models that explore the specific economic features of this industry. We need careful empirical studies that recognize the unique features of the industry.'[41]

1.3 Purpose of study

The purpose of this study is to provide a substantial contribution to closing the aforementioned research gap. To this end, the two core research issues are

---

[37] Cf. European Commission (ed.) (07.11.2006); and Oxera (ed.) (2007), p. i. The methodology is to be applied for the first time in the second half of 2007, and subsequently in the following three years.
[38] Refer to section 3.2 for a definition of clearing-related direct and indirect costs.
[39] Details on the clearing services provided by CCPs and the associated micro- and macroeconomic benefits are outlined in Chapter 2.
[40] Milne (2007), p. 2946.   [41] Milne (2007), p. 2947.

the efficiency of CCP clearing and clearing industry structure. It is the research objective to determine the impact that different cross-border integration and harmonisation initiatives between CCPs have on the efficiency of clearing. For the purpose of this study, these integration and harmonisation initiatives are referred to as 'network strategies'. The results of this investigation allow conclusions to be drawn with respect to the most preferable future clearing industry structure.

Clear-cut definitions designed to avoid any further confusion about CCP and CSD/ICSD issues, together with a concise characterisation and descriptive analysis of the current state of the clearing industry, set the stage for the following analytical objectives:

(i) Examine the efficiency of clearing:
- develop a method to assess the efficiency of CCP clearing;[42]
- identify, classify and analyse the clearing-related direct and indirect transaction costs that market participants have to bear;
- generate insight into the nature and dynamics of these costs from the perspective of different market participants;
- provide a detailed qualitative and quantitative analysis of direct and indirect clearing costs to enable benchmarking to other market infrastructure-related costs, such as trading and settlement.

(ii) Provide a characterisation of the clearing industry structure:
- identify and analyse characteristics of the current clearing industry structure.
- classify archetypes of different network strategies;
- provide an overview of selected network strategies in the clearing industry;
- define potential demand- and supply-side scale effects in clearing;
- collect evidence for the existence of demand- and supply-side scale effects in clearing.

(iii) Research the impact of different network strategies on the efficiency of clearing:
- develop an innovative framework for analysis that integrates the perspectives of different market participants and provides a graphical illustration of the complex relationships between economies of scale and scope, and network effects in clearing, their impact on transaction costs and industry efficiency;

---

[42] The term 'clearing' as used throughout this study refers to services provided by CCPs.

- analyse the magnitude of demand- and supply-side scale effects inherent to different network strategies in the clearing industry;
- examine whether these demand- and supply-side scale effects translate into an equally great transaction cost reduction;
- classify the efficiency impact of different network strategies in the clearing industry;
- take into account other relevant dynamics to discern whether any particular network strategy will reduce costs as well as maximise profits for the different market participants;
- quantify the efficiency impact of different network strategies.

These analyses serve to identify the most preferable future clearing industry structure and to deliver recommendations on the industry's future development.

The two core issues of research are efficiency of clearing and industry structure. Clear-cut definitions together with a concise characterisation and descriptive analysis of the current state of the clearing industry set the stage for the following analytical objectives: besides defining the efficiency of clearing and identifying ways in which to measure it, this study aims to determine the efficiency impact of various cross-border 'network strategies', i.e. integration and harmonisation initiatives between CCPs, within the clearing industry. An assessment of this impact serves to identify the most preferable future clearing industry structure. The research primarily focuses on analysing the European exchange-traded derivatives clearing industry. In a final step, the research results are applied to European exchange-traded cash equities clearing as well as to Europe with respect to its global positioning.

1.4 Focus area of research

Action to promote financial integration in the field of clearing and settlement needs to be taken urgently. In a fast-evolving global financial system, there is a window of opportunity to raise the euro area financial infrastructure to the highest levels of efficiency, competitiveness, sophistication and completeness. The window of opportunity was opened by the euro, but will not remain open forever. The shape of the euro financial system is likely to be determined in the next few years and remain crystallised in that shape for a very long time.[43]

---

[43] Tumpel-Gugerell (2006).

This section briefly outlines the rationale for choosing to focus the research on the exchange-traded derivatives clearing industry and on Europe.

The research centres on exchange-traded derivatives clearing because CCPs have traditionally played a more significant role in this area than in cash equities markets due to the characteristics of derivative trades.[44] CCPs thus have a much longer history in the context of derivatives clearing. The rationale for focusing on derivatives clearing further lies in the enhanced electronic and global market structure related to derivatives trading and clearing, which significantly increases cross-border flows.[45] The rapid growth of exchange-traded derivatives in the past decade has been accompanied by an increasing internationalisation of the markets and their clearing arrangements.[46] Institutional and individual traders worldwide continue to expand their use of derivatives instruments. Institutional investors in particular are increasingly trading derivatives, such as single stock futures or options, in lieu of the respective underlying stock.[47] Derivatives markets are therefore growing faster than stock market activity. The daily liquidity of many equity derivatives is more than three times higher than the trading volume of the underlying stock, and the derivatives trading volumes continue to grow faster than the securities trading volumes.[48] The exchange-traded volume of derivative financial instruments, i.e. futures and options on interest rates, exchange rates, cash equities and equity indices, has consequently grown enormously over the past decade.[49] It is therefore useful to study derivatives clearing and subsequently apply the findings to cash equities clearing. The examination of clearing for cash equities markets will benefit from the derivatives clearing analysis.[50]

Despite the fact that the US clearing industry is often looked at as a model for Europe,[51] it is in some respects still more fragmented and less integrated than its European counterpart.[52] This is one of the reasons why Europe was chosen as focus area for the study. Additionally, in Europe, the cross-border integration and harmonisation of the clearing industry has been spurred on

---

[44] Details regarding the role of a CCP in cash equities and derivatives markets are outlined in Chapter 2.
[45] Cf. Hasan/Malkamäki/Schmiedel (2002), p. 12.
[46] Cf. Bank for International Settlements (ed.) (1997a), p. 5.
[47] Cf. Deutsche Börse Group (ed.) (2005a), p. 20.   [48] Cf. Deutsche Börse Group (ed.) (2005a), p. 20.
[49] Cf. Bank for International Settlements (ed.) (1997a), p. 1. Note that the analysis does not cover clearing services provided for over-the-counter (OTC) derivatives trades. CCP services have only recently been introduced to OTC markets. Cf. Bank for International Settlements (ed.) (2004), p. 1. Additionally, the study focuses on financial derivatives and does not include derivatives on commodities such as sugar, cocoa, gold, etc.
[50] Cf. LCH.Clearnet (ed.) (2004a), p. 2.   [51] Cf. Corporation of London (ed.) (2005), p. 19.
[52] Cf. Hart/Russo/Schönenberger (2002), p. 8. For more information on the European and American clearing industry, refer to section 2.5.2.

by the introduction of the euro and the ongoing process of European economic integration, as outlined in section 1.1. Particularly the launch and implementation of the Code have lent new momentum for the European clearing industry,[53] which further underlines the vigour with which Europe is currently pursuing a fundamental restructuring of its clearing industry. These events serve as unique catalysts; comparable drivers are absent in the US.[54]

1.5 Structure of study

This section provides a detailed outline of the study's structure, including the sequence in which the various analyses will be conducted.

The study consists of nine main chapters (Chapters 2 to 10). **Chapter 2** sets the stage for the research by providing relevant definitions of clearing, indicating the value-added of CCP clearing and delivering insight into the various stakeholders in clearing. An overview of the structural set-up of the European and US clearing industries follows.

Chapter 3 defines the two core issues of research: the efficiency of clearing and the structure of the clearing industry. For the purpose of this study, the efficiency is measured by the transaction costs that clearing members have to bear. The transaction costs of derivatives clearing are defined and systematised to facilitate the analysis. The clearing industry structure is researched in terms of the different integration and harmonisation initiatives between clearing houses, with emphasis on certain inter-institutional arrangements called 'network strategies'. Four archetypes of network strategies are presented, followed by an overview of selected network strategies between clearing houses from 1973 to 2006.

A comprehensive empirical study was conducted to obtain insight into the transaction costs of clearing as well as to derive a basis for analysing the impact that network strategies have on clearing costs. **Chapter 4** introduces the empirical study by describing the underlying data, the method of data collection and the structure and component parts. The data treatment and quality of the survey are also discussed. The results of the empirical study are presented in Chapters 5 and 8.

---

[53] Cf. McCreevy (2006b), p. 2.
[54] Cf. Hart/Russo/Schönenberger (2002), p. 6; and Sabatini (2003), p. 1.

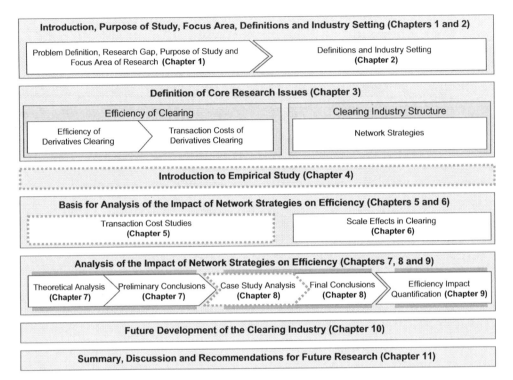

Figure 1.1.   Layout of the study

To evaluate the impact of network strategies on efficiency, it is first necessary to learn more about the transaction costs as well as the demand- and supply-side scale effects in clearing. To this end, **Chapter 5** examines various aspects of European derivatives clearing costs, presents findings from the empirical study and provides a number of quantitative and qualitative transaction cost analyses. **Chapter 6** classifies potential demand- and supply-side scale effects in clearing and furnishes evidence of their existence.

A three-step analysis of the impact of network strategies on the efficiency of European clearing comes next: **Chapter 7** establishes an original framework for it. The framework builds on the findings of the previous chapters and consists of four matrices. These provide the foundation for an assessment of the impact of various network strategies on efficiency. The matrices also take into account other dynamics impacting the industry structures. It is thereby revealed that although some scenarios are cost-efficient, they are not necessarily profit-maximising for all clearing members. The analysis conducted in this chapter delivers preliminary findings on the impact of network strategies on the efficiency of clearing. **Chapter 8** compares these conclusions with the case study findings. Final conclusions are then drawn regarding the impact of network strategies on the efficiency of European clearing. Based on these findings, a quantitative assessment of the efficiency impact of European network strategies is presented in **Chapter 9**.

Based on the impact assessment of the different network strategies on the efficiency of European clearing, **Chapter 10** endeavours to determine the most preferable future European industry structure and delivers recommendations for its development. Additionally, the research results are applied to European exchange-traded cash equities clearing as well as to Europe with respect to its global positioning.

Chapter 11 recapitulates the most important findings of this study and closes with a critical discussion of the research results. The study concludes with recommendations for further research.

2   Setting the stage – definitions and industry setting

The purpose of this chapter is to set the stage for the research conducted in this study. As relevant definitions are a prerequisite for any thorough analysis, the first step is to clarify the terminology used throughout this study (section 2.1). Next, the value-added of clearing for individual market participants (microeconomic view) and for capital markets as a whole (macroeconomic view) and according to different asset classes (cash equities and derivatives) is outlined in section 2.2.

At this juncture, the so-called 'Value Provision Network' is introduced to illuminate the structural set-up of the clearing industry, including the different layers of access to the market infrastructure (section 2.3). The network consists of the clearing house and market participants, both with direct (the so-called 'clearing members') and indirect access to the CCP (the so-called 'non-clearing members'), whose access to the clearing house takes place through intermediaries). An understanding of the Value Provision Network is critical for grasping the true underlying mechanisms of the clearing industry, which influence the structural set-up and competitive dynamics relevant for the future development of the industry.

Once this has been provided, the different stakeholders in clearing are introduced (section 2.4), followed by an explanation and comparison of the current clearing industry structures in Europe and the United States (section 2.5). A final step provides a summary of this chapter (section 2.6).

While the remainder of this study primarily analyses the European exchange-traded derivatives clearing industry and its efficiency, the definitions provided in Chapter 2 apply to both securities and derivatives clearing. Particularities of securities versus derivatives clearing are identified and explained.

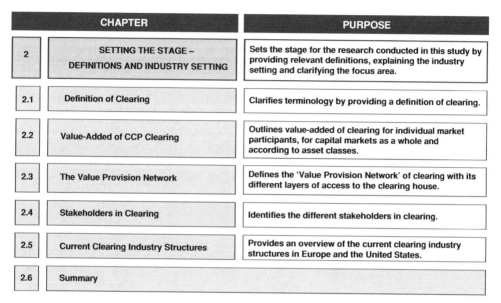

Figure 2.1   Structure of Chapter 2

2.1 Definition of clearing

Paradoxically, the term 'clearing' is used often, defined rarely and is, as a result, far from always clear.[1]

The precise definition of the term 'clearing', including the composition of the value chain and the related services, has been a matter of considerable debate among market participants, regulators and policymakers.[2] This section establishes a definition for the purpose of this study.[3] This definition is presented according to four different perspectives:

- The *process view* refers to clearing as a process that constitutes a vital part of the life cycle of a trade (section 2.1.1).

---

[1] Bressand/Distler (2001), p. 6.

[2] Cf. London Economics (ed.) (2005), p. 3; and European Commission (ed.) (2005), p. 5. Through its Clearing and Settlement Advisory and Monitoring Expert Group (the so-called CESAME Group), the European Commission is currently in the process of establishing a final report on definitions. Cf. CESAME Group (ed.) (2006), p. 15. The CESAME Group holds a mandate from the European Commission to monitor and provide advice on European clearing and settlement. For details, refer to CESAME Group (ed.) (2004).

[3] The provided definition is consistent with and builds upon the view of important industry bodies and policymakers, as expressed in EACH (ed.) (2004c); European Commission (ed.) (2005); and European Commission (ed.) (2006d).

- The *functional view* focuses on clearing as a service and details the various value chain components (section 2.1.2).
- The *structural view* concentrates on identifying the types and roles of typical clearing service providers (section 2.1.3).
- The *institutional view* builds on the institutional characteristics of clearing (section 2.1.4).

In the context of financial services, clearing can refer to the processing of payment instruments or financial product transactions. Because this study focuses on the clearing of financial transactions, the definition of clearing used here refers exclusively to securities and derivatives transactions.[4] The following section provides a definition of securities and derivatives clearing according to each of the views outlined above.

2.1.1 Process view

Clearing constitutes a vital part of the life cycle of a trade. This life cycle consists of execution, clearing and settlement. By executing a trade, buyers and sellers enter into a specific legal obligation to buy or sell securities or, in the case of derivatives, another underlying. There are two sides to every trade: the buy position and the sell position.[5]

Settlement refers to the fulfilment of the legal obligation. In the trading of securities, fulfilment occurs when the ownership of the securities is exchanged for cash or vice versa. In the trading of derivatives, the legal obligation is fulfilled when the duration of a contract expires or when a close-out of the position occurs (i.e. an offsetting sell contract for the holder of a buy contract is entered into and vice versa).[6] The process that takes place between execution and settlement, i.e. during the respective time lag, is referred to as clearing.[7] Whereas in the context of trading securities, this time lag is usually minimal (between one and five days), it can be substantially longer in derivatives trading (from one day up to several decades). During this time lag, trades need to be processed, managed, monitored and ultimately prepared for settlement.

---

[4] For information on the parallels between derivatives clearing and clearing of payment instruments, refer to Kroszner (1999), pp. 16–17. Also see Bank for International Settlements (ed.) (2000a), pp. 6–8 for further details.

[5] Note that the term 'position' is commonly employed with reference to derivatives trades, whereas in the context of securities trades, the term 'transaction' is used.

[6] Cf. Edwards (1983), p. 370.   [7] Cf. Lannoo/Levin (2001), p. 3; and EACH (ed.) (2004c), p. 5.

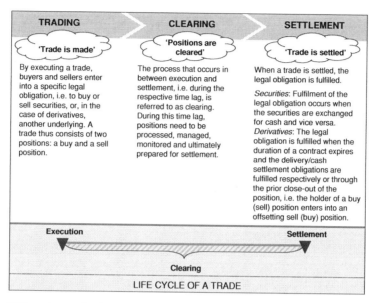

Figure 2.2 Process view on clearing
Source: Author's own.

2.1.2 Functional view

The functional view focuses on clearing as a service and details the various value chain components. The term 'clearing' originates from the expression 'to clear' (lat. clarus), which refers to the balancing of accounts with another party, i.e. clearing one's debts. In reality, however, clearing usually comprises a much greater scope of services. The number of services offered within the clearing value chain generally depends on the characteristics of the cleared market and product and the provider offering these services.[8] The scope and type of clearing services available can be classified as follows (see Figure 2.3):

- basic clearing services (section 2.1.2.1);
- value-added clearing services in general, with unique CCP services in particular (section 2.1.2.2); and
- complementary clearing services (section 2.1.2.3).

Each of these clearing service levels has a different scope and comprises different functions, which are detailed in the next sections.

---

[8] For details on different providers of clearing services and the scope of their services offered, refer to section 2.1.3.

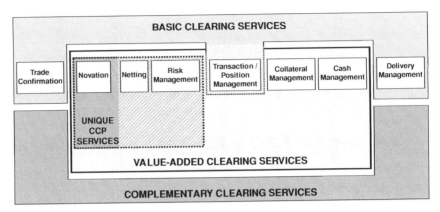

Figure 2.3   Functional view on clearing
Source: Author's own.

2.1.2.1 Basic clearing services

Clearing refers to the process that takes place between the execution of a trade and its settlement. The linking of trading and settlement processes creates the need for a number of clearing services, which are essential to the life cycle of a trade, including trade confirmation, transaction/position management and delivery management. These services are categorised as basic clearing services.

2.1.2.1.1 *Trade confirmation*

Trading entails a specific legal obligation between a seller and a buyer. Once this obligation has been entered into (through the execution of a trade), the trade proceeds to the clearing process. The first step in the clearing process is to assess the consistency of the buyer's and seller's terms of trade in order to prevent any unintentional errors.[9] This service is referred to as trade confirmation.[10] Providing trade confirmation means to compare the trade details of the sell and buy instructions in order to identify and link the related transactions. This commonly includes identifying the security or type of contract, the quantity of the security or other underlying, the invoice price and the settlement, delivery or expiry date.[11]

---

[9] Cf. Moser (1998), p. 4; Bank for International Settlements (ed.) (2001), p. 9; Giovannini Group (ed.) (2001), p. 4; Kröpfl (2003), p. 17; Iori (2004), p. 8; NERA Economic Consulting (ed.) (2004), p. 7; and Linciano/Siciliano/Trovatore (2005), p. 4.

[10] Cf. Bank for International Settlements (ed.) (2001), p. 9; and Guadamillas/Keppler (2001), p. 7.

[11] Cf. Moser (1998), p. 4; and Iori (2004), p. 8.

2.1.2.1.2 Transaction/position management

Positions need to be processed and managed until the respective legal obligations are successfully fulfilled. The need for and intensity of this management strongly depends on the type of asset class. It is for this reason that transaction/position management can either be classified as a basic clearing service or as a value-added clearing service – depending on the scope of managerial services offered.

As outlined earlier, in the context of securities transactions, the legal obligation is usually fulfilled within a very short time frame, i.e. the standard settlement period, which is a predetermined date as close as possible to the trade day (T + 1, T + 2, T + 3, etc.).[12] Fulfilment of the legal obligation for derivatives positions, on the other hand, may require much longer time frames.

Important managerial services provided between the execution and fulfilment of the legal obligation include corporate action services during this period[13] as well as any previously announced transfer of pending obligations to another counterparty (e.g. position transfers, give-up and take-up services).[14] A counterpart or counterparty is the contracting party in a trade.[15]

The standardisation of exchange-traded derivatives enables previously established sell (short) or purchase (long) positions to be offset via appropriate opposite positions (close-out).[16] In this case, the actual fulfilment of the contract, i.e. the delivery or purchase of the underlying, is no longer necessary.[17] When derivatives are traded, there always remain a number of contracts – both bought and sold – that are not closed out, settled or delivered on any given day and thus remain open.[18] The total number of outstanding options and/or futures contracts that are held by counterparties at the end of

---

[12] T = the day on which the trade is made. 1, 2, 3, etc. stand for the number of elapsed business days before the legal obligation is fulfilled.

[13] 'Corporate actions covers a wide range of activities including the collection of interest and dividends from the issuer, the allocation of interest and dividends to the legal owner of the securities, and the evaluation and correct processing of issuers' corporate transactions (stock splits, capital increases, rights, spin-offs, etc.) for the benefit of the legal owner of the financial instrument in question. These transactions do not have to be limited to cash securities only, as they may also have an impact on derivatives or other financial products.' EACH (ed.) (2004c), p. 4.

[14] Cf. EACH (ed.) (2004c), p. 5. When a so-called 'give-up' occurs, the counterparty A executing a trade relinquishes the trade to another counterparty B. This is done because the executing counterparty A placed the trade on behalf of the other counterparty B as if B had actually executed the trade. Reasons for this might include capitalisation issues on the part of counterparty B, i.e. a thin capitalisation prevents B from maintaining a large order. Cf. Moser (1998), p. 4. However, various other reasons related to market access customer relationships, etc. on the part of counterparty B can motivate a give-up. The term 'take-up' refers to the reverse process on the part of B; whereas A gives up the trade to B, counterparty B takes up the trade from counterparty A.

[15] Cf. Eurex (ed.) (2003a), p. 65.   [16] Cf. Eurex (ed.) (2003b), p. 11.

[17] Cf. Eurex (ed.) (2003b), p. 11.   [18] Cf. Loader (2004), p. 215.

each trading day is referred to as 'open interest'.[19] Open interest of exchange-traded derivatives is held at and managed by the clearing house. Transaction management is particularly important in this context and usually comprises additional value-added services related to the exercise of option positions and expiry of future positions. These additional services may also entail the issuance of daily reports pertaining to transactions, modifications and exposure components.[20]

2.1.2.1.3 Delivery management

Delivery management constitutes the final service within the clearing cycle. It is the process of preparing the settlement instructions[21] for securities or cash (which can originate from cash equities, derivatives, bond or repurchase agreement (repo) trades or swap contracts) or, in the case of derivatives, another underlying. Settlement instructions are then sent to the respective settlement institutions.[22] It should be taken into account that settlement instructions only result from derivatives transactions if a position has not been closed out prior to the expiry of the contract.

2.1.2.2 Value-added clearing services

[Clearing] is what must take place before [settlement] is undergone, in order to enable a proper exchange of 'good securities' for 'good money'. 'Enabling' however can also mean 'adding value'.[23]

In addition to the basic clearing services described earlier, clearing often comprises a much greater spectrum of services. Whereas these additional services are not essential to the life cycle of a trade, they offer important value-added to the trade's counterparties. These services are therefore referred to as value-added clearing services. These comprise unique CCP services, such as novation, netting and risk management, as well as transaction/position management, collateral management and cash management. The scope of netting and risk management services that a CCP can offer is unique. Nonetheless, other clearing service providers can also offer these services, albeit in a more

---

[19] Open interest is not the same as the traded volume of options and futures contracts. For each seller of a futures contract, there must be a buyer. Thus, a seller and a buyer combine to create one contract. Volume represents the total number of contracts that have changed hands in a given product and during a given period. In contrast to the volume, the open interest relates to a certain fixed point in time. For example, if the parties to a trade initiate a new contract, open interest and volume will increase by one contract each. If a position is closed out, open interest will decline by one contract and volume will increase by one. On the other hand, if a trader passes off his or her open position to another trader, the open interest will not change and volume will increase by one.

[20] Cf. EACH (ed.) (2004c), p. 5.   [21] Cf. Schiereck (1996a), p. 189.
[22] Cf. EACH (ed.) (2004c), p. 5.   [23] Bressand/Distler (2001), p. 6.

limited capacity. This is why netting and risk management services can either be classified as value-added clearing services or as unique CCP services – depending on the type of service provider.

2.1.2.2.1 Unique CCP services

Due to the nature of derivatives products (especially the leverage effect)[24] and the potentially significant time lag between execution and settlement of derivatives (which can lead to a build-up of large unsettled exposures between market participants),[25] the evolution of derivatives clearing services has been shaped by the counterparties' desire to control their risk of losses from non-performance.[26] This desire led to the introduction of the so-called central counterparty (CCP): '[a]n entity that interposes itself between the counterparties to trades, acting as the buyer to every seller and the seller to every buyer.'[27]

Compared to the market structure of bilateral relationships between counterparties, CCPs offer a number of important clearing services. Some of these services are unique to the CCP structure in terms of their scope and nature; they are therefore referred to as 'unique' CCP services. Although CCPs have long been solely associated with derivatives clearing services,[28] their use in exchange-traded securities markets has also become common. Central counterparty clearing has become an integral part of modern clearing services[29] and forms a core part of the financial market infrastructure in most developed economies.[30]

2.1.2.2.1.1 Novation. Novation is a crucial unique CCP service. It refers to the legal process of replacing the original counterparties to a trade with a single (thus central) counterparty to both sides of the transaction.[31]

Figure 2.4 illustrates the process by which the CCP interposes itself between counterparties A and B to assume their rights and legal obligations, thereby becoming the buyer to every seller and the seller to every buyer. The process of novation replaces the original bilateral contractual obligations by new

---

[24] The leverage effect of derivatives signifies the effect to which the value of a derivative position is greater than the value of the underlying. Cf. Rettberg/Zwätz (1995), p. 101.

[25] Cf. Knott/Mills (2002), p. 162.

[26] Cf. Moser (1998), p. 7; Knott/Mills (2002), p. 162; and Ripatti (2004), p. 4.

[27] Bank for International Settlements (ed.) (2001), p. 45.

[28] Cf. Bank for International Settlements (ed.) (2004), p. 6.

[29] Cf. Ripatti (2004), p. 4.   [30] Cf. Knott/Mills (2002), p. 162.

[31] Cf. Giovannini Group (ed.) (2001), p. 12; Lannoo/Levin (2003), p. 3; Wright (2003), p. 2; Ripatti (2004), p. 5; and BNP Paribas Securities Services (ed.) (2005), p. 5.

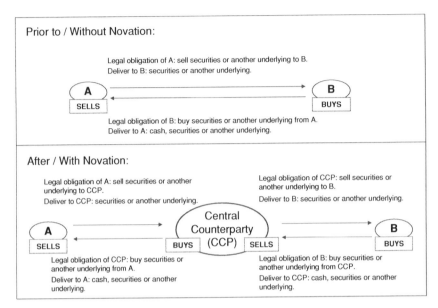

Figure 2.4 Legal relationship between counterparties to a trade prior to and after novation
Source: Author's own.

obligations with the CCP.[32] Novation entails that the CCP assumes the associated risks of counterparty default.[33] As a result, bilateral counterparty risk (of variable quality) is replaced with a (high quality)[34] counterparty risk against the CCP.[35] Through *novation*, central counterparty clearing helps to maintain anonymity when the trade execution process itself is anonymous.[36]

2.1.2.2.1.2 Netting. Originally, the principal benefit provided by CCPs was the removal of counterparty risk. This type of credit intermediation is still part of the CCP's functionality. But the name of today's game is far more about managing the process of netting.[37]

---

[32] Cf. Knott/Mills (2002), p. 162; Citigroup (ed.) (2003), p. 35; Lannoo/Levin (2003), p. 3; Loader (2004), p. 214; NERA Economic Consulting (Ed.) (2004), p. 10; and Bank for International Settlements (ed.) (2004), p. 72.

[33] A default is the failure to satisfy an obligation on time.

[34] This is naturally only true under the assumption that CCPs usually fulfil the criteria of high creditworthiness.

[35] Cf. Knott/Mills (2002), p. 162; and Ripatti (2004), p. 5.

[36] Cf. Giovannini Group (ed.) (2001), p. 12; Ferscha/Potthoff (2002), p. 5; NERA Economic Consulting (ed.) (2004), p. 10; Loader (2004), p. 19; Hardy (2004), p. 57; Linciano/Siciliano/Trovatore (2005), p. 4; BNP Paribas Securities Services (ed.) (2005), p. 5; and Hachmeister/Schiereck (2006), p. 6. It should be noted that CCPs do not always operate under conditions of anonymity – some OTC trades are cleared through a CCP, but both parties are known to each other.

[37] Hardy (2004), p. 57.

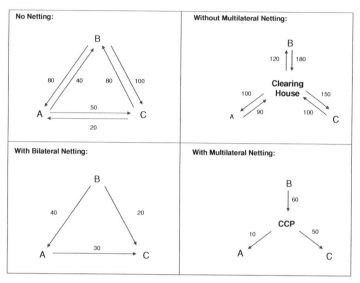

Figure 2.5 The exchange of payments arising from financial transactions
Source: Based on Hills *et al.* (1999), p. 124.

When a CCP is involved in the clearing process, novation is usually followed by netting. In securities markets, the same security is often sold back and forth between market participants. As a result of these transactions, a number of exposures can arise; these might offset one another completely or partially. The same applies to derivatives trading, where market participants commonly maintain a number of offsetting positions with the same underlying and the same attributes. When many counterparties are replaced by one central counterparty by means of novation, these offsetting positions can be netted off against each other,[38] thereby reducing the overall number of positions.[39]

There are two types of netting services: simple bilateral and more sophisticated multilateral netting (see Figure 2.5). **Bilateral netting** allows amounts owed between two counterparties to be combined into a single net amount payable from one party to the other.[40] Bilateral netting therefore consolidates the flows between each pair of counterparties into one single net obligation.[41]

Multilateral netting means that the CCP nets all offsetting positions of its counterparties and reduces all outstanding residuals to a single debit/credit

[38] Cf. Bank for International Settlements (ed.) (1998), p. 43.
[39] Cf. NERA Economic Consulting (ed.) (2004), p. 10; and Van Cayseele/Wuyts (2005), p. 3.
[40] Cf. Gizycki/Gray (1994), p. 1.
[41] Cf. Ripatti (2004), p. 5. With bilateral netting, two counterparties agree to net with one another. They sign a master agreement specifying the types of netting to be performed as well as the existing and future contracts that will be affected. Bilateral netting is common in OTC derivatives markets.

between itself and each counterparty (rather than a multiplicity of bilateral exposures between the original counterparties to a trade).[42] This multilateral net position encompasses the bilateral net position between each clearing member and the clearing house.[43] The scope for multilateral netting is greatest in markets where a number of firms trade intensively among each other, with each firm both extending and receiving credit, creating a web of bilateral exposures.[44] The value of being able to net all positions into a single position naturally becomes more pronounced as volumes grow.[45]

An additional classification further distinguishes two netting levels according to their varying degrees of legal enforceability. Unfortunately, no universal definition has yet emerged for either netting level. 'This is due, in part, to the fact that terms tend to be used loosely in the markets and various forms have been developed to accommodate specific types of transactions.'[46] For the purpose of this study, these two netting levels are classified as 'type1 netting' and 'type2 netting'. Whereas **type1 netting** signifies the legally enforceable dissolution of gross positions into one single net obligation, **type2 netting** neither satisfies nor discharges the original individual obligations.[47] With type2 netting, the offsetting positions are therefore not extinguished, but funds or securities transfer instructions are settled on a net basis.[48] Whereas both netting levels provide significant efficiency gains to users, the legal enforceability of netting levels is of crucial importance in the event of counterparty (i.e. member of a CCP) default.[49] Type1 netting, as distinct from type2 netting, must therefore provide for 'contract liquidation procedures in the event that one of the parties defaults under a contract or becomes bankrupt'.[50]

In the context of derivatives clearing, the most prominent form of type1 netting is close-out netting.[51] Close-out netting signifies the legally enforceable consolidation of individual trades into net amounts of securities, cash or other

[42] Cf. Hanley/McCann/Moser (1996), p. 1; Moser (1998), p. 5; Bank for International Settlements (ed.) (1998), p. 43; King (2000), p. 32; Giovannini Group (ed.) (2001), p. 12; and Ripatti (2004), p. 5.

[43] Cf. Moser (1998), p. 5; Bank for International Settlements (ed.) (1998), p. 43; Ripatti (2004), p. 5; NERA Economic Consulting (ed.) (2004), p. 10; and Linciano/Siciliano/Trovatore (2005), p. 4.

[44] Cf. Hills et al. (1999), p. 125.   [45] Cf. Bressand/Distler (2001), p. 5.

[46] Huang (2006), p. 62.

[47] The type of netting arrangement that neither satisfies nor discharges the original individual obligations is often also referred to as 'position netting' or 'payment netting', again depending on the type of transaction and the type of clearing service provider.

[48] Cf. Bank for International Settlements (ed.) (2001), p. 38.

[49] A clearing member is an entity which may use the services of a clearing service provider. For details regarding clearing members and their clients, refer to section 2.3.

[50] New York Foreign Exchange Committee (ed.) (1997), p. 4.

[51] Other forms of a legally enforceable dissolution of gross positions into one single net obligation are exposure netting, trade netting or obligation netting; depending on the type of transaction and the type of clearing service provider. Cf. Bank for International Settlements (ed.) (1998), pp. 21 and 41; and Bank for International Settlements (ed.) (2001), p. 38.

underlyings. The offsetting positions with the same underlying and the same attributes, such as a contracting party, security or trading currency, are thus dissolved into one single net obligation in either cash or cash and securities or another underlying.[52]

Important efficiency gains can also be realised through type2 netting. During the time a derivatives position is open at the clearing house, the value of the positions is constantly recalculated and adapted to market movements, which can result in certain payment obligations.[53] Position netting then reduces collateral requirements by taking offsetting positions into account;[54] it is an agreement that nets payments across multiple contracts,[55] but keeps each contract distinct.[56] Without such netting, total credit risk exposures[57] would grow in proportion to the respective counterparty's gross number of trades.[58]

Another prominent form of type2 netting is settlement netting, which plays a crucial role in securities clearing.[59] Settlement netting encompasses the netting of delivery instructions for cash or securities deliveries[60] or the delivery of another underlying. It thus refers to the netting of delivery instructions, which neither satisfies nor discharges the original individual obligations.[61] Settlement netting services bring about significant efficiency gains by reducing the number of settlement processes.[62] In exchange-traded derivatives markets, most positions are closed out prior to expiration[63] and are thus not eligible for the settlement process that normally proceeds when the duration of the contract expires.

---

[52] Cf. EACH (ed.) (2004c), p. 5.
[53] For more details, refer to the explanation of risk management services.
[54] Cf. OM Group (ed.) (2002), p. 1.   [55] Cf. Bank for International Settlements (ed.) (1998), p. 43.
[56] Cf. Tsetsekos/Varangis (1997), p. 9. Position netting reduces collateral requirements because the clearing house often only charges margin on the net (and not gross) positions of a clearing member. The term 'margin' refers to the collateral that has to be deposited at the clearing house for each transaction and serves risk management purposes. Margins, cross-margining and risk management are explained in more detail in the following.
[57] Exposure is the maximum loss from default by a counterparty.
[58] Cf. Bliss/Kaufman (2005), p. 10.   [59] Cf. King (2000), p. 89.
[60] Cf. Bank for International Settlements (ed.) (2001), p. 45; Eurex (ed.) (2006), p. 7; Ripatti (2004), p. 5; Linciano/Siciliano/Trovatore (2005), p. 4; and NERA Economic Consulting (ed.) (2004), p. 78.
[61] Cf. Bank for International Settlements (ed.) (1989), p. 27.
[62] Cf. King (2000), p. 89. 'Netting means fewer trades proceed to settlement. Experience suggests that reductions of 95 per cent or more in the volume of trades proceeding to settlement can be achieved in the equity markets and 70 per cent or more in the fixed income markets. Moreover, those trades that are settled can be processed internally within a CSD/ICSD settlement platform, irrespective of the preference of the counterparty. This means CCPs facilitate cross-border trading by enabling trades to settle at the lower costs typically achieved in domestic markets.' LCH.Clearnet (ed.) (2003a), p. 31.
[63] Note that the same does not apply to OTC derivatives. Positions resulting from OTC transactions are seldom closed out prior to maturity, as doing so requires the consent of both counterparties. The negotiation of such a close-out is consequently a time-consuming process. Cf. Bank for International Settlements (ed.) (1997a), p. 6; and Bank for International Settlements (ed.) (1998), p. 9.

2.1.2.2.1.3 Risk management. The information about the full portfolio of positions provided by transaction/position management is also required for risk management processes. Risk management is a crucial part of the clearing services value chain.[64] Positions managed and processed by a clearing house are associated with specific risks inherent to the different product types. The exact risks a CCP must manage depend on the product types it processes and the specific terms of its contracts with participants as well as the scope of services offered.[65]

CCPs typically incorporate three tiers of financial safeguards in order to control the risks they face,[66] which may vary in their specific constitution:[67]

- Members of a CCP are subject to minimum financial and capital adequacy requirements as well as periodic monitoring of their risk management policies.[68] This serves to reduce the likelihood of a participant's default.[69]

- The clearing house imposes a margining regime to ensure that the obligations of both the clearing members and their customers are collateralised.[70] Margining regimes are designed to cover a default in normal market conditions.[71]

- There are clearly defined and transparent emergency rules and procedures as well as financial back-up arrangements to address default[72] by a clearing house member. These measures include the instalment of supplemental clearing house resources (e.g. set-up of a default fund or the instalment of insurance policies).[73] A CCP's total resources should be sufficient to

---

[64] Cf. Green (2000), p. 12.

[65] Nonetheless, all CCPs are exposed to a common set of risks, which have to be managed effectively. There is, for example, the risk that participants will not settle the full value of their obligations at any time (counterparty credit risk). Cf. Kahn/McAndrews/Roberds (1999), p. 3. Another risk is that participants will settle obligations late (liquidity risk). For more details and further types of risk to which a CCP is exposed, refer to Bank for International Settlements (ed.) (2004), p. 8; and Ripatti (2004), p. 15. Details on the risks that arise from the CCP structure for the market participants and the financial market as a whole are specified in sections 2.2.1 and 2.2.2.

[66] Cf. Dale (1998a), pp. 9–12; EACH (ed.) (2004c), p. 5; and Loader (2004), p. 21.

[67] Further details on how CCPs can most effectively manage the specific risks they encounter can be found in Bank for International Settlements (ed.) (2004).

[68] By imposing rules on the quality of its membership, the clearing house achieves a degree of risk control. The structure of clearing service provision, including membership criteria and common structures among CCPs for admission to direct participation in the clearing process is detailed in section 2.2.3.

[69] Cf. Bank for International Settlements (ed.) (2004), p. 14.

[70] For details on the structure of the Value Provision Network, clearing members and their customers, refer to section 2.3.

[71] Cf. Bank for International Settlements (ed.) (2004), p. 16.

[72] A default is the failure to satisfy an obligation on time. A clearing house may specify certain other events, e.g. insolvency, as constituting default for the purpose of triggering its default procedures. Cf. Bank for International Settlements (ed.) (2004), pp. 70–71.

[73] For details on supplemental clearing house resources, refer to Bank for International Settlements (ed.) (1997a), p. 26; and Bank for International Settlements (ed.) (2004), p. 20.

cover a default that occurs in abnormal (extreme but plausible) market conditions.[74]

While participation requirements serve to reduce the likelihood of a participant's default, they cannot eliminate the possibility of default. Many clearing service providers require participants to post collateral to cover exposures in order to limit losses and liquidity pressures in the event of participant default. 'Margin' generally refers to the cash and collateral used to secure an obligation, either realised or potential.[75] Although margins alone may be insufficient to protect CCPs from rare extreme but plausible events either,[76] they generally constitute a crucial element of a CCP's risk controls.

Margining encompasses the entire process of measuring, calculating and administering the cash and collateral that must be put up to cover open positions.[77] The provision of margin is intended to ensure that all financial commitments related to the open positions of a clearing member can be liquidated within a very short period of time once default has occurred. 'The margin system is the clearinghouse's first line of defense against default risk.'[78] Margin levels are usually designed to protect the clearing house against losses resulting from typical price movements over one or more days[79] and cover potential price movements in normal market conditions.[80] Clearing houses differentiate and calculate various margin types, most importantly the so-called 'initial margin' and 'variation margin'. The two margin types can be differentiated according to their time reference. Whereas the initial margin is set to cover the potential future risks inherent to a traded contract, the variation margin is set to cover risks resulting from the past events inherent to an open position.

Initial margin is the primary layer of protection, intended to insulate the CCP against the risk of non-performance as well as the possibility that shifting market prices will leave the counterparty with a credit risk.[81] Market volatility and the specific counterparty risk usually determine the initial margin.[82] Clearing members are required to place an initial margin in an account with

---

[74] Cf. Bank for International Settlements (ed.) (2004), p. 16.

[75] Cf. NERA Economic Consulting (ed.) (2004), p. 104.   [76] Cf. Knott/Mills (2002), p. 162.

[77] Cf. Eurex (ed.) (2003b), p. 14.   [78] Bates/Craine (1999), p. 248.

[79] Cf. Knott/Mills (2002), p. 162; and Loader (2004), p. 21. For more details on the determination of margin levels, refer to Phillips/Tosini (1982); Figlewski (1984); Gay/Hunter/Kolb (1986); Edwards/Neftci (1988); Warshawsky (1989); Fenn/Kupiec (1993); Gemmill (1994); Kupiec (1997); Longin (1999); Cotter (2001); Day/Lewis (2004); and Cotter/Dowd (2005). Edwards (1983) describes the structure and administration of margin collection.

[80] The definitions of normal markets can vary; one possibility is to define normal market conditions as those observed 99 out of 100 days. However, the appropriate amount of data used to determine that level will vary from market to market and over time.

[81] Cf. Knott/Mills (2002), p. 163; and Loader (2004), p. 211.   [82] Cf. Mogford (2005), pp. 34–7.

the CCP as soon as possible after trade execution (according to the clearing house's risk management standards).[83] Margin requirements can generally be collected based on either net positions or gross positions[84] depending on the scope of netting services offered. Another commonly used methodology to calculate margin requirements also takes correlations into account. This methodology is referred to as cross-margining. **Cross-margining** is based on the idea that certain inter-market trading positions with offsetting risk characteristics can be margined together as a single portfolio.[85] It usually includes financial products showing 50 to 100 per cent price correlation, i.e. all derivatives of the same underlying instrument and cross-margining for securities showing a lower but substantial correlation among each other, such as derivatives products whose underlying instruments possess the same kind of price risk.[86]

Variation margin is a payment made when the market price of a transaction has changed.[87] It is therefore a risk management tool to cover the latest exposure. Variation margin is called for when positions are revalued during the course of a trade (until fulfilment of the legal obligation) using the marking-to-market procedure.[88] This revaluation of positions occurs daily or intra-daily.

---

[83] Cf. Harris (2003), p. 156. Common practice is to collect initial margin at least once a day and more often (intra-day) in case of high exposure. Some CCPs even only novate transactions once they have received the initial margin payment. By increasing the initial margin, excesses in risk accumulation in the market can be avoided and the impact of potential defaults can be reduced. Cf. Mogford (2005), pp. 34–7. The challenge faced by CCPs is to set the initial margin at a level sufficient to provide protection against all but the most extreme and predictable price moves, but not so high as to damage market liquidity or discourage use of the CCP. Cf. Knott/Mills (2002), p. 166. Adrangi/Chatrath (1999) investigate the impact of margin requirements on the trading activity and volatility in futures markets. Also refer to Wendt (2006) for issues related to intra-day margin collection.

[84] Under a net margin system, margin is charged for net long or net short positions. Cf. Bank for International Settlements (ed.) (2004), p. 25.

[85] Cf. Dale (1998a), p. 25.

[86] If an account holds a number of positions that are based on the same underlying instrument, it is possible that the risk components of these positions partially offset each other. A typical example of this is a spread in which the risk of a call (put) that was sold is to a large extent neutralised by the simultaneous purchase of a call (put). Cf. Eurex (ed.) (2003b), p. 44. In a highly liquid market, such positions with counterbalancing risks exist because the prices of options and futures on the same underlying instrument are essentially driven by the same factors: the price and the volatility of the underlying instrument as well as the trend in interest rates. Cf. Eurex (ed.) (2003b), p. 44.

[87] Cf. Bernanke (1990), p. 137; Knott/Mills (2002), p. 163; and Loader (2004), p. 211.

[88] Cf. Ripatti (2004), p. 5. The expression 'mark-to-market' refers to the process of revaluing positions on a continuous basis, at least once a day or intra-daily as close as possible to real-time. Its value is the difference between the closing price from the previous day and the current closing price. Generally, marks are either the most recent market-determined price for each contract or, at the contract's termination, the cash-market price of the underlying asset. Increases in settlement prices produce gains for long positions and losses for short positions. Conversely, decreases in settlement prices result in losses to long positions and gains to short positions. The respective profits or losses can then be settled accordingly. Cf. Fishe/Goldberg (1986), p. 262; Weiss (1993), p. 336; and Hull (2001), pp. 33–4.

Margin calls are then issued in the form of cash.[89] Due to this continuous marking-to-market of positions, variation margin payments are in effect a settlement of unrealised profit or loss.

As explained above, the employment of margins is but one component in a CCP's risk management package.[90] CCPs need to assess the losses they could face on occasions when margin proves insufficient[91] and ensure that they can meet these losses from extreme but plausible events by other means.[92]

2.1.2.2.2 Collateral management

The term 'collateral' refers to assets that are delivered by the counterparties to secure their trades.[93] 'Collateral management is the process used to control counterparty assets against the exposure calculated as part of the risk management process.'[94] Most importantly, collateral management ensures that margin requirements are covered by available collateral. If there is a collateral shortfall, a collateral call is generated. If there is collateral excess, a collateral release is generated (automated or upon member request). It further involves the functions of processing new collateral and evaluating the value on a daily or ongoing basis. The evaluation of collateral can be complex. Collateral needs to be evaluated on an ongoing basis to ensure adequate coverage of risk exposure.[95]

---

[89] Cf. EACH (ed.) (2004c), p. 5. Note that collateral is deposited as initial margin payment; variation margin is usually deposited in cash only. For methodologies to calculate collateral value ('haircuts'), refer to García/Gençay (2006). For details on the legal aspects concerning collateralisation, refer to Clarke/Naumowicz (1999).

[90] Risk management of a CCP can feature many additional components, rules and regulations. A common feature in the context of derivatives trading is the employment of position limits, which are set by either the exchange or clearing house. Position limits constrain 'the number of contracts or the percentage of total open interest in a contract that a single client (or single clearing firm) can hold.' Bank for International Settlements (ed.) (1997a), p. 26.

[91] For details on the efficiency of margining systems, refer to Kupiec/White (1996).

[92] Cf. Knott/Mills (2002), p. 162. Effective risk management therefore requires CCPs to have access to additional default resources. Often a default fund (also referred to as compensation or guarantee fund) serves as financial back-up once a default by a clearing house member has occurred. Whereas a margin deposit is usually only available to cover the losses of the participant posting the margin, a default fund may also be used to refer to a CCP's resources available to cover losses (resulting from default of a clearing member), that is resources posted by one participant that may be used to cover losses caused by the default of another participant. This fund serves to compensate non-defaulting participants from losses they may suffer in the event that one or more participants default on their obligation to the CCP. Default funds are typically composed of cash or high-quality liquid securities and are often calculated using either a static or dynamic formula based on the volume of the participant's settlement activity, risk of the CCP's clearing members or other benchmark figures. Liquidity demands resulting from clearing member default are thus primarily met with default fund assets. However, committed bank credit lines ensure the short-term needs until assets in the guarantee funds can be liquidated. Cash, securities or other financial support often further augment the resources of a default fund.

[93] Cf. NERA Economic Consulting (ed.) (2004), p. 102.   [94] EACH (ed.) (2004c), p. 4.

[95] Cf. EACH (ed.) (2004c), p. 5.

2.1.2.2.3 *Cash management*

Cash management provides important services for the smooth functioning of the clearing house, which is highly relevant for risk management, as well as services valuable to users. Cash management comprises operational and treasury management. Operational cash management includes the processing of cash instructions from netting, premium payments, realised profit and loss (P&L) cash instructions, fines and fees, unrealised P&L, income events or margin calls. Sources can be regular trading and clearing activities, corporate actions, P&L adjustments or margins. Treasury management may include the following services (some of which might require a banking licence and are thus not provided by all CCPs): realignment of the CCP's cash positions, interest payments on cash collateral deposited by users, investment of the CCP's long positions and liquidity management.

2.1.2.3 Complementary clearing services

The final category of clearing services is complementary clearing services. Whereas these services are neither suited nor required to maintain the life cycle of a trade, they constitute an important additional value provision. Despite the fact that there is a significant value-added inherent to these services, CCPs only rarely engage in the provision of these services (or only to a limited extent).[96] Therefore, and due to their status as 'add-on features', they are classified as complementary clearing services. Complementary clearing services can comprise a significant number of different services, such as:

- single interface and access to many markets and various CCPs (including centralised collateral and cash management services);
- technical and operational support;
- risk management and services across multiple asset classes and CCPs;
- accounting and regulatory information provision;
- regulatory reporting services;
- book-keeping services;
- sophisticated and flexible customer account structure and management solutions (i.e. establishment of customised sub-account structures);
- facilitation of fungibility[97] of products (despite the fact that products may not be fungible at the respective different CCPs);

---

[96] Refer to section 2.1.3 for the typical clearing service providers for different types of clearing service.

[97] Fungibility is the inter-changeability of exchange-traded derivatives contracts and other instruments dependent upon identical terms. It is a prerequisite for allowing buyers and sellers to close-out a position through a closing transaction in an identical contract. The standardisation of exchange-traded financial derivatives enables previously established sell or purchase positions to be offset via appropriate opposite transactions. If the traded good is standardised and market participants have created offsetting

- provision of credit lines; securities lending;
- provision of sophisticated risk management tools;
- interest calculations; and
- multiple account reporting and consolidation levels.

2.1.3 Structural view

'Clearing and settlement' tends to be mentioned in one breath as the salt-and-pepper for the securities industry cuisine, but practices vary within each market and separating these ingredients can be as difficult as isolating the different spices in an Indian curry dish.[98]

While the functional view focuses on clearing as a service and details the various value-chain components, the structural view focuses on identifying the different types and roles of clearing service providers. A first step identifies clearing service providers according to the process view on clearing and presents the entities whose main functions serve the purpose of supporting the process of trading, clearing or settlement. A second step defines clearing service providers according to function, i.e. the type of clearing services provided by these different entities.

Figure 2.6 shows the various types of entity performing core functions in the trading, clearing and settlement process. Trading takes place on various kinds of marketplaces, such as over-the-counter (OTC),[99] through an alternative execution venue (AEV)[100] or regulated exchange.

The clearing process is typically supported by banks/brokers, clearing houses and/or CCPs.[101] A clearing house carries out the designated function of clearing transactions;[102] it can also be referred to as a clearing corporation or clearing organisation.[103] It is a central location or central processing mechanism through which financial institutions agree to exchange instructions or

---

exposures, a CCP can make settlement by offset feasible, because it is the counterparty to every trade. Cf. Hills *et al.* (1999), p. 124.

[98] Bressand/Distler (2001), p. 6.

[99] OTC trades are negotiated bilaterally, usually between banks/brokers.

[100] Alternative execution venues permit the trading of financial products outside of regulated exchanges. These venues include the so-called Electronic Communication Network (ECN), Alternative Trading Systems (ATS) and the Multilateral Trading Facility (MTF). ECNs constitute, maintain or provide systems for bringing together buyers and sellers for the electronic execution of trades. Cf. SEC (ed.) (1998). On the other hand, ATS and MTF are 'essentially pure agency broker dealers that primarily use technology to bring together investors and liquidity providers'. Instinet (ed.) (2007), p. 2.

[101] Cf. EACH (ed.) (2004c), p. 2.

[102] Cf. Bank for International Settlements (ed.) (1997a), p. 1; Bank for International Settlements (ed.) (1998), p. 41; Hart/Russo/Schönenberger (2002), p. 59; and Lannoo/Levin (2003), p. 3.

[103] Cf. Loader (2005), p. 35.

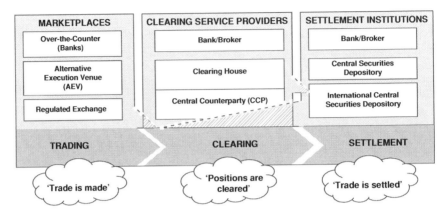

Figure 2.6   Structural view on clearing – clearing service providers according to process
Source: Author's own.

other financial obligations.[104] Not all clearing houses act as CCPs. They can provide basic clearing services without becoming principals to transactions, in which case the clearing house simply plays an agency role. A clearing house assumes the role of a CCP when it performs novation. The focus of this study is on clearing houses that act as CCPs, which form an integral part of modern financial market infrastructure;[105] therefore, the terms 'clearing house' and 'CCP' will be used interchangeably for the purpose of this study.[106] The settlement process is typically supported by settlement institutions, which can be banks/brokers, Central Securities Depositories (CSDs) and/or International Central Securities Depositories (ICSDs).

Figure 2.6 suggests that whereas the different entities service different parts of a trade's life cycle, i.e. either trading, clearing or settlement, each of them potentially provides services other than the ones they were originally designated to support. This means that marketplaces and settlement institutions can provide certain clearing services, whereas CCPs might effectuate settlement in some instances. It is consequently not possible to draw a sharp line between the different service providers' services. With the further sophistication of technology and system advancements, this line is growing even fuzzier. Whereas clearing functions are mainly performed by CCPs, they can also be performed by other entities.[107] The main difference lies in the type and scope of clearing services provided by the different entities. The value chain can thus

[104] Cf. NERA Economic Consulting (ed.) (2004), p. 102.   [105] For details, refer to section 2.2.
[106] This is coherent with terminology used by EACH (ed.) (2004c), p. 1; and European Commission (ed.)
       (2006c), p. 8.
[107] Cf. EACH (ed.) (2004c), p. 6.

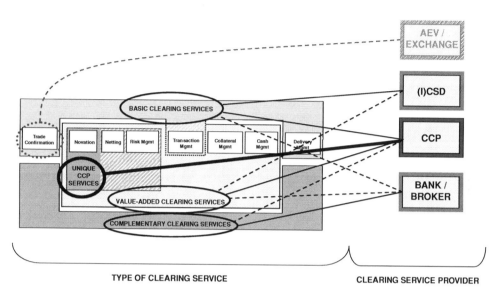

TYPE OF CLEARING SERVICE   CLEARING SERVICE PROVIDER

Figure 2.7 Structural view on clearing – clearing service providers according to function
Source: Author's own.

vary in structure. Its scope depends to a large extent on the characteristics of products cleared (type of marketplace, asset class, volumes, standardisation, etc.), the nature of market participants and domestic market conventions.

In the following, the type and scope of clearing services provided by banks/brokers, CCPs and other entities, whose main function is actually to support the process of trading or settlement, is summarised. Figure 2.7 provides a graphical illustration.

2.1.3.1 Alternative execution venues/exchanges as clearing service providers

Once a trade is executed, the first step in the clearing process is to ensure that counterparties agree to the terms of the trade.

This process of trade confirmation can take place in a variety of ways, and the trading mechanism itself often determines how it occurs. Thus, for example, an electronic trading system automatically produces a confirmed trade between the two counterparties. Other trades are confirmed by exchanges, clearing corporations, trade associations, etc., based on data submitted to them by the counterparties.[108]

Matched trades requiring confirmation are generally received in different formats, depending on the type of marketplace. Trades can be matched

---

[108] Bank for International Settlements (ed.) (2001), p. 37.

on-exchange or off-exchange (OTC trades or via AEVs). On-exchange transactions are often executed on an electronic order book, typically pre-matched by the same trading system and then automatically forwarded for clearing. AEVs or exchanges do not perform any clearing services beyond confirming trades. As additional basic clearing services are required to maintain the life cycle of a trade, AEVs and exchanges do not classify as 'true' clearing service providers.

2.1.3.2 CSDs and ICSDs as clearing service providers

Particularly in securities markets, CSDs and ICSDs[109] have long assumed the role of an integrated clearing and settlement service provider. The type of clearing services they provide tend to be limited to basic clearing services, i.e. those necessary to maintain the life cycle of a trade and to enable settlement. However, many CSDs/ICSDs offer a broader value proposition to their customers, including value-added clearing services, such as collateral and/or cash management and sophisticated transaction/position management services. For corporate action services, the respective functionality can either be built into the CCP or outsourced to a CSD or ICSD. CSDs/ICSDs can also perform risk management to evaluate and manage all relevant sources of risk in order to reduce the probability of default.[110] Additionally: 'most settlement systems use some forms of netting, if only on the money side where participants' cash debits and credits are aggregated into a single, end-of-day position. Some systems net both cash and securities positions, others carry any unsettled securities position forward to the next business day.'[111] The scope of clearing services offered by CSDs/ICSDs ultimately depends on the organisation of the market infrastructure. When no CCP is involved, CSDs/ICSDs can assume basic and value-added clearing services as outlined, but they do not

---

[109] Settlement and custody are required after two counterparties have decided to transfer ownership of a security from one party to another, and involve the transfer of cash as payment of the security. The final phase of a securities transaction once settlement occurs consists in the custody service. Custody refers to the safekeeping of assets and the administration of these securities on behalf of intermediaries and investors. It is mostly related to dematerialised securities held in a book-entry system, and performed by what is usually called a Central Securities Depository or CSD. CSDs hold securities centrally on behalf of their members to speed up the process of settlement, as the selling party does not have to physically send the securities to the buying party. The service also helps to reduce the loss of securities. A CSD service is usually sufficient for local investors, whereas foreign investors who invest in several markets (and are unable or unwilling to acquire expertise sufficient to exercise the obligations and rights connected with holding a security in different jurisdictions) are often served by custodians or International Central Securities Depositories (ICSDs). They act as the interface to all markets in which the investor wants to invest, either by having its own branches or by using local custodians. Cf. Horn (2002), p. 11; Lannoo/Levin (2003), p. 4; Loader (2004), p. 2; Linciano/Siciliano/Trovatore (2005), p. 5; and Deutsche Börse Group (ed.) (2005a), p. 7. For more details on CSDs/ICSDs, settlement and custody, refer to Lannoo/Levin (2001); Simmons (2002); and Kröpfl (2003).

[110] Cf. EACH (ed.) (2004c), p. 1.   [111] Bressand/Distler (2001), p. 5.

provide unique CCP services. When a CCP that provides basic and value-added clearing services is involved, however, the clearing services provided by CSDs/ICSDs might be limited to 'validating and matching the delivery instructions; the result of which is forwarded to settlement.'[112]

2.1.3.3 CCPs as clearing service providers

Of the many different types of clearing service provider, the central counterparty structure has been the most important innovation in terms of value-added clearing services.[113] CCPs not only offer the full scope of basic clearing services, but also a complete range of value-added clearing services, including unique CCP services. As a CCP assumes a unique role through novation, the benefits of its value-added services are immense, especially its netting and risk management services. A CCP's risk management service is sophisticated in its assumption of risk by novation, the provision of a central performance guarantee, centralised risk management and controls.[114] Risk management also entails that unrealised P&L processes are executed at least on a daily basis.[115] This service provides the latest overall position information (and thus P&L results) at any time during the day, based on the pending trades and contracts in the system. The user is thus provided with an overall, up-to-date and consistent view of his or her entire portfolio. 'The other benefits CCPs can provide depend on the types of functions they offer, but chief among them is netting.'[116]

Another unique benefit offered by CCPs is the facilitation of straight-through processing (STP).[117] Contracts traded on an exchange are then executed with a central counterparty that processes all transactions/positions and guarantees performance.[118] CCPs can thus offer sophisticated position management. They enable users to monitor daily position movements, acquire

---

[112] EACH (ed.) (2004c), p. 3. EACH (ed.) (2004c) denominates such a limited provision of basic clearing services as 'CSD Clearing'; CCP clearing services are provided prior to the clearing performed by CSDs/ICSDs.

[113] Refer to section 2.2 regarding the microeconomic and macroeconomic benefits associated with the employment of CCPs.

[114] Cf. Hardy (2004), p. 58.

[115] These P&L processes are referred to as 'unrealised' because the gains or losses constitute book values only until the final settlement or close-out of the positions has occurred.

[116] Bressand/Distler (2001), p. 4. Also refer to Hardy (2004), p. 57.

[117] Cf. Deutsche Börse Group (ed.) (2002), p. 34. STP is the capture of trade details directly from front-end trading systems and the completely automated processing thereof without the need for reformatting data. Cf. Bank for International Settlements (ed.) (1998), p. 44. It includes the seamless electronic transmission of information and data utilising standardised technologies and infrastructure, and thus refers to the full automation of the trading process between buyer and seller. Cf. Accenture (ed.) (2001), p. 23.

[118] Cf. Ripatti (2004), p. 4.

up-to-date position balances per contract, make inquiries about current and historical positions, etc.[119]

Whereas CSDs/ICSDs can provide certain clearing services, CCPs also provide services that effectuate settlement (as suggested in Figure 2.6), which is the fulfilment of the legal obligations that accompany a trade. The settlement of an open position can be effected through a CCP by means of netting[120] (close-out netting). Finally, although some CCPs provide some complementary clearing services, these tend to be provided by banks/brokers.

2.1.3.4 Banks/brokers as clearing service providers

Banks/brokers can act as clearing service providers and perform clearing services for:

- internal transactions (basic clearing services);
- trades executed in OTC markets, on a non-electronic exchange or an AEV (basic clearing services; possibly also value-added and complementary clearing services); and
- their proprietary and customer trades in their role as members of a CCP (complementary clearing services).[121]

When a bank/broker executes internal transactions, it performs basic clearing services that maintain the life cycle of a trade. When the trade is executed either off-exchange (OTC) or on a non-electronic exchange, the counterparties may match the trades manually between themselves, or use a semi-automated matching service.[122]

In over-the-counter markets, counterparties must submit the terms of the trade to each other for verification by some mechanism, be it fax, SWIFT message, or perhaps some specialised electronic messaging and matching service. While this process is occurring, the back offices of the direct counterparties to the trade also issue settlement instructions, which central securities depositories typically require to match before they effect any settlements.[123]

Particularly in markets where no CCP is involved, banks/brokers can extend their basic clearing services to include value-added and complementary clearing services, which are provided for proprietary as well as customer trades.

The scope and type of value-added and complementary clearing services offered by banks/brokers for OTC, non-electronic exchange or AEV trades ultimately depends on various factors; the most important are the

---

[119] Cf. Eurex (ed.) (2003a), p. 32.   [120] Cf. EACH (ed.) (2004c), p. 2.
[121] For details on the structure of the Value Provision Network, refer to section 2.3.
[122] Cf. NERA Economic Consulting (ed.) (2004), p. 9; and Linciano/Siciliano/Trovatore (2005), p. 4.
[123] Bank for International Settlements (ed.) (2001), p. 37.

characteristics of the traded products (e.g. level of standardisation, traded volumes, etc.) as well as the particularities of the banks'/brokers' business (such as total volumes processed, type of customers, etc.). Whereas banks/brokers might offer basic, value-added and complementary clearing services for trades executed in OTC markets, on a non-electronic exchange or an AEV, they do not provide unique CCP services.

The CCP model differs from a bilateral or decentralised market in which participants retain credit exposures to their trading counterparties (or their guarantors) until the transaction is complete.[124] In a bilateral market, each counterparty has a legal relationship with as well as a separate gross exposure to each of its counterparties.[125] Although the scope of netting and risk management services offered by a bank/broker does not include the unique benefits associated with a CCP structure,[126] they provide important value by offering unique banking services[127] and complementary clearing services. Finally, when banks/brokers are members of a CCP, they often perform complementary clearing services for their proprietary and customer trades.

2.1.4 Institutional view

The institutional view focuses on the institutional characteristics of clearing. These can take a variety of forms. The two most typical are clearing houses organised as departments or subsidiaries of their affiliated exchange(s) or operating as independent entities (see Figure 2.8).

A clearing house organised as a department of its affiliated exchange(s) is said to be 'vertically integrated'.[128] Vertical integration is the process whereby exchange organisations consolidate the activities that take place at various points in the value chain, such as the integration of trading, clearing and settlement services within a single entity or group of entities.[129]

So-called 'horizontal clearing' or 'horizontal integration', on the other hand, refers to separate ownership and operation of exchanges, clearing houses and

---

[124] Cf. Hills *et al.* (1999), p. 122.   [125] Cf. Hills *et al.* (1999), p. 124.

[126] With bilateral netting, two counterparties agree to net with one another. They sign a master agreement specifying the types of netting to be performed as well as the existing and future contracts that will be affected. Whereas banks/brokers commonly offer bilateral netting in the OTC derivatives markets, they are unable to offer the unique benefits of multilateral netting provided by a CCP.

[127] As outlined in section 2.1.2.2, some treasury management services require a banking licence and are thus not provided by all CCPs.

[128] Cf. Hart/Russo/Schönenberger (2002), p. 29; Rochet (2005), p. 2; and Direction Générale du Trésor et de la Politique Économique (ed.) (2006), p. 7.

[129] Cf. London Economics (ed.) (2005), pp. 9 and 13; Wright (2005), p. 9; and Lambe (2005), p. 18. An organisation integrated in this way is often also referred to as a 'vertical silo'.

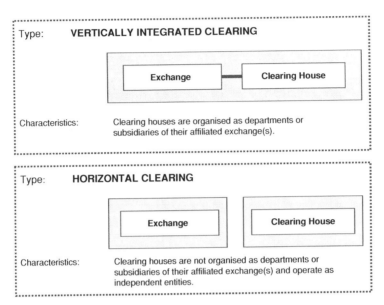

Figure 2.8   Institutional view on clearing
Source: Author's own.

settlement institutions.[130] Horizontally integrated clearing houses operate as independent legal entities. Horizontal integration serves to consolidate entities that perform the same functions, i.e. providing trading, clearing or settlement services. Horizontally integrated clearing houses are typically governed by the exchanges for which they provide clearing services and/or their (largest) clearing members. Clearing houses whose members have a stake in or control the ownership or governance of a CCP are classified as user-owned or user-governed.

Finally, some clearing houses provide services to only one exchange; others serve a group of exchanges.[131] Despite these organisational differences, clearing houses typically have a core set of common features.[132] Although the clearing house does not make the rules and regulations pertaining to carrying out transactions, it does establish the rules for clearing, in accordance with the regulatory requirements and the exchange specifications.

There has been an ongoing discussion regarding the general benefits, drawbacks and preferability of horizontal over vertical integration. Refer to section 2.5 for details on this debate.

---

[130] Cf. Direction Générale du Trésor et de la Politique Économique (ed.) (2006), p. 7.
[131] Cf. Bank for International Settlements (ed.) (1997a), p. 11.
[132] Cf. Bank for International Settlements (ed.) (1997a), p. 11.

2.2 Value-added of CCP clearing

The benefits of clearing, particularly risk mitigation and increased efficiency, are appreciated by our clients and will create substantial benefits to the marketplace as a whole. Marco Strimer (CEO SIS x-clear).[133]

This section outlines why CCP clearing has become such an integral part of modern clearing services;[134] it now forms a core part of the financial market infrastructure in most developed economies.[135] Its benefits and limitations are described from three vantage points. From a microeconomic perspective (section 2.2.1), CCPs provide benefits and value-added for individual market participants. In macroeconomic terms (section 2.2.2), clearing plays a vital role by facilitating the smooth and frictionless functioning of capital markets, thus increasing their efficiency. Finally, the asset class view revisits the benefits of CCPs for securities and derivatives markets (section 2.2.3).

2.2.1 Microeconomic view

The services offered by CCPs translate into a number of benefits to market participants:[136]

- trading benefits;
- risk reduction;
- capital efficiency;
- balance sheet benefits;
- operational efficiency; and
- settlement benefits.

These benefits result from the services performed by a CCP; their effects are briefly summarised in the following. As outlined in section 2.1.2.2, CCP clearing helps to maintain anonymity through novation, if the trade execution process itself is anonymous. This is a valuable service for market participants who fear a market impact as a result of their trading activities.[137] Remaining anonymous is also preferable to firms that do not want to reveal that they are large sellers or buyers[138] or that they are active in a particular market.

---

[133] SWX Swiss Exchange (ed.) (03.03.2006).   [134] Cf. Ripatti (2004), p. 4.
[135] Cf. Knott/Mills (2002), p. 162.
[136] Cf. Deutsche Börse Group (ed.) (10.02.2003); Wright (2004), SWX Swiss Exchange (ed.) (03.03.2006); Kroszner (2006); and Tumpel-Gugerell (2006).
[137] Cf. Ripatti (2004), p. 12. Also refer to Hachmeister/Schiereck (2006) for an analysis of the impact of post-trade anonymity on liquidity and informed trading in an order-driven market.
[138] Cf. Hills et al. (1999), p. 125.

Furthermore, due to the reallocation of counterparty risk to the CCP, market participants can trade without having to assess the creditworthiness of the original counterparty to a trade.[139] As novation entails exposure to a standard credit risk, the associated credit monitoring and collateral management processes become less complex, which in turn reduces legal as well as operational costs.[140] Market participants also benefit from novation in that it enables open interest (derivatives) to be centrally held, thus facilitating the close-out of open positions.[141]

Netting and risk management services also furnish trading benefits by reducing the amount of capital that is tied up at the clearing house. These services free up resources, credit lines and cash flow and increase the volume of business that can be supported on a given capital base.[142] Netting enables the efficient use of capital, because each outstanding position generates a need for capital, margin or collateral. Reducing the number of outstanding positions thus translates into diminished costs of capital.[143] The offsetting of all gross positions against each other so that all outstanding positions are converted into a single debit or credit between the CCP and another party[144] also offers higher levels of automation, which helps to minimise operational costs.[145]

The **risk management** services performed by a CCP offer a number of benefits, such as the mutualisation of all or part of the risk of default,[146] centralised and transparent risk management and continuous exposure monitoring (including the revaluation of positions on a daily or intra-daily basis using mark-to-market). Posting margin on net positions reduces opportunity costs to users and entails balance sheet benefits by enabling a more efficient use of collateral.[147] Mark-to-market and collateralisation disciplines also create savings at the operational level, free up credit lines and reduce collateral

---

[139] Cf. Hills *et al.* (1999), p. 126; Ripatti (2004), p. 12; and Mogford (2005), pp. 34–7.
[140] Cf. Murawski (2002), p. 3; and LCH.Clearnet (ed.) (2003a), p. 31.   [141] Cf. Book (2001), p. 62.
[142] Cf. LCH.Clearnet (ed.) (2003a), p. 29; and Bliss/Kaufman (2005), p. 11.
[143] Cf. Hardy (2004), p. 58.   [144] Cf. Van Cayseele/Wuyts (2005), p. 3.
[145] Cf. Bressand/Distler (2001), p. 4.   [146] Cf. Moskow (2006).
[147] 'While use of a CCP has no impact on losses arising from market risk, it can reduce the potential for losses arising from credit and operational risk. Use of a CCP offers two credit exposure enhancements. First, it facilitates multilateral exposure netting, which typically reduces overall credit exposure. Secondly, it consolidates bilateral exposures into a single low risk exposure with the CCP. The effects of the reduced credit exposure can be seen on both sides of the balance sheet. The absolute value of exposure to trading counterparties falls on the asset side of the balance sheet, while the allocation of capital to support those assets falls on the liability side. It follows that the increase in revenue arising from a reduction in expected credit losses (and lower operational costs) divided by the reduction in capital necessary to support unexpected credit losses will lead to an improvement in return on capital. When the opportunity cost of the capital released in this way is taken into account, the increased net profit will also show an improved risk-adjusted return on capital (RAROC). Firms may also elect to retain the released capital and thereby improve their credit standing, resulting in the reduction of funding costs and increased

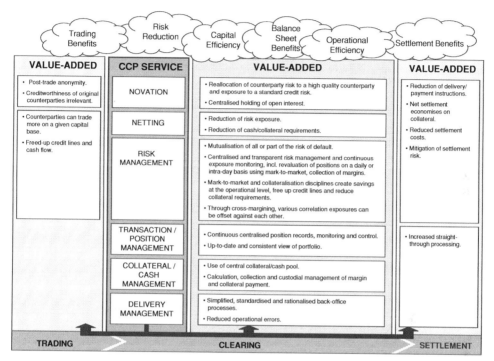

Figure 2.9   Microeconomic benefits of CCP clearing
Source: Author's own.

requirements.[148] Finally, cross-margining allows various correlation exposures to be offset against each other; through the use of a central pool of collateral, the amount of tied-up capital at the clearing facility is reduced.[149]

Additional benefits are offered through sophisticated **transaction/position management**, which allows for continuous centralised position records, monitoring and control as well as an up-to-date and consistent view of the portfolio. Simplified, standardised and rationalised back-office processes result from the use of a central **collateral/cash** pool and the calculation, collection and custodial management of margin and collateral payment;[150] **delivery management**

client trading volume, making a different but equally significant contribution to profitability. Improved reserves can also assist in maintaining or enhancing credit ratings.' LCH.Clearnet (ed.) (2003a), p. 30.

[148] Cf. LCH.Clearnet (ed.) (2003a), p. 31.
[149] Cross-margining could, for example, also further allow traders to use positive cash flow generated in the futures market to cover losses in the equity market and accrued profits on equity options to reduce margin required on offsetting futures positions. Cf. Dale (1998a), p. 25. Also refer to Parkinson *et al.* (1992), p. 184.
[150] Cf. LCH.Clearnet (ed.) (2003a), p. 29.

services offer many of the same benefits. By standardising processes, documentation and systems as well as processing trades through a single channel, STP can be increased and operational errors reduced.[151]

Finally, CCP services result in settlement benefits. A considerable reduction in the value and volume of trades eligible for settlement can be achieved by netting.[152] The reduced number of delivery/payment instructions translates into lower settlement costs[153] and a reduced administrative burden.[154] Additionally, the adoption of procedures like 'delivery versus payment' (DVP) mitigates settlement risk.[155]

Not all markets are necessarily suitable for central counterparty clearing. Its potential benefits come at a cost and it is simply not available in some markets.[156] The trade-off between potential costs and benefits to market participants determines the suitability of a CCP for a given market.[157] This balance depends on factors such as the volume and value of transactions, trading patterns among counterparties, the characteristics of the traded goods, the credit quality of market participants and the opportunity costs associated with settlement liquidity.

2.2.2 Macroeconomic view

Clearing and settlement systems are critical to the stability of the financial system, a system that is increasingly interconnected and global in scope.[158]

Central counterparty clearing creates value-added not only for individual market participants, but for capital markets as a whole. 'Central Counterparties are among the crucial building blocks of any well-organised financial system. They facilitate the allocation of resources and their deployment within a financial system.'[159] The following section briefly explains how the efficiency of capital markets can be affected by CCPs.[160] CCPs impact the allocation of

---

[151] Cf. DTCC (ed.) (2000a), p. 4.
[152] Cf. Milne (2002), p. 6. Net settlement systems can also economise on collateral; in situations where collateral is needed to effect settlement, a net settlement system may require less collateral than a gross settlement system. Cf. Kahn/McAndrews/Roberds (1999), pp. 27–31. Green (1997) shows that a net settlement system can improve welfare by allowing agents' original obligations to be replaced with a set of enforceable net claims.
[153] Cf. Bressand/Distler (2001), p. 4; and Hardy (2004), p. 58.
[154] Cf. LCH.Clearnet (ed.) (2003a), p. 29.   [155] Cf. Moskow (2006).
[156] Cf. Hills et al. (1999), p. 123; Lee (2000), p. 35; Bank for International Settlements (ed.) (2001), p. 11; Ripatti (2004), p. 8; and Moskow (2006).
[157] Cf. DTCC (ed.) (2000b), p. 1.   [158] Bliss/Steigerwald (2006), p. 22.
[159] Blattner (2003), p. 1.
[160] Efficient capital markets are both allocationally and operationally efficient. In an allocationally efficient market, scarce savings are optimally allocated to productive investments in a way that benefits the

risk and capital and can positively influence market liquidity; these aspects are detailed in the following.[161]

2.2.2.1 Allocation of risk

Whereas the CCP structure offers significant benefits and risk-reducing attributes,[162] the funnelling of market activity through one institution concentrates risk as well as the responsibility for risk management.[163] By definition, CCPs have a higher concentration of risk than the single participants of a decentralised market. This concentration poses both advantages and dangers for capital markets.

A CCP itself does not remove credit risk from a market; rather, it re-allocates counterparty risk, replacing a firm's exposure to bilateral credit risk (of variable quality) with the standard credit risk of the CCP.[164] As outlined above, CCPs thus enable market participants to trade without having to worry about the creditworthiness of individual counterparties.[165] Due to novation, CCPs can manage and redistribute counterparty credit risk more efficiently than individual market participants.[166] Moreover, multilateral netting performed by a CCP substantially reduces the potential losses in the event of participant default[167] and permits the size of the credit risk exposures to grow at lower rates than the market as a whole.[168] Pooling risk management facilities at the CCP further benefits capital markets through risk management specialisation effects: it is more efficient to have one party collect the information and monitor the other parties rather than having all parties monitor each other.[169]

One potential threat associated with high risk concentration in markets is that an unsuitable system configuration or weak supervision will have a higher impact on the market than the deficiencies of any one participant. Faulty CCP risk management has the potential to severely disrupt the markets as well as other components of the settlement systems for instruments traded in the respective markets. These disruptions could spill over into payment systems and other settlement systems and negatively influence the stability

---

market as a whole. Operational efficiency is achieved if the costs for transferring funds are minimised. Cf. Copeland/Weston (1998), pp. 330–31. Refer to section 3.1 for more details.

[161] Also refer to McPartland (2005) regarding the question of how clearing systems support a sound financial system.

[162] Cf. Competition Commission (ed.) (2005), p. 27.

[163] Cf. Hanley/McCann/Moser (1996), p. 1; and Knott/Mills (2002), p. 163.

[164] Cf. Hills et al. (1999), p. 126.   [165] Cf. Russo/Terol (2000), p. 8; and Ripatti (2004), p. 12.

[166] Cf. Ripatti (2004), p. 12.   [167] Cf. Bank for International Settlements (ed.) (2001), p. 11.

[168] Cf. Bliss/Kaufman (2005), p. 11.

[169] Cf. Dale (1998b), p. 296. Also refer to Diamond (1984) for an analysis of delegated monitoring by a financial intermediary.

of a financial market.[170] The effectiveness of a CCP's risk management and sufficient levels of financial resources are therefore crucial for the stability of the markets, which are served by the CCP infrastructure.[171] The CCP's design will ultimately determine its ability to withstand market disruptions, which may carry systemic implications.[172] Consequently, a CCP's ability to monitor and control the credit, liquidity, legal and operational risks it incurs as well as to absorb losses is essential for the sound functioning of the markets it serves.

2.2.2.2 Allocation of capital

Clearing service provision can also positively impact the allocation of capital within markets. The services of netting and cross-margining provided by a CCP minimise the amount of collateral that has to be deposited at the clearing house for risk management purposes. The level of capital required to support risk management is therefore optimised. This results in balance sheet benefits for investors, which enhances the overall market quality. These benefits include an increased return on capital via cost reduction and improved credit standing (firms may elect to retain the released capital and thereby improve their credit standing).[173] When the level of capital required to support risk management is optimised, counterparties can execute more trades on a given capital base.[174] Since equity capital is relatively expensive and collateral is scarce, this can have a positive effect on the size of the market as well as the size of counterparties in the market.[175]

2.2.2.3 Market liquidity

CCPs can contribute to a market's liquidity by ensuring post-trade anonymity,[176] 'keeping the cost of trade completion as low as possible',[177]

---

[170] Cf. Knott/Mills (2002), p. 164. Whether the fact that a CCP serves multiple markets results in serious systemic consequences in the event of a risk management failure is, nonetheless, a matter of debate, and has neither been proved nor disproved in reality. As such, a CCP has the potential to either reduce or increase the systemic risk in a market. For more details refer to Gemmill (1994); Corrigan (1996); Labrecque (1996); Dale (1998a); Hills et al. (1999); Knott/Mills (2002); and Iori (2004). Regarding the question of whether the globalisation of financial markets has changed the nature and potential vulnerability of the financial system to systemic risk, refer to Eisenbeis (1997). Fortunately, CCP failures have been extremely rare, although the examples of Paris in 1973, Kuala Lumpur in 1983 and Hong Kong in 1987 demonstrate that they can occur. Refer to Hills et al. (1999) for further details.

[171] Cf. Knott/Mills (2002), p. 172; and Bank for International Settlements (ed.) (2004), p. 1.

[172] Cf. Hanley/McCann/Moser (1996), p. 1.   [173] Cf. Ripatti (2004), p. 10.

[174] Cf. Bliss/Kaufman (2005), p. 11.

[175] Cf. Bliss/Kaufman (2005), p. 10. For more details on the impact of netting and CCPs on the allocation of capital, refer to: Green (1997); and Kahn/McAndrews/Roberds (1999).

[176] For more details on the effect of post-trade anonymity on liquidity, refer to Hachmeister/Schiereck (2006).

[177] Bernanke (1990), p. 140.

reducing risks to its participants[178] and providing multilateral netting.[179] Through novation, a CCP creates more certainty in trading.[180] With lower counterparty risk and an optimised level of capital created by multilateral netting, market participants using a CCP may be encouraged to trade more and establish larger positions.[181] The effects on liquidity can be substantial, especially if the size of the counterparty exposures is actually a limiting factor for trade, although this need not always be the case.[182] The positive effects of risk redistribution become more evident when the market is turbulent and risks increase:[183] in volatile markets, participants might stop trading. Some of those who cease trading during times of market turbulence would probably have continued had they had a known and secure counterparty to trade with. A central counterparty can thus contribute to more stable market liquidity.

On the other hand, CCPs can also have a negative impact on a market's liquidity if exorbitant margin requirements are imposed or if the financial integrity of a clearing house is in question. Empirical evidence suggests that exorbitant margins can have a detrimental effect on market activity.[184] A dilemma for clearing houses in setting margins is how to balance prudence against the higher cost to members – the challenge for CCPs is to set the initial margin at a level sufficient to provide protection against all but the most extreme price moves, but not so high as to damage market liquidity or discourage the use of the CCP.[185]

2.2.3 Asset class view

Trades executed in securities or derivatives markets possess different particularities and dynamics; the markets themselves also have unique characteristics. The following section provides a brief overview of the value-added of CCPs for securities versus derivatives markets (see Figure 2.10).

As outlined above, CCPs have traditionally played a more significant role in derivatives than in securities markets, because the latter particularly demands

---

[178] Cf. Kroszner (2000), p. 6.
[179] Cf. Bank for International Settlements (ed.) (2004), p. 1; and Citigroup (ed.) (2006), p. 1.
[180] Cf. Moser (1998), p. 7; and Ripatti (2004), p. 5.
[181] Cf. Hills *et al.* (1999), p. 125; Knott/Mills (2002), p. 164; LCH.Clearnet (ed.) (2003a), p. 29; Ripatti (2004), p. 28; and Bliss/Kaufman (2005), p. 11. As a result of established practice, or in some cases regulations, market participants often limit their trading volumes to a certain percentage of their balance sheet. In these cases, the netting effect increases the participants' scope for action. Cf. Riksbank (ed.) (2002), p. 50.
[182] Cf. Riksbank (ed.) (2002), p. 52.   [183] Cf. Riksbank (ed.) (2002), p. 51.
[184] Cf. Telser (1981), p. 252; and Knott/Mills (2002), p. 166. Additional studies on the effect of margins on trading include Fishe/Goldberg (1986); Hartzmark (1986); Kalavathi/Shanker (1991); and Hardouvelis/Kim (1995).
[185] Cf. Kahl/Rutz/Sinquefield (1985), p. 107; and Knott/Mills (2002), pp. 166–7.

ASSET CLASS	TRADE AND MARKET CHARACTERISTICS	COUNTERPARTIES' INTEREST	CCPs' VALUE-ADDED
SECURITIES	Immediacy of Trade Lifecycle	• Minimise settlement cycle at lowest cost. • Reduce cash/collateral requirements.	• Increased straight-through processing (STP). • Netting, margining.
	Settlement Risk	• Mitigate settlement risk. • Reduce operational costs and risks.	• Netting, margining. • Delivery management.
	Large Number of Small Counterparties	• Exposure to high quality counterparties.	• Novation.
	Increasing TurnOver Ratio	• Reduce settlement instructions. • Optimise use of collateral. • Post-trade anonymity.	• Netting. • Margining, cash/collateral management. • Novation.
	Increasing Cross-Border Trades	• Reduce intermediary costs. • Minimise settlement cycle. • Reduce errors due to manual intervention.	• Netting. • Increased STP. • Delivery, cash/collateral management.
DERIVATIVES	Time Lag between Execution and Settlement	• Eliminate counterparty risk. • Manage risk of price fluctuations (replacement cost risk). • Possibility for close-out prior to maturity/expiration of contract. • Continuous position monitoring and control. • Reduce delivery errors.	• Novation. • Margining. • Centralised holding of open interest. • Transaction and risk management. • Facilitation of STP, delivery management.
	Large Exposures	• Control and limit exposures. • Eliminate counterparty credit risk. • Sophisticated risk management.	• Netting, margining. • Novation. • Risk management.
	Collateral Intense	• Reduce cash/collateral requirements. • Free up credit lines. • Efficient cash/collateral management.	• Netting, margining. • Risk management. • Cash/collateral management.
	High Volume Global Growth Market	• Post-trade anonymity. • Optimise use of cash/collateral. • Simplify, standardise and rationalise back-office processes. • Reduce operational errors.	• Novation. • Netting, margining, risk management. • Cash/collateral management. • Delivery management.

Figure 2.10   Asset class view on the value-added of CCP clearing
Source: Author's own.

efficient risk reduction. Securities transactions are processed and settled as fast as technological, legal and regulatory restrictions will allow; the time frame usually consists of a few days.[186] Because these transactions only remain with the clearing house for a relatively short period of time,[187] the need for risk management and transaction monitoring and management is relatively modest. Once a securities trade has been executed, the primary objective is to fulfil the legal obligations as immediately, efficiently and securely as possible, optimising the use of collateral required for securing the trade. The focus has therefore traditionally been on settlement rather than on clearing. The main value-added of CCPs in the context of securities processing is doubtlessly their

---

[186] Cf. Bliss/Steigerwald (2006), p. 23.
[187] The time lag between the trade execution (T) and the settlement date is commonly referred to as the 'settlement cycle'. The settlement cycle is measured relative to the trade date, i.e. if settlement occurs on the third business day following T, the settlement cycle is referred to as T + 3. Cf. Bank for International Settlements (ed.) (2001), p. 49.

provision of netting services and facilitation of STP. Furthermore, given that securities markets in most developed countries are characterised by a large number of small counterparties, an increasing turnover ratio[188] and a growing number of cross-border trades (which reflects the increasing integration of global markets), the CCPs' additional services provide important value-added for the counterparties (see Figure 2.10 for details).[189]

By contrast, the fulfilment of the legal obligation in derivatives trading can be a matter of much longer time frames – months and years rather than days.[190] Large unsettled exposures may consequently build up between counterparties,[191] which underscores the need for enhanced risk management.[192] CCPs were therefore originally established to protect market participants from counterparty risk in exchange-traded derivatives markets.[193] The elimination of counterparty risk through novation, as well as the benefits of netting, margining, sophisticated risk management and position control through a CCP, is thus highly advantageous. Derivatives markets further benefit from the centralised holding and management of open interest at a clearing house, which allows for the fungibility of products and enhances liquidity.[194] Closing out positions prior to maturity is often attractive, particularly in futures markets, where the purpose of the trade is to take on price risk rather than to receive or deliver the underlying instrument.[195] In securities markets, on the other hand, market participants are typically keen to obtain or deliver the underlying instrument.[196] The actual fulfilment of the legal obligation, i.e. the delivery or purchase of the underlying, can therefore be avoided in derivatives markets.[197] Only the profit or loss arising from the difference between the entry and exit price remains.[198] Closing out can stimulate the market to expand further.[199] The multilateral netting provided by CCPs has had an important impact on the structure of derivatives markets. In fact, without the services provided by CCPs, the current large size, liquidity and concentration of the worldwide exchange-traded derivatives markets would likely not exist.[200]

---

[188] The turnover ratio refers to the time required to circulate a given volume of securities.
[189] Cf. Bank for International Settlements (ed.) (2001), p. 1; and Lannoo/Levin (2003), p. 5.
[190] Of course, the time lag is minimal when day traders engage in derivatives trades, because they close-out all of their open positions at the end of each trading day.
[191] Cf. Knott/Mills (2002), p. 162.   [192] Cf. Riksbank (ed.) (2002), p. 48.
[193] Cf. Knott/Mills (2002), p. 162; and Ripatti (2004), p. 4.
[194] Cf. Bank for International Settlements (ed.) (1998), p. 9.
[195] Cf. Hills *et al.* (1999), p. 125.   [196] Cf. Hills *et al.* (1999), p. 125.
[197] Cf. Eurex (ed.) (2003b), p. 11.   [198] Cf. Eurex (ed.) (2003b), p. 11.
[199] Cf. Bliss/Kaufman (2005), p. 8.   [200] Cf. Bliss/Kaufman (2005), p. 8.

2.3 The Value Provision Network

Clearing services are usually offered in a tiered structure.[201] This section explains the structural set-up of the clearing industry, including the different layers of access to the market infrastructure. For the purpose of this study, this network, i.e. the clearing house and its customers, both direct (the 'clearing members') and indirect (the 'non-clearing members', which only have access to the clearing house through clearing members), is referred to as the Value Provision Network (VPN). The structure of the VPN is presented first (section 2.3.1), and then the different types of clearing member are identified and categorised (section 2.3.2).

2.3.1 Structure of the Value Provision Network

The fact that CCPs only grant membership to a subset of market participants accounts for the tiered structure of clearing service provision.[202] Consequently, not every trading member on an exchange is also a clearing member of the respective clearing house. By exercising selectivity, the clearing house ensures that direct participation in the clearing process is only granted to the most creditworthy subset of market participants. The practice lends the VPN its two-tiered structure. The first level comprises the clearing house and market participants with direct access to the CCP; the second level involves participants with indirect access, i.e. those requiring the use of an intermediary (see Figure 2.11). The research focus of this study is on the first level of the VPN.

The group of market participants occupying the **first level of the VPN** enjoys direct access to a clearing house and is commonly referred to as 'clearing member' (CMs), clearers or clearing firms.[203] There are two categories of clearing members:[204] general clearing members and individual clearing members. A general clearing member (GCM) is allowed to clear its own transactions (proprietary activity) as well as those of its customers and exchange participants not holding a clearing licence (agency activity). An exchange participant that does not hold a clearing licence is referred to as a non-clearing member

---

[201] Cf. Bank for International Settlements (ed.) (1997a), p. 12; and Hart/Russo/Schönenberger (2002), p. 13.
[202] Cf. Bank for International Settlements (ed.) (2004), p. 7; and Deutsche Börse Group (ed.) (2005a), p. 34.
[203] Cf. Loader (2005), p. 35.
[204] Variations of these two types of clearing member may exist.

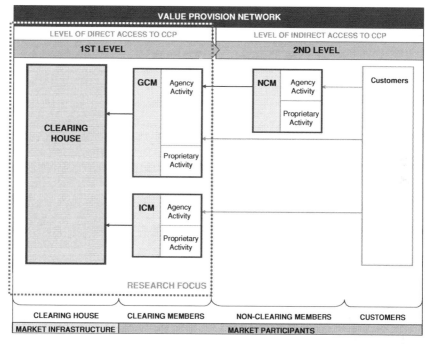

Figure 2.11   The Value Provision Network of clearing
Source: Author's own.

(NCM). An individual clearing member (ICM), on the other hand, is qualified to clear its own (proprietary activity) and its customers' transactions (agency activity), but it is not allowed to provide clearing services to NCMs.

Clearing members must comply with the various membership requirements set by the clearing house (regarding minimum net capital, regulatory authorisation requirements, fulfilment of additional operational requirements, etc.). The broader the scope of the clearing membership, the more stringent the membership requirements generally are: applicants for the GCM status must therefore, for example, comply with higher net capital requirements than ICM applicants.[205]

Within the **second level of the VPN**, market participants have no direct access to the clearing house. So-called non-clearing members are members of the clearing house's affiliated exchange(s), but do not hold a clearing

---

[205] For details on the legal relationships between CCPs and clearing members as well as regulatory issues regarding CCPs, refer to Huang (2006), pp. 117–95.

licence. NCMs may either not be eligible for or may not desire direct membership in the CCP.[206] NCMs must therefore become customers of a GCM to effect clearing.[207] The GCM consequently acts as the NCM's clearing intermediary.[208] The second level of the VPN also comprises other customers, i.e. individuals or firms that are not members of the clearing house's affiliated exchange(s).[209]

To summarise, clearing members and non-clearing members alike can engage in agency activity or proprietary (prop.) activity. Agency activity refers to services provided to NCMs and customers, whereas prop. activity refers to servicing one's own transactions. From the perspective of a GCM, agency activity comprises servicing the individuals and firms that are not members of the clearing house's affiliated exchange(s) as well as NCMs. From the perspective of an ICM, agency activity is limited to servicing the individuals and firms that are not members of the clearing house's affiliated exchange(s). An NCM, on the other hand, can only provide trade execution services to individuals and firms that are not exchange members; to clear the trades, it has to establish a relationship with a GCM.

2.3.2 Clearing member types

In most markets, tiered relationships that are often varied and complex have developed between the firms that provide clearing and the ultimate parties trading in the market.[210]

As the research focus of this study is on the first level of the VPN, this section identifies and groups different types of clearing members according to their business focus. Consequently, for the purpose of this research, clearing

---

[206] Cf. BNP Paribas Securities Services (ed.) (2005), p. 6.

[207] Cf. Bank for International Settlements (ed.) (1997a), p. 1; and Hart/Russo/Schönenberger (2002), p. 13.

[208] Non-clearing members are often exposed to counterparty credit risk vis-à-vis their GCM and vice versa. Where many market participants rely on the same GCM, counterparty risk and responsibility for risk management may be concentrated to a significant degree in that clearing member. Thus, a risk management failure perpetrated by such a GCM could have effects similar to a risk management failure by a CCP. Cf. Bank for International Settlements (ed.) (2004), p. 7.

[209] When such a non-member of the exchange (e.g. a retail client) executes a trade: 'the clearing of that trade can take place through different paths . . . The retail client might choose to have its trade executed by a firm that is a clearing firm; the trade might then be executed and cleared through that one firm. Alternatively, the retail client might desire to have its trade executed by a non-clearing exchange member. That firm would be able to provide trade execution services to the client, but it would have established a relationship with a member of the clearing house for the provision of clearing services.' (Bank for International Settlements (ed.) (1997a), p. 12).

[210] Bank for International Settlements (ed.) (1997a), p. 12.

	PROP. FOCUS ICMs/GCMs	AGENCY FOCUS ICMs/GCMs
REGIONAL FOCUS (LOW VOL. CLEARER) Typical: 3rd Tier Players	CM_{PR}	CM_{AR}
REGIONAL-TO-GLOBAL FOCUS (MEDIUM VOL. CLEARER) Typical: 2nd Tier Players	CM_{PR-G}	CM_{AR-G}
GLOBAL FOCUS (HIGH VOL. CLEARER) Typical: 1st Tier Players	CM_{PG}	CM_{AG}

Figure 2.12   Typical clearing member types classified by their business focus
Source: Author's own.

members are distinguished according to the following characteristics: those whose activity has a 'regional focus', a 'regional-to-global focus' or a 'global focus'. In each case, the member can focus its business on prop. or agency transactions (see Figure 2.12).[211] The analyses conducted in the remainder of this study are performed according to this classification. It thus remains to be seen whether the different clearing member types are asymmetrically affected by the various network strategies.

In reality, most clearing members engage in both agency and prop. activity. In this case, the two activity types refer to the main revenue-contributing areas within the firm. In large investment banks, both areas can be important sources of revenue. Whether or not this results in areas of conflict is subject to further analysis. Classification according to these two focus areas ultimately results in the differentiation of six clearing member types:

- regionally active clearing members with a prop. focus (CM_{PR});
- regionally active clearing members with an agency focus (CM_{AR});
- regionally-to-globally active clearing members with a prop. focus (CM_{PR-G});
- regionally-to-globally active clearing members with an agency focus (CM_{AR-G});
- globally active clearing members with a prop. focus (CM_{PG}); and
- globally active clearing members with an agency focus (CM_{AG}).

A **regionally active** clearing member (CM_{PR}/CM_{AR}) is defined as a clearer whose focus of activity lies within its regional home market. This kind of

[211] The identification of these three broad categories is broadly consistent with the system used by the London Investment Banking Association (LIBA) to differentiate firms active in settlement. Cf. LIBA (ed.) (2004), p. 6.

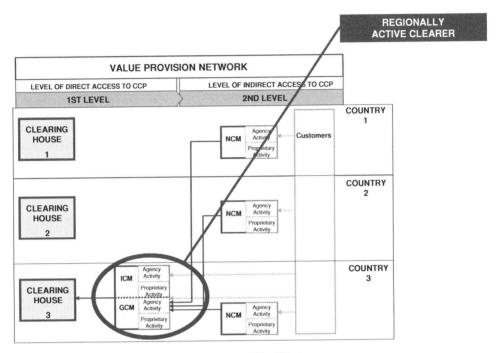

Figure 2.13   Classification of regionally active clearers (CM$_{PR}$/CM$_{AR}$)
Source: Author's own.

clearing member maintains a single clearing membership, which is with its domestic clearing house (see Figure 2.13). Regionally focused clearing members are assumed to have no interest in being active in any additional (foreign) markets or products. A regionally focused clearer can be a GCM or an ICM, with either a prop. or an agency focus. When a regionally active clearing member acts as an ICM, other domestic and/or non-domestic customers can use this clearer as an intermediary to the domestic clearing house. When a regionally active clearing member acts as a GCM, other domestic and/or non-domestic NCMs and/or other customers can use this clearer as an intermediary to the domestic clearing house.

On the other hand, **regionally-to-globally active** clearing members (CM$_{PR-G}$/CM$_{AR-G}$) are defined as being active (or interested in becoming active) in many markets. Clearing members with a regional-to-global focus maintain a single direct clearing membership, which is with their domestic clearing house (see Figure 2.14), while acting as NCMs in other (foreign) markets. To clear their transactions in these other (foreign) markets, these clearers utilise one or several other GCMs as clearing intermediaries. Within

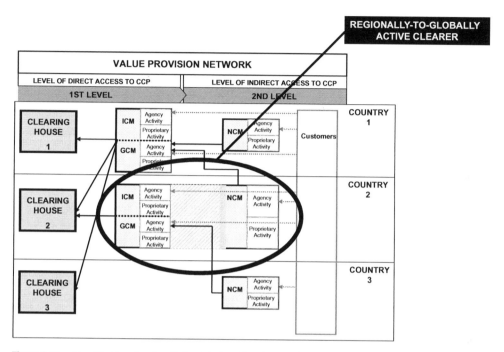

Figure 2.14   Classification of regionally-to-globally active clearers (CM$_{PR-G}$/CM$_{AR-G}$)
Source: Author's own.

its domestic home market, the regionally focused clearer can be a GCM or an ICM, with either a prop. or an agency focus. When a regionally-to-globally active clearing member acts as an ICM, other domestic and/or non-domestic customers can use this clearer as an intermediary to the domestic clearing house and to other CCPs to which the clearer is indirectly connected. When this type of clearing member acts as a GCM, other domestic and/or non-domestic NCMs and/or other customers can employ it as an intermediary to the domestic clearing house and to other CCPs to which the clearer is indirectly connected.

Finally, **globally active** clearing members (CM$_{PG}$/CM$_{AG}$) are defined as being active in all of the world's major financial markets, with direct access to each of the many clearing houses. The globally active clearer can assume the role of a GCM or an ICM of the respective clearing houses, with either a prop. or an agency focus. The globally active clearer holds a direct clearing membership with all of the major clearing houses, because its core value proposition is single access to many markets. When it acts as a GCM, other domestic and/or non-domestic NCMs and/or other customers can use it as an

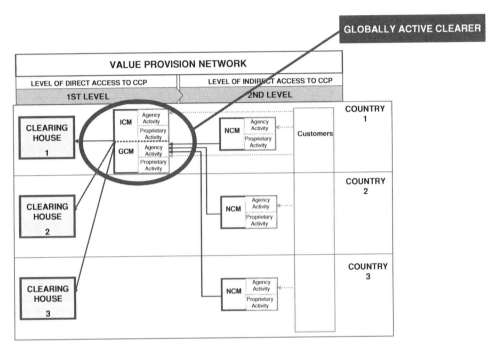

Figure 2.15   Classification of globally active clearers (CM_{PG}/CM_{AG})
Source: Author's own.

intermediary to the domestic clearing house and to all other CCPs to which the clearer is directly connected. When a globally active clearing member acts as an ICM, other domestic and/or non-domestic customers can use this clearer as an intermediary to the domestic clearing house and to other CCPs to which the clearer is directly connected.

The various clearing member types can be further classified with respect to the size of their business, i.e. its cleared market share within a defined economic area (e.g. Europe, the USA, etc.). For this purpose, three volume groups are defined, representing low, medium and high volume clearers. For the minimum and maximum market share associated with the different groups, see Figure 2.16.[212]

A regional focus of activity is typically associated with low volume clearing members, whereas a regional-to-global focus is considered characteristic for medium volume clearers. Globally active clearers are synonymous with high volume clearing members. For the purpose of this study, the

---

[212] The market share categorisation is based on information provided by Eurex Clearing AG. The final categories were further scrutinised by three interviewed experts.

	MINIMUM CLEARED MARKET SHARE		MAXIMUM CLEARED MARKET SHARE
LOW VOLUME CLEARER (REGIONAL FOCUS) Typical: 3rd Tier Players	0.01%	–	0.30%
MEDIUM VOLUME CLEARER (REGIONAL-to-GLOBAL FOCUS) Typical: 2nd Tier Players	0.31%	–	2.00%
HIGH VOLUME CLEARER (GLOBAL FOCUS) Typical: 1st Tier Players	2.01%	–	> 2.01%

Figure 2.16 Typical clearing member types classified by cleared market share
Source: Author's own.

focus of activity and the respective clearing volume level will be considered synonymous.[213]

2.4 Stakeholders in clearing

Clearing stakeholders comprise various groups with divergent interests that can sometimes lead to conflict. Stakeholders generally pursue either public or private interests. Those pursuing private interests include providers of clearing services, owners and other market infrastructure providers. Stakeholders pursuing public interests include regulators, policymakers and central banks.

Regulators pay attention to clearing issues in their efforts to strengthen the international financial infrastructure and reduce the financial sector's vulnerability to external shocks.[214] From the regulators' perspective, the massive advances in product design and risk allocation have heightened the threat of systemic risk.[215] Cross-border elements add even more complexity to risk

---

[213] In reality, clearing members do not always fit into the defined groups – the volume cleared by a clearing member with a global focus could, for example, classify it as a medium volume clearer rather than a high volume clearer. Nonetheless, for the purpose of simplicity and clarity, this research excludes such exceptions.

[214] Since the Barings collapse and the extraordinary expansion of derivatives markets worldwide, regulators have become concerned about risk management techniques regarding the clearing of exchange-traded derivatives, underlining the increasing systemic sensitivity of clearing procedures in this area. Cf. Hanley/McCann/Moser (1996), p. 1; and Dale (1998a), p. 6.

[215] Cf. Hanley/McCann/Moser (1996), p. 3; and Hart/Russo/Schönenberger (2002), p. 5.

management.[216] As the nature of CCPs' businesses grows increasingly complex due to expansion into new markets as well as more centralised by virtue of consolidation,[217] antitrust authorities are becoming concerned with the competitive situation of CCPs;[218] regulators are also taking careful note of the risks that clearing houses have to manage. For similar reasons, other financial market **policymakers** have convened to establish appropriate standards for the design, operation and oversight of CCPs.[219] 'In recent years, public policymakers have demonstrated growing interest and concern about the effectiveness of CCP risk management.'[220] As clearing houses are critical for the performance of the economy, public policymakers are striving to ensure that these systems function well when confronted by a variety of stresses.[221] **Central banks** have an interest in smoothly functioning clearing procedures for three reasons:[222] Firstly, CCPs can enhance financial stability when they are working properly. Secondly, links between CCPs operating in different countries can foster financial integration across borders. Thirdly, because clearing houses use payment systems and other infrastructures operated by central banks to carry out their activities,[223] rigorous management of the risks associated with multilateral clearing facilities is consequently of vital interest to central banks. Given their role as the lender of last resort, these banks are required to exercise vigilance in all areas that could threaten the viability of the world's financial markets.[224] Central banks therefore have a core interest in understanding the ways in which the increasing use of CCP services alter the distribution of risk as well as affect the likelihood of systemic risk within financial markets.[225] In addition, due to the potential impact a major disruption could have on two of their key responsibilities, the implementation of monetary policy and the smooth functioning of payment systems, central banks know the importance of smoothly functioning clearing for overall stability.[226]

Stakeholders pursuing private interests include the providers of clearing services (as outlined in section 2.1.3), owners, users (with either direct or indirect access to the CCP) and other market infrastructure providers such as marketplaces and settlement institutions. The roles and functions of the respective entities can overlap, i.e. providers can be both owners and users (which would be the case in a user-owned clearing house, i.e. a CCP owned

---

[216] Cf. Bank for International Settlements (ed.) (1997a), p. 5.
[217] Cf. Knott/Mills (2002), p. 172.   [218] Cf. European Commission (ed.) (2006a), p. 32.
[219] Cf. Moskow (2006).   [220] Kroszner (2006).   [221] Cf. Moskow (2006).
[222] Cf. Trichet (2006).   [223] Cf. Trichet (2006).
[224] Cf. Hanley/McCann/Moser (1996), p. 3.
[225] Cf. Hills et al. (1999), p. 122; Parkinson (2001), p. 28; and Tumpel-Gugerell (2006).
[226] Cf. Ripatti (2004), p. 22; and Trichet (2006).

by banks/brokers that are also clearing members of the CCP); or other market infrastructure providers can also assume the role of providers. This kind of overlap can result in divergent stakeholder interests and areas of conflict. **Providers** of clearing services generally strive to tailor their service and product offers to best meet the needs of their customers as well as fulfil their own strategic and business purposes. Their focus of attention and business strategy largely depends on their corporate and governance structures. **Owners** of clearing service providers can either be the providers themselves, such as banks/brokers or CSDs/ICSDs that provide clearing services, or some other third party. As outlined above, clearing houses are either horizontally or vertically integrated. A horizontally integrated clearing house, which is governed by its users, pursues the strategy that best supports the strategic and business purposes of its largest owners. A vertically integrated clearing house, on the other hand, generally adheres to the strategic and business needs of the respective exchange(s).

Users with direct access to the CCP represent an important stakeholder group in clearing. As outlined above, they can depend on clearing for their own proprietary activities as well as for their agency activities. Generally, the larger the volumes cleared by a direct member, the greater the stake the member has in the development of the clearing house. Clearing is of particular relevance for members with an agency focus, such as bankers/brokers, because it then becomes part of the clearer's own value proposition towards its customers. In this case, the provision of clearing services is of important strategic value to the positioning of the bank/broker. Clearing commissions provide an important source of revenue and can generate synergies in investment and operating expenses. Global (investment) banks, brokers and futures commission merchants (FCMs)[227] therefore represent a powerful group of stakeholders with a strong lobby for putting in their vote regarding the development of clearing.

Users with indirect access are also stakeholders in clearing in that they rely on the efficient and safe functioning of clearing to process their trades. Finally, other **market infrastructure providers**, such as marketplaces and settlement institutions, are stakeholders in clearing with heterogeneous interests. Exchange organisations or AEVs can be owners and/or rely on clearing service providers for the efficient and safe processing of their trades. As such, they are interested in receiving the best price with the lowest possible technical

---

[227] An FCM is, under US law, '[a]n individual or organization accepting orders to buy or sell futures or futures options.' www.investorwords.com. For details, see: Burns (2005); and Burns/Acworth (2006). Also refer to www.cftc.gov/opa/glossary/opaglossary_f.htm.

investments[228] and enhanced service quality. As owners, they are also interested in the efficiency and profitability of their vertically integrated institution. In such an integrated structure, the provision of clearing services is of important strategic value to the positioning of exchanges. Clearing fees provide additional revenue and generate synergies in investment and operating expenses.

CSDs/ICSDs can themselves be clearing providers and/or rely on other clearing service providers for efficient and safe trade processing and transmission of settlement instructions. The decision to add clearing to their services portfolio can have significant strategic value for all of these institutions with respect to their positioning in the industry. In addition, clearing fees provide additional revenue and generate synergies in investment and operating expenses.

The stakeholders' partly divergent interests can complicate their interaction and sometimes lead to conflicting goals, particularly between providers, owners and users of clearing services. When these different stakeholder groups overlap and owners, for example, also use a CCP, this can give rise to conflicting interests. Whilst owners usually strive to maximise return, users are interested in the lowest possible fees. Other areas of conflict result from the different types and roles of clearing service providers (see section 2.1.3). For example, a bank/broker can also be a clearing member of a CCP (and thus a user of clearing services) as well as being a provider of clearing services to other market participants. Conflicting goals can also exist within the different user groups, when, for example, banks have an equally great focus on clearing both their prop. and agency business. These areas of conflict and their impact on different integration and harmonisation initiatives in the clearing industry are further examined in the remainder of this study.

2.5 Current clearing industry structures

Practices and procedures concerning clearing and central counterparty services are currently undergoing a process of evolution in Europe and in the United States. These innovations present numerous challenges.[229]

Competing institutional structures coexist in the European and US clearing industries.[230] Some clearing houses are vertically integrated, whereas others

---

[228] Cf. Ripatti (2004), p. 27.   [229] Hart/Russo/Schönenberger (2002), p. 7.

[230] The focus of this study is on analysing the European clearing industry. An overview of the US clearing industry is included because any effort to integrate and harmonise the European clearing industry will ultimately be global in scope. Therefore, and because the US clearing industry is often referred to as

operate in horizontal structures. There has been an ongoing public discussion regarding the general benefits, drawbacks and preferability of horizontal over vertical integration.[231] Whereas vertical integration is seen to offer a number of benefits, it is not without potential drawbacks. Some of the commonly mentioned positive aspects include increased speed of processing due to reduced interfaces, increased safety, ease of risk management and enhanced legal certainty; all of these features can serve to improve efficiency.[232] One often-cited possible drawback of vertical integration is the limited choice for users when the selection of a clearing house is preconditioned. Advocates of the horizontal model even argue that the vertical model effectively locks users into a package of services, thus restricting possible competition from other providers.[233] Market participants also fear reduced price transparency, which would enable a vertical subsidisation of operations and ultimately lead to higher clearing costs.[234]

Very little research has been done on this issue and despite the ubiquitous criticism of vertical structures, no definite and widely agreed recommendation has yet been made as to which model should prevail. The European Commission has so far refused to endorse a certain form of integration, claiming that it should be left to market forces ultimately to determine the structure.[235] Literature has so far provided evidence that supports both the opposing views of the 'horizontalists' and the 'verticalists'.

Serifsoy (2007) finds no evidence that vertical integration is more efficient or productive than other business models. However, the author concludes that vertically integrated entities seem to possess a substantially stronger factor productivity growth than other business models. Köppl/Monnet (2007) conclude that vertical silos can prevent the full realisation of efficiency gains from horizontal consolidation of trading and settlement platforms. While Baur (2006) focuses his analysis on trading and settlement, the author finds a lack of clear evidence that vertical integration leads to lower prices of trading, clearing and settlement. Tapking/Yang (2004) contend that whereas horizontal integration of settlement systems is preferable to vertical integration, vertical integration is still better than no integration at all. The European Banking

---

a role model for Europe, current US industry structures are briefly outlined, whereas other regions (such as the Asian clearing industry) are not covered.

[231] Refer to Scott (2003), pp. 3–5, for details on this discussion. For examples of vertical and horizontal integration in Europe and the US, refer to Hart/Russo/Schönenberger (2002), pp. 31–6.

[232] Cf. Schmiedel/Malkamäki/Tarkka (2002), p. 14; Lannoo/Levin (2003), p. 4; and Serifsoy/Weiß (2005), p. 10.

[233] Cf. Werner (2003), p. 22.

[234] Cf. Lannoo/Levin (2003), p. 4. Deutsche Börse Group (ed.) (2002), p. 31, considers this allegation to be unfounded.

[235] Cf. European Commission (ed.) (2004), p. 11.

Federation (ed.) (2004), on the other hand, sees a positive impact on the market by utilising vertically integrated structures. Milne (2002) supports the standpoint of the European Commission by concluding that the market should determine whether vertical or horizontal integration ought to prevail. Scott (2003) finds the vertical/horizontal debate to be misleading insofar as it gives the illusion that incumbent clearing houses represent pure bipolar vertical or horizontal forms.[236] Scott's (2003) research suggests that clearing houses are constituted from multiple inter-organisational business configurations, and that some are in fact vertical, whilst others are more horizontal, depending on the business/product line analysed.

The heterogeneity of existing industry structures supports that stakeholders harbour no general preference for one structure over the other. This chapter summarises the most important structural and institutional characteristics of the current European and American clearing industries.[237] Understanding these set-ups and characteristics is crucial for the remainder of the study, because current industry structures are the framework for any harmonisation or integration initiative. Such initiatives can potentially transform and impact the structure and characteristics of the clearing industry.

2.5.1 Europe

Although CCPs have long been a standard feature in most European exchange-traded derivatives markets,[238] few clearing houses have traditionally acted as CCPs for the securities markets there. This is due to the relatively low volume and value of the transactions.[239] The introduction of the euro as well as the integration and expansion of European securities markets in both size and volume has created a growing demand for CCP services.[240] The implementation of electronic trading systems, in which the anonymity of counterparties is becoming increasingly relevant, has further spurred demand.[241] Today, most of Europe's major markets have established central counterparty clearing houses for the securities and derivatives markets, thus providing for cross-product clearing.[242] European CCPs traditionally confined their services to

---

[236] Cf. Scott (2003), p. 20.
[237] For a brief summary of the history of clearing, refer to Schwartz/Francioni (2004), pp. 265–7.
[238] Cf. Bank for International Settlements (ed.) (2004), p. 6.
[239] Cf. Lannoo/Levin (2003), p. 5.
[240] Cf. Hart/Russo/Schönenberger (2002), p. 7; and Ripatti (2004), p. 3.
[241] Cf. Corporation of London (ed.) (2005), p. 11.
[242] Cf. Hart/Russo/Schönenberger (2002), p. 19; NERA Economic Consulting (ed.) (2004), p. 17; and Tumpel-Gugerell (2006).

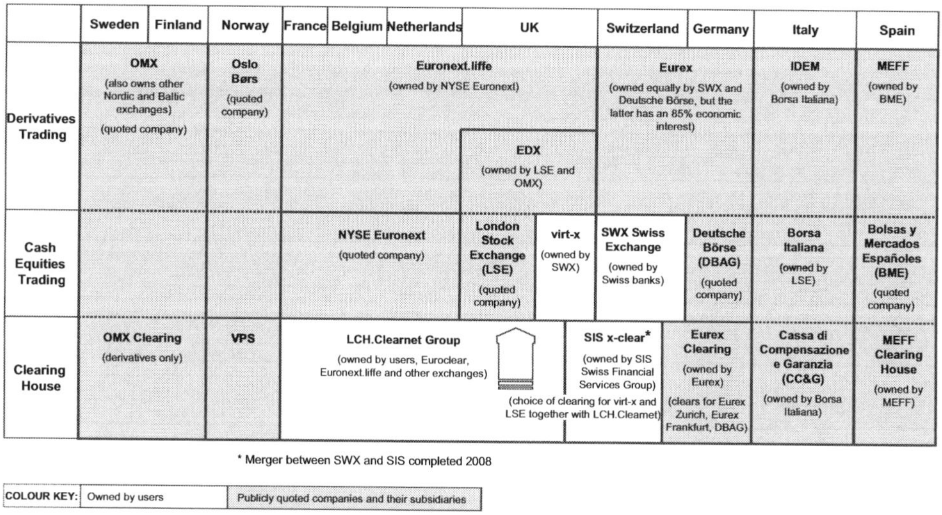

	Sweden	Finland	Norway	France	Belgium	Netherlands	UK	Switzerland	Germany	Italy	Spain
Derivatives Trading	**OMX** (also owns other Nordic and Baltic exchanges) (quoted company)		**Oslo Børs** (quoted company)	**Euronext.liffe** (owned by NYSE Euronext) / **EDX** (owned by LSE and OMX)				**Eurex** (owned equally by SWX and Deutsche Börse, but the latter has an 85% economic interest)		**IDEM** (owned by Borsa Italiana)	**MEFF** (owned by BME)
Cash Equities Trading				**NYSE Euronext** (quoted company)			**London Stock Exchange (LSE)** (quoted company) / **virt-x** (owned by SWX)	**SWX Swiss Exchange** (owned by Swiss banks)	**Deutsche Börse (DBAG)** (quoted company)	**Borsa Italiana** (owned by LSE)	**Bolsas y Mercados Españoles (BME)** (quoted company)
Clearing House	**OMX Clearing** (derivatives only)		**VPS**	**LCH.Clearnet Group** (owned by users, Euroclear, Euronext.liffe and other exchanges)			**SIS x-clear*** (owned by SIS Swiss Financial Services Group) (choice of clearing for virt-x and LSE together with LCH.Clearnet)		**Eurex Clearing** (owned by Eurex) (clears for Eurex Zurich, Eurex Frankfurt, DBAG)	**Cassa di Compensazione e Garanzia (CC&G)** (owned by Borsa Italiana)	**MEFF Clearing House** (owned by MEFF)

* Merger between SWX and SIS completed 2008

COLOUR KEY: Owned by users   Publicly quoted companies and their subsidiaries

Figure 2.17 Overview of principal financial market infrastructures in selected European countries
Source: Based on Corporation of London (ed.) (2005), p. 14.

single countries, establishing infrastructures and services that were tailored to serve best the demands of local markets;[243] each national system thus inevitably developed differently.[244] Due to the integration and expansion of European securities markets and the continuing global growth of derivatives markets, paired with the advance of electronic markets, the European clearing industry has become increasingly interlinked.[245] Besides broadening the scope of clearing services offered, European clearing houses have also started to consolidate both vertically and horizontally[246] over the past decade. From 1998 to 2005, the number of European CCPs decreased from thirteen to seven.[247] Despite the ongoing integration and consolidation processes, however, the structure of clearing – including the practices, processes and services offered by providers – still varies widely across Europe. National structures continue to be the product of traditional market practices as well as regulatory and customer influence.[248]

Figure 2.17 provides an overview of the principal financial market infrastructures in selected European countries. Whereas it illustrates that many

[243] Cf. Hart/Russo/Schönenberger (2002), p. 31.   [244] Cf. European Commission (ed.) (28.04.2004).
[245] Cf. Tumpel-Gugerell (2006).
[246] Cf. NERA Economic Consulting (ed.) (2004), p. 38; and Tumpel-Gugerell (2006).
[247] Cf. Rosati/Russo (2007), p. 6.   [248] Cf. Hanley/McCann/Moser (1996), p. 3.

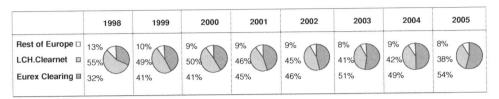

	1998	1999	2000	2001	2002	2003	2004	2005
Rest of Europe □	13%	10%	9%	9%	9%	8%	9%	8%
LCH.Clearnet ▣	55%	49%	50%	46%	45%	41%	42%	38%
Eurex Clearing ▣	32%	41%	41%	45%	46%	51%	49%	54%

Figure 2.18 European clearing industry – market share distribution of exchange-traded derivatives volumes from 1998 to 2005[249]
Source: Author's own; clearing houses' derivatives volumes provided by FOW (ed.) (2001); and FOW (ed.) (2006).

European clearing houses operate as part of a publicly quoted and vertically integrated structure – Europe's two major clearing houses, Eurex Clearing and LCH.Clearnet Group, could hardly differ more in terms of their institutional structure and ownership. Eurex Clearing is a subsidiary of the Eurex exchanges (equally owned by Deutsche Börse and SWX Swiss Exchange). As one of its parent companies, Deutsche Börse, holds 85 per cent economic interest in Eurex, the clearing house is thus classified as forming part of a vertically integrated, publicly quoted structure.[250] LCH.Clearnet Group, on the other hand, provides for horizontal clearing;[251] it is owned and governed by its clearing members, the ICSD Euroclear and its affiliated exchanges. In addition to these major CCPs, there exist a number of smaller ones, such as OMX Clearing and VPS in the Nordic markets, CC&G in Italy, MEFF in Spain and SIS x-clear in the Swiss and UK markets.[252]

The current European VPN thus contains a number of clearing houses, two of which dominate the European market in terms of their cleared market share. Figure 2.18 illustrates the market share in European derivatives clearing for LCH.Clearnet, Eurex Clearing and the rest of Europe.[253] It shows that from 1998 to 2005, LCH.Clearnet and Eurex Clearing maintained a combined European market share of roughly 90 per cent. Another 8 to 9 per cent of

---

[249] Volumes of LCH. Clearnet Group prior to the merger of Clearnet and LCH in 2003 reflect the combined volumes of the two component CCPs.

[250] Refer to section 8.1.2.1.1 for details on the institutional structure of Eurex Clearing.

[251] Whether or not the institutional structure of LCH.Clearnet qualifies as a purely horizontal model can be debated. One of its affiliated exchanges (Euronext.liffe) has traditionally held a significant stake in the clearing house; despite a cap on Euronext.liffe's voting rights, it could be argued that the LCH.Clearnet model does not qualify as a purely horizontal model. Refer to section 8.2.1.1.1 for details on the current institutional structure of LCH.Clearnet.

[252] For details regarding the structure and development of the European clearing industry, refer to Hart/Russo/Schönenberger (2002); Corporation of London (ed.) (2005), pp. 13–18; and London Economics (ed.) (2005).

[253] The 'rest of Europe' includes the following clearing houses: OMX Clearing, MEFF, CC&G, VPS (formerly NOS), KDPW (Warsaw-based Clearing House), ADECH (Athens Derivatives Exchange Clearing House), KELER (Budapest-based clearing house) and CCP.A (CCP Austria).

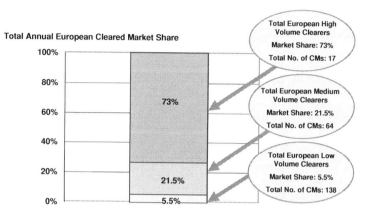

Figure 2.19   European derivatives clearing industry – average annual market share distribution of different clearing member types
Source: Author's estimates.[254]

European exchange-traded derivatives are cleared by OMX Clearing, MEFF and CC&G. Consequently, in European derivatives clearing, the vast majority of trades (roughly 98 to 99 per cent) are cleared through a small number of clearing houses (LCH.Clearnet, Eurex Clearing, OMX Clearing, MEFF and CC&G). However, an equally great number of CCPs with a minimal market share operate in parallel at the local level.[255]

In addition to these structural characteristics, another particularity of the first level of the European VPN concerns the clearing members. Figure 2.19 shows that a relatively small number of European high volume clearers account for the bulk of the total annual European cleared market share, i.e. roughly seventeen high volume clearers account for 73 per cent of the market share.[256] Furthermore, it is estimated that of these seventeen high volume clearers, the nine largest account for roughly 50 per cent of the European cleared market share.

[254] The total number of European clearing members is based on publicly available information on clearing members of Eurex Clearing, LCH.Clearnet, OMX Clearing, MEFF and CC&G. Note that institutions are counted and not legal entities – for example: at Eurex Clearing, two legal entities of Morgan Stanley are clearing members; Morgan Stanley & Co. International Plc and Morgan Stanley Bank AG (refer to www.eurexchange.com/documents/lists/members_en.html). For the purpose of this study, Morgan Stanley is counted as one European clearing member. Market share estimates are based on information provided by Eurex Clearing and draw upon the insight provided by the publicly available information on clearing membership.

[255] The comparisons of the European market share and the number of clearing houses apply to derivatives clearing. The Value Provision Network for European securities clearing industry has a similar structure.

[256] With ongoing consolidation among these high volume clearers, the concentration of the European cleared market share will further advance. In 2006, for example, UBS bought ABN Amro's brokerage unit. Cf. UBS (ed.) (25.05.2006). In early 2007, Société Générale and Calyon entered into negotiations to merge their brokerage activities, currently carried out by Fimat and Calyon Financial, respectively. Cf. Société Générale/Calyon (eds.) (08.01.2007).

These structural particularities have important implications with regard to the competitive dynamics within the European VPN, whose high volume clearers are thereby provided with an important lobby and strong negotiating power towards European clearing houses.

2.5.2 United States

The US clearing industry is often viewed as a benchmark for gauging the efficiency of the European industry landscape.[257]

One of the main arguments articulated in this debate is that the creation of a single CCP in Europe would create clearing arrangements that mirror those in the US, where clearing arrangements are more consolidated, and therefore more cost-effective, than in Europe. However, a critical comparison between the US and European cases leads to different conclusions in the case of derivatives. On the one hand, it shows that the main features of CCPs in the two currency areas are not fundamentally different. On the other hand, when looking at the level of consolidation, the situation is far more complex than is commonly thought. In particular, it may be argued that, in some respects (including regulatory aspects), clearing arrangements in the US are less integrated than those in Europe.[258]

In Europe, it is common for clearing houses to offer a multitude of products and asset classes, including securities and derivatives, but the practice is not easily replicable for a US clearing house. The reason for this is that the US regulatory structure has evolved towards supporting a hybrid industry structure,[259] whose regulation is split between the Securities and Exchange Commission (SEC) and the Commodity Futures Trading Commission (CFTC).[260] Whereas the market infrastructure (i.e. exchanges, clearing houses and settlement institutions) necessary to support trades and market participants active in securities or options are regulated by the SEC, the futures market infrastructure and market participants active in futures are overseen by the CFTC. The Options Clearing Corporation (OCC) is the sole American clearing house operating under the regulation of both the SEC and CFTC. The most significant differences regarding the industry structures that have evolved under SEC and CFTC regulation are attributable to the two authorities' differing approaches to market regulation and oversight.[261]

---

[257] Cf. Corporation of London (ed.) (2005), p. 19.   [258] Hart/Russo/Schönenberger (2002), p. 8.
[259] Cf. Moskow (2006).   [260] See DeWaal (2005a); and DeWaal (2005b).
[261] For details regarding the structure and development of the US clearing industry, refer to Davidson III (1996); Moser (1998); Hart/Russo/Schönenberger (2002); Corporation of London (ed.) (2005), pp. 19–20; Securities Industry Association (ed.) (2005); and Kroszner (2006). Harvard Research Group (ed.) (2003) identifies barriers to US clearing and settlement efficiency.

Under the jurisdiction of the SEC, which generally employs a more rigorous approach, a centralised clearing structure has evolved. In 1975, Congress directed the SEC to facilitate the establishment of a 'national market system'.[262] A twenty-year process began that led to the gradual absorption of previously vertically integrated CCPs and CSDs into a centralised structure.[263] Today, clearing for securities is centrally provided by the Depository Trust and Clearing Corporation (DTCC) and its subsidiaries,[264] while clearing for options is centrally provided by the OCC. While the SEC has favoured centralised clearing and settlement arrangements since Congress's policy mandate,[265] '[a]ny trading space wishing to clear and settle without going directly to the national infrastructures is free to do so as long as it meets the standards set by the SEC. In addition, any organisation can apply for approval and registration as a clearing agency'.[266]

Although clearing under SEC regulation is currently centralised, there have been instances of exchanges seeking ways in which to compete with DTCC through vertically integrated structures. For example, in the context of NASDAQ's acquisition of the BSE Group (the holding company of the Boston Stock Exchange) in 2007, the exchange announced its plan to revive BSE's dormant clearing agency licence to clear its trades rather than relying on DTCC.[267] The Philadelphia Stock Exchange (PHLX), which was also acquired by NASDAQ later that year, likewise holds a stock clearing licence that is currently dormant.

There is no such policy mandate for the CFTC-regulated futures industry.[268] The clearing industry structure for futures differs in that there exist a multitude of clearing houses, most of which operate in vertically integrated structures (see Figure 2.20).[269] Within the US futures industry, one major exchange with an integrated clearing house dominates the market: the CME Group, which was created in 2007 through a merger of the Chicago Mercantile Exchange (CME) and the Chicago Board of Trade (CBOT).[270] Whereas both exchanges

---

[262] Cf. Moskow (2006).
[263] For details of the process, refer to Securities Industry Association (ed.) (2005), pp. 2–4; and Donald (2007), pp. 101–14.
[264] Through its subsidiary the National Securities Clearing Corporation (NSCC), DTCC also provides securities settlement services. NSCC is the single CSD serving US securities markets. For details, refer to www.dtcc.com.
[265] Cf. Moskow (2006).   [266] Securities Industry Association (ed.) (2005), p. 3.
[267] Cf. NASDAQ (ed.) (02.10.2007).   [268] Cf. Moskow (2006).   [269] Cf. Young (2007), p. 82.
[270] On 17 October 2006, the CME and CBOT announced their intention to merge; ICE subsequently launched a counter offer to merge with CBOT on 15 March 2007, which was ultimately rejected. On 9 July 2007, CME and CBOT completed the merger.

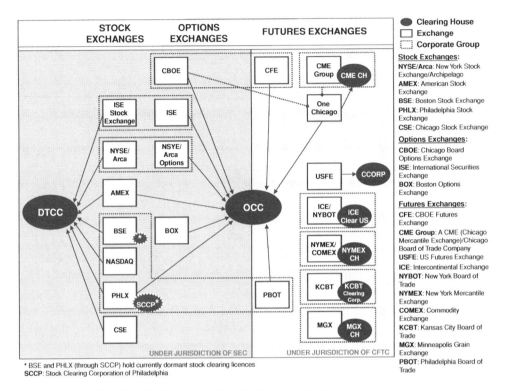

Figure 2.20   Overview of principal financial market infrastructure in the US
Source: Based on Bourse Consult (ed.) (2006).

had historically employed different clearing houses,[271] CBOT decided to transfer its clearing to the CME Clearing House in 2004.[272]

2.5.3 Comparing Europe and the United States

When comparing the European and US clearing industries, it is important to take into account the structural differences; particularly the US's fragmentation into a SEC- and CFTC-regulated market infrastructure. Due to the pressures of globalisation, technological innovations and a changing regulatory environment, a harmonisation and integration of both the US and European clearing industries is currently far from complete.[273]

---

[271] CME operates vertically integrated structures, thus employing its own clearing house. CBOT previously had a long-standing relationship with the Board of Trade Clearing Corporation (BOTCC, later CCorp).

[272] For details, refer to section 8.1.2.2.

[273] Cf. London Economics (ed.) (2005), p. 1.

No. of Cleared Contracts

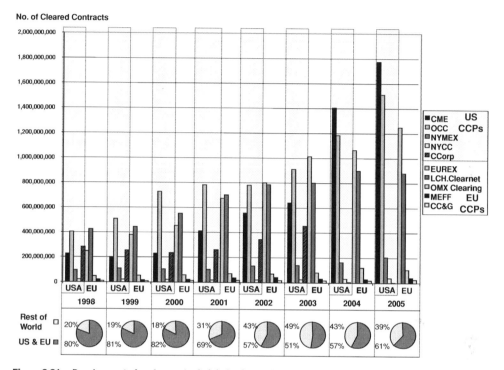

Figure 2.21   Development of exchange-traded derivatives volumes (single counted) at the largest US-American
and European CCPs from 1998 to 2005[274]
Source: Based on FOW (ed.) (2001); FOW (ed.) (2003); and FOW (ed.) (2006).

Cleared volumes are another factor that should be considered when comparing the clearing industries on both sides of the Atlantic.[275] Whereas the US
domestic securities market is still by far larger than its European equivalent,[276]
the same is not true regarding exchange-traded derivatives volumes.
Figure 2.21 charts the development of exchange-traded derivatives volumes at
the largest American and European clearing houses from 1998 to 2005. Two
important facts become apparent: American and European CCPs have long
been competing head to head, and the combined market share of their five
respective major clearing houses has accounted for roughly 60 to 80 per cent

[274] NYCC (New York Clearing Corporation) is today ICE Clear US. LCH.Clearnet volumes reflect the two
component CCPs (LCH and Clearnet) of the LCH.Clearnet Group. The 'rest of world' does not include
volumes cleared by the Korea Exchange's clearing house.

[275] Cf. Zentraler Kreditausschuss (ed.) (2004), p. 3.

[276] Cf. Corporation of London (ed.) (2005), p. 19. In 2006, the total number of trades in equity shares
in the US was more than five times higher than in Europe (2.582 million versus 480 million) (World
Federation of Exchanges statistics, www.world-exchanges.org).

of total worldwide exchange-traded derivatives volumes over the past decade. The rapid growth of cross-border trading, which spans many clearing systems and increases global interdependence, underscores the fact that the clearing industry is ultimately global in coverage.

Finally, recent merger and acquisition initiatives among European and American stock and derivatives exchanges are likely to spur further the debate on the efficiency and structure of the European and American clearing industries. The impact on cross-Atlantic clearing has yet to be seen: on 4 April 2007, NYSE Group and Euronext merged to create NYSE Euronext. On 27 July 2007, stockholders of the ISE voted to approve a merger agreement with Eurex. On 20 September 2007, NASDAQ, Borse Dubai and OMX announced a series of corporate transactions that will culminate in NASDAQ and OMX forming the NASDAQ OMX Group.[277]

2.6 Summary

This chapter set the stage for the research conducted in this study by providing relevant definitions of clearing, indicating the value-added of CCP clearing and delivering insight into the various stakeholders in clearing. An overview of the structural set-up of the European and US clearing industries followed.

The definition of clearing used for the purpose of this study encompasses four different perspectives:

- The process view refers to clearing as a process that constitutes a vital part of the life cycle of a trade, as it occurs during the time lag between execution and settlement of a trade.
- The functional view focuses on clearing as a service. It identifies the following value chain components: basic clearing services, value-added clearing services in general (with unique CCP services in particular) and complementary clearing services. Each of these clearing service levels has a different scope and comprises different functions.
- The structural view identifies the different types and roles of clearing service providers. Typical clearing service providers include CSDs/ICSDs, clearing houses and banks/brokers. CSDs/ICSDs usually only provide basic clearing services. Most clearing houses today act as a so-called central counterparty (CCP).[278] They provide a much greater spectrum of services with respect

---

[277] For details on the transactions, refer to the companies' websites.

[278] The focus of this study is on clearing houses that act as CCPs. Therefore, the terms 'clearing house' and 'CCP' will be used interchangeably throughout this study.

to value-added clearing services, including unique CCP services. While market participants benefit significantly from clearing services provided by CCPs, complementary clearing services also play an important role. These services are not required to maintain the life cycle of a trade, but many market participants benefit enormously from them. Nonetheless, today's CCPs rarely provide a full range of complementary clearing services. These clearing services are usually delivered by banks/brokers.

• Finally, the institutional view focuses on the institutional characteristics of clearing. The two most typical forms are clearing houses organised as departments or subsidiaries of their affiliated exchange(s) (i.e. vertical clearing) or operating as independent entities (i.e. horizontal clearing).

CCP clearing constitutes the core of modern financial market infrastructure. These clearing services not only benefit individual market participants, but markets as a whole, by increasing the efficiency of capital markets. CCPs have traditionally played a more significant role in derivatives markets than in securities markets due to their different particularities, dynamics and unique characteristics. Nonetheless, the use of CCPs in securities markets has been increasing.

A starting point for the study was provided by identifying and characterising the tiered structure in which the provision of clearing services usually takes place: the so-called Value Provision Network (VPN). The VPN consists of two levels of access to the clearing house: direct and indirect. The research focus of this study is on the first level of direct access. To this end, six different clearing member types were differentiated according to their focus of activity and average European cleared market share: regionally active (low volume) clearers with a prop. or an agency focus (CM_{PR}/CM_{AR}), regionally-to-globally active (medium volume) clearers with a prop. or an agency focus (CM_{PR-G}/CM_{AR-G}) and globally active (high volume) clearers with a prop. or an agency focus (CM_{PG}/CM_{AG}). The analyses conducted in the remainder of this study are performed according to this classification. It thus remains to be seen whether the different clearing member types are asymmetrically affected by the various network strategies.

Stakeholders in clearing comprise various groups with divergent interests that can sometimes lead to conflict. Stakeholders generally pursue either public or private interests. Those pursuing private interests include providers of clearing services, owners and other market infrastructure providers. Stakeholders pursuing public interests include regulators, policymakers and central banks.

Although the analytical focus of this study is on the European clearing industry, a brief overview of the US clearing industry was included in this chapter, because any effort to integrate and harmonise the European clearing industry will ultimately be global in scope. Furthermore, as the US clearing industry is often referred to as a role model for Europe, current US industry structures were briefly outlined. This overview showed that competing institutional structures coexist in the European and US clearing industries. Some clearing houses are vertically integrated, whereas others operate in horizontal structures. It is clear that American and European CCPs have long been competing head to head; the combined market share of their five respective major CCPs has accounted for roughly 60 to 80 per cent of total worldwide exchange-traded derivatives volumes over the past decade. The overview also revealed that in some respects, clearing arrangements in the US are less integrated than those in Europe.

With respect to the current structure of the European VPN, the following particularities were revealed: firstly, while there are a number of CCPs, two of them dominate the European market (LCH.Clearnet and Eurex Clearing). Secondly, a relatively small number of European high volume clearers account for the majority of the total annual European cleared market share (i.e. approximately seventeen clearers account for over 70 per cent of the market share). Furthermore, of these seventeen high volume clearers, the nine largest account for roughly 50 per cent of the European cleared market share. These structural particularities have important implications with regard to the competitive dynamics within the European VPN, whose high volume clearers are thereby provided with an important lobby and strong negotiating power towards European clearing houses.

The purpose of this study is to determine the efficiency impact of various network strategies within the clearing industry. Chapter 3 therefore defines the core issues of research: efficiency of clearing and industry structure.

3 Defining the core issues – efficiency and network strategies

The previous chapter set the stage for the research on efficiency of clearing and industry structure. This chapter examines these two issues in greater depth. The first step is to outline the various dimensions of 'efficiency', to explain the related analytical concepts and to identify the efficiency criterion used for the purpose of this study (section 3.1). The central criterion for determining the efficiency of clearing is operational efficiency, which is influenced by transaction costs. In section 3.2, this criterion is further explained and systematised, and a definition of clearing-related transaction costs is provided.

There are numerous ways to reduce the transaction costs (thus increasing the efficiency) of clearing. This study focuses on analysing the impact that certain network strategies between clearing houses have on transaction costs. These integration and harmonisation initiatives can potentially impact both the direct and indirect costs of clearing. This chapter (section 3.3) includes a definition and classification of different network strategies, followed by an overview of selected initiatives between clearing houses from 1973 to 2006. These steps lay the groundwork for the study's ultimate research objective.

3.1 Efficiency of derivatives clearing

Throughout economic literature, the term 'efficiency' is used in a variety of different contexts and denotations. Efficiency and its respective indicators can generally be employed to describe and evaluate different analytical concepts.[1] The purpose of this study is to determine the efficiency impact

---

[1] Note the difference between the terms 'efficiency' and 'effectiveness'. Whereas effectiveness is a criterion employed to measure the achievement of certain output objectives (doing the right things), efficiency describes the relationship between output and input factors (doing things right). Cf. Thommen/Achleitner (2006), pp. 110–11. In this respect, effectiveness is a more generally valid measure and efficiency is a measure better suited for detailed analysis. Effectiveness is appropriate for describing the

CHAPTER		PURPOSE
3	DEFINING THE CORE ISSUES – EFFICIENCY AND NETWORK STRATEGIES	Provides definitions of the two core research issues, which are industry efficiency and industry structure.
INDUSTRY EFFICIENCY		
3.1	Efficiency of Derivatives Clearing	Outlines the different dimensions of efficiency and identifies the efficiency criteria used in this study.
3.2	Transaction Costs of Derivatives Clearing	Provides a definition of clearing-related transaction costs, which can be divided into direct and indirect costs.
INDUSTRY STRUCTURE		
3.3	Network Strategies	Provides a classification of different network strategies and an overview of such agreements between CCPs from 1973 to 2006.
3.4	Summary	

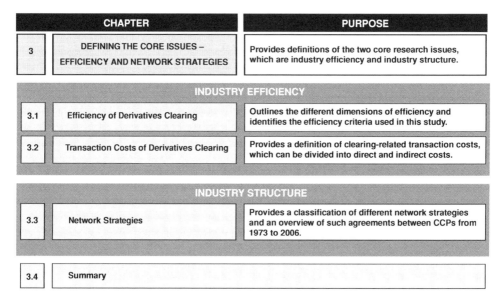

Figure 3.1   Structure of Chapter 3

of certain institutional arrangements, i.e. network strategies, on the provision of European exchange-traded derivatives clearing services – particularly in the context of the challenges created by the integration of the European capital markets into a global setting. To determine the efficiency impact of certain institutional arrangements between European CCPs, it is fundamental to identify and define suitable criteria for measuring and assessing it. To this end, the following section outlines the different dimensions of an efficiency analysis, explains the related analytical concepts (section 3.1.1) and identifies the efficiency criterion used for the purpose of this study (section 3.1.2).

3.1.1 General efficiency criteria

In economics, the efficiency of a market refers to its ability to allocate optimally scarce savings to productive investments in a way that benefits the market as a whole. The allocation of resources generated by the market is said to be efficient if no alternative would make a certain individual better off without making another individual worse off.[2] The concept of allocational efficiency

overall suitability of a specific package of measures, but does not allow individual measures to be ranked. Efficiency, on the other hand, allows single measures to be evaluated and thus enables a ranking. Cf. Corsten (ed.) (2000), p. 207.

[2] Cf. Stiglitz (1981), p. 235. Efficient allocation of resources is also referred to as 'Pareto Optimal', tracing back to the Italian economist Vilfredo Pareto (1848–1923), one of the founders of welfare analysis.

is widely employed in economic literature to measure the ability of financial markets to allocate resources to the highest yield investment alternatives.[3] An allocationally efficient situation can therefore be defined as optimal attainment of a given objective. Allocational efficiency is thus the overall objective of all financial market activity. It therefore follows that allocational efficiency is also the objective of clearing service provision. To determine how clearing services can be provided in an allocationally efficient manner, suitable criteria for measuring and classifying efficiency must first be established. Further, it is necessary to define the economic entity relevant for the analysis as well as its pursued objectives.

The examination of efficiency in financial markets has mainly focused on analysing the efficiency of exchanges (both securities and derivatives). With respect to securities exchange efficiency, this analysis revealed that the contribution of exchanges to an allocationally efficient market is mainly determined by information and operational efficiency.[4] Both are preconditions for achieving allocational efficiency.[5] Information efficiency, as defined by Fama (1976), is said to exist in markets in which prices reflect all available information promptly and correctly.[6] Operational efficiency measures the efficiency of the employed market mechanism.[7]

To the best of the author's knowledge, no studies evaluating the efficiency of derivatives clearing have been conducted to date, and thus no classification of efficiency criteria has yet been established.[8] The following therefore provides a definition of the criteria that will be employed to determine the contribution of clearing to an allocationally efficient market. As detailed in section 2.2.2, clearing can contribute to the smooth and frictionless functioning of capital markets and thereby increase allocational efficiency. One precondition for an allocationally efficient market is operational efficiency. An operationally efficient market is one in which buyers and sellers of financial products can

---

[3] See, e.g. Kohl *et al.* (1974), pp. 16–17; Francis (1976), p. 68; and West (1986), p. 21.

[4] Refer to West (1975); Schmidt (1977); Uhlir (1990); Gerke/Rapp (1994); and Bortenlänger (1996) for further analyses regarding efficiency criteria for securities markets. Refer to Fama (1970), pp. 383–417, for a summary of the early literature on efficient markets and to Fama (1991), pp. 1575–617, regarding empirical studies on the subject of information efficiency.

[5] Cf. West (1975), p. 32.

[6] Cf. Fama (1976), p. 133. 'While the view that markets process information efficiently is still the dominant paradigm in finance theory, equity markets exhibit, however, some empirical "anomalies" that seem to contradict this view.' Moerschen/Schiereck (2005), p. 123. For an exploration of such irregularities, refer to Moerschen/Schiereck (2005).

[7] Cf. West/Tiniç (1974), p. 15.

[8] The focus of past studies has mainly been on the question of whether a CCP has in place the mechanisms to review periodically service levels, costs, pricing and operational reliability. Cf. Bank for International Settlements (ed.) (2004), p. 48.

purchase transaction services 'at prices that are as low as possible, given the costs associated with having these services provided'.[9] When analysing the efficiency of derivatives transaction services, it is important to bear in mind that the main contribution of derivatives markets lies in the allocation of risk. Allocational efficiency in the context of derivatives markets therefore also accounts for their contribution and ability to transfer risk.[10] Other relevant efficiency criteria for analysing financial markets, such as information efficiency and hedging effectiveness, are not applicable to clearing.

Operational efficiency is the central criterion used in this analysis to assess clearing industry efficiency; efficiency criteria related to the transfer of risk are set aside. A definition of and further details on operational efficiency are provided in the following section.

3.1.2 Operational efficiency and transaction cost theory

As specified above, an operationally efficient market is one in which buyers and sellers of financial products can purchase transaction services (here: clearing services) at prices that are as low as possible, given the costs associated with having these services provided.[11] The most important factors influencing operational efficiency are the so-called transaction costs.[12] To increase the operational efficiency of a market, it is necessary to minimise these costs.[13]

Transaction cost theory,[14] as developed primarily by the economists Coase and Williamson, suggests that economic organisations emerge from

---

[9] West/Tiniç (1979), p. 92. Also see West (1986), p. 24. Similar definitions can be found in Friend (1966), p. 328; Friend (1972), p. 213; Kohl *et al.* (1974), p. 16; West (1975), p. 31; Schmidt (1977), pp. 31–2; Burns (1983), p. 51; Schulte (1992), p. 23; Kress (1996), pp. 43–4; Copeland/Weston (1998), p. 331; and Gomber (2000), p. 14. Note that these definitions all relate to the purchase of transaction services, i.e. the price buyers and sellers of a security have to pay for executing their trade. For the purpose of this study, this definition of operational efficiency is transferred to the purchase of clearing services.

[10] Cf. Bessler (1989), pp. 99–100. Refer to Edwards (1981); Burns (1983); and Bessler (1989) for further analyses on efficiency criteria for derivatives markets.

[11] Operational efficiency is often also referred to as internal efficiency. Cf. West/Tiniç (1974), p. 15.

[12] Schmidt (1983) distinguishes four different cost categories relevant for the analysis of secondary markets. These are costs for transaction services, administration and safekeeping costs, information costs and the costs of immediate execution. Cf. Schmidt (1983), p. 188; and Schmidt (1988), p. 7.

[13] Cf. Hagermann (1973), p. 846.

[14] Picot (1985) defines a transaction as the exchange of property rights. Cf. Picot (1985), p. 224. Also refer to Picot/Dietl (1990), p. 178. Throughout this study, the term 'transaction' is consistently used to describe the business conducted between two parties, i.e. the buy-side and the sell-side. As the term also describes the exchange of a property right, the definition is compatible with the one used in the context of transaction cost theory. Note that the term 'transaction cost' is used dichotomously in two streams of economic literature. According to Allen (2000), one stream relates to property rights literature and

cost-minimising behaviour in a world of limited information and op-portunism.[15] The theory originates in Coase's (1937) assumption that trans-action costs constitute the basic reason for the existence of firms.[16] Transac-tion cost theory was developed to facilitate an analysis of 'the comparative costs of planning, adapting, and monitoring task completion under alter-native governance structures'.[17] The unit of analysis is a transaction, which 'occurs when a good or service is transferred across a technologically separable interface'.[18]

Transaction costs arise for *ex ante* reasons (drafting, negotiating and safe-guarding agreements between the parties to a transaction) as well as for *ex post* reasons (maladaptation, haggling, establishment, operational and bond-ing costs). Williamson (1985) argues that two human and three environmental factors trigger transaction costs. The two human factors are bounded ratio-nality and opportunism.[19] Bounded rationality refers to the general human inability or lack of resources to consider every state-contingent outcome asso-ciated with a transaction that might arise. Opportunism refers to the human practice of acting to further self-interests. The three environmental factors are uncertainty, small numbers and asset specificity. Uncertainty exacerbates the problems that arise from bounded rationality and opportunism. Secondly, if marketplaces contain only a small number of players, it may be difficult for a party to a transaction to discipline other parties by withdrawing or seeking alternate players in the marketplace. Thirdly, the value of an asset may be tied to a particular transaction that it supports. The party that is invested in the asset will incur a loss if the non-invested party withdraws from the transaction.[20]

Three dimensions of a transaction mainly affect the type of gover-nance structure chosen for the transaction: asset specificity, uncertainty and frequency. As asset specificity and uncertainty increase, the risk of

the other pertains to neoclassical economic literature. In property rights literature, transaction costs are defined as the costs of establishing and maintaining property rights. The neoclassical definition centres on the costs of trading across a market. Cf. Allen (2000), p. 893. The property rights literature begins with Coase and is further detailed in the following. The neoclassical literature on transaction costs starts with Hicks (1935) and defines transaction costs more narrowly. This approach to transaction costs dominates in finance and pure theory. Refer to Allen (2000), pp. 895–903, for further details on the differences between the two streams of literature.

[15] For literature referring to the basics of transaction cost theory, see Coase (1937); Williamson (1979); Williamson (1981); Bössmann (1981); Picot (1982); Williamson (1985); Hax (1991); Picot (1991b); Fischer (1992); and Schmidt (1992).

[16] Cf. Coase (1937), pp. 386–405.   [17] Williamson (1985), p. 2.

[18] Williamson (1985), p. 1.   [19] Cf. Williamson (1985), p. 44.

[20] The possibility (threat) of this party acting opportunistically leads to the so-called 'hold-up' problem.

opportunism increases. Thus, decision-makers are more likely to choose a hierarchical (firm-based) governance structure. As frequency increases, the comparative advantage of using market governance structures decreases because the costs of hierarchical governance structures can be amortised across more instances of the transaction.

Transaction costs of clearing are defined as the total costs a market participant has to bear for using a certain institutional structure providing clearing services. It is assumed that market participants want to minimise these transaction costs. Transaction costs are thus the criterion for evaluating and choosing between different institutional arrangements.[21] The institutional arrangement entailing the lowest transaction costs is preferred.[22]

The economic entity relevant for the efficiency analysis is the view of clearing houses' direct customers, i.e. the clearing member view.[23] Clearing members include those allowed to clear their own transactions as well as their customers' (GCMs) and those allowed to clear only their own transactions (ICMs). The interaction between clearing houses and clearing members necessitates a continuous coordination between both parties, which incurs costs. Transaction cost theory enables a structured analysis of these costs and provides a model for analysing institutional arrangements[24] between clearing houses (i.e. network strategies). A comparison of the efficiency impact of different network strategies is therefore based on the analysis of the inherent transaction cost impact.

> The central criterion for determining the efficiency of clearing is operational efficiency, which is influenced by transaction costs. To increase the (operational) efficiency of clearing, it is necessary to minimise clearing members' transaction costs.[25] The efficiency of the clearing industry is thus increased when the transaction costs that clearing members have to bear are reduced (and vice versa).

---

[21] Cf. Picot/Reichwald/Wigand (1996), p. 41.   [22] Cf. Picot/Dietl (1990), p. 183.

[23] A similar approach is often chosen to analyse the efficiency of financial exchange markets, i.e. through adopting the view of large institutional investors. Their pursued objective in the context of securities trading can be subcategorised into the goal of minimising transaction costs, maximising order fulfilment and transparency, liquidity and information efficiency. For details, refer to the studies by Schiereck (1995) and Averdiek-Bolwin (1998).

[24] Cf. Picot/Dietl (1990), p. 178.

[25] Kröpfl (2003) employs a similar approach when analysing the efficiency of securities settlement and custody services in defining efficiency as the minimisation of transaction costs. Lattemann/Neumann (2002), pp. 6–8, also suggest using transaction costs to measure the efficiency of securities settlement and custody services.

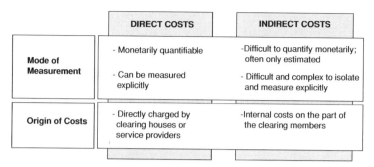

Figure 3.2   Categorisation of clearing-related transaction costs
Source: Author's own.

3.2 Transaction costs of derivatives clearing

For the purpose of assessing the impact that certain network strategies between CCPs have on the efficiency of clearing, it is first necessary to establish a categorisation of clearing-related transaction costs.[26] Transaction costs are therefore categorised along two dimensions: the mode of measurement and the origin of costs (see Figure 3.2).

The mode of measurement refers to whether or not costs are monetarily quantifiable. Monetarily quantifiable costs are referred to as direct costs. When analysing institutional arrangements based on transaction cost theory, however, it is important to take all transaction-related endeavours into account, and not just the monetarily quantifiable costs.[27] For the purpose of this study, these costs will be referred to as indirect costs.[28] Whereas direct costs are monetarily quantifiable and can thus be measured explicitly, indirect costs are difficult to quantify monetarily and can often only be estimated.[29] Measuring and isolating indirect costs explicitly is therefore a difficult and highly complex task.

Both kinds of cost are borne by clearing members. Direct costs refer to clearing house or service provider charges,[30] whereas indirect costs comprise internal costs, such as cost of capital, risk management costs, information

[26] For simplicity's sake, the transaction costs of clearing are also referred to as 'costs' in this analysis.

[27] Cf. Picot (1985), p. 224.

[28] The categorisation of 'direct' and 'indirect' costs is established with reference to the terminology used by communication of the European Commission and the Giovannini Group. Cf. Giovannini Group (ed.) (2001), p. 36; and European Commission (ed.) (2006a), pp. 2–3.

[29] Cf. Oxera (ed.) (2007), p. iii.

[30] Refer to section 3.2.1 for a definition of clearing-related service providers.

technology (IT) costs and back-office costs.[31] In other words, there are two direct cost categories and four indirect cost categories.[32] The 'all-in' costs of clearing refer to the sum of all direct and indirect costs.

A commonly employed categorisation of transaction costs in economic literature distinguishes the following five cost components:[33]

- cost of initiating contracts, especially information and search costs;
- cost of completing contracts, contracting and decision costs;
- cost of executing contracts, management and coordination costs;
- cost of control, i.e. control and enforcement of legal obligations; and
- cost of adaptations to contracts.

Although the transaction costs related to clearing can be arranged to match this categorisation, the classification schema presented in Figure 3.3 better suits the research objective of this study. Appendices 1 and 2 provide a matrix overview of clearing-related transaction costs. The figures compare the classification schema presented in Figure 3.3 to the five general transaction cost categories that are commonly employed throughout economic literature. The figures show that while this widespread categorisation can be used to analyse clearing costs, it is not suited for conducting a structured and accessible analysis. This study therefore utilises the more specific classification relevant to clearing services, as detailed in Figure 3.3.

The interaction between a clearing house and its members and non-members incurs transaction costs. Generally, costs related to clearing arise in different parts of the Value Provision Network (VPN). Figure 3.4 provides an overview of the different levels of transaction costs in the VPN.

---

[31] Cost categories were established in cooperation with seven industry experts from various institutions, which were consulted prior to conducting the first interview. Refer to Chapter 4 for details of the empirical study. In the context of the conducted interviews with clearing members, interviewees were also asked for their accordance with the defined cost types and cost categories. Out of twenty-one interviewed clearing members, fifteen agreed to the classification of cost types and cost categories. Whereas five respondents generally approved the classification, they suggested including different additional cost categories; one interviewee was not sure whether or not he agreed. For the purpose of gathering comprehensive information from clearing members, no additional cost categories were included during the phase of conducting the interviews, as this would have resulted in interviews being difficult to compare. Nonetheless, suggestions by interviewees for additional cost categories will be briefly referred to in section 5.1.

[32] Cost types and cost categories, as defined for the purpose of this study, are not fully compatible with the definition employed by the European Commission. The Commission differentiates three main cost categories, i.e. direct, indirect and opportunity costs. Opportunity costs are regarded as a separate cost type. Opportunity costs resemble the 'cost of capital' in this study. Further, the European Commission applies a more narrow definition of indirect costs, by classifying back-office costs as a sole indirect cost category. Cf. European Commission (ed.) (2006a), pp. 2–3.

[33] Cf. Coase (1937), pp. 390–91; Picot (1985), p. 224; Richter (1990), p. 577; Picot (1991a), p. 344; Richter (1994), pp. 6–7; and Dyer (1997), p. 536.

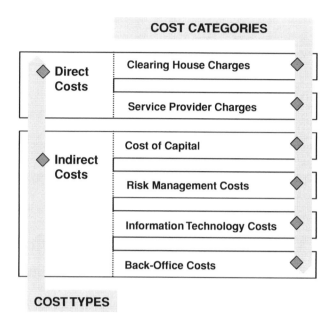

Figure 3.3   Cost types and categories
Source: Author's own.

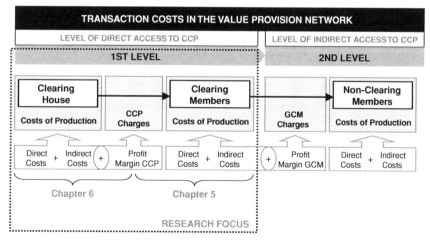

Figure 3.4   Transaction costs in the Value Provision Network
Source: Author's own.

The 'first level' of costs refers to those occurring on the first level of the VPN, i.e. those borne by the producer of the service, the clearing house and its direct customers, the clearing members. As outlined above, this research examines both the direct and indirect costs that clearing members have to bear in order to clear their transactions. To analyse these costs, it is crucial to include the clearing house's costs of production, as these translate into direct costs for the clearing members.[34] Costs of production have divergent meanings for different clearing members. For a clearing member with a proprietary focus, costs of production refer to the costs of doing business, i.e. the total costs related to clearing its own transactions. Costs of production from the perspective of a clearing member with agency focus, on the other hand, mean the internal costs for producing the service it provides to its customers.[35]

This study focuses on the first level of transaction costs for different reasons. Firstly, this analysis serves to assess the efficiency impact of different network strategies. Secondly, a detailed and comprehensive analysis of the second level of transaction costs exceeds the scope of this study.[36] Although the research focus lies on the first level of costs, it is important to have a basic understanding of both cost levels to truly comprehend the full impact network strategies can have on the efficiency of clearing and the structure of the VPN. Throughout the research, information on and analysis of the second level will thus be provided, albeit with a more narrow scope.

3.2.1 Direct transaction costs

Direct transaction costs are clearing-related costs that are monetarily quantifiable and can be measured explicitly. This cost type comprises two cost categories – clearing house charges and service provider charges (see Figure 3.5). Service providers for clearing members, as defined for the purpose of

---

[34] An analysis of the costs of production for clearing houses is provided in Chapter 6; an analysis of the direct and indirect costs for clearing members is provided in Chapter 5.

[35] Both perspectives are elaborated in more detail in the following chapters.

[36] As non-clearing members need to establish an account relationship through another party to effect clearing, the transaction costs they have to bear significantly depend on the fees charged by their respective GCM(s). Because these costs are highly dependent on the internal calculations and pricing policy of the clearing intermediary involved, they are difficult to analyse. The same applies to other customers, i.e. individuals or firms that are not members of the clearing house's affiliated exchange(s), whose view is not included in this study for similar reasons. Again, it is more relevant here to analyse the costs of production for clearing members, i.e. the first level of costs, because such an analysis serves to provide insight into the costs that these other customers have to bear.

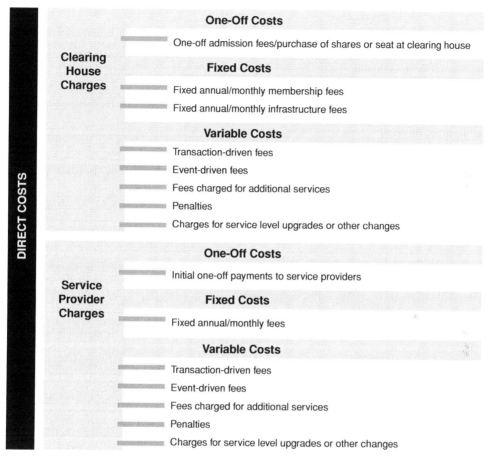

Figure 3.5 Categorisation of direct transaction costs
Source: Based on Eurex Clearing price list; LCH.Clearnet website; and FOW (ed.) (2006).

this study, include back-office vendors, telecommunications companies, (correspondence) banks,[37] settlement institutions and other GCMs; all of these entities sell different clearing-related (supporting) services. Clearing members usually have to bear one-off costs for establishing their initial relationship to a clearing house and service providers, together with any recurring fees charged by clearing houses and service providers. These charges commonly have fixed and variable components.[38]

---

[37] Clearing members are required to operate accounts for settlement. The accepted banks are predefined in the rules and regulations of the respective clearing house.

[38] Direct costs, which are not taken into account in this study, result from the charges from acquiring hardware and paying software licence fees and regulatory fees.

3.2.1.1 Clearing house charges

Depending on their institutional structure, some clearing houses impose a **one-off** admission fee on members; others require the upfront purchase of a certain number of shares, memberships or seats at the clearing house. One-off admission fees can vary according to the clearing membership level, i.e. according to whether clearing members can clear their own transactions and those of their customers (GCMs) or are allowed to clear only their own transactions (ICMs).

Fixed costs include all recurring annual or monthly fees charged by clearing houses, such as minimum transaction charges, membership or clearing licence fees. Another fixed fee component charged by clearing houses relates to infrastructure fees (which are often also referred to as 'communication' fees). Infrastructure fees are paid for connecting a specific clearing member location to the clearing house – either through the internet or via dedicated telecommunication lines. These lines are commonly leased to clearing members for the duration of their particular clearing member status. Charges for line fees can depend on the bandwidth size, connection type, i.e. internet versus dedicated lines, or geographical location. Line fees commonly cover the usage and initial installation of the line(s). Some clearing houses outsource this service to designated telecommunications companies, which then charge clearing members directly.[39] Infrastructure fees can also include additional charges for workstations, servers, back-office and information services link-ups.

Clearing house charges that translate into **variable costs** to clearing members can be itemised as follows: transaction-driven fees, event-driven fees, fees charged for additional services, penalties and fees charged for service level upgrades, other services or infrastructure changes. Among the most commonly observed and discussed direct costs associated with the use of a CCP are the transaction-driven fees. Clearing house fees are commonly charged to each side (i.e. both the buy and sell sides) of a contract. Different fee levels are usually set for each exchange or execution platform or venue eligible for clearing at the respective CCP. The most significant difference among transaction-driven fees is their varying base of reference. Vertically integrated clearing houses often charge so-called 'all-in' fees, which cover both the trading and clearing fee per contract, rather than charging a separate clearing

---

[39] In such cases, line fees are part of the service provider charges and not part of the clearing house charges.

fee.[40] Fees may further vary according to product or product groups (e.g. individual equity, stock index, interest rate, etc.), member type[41] or business type (prop. versus agency business). Finally, transaction-driven fees may be eligible for discount schemes or rebates. A tiered fee structure allows fees to be discounted on an aggregated basis, i.e. according to the trade size (number of contracts per trade) or volume thresholds.[42] Depending on the institutional structure, clearing houses may employ a policy that entails the refunding of part of the transaction-driven fees to members at the end of a financial year.

Event-driven fees result from any 'event' affecting an open position. These fees may thus be charged for option exercises,[43] assignments and adjustments or futures contracts tendered, assigned or cash settled. Therefore, the amount of event-driven fees clearing members have to bear heavily depends on the product portfolio they clear. Clearing houses also charge variable fees for additional services,[44] which can, for example, include the service provision for give-up executions, allocations, claims, transfers, specialised account structures or reports.

Clearing houses may also charge penalties, e.g. for delayed payments or deliveries. The fees commonly involve the refunding of the costs covered by a clearing house when a clearing member issues a late payment or delivery. Additionally, clearing houses sometimes charge a fixed fee per product and day late, requiring a daily interest payment on the outstanding amount to be paid or delivered.[45] Last but not least, variable costs may include possible charges for service level upgrades, such as non-gratuitous network or bandwidth upgrades (insofar as this service has not been outsourced to another service provider).

These fixed and variable components represent a catalogue of various possible clearing house charges; the ultimate scope and type of fees depend on

---

[40] In Europe, Eurex Clearing and OMX Clearing charge an all-in fee, whereas LCH.Clearnet, MEFF and CC&G charge a separate clearing fee.

[41] US clearing houses typically categorise different member types; each member type usually corresponds to individual fee levels. See, e.g. www.cme.com.

[42] Volume thresholds may, for example, refer to daily volume levels, accounting months or yearly cleared contracts.

[43] Note that when exercising an option, the exercise fee is only paid by the buyer.

[44] The definition of which services command additional charges and which are included in the transaction fee differs from one clearing house to another.

[45] This daily interest payment can be calculated on top of a standard reference interest rate, such as the European Central Bank's overnight lending interest rate, or the commercially available money market interest rate.

several factors, such as the clearing house's regulatory environment, institutional structure and general pricing policy.

3.2.1.2 Service provider charges

Service provider charges also consist of one-off, variable and fixed costs. As outlined above, service providers comprise back-office vendors, telecommunications companies, (correspondence) banks, settlement institutions and other GCMs. The number and type of service providers employed usually depend on the relative size of a clearing member. Isolating the clearing-related amount from the overall service provider charges is often difficult, as service providers are commonly employed to provide a variety of internal support services for their clients and not merely those related to clearing.

Back-office vendors are firms providing the financial community with specialised software solutions.[46] Clearing members commonly require their services to integrate the different IT structures from various clearing house interfaces and to customise applications. The back-office solutions provided by these vendors are designed to facilitate processing with various interfaces. Clearing members often employ vendor technology to consolidate their back-office applications into a single user interface, which can lead to improved risk monitoring and scalability.[47] Adaptation of internal systems also becomes necessary when clearing members perform a broad range of clearing services.[48] Such services can include the replication of certain clearing house processes for their clients when data and reports provided by a CCP are incompatible with a clearer's internal processing system. GCMs in particular often require a more detailed internal risk reporting or account structure to serve their clients better, and thus incur costs for this replication. Back-office vendors provide for the necessary system adaptation.[49] They usually charge initial one-off, fixed annual or monthly payments, as well as fees for additional services.

---

[46] A general distinction differentiates front- and back-office vendors. Technology from front-office vendors allows, for example, the loading of various exchanges' screens on to a single platform, and enables customers to search electronically for the best price (best execution) for a trade and choose the exchange with the lowest fees. Cf. Cohen (2005), p. 20.

[47] Scalability refers to the ability of a hardware or software system to adapt to an increase in size or capability.

[48] Cf. Bank for International Settlements (ed.) (2004), p. 6.

[49] Additionally, vendor technology supports the automatic management of services, such as give-ups, reducing manual intervention through monitoring the clearing status of transactions and monitoring margins via a single interface. At the same time, clearing houses update and replace their software and systems periodically, typically on a replacement cycle of five to seven years. Cf. Group of Thirty (ed.) (2003), p. 5. Vendors can facilitate these updates and replacements to clearing members.

Additional charges from service providers may stem from the aforementioned outsourcing of technical infrastructure provision to telecommunications companies, which may charge recurring fixed fees as well as possible fees for service level upgrades or other changes and infrastructure adaptations.

Dealing with a CCP also entails costs for the banking intermediaries. Clearing houses usually demand that all clearing members hold dedicated accounts for the physical delivery of an underlying and cash payments. This requirement entails administrative costs stemming from the maintenance of margin accounts and the calling and calculation of margin requirements.[50] Clearing members that choose not to open an account at such a dedicated bank can utilise the services of a so-called 'correspondence' bank. The clearing member can use the correspondence bank's account at a central bank; the correspondence bank in turn charges fees for this intermediary service.

A fourth category of clearing-related service provider concerns those involved with custody and enabling settlement. As outlined above, these institutions most importantly comprise CSDs and ICSDs. Clearing members need to hold accounts with CSDs/ICSDs and custodians in order to hold and manage collateral, which is employed for margin payments, or physical delivery of positions. Holding accounts and moving collateral translates into fixed and variable costs for clearing members. Due to the limited scope of this study, costs related to settlement and custody services will not be explored and analysed in detail.[51]

Finally, service providers for clearing members can also include other GCMs. As outlined in section 2.3.2, not all clearing members are necessarily members of all the clearing houses relevant for the markets in which they are active. In such cases, clearing members employ the service of other GCMs to clear their transactions, thus acting as NCMs in these other markets. However, clearing members can also employ third-party GCMs as service providers for functions and processes they would otherwise perform internally. This kind of outsourcing can relate to single services, such as regulatory reporting, or complete functional areas, such as back-office functions. Utilising the services of other clearers translates into fixed and variable costs for clearing members.

---

[50] Cf. NERA Economic Consulting (ed.) (2004), p. 11.
[51] Refer to Kröpfl (2003) for an in-depth analysis of transaction costs related to settlement and custody services.

3.2.2 Indirect transaction costs

Clearing services costs entail not only those fees directly charged by clearing houses or service providers, but also any additional internal costs related to the use of the CCP infrastructure and services. These costs are difficult to isolate and measure explicitly; they are therefore referred to as indirect transaction costs. Because these costs are difficult to quantify monetarily, they can often only be estimated. For the purpose of this study, they are categorised as cost of capital, risk management costs, IT costs and back-office costs. In the following, each cost category is defined briefly and its mode of measurement for the purpose of this study is determined.

3.2.2.1 Cost of capital

Utilising clearing services entails the cost of capital that is lodged at the clearing house and tied to the clearing process.[52] The cost of capital is the expected return foregone by the clearing member by bypassing other investment alternatives, i.e. investing its capital elsewhere instead of having to dedicate it to the purpose of clearing. The cost of capital is therefore an opportunity cost, and is commonly also referred to as the opportunity cost of capital.[53] Opportunity costs are transaction costs associated with missed trading[54] or investment opportunities. Opportunity costs thus result from not allocating capital to its most productive investment.[55]

The measurement of the opportunity cost of capital is problematic in that its true measure can be calculated only if it is known how an investment would have performed had it been executed at desired times across an investment horizon.[56] Because this desired investment was not in fact executed, however, the opportunity costs are inherently unobservable and differ from member to member. Nevertheless, one can monitor the theoretical performance of (unexecuted) desired investments by tracking an investment benchmark that reflects the desired investment and thereby estimate the opportunity cost of

---

[52] Cf. NERA Economic Consulting (ed.) (2004), p. 11.
[53] Cf. Brealey/Myers (2000), p. 19.   [54] Cf. Keim/Madhavan (1998), p. 54.
[55] Whether or not opportunity costs should be qualified as another form of transaction cost is debated. Some authors define these as part of transaction costs. Cf. Neus (1998), p. 84; and Collins/Fabozzi (1991), p. 28. Other authors criticise this definition, claiming that because opportunity costs can be illustrated as the difference between two alternatives for action, they should not be defined as a separate category. Further, in order to assess the opportunity costs of an alternative, it is necessary to have knowledge about 'better' alternatives. A rational individual would in this case choose the better alternative.
[56] Refer to Bufka/Schiereck/Zinn (1999); and Bufka/Schiereck (1999); who analyse the suitability of pragmatic approaches to determine the divisional cost of capital for multi-industry firms.

INDIRECT COSTS

Cost of Capital

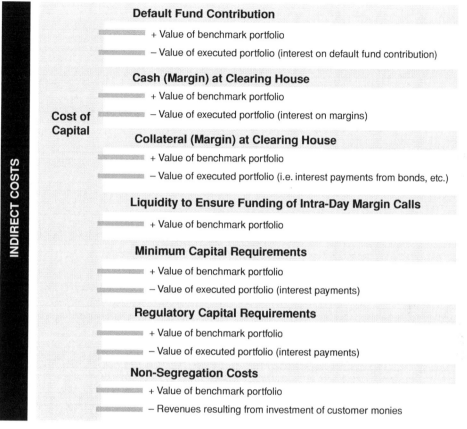

Default Fund Contribution

+ Value of benchmark portfolio

− Value of executed portfolio (interest on default fund contribution)

Cash (Margin) at Clearing House

+ Value of benchmark portfolio

− Value of executed portfolio (interest on margins)

Collateral (Margin) at Clearing House

+ Value of benchmark portfolio

− Value of executed portfolio (i.e. interest payments from bonds, etc.)

Liquidity to Ensure Funding of Intra-Day Margin Calls

+ Value of benchmark portfolio

Minimum Capital Requirements

+ Value of benchmark portfolio

− Value of executed portfolio (interest payments)

Regulatory Capital Requirements

+ Value of benchmark portfolio

− Value of executed portfolio (interest payments)

Non-Segregation Costs

+ Value of benchmark portfolio

− Revenues resulting from investment of customer monies

Figure 3.6   Categorisation of clearing-related cost of capital
Source: Author's own.

capital.[57] The opportunity cost of capital is neither fixed nor directly measurable; it is generally defined as the difference between the performance of an actual investment and the performance of a desired investment, adjusted for fixed costs and execution costs.[58] Due to the complex nature of this calculation, adjustments for fixed and execution costs are not made in this study. To simplify the terminology, the opportunity cost of capital is referred to as 'cost of capital'.

Capital is lodged at the clearing house or tied to the clearing process for different purposes. These purposes comprise possible default fund

---

[57] Cf. Collins/Fabozzi (1991), p. 29.   [58] Cf. Collins/Fabozzi (1991), pp. 27, 28.

contributions, margin payments in cash or collateral, liquidity tied to the clearing process or clearing-related funding efforts. For the purpose of this study, the cost of capital related to clearing is defined as the value of an investment benchmark portfolio minus the value of the executed portfolio,[59] if applicable. The cost of capital a clearing member has to bear in compliance with a clearing house's risk management requirements can be regarded as an offset for the risk assumed by the CCP for the clearing members and for the savings in risk management gained from utilising the services of a CCP.[60] In helping to manage counterparty risk and by providing netting services, CCPs can allow market participants to economise on collateral with regard to what they would otherwise need to hold to ensure equivalent protection in bilaterally cleared markets.[61] A correct calculation of the cost of capital would thus also have to take these aspects into account. Again, due to the complexity of this calculation, its various factors are not explicitly taken into account for the remainder of this analysis.

As detailed in Chapter 2, clearing houses are exposed to a common set of risks that have to be managed effectively. Clearing houses therefore employ three tiers of financial safeguards to control these risks. These safeguards usually consist of a default fund, a margining regime that collateralises the obligations of both the clearing members and their customers and the imposition of minimum financial and capital adequacy requirements on clearing members. These risk-management measures translate into cost of capital for clearing members.[62] Generally, cost of capital can be reduced by CCP interest payments on capital lodged at the clearing house or through interest payments from bonds, etc.

If applicable, the contribution to a clearing house's default fund is a one-off fixed payment prerequisite to becoming a clearing member. The appropriateness of the clearing fund contribution is re-calculated and readjusted on a regular basis by the clearing house. Different indices can be used to determine the value of the investment benchmark portfolio depending on the type of

---

[59] The value of the executed portfolio refers to the return on investment received by the clearing member for the respective amount of capital tied to certain clearing-related purposes.

[60] Further, the opportunity cost of capital clearing members have to bear can also be regarded as compensation for the opportunity costs they would have had to bear if they had not used a CCP. Not transacting (i.e. in case of difficult market conditions) represents an opportunity cost. Cf. Collins/Fabozzi (1991), p. 29. A CCP usually guarantees the execution of transactions even under difficult market conditions, thus eliminating these potential opportunity costs.

[61] Cf. Knott/Mills (2002), p. 163.

[62] Not only clearing members, but also NCMs have to bear the cost of capital related to financial safeguards, i.e. margin collected from the clearing house, and financial safeguards as required by the GCMs.

funding used for the default fund contribution.[63] The payment of interest on default fund contributions reduces the cost of capital.

Margin payments constitute another important financial safeguard for clearing houses. The index used to determine the value of the benchmark portfolio again depends on the nature of the margin payments.[64] Generally, the level of margin payments is reduced by the netting and cross-margining services offered by clearing houses. Especially for large transaction volumes, netting offers huge cost savings, because participants need not hold the respective balance of cash or securities throughout the day.[65] The cost of margin payments additionally depends on the range of instruments accepted as collateral and whether the clearing member receives interest payments on any portion of the margin deposits.[66] Lastly, the cost is affected by 'haircuts' applied to securities deposited at the clearing house.[67]

Similar to the cost of capital resulting from margin payments, cost of capital is also incurred according to the amount of estimated average liquidity tied to ensuring the funding of intra-day margin calls, as the respective amount of liquidity cannot otherwise be invested. Additional cost of capital related to intra-day margin calls can result from exchange rate funding. The necessity for exchange rate funding arises if margin is required in a currency that is not the clearing member's 'home currency'. Banks charge fees for the provision of exchange rate funding.

As mentioned above, clearing houses impose minimum financial and capital adequacy requirements on clearing members that translate into cost of capital. Cost of capital results from imposed restrictions on the investment alternatives for minimum capital requirements and regulatory capital, resulting in the clearing member foregoing the expected return by bypassing other investment alternatives. Additional costs can emerge if a clearing member does not possess the required equity capital *ex ante* and funding becomes

---

[63] In case of a guarantee, a six-month to one-year interest rate can be employed, depending on the nature of the guarantee. Additionally, it has to be taken into account that guarantees incur further costs, such as fee payments to the respective guarantor, or are related to larger 'haircuts', which a clearing house might apply to a guarantee as opposed to cash or securities deposits. 'Haircuts' on guarantees are usually larger due to the uncertainty of the clearing house's final ability to convert the guarantee into cash. In case of funding through cash and/or securities, a three-month interest rate could, for example, be utilised as a benchmark.

[64] In case of a cash margin deposit, a short-term interest rate can be employed, such as the European Central Bank's (ECB) overnight lending rate. In case of collateral deposited for margin purposes, different benchmark indexes can be utilised – such as the repo. rate for bonds; for other collateral, the ECB overnight lending rate can be used.

[65] Cf. Werner (2003), p. 23.   [66] Cf. NERA Economic Consulting (ed.) (2004), p. 18.

[67] Cf. NERA Economic Consulting (ed.) (2004), p. 80.

necessary. As the sole purpose of this funding relates to using the respective clearing house infrastructure, cost of capital is incurred for the amount of equity raised. The same applies if a clearing member does not fulfil regulatory capital requirements *ex ante* and requires funding.[68] Regulatory counterparty capital refers to the capital held by clearing members to meet legislative and regulatory requirements. The relevant criteria are established by national regulators rather than by clearing houses.[69] Where a clearing house acts as a CCP to several markets that are subject to identical or highly correlated risks, the benefit of netting may extend to market risk.[70] This creates the possibility of margin offsets where firms are long in one market and short in another (i.e. margin against a long position in a bond futures contract might be offset against margin against a matching short position in repo.).[71] To the extent that supervisors recognise these offsets, which reduce the financial liabilities of a clearing member when a CCP is involved but not otherwise, regulatory capital requirements may be lower.[72] Regulators may also recognise the reduction in counterparty risk by allowing clearing members to hold less capital than if they were exposed directly to other market participants.[73]

Finally, cost of capital can result from non-segregated customer accounts. Segregation is the optional or compulsory separation of the collateral held by a clearing member on its own behalf from the collateral it holds on behalf of its customers.[74] In the former scenario, the cash and securities are kept in proprietary accounts – as opposed to the cash and securities held on behalf of its customers.[75] If the accounts are segregated, a clearing member may utilise its customers' collateral for a margin deposit at the clearing house. In the case of non-segregated accounts, a clearing member must bear the costs of funding, i.e. has to fund the customer's margin requirement; or (if funding is not required because the clearer has sufficient collateral available) the clearer

---

[68] Isolating the cost of capital related to regulatory capital requirements is difficult, because a clearing member will usually utilise the respective banking or financial intermediary licence for various business purposes, and not only those related to its clearing member status.

[69] The utilised benchmark index to establish the cost of capital related to clearing house and regulatory capital requirements depends on the type of funding. In case of a guarantee, a six-month to one-year interest rate can be employed. In case of a capital increase, the return on equity can be measured.

[70] Cf. Hills *et al.* (1999), p. 125.   [71] Cf. Hills *et al.* (1999), p. 125.

[72] Cf. Hills *et al.* (1999), p. 125. Basel II, with its handling of, e.g. operational risk, could therefore prove to be a major incentive to a wider establishment of CCP clearing. Cf. Ripatti (2004), p. 12.

[73] Cf. Knott/Mills (2002), p. 163.

[74] Cf. Keler (ed.) (1998), p. 66. The rationale behind this requirement is to ensure that a clearing member cannot use client collateral for its own business and that such collateral is protected from the member's general creditors in the event of insolvency.

[75] An account in which the cash or securities, held by the participant on behalf of all (or at least several) of its customers, is kept is called an omnibus customer account. Cf. Keler (ed.) (1998), p. 64.

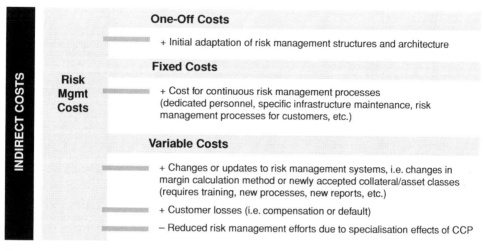

INDIRECT COSTS

Risk Mgmt Costs

One-Off Costs

+ Initial adaptation of risk management structures and architecture

Fixed Costs

+ Cost for continuous risk management processes (dedicated personnel, specific infrastructure maintenance, risk management processes for customers, etc.)

Variable Costs

+ Changes or updates to risk management systems, i.e. changes in margin calculation method or newly accepted collateral/asset classes (requires training, new processes, new reports, etc.)

+ Customer losses (i.e. compensation or default)

− Reduced risk management efforts due to specialisation effects of CCP

Figure 3.7   Categorisation of clearing-related risk management costs
Source: Author's own.

must bear the cost of capital of these margin payments. The resulting cost of capital is mitigated by revenues resulting from the investment of customer monies.

3.2.2.2 Risk management costs

The second category of indirect costs relates to internal risk management costs, which are borne by clearing members. Risk management costs comprise one-off, fixed and variable cost components.

One-off costs arise for the initial adaptation of internal risk management structures and architecture to align with a clearing house's structure, processes and risk methodology. **Fixed costs** comprise costs for continuous risk management processes, i.e. the monitoring of transactions and positions. This involves the employment of dedicated personnel[76] and the maintenance of specific infrastructure, which is either developed internally or acquired externally.[77] A clearing member (GCM) incurs further costs related to executing risk management processes for its customers (and NCMs), i.e. maintenance of margin

---

[76] Note that personnel costs are step costs. These costs are fixed for a given range of cleared volume, but increase to a higher level once a critical volume threshold is reached.

[77] In the event that a clearing member utilises third-party risk management software and infrastructure, the fees paid for this service are attributed to the cost category 'service provider charges'.

accounts and the calling and calculation of margin requirements[78] as well as the ongoing risk monitoring of its customers' positions.[79]

Variable costs arise from changes or updates of the risk management system, i.e. changes in the margin calculation method, or newly accepted asset classes as collateral, which involves the costs of implementing the new process, the potentially new system and adapting it to current structures. Such updates also often require the training of dedicated risk management personnel, which involves more costs. Finally, variable risk management costs can stem from customer losses. These costs arise when a clearing member compensates its customers for incorrect transaction processing or for NCM defaults. In the case of a default, the GCM is liable for any losses not covered by margin payments or other securities deposited by the respective NCM.

As mentioned above, using a CCP can reduce indirect costs, including those associated with counterparty risk management and processing.[80] A CCP that functions well can reduce transaction costs and the cost of risk bearing.[81] One dimension of risk management entails collecting information on the counterparties, which is costly for an investor. Clearing a transaction through a CCP eliminates the need for this step. The CCP redistributes counterparty risk by replacing the individual counterparties' exposure to bilateral credit risk (of variable quality) with the standard credit risk on the CCP.[82] This redistribution reduces transaction costs by improving the monitoring of risk, i.e. by improving the information available to those at risk or their agents. Clearing members may also reduce the amount of resources spent on monitoring individual counterparties, insofar as their actual counterparty is the CCP.[83] The risk redistribution further reduces transaction costs by improving the alignment of risk and reward in the market and thus improving incentives for market participants to control and monitor risk. Finally, the redistribution increases transparency and predictability, so that it becomes clear where potential losses will fall; when this is unclear, asymmetric information on exposure to risk has the potential to create systemic problems.[84] As illustrated by the mechanisms described above, CCPs clearly offer substantial savings

---

[78] Cf. NERA Economic Consulting (ed.) (2004), p. 11.

[79] It can generally be assumed that a GCM has to bear higher risk management costs than an ICM. This is due to the nature of its business – a GCM has to manage risk for its proprietary business as well as for the business conducted by its NCMs. In this case, risk management becomes more complex. A GCM's risk management effort further depends on the quality, in terms of creditworthiness, of its NCMs. The less creditworthy an NCM is, the higher the risk management effort for the GCM becomes.

[80] Cf. NERA Economic Consulting (ed.) (2004), p. 17.

[81] Cf. Hills *et al.* (1999), p. 133.   [82] Cf. Hills *et al.* (1999), p. 126.

[83] Cf. Knott/Mills (2002), p. 163.   [84] Cf. Hills *et al.* (1999), p. 127.

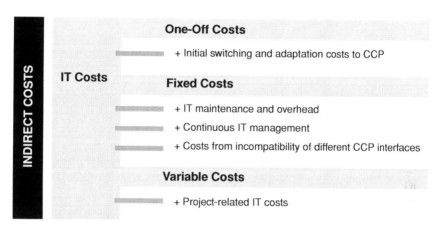

Figure 3.8   Categorisation of clearing-related information technology costs
Source: Author's own.

vis-à-vis risk management costs. However, due to the complexity of measuring and quantifying the actual savings, this analysis will not go into further detail. One reason for the difficulty in gauging the overall cost reductions is that clearing members commonly allocate risk management over different internal business areas and departments. For the purpose of this study, the indicator for quantifying risk management costs is personnel costs; infrastructure, software costs and customer losses are not considered here.

3.2.2.3 Information technology costs

A third category of indirect costs relates to the connectivity between clearing members and clearing houses. Connectivity to clearing houses involves costs referred to as information technology (IT) costs, which stem from the internal management of different interfaces to clearing houses on the part of the clearing members.[85] IT costs comprise one-off, fixed and variable cost components.

One-off IT costs result from the initial conversion to and integration of a new clearing house interface and technology. These costs comprise the requisite internal integration effort and adaptation processes.[86]

---

[85] This classification is based on Lannoo/Levin's (2001), p. 14 classification of interface costs as indirect transaction costs of securities clearing and settlement. For the purpose of this study, a broader terminology is employed by referring to this cost category as IT costs.

[86] In most cases, vendors are hired as intermediaries to ensure a user-friendly integration of interfaces into existing interface management technology. The respective fees charged by vendors for these services are categorised as direct transaction costs, which were detailed in section 3.2.1.

Fixed costs subsume the IT-related maintenance and overheads. Overheads include server locations, back-up sites and personnel costs. IT and interface management, including the ongoing need to manage and adapt various incompatible clearing house interfaces, incur additional fixed costs. As outlined above, IT costs increase with the number of interfaces managed by a clearing member. Generally, the more interfaces in play, the more complex and costly it becomes to clear transactions.[87] Significant costs can incur from the operation of various different systems, due to clearing houses using incompatible IT and interfaces for clearing.[88] Clearing members that are connected to several CCPs thus have to ensure that their communications network can interface with a variety of networks employing widely differing technology and standards. Clearing house services mostly rely on proprietary standards, i.e. systems that clearing members have developed in-house, which vary widely across the industry.[89] Alternatively, clearing members may opt for a vendor solution to connect to different clearing houses and markets[90] and to integrate originally incompatible clearing house technology into a harmonised systems environment. Consequently, the more standardised the clearing house IT and interfaces are, the more clearing members can save on IT costs.[91]

Variable IT costs stem from clearing house projects, which might involve new software releases, connecting and integrating new platforms, products and markets, rebuilding or changing the core clearing system, IT upgrades or other clearing house projects.

3.2.2.4 Back-office costs

The fourth and final category of indirect costs is back-office costs.[92] Back-office costs comprise one-off, fixed and variable cost components. **One-off back-office costs** include the initial costs of connecting to a clearing house, which can comprise initial informational, search and contracting costs. These costs include the compilation of necessary data and information, consultations with vendors regarding the integration of IT structures, business case calculation

---

[87] Cf. Davison (2005), pp. 10–11.
[88] Cf. Barnes (2005), p. 51. If a customer has to connect to ten different platforms and handle ten different ways of post-trade processing, this can imply significant costs.
[89] Cf. Steele (2005), p. 26.
[90] Fees paid for the use of a vendor system then translate into service provider charges.
[91] Cf. Grant (2005), p. 16.
[92] This classification is based on Lannoo/Levin's (2001) and Kröpfl's (2003) classification of back-office costs as transaction cost of securities clearing and settlement. Cf. Lannoo/Levin (2003), p. 14; and Kröpfl (2003), p. 149.

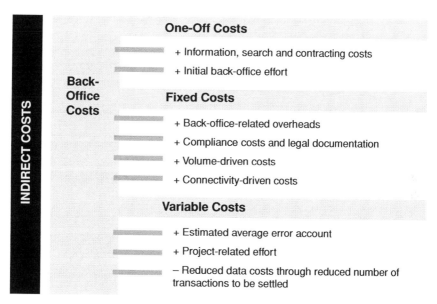

Figure 3.9   Categorisation of clearing-related back-office costs
Source: Author's own.

vis-à-vis the utilisation of the respective CCP and obtaining a legal opinion on contracts from either in-house counsel or from an external law firm.

Additionally, one-off costs comprise the requisite initial back-office effort. Clearing membership is contingent upon the fulfilment of a number of pre-defined admission criteria, which carries costs. Some clearing houses require their clearing members to acquire a certain legal status which eventually involves costs related to obtaining approval from a regulatory agency. More-over, potential clearing members are commonly required to satisfy specified operational procedures defined by the clearing house in order to establish their ability to meet the day-to-day operational requirements of the CCP. Clearing members must also furnish certain data upon admission to the clearing house. The newly integrated structure requires training, setting up specific account structures and opening accounts at (correspondence) banks according to the clearing house's rules and regulations. These efforts all translate into costs.

Fixed back-office costs can be categorised into four distinct groups: back-office-related overheads, compliance costs and legal documentation, volume-driven costs and connectivity-driven costs. Overhead costs encom-pass premises and office infrastructure costs as well as personnel costs, which may include engaging experts on specific markets. Compliance costs and legal documentation refer to back-office costs resulting from efforts to comply with regulatory oversight.

Volume-driven costs refer to costs that are highly dependent on the processed volume.[93] The requisite position management translates into increased back-office effort, i.e. corporate actions processing, expiries and deliveries, settlement processing, etc. Connectivity-driven costs depend on the number of connected interfaces.[94] Back-office costs are affected by the connection to different interfaces in that the variety augments the complexity of processes and management, and potentially requires a greater amount of manual interaction. These costs climb with the need to apply specific accounting principles, manage accounts at various (correspondence) banks and, most importantly, continuously reconcile both internal and external data, such as profit and loss and transaction reports.

It is important to understand the difference between the volume-driven and connectivity-driven cost components. Whereas volume-driven back-office costs can only be reduced by more efficient processing, i.e. through enhanced STP, connectivity-driven costs can only be reduced via a harmonisation or integration of interfaces.[95] Back-office costs escalate significantly due to the inefficient transaction processing commonly found in fax, paper-based and proprietary systems. The inefficiency, which is caused by duplication of connectivity and operational costs, leads to higher risks and costs.[96] The more standardised the process for the valuation of securities, margin calls and payments of dividends, the higher the reduction in back-office costs.[97] The use of old technology and manual processes in back-office systems translates into expensive operations with high failure rates and augmented risk. Another source of complexity and contributor to back-office costs is the plethora of different rules and conflicting laws in Europe.[98]

Variable back-office costs include error account and project-related costs. The error account settles losses resulting from failed deliveries or payments.[99]

---

[93] Volume-driven costs are defined as fixed costs, because personnel costs are employed as a mode of measurement in this study. The number of employed back-office staff depends on the overall back-office effort on the part of the clearing member, and is unlikely to be impacted by short-term variations of the number of contracts cleared. Nonetheless, while these costs are fixed for a given range of cleared volume, they can increase once a critical volume threshold is reached (step costs).

[94] Note that systems costs related to various interfaces are classified as IT costs.

[95] An integration of interfaces has no impact on volume-driven back-office costs and possibly also encompasses a reduction of (correspondence) bank interfaces. If a single bank account could be used to process transactions cleared at different clearing houses, this would reduce back-office costs.

[96] Cf. Barnes (2005), p. 51.

[97] Cf. Hills *et al.* (1999), p. 125.   [98] Cf. Deutsche Börse Group (ed.) (2002), p. 27.

[99] If a clearing member operates the back-office as a profit centre, the error account is booked there; otherwise, it is commonly credited to the institution's trading accounts.

The elimination of poor data, manual processes and weak communications that typically cause such failures could obviate the need for an error account and thus result in (significant) savings.[100] Additionally, real-time settlement information,[101] as well as the harmonisation of operating hours and settlement deadlines,[102] can improve the ability of clearing members to prevent failures. The error rate climbs dramatically in the absence of STP. A lack of STP can lead to a high degree of manual intervention being required. At its most sophisticated form, automation allows for the elimination of manual intervention altogether. Variable back-office costs also stem from efforts related to clearing house projects.[103]

Utilising a CCP structure can reduce back-office costs, including processing and data costs, which are dependent on the number of transactions forwarded to settlement. Multilateral netting substantially reduces the number of transactions available for settlement and therefore lessens operational costs.[104] In addition, netting decreases the number of individual contractual obligations, which serves to streamline customer books and balance sheets and reduce the complexity of back-office processes. Due to the complexity of measuring and quantifying the savings from the reductions in back-office costs, these savings are not analysed in the context of this study. For the purpose of this study, the indicator for quantifying back-office costs is personnel costs; an estimation of the average error account is not part of the study.

3.3 Network strategies

There are two main advantages to be gained from consolidation in the clearing industry: explicit cost reductions through economies of scale as well as internal cost reductions for customers by virtue of fewer interfaces having to be supported.[105]

As indicated above, there are numerous opportunities to reduce clearing costs. For the purpose of this study, the research focus lies on analysing the impact that certain integration and harmonisation initiatives between clearing houses can have on the transaction costs of clearing. These integration and harmonisation initiatives are referred to as network strategies. Network

---

[100] Cf. Group of Thirty (ed.) (2003), p. 5.
[101] Cf. NERA Economic Consulting (ed.) (2004), p. 84.   [102] Cf. Barnes (2005), p. 51.
[103] Project-related back-office costs are classified as a variable component, because the effort most likely includes the relocation of staff internally to the project and/or the hiring of external consultants. Project-related costs are elevated if the project entails exposure to new regulatory environments.
[104] Cf. Ripatti (2004), p. 12.   [105] Statement made by interviewed exchange representative.

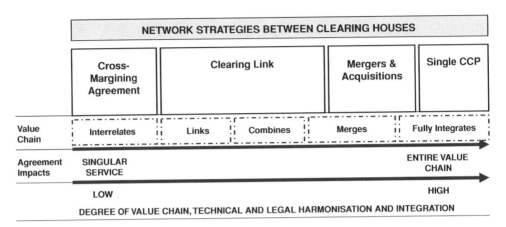

Figure 3.10 Classification of network strategies between clearing houses
Source: Author's own.

strategies between clearing houses can potentially impact both direct and indirect costs. Whereas this effect is analysed in detail in the remainder of the study, the following section begins by providing a definition and classification of the different network strategies to be analysed (section 3.3.1), followed by an overview of selected network initiatives between clearing houses from 1973 to 2006 (section 3.3.2).

3.3.1 Classification of network strategies

The term 'network strategies' refers to different forms of cooperative, i.e. institutional, arrangements between two or more clearing houses. Following a brief classification of different network strategies, the nature and characteristics of each strategy as well as its impact on the structure of the VPN is explained.

Figure 3.10 provides a classification of the different network strategies that are analysed in this study. Network strategies can be differentiated according to the related degree of value chain, technical and legal harmonisation[106] as well as integration.[107] Depending on the type of strategy employed, the clearing houses' value chain interrelates, links, combines, merges or is fully integrated. Network strategies can be restricted to singular services or can comprise the CCPs' entire value chain. The associated degree of harmonisation and

---

[106] Harmonisation means the alignment of standards, practices and processes.
[107] Integration refers to the merging of standards, practices and processes, resulting in a single structure.

integration ranges from low to very high. The greater the degree of value chain integration, the more the clearing houses' level of autonomy declines, i.e. the higher the level of inter-organisational dependencies between the partners.[108] Also, the higher the level of integration through a certain initiative, the stronger the potential effect of any given initiative on the structure of the Value Provision Network.

3.3.1.1 Cross-margining agreements

The weakest form of cooperation between clearing houses is the establishment of a cross-margining agreement. Cross-margining agreements refer to contractual agreements between clearing houses for jointly margining transactions in designated products.[109] The underlying concept is identical to the cross-margining of different products within a single clearing house, as outlined in section 2.1.2.2.

Cross-margining is based on the idea that certain inter-market trading positions with offsetting risk characteristics can be margined together as a single portfolio. Cross-margining agreements replicate the margin offsets that would be available to clearing members of the partnering clearing houses if certain products were cleared through the same clearing house. Offsetting exposures on both clearing houses are consequently netted across the correlated products for the purpose of calculating margin requirements.

Cross-margining agreements are either limited to designated products or extend to the complete product portfolio of the partnering clearing houses.[110] A cross-margining agreement usually serves to interrelate two clearing houses, but can extend to several clearing houses.

Cross-margining programs have long been recognized for both enhancing the safety and soundness of clearing systems and for allowing members to optimize their capital usage by viewing their positions at different clearing organizations as combined portfolio. Various risk management benefits result, including providing clearing organizations with more complete data concerning the true risk of inter-market positions and enhanced sharing of collateral resources.[111]

For the purpose of this study, two archetypes of cross-margining agreement are classified and distinguished according to their functional set-up: the so-called 'one-pot' and 'two-pot' approaches (see Figure 3.11).

---

[108] Cf. Contractor/Lorange (1988), p. 7.   [109] Cf. National Futures Association (2006).
[110] Clearing houses usually limit cross-margining agreements to selected products that are economically correlated. Cf. Hart/Russo/Schönenberger (2002), p. 26.
[111] DTCC (2002).

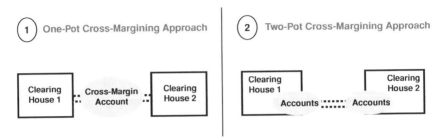

Figure 3.11   Classification of cross-margining agreements according to their functional set-up
Source: Author's own.

The **one-pot cross-margining approach** refers to a set-up whereby the two partnering clearing houses set up a joint account into which the required margin on the eligible contracts is deposited.[112] All of the margin requirements and deposits are put into this one pot, i.e. the cross-margin account, and the clearing houses co-own the account. A previously established agreement determines the applicable margin offsets.[113] Management of the account is usually centralised and conducted by one elected clearing house, which applies its risk management programme and calculates the applicable margin. In the event of a default, the clearing houses divide up the deposits in the cross-margin account according to a predetermined procedure.[114] Each clearing house can usually only access funds according to jointly determined instructions.[115] Implementing and operating one-pot cross-margining agreements is usually cumbersome for clearing houses, because they involve additional effort. The more manual intervention such a set-up requires, the higher the related complexity.

With the **two-pot cross-margining approach**, the partnering clearing houses hold the margin for the eligible positions in separate accounts at their respective CCPs. The accounts at each partnering clearing house are treated as though the positions were internally available in terms of margin offsets granted. Margin owed is thus calculated separately by each clearing house and each clearing house continues to operate its own risk management programme. In the event of a default, a previously established loss-sharing agreement applies. The agreement is intended to leave the partnering clearing

---

[112] Cf. Hart/Russo/Schönenberger (2002), p. 25.
[113] Margin offsets granted are reviewed regularly in both cross-margining approaches.
[114] The exact default procedure of handling the cross-margining account is complicated and involves legal details that cannot be addressed in the context of this study.
[115] Cf. Hart/Russo/Schönenberger (2002), p. 25.

houses no worse off in terms of financial resources available in a default situation than for internal offsets. This means that in case the defaulting clearing member's account is in profit at one clearing house (in terms of margin provided versus losses), then this amount would be used to offset any losses facing the other clearing house.[116] Even though the two-pot approach to the technical processing of the cross-margining is simpler than the one-pot method, in the event of a default, two-pot approaches increase complexity and give rise to a number of tricky legal details, especially in the case of cross-border agreements.[117]

For the clearing members, both approaches can either function automatically or require the manual selection of positions available for cross-margining. Clearing members generally prefer to manage actively their positions, i.e. manually select the transactions that will be made eligible for cross-margining.[118]

The outlined archetypes of cross-margining agreements show that this network strategy is limited to a singular service, i.e. the interrelation of the partnering clearing houses' value chains, affecting margining and related processes and functions. Cross-margining agreements thus involve a low degree of value chain, technical and legal harmonisation as well as integration.

3.3.1.2 Clearing links

The second type of network strategy that can be employed by clearing houses is the creation of **clearing links**. Links between clearing houses allow clearing members to benefit from expanded clearing opportunities through their established clearing membership. The most important feature of a clearing link is that the established relationship between a clearing house and its clearing members remains largely unchanged.

Following a definition employed by the Bank for International Settlements (1997b) and Hills and Young (1998), the clearing house at which a clearer maintains a membership is referred to as the 'home clearing house'. The clearing house with which the clearer has no direct relationship is called the

---

[116] Cf. Financial Services Authority (ed.) (2006), p. 23.

[117] Refer to Hart/Russo/Schönenberger (2002) for details on such issues and risks inherent to cross-margining agreements.

[118] In case of clearing houses automatically making all of their clearing members' transactions (in products eligible for cross-margining with the partner clearing house) available for cross-margining, clearing members might actually be worse off than they would be without the cross-margining agreement.

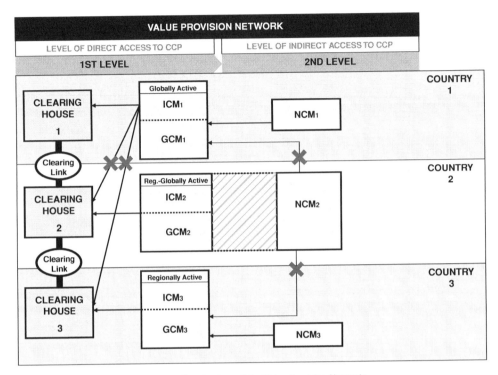

Figure 3.12   Clearing links' impact on the structure of the Value Provision Network
Source: Author's own.

'away clearing house'.[119] For globally active clearers who are by definition a member of several clearing houses, the 'home clearing house' refers to the CCP located in the clearer's country of origin. All other CCPs at which the clearer holds a direct membership are referred to as 'away clearing houses'.

Clearing members benefit from expanded clearing opportunities, because additional products – originally cleared through the away clearing house – become available for clearing through the link, and the clearing members can continue to utilise the existing infrastructure of their home clearing house. Figure 3.12 illustrates how globally as well as regionally-to-globally active clearing members benefit from clearing links. Links eliminate the need for clearers to become members of, or to appoint intermediaries in, the away clearing house.[120] Links also give clearers the choice of accessing clearing services through either one of the partnering clearing houses. A link usually

---

[119] Similarly, the primary exchange for the trading of contracts subject to the link is the 'home exchange'; the 'away exchange' refers to any other exchange(s) involved in the link set-up. Cf. Hills/Young (1998), p. 161.
[120] Cf. The Clearing Corporation (ed.) (2004), p. 6.

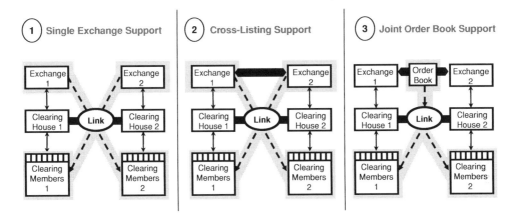

Figure 3.13   Classification of clearing links according to their business purpose
Source: Based on Eurex/The Clearing Corporation (eds.) (2004a), p. 3.

serves to interrelate two clearing houses, but can extend to link several clearing houses. The way and extent to which clearing links affect the VPN is analysed in greater detail in the remainder of the study.

For the purpose of this research, clearing links are classified and distinguished according to their business purpose and functional set-up.[121]

Hills and Young (1998) differentiate three types of link: links for joint clearing of a contract traded on a single exchange, links to support cross-listing arrangements and links to support joint electronic order books.[122] This typology allows the links to be classified according to their business purpose (see Figure 3.13).

When a clearing link serves the purpose of **supporting a single exchange**, clearing members can clear products at the away exchange through their existing membership with their home clearing house.[123] Single exchange support does not necessarily imply the restriction of the link functionality to one

---

[121] Clearing links can additionally be distinguished according to the access and distribution of the open interest of the link-affected products. Generally, links can be set up with a split open interest, i.e. the home clearing house is the sole holder of the open interest, or with a consolidated open interest pool, in which case the partnering clearing houses are equal holders of the open interest. For the purpose of this study, this distinction is not separately classified, but analysed as part of the defined archetypes.

[122] Cf. Hills/Young (1998), p. 161.

[123] With reference to Figure 3.14, Exchange 1 is the home exchange for products originally traded on this exchange, and cleared through Clearing House 1. The home clearing house for Clearing Members 1 is thus Clearing House 1. The home clearing house for Clearing Members 2 is consequently Clearing House 2. From the perspective of Clearing Members 2, Clearing House 1 is the away clearing house; from the perspective of Clearing Members 1, Clearing House 2 is the away clearing house. Prior to the introduction of the link, Clearing Members 2 were required to either employ an intermediary to clear the products traded on Exchange 1, or to themselves become clearing members of Clearing House 1.

exchange; if the link works in both directions, it serves to benefit both part-nering clearing houses. The link therefore provides 'Clearing Members 1' with expanded clearing opportunities, as 'Clearing House 1' is now able to clear products traded on 'Exchange 1' as well as products traded on 'Exchange 2' (Figure 3.13). 'Clearing Members 2' benefit because 'Clearing House 2' is now able to clear products traded on 'Exchange 2' as well as products traded on 'Exchange 1'. The purpose of this kind of link is to facilitate access to the home exchange's products.

Note that this business purpose corresponds to the exchange perspective rather than to the clearing house perspective. Clearing houses engage in links to enlarge the scale and scope of the clearing opportunities they offer at reduced costs. A link can reduce the costs of systems development and operation faced by clearing houses, because it enables the partners to share these expenses.[124]

Depending on the link structure, the network strategy can lead to an unequal distribution of benefits for the partners. Whereas the away clearing house can benefit greatly from a link, as it can thereby offer broadened clearing oppor-tunities to its clearing members, the home clearing house may find itself at a disadvantage. The reasons for this are twofold: by extending trading opportu-nities without imposing all of the costs normally associated with establishing clearing relationships, links can deepen the liquidity in markets.[125] Should the link truly lead to an increase in volumes generated by members of the away clearing house, the home clearing house is initially unable to partake of these revenues. Secondly, the implementation of a link enables members of the away clearing house to clear the additional link products without the need to employ an intermediary. The introduction of a link can thus lead to a reduc-tion of volumes cleared through the home clearing house if globally as well as regionally-to-globally active clearers of the away clearing house cancel their intermediary relationship with 'Clearing Members 1'. This unequal distribu-tion of profits can be remedied by mechanisms existing within the contractual structures of the link set-up. Links can be structured to compensate partners for unequal distribution of profits.

The logic of a link **supporting cross-listed products** works in a similar manner. A product launched by one exchange (the 'home exchange', which is the primary exchange for trading the contract subject to the link) can also be traded on another exchange (the 'away exchange') if the product is listed on both exchanges. This is referred to as the 'cross-listing' of products. The away

---

[124] Cf. Bank for International Settlements (ed.) (2004), p. 40.
[125] Cf. Bank for International Settlements (ed.) (2004), p. 40.

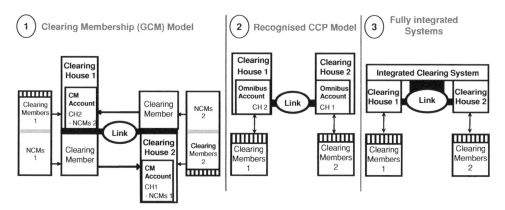

Figure 3.14   Classification of clearing links according to their functional set-up
Source: Author's own.

exchange is commonly located in a different country and time zone, resulting in an extension of trading hours for the respective products.[126] Clearing links supporting cross-listed products enable these contracts to be traded on away exchanges in different time zones, but be cleared at the clearing members' home clearing house.[127] In other words, clearing members benefit from being able to clear the contracts at their home clearing house throughout the entire trading day, regardless of where the underlying transactions are executed.

Finally, links between clearing houses can serve to **support a joint order book** between exchanges.[128] These links enable clearing members to clear all contracts traded through the joint order book at their respective home clearing house. Clearing links can further be distinguished according to their functional set-up.[129] The functional set-up and technical sophistication of links generally varies. Figure 3.14 illustrates three archetypes of a link set-up.

---

[126] Exchanges usually employ cross-listing for liquid, popular contracts. Cross-listing consequently enables trading to take place when the home exchange is closed. Cf. Hills/Young (1998), p. 161.

[127] Cf. Hills/Young (1998), p. 160.

[128] The creation of a joint order book either refers to the establishment of common trading platforms between different exchanges, i.e. replacing separate structures with a joint platform, or to exchanges engaging in joint ventures to enter new markets. The joint order book then relates to a newly created venture that does not affect incumbent trading platforms.

[129] The Bank for International Settlements (ed.) (1997b) differentiates between two types of link; clearing links and mutual offset systems. In contrast to a clearing link, a mutual offset system allows clearing members to choose the clearing house with which they want to hold their positions. Positions thus can, but need not be, transferred from one clearing house to another. Cf. Bank for International Settlements (ed.) (1997b), p. 34; Chicago Mercantile Exchange (ed.) (2003), p. 77; and McPartland (2003b). Mutual offset systems require that both clearing houses recognise each other as clearing houses, mirroring the transactions of the partner CCP. For the purpose of this study, mutual offset systems are not analysed separately. For further details on the functioning of mutual offset systems, refer to McPartland (2003b).

'The different types of links can be distinguished according to the degree to which the systems of the linked CCPs are integrated and whether the obligations of the CCPs to their clearing participants are shifted. In the most straightforward type of link, one CCP becomes a clearing participant of another CCP without any further integration of systems.'[130] When a **Clearing Membership (GCM) Model** set-up is chosen, each product available for clearing through the link remains under the responsibility of the home clearing house. The home clearing house is thus the counterparty in all transactions involving the particular link products. The away clearing house acts in the role of a clearing member to the home clearing house, and vice versa if the link functions in both directions. The rules and regulations applying to clearing members of the respective CCPs form the general basis for the functional set-up of the link. Consequently, the away clearing house, which acts as a clearing member, can, for example, be obliged to provide margins and contributions to the clearing fund according to the rules of the home clearing house. Depending on the details of the functional link set-up, the away clearing house can be granted privileges that are not available to the regular clearing member firms.[131] In this case, the away clearing house becomes a 'special' clearing member of the home clearing house, implying that the clearing house is exempt from certain routine clearing processes; however, specialised processes that do not apply to regular clearing members might be mandatory for the away clearing house.[132] Whereas this set-up is easiest in terms of functional implementation and the interlinking of systems, it entails a number of limitations and drawbacks. For one thing, it is usually not possible to net obligations in a link that works in both directions; many clearing houses limit membership to firms with a bank or broker licence, which in turn implies that the partnering clearing house needs to be in possession of such a licence.[133] Furthermore, the away clearing house, acting as a (specialised) clearing member, has to enter into additional contracts with its clearing members, because these now become NCMs from the perspective of the linked home clearing house.[134]

The second archetype of a link set-up is the **Recognised CCP Model**. As the denomination suggests, the partnering clearing houses participate in each other's systems as equals.[135] As opposed to the cross-clearing membership type

---

[130] Bank for International Settlements (ed.) (2004), pp. 40–41.
[131] Cf. McPartland (2003a).   [132] Cf. McPartland (2003a).
[133] Applying for these licences involves a significant effort and is also often a tedious and expensive process.
[134] This also requires the respective clearing members, now considered NCMs, to enter into new or additional contracts with their customers.
[135] Cf. Bank for International Settlements (ed.) (2004), p. 43.

of link, both clearing houses may act in their role as clearing house at any time. The basis for the cooperation between the partners is thus not their respective rules and regulations, but a dedicated contractual framework – the clearing link agreement. This defines, amongst other things, the responsibilities and obligations of each partner, as well as the risk management approach. Each clearing house reflects the positions of the partner clearing house in the form of an omnibus account.[136] This means that the opening of a position at one CCP can automatically lead to the creation of an equal and opposite position at the linked CCP.[137] A more common handling, which serves to reduce the complexity of such processing, is to create equal and opposite positions of the net balance at predetermined times, i.e. at regular intervals (e.g. every five to ten minutes) or once at the end of the trading day.

The existing relationships between each clearing house and its clearing members do not change. This type of link set-up requires a greater level of functional, technical and legal harmonisation and integration in comparison with the first model. Obligations between the involved clearing houses and between the clearing members and their home clearing house are usually separated. However, in terms of risk management,[138] each clearing house has to bear its own risk as well as that of the other clearing house, which is not covered in the event that the other clearing house defaults. Therefore, clearing houses using this kind of link set-up commonly implement credit support mechanisms to deal with the risks related to variation margin obligations between the clearing houses.[139]

The third archetype of a functional link set-up refers to the **fully integrated systems** of the partnering clearing houses.

In the most integrated form of link, the CCPs effectively merge their systems to offer a single clearing platform. The participant of one CCP will continue its relationship with that CCP, but all risk management is effected by the wholly integrated systems of the linked CCPs. The participation, default, margin requirements, financial resources and operational requirements to which CCP participants are subject become harmonised

---

[136] An omnibus account is an account maintaining the positions of multiple clients. Cf. Loader (2004), p. 214. Each omnibus account, maintained on the books of a home clearing house for the away clearing house, contains one or more omnibus sub-accounts. Each such omnibus sub-account reflects positions submitted by the clearing members of the away clearing house.

[137] Cf. Bank for International Settlements (ed.) (2004), p. 43.

[138] Regarding a more detailed assessment of the risks involved with clearing links, refer to Hills/Young (1998); Bank for International Settlements (ed.) (2004); and Euronext (ed.) (2005).

[139] Clearing houses using this kind of link set-up commonly implement sufficient and irrevocable credit support mechanisms to deal with the risks related to variation margin obligations between the clearing houses. Mechanisms employed include the implementation of credit lines, letters of credit, guarantees or insurances.

and may thus differ from the requirements in place at one or both of the CCPs prior to the link.[140]

Integrating systems requires a high degree of value chain integration, especially in terms of functional, technical and legal harmonisation as well as integration. This type of set-up is thus the most difficult type of link to implement, because it entails a significant integration effort from the involved clearing houses. Clearing members are impacted because they need to integrate the related updates and changes to rules, regulations and processes.

To summarise, there are several kinds of clearing link design, each with a particular degree of value chain integration and functionality. The classification of links served to clarify that links involve a varying degree of integration depending on their specific purpose and functional set-up. The provided definitions refer to theoretical archetypes of clearing links; in reality, however, additional clearing link designs might exist.

3.3.1.3 Mergers and acquisitions

Whereas cross-margining agreements have the character of relatively straightforward contractual arrangements, links are more akin to strategic alliances or joint ventures. Despite the relatively high degree of integration related to links with fully integrated systems, both scenarios nonetheless enable the partners to maintain their economic and legal independence.[141] The third type of network strategy between clearing houses – mergers and acquisitions (M&A) – refers to cooperation scenarios that entail the loss of economic and legal independence of one or all partners.

Acquisitions refer to transactions that involve either the purchase of shareholdings in the partner clearing house or the purchase of the entire clearing entity. A full acquisition results in the full integration of the purchased entity and its value chain into the acquirer's existing company structure; the acquired enterprise loses its identity. Mergers occur when partners join together to form a new legal entity, with or without prior shareholding.[142]

Figure 3.15 illustrates how globally as well as regionally-to-globally active clearing members benefit from mergers and acquisitions between clearing houses when both value chains are fully integrated. In the context of mergers, both clearing houses integrate, but usually maintain part of their old identity (e.g. name, logo, etc.). A merger thus does not necessarily result in the full

---

[140] Bank for International Settlements (ed.) (2004), p. 43.
[141] Refer to Knoppe (1997), p. 43, for details on strategic alliances within the financial industry.
[142] Cf. Wöhe (1996), p. 943; and Achleitner (2001), p. 141.

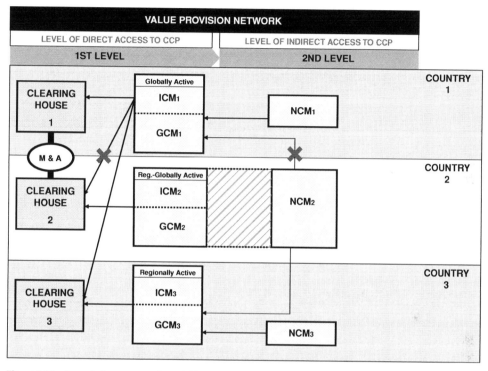

Figure 3.15   Impact of mergers and acquisitions on the structure of the Value Provision Network
Source: Author's own.

integration of both value chains. The way and extent in which mergers and acquisitions affect the Value Provision Network is analysed in greater detail in the remainder of the study.

3.3.1.4 Single central counterparty

The final type of network strategy and the strongest form of cooperation between clearing houses is the Single CCP. This strategy derives from the previously explained mergers and acquisitions scenario, resulting in a full consolidation of market infrastructure. The Single CCP scenario thus stands for mergers and acquisitions initiatives that lead to the creation of a single clearing entity for a defined asset class,[143] and within a defined economic area.[144] Depending on the market structure, the creation of a single clearing

---

[143] A Single CCP solution can thus be sought for the clearing of securities, financial derivatives, energy derivatives or any relevant subcategory thereof.

[144] An economic area can refer to a country, a continent or any other predefined economic region, such as the European Union.

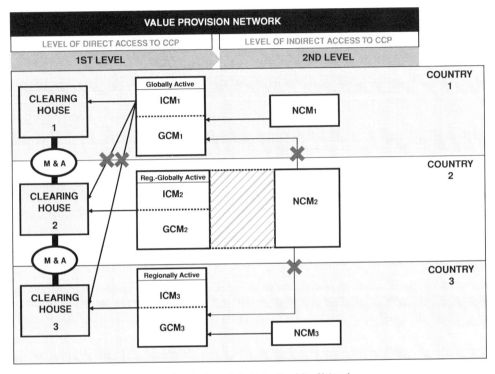

Figure 3.16   Single CCP's impact on the structure of the Value Provision Network
Source: Author's own.

house can involve two or several CCPs. This network strategy implies the full integration of the partnering clearing houses' entire value chains, as well as technical and legal harmonisation and integration.[145]

Figure 3.16 illustrates how globally as well as regionally-to-globally active clearing members benefit from the creation of a Single CCP. The way and extent to which a Single CCP affects the VPN is analysed in greater detail in the remainder of the study.

Note that the provided classification of network strategies refers to theoretical archetypes. In reality, integration and harmonisation initiatives between clearing houses commonly involve the characteristics of several different archetypical set-ups. Cross-margining agreements have, for example, some of the same implications for clearing houses as links, because the partners rely

---

[145] Note that the outlined network strategies refer to theoretical archetypes used for the purpose of this study; in reality a merger might have more the characteristics of a link, and a Single CCP might not necessarily involve the full integration of the entire value chain.

on each other's risk management systems when viewing a clearing member's positions and supporting margin as a single portfolio.[146] On the other hand, clearing links often include some form of cross-margining agreement, and the scenario of fully integrated systems embraces characteristics of a mergers and acquisitions strategy. Finally, acquisitions might only lead to a weak form of integration and harmonisation, and mergers can in reality more closely resemble a clearing link structure.

3.3.2 Overview of network initiatives from 1973 to 2006

Whereas the previous section detailed and classified network strategies between clearing houses, this section provides an overview of selected network initiatives from 1973 to 2006. Numerous cooperative agreements in the form of cross-margining agreements, links, mergers and acquisitions as well as Single CCP initiatives have been announced and established over the years. The overview focuses on initiatives between major derivatives clearing houses, which were selected according to data availability.

Figure 3.17 provides an overview of cross-margining agreements and clearing links. The overview of cross-margining agreements suggests that this type of network strategy has mainly been utilised on a domestic basis, whereas most clearing links were subject to partners cooperating across borders.

The set-up of the selected cross-margining agreements varies. The agreement between the CME, OCC, BOTCC (today called CCorp) and NYCC (today called ICE Clear US), for example, utilises a one-pot approach.[147] The agreement was established in 1989 and included the BOTCC, which joined after the CME and OCC had started it, and was then later joined by the NYCC.

The Government Securities Clearing Corporation (GSCC, which today is part of DTCC) and NYCC cross-margining agreement from 1999, on the other hand, relies on a two-pot approach.[148] The CME and LCH agreement, announced in 2000, also constitutes a two-pot cross-margining approach.[149]

As outlined in the previous section, there are different types of clearing link, all with varying degrees of value chain integration. One of the most renowned links was also among the earliest initiatives – the clearing link between CME and the Singapore Exchange (SGX, formerly SIMEX); established in 1984, it is

---

[146] Cf. Bank for International Settlements (ed.) (2004), p. 41.
[147] Cf. Chicago Mercantile Exchange (ed.) (2003), p. 77.
[148] Cf. Chicago Mercantile Exchange (ed.) (2003), p. 78.
[149] Cf. Financial Services Authority (ed.) (2006), p. 23.

Year	Partnering Clearing Houses	Status
Cross-Margining Agreements		
1988	CME and OCC	I
1989	BOTCC joined CME and OCC agreement, later followed by NYCC	I
1990	ICC and OCC	I
1993	ICC, OCC and CME trilateral agreement	I
1996	BOTCC and CCOS	I
1999	CME and BOTCC	I
1999	GSCC and NYCC	I
2000	CME and LCH	I
2001	BOTCC and GSCC	I
2001	OCC and DTCC	I
2002	GSCC and CME	I
2002	GSCC and BrokerTec Clearing Company	I
2002	CME and NYMEX Clearing	I
Clearing Links		
1976	LCH and Clearnet (formerly ICCH and MATIF)	I
1984	CME and SIMEX	I
1987	OCC and Amsterdam Clearing Corporation	I
1989	OM and OM London Exchange (OMLX)	I
1995	SIMEX and LCH	I
1995	TIFFE and LCH	I
1997	DTB and MATIF (Euro Alliance)	F
1997	LCH and BOTCC	I
1997	DTB and SIMEX	F
1997	OM, OMLX and NOS	I
1997	OM, OMLX and SOM	I
2001	OM and FUTOP	I
2001	CME and MEFF	I
2002	CC&G and Clearnet	I
2003	LCH.Clearnet and SIS x-clear	I
2003	Eurex and CCorp	I
2004	Stockholmsbörsen and LCH.Clearnet	I

Network Initiatives between Clearing Houses

Figure 3.17   Selection of cross-margining agreements and clearing links (status: I = Implemented; F = Failed)[150]
Source: Author's own.

still in use.[151] From a business purpose perspective, it supports cross-listing, and from a functional perspective, it is constructed as a Clearing Membership (GCM) Model.[152] This link supports the cross-listing of the following futures contracts: Eurodollar, Euroyen TIBOR, Euroyen LIBOR and Japanese Government Bonds. It allows clearing members to choose the clearing house with which they hold positions in the respective contracts. Positions can, but need

---

[150] The status does not indicate whether or not the outlined network initiatives are still in place.
[151] For more details on the link, refer to Lee (1998), pp. 76–96.   [152] Cf. McPartland (2003a).

not, be transferred from one clearing house to another.[153] Members of the CME can thus open a Eurodollar Futures position on SGX and have it cleared at the CME, and vice versa.[154]

An example of a different type of link is the set-up established by the 1997 linkage between OM (today OMX), OM London Exchange (OMLX, today replaced by EDX London and LCH.Clearnet) and the Norwegian Futures and Options Clearing House (NOS). This structure, named 'Linked Exchanges and Clearing' (LEC), was later joined by the Finnish Securities and Derivatives Exchange Clearing House (SOM) and the Danish FUTOP clearing house. It served to support a joint order book between OM and OMLX for most of the products traded on the respective exchanges; between OM, OMLX and NOS for Norwegian and Swedish equity futures and options; between OM, OMLX and SOM for Finnish equity derivatives, bond and interest rate derivatives;[155] and between OM and FUTOP for Finnish equity-related derivatives. From a functional perspective, it resembles the fully integrated systems set-up. The LEC link set-up is still operating at the time of writing.

Finally, an example of a link constructed to support a single exchange is the one established between LCH.Clearnet and SIS x-clear to support the London-based exchange virt-x. Both interlinked clearing houses clear the full range of products traded on the exchange, allowing members the choice of clearing location. According to the functional set-up, the link resembles the Recognised CCP Model.

Figure 3.18 lists various mergers and acquisitions initiatives and also presents different attempts to create a Single CCP. Whereas links are used to cooperate across borders, mergers and acquisitions have been used in both contexts – domestic partnerships as well as cross-border consolidation. Mergers have primarily served to consolidate domestic market infrastructure, but clearing houses have shown an early interest in integrating on an international basis, as demonstrated by OCC's attempted acquisition of the London-based International Commodities Clearing House (ICCH) in the early 1980s. Within Europe, clearing house partnerships increasingly tend to strive for regional integration. In 1998, the Swiss Soffex and the German Deutsche Terminbörse (DTB) merged, which included the formation of a common clearing house (Eurex Clearing). This was followed by the merger of the Belgian, French and Dutch CCPs to form the Paris-based Clearnet in 2001. The latest example of a

---

[153] Cf. Bank for International Settlements (ed.) (1997b), p. 34.

[154] The CME/SGX link is the typical example of a link operating as a mutual offset system. Cf. Thackray (1997).

[155] Cf. Hills/Young (1998), p. 161.

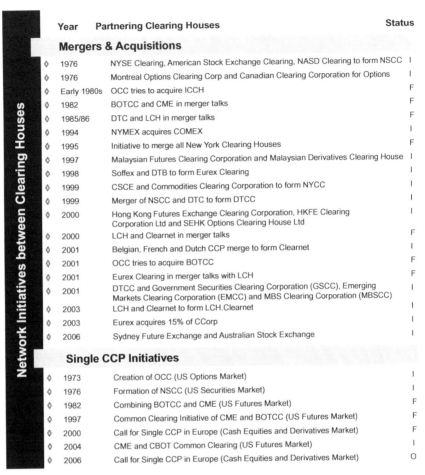

Year	Partnering Clearing Houses	Status
Mergers & Acquisitions		
1976	NYSE Clearing, American Stock Exchange Clearing, NASD Clearing to form NSCC	I
1976	Montreal Options Clearing Corp and Canadian Clearing Corporation for Options	I
Early 1980s	OCC tries to acquire ICCH	F
1982	BOTCC and CME in merger talks	F
1985/86	DTC and LCH in merger talks	F
1994	NYMEX acquires COMEX	I
1995	Initiative to merge all New York Clearing Houses	F
1997	Malaysian Futures Clearing Corporation and Malaysian Derivatives Clearing House	I
1998	Soffex and DTB to form Eurex Clearing	I
1999	CSCE and Commodities Clearing Corporation to form NYCC	I
1999	Merger of NSCC and DTC to form DTCC	I
2000	Hong Kong Futures Exchange Clearing Corporation, HKFE Clearing Corporation Ltd and SEHK Options Clearing House Ltd	I
2000	LCH and Clearnet in merger talks	F
2001	Belgian, French and Dutch CCP merge to form Clearnet	I
2001	OCC tries to acquire BOTCC	F
2001	Eurex Clearing in merger talks with LCH	F
2001	DTCC and Government Securities Clearing Corporation (GSCC), Emerging Markets Clearing Corporation (EMCC) and MBS Clearing Corporation (MBSCC)	I
2003	LCH and Clearnet to form LCH.Clearnet	I
2003	Eurex acquires 15% of CCorp	I
2006	Sydney Future Exchange and Australian Stock Exchange	I
Single CCP Initiatives		
1973	Creation of OCC (US Options Market)	I
1976	Formation of NSCC (US Securities Market)	I
1982	Combining BOTCC and CME (US Futures Market)	F
1997	Common Clearing Initiative of CME and BOTCC (US Futures Market)	F
2000	Call for Single CCP in Europe (Cash Equities and Derivatives Market)	F
2004	CME and CBOT Common Clearing (US Futures Market)	I
2006	Call for Single CCP in Europe (Cash Equities and Derivatives Market)	O

Network Initiatives between Clearing Houses

Figure 3.18 Selection of mergers and acquisition and single CCP initiatives (status: I = Implemented; F = Failed; O = Open)[156]
Source: Author's own.

European merger initiative is the combination of the UK's LCH and Clearnet, resulting in LCH.Clearnet.

The idea to create a Single CCP solution for certain markets and economic areas is not new either. It has been attempted successfully and unsuccessfully at various times throughout the last thirty years within the US and Europe. Although at first sight, the overview suggests that clearing houses have been relatively eager to engage in such initiatives, it should be noted that except

---

[156] The status does not indicate whether or not the outlined network initiatives are still in place.

for the implementation of a common clearing solution between CME and CBOT in 2004 – which effectively created a dominant (although literally not single) CCP for the US futures market – none of the other Single CCP initiatives was driven by nor initiated by clearing houses. These initiatives were in fact promoted by regulators, policymakers or market participants. Out of seven initiatives – five in the US and two in Europe – three initiatives were implemented and three failed. The outcome of one initiative is currently still in progress, which is the 2006 initiative calling for a Single European CCP.[157]

To summarise, the overview of network initiatives from 1973 to 2006 shows that US clearing houses were more active in engaging in network strategies than European CCPs.[158] Further, the examples indicate that the higher the level of integration through selected initiatives, the more difficult it is to successfully implement the network strategy (and the higher the failure rate).

3.4 Summary

This chapter served to define the two core issues of research: efficiency of clearing and network strategies. The central criterion for determining the efficiency of clearing is operational efficiency, which is influenced by transaction costs. The economic entity relevant for the cost analysis is the clearing member view. The efficiency of clearing is thus increased when the transaction costs that clearing members have to bear are reduced (and vice versa).

Transaction costs of clearing comprise direct and indirect costs. Monetarily quantifiable costs are referred to as direct costs. This cost type comprises two cost categories – clearing house charges and service provider charges. Indirect costs are difficult to quantify monetarily and can often only be estimated. Measuring and isolating them is therefore a difficult and highly complex task. For the purpose of this study, indirect costs were categorised as cost of capital, risk management costs, IT costs and back-office costs.

Transaction costs can be impacted by network strategies between clearing houses. Network strategies can be differentiated according to the related degree

---

[157] Details on Single CCP initiatives are outlined in section 8.3.

[158] This could be due to different reasons. It could be argued that there is generally less need for cross-margining agreements in Europe, as European clearing houses clear cash equities, options and futures; or, put another way, the products cleared by the different European clearing houses might be less suited for cross-margining. A final assessment of the reasons that US clearing houses were more active than European CCPs in engaging in network strategies would require a more detailed analysis, which is beyond the scope of this study.

of value chain, technical and legal harmonisation as well as integration. For the purpose of this study, four network strategies were distinguished: cross-margining agreements, clearing links, mergers and acquisitions and a Single CCP. The associated degree of harmonisation and integration ranges from low to very high. The greater the degree of value chain integration, the more the clearing houses' level of autonomy declines, i.e. the higher the level of inter-organisational dependencies between the partners. In addition, the higher the level of integration through a certain initiative, the stronger the potential effect of any given initiative on the structure of the Value Provision Network.

The overview of selected network initiatives from 1973 to 2006 shows that US clearing houses were more active in engaging in network strategies than their European counterparts. Finally, the examples suggest that the higher the level of integration, the more difficult it is to successfully implement a given network strategy.

The purpose of this study is to determine the efficiency impact of these various network strategies. Due to the lack of existing research on the issues of efficiency of clearing and network strategies, it was necessary to conduct an original empirical study. Chapter 4 outlines the structure and component parts of this empirical study, including the methods of data collection and treatment.

4 Collecting empirical insights – introduction to the empirical study

To gain insight into the practical relevance and nature of the different cost categories for various clearing member types as well as to derive a basis for analysing the impact network strategies have on clearing costs, the author conducted a comprehensive original empirical study. The original study was also necessary because relevant cost data is not publicly available, and published evidence is scarce at best. Additionally, as the European Commission has observed, '[t]he pricing of post-trading services is complex. Several studies have attempted to shed some light'.[1] Nonetheless, as outlined in section 1.2, none of these studies delivers a universally accepted and accurate description of clearing costs.[2]

This study's original empirical component therefore serves to provide the necessary basis for analysing the costs of derivatives clearing in general and the efficiency impact of European network strategies in particular. The aim of this chapter is fivefold: to describe the underlying data (section 4.1); to detail the method of data collection and explain the process and timeline of the empirical study (section 4.2); to present the study's structure and component parts (section 4.3); to describe the data treatment and interpretation (section 4.4); and to discuss the quality of the expert inquiry (section 4.5). Finally, a summary is provided on the purpose and use of the empirical insights (section 4.6).

4.1 Underlying data

The empirical study consists of seventy-nine interviews conducted with various stakeholders in clearing. As outlined above, the development of the clearing industry is of importance to all clearing stakeholders, which constitute a heterogeneous group. Although the focus of this research is on determining

---

[1] European Commission (ed.) (2006e), p. 1.   [2] Cf. European Commission (ed.) (2006e), p. 1.

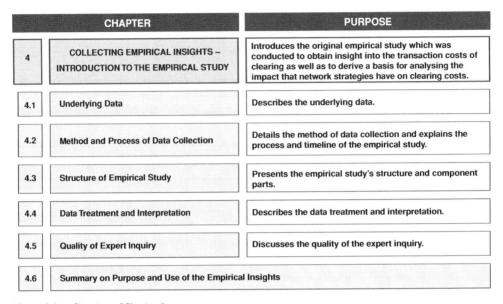

Figure 4.1   Structure of Chapter 4

the costs of clearing from the perspective of European-based clearing member firms, a restructuring of the European clearing industry ultimately requires the involvement, cooperation and support of all of the different stakeholders. Consequently, it was considered necessary to include representatives from the various public and private stakeholders in the sample in order to achieve a more comprehensive view on integration and harmonisation initiatives within the clearing industry. Potential respondents were consciously selected[3] because the nature of the empirical study required detailed insight into the subject of clearing, both from a cost management and a more strategic perspective; seniority was thus considered a prerequisite. The conscious selection of individuals with a suitable background also served to reduce the number of rejections that a random selection or inquiry within firms might have incurred. On the other hand, such a conscious selection of respondents entails a lengthy and time-consuming process: firstly, a long list of public and private stakeholder entities in clearing was compiled; secondly, suitable individuals within these entities were identified; and thirdly, relevant contact information was collected. The conscious selection process led to a high positive response rate of suitable respondents, but was not without inherent limitations. The

---

[3]   The selection process to find interviewees can be either random or conscious. Refer to Schnell/Hill/Esser (2005), pp. 297–300, for details on the advantages and disadvantages of both methods.

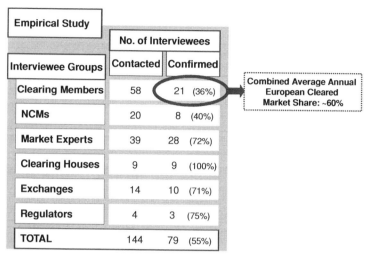

Figure 4.2 Empirical study – positive response rate of contacted individuals according to interviewee groups
Source: Author's own.

maximum number of identifiable suitable individuals within stakeholder entities as well as access to relevant personalised contact information both posed
limitations. Time and cost issues also came into play, because the data was
mainly collected via interviews held in person.[4] In the end, 144 individuals
representing different stakeholder groups were contacted.

Figure 4.2 provides an overview of the response rate and divides the contacted individuals into six so-called 'interviewee groups': clearing members,
non-clearing members (NCMs), market experts, clearing houses, exchanges
and regulators.

The **clearing member** respondents, who were critical for obtaining detailed
and diversified insight into the costs of European derivatives clearing, represented the core interviewee group. The individuals representing clearing member firms constituted a representative sample of the first level of the European
VPN. The list of clearing members is publicly available on the European
clearing houses' websites. For the purpose of this study, the focus was put
on contacting clearing members of LCH.Clearnet Group and Eurex Clearing.
A total of fifty-eight individuals were contacted: twenty-one represent high
volume clearers, thirteen represent medium volume clearers and twenty-four
represent low volume clearers. Positive response rates were as follows:

---

[4] For the reasons for conducting personal interviews and for details on the process of data collection, refer
to section 4.2.

- high volume clearers: twenty-one contacted; thirteen confirmed (i.e. sixty-two per cent);
- medium volume clearers: thirteen contacted; five confirmed (i.e. 38 per cent); and
- low volume clearers: twenty-four contacted; three confirmed (i.e. 13 per cent).

The high positive response rate on the part of high volume clearers suggests that this group is highly interested in the subject of this research. Indeed, many of the individuals contacted from this group had been actively engaged in restructuring the European clearing industry through participation in interest groups, lobbying activities, publication of articles or papers, speeches and panel participation at international industry conferences, interviews in relevant publications, etc. Some representatives of medium volume clearers had also publicly pronounced their interest in the issues of clearing efficiency and the future structure of the industry, but the same cannot be said about the individuals representing low volume clearers contacted for the study. The disparity may in part be explained by the fact that most high and many medium volume clearers employ dedicated managers, to whom the issue of clearing is of strategic value. On the other hand, most low volume clearers tend to be much smaller in size; they consequently tend to have leaner management teams that are devoid of managers with a strategic interest and detailed cost view on clearing. Clearing is, after all, more of operational than strategic importance for most low volume clearers.[5] Additional factors might have influenced the response rates of the different clearing member types.

Whereas twenty-one clearing members were ultimately interviewed, the above-mentioned response rates show that the empirical study is biased towards the view of high volume clearers. The combined European cleared market share in exchange-traded derivatives[6] of the twenty-one interviewed clearing members equals roughly 60 per cent.[7]

The comparatively large number of **NCM** representatives (eight out of twenty) who agreed to contribute to the empirical study was surprising at first. As NCMs only have indirect access to the clearing house, it was assumed that entities with direct access to the CCP would generally be more concerned about the transaction costs associated with clearing. The possible reasons and

[5] Details regarding the relevance of clearing costs and the impact of different network strategies on the different clearing member types are analysed in the remainder of this study.

[6] This estimate refers to Europe's five major derivatives clearing houses: LCH.Clearnet, Eurex Clearing, OMX Clearing, MEFF and CC&G.

[7] The estimate of combined European cleared market share is based on information provided by Eurex Clearing AG. LCH.Clearnet refused to comment on the correctness of the estimate.

Empirical Study – Number of Interviewees per Location						
TOTAL	Clearing Members	NCMs	Market Experts	Clearing Houses	Exchanges	Regulators
79	21	8	28	9	10	3
London: 27 EU: 17 US: 35	London: 9 EU: 7 US: 5	London: 5 EU: 0 US: 3	London: 9 EU: 4 US: 15	London: 1 EU: 2 US: 6	London: 2 EU: 3 US: 5	London: 1 EU: 1 US: 1

Figure 4.3   Empirical study – number of interviewees by group and location[8]
Source: Author's own

driving factors for the interest shown by NCMs in the subject of the research are further analysed in the remainder of the study.

The group of **market experts** encompasses a variety of different stakeholders, such as former executives of clearing houses, exchanges and financial service providers, as well as former regulators. Representatives of banks/brokers (which are not clearing members of European derivatives clearing houses), interest groups, industry associations, academics, lawyers and central bankers are also included in this interviewee group. As the contacted individuals were carefully selected with regard to their background and interest in the research area, this explains their willingness (and high positive response rate) to contribute to the empirical study.

Finally – and not surprisingly – **clearing houses**, **exchanges** and **regulators** all showed great interest in the focus area of the research. As outlined in section 2.4, these stakeholders have a natural interest and significant stake in the core issues analysed in this study. The only group of private stakeholders deliberately excluded from the empirical study was CSDs/ICSDs, because they generally play a less important role in the life cycle of a derivatives trade and because their current focus is on the consolidation of the securities settlement industry. Because this analysis centres on the integration and harmonisation of European CCP clearing, these stakeholders were not asked to participate in the empirical research.[9]

The individuals who contributed to the empirical study were located in Continental Europe (Belgium, France, Germany and Switzerland), London and the US (Chicago, New York and Washington). Figure 4.3 shows the number of interviewees per group and by location.

---

[8] EU: Continental Europe representing Belgium, France, Germany and Switzerland.
[9] Another group of public stakeholders that did not provide input to the research is European policymakers. Although four policymakers were contacted and two of them provided feedback on the research goal and structure of this study, a formal interview ultimately did not take place.

The rationale for including these different European interviewee locations was twofold: firstly, it was felt that the most important home markets of Europe's two major CCPs (Eurex Clearing and LCH.Clearnet) should be included in the study. Secondly, a large number of suitable experts and professionals in clearing turned out to be located in London; this is reflected in the fact that more interviews were conducted in London than in Continental Europe. The US was included because any effort to integrate and harmonise the European clearing industry will ultimately be global in scope. Therefore, and because the US clearing industry is often referred to as a role model for Europe, it was considered necessary to include US-based interviewees. Furthermore, for some of the selected clearing member firms, the management concerned with the strategic and cost issues of clearing happens to be located in the US. The five clearing member representatives based in the US are all clearers maintaining a direct clearing relationship with LCH.Clearnet and/or Eurex Clearing through their European subsidiaries.

4.2 Method and process of data collection

To generate the empirical data, an expert-interview-based approach was employed to obtain qualitative insights; the interviews were complemented with quantitative data from a questionnaire. At the initial contact, stakeholders were asked to give an interview. The data-gathering approach was to firstly conduct an interview in person and then distribute the questionnaire at the end of the interview. The rationale for pursuing this approach (rather than a purely questionnaire-based approach or sending out the questionnaire prior to the interview) was based on the partially explorative angle of this research, the nature of the respondents and the type of empirical insight desired.

Whereas a purely questionnaire-based approach might have generated a larger sample size, this approach was not suited to this study's research objective. Due to the complexity of the research question and the general lack of publicly available studies, data and insight, a semi-structured approach was chosen to afford more flexibility as well as the ability to actively steer the course of the investigation. This enabled greater responsiveness to the respondent's background and his or her feedback.

Seniority was a prerequisite in the selection of interviewees. Most of the individuals who participated in the empirical study were thus senior managers in the first or second management level. It was assumed that these managers generally have neither the time nor inclination to fill out questionnaires;

it was also supposed that these managers would see no particular reason and would thus most likely not be willing to delegate the completion of the questionnaire to their team. Prior interaction was therefore considered essential for conveying the benefits of contributing to the research and to enhance the interviewees' understanding of the nature and purpose of this study. It was hoped that this would serve to encourage the respondents to provide further input (i.e. beyond the expert interview) as well as facilitate the collection of quantitative cost data. Ultimately, however, the greatest hurdle was presented by the strictly confidential nature of the cost data that was sought from clearing members. Managers were expected to be unwilling to agree to the release of such sensitive data to an unknown third party. It was therefore considered essential to establish a personal relationship with the interviewees beforehand in order to reassure them of the anonymity and confidential treatment of any submitted data prior to asking for concrete cost data and distributing the questionnaire. However, even then, the undertaking of collecting clearing cost data was prone to difficulties.

Ultimately, the author conducted seventy-nine interviews. Although the majority of interviews were one-on-one, three interviews with two respondents and two interviews with three respondents were conducted. All interviews but one were conducted orally,[10] with 94 per cent of all interviews (seventy-four of seventy-nine) held in person with the author of this study. Four interviews were conducted via phone by the author and one in written form via e-mail. The majority of interviews, namely sixty-three out of seventy-nine, were conducted in English. The remaining sixteen interviews were conducted in German.

The process of data collection took place over a period of three-and-a-half months, according to the following timeline: from early February to early March 2006, interviews with London-based respondents proceeded. The interviews with respondents based in Continental Europe were conducted thereafter. Finally, from early April to early May 2006, US-based participants were interviewed. In May 2006, further interviews with respondents based in Continental Europe were performed.

The interviews took between thirty minutes and two-and-a-half hours, depending on the time granted for the interview as well as the particular respondent's manner of expression and knowledge of the issues. The majority of interviews took place once, although in some cases, follow-up questions

---

[10] In one case, the interview guide was sent electronically to the respondent, who then provided written answers to selected questions.

were asked subsequent to the interview, or additional information was provided via phone or e-mail. Prior to the interview process, the respondents were assured of the anonymity of their participation, i.e. that no information, be it quantitative or qualitative in nature, would be published in a way that would identify or provide a direct reference to their person and/or company. Any input provided by the interviewees was therefore made anonymous; the completed questionnaires and interview transcripts are therefore not publicly available. Whenever an interviewee is identified by name in the remainder of this study, prior consent was obtained from the respective individual. Any views expressed by the interviewees are their own and do not necessarily represent the official stance of their organisation. The interviewees are not associated with the final conclusions of this study. The findings of this study do not necessarily reflect the views of the individuals interviewed in the context of this study.

The majority of the oral interviews were recorded on tape or digitally (sixty-five out of seventy-eight). In thirteen cases, the interviews were not taped. In six of these cases, the interviewees declined to have the conversation taped; the other seven interviews could not be taped for other reasons (in most cases, the meeting location was not amenable to tape recording, i.e. too much ambient noise was present or the dynamics of the interview precluded asking to tape the interview). In addition to recording the interviews wherever possible, the interviewer also took notes.

4.3 Structure of empirical study

As indicated before, the empirical data collection mainly consisted of an expert-interview-based approach. In a second step, the qualitative insights provided in the interviews were complemented with quantitative data from the questionnaire. Although it was clear *ex ante* that this undertaking contained a high likelihood of failure, i.e. that the interviewees were not likely to respond to the questionnaire, it was nonetheless attempted. The main purpose of the questionnaire was to collect concrete quantitative cost data from clearing members and subsequently conduct comparative assessments of the impact of different network strategies on the transaction costs of clearing.[11]

---

[11] Overall, the questionnaire consisted of five parts: Part 1 comprised closed questions concerning the general relevance of CCP clearing; Part 2 asked for concrete cost data and concerned the transaction cost analysis of derivatives clearing; Part 3 contained closed questions related to analysing demand- and

The strict confidentiality of cost data accounted for the presumption of a low response rate. The attempt to collect quantitative cost data from clearing members through the questionnaire did indeed fail, as expected. For competitive reasons, banks and brokers acting as clearing members were understandably not willing to voluntarily release any such information to an outside third party – not even under reassurance of strict non-disclosure and academic purposes. Only five clearing members returned the questionnaire, but none provided concrete cost data.[12] Nonetheless, the few questionnaires that were partially filled out served to provide helpful insight regarding the case study assessment in Chapter 8.[13]

Because the likelihood of failing to gather quantitative cost data via the questionnaire was expected *ex ante*, a 'workaround' enabling a cost calculation was devised. The workaround consisted of collecting qualitative information in the interviews that could be used as a basis for deriving quantitative clearing costs in a subsequent step. This objective was consequently taken into account in the determination of the structure and questions for the interview guide. The interviews were semi-standardised. An interview guide tailored to each of the different interviewee groups as well as to the particular experiences and background of the respondents was developed. Adaptations were also made with respect to the interviewees' location; a subset of specific questions concerned only US-based respondents, whereas other questions were only relevant to interviewees based in Continental Europe and London. Depending on the particular experience, knowledge and background of the respondents, certain questions were not posed if it became clear that the interviewees would be unable to answer them. The number of questions consequently varied slightly and the order was generally not fixed (i.e. the order was adapted according to the answers provided by an interviewee). The interview guide covered questions related to the following issues:[14]

---

supply-side scale effects; Part 4 consisted of closed questions pertaining to different industry initiatives; and Part 5 solicited basic respondent information.

[12] Prior to the distribution of the questionnaire, eight test runs were conducted. Representatives of two banks and two clearing houses as well as four market experts participated in the test runs. All representatives provided positive feedback on the structure, length, style and clarity of the questionnaire. Respondents also indicated that they would be willing to fill out the questionnaire – including the part asking for cost data. Despite the positive test runs, the final response rate was as low as predicted. The bank representatives who had previously confirmed their willingness to return the completed questionnaire (including the cost data part) ultimately failed to return the questionnaire at all, even partially filled out. Whereas one bank did not provide reasons for this, the other specified that the questionnaire could not be returned due to reasons of confidentiality.

[13] Refer to Appendix 4 for the questionnaire.   [14] Refer to Appendix 5 for a sample interview guide.

1. Introductory Questions.
2. Transaction Cost Analysis.
3. Network Strategies.
4. Efficiency Impact of Network Strategies.
5. Case Studies of Network Strategies.
6. Future Development of Clearing and Global Outlook.

Although the approach of establishing a personal relationship with the interviewees to reassure them of the anonymity and confidential treatment of submitted data prior to asking for concrete cost data did not boost response rates to the questionnaire, it did help to ensure that respondents provided helpful feedback. This was particularly relevant for the critique of the author's qualitative and quantitative research results subsequent to the interview process.

4.4 Data treatment and interpretation

Prior to the data treatment, all seventy-nine interviews were transcribed. For those conversations that were not taped, an interview protocol was established; the taped interviews were transcribed verbatim. For data treatment, the procedure suggested by Schmidt (1997) was used, consisting of the following four steps:[15]

1. Establish categories for interview analysis.
2. Code interviews.
3. Provide quantitative overview (frequency of occurrence).
4. Interpretation.

The objective of the data treatment was to identify response patterns, similarities and varieties in the answers provided in the expert interviews in order to facilitate the interpretation of the collected data.[16] To this end, **categories** for analysing the contents of the interviews were developed according to the procedure suggested by Mayring (2007).[17] This procedure follows a three-step approach. The first step summarises the collected data, structured according to the most important contents of the interviews and utilising an interview synopsis table. The second step consists of a clarifying text analysis that elucidates ambiguous terms used by interviewees by taking into account additional material such as other interview passages or information on the

---

[15] Cf. Schmidt (1997), pp. 544–66.   [16] Cf. Mühlfeld *et al.* (1981), p. 334.
[17] Cf. Mayring (2007), pp. 59–100.

respondents' background, i.e. company, responsibilities, industry experience, etc. In step three, the categories for the final interview analysis are subsequently established. These categories are differentiated according to different category values. Categories and category values were defined based on the structure of the interview guide and the research questions of this study.

The categories and category values are then used as the basis for the process of **coding** the interviews. Coding enables the reduction of the collected data to short and comparable codes, and includes the establishment of a coding outline and the actual process of attributing data to the employed codes. Due to the large amount of text, coding was carried out with the support of special data analysis software (QSR NVIVO 2.0).

The third step of the data treatment consists of summarising the coding results, i.e. the provision of a **quantitative overview** of the frequency of occurrence of certain codes. For the purpose of this study, this overview is provided in the form of bar graphs. These graphs illustrate, for example, the number of respondents supporting or opposing a particular concept or idea. These quantitative overviews establish the basis for a further qualitative data analysis and interpretation. The quantitative overviews thus do not represent the results of the empirical study, but constitute a supporting step to facilitate further data interpretation.[18] Whereas the use of such quantitative overviews in the context of qualitative expert interviews can be controversially discussed,[19] they were helpful for data interpretation in this study. The reason for this is that due to the relatively large sample size, the quantitative overviews highlight controversial opinions and areas of conflict, and generally help to increase the transparency of interviewees' responses.[20]

The final step of data treatment consists of **data interpretation**. The interpretation was conducted along the lines of interviewee groups and/or interviewee location, depending on the category under analysis. This permitted the identification of regional particularities and yielded a better understanding of the dynamics among different stakeholder groups. The process also revealed the origins of possibly vested interests and divergent opinions. In some cases, further distinctions were made according to the interviewees' industry experience and seniority, their position within a firm and the background and nature of the organisation they represent (such as cleared volumes, nature of business, etc.).

---

[18] Cf. Schmidt (1997), p. 560.   [19] Cf. Schmidt (1997), p. 562.

[20] Not all coding results are presented in a quantitative overview, however. A quantitative overview is provided only when it is considered instrumental for a better understanding or for the further interpretation of the data.

4.5 Quality of expert inquiry

Measuring the quality of expert inquiries was based on methods that are applied in quantitative studies. These methods are rooted in the classical test theory, as used in psychology.[21] The quality can be described in terms of validity, reliability and objectivity.[22] These concepts have been adapted and expanded to qualitative research, although reference to reliability and objectivity is hardly ever made; it is more common to refer to different criteria of validity.[23] Reliability and objectivity thus rather correspond to the validity of interpretation in the context of qualitative research.[24] Validity of interpretation refers to the fact that the results of a qualitative survey are independent from the interviewer, i.e. that different researchers using the same methods and approach produce similar research results. To enhance the validity of interpretation for this empirical study, the underlying data, method and process of data collection, structure of empirical study, data treatment and interpretation were accurately documented in the previous sections. Systematic and structured categorising, coding and interpretation of the data were used to circumvent random or intuitive interpretations.

The criteria of internal and external validity are important in data interpretation:[25] Results of a study are considered internally valid if they can be interpreted without ambiguity, whereas external validity pertains to the extent to which the results of the study can be generalised. Generally, the internal validity of research results decreases with an increasing number of plausible alternative interpretations.[26] To account for internal validity, the process of deriving certain interpretations is outlined in the study; in this context, explicit reference is made to areas of conflict and controversial opinions among respondents; these areas are identified and analysed. Whenever research results could be interpreted in various plausible ways, these different interpretations are outlined.

An important element in determining external validity concerns the concept of so-called 'construct validity', which relates to the adequate explanation of constructs employed in the research. Interview questions, for example, should be posed in such a way that they are correctly understood by the respondents so that the answers will contain the sought-after information. A variety of measures were taken to ensure construct validity: four test interviews

---

[21] Cf. Lamnek (1995), p. 152.   [22] Cf. Friedrichs (1990), pp. 85–103.
[23] Cf. Bortz/Döring (2002), pp. 326–9.   [24] Cf. Bortz/Döring (2002), p. 327.
[25] Cf. Bortz/Döring (2002), p. 335.   [26] Cf. Bortz/Döring (2002), p. 57.

were held with bank, exchange and clearing house representatives to check the quality of the interview guide in terms of clarity and comprehensibility of the questions in general, and the language, terms and expressions used in particular. Interviewees were also given the opportunity to receive the interview guide in advance (although few respondents requested the documents prior to the interview). Finally, during the interview itself, questions were formulated so as to ensure that the interviewee understood them correctly; the research-specific terms used during the interview were defined as necessary.

The extent to which the results of qualitative studies can be generalised (external validity) is problematic, in part due to the inherent characteristics of qualitative studies.[27] As outlined above, the sample of respondents was chosen to provide a cross-section of stakeholders in European clearing. Particular efforts were made to obtain a representative selection of clearing members, because their perspective is of particular importance to the study at hand; clearing costs are analysed from the perspective of clearing members. The fact that the clearing members who were interviewed have a combined European cleared market share of roughly 60 per cent strengthens the external validity. Nonetheless, as outlined above, due to a low positive response rate from medium and low volume clearers, the expert inquiry was biased towards the high volume clearers.

Additionally, it must be noted that the data interpretation utilises and refers to archetypes of particular clearing members (as defined in section 2.3.2). Although these aspects are accounted for in the data interpretation, the research results cannot be generalised to apply to the perspective of every single European clearing member or stakeholder. External validity of the research results is thus only furnished insofar as a clearing member matches the defined archetypes. The constraints or limits of the external validity of the research results are further detailed within the remainder of the study; explicit reference is made with regard to which particular research results can be generalised.

4.6 Summary on purpose and use of the empirical insights

In the following, a summary on the purpose as well as an overview on the use of the collected empirical insights is provided. Figure 4.4 illustrates the dual approach pursued (i.e. expert interviews and questionnaire) and the objectives

---

[27] Refer to Bortz/Döring (2002), pp. 336–7, for details.

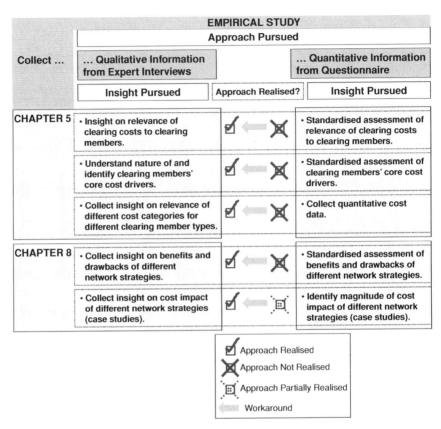

Figure 4.4   Empirical study – insight pursued by interviews and questionnaire
Source: Author's own.

(insight) sought by each approach (together with an indication of whether or not the respective approach was realised). It also shows which chapters contain the collected empirical insights, research results and interpretation.

This chapter introduced the author's empirical study. The results of the empirical study are then presented in Chapters 5 and 8. To evaluate the impact of network strategies on efficiency, it is necessary to learn more about the transaction costs of clearing. To this end, Chapter 5 examines various aspects of European derivatives clearing costs, presents findings from the empirical study and provides a number of quantitative and qualitative transaction cost analyses.

5 Analysing costs of derivatives clearing – transaction cost studies

As outlined above, one of this study's core research issues is the efficiency of clearing. The central criterion for determining the efficiency of clearing is operational efficiency, which is influenced by transaction costs. The economic entity relevant for the cost analysis is the clearing member view. The purpose of this study is to determine the efficiency impact of different network strategies. To accomplish this, it is first necessary to examine the transaction costs of clearing from the perspective of different clearing member types. Due to a lack of existing research and data on this topic, an original empirical study was conducted, whose findings are presented in this chapter (section 5.1). This research is unique in that it is the first study providing a comprehensive analysis of derivatives clearing costs, including both direct and indirect costs.

In a first step, findings from the empirical study are presented that serve to clarify clearing members' general perceptions of clearing costs (section 5.1.1); these findings also demonstrate the concrete relevance of the various direct and indirect cost categories (section 5.1.2). A second step identifies the core cost drivers for different clearing member types (section 5.1.3). An analysis of the interviewed clearing members' backgrounds shows that various factors can influence the way in which direct and indirect costs are perceived and reveals the ultimate importance of the different cost categories (section 5.1.4).

To provide a deeper understanding of European derivatives clearing costs, additional cost analyses are conducted (section 5.2). These cost analyses include a comparison of per-contract fees charged by major clearing houses (section 5.2.1), an analysis of volume discount schemes of these clearing houses (section 5.2.2), a quantitative estimate of total European industry costs in 2005 (section 5.2.3) and an assessment of average direct and indirect costs for different clearing member types (section 5.2.4). In the next section, a more detailed exploration of clearing members' unit costs is provided (section 5.2.5). Derivatives clearing costs are then compared to other market infrastructure costs (such as derivatives trading costs as well as securities trading, clearing and settlement costs) to assess their relative significance

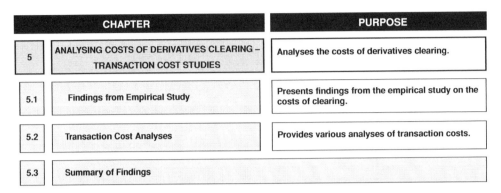

Figure 5.1   Structure of Chapter 5

(section 5.2.6). After that, insights obtained from the expert inquiry on the various opportunities for reducing clearing costs for clearing members are summarised (section 5.2.7). Although the focus of the cost analyses is on the first level of transaction costs, non-clearing members' perspectives on clearing costs are briefly summarised (section 5.2.8) and cost reduction opportunities for non-clearing members are identified (section 5.2.9). In a final step, the findings on transaction costs of European derivatives clearing are summarised (section 5.3), which then serves as input for the remainder of the study.

While transaction cost studies are notoriously difficult and controversial,[1] the limitations and sensitive assumptions associated with the findings and analyses presented in sections 5.1 and 5.2 are explicitly mentioned and explained throughout the text.

5.1 Findings from empirical study

As a firm we most definitely analyse these costs very, very closely indeed, very closely.[2]

We are not really interested in driving the costs down. We are just interested in making more money![3]

The empirical research provided insight as to what role the cost of derivatives clearing plays in reality, i.e. whether managers care about these costs, how they look at the different cost categories and how they deal with these internally on the part of the clearing members. Findings from the interviews also enabled

---

[1] Cf. European Commission (ed.) (02.08.2007).
[2] Statement made by interviewed clearing member representative.
[3] Statement made by interviewed clearing member representative.

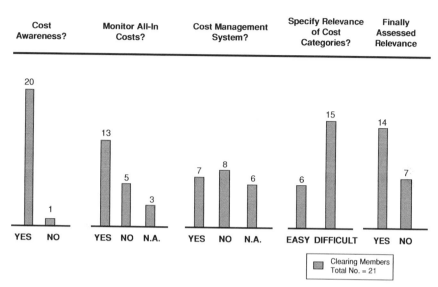

Figure 5.2   Clearing members' perception of transaction costs of derivatives clearing
Source: Author's own.

a classification of the different direct and indirect cost categories' significance and thus revealed clearing members' core cost drivers.

5.1.1 Relevance of clearing costs to clearing members

In order to determine clearing members' general perceptions of costs, interviewees were asked whether they had any awareness of clearing costs and, if so, whether they monitored the all-in costs of clearing and employed a cost management system for this purpose. Finally, they were asked to specify the relevance of each cost category as a percentage, with the all-in costs equalling 100 per cent. Figure 5.2 provides an overview of their responses to these questions.

Almost all of the interviewees, i.e. twenty out of twenty-one, stated that clearing costs do matter to them. Only one clearing member expressed indifference towards the costs. A majority (thirteen versus five) claimed to regularly monitor the all-in costs of clearing. Three respondents did not specify. Responses were diverse regarding the employment of a cost management system to manage and monitor these costs: eight clearing members confirmed the use of a cost management system, while seven claimed to lack such a standardised approach to monitoring clearing costs. The remaining six interviewees

INFLUENCING FACTORS	1.	**Product Attributes**	• Exotic, new or niche products • Illiquid products	• Standardised products • Highly liquid products
	2.	**Market Characteristics**	• Low volume market • Retail focus	• High volume market • Institutional focus
	3.	**Nature of Trade**	• Complex strategy trades • Hedging • Large overnight positions	• Plain vanilla trades • Day trading • No overnight positions
	4.	**Business Focus**	• Agency business	• Proprietary business

LOW   HIGH
LEVEL OF COST AWARENESS

Figure 5.3   Factors influencing the level of cost awareness
Source: Author's own.

did not elaborate on this issue. Clearing members were then asked to rank the relevance of each cost category (clearing house charges, service provider charges, cost of capital, risk management costs, IT costs and back-office costs) in terms of percentages, with the all-in costs adding up to 100 per cent. Surprisingly, most clearing members (fifteen out of twenty-one) considered this task difficult to complete. Only six respondents were able to assign percentages to each cost category without difficulty. Of the fifteen clearers who found this difficult, eight were nonetheless able to ultimately assign percentages and complete this task. This resulted in a total of fourteen clearing members who finally assessed the relevance of each cost category. Seven clearers were unable to assign percentages, but gave more general feedback on the issue without providing specific cost details.

5.1.1.1 Cost awareness

Although the majority of respondents considered themselves as being aware of clearing costs, the answers given revealed that the level of cost awareness and the general perception of clearing costs depend on a variety of influencing factors. These factors can be grouped by topics as follows (see Figure 5.3): attributes of cleared products, market characteristics, nature of trade and business focus of clearing members.

Regarding **product attributes**, cost awareness can be correlated with a product's life cycle. In the early stages, the product is usually characterised by low market demand as well as a lack of standardised processes for clearing it.

Therefore, the clearing of exotic, new or niche products often requires some form of manual interaction, and is thus complex and labour intensive. The clearing house and clearing members both have to adapt IT and back-office processes, which involves costs. At this stage, clearing members are more concerned with the general availability and processability of a certain product than they are with the associated costs. The same is true for illiquid products, where being able to close a position is the primary concern.[4] On the other hand, established products benefit from implemented and proven back-office processes and IT infrastructures on the part of the clearing house and clearing members. Standardised products usually also benefit from straight-through processing. Highly liquid products indicate a high number of contracts traded, which are thus available for clearing. With such products, scale is critical; consequently, clearing members are highly cost sensitive. Whereas cost awareness may be fairly low for complex or exotic new products, the same is not necessarily true for all new products. If a new product is simply a variant of an existing product,[5] clearing costs are likely to matter quite a bit and can determine the success or failure of a new product launch.[6]

Market characteristics also influence the level of cost awareness. Markets with a low number of contracts traded are less likely to be in the centre of cost considerations. On the other hand, cost awareness is high with reference to high volume markets. In these markets:

Clearing costs can restrict the volume of trading of a broker or a bank . . . The clearest example of that are the so-called black-box traders, who trade through an automated system, doing arbitrage of various kinds, or some kind of programmatic trading. Many of those systems are designed to do small trades, but do them very often. So they make very small margins, they try to do it at low risk, but they do lots and lots of them, looking for arbitrage opportunities – electronically looking for those opportunities. In those circumstances, the cost of clearing . . . has a direct impact on the output of the trading model they use.[7]

For similar reasons, within markets that are characterised by a high involvement of institutional traders, awareness of clearing costs is high, because small

---

[4] Cf. interviews.

[5] An example is the launch of CME's E-Mini S&P 500 Future in 1997, a variant of the S&P 500 Future, which began trading in 1982. With identical contract specifications, the so-called 'E-Mini' product is merely distinguished by its lower contract value.

[6] In accord with the respective exchange, many clearing houses therefore offer discount clearing rates for new products. See as an example OCC's standard approach to discounts for new products at www.theocc.com/about/schedule.jsp.

[7] Interview with Peter Cox.

margins matter a lot. On the other hand, retail trades are hardly ever conceptualised to make money out of fractions, and are thus less price sensitive to the overhead cost of the trade. Markets with a retail focus are therefore likely to be less concerned with clearing costs.

A third factor influencing the level of awareness of clearing costs is the **nature of the trade**. So-called 'plain vanilla' derivatives are easy to process and, consequently, the willingness to accept high costs for these trades is low, i.e. cost awareness is high. On the contrary, complex strategy trades can be more difficult to process. Note that this is not necessarily true for all complex trades. Cost awareness is low when the clearing costs are low compared to the risks and profit margin of the respective strategy trade. However, if clearing costs are very high compared with the risks and profit margin of a certain trade, cost awareness is also very high – in that circumstance, clearing costs can affect whether or not the respective trade is executed at all:

One more thing about cost sensitivity in the derivatives markets – there are derivative strategies which do not make sense if your clearing and settlement costs are significant. It is a similar sort of story to black-box trading, but it is where you are trying to trade very, very big positions in a strategy package, which has very low risk and low margin. The strategy is designed to have a very slim margin, but to be done in a very big block. In those circumstances, if you pay clearing costs at a per-contract basis, your clearing costs are very high compared to your risks and profit margin in the whole strategy. As a result, clearing houses in recent times have had to come up with special deals for block trades, because the old per-contract pricing in derivatives markets doesn't work for those kinds of trades. Initially, they were being done OTC, because they couldn't be put through a clearing house. It wasn't worth doing.[8]

Another factor concerning the nature of the trade is related to the purpose of engaging in a certain derivatives position. When trades are done for hedging purposes, this usually implies that the positions are open for longer than one day, resulting in overnight positions. The longer a position is open, the more value a clearing member gets out of the per-contract clearing fee. Those clearing members carrying large overnight positions are less cost sensitive.[9] In contrast, the market participants that trade multiple contracts per day – and for whom the cents or pence will eventually add up – are very sensitive to clearing costs.[10]

Finally, the level of cost awareness and the perceived significance of clearing costs depend on the **business focus** of market participants, i.e. whether the focus is on proprietary or agency business. Whereas clearing members with a

---

[8] Interview with Peter Cox.   [9] Cf. interviews.   [10] Cf. interviews.

prop. focus are highly cost sensitive, the opposite is true for clearing members with an agency focus. A manager of an investment bank illustrates it like this:

Well, I have two hats in this. As a proprietary organisation we do an awful lot of business and from an overall P&L point of view – yes, we are sensitive to costs. That is one side of it. On the client side, it is pass-through. Do I think that if you dropped the LCH fees from 3 pence to 2 pence, it would make any difference to the volume? No, I don't think so. I think it would be entirely insensitive to that. I think we would be happy and all the major trading prop houses would be happy, because we'd have more P&L, but would we do more business as a result? No, I don't think so. It doesn't make a difference from that point of view.[11]

Most respondents answered the question of cost awareness from both prop. and agency perspectives. Solely the interviewee expressing indifference towards clearing costs responded from a purely agency perspective,[12] even though his company engages in both prop. and agency business.

5.1.1.2 Monitoring of all-in costs

Although nearly all of the clearing members in the study claimed to be generally concerned about the costs of clearing, only 65 per cent of those actually monitor their all-in costs. Another 25 per cent focus exclusively on the monitoring and management of direct costs, excluding indirect cost components. The interviews revealed that the reasons for not monitoring the all-in costs are largely due to peculiarities of the respective clearing member's corporate structure. Generally, the more complex a company's structure, the more difficult the task of consolidating the all-in costs of clearing. Due to the common separation of management responsibilities for a company's proprietary and agency businesses, the monitoring of direct and indirect clearing-related costs is often performed by different people in different departments within an organisation. In order to calculate the all-in costs, information must be collected from throughout the company; input from the prop. and agency sides as well as from the treasury department is necessary. If these areas of responsibility are diffused across different financial centres, obtaining the complete picture becomes even more complex and involves significant internal effort. In addition, any discord between the different parts of the company or lack of

[11] Statement made by interviewed clearing member representative.
[12] Although the respondent repeatedly claimed to be unconcerned about reducing clearing costs, he did define as a business objective to enhance internal processing and leverage the back-office and IT infrastructure.

transparent information sharing within the firm further complicates the task of managing and monitoring the all-in costs of clearing.[13]

5.1.1.3 Employment of a cost management system

Of the thirteen clearing members claiming to monitor all-in costs, seven employ a cost management system that supports the monitoring and management of clearing costs. Six respondents monitor all-in costs without the support of a dedicated management or database tool. Although these interviewees admitted to not having a dedicated system in place, they all claimed to regularly monitor all-in costs of clearing by other means. No evidence was found as to whether or not the clearing members tend to calculate the unit costs on the basis of the all-in clearing costs. Two clearing members explicitly referred to their unit costs of clearing, but the majority of respondents were vague on the subject. One clearing member explained that he did not calculate the unit cost based on all-in cost data:

> We look at our direct costs on a direct per-lot basis, whereas we look at our indirect costs on an overall basis. And we don't tend to work out how much these costs are on a per-lot basis. Regarding our indirect costs, we know what the cost is over the year for the business we are doing and that is where we can try and save money or where we can spend more money, depending on the business.[14]

5.1.1.4 Ability to assess relevance of cost categories

The empirical findings suggest that at least thirteen of the twenty-one interviewed clearing members had very detailed knowledge of their clearing costs, as they claimed to monitor these costs. Surprisingly, when asked to assess the relevance of the different cost categories, only six respondents were able to do so with ease, whereas the majority, i.e. fifteen out of twenty-one, found it difficult to provide concrete details. It is also surprising that of the seven respondents claiming to employ a cost management system, only three found it easy to recount details of their cost structure. The other four respondents had difficulty providing details; two of which were eventually able to comment upon the relevance of each cost category. The remaining two remained unable to specify further. The six clearing members that considered the task easy had previously all indicated that they monitored all-in costs; some with and others without the aid of a dedicated tool. The existence of a cost management system therefore does not seem to guarantee familiarity with the

---

[13] Cf. interviews.
[14] Statement made by interviewed clearing member representative.

individual cost categories. Rather, the ability and willingness of respondents to provide details on the relevance of different cost categories was influenced by individual characteristics, such as:

• Management position.
• Industry experience.
• Willingness to share knowledge.
• Other reasons.

When analysing the interviewees' background, it became obvious that the higher their position in the corporate hierarchy and the greater their industry experience, the more concrete insight they had on the issue of clearing-related costs. It seems logical to assume that the higher up the management chain an individual is, the easier it should be to obtain access to relevant cost data. Some interviewees might have known more about clearing costs than they were willing to share for reasons of confidentiality. This possibility is strongly supported by the fact that some respondents were not willing to fill out the quantitative part of the questionnaire for reasons of secrecy.[15] In addition, there could have been other reasons for the difficulty the majority of clearing member representatives had in providing concrete details on the components of their firms' all-in costs.

5.1.2 Direct versus indirect clearing costs

While only fourteen out of twenty-one clearing members were willing or able to provide a detailed assessment of costs, all of them voiced an opinion on which cost type (i.e. direct versus indirect) is the strongest transaction cost driver. The other interviewee groups in the study were similarly questioned about their perceptions of the clearing industry and its related issues. The question asked was:

What do you consider the core driver of clearing-related transaction costs clearing members have to bear – direct or indirect costs?

Similar to the majority of clearing members, the other respondent groups also considered it difficult to specify the relevance of the different cost categories. Many interviewees refused to provide details, believing themselves incapable of answering this question accurately. Nonetheless, almost 50 per cent of all interviewees (thirty-nine out of seventy-nine) ultimately issued an opinion on which cost type is most relevant to clearing members. The remaining

---

[15] Refer to Chapter 4 for details on the empirical study and the questionnaire.

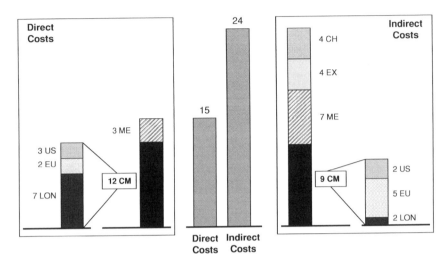

Figure 5.4   Interviewees' assessment of clearing members' strongest transaction cost drivers[16]
Source: Author's own.

either felt that they did not know, had no clear opinion, refused to answer, did not specify their opinion or, in the case of the regulator group, were not asked to perform the assessment. Figure 5.4 provides an overview of how the interviewees answered this question.

At first sight, the answer seems unambiguous – twenty-four interviewees identified indirect costs to be the core driver of the clearing-related transaction costs that clearing members have to bear; only fifteen respondents cited direct costs. However, when the responses are analysed more closely, the picture becomes less distinct. Whereas a small majority of clearing members (twelve versus nine) singled out direct costs as core cost drivers, the vast majority of the other interviewees (fourteen versus three) identified indirect costs as being most significant.[17] In order to interpret the above results, it is thus necessary to analyse the answers group by group.

5.1.2.1 Clearing members' view

Naturally, the group with the highest level of insight into the issue turned out to be the clearing members themselves. Their responses yield no single

---

[16] Interviewee groups: CM = clearing member; ME = market expert; EX = exchange; CH = clearing house. Interviewee locations: US = United States; EU = Continental Europe; LON = London.

[17] NCMs are not included in the above figure, because they had been asked to identify their own most important cost driver. Not surprisingly, they unanimously viewed direct costs as the most significant cost category.

clear-cut answer, however. A look at the feedback provided by the six clearing members who found it easy to assess the relevance of cost types brings no resolution, as three of them identified direct costs and three identified indirect costs as the core cost driver. To understand why an almost equal number of respondents (twelve versus nine) viewed direct and indirect costs as core drivers, it is essential to consider additional factors when interpreting the results. An analysis of the respondents' backgrounds reveals that the following aspects influence the way in which cost types are perceived:
- management position and industry experience;
- business focus of clearer and area of responsibility of interviewee; and
- geographical location.

All of these factors are interrelated. As outlined above, the interviewees' **management position and industry experience** were found to affect their level of knowledge about clearing costs. The higher their management position and the greater their industry experience, the easier it was for them to provide a well-informed answer. Secondly, the business focus of the clearer as well as the respondent's area of responsibility can influence her or his perceptions and answers. The interviews showed that when the clearer's focus is on proprietary business, direct costs are more relevant. In contrast, when the focus is on agency business, indirect costs are perceived as the core cost drivers.

For an agency focused clearing member: 'It doesn't really matter . . . whether the clearing house charges one euro or ten euros, because those fees are built into our price environment.'[18]

From a proprietary point of view, it looks a bit different . . . because it is not a direct cost to us if we pass them on to our clients. But from a proprietary point of view, it is a significant proportion of our direct costs.[19]

It is thus clear that the issues of perspective and **business focus** were central factors in determining the clearing members' responses vis-à-vis the core cost drivers in clearing. This suggests another influencing factor: the greater the focus on prop. business, the more likely a clearing member is to engage in lobbying efforts to reduce direct costs. The reason for this is obvious: whereas clearing members have a large degree of control over their indirect costs, direct costs are more difficult to manage. In order to reduce direct costs, firms have to engage in lobbying activities.[20] They have no other avenue for reining in

---

[18] Interview with Steve G. Martin.
[19] Statement made by interviewed clearing member representative.
[20] Engaging in lobbying efforts usually involves participation in relevant interest groups and industry associations.

this cost type. But did participation in lobbying or interest group activities influence the interviewees' responses? And if so, how?

Lobbying efforts are by definition designed to help interest groups reach certain objectives. Any form of communication must thus support the lobbying efforts, i.e. adhere to the 'party line'. Engaging in lobbying efforts could potentially have influenced the interviewees' responses in two ways. It could have had a positive effect, substantiating the cost analysis, or it could have had a negative effect, weakening the response. On the positive side, the greater a firm's engagement in lobbying activities and/or interest groups, the more likely it is that it has thoroughly analysed its clearing costs. A negative effect results if the interviewees' own perception of clearing costs does not correspond to the party line. Four clearing member representatives acknowledged that their personal view on the relevance of certain cost types differs from the official stance taken by their respective companies.

When viewing Figure 5.4, it is thus crucial to keep in mind that the responses of the 'highly knowledgeable' interviewees (i.e. those in senior management or whose companies are highly involved in interest group or lobbying activities, etc.)[21] might have been biased due to adherence to company policy. On the other hand, the responses of the 'less knowledgeable' interviewees (i.e. those holding lower management positions or whose companies have no involvement in interest group or lobbying activities, etc.)[22] could have been affected either by their lack of access to cost data or by the fact that whereas '[t]he fees charged by clearing houses and intermediaries are very clearly seen; they [the clearing members] get an invoice for them and so they are very obvious',[23] indirect costs are generally more difficult to monitor and quantify.

Finally, the analysis of the interviews revealed a possible correlation between the **geographical location** of a clearing member and the perception of cost types. Whereas the majority of London-based clearing members identified direct costs as the core cost driver, the majority of interviewees based in Continental Europe considered indirect costs as most relevant. These findings are difficult to interpret, but they could indicate that, for various reasons, indirect costs are higher in Continental Europe. Alternatively, this response

---

[21] Twelve clearing members are classified as 'highly knowledgeable'. From this group, four clearing members identified indirect costs as the core cost driver, whereas eight deemed direct costs most significant.

[22] Nine clearing members were classified as 'less knowledgeable'. Five of these considered indirect costs as the core cost driver and four regarded direct costs as the most important driver.

[23] Interview with Peter Cox.

pattern could simply be due to the interviewees' individual backgrounds, differences in the companies' business focus (i.e. the proprietary trading part of clearers tending to be located in London rather than in Continental Europe) or other factors.

5.1.2.2 Other interviewee groups' views

The other interviewee groups' comments regarding the core cost drivers should not be overestimated; they have considerably less information about the matter than clearing members. Nonetheless, it is striking that a clear majority identified indirect costs as the core cost driver. Again, in order to interpret the responses, it is crucial to take the respondents' backgrounds into account: Naturally, one would expect clearing houses to identify indirect costs as the main cost driver rather than *quasi* accusing themselves of charging excessive fees. Exchanges will also be more likely to cite indirect costs rather than fees to ward off scrutiny of their own fee structure. This inference is not meant to suggest that the answers provided by clearing houses and exchanges are not truthful, but simply to underscore the importance of keeping in mind the interviewees' background when analysing their responses. The group of market experts is heterogeneous. Seven market experts identified indirect costs, whereas three cited direct costs as the core cost driver.

5.1.2.3 Conclusions from Figure 5.4

The findings presented in Figure 5.4 deliver no clear-cut conclusion with regard to the strongest cost driver. Although at first glance the results seem to suggest that indirect costs are perceived as the strongest driver, a closer interpretation of the responses suggests that this is not necessarily the case. It becomes clear that no unequivocally 'true' answer emerges to the query of which type of costs constitutes the core driver. In the end, perceptions were shown to be highly dependent on a variety of factors, most importantly on the business focus of the respective clearing member.

5.1.3 Clearing members' core cost drivers

To obtain deeper insight into the relevance of the different cost categories and cost types, further analysis was conducted. As described above, clearing members were asked to specify the relevance of each cost category in terms of percentages, with 100 per cent equalling the all-in clearing costs.

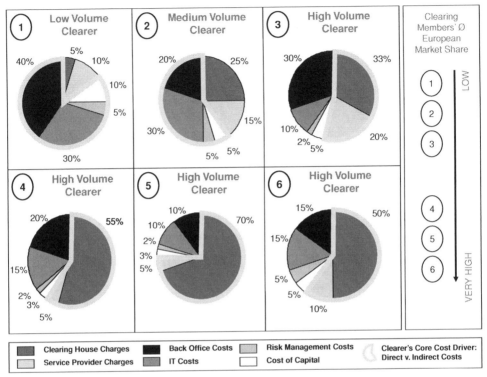

Figure 5.5   Composition of all-in clearing costs for six interviewed benchmark clearing members
Note: Ø = average
Source: Author's own.

As mentioned above, fourteen clearing members provided details on the different cost categories. Of those fourteen, only seven assigned percentages to all of the cost categories – the results of which were converted into pie charts. The other clearers either provided qualitative information about the cost categories without assigning percentages, or provided percentages for only some of the cost categories. Of the seven clearing members who gave complete information, six were classified as 'highly knowledgeable', and one as 'less knowledgeable'. For the purpose of coherence, only the six charts of the 'highly knowledgeable' clearing members were included in Figure 5.5 for further analysis.

Figure 5.5 provides an overview of the different clearing members' assessment of costs, represented by one pie chart per interviewee. Each pie chart represents 100 per cent of a clearing member's all-in clearing costs. The order of the pie charts has been arranged according to the estimated European market share of each clearing member,[24] from low volume clearers to very high volume clearers.[25] The combined European market share of these six benchmark clearers adds up to an estimated 22.8 per cent.

For example, Clearing Member 2 is classified as a medium volume clearer due to his estimated market share. Clearing Member 2's all-in costs are broken down as follows: clearing house charges, 25 per cent; service provider charges, 15 per cent; cost of capital, 5 per cent; risk management costs, 5 per cent; IT costs, 30 per cent; and back-office costs, 20 per cent. The framed part of the pie represents the core cost driver for the respective clearing member, i.e. direct versus indirect costs. This means that for Clearing Member 2, indirect costs, comprising 60 per cent of total clearing costs, are the core cost driver.

When interpreting Figure 5.5, the following caveat applies: the above pie charts were created ad hoc during the interviews. Therefore, it cannot be assumed with certainty that the classification of the different cost categories is based on a detailed cost calculation. On the other hand, only the feedback provided by clearing members classified as highly knowledgeable was used to create the charts. Therefore, although the charts were established spontaneously, the interviewees were well suited to provide input for this task. Whereas several examples are available for high volume clearers, only two diagrams pertain to low and medium volume clearers (one apiece). This is simply due to the fact that very few low and medium volume clearing members were available for an interview,[26] with the consequence that the interview results are biased towards the perceptions of high volume clearing members.

Despite these limitations, the analysis provides some important insights: the core cost driver for low and medium volume clearers is indirect costs, whereas the core cost driver for high volume clearing members is direct costs. It is obvious that the higher the cleared volume, i.e. the higher the market share, the more relevant becomes the volume-driven variable cost component and the less relevant becomes the fixed cost component. An increasing scale allows clearing members to leverage their internal infrastructure, thus reducing the significance of indirect costs. Hence, the more volume cleared, the higher the

[24] The European market share refers to the combined cleared market share of derivatives contracts cleared through Eurex Clearing, LCH.Clearnet, OMX Clearing, MEFF and CC&G. An estimate of the market share of each clearing member is based on information provided by Eurex Clearing, which was extended and adapted to an estimate of an overall European market share. These conclusions from the Eurex Clearing data were derived with the support of market experts. The reference date for all estimates is 2005.

[25] Refer to section 2.3.2 for details on the classification of low, medium and high volume clearing members.

[26] Refer to Chapter 4 for details on the response rates of the different interviewee groups.

	LOW / MEDIUM VOLUME	HIGH VOLUME
	CLEARING MEMBERS	
PROP. PERSPECTIVE	Significant P&L effects can be realised through ...	
	1. Increasing internal efficiency	1. Engaging in lobbying activities and putting pressure on clearing houses to reduce fees
	2. Benefiting from improvement of operational and process efficiency through industry initiatives	
	(INDIRECT COST REDUCTIONS)	(DIRECT COST REDUCTIONS)
AGENCY PERSPECTIVE	Significant profit margin impacts can be realised through ...	
	1. Increasing internal efficiency	1. Increasing internal efficiency
	2. Benefiting from improvement of operational and process efficiency through industry initiatives	2. Benefiting from improvement of operational and process efficiency through industry initiatives
	(INDIRECT COST REDUCTIONS)	(INDIRECT COST REDUCTIONS)
CORE COST DRIVER:	**INDIRECT COSTS**	**DIRECT COSTS**

Figure 5.6   Clearing members' focus area in terms of cost reductions
Source: Author's own.

importance of direct costs.[27] These findings suggest the existence of economies of scale on the part of the clearing members.[28]

Taking into account the prop. and agency perspective shows that this fact has different implications. Figure 5.6 provides an overview of the interviewed clearing members' focus area in terms of cost reductions, depending on their perspective. The findings reveal that the previous assumption, that the prop. perspective implies a high significance of direct costs whereas the agency perspective implies a high relevance of indirect costs, does not apply to all clearing members. The inference is only valid for high volume clearing members.

For low and medium volume clearers with either an agency or prop. perspective, the core cost driver is indirect costs. Reducing direct costs for low and medium volume clearers will have a small to medium positive impact at best. From a prop. perspective, significant profit and loss (P&L) effects can only be realised if these clearers overhaul their internal efficiency or benefit from improvements in operational and process efficiency undertaken by

---

[27] Note the peculiarity that although Clearing Member 5 clears less contracts than Clearing Member 6, indirect costs only account for 30 per cent of his all-in costs, whereas for Clearing Member 6, indirect costs account for 40 per cent of all-in costs. The provided data thus suggests that Clearing Member 5 operates more efficiently. On the other hand, the pie charts should not be over-interpreted, due to the aforementioned limitations.

[28] Evidence for the existence of economies of scale on the part of investment banks is also provided by Smith (2001), p. 9; and Mainelli (2004).

their clearing houses. The same is true from an agency perspective: in order to impact positively their profit margin, they need to reduce indirect costs through internal measures or depend on industry initiatives.

For high volume clearing members, direct costs are the core cost driver. This is important from a prop. perspective, because fees charged by clearing houses and service providers exert a direct, negative P&L effect on the clearing member. As outlined above, in order to tackle their largest P&L contributor, these clearers need to engage in lobbying activities. On the other hand, if direct costs are the largest cost component from an agency perspective, the clearing member benefits, because it can pass those charges on to its customers.

The other costs, the direct costs, we don't actually worry too much about it. We pass those on to our clients. They don't really affect our bottom line.[29]

The only way in which a high volume clearing member with agency focus can positively impact its profit margin is thus by increasing its internal efficiency or realising efficiency gains through industry initiatives.

Our commissions have been driven down and we are under criticism and competitive pressure for commissions. We need to harmonise and make our own organisation more efficient.[30]

A reduction of clearing house fees only has a positive P&L impact on the clearer if it is able to retain the fee reductions without passing them on to its customers. Whether or not this is possible depends on the level of competition between clearers as well as on the amount of pressure exerted by their customers to reduce commissions.

Obviously we are sensitive to clients only to the extent that we are passing the charges through to the clients and they obviously are eager to encourage us to try and get the costs down.[31]

In this case, although direct costs constitute the core cost driver for the high volume clearers, due to their agency perspective, they are less concerned with the reduction of these direct costs than they are with the elimination of operational inefficiencies to increase their profit margin.

The analysis of Figures 5.5 and 5.6 thus revealed that there is an important fourth factor influencing the way in which cost types are perceived, which is the cleared volume. To summarise, the perception of clearing-related cost types

---

[29] Statement made by interviewed clearing member representative.
[30] Interview with John Mathias.
[31] Statement made by interviewed clearing member representative.

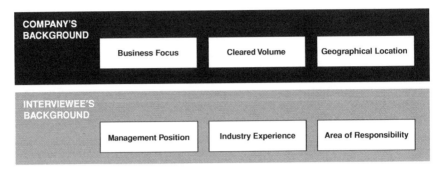

Figure 5.7   Key factors influencing perception of cost types
Source: Author's own.

greatly depends on the respective company (its cleared volume, business focus and geographical location) and interviewee backgrounds (management position, industry experience and area of responsibility). Figure 5.7 summarises these key factors.

5.1.4 Cost categories revised

The analysis of the pie charts in Figure 5.5 delivers another important insight with regard to clearing members, which is that clearing house fees are perceived as the core direct cost driver, whereas back-office and IT costs constitute the most important indirect cost categories. This insight is supported by the other interviewed clearing members.[32] Concerning indirect costs, the relevance of cost of capital and risk management costs is generally perceived as low. In the following, insights from the interviews on the cost categories are briefly described.

5.1.4.1 Direct costs

Most interviewed clearing members regarded the fees charged by clearing houses as significantly more important than clearing-related service provider fees. Nonetheless, if clearers rely on the intermediary services of one or several other GCMs to connect to clearing houses with which they do not hold a direct membership, service provider charges can be significantly higher. High volume clearing members conducting a large-scale business are likely to

---

[32] Note that the findings from the cost analysis represent a snapshot. Interviewees revealed that the relevance of the different cost categories has changed over time. Automation has been a key factor in this regard; the increase of derivatives volumes over the past years has not been matched by a corresponding increase in staffing level, thanks to automation. Cf. interviews.

benefit generally from their size; being in a good negotiating position vis-à-vis third-party service providers enables them to drive down costs.[33] Further details and analysis of the fee structures of different clearing houses is provided in sections 5.2.1 and 5.2.2.

5.1.4.2 Cost of capital

Analysing the cost of capital yields some interesting insights. Although none of the interviewed clearing members regarded this cost category as a significant cost driver, it encompasses some important aspects.

You can divide the world into two primary groups, those that are collateral rich and those that are collateral poor.[34]

The collateral poor tend to be the large trading houses, such as arcades,[35] with a high proportion of day trading and low capital backing.[36] As outlined above, the empirical research is biased towards the view of high volume clearing members – the collateral rich. Although the interviewed low and medium volume clearing members concurred with the high volume clearers by assigning low importance to the cost of capital, a more diversified group of interviewed clearing members might have led to a different evaluation. Furthermore, besides depending on the capital structure of the clearer, the perception of cost of capital is influenced by the interviewee's management position as well as the nature of the clearing member's business. Calculating, analysing and understanding the true cost of capital related to clearing is difficult, because it requires the individual to have knowledge about the internal rates charged by the treasury department as well as the ability to evaluate opportunities for alternative, more beneficial uses of the capital that is tied up in the clearing house. Generally, the higher up in management and the more concerned the respondent is with the strategic and financial development of his or her firm, the more likely he or she will be able to provide a comprehensive assessment of the cost of capital.[37] The evaluation of the cost of capital depends on the characteristics of the clearing member's business perspective (i.e. prop. versus agency) and whether the firm holds overnight positions or is flat at the end of each business day, because holding open positions requires more capital.[38]

---

[33] Cf. interviews.
[34] Statement made by interviewed clearing member representative.
[35] Trading arcades are firms that offer individual traders access to trading platforms and clearing services. Arcades offer traders a place where they can work together, rent a desk and trade for their own account at reduced commissions through the combined high volume trading activity.
[36] Cf. interviews.   [37] Cf. interviews.   [38] Cf. interviews.

Relatively speaking, collateral isn't that expensive for large clearing members to obtain . . . You receive the collateral from the customers, and to the extent that you are an intermediary, you have to lodge it somewhere. The clearing house is a legitimate and well-trusted place to lodge it, so it is very convenient to just hold collateral there as opposed to other things you could do with it – as compared to other things that require an amount of work.[39]

Capital costs related to a clearing member's agency business are usually lower than the capital costs related to its proprietary business.[40] Although clearing members incur capital costs, i.e. default fund contributions and regulatory capital requirements, from both perspectives, they mainly incur capital costs related to customers' margin requirements in the event that time lags arise between the margin call from the clearing house and the moment the clearing member can collect margin from the respective customers. In the case of proprietary transactions, the clearing member itself has to provide the margin collateral, thus incurring capital costs related to margin payments. Clearing members with an agency focus and a collateral-poor customer base will be concerned with opportunities to reduce the cost of capital to the extent that customers can use their money more efficiently, which theoretically enables them to trade more, translating into higher fee income for the clearer.[41]

Nonetheless, the interviewed clearing members' general perception of the relevance of the cost of capital was marginal:

The cost of funding for us as a bank is actually relatively low. I guess it is different for us . . . than for a small broker. If we got 20 million additional less in margins – does that make that much difference to our P&L? Hardly![42]

The interviewees' assessment of the low relevance of cost of capital was mainly based on the following arguments:
• collateral-rich clearers have enough capital available;
• clearing houses can serve as a cheap form of custody; and
• clearing houses pay interest on most collateral.
The collateral-rich clearing members usually have large bond portfolios in place, regardless of their clearing-related capital requirements. These bonds can be deposited at a custodian, but the custodian commonly charges for custody services. Leaving the bonds with the clearing house can thus be a cheap form of custody – from that perspective, the marginal cost of collateral is zero.[43]

---

[39] Interview with John P. Davidson III.   [40] Cf. interviews.   [41] Cf. interviews.
[42] Statement made by interviewed clearing member representative.   [43] Cf. interviews.

As for the money we put up to cover our margins, we use non-cash collateral where possible, just to use the bank's normal inventory. So we have sufficient securities which we can stick to Eurex or LCH.Clearnet, just as easily as putting them at Euroclear or Crest. That doesn't cost us anything.[44]

This is one important reason why collateral-rich clearing members appear to be so comfortable with keeping excess collateral at the clearing house.[45] Doing so allows them to reduce the operational burden of constantly adapting their collateral lodged at the clearing house.[46] What is more, many clearing houses pay interest on the deposited cash. Generally, clearing members will endeavour to put up assets as clearing fund deposits or margin deposits that are interest bearing to begin with, and try to minimise those that are not. Despite the fact that interest paid on cash is usually below the market rates, this disadvantage is thought to be outweighed by the convenience of leaving it in one place rather than shifting it around on a daily basis to obtain the best rates.

Finally, although the clearing members generally perceived the cost of capital as only marginally relevant, they nonetheless pointed out the impact that industry initiatives and improvements in collateral management had made, including netting opportunities, types of collateral accepted by the clearing house, cross-margining possibilities, automation and the level of interest rates paid on deposited cash. Interviewees agreed that without these improvements, cost of capital would likely be a much more significant cost category.

5.1.4.3 Risk management costs

There are several reasons for risk management costs being perceived as less important by interviewees. Firstly, risk management commonly covers several different areas and products within a company, resulting in one team covering several or all of the businesses in which the clearing member is active. If risk management is performed for several businesses and functions combined, then separating out the personnel costs of clearing-related risk management becomes very difficult. Furthermore, the risk management function is to a large degree supported and conducted by specialised risk management tools. Compared to other costs, the use of such tools is considered relatively cheap.[47] Difficulties in assessing the risk management costs also stem from the fact that the systems and tools are used for both trading- and clearing-related

---

[44] Statement made by interviewed clearing member representative.
[45] Keeping 'excess collateral' refers to a clearer lodging more collateral at the clearing house than is actually required by the CCP.
[46] Cf. interviews.   [47] Cf. interviews.

risk management functions.[48] Whereas risk management of prop. positions relies to a great extent on electronic risk management tools, risk management of agency positions can involve a higher degree of manual oversight. The significance of risk management costs further depends on the nature of the trades: when positions are held overnight, a higher degree of continuous risk management effort is necessary. If clearing members apply a conservative approach to risk management,[49] the effort in terms of manual customer risk oversight is considered marginal.[50] Although the significance of risk management costs was classified as low by all interviewees, some respondents pointed out that risk management costs are expected to rise in the future due to regulatory initiatives, such as Basel II and the Markets in Financial Instruments Directive (MiFID),[51] or the addition of new client segments, both of which would entail more risk management effort.[52] Either scenario could lead to more investment in risk management as well as a greater focus on this cost category.[53]

5.1.4.4 Information technology costs

Naturally, the significance of IT costs increases with the replacement of manual labour by automation. It is obvious that the more markets a clearing member is connected to, the higher its IT expenditures will generally be. This is due to the varying technology and systems employed by the different clearing houses. Depending on its size, the clearing member will decide whether it prefers to automate all of its clearing house interfaces or to implement semi-automated solutions: interviewees stated that expensive software solutions often do not make economic sense for very low volume markets. IT costs climb further with demands for flexibility of infrastructure and custom-tailored solutions; flexibility always translates into greater IT costs.[54] The interviews underscored the importance of a prop. versus an agency focus when evaluating the relevance of IT expenditures. All clearing members incur costs for in-house or vendor solutions, software licence fees, and the ongoing maintenance and management of the clearing house interfaces, which can be substantial.[55]

---

[48] Cf. interviews.

[49] Applying a conservative approach to risk management includes, e.g. putting customers through rigorous checks before they can obtain clearing services from a certain clearer. However, this approach can impede efforts to minimise day-to-day risk management efforts.

[50] Cf. interviews.

[51] Cf. interviews. For details on the impact of MiFID, refer to Casey/Lannoo (2006a); Casey/Lannoo (2006b); Deutsche Börse Group (ed.) (2007b); and www.fsa.gov.uk. For details on Basel II, refer to Bank for International Settlements (ed.) (2006).

[52] Cf. interviews.   [53] Cf. interviews.   [54] Cf. interviews.

[55] The ongoing maintenance of clearing house interfaces includes updates on the infrastructure related to operational processes (such as margin calculations, batch processes, etc.) as well as the costs associated

Our IT spending is ridiculously high because of all the exchanges having different APIs. If they do three releases a year and there are forty exchanges we are members of, that requires many bodies full-time just to do the testing. Further, we incur costs as a result of our vendors changing things as well as hook-ups if they don't get it right the first time. That is a massive cost across the industry, absolutely huge![56]

Another important cost concerns project management and implementation. Projects can revolve around the entrance into new markets, the clearing of new products, new service offerings, agreements between different clearing houses and any other initiative launched by clearing houses. Whereas clearing members with a prop. focus are free to decide whether or not to pursue, support or postpone an elective clearing house initiative at their leisure, clearing members with an agency focus are under greater pressure to implement new initiatives in order to satisfy their customers and maintain their market position as service providers.

Every exchange we clear brings 2–3 new things a year, and we clear 40 exchanges, so that makes 120 initiatives we need to look at based on what our clients want and pay fees to enhance the system to support it and then nobody does any business on it – that is all wasted. That is a cost![57]

If it then turns out that there is no market demand to support a certain initiative, the costs incurred from adapting and enhancing systems on the part of the clearing member are not balanced by any benefits, such as more transactions cleared or even a mere increase in customer satisfaction. Clearers with an agency focus are saddled with additional costs stemming from their need to manage customer relations, because this often involves a great deal of manual intervention. Standardised IT systems can hardly ever provide completely automated solutions. Clearers therefore often employ their own IT system, which can be based on a back-office vendor's software that is then developed further and adapted to specific requirements. However, this software is often based on old versions of the vendor software; upgrades are often put off until the last minute due to the expense. These IT systems are then largely proprietary and it is very difficult actually to share data among clearing intermediaries – if at all; data sharing almost never occurs in real

---

with release management. Every clearing house launches roughly one new release of its software every year. Implementing the respective software updates can involve manual work, such as testing the software. Depending on the number of clearing houses a clearer is connected to, keeping up with that flow of updates can involve huge maintenance efforts – especially if proprietary systems are employed.

[56] Statement made by interviewed clearing member representative.

[57] Statement made by interviewed clearing member representative.

time due to the complexity of the systems.[58] This causes IT costs to rise even further.

5.1.4.5 Back-office costs

As outlined above, the interviewed clearing members unanimously regarded back-office and IT costs as the core drivers of indirect costs, because these areas require continuous investment. Opinions differed as to which category was more significant. Respondents identified the level of back-office costs as largely dependent on the degree of STP versus manual intervention required. Further costs can arise from the need to employ different expert teams for different markets, i.e. the 'cost of expertise'. High STP rates minimise failure rates, whereas manual labour is error-prone and can translate into huge costs. Although these aspects are important from both the agency and proprietary perspectives, clearing members engaging in agency business require more manual intervention, which brings additional costs; the management of customer relations (including account and sub-account structures, etc.) sometimes has to be done manually to some degree, which results in a head-count-intensive back-office. Back-office costs are also impacted by the number of markets in which a clearing member is active, as well as the degree of specialist knowledge required.

5.2 Transaction cost analyses

When people are getting price sensitive, the fees charged by clearing houses and intermediaries are the costs that people look at.[59]

My own feeling is that the clearing fees and the other fees are really noise.[60]

Whereas the previous section served to deliver insights into the relevance of the different cost categories and identified the core cost drivers for different clearing member types, this section focuses on providing a deeper understanding of the costs related to derivatives clearing. For this purpose, the following qualitative and quantitative cost analyses are conducted:

- comparison of per-contract fees charged by major clearing houses (section 5.2.1);
- analysis of clearing houses' volume discount schemes (section 5.2.2);
- estimate of total European clearing industry costs in 2005 (section 5.2.3);

---

[58] Cf. interviews.   [59] Interview with Peter Cox.
[60] Statement made by interviewed market expert.

- assessment of clearing members' average direct and indirect costs (section 5.2.4);
- analysis of clearing members' unit costs (section 5.2.5);
- benchmarking of derivatives clearing versus other market infrastructure costs (section 5.2.6);
- identification of cost reduction scenarios for clearing members (section 5.2.7);
- presentation of non-clearing members' perspectives (section 5.2.8); and
- introduction of cost reduction scenarios for non-clearing members (section 5.2.9).

5.2.1 Clearing house fees

The comparison of clearing house fees is valuable for different reasons. Firstly, the previous section showed that as the core driver of clearing costs, clearing house fees have great relevance for high volume clearing members with a prop. focus; but the fees ultimately represent an important cost component for all clearing member types. Secondly, clearing house charges constitute the basis for the subsequent analyses, such as the estimate of total European clearing industry costs (section 5.2.3),[61] which in turn allows for conclusions on the average direct and indirect costs of the various low, medium and high volume clearing member types (section 5.2.4) and their unit costs (section 5.2.5).

For the comparison of per-contract fees, the major European clearing houses (Eurex Clearing, LCH.Clearnet, OMX Clearing, MEFF and CC&G) were chosen to constitute the peer group to be benchmarked against the two largest US derivatives clearing houses, the CME and the OCC. For the purpose of this analysis, fees are not compared on a per-contract basis, but with reference to a hedged amount of €500,000. The fee levels presented in the following thus signify the charges for a single derivatives transaction worth €500,000.[62] The reference date for the analysis was 29 September 2006.[63]

---

[61] Clearing house charges constitute the only publicly available information on the transaction costs of derivatives clearing. As interviewees refused to provide quantitative details on their direct and indirect costs, any further cost calculation must therefore be based on publicly available data.

[62] This type of analysis facilitates the comparison of the per-contract fees charged by clearing houses by equalising the different contract values. Although it can be assumed that the contract value is at least to some extent reflected in the fee levels set by clearing houses, a comparison of per-contract fees runs the risk of yielding incommensurable results.

[63] 29 September 2006 thus served as the reference date for exchange rates and the value of the respective underlying.

The fee levels of three different product groups, i.e. equity, equity index and interest rate products, are compared. For each product group, benchmark products were chosen according to comparability and volume within the respective product group. In other words, whenever possible, the products with the highest number of contracts cleared were selected as benchmark products.[64] The fees specified have been rounded down or up to the nearest integral number.[65] Comparing clearing fees is problematic when all-in fees (comprising trading and clearing fees) are charged by clearing houses or exchanges. As this is indeed the case for Eurex Clearing and OMX,[66] the following workaround was implemented: in order to ensure comparability with the fee levels of Eurex Clearing and OMX, trading fees were included in the analysis. Whereas the OMX fees thus represent the combined charges for trading and clearing, an artificial fee split was developed to separate the trading and clearing components out of the all-in fees charged by Eurex.[67] Despite the inclusion of trading fees, the focus of the analysis is on the fees charged by clearing houses. Note that whenever reference is made to Eurex's clearing fee in the following analysis, this fee represents an artificial estimate. Should Eurex decide to separate its combined fee into trading and clearing components at any point in the future, it must be assumed that this will result in entirely different clearing fees. For a comprehensive overview of all fees and details on the calculation, refer to Appendix 6. Following a brief description of the benchmark analysis of equity, equity index and interest rate fees, the findings are summarised and interpreted.

---

[64] Based on the assumption that the highest volume products enjoy the most competitive pricing and are thus best suited for a benchmark analysis, they were selected as benchmark products whenever possible. For the purpose of this analysis, the results of the comparison of benchmark products are generalised according to the respective product category. It should be taken into account that this generalisation of results might not be applicable to all products within a specific product category.

[65] Decimal places 0.1 to 0.4 were rounded down; decimal places 0.5 to 0.9 were rounded up.

[66] Furthermore, OneChicago charges all-in fees for single stock futures and Euronext.liffe charged an all-in fee for equity derivatives traded on the Amsterdam market and cleared through LCH.Clearnet until November 2006. Since then, Euronext.liffe and LCH.Clearnet have charged separate trading and clearing fees.

[67] Eurex and the Clearing Corporation planned to charge a link fee of €0.05 for the clearing of the Eurex's CFTC-approved euro-denominated products. The average transaction fee for these products is approximately €0.30. It is assumed that the value of the link fee approximately resembles the stand-alone value of Eurex's clearing service. For the purpose of this analysis, the clearing and trading fees are thus assumed to be equivalent to 17 and 83 per cent of the all-in fee, respectively. Note that this calculation serves the purpose of approximation only. The average transaction fee of €0.30 includes both a trading and a clearing fee component. Calculating the exact fee split would thus require taking this factor into account.

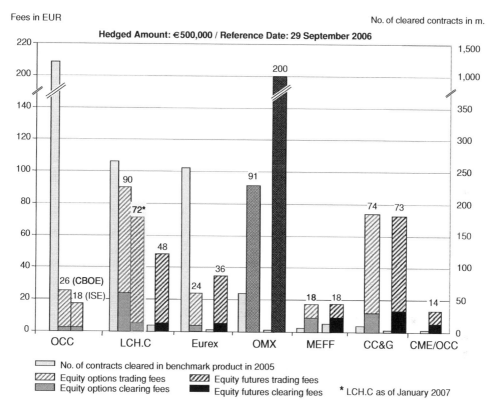

Figure 5.8 Clearing and trading fees for €500,000 hedge in equity options or equity futures[68]
Source: Author's own; based on clearing houses' published fee schedules.

Figure 5.8 provides an overview of clearing and trading fees for a €500,000 hedge in individual equity options or single stock futures. The left axis displays the respective fees charged for the transaction in euros. The right axis refers to the number of cleared contracts in millions of contracts, i.e. the volume of individual equity options and single stock futures cleared through the respective clearing house in 2005.[69] The sequence of the clearing houses as presented in the figure is sorted by these cleared volumes. The volume

---

[68] Single stock futures traded on OneChicago can be cleared at the CME or OCC. Whilst OneChicago charges all-in fees for single stock futures, the assumed fee split is artificial and based on estimates from expert interviews.

[69] The volume of cleared products is exhibited on an annual basis rather than on a monthly basis because clearing houses are more likely regularly to review their pricing structure with reference to annual figures rather than to any short-term data.

information is included in the analysis to evaluate whether or not clearing houses tend to translate higher volumes in benchmark products into lower fees.[70]

A comparison of the trading and clearing fees charged for a €500,000 hedge in individual equity derivatives reveals that trading fees are generally higher than clearing fees. The significant variation of total fees within the peer group is largely due to the different trading fees charged by the exchanges rather than to substantial differences in clearing house fees. The clearing of the equity options hedge is cheapest at the OCC and Eurex Clearing (ECAG), with the OCC charging approximately €3 and ECAG claiming €4. At €9, MEFF's are roughly twice as high as ECAG's clearing fees; at €12, CC&G charges are triple their fee. At the reference date, LCH.Clearnet's clearing fees were at a non-competitive level, with €24 charged for the hedge. On 27 September 2006, the firm announced a reduction of these clearing fees as of January 2007,[71] resulting in charges that were more in line with those of its peers (i.e. €6 for the hedge in equity options).

For the hedge in single stock futures, Eurex Clearing, LCH.Clearnet and the CME/OCC each charge clearing fees of roughly €6, while MEFF charges €9 and CC&G €13. It is apparent that OMX charges the highest all-in fees for both equity options and single stock futures. Whereas its charges for equity options are on a par with the combined trading and 'old' clearing fees charged by Euronext.liffe and LCH.Clearnet, fees charged for single stock futures appear to be extraordinarily high. At €200, its fees are roughly three times higher than those charged by CC&G and IDEM (the Italian derivatives exchange) as well as fourteen times higher than OneChicago's combined clearing and trading fees.

Figure 5.9 exhibits clearing and trading fees for a €500,000 hedge in index options or index futures.[72] Clearing the hedge in index options is cheapest in the US; the OCC charges 13 cents. In Europe, LCH.Clearnet offers the most competitive rate at 25 cents. Eurex Clearing charges more than twice as much, i.e. 65 cents for the hedge in index options. Lastly, CC&G charges €1.56 for clearing services.

---

[70] This helps to provide first evidence of the existence of economies of scale on the part of the clearing houses. Note that a final conclusion on this issue is not possible without taking into account the production costs of clearing houses. A more detailed analysis of clearing house production costs and the existence of economies of scale is provided in Chapter 6.

[71] Cf. LCH.Clearnet (ed.) (27.09.2006).

[72] Refer to Appendix 6 for details on which products were chosen for the benchmark analysis.

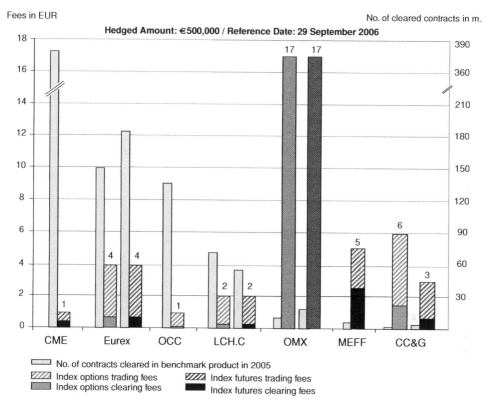

Figure 5.9   Clearing and trading fees for €500,000 hedge in index options or index futures
Source: Author's own; based on clearing houses' published fee schedules.

An analysis of the fees for the hedge in index futures reveals that clearing is cheapest in Europe, with 25 cents charged by LCH.Clearnet. The CME charges 30 cents for clearing the hedge, Eurex Clearing and CC&G both demand 65 cents and MEFF asks €2.50. The combined trading and clearing fees charged by OMX are again well above the levels charged by its peer group, with €17 charged for both the hedge in index options or index futures.

Finally, the fees charged for a €500,000 hedge in interest rate futures are compared. Figure 5.10 provides an overview of relevant fees for cash settled and physically delivered interest rate futures.[73] The analysis shows that the clearing of physically delivered interest rate products is cheapest in Europe, with Eurex Clearing charging 17 cents for the €500,000 hedge. At 30 cents, the

---

[73] Refer to Appendix 6 for details on which products were chosen for the benchmark analysis.

Fees in EUR

No. of cleared contracts in m.

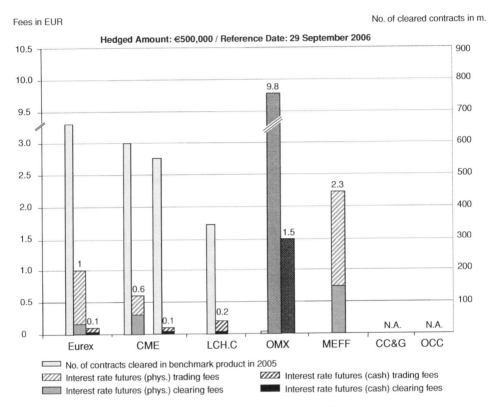

Figure 5.10   Clearing and trading fees for €500,000 hedge in interest rate futures
Source: Author's own; based on clearing houses' published fee schedules.

CME charges almost twice as much for clearing the hedge in T-bond futures; MEFF prices the clearing of its product at 75 cents.[74] Clearing the hedge in cash settled interest rate derivatives is generally cheaper. The cheapest fees are offered in Europe, with Eurex Clearing and LCH.Clearnet both charging 2 cents for the hedge. The CME's clearing fees are double the amount at 4 cents. The all-in fees charged by OMX are above the combined trading and clearing fees of its peers; its fees for physically delivered interest rate futures are roughly ten times higher than the fees charged by Eurex and roughly four times higher than those charged by MEFF. At €1.50, cash settled interest rate futures are seven-and-a-half times more expensive than products traded at Euronext.liffe and cleared through LCH.Clearnet.

---

[74] The inclusion of MEFF's product, the Bono 10, is for the purpose of enlarging the peer group only. In 2005, not a single contract was traded in interest rate products at MEFF.

To summarise, the benchmark analysis yielded a number of insights. Firstly, trading fees are in all cases higher than clearing fees. Secondly, the most economical way to execute the hedge is in the form of interest rate derivatives. Hedging in index derivatives is more expensive, but hedging in individual equity derivatives is the most expensive of all.[75] Further, the comparison of fee levels charged by the different European and US clearing houses revealed that with respect to four of the six benchmarked product types, European clearing houses charged lower fees than their US counterparts. However, US clearing houses offer the lowest rates in equity options and index options clearing. In fact, given the disparity between volumes cleared in the US in certain products, such as by the OCC in equity options and by the CME in index futures, and the largest European CCPs, it is surprising that the difference in fees is not greater. It should be taken into account, however, that it is common practice amongst American clearing houses to grant rebates and/or (annual) discounts to certain clearing member types. Such reductions were not taken into account, which distorts any final conclusions.

The analysis also serves to illuminate and provide a snapshot of the pricing structure of the benchmarked clearing houses. High volumes do not always seem to translate into lower fees, suggesting that there is room for the reduction of per-contract clearing fees. Eurex Clearing offers competitive pricing for the clearing of equity options, single stock futures and interest rate derivatives.[76] Although the fee split is artificial, its fees for clearing index options and index futures nonetheless appear to be too high.[77] LCH.Clearnet's fees for single stock futures, index derivatives and cash-settled interest rate products are competitive.[78] Despite the reduction in clearing fees for equity options, these charges still seem excessive.[79] Whereas the clearing fees charged by the CME and OCC for the clearing of single stock futures traded on OneChicago

---

[75] These results are not surprising, because the pricing of derivatives is usually based on a per-contract level. Due to the very high value of one interest rate contract as compared to one index, or individual equity contract, a smaller number of contracts is needed for hedging a certain amount in interest rate derivatives – which in turn results in lower fees charged for the transaction.

[76] An analysis of combined trading and clearing fees, on the other hand, suggests that the all-in fees charged by Eurex could be lower for equity futures and physically delivered interest rate derivatives.

[77] In index options, LCH.Clearnet charges half of Eurex's clearing fees, although Eurex clears double the volume. In index futures, Eurex's clearing fee levels are equal to clearing fees charged by CC&G, albeit with a volume of cleared contracts that is roughly thirty-seven times higher.

[78] An analysis of the combined trading and clearing fees indicates that the trading fees charged by Euronext.liffe for single stock futures could be lower.

[79] With more volume cleared in equity options than Eurex, LCH.Clearnet's new fee is still one-and-a-half times higher than that of Eurex. There is room for improvement with regard to Euronext.liffe's trading fee; despite volumes that are approximately twenty-two times higher than those of CC&G and IDEM, its all-in fees are merely 3 per cent lower.

are competitive, the CME's fees for clearing index futures and interest rate derivatives appear over-priced.[80] The fees charged by the OCC for individual equity and index options seem reasonable, but not remarkably so.[81] Taking into account the comparatively low volumes cleared at MEFF and CC&G, both clearing houses' fees are generally at very competitive levels.[82] The combined trading and clearing fees charged by OMX for equity options and cash-settled interest rate derivatives are relatively high, but within the scope of the peer group. However, the fees charged for single stock futures, index derivatives and physically delivered interest rate products are non-competitive.

Overall, the comparative analysis of per-contract fees charged by the major horizontally and vertically integrated European and US clearing houses produced no clear winner in terms of the most competitive fee levels.

5.2.2 Clearing houses' volume discount schemes

As outlined above, the second focus of the cost analysis is on investigating the clearing houses' volume discount schemes. The purpose of the analysis is to discover which clearing member types – i.e. low, medium or high volume clearers – receive preferential treatment from clearing houses; this serves further to explore particularities of the current structure of the Value Provision Network.

Not all clearing houses grant volume discounts, though. Figure 5.11 specifies which of the benchmarked clearing houses employ volume discounts, and in which product categories. It also identifies the criterion used by the clearing house to determine the discounts. When clearing houses utilise the 'trade size' as a criterion for discounts, this refers to the number of contracts per transaction. Other criteria employed are volume thresholds, i.e. a determination of the minimum number of contracts cleared, either on a daily or monthly basis. Usually, volume discounts either translate into reduced per-transaction fees or fee caps.[83]

---

[80] Even though CME's cleared volumes of index futures are roughly seven times higher than those of LCH.Clearnet, CME's clearing fee is still higher. Taking the trading fees into account changes the result of the analysis, though – CME's combined trading and clearing fee for index futures is the cheapest rate offered. The same applies to the all-in fees for interest rate products charged by CME; these are at very competitive levels.

[81] At first sight, the fees charged for the clearing of equity options seem to be too high, because they are at roughly the same level as those charged by Eurex, albeit with five times higher volumes cleared at the OCC. However, the OCC provides refunds, fee reductions and discounts to its members on an annual basis, which can ultimately lead to a significant reduction of the per-contract fee.

[82] Taking the trading fees into account suggests that fees charged by IDEM for equity options and single stock futures could be lower in comparison with its peers.

[83] Volume discounts can also be granted through annual refunds and discounts.

	Eurex	LCH.C	OMX	MEFF	CC&G	CME	OCC
Equity Options	NO	**YES**	**YES**	NO	**YES**	N.A.	**YES**
CRITERION:		Trade Size	Trade Size		Trade Size		Trade Size
Single Stock Futures*	NO	NO	**YES**	NO	**YES**	**YES**	
CRITERION:			Trade Size		Trade Size	Unspecified	
Index Options	NO	NO	**YES**	NO	NO	N.A.	**YES**
CRITERION:			Monthly Contracts				Trade Size
Index Futures	NO	NO	NO	NO	NO	NO	N.A.
CRITERION:							
Interest Rate Futures	NO	NO	NO	NO	N.A.	**YES**	N.A.
CRITERION:						Daily Contracts	

* Cleared through CME or OCC

Figure 5.11   Clearing houses' volume discounts in benchmark products, as of September 2006
Source: Author's own; compilation based on clearing houses' websites.[84]

The overview shows that except for ECAG and MEFF, all of the other benchmarked clearing houses employ volume discounts.[85] Volume discounts are granted for the clearing of equity options, single stock futures, index options and interest rate future contracts. None of the clearing houses applies a volume-based discount scheme for index futures.

Whether or not clearing members generally welcome the implementation of discount schemes again depends on their perspective and business focus. Clearing members with a prop. focus welcome any reduction in fees charged by clearing houses; members with an agency focus, however, are often dismissive of such discounts, because the schemes tend to augment the complexity of calculating the fees charged to customers. The need to monitor and track discount levels translates into increased back-office costs.

From a proprietary point of view, I quite like fee caps, because we always hit them. But it doesn't benefit me as an individual from a client point of view. Then yes, it just becomes a pain![86]

[84] The key according to which annual refunds are granted by the OCC is not publicly available. Therefore, the OCC's annual refund policy is not included in the overview.

[85] Note that the volume discounts specified for the CME refer to the Equity/Clearing Member pricing and that the discount scheme of OMX concerns combined trading and clearing fees.

[86] Statement made by interviewed clearing member representative.

		LCH.C	OMX	CC&G	CME	OCC
Equity Options	Product:	Traded in Paris	Traded in SEK, EUR or DKK	Equity Options	N.A.	Equity Options
	Criterion:	Trade Size	Trade Size	Trade Size		Trade Size
	Discount Level (No. of contracts) Rate of Reduction:	(1) 1–6,000 (2) > 6,000 } –97%	(1) 1–2,000 (2) 2,001–10,000 } –10% (3) > 10,000 } –75%	(1) 1–1,000 (2) > 1,000 } –75%		(1) 1–500 } –20% (2) 501–1,000 } –40% (3) 1,001–2,000 } (4) > 2,000 > 40%
	Applicable Member Type:	**VERY HIGH VOLUME**	**VERY HIGH VOLUME**	**VERY HIGH VOLUME**		**HIGH VOLUME**
Single Stock Futures (SSF)	Product:	N.A.	Traded in SEK or DKK	SSF	Single Stock Futures	
	Criterion:		Trade Size	Trade Size	Unspecified	
	Discount Level Rate of Reduction:		(1) 1–2,000 (2) > 2,000 } –50%	(1) 1–1,000 (2) > 1,000 } –50%	Unspecified	
	Applicable Member Type:		**VERY HIGH VOLUME**	**VERY HIGH VOLUME**	**UNSPECIFIED**	
Index Options	Product:	N.A.	Traded in SEK or EUR	N.A.	N.A.	Index Options
	Criterion:		Monthly Contracts			Trade Size
	Discount Level Rate of Reduction:		(1) 1–21,000 (2) > 21,000 } –43%			(1) 1–500 } –20% (2) 501–1,000 } –40% (3) 1,001–2,000 } (4) > 2,000 > 40%
	Applicable Member Type:		**HIGH VOLUME**			**HIGH VOLUME**
Interest Rate Products	Product:	N.A.	N.A.	N.A.	CME Futures or Options on Futures	N.A.
	Criterion:				Daily Contracts	
	Discount Level Rate of Reduction:				(1) 1–15,000 (2) 15,001–30,000 } –33% (3) > 30,000 } –66%	
	Applicable Member Type:				**MED./HIGH VOLUME**	

Figure 5.12   Clearing houses' volume discounts and benefiting clearing member types
Source: Author's own; compilation based on clearing houses' websites.[87]

Even though the clearing houses are trying to do you a favour by doing this tiered structure, it doesn't reduce your costs; it actually increases your costs, because you have to track these and pass them on to the customer. So that is a very big issue for us.[88]

Figure 5.12 details the discount schemes employed by the clearing houses, specifies the benefiting clearing member types and allows conclusions as to whether or not the potential savings through volume discounts are substantial.

The overview shows that clearing houses tend to give high volume clearers preferential treatment through discounts. Medium volume clearers hardly ever benefit, and low volume clearers are not eligible for discounts at all. Out

---

[87] Identification of applicable clearing member types is based on estimates that take into account the following information: the number of cleared contracts per year/month/day eligible for discounts; minimum and maximum market share thresholds as defined for low/medium/high volume clearers; and information on average contracts per cleared trade as published by clearing houses.

[88] Statement made by interviewed clearing member representative.

of ten relevant discount schemes, only one initiative allows medium volume clearing members to benefit from fee reductions, three schemes benefit merely high volume clearers, and five initiatives are solely applicable to very high volume clearing members.[89] Given that the high and very high volume clearing members are the clearing houses' most important customers, these findings are not surprising; the clearing houses will logically aim to satisfy them. Those types of clearer also have the greatest lobbying power, which ensures that their voice is heard. A clearing house's governance and ownership structures also impact the ultimate influence that different types of clearer can exert over the CCP.

The analysis also shows that the potential savings from discount schemes can be substantial – on average, clearing members can save 50 per cent or even much more in some cases. Findings suggest that benefits from preferential pricing can translate into a competitive advantage for the respective high volume clearing members.

To summarise, not all clearing houses provide volume discounts, but those that do penalise low and medium volume clearing members; the CCPs tailor their discount schemes to their high and very high volume clients. Fee caps and rebates mainly benefit the high volume clearers with a prop. focus; whether or not NCMs and other customers benefit from such schemes depends on whether clearing members undertake the arduous monitoring and tracking effort required to pass on these savings.

5.2.3 Total European clearing industry costs in 2005

To enable a deeper understanding of the true costs related to European derivatives clearing and to provide a basis for analysing the impact that certain network strategies between clearing houses have on transaction costs, the third step of the cost analysis provides an estimate of the total European clearing industry costs in 2005. The estimated figure represents the sum of all direct and indirect costs borne by European clearing members in 2005 for clearing exchange-traded derivatives transactions through Eurex Clearing, LCH.Clearnet, OMX Clearing, MEFF and CC&G. The calculation of costs is based on insights from the empirical study (particularly information on the composition of all-in clearing costs for different benchmark clearing member types; see Figure 5.5), confidential information provided by Eurex Clearing, as well as publicly available data on clearing houses' cleared volumes,

---

[89] One initiative could not be specified due to a lack of publicly available information.

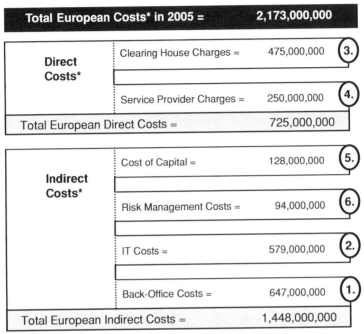

Total European Costs* in 2005 =	2,173,000,000	
Direct Costs*	Clearing House Charges =	475,000,000	3.
	Service Provider Charges =	250,000,000	4.
Total European Direct Costs =	725,000,000	
Indirect Costs*	Cost of Capital =	128,000,000	5.
	Risk Management Costs =	94,000,000	6.
	IT Costs =	579,000,000	2.
	Back-Office Costs =	647,000,000	1.
Total European Indirect Costs =	1,448,000,000	

* Costs in EUR

Figure 5.13 Total European derivatives clearing costs in 2005
Source: Author's own.

per-transaction fees, other fees charged, communication and network charges. This resulted in the calculation of direct and indirect cost estimates for the benchmark clearing members. This data was subsequently used to calculate the total industry costs. For details on the quantitative analysis and the underlying assumptions, refer to Appendix 7.

Following the presentation of the quantitative results, the shortcomings and limitations of the analysis are outlined. A more detailed interpretation of the cost estimates is provided in section 5.2.6.

Figure 5.13 outlines the quantitative results of the analysis.[90] The total European costs of derivatives clearing amounted to roughly €2.173 billion in 2005. This figure correlates to the first level of transaction costs, thus representing all direct and indirect costs that the 219 European clearing members had to bear in the first place. Note that some of these direct and indirect costs are redistributed within the Value Provision Network, as they are ultimately

[90] Figures are rounded to millions of euros; €100,000 to €499,000 are rounded down, whereas €500,000 to €999,000 are rounded up.

passed on (either directly or indirectly, as part of the commissions) by clearers to their respective NCMs and/or other customers.

At €725 million, direct costs represent 33 per cent of total industry costs, whereas indirect costs of roughly €1.448 billion amount to 67 per cent of total costs. The most significant cost categories in 2005 were back-office costs, with estimated annual costs of €647 million, followed by IT costs of €579 million; clearing house charges accounted for €475 million and service provider charges came to €250 million. At the lower end of the spectrum, capital costs and risk management costs added up to approximately €128 million and €94 million, respectively.

The underlying data on individual benchmark clearing members' costs was cross-checked with interviewees representing three of the selected clearing members. Some limitations in the data were thereby uncovered, mainly resulting from a mismatch of clearing-related costs as defined in section 3.2 and the input received from the interviewed clearing members.

The interviewees' perception of the different cost categories is outlined in section 5.1 and explains why certain cost categories (such as the cost of capital and risk management costs) were structurally underestimated in terms of their significance by the interviewed clearing members. Other factors also impacted the results of the cost analysis, mainly affecting the indirect cost categories. All of these factors are detailed in the following paragraphs. Whereas the validation of the data on clearing house charges revealed that the above-mentioned figure is in the right magnitude (see Appendix 7 for details), several caveats apply to the interpretation of the indirect cost estimates.[91]

The estimated €94 million in risk management costs represents the personnel costs pertaining to the basic continuous risk management processes related to monitoring proprietary and agency positions, but they do not cover the personnel costs arising from sophisticated risk management processes. Particularly high volume clearing members typically incur costs resulting from dedicated risk management processes, which go beyond pure position monitoring. The figure thus underestimates the effort and costs related to such sophisticated risk management processes. As outlined above, the difficulties associated with the correct evaluation of risk management costs have various causes. Risk management commonly covers several different markets and products within a company; the responsibility for risk management can also reside in (geographically) distinct departments and is not necessarily relegated to one individual manager. Depending on the clearer's set-up, risk

---

[91] These caveats were identified with the help of interviewees.

management costs might not be reallocated internally, which makes it even more difficult for clearing managers to gain a true understanding of these costs. Clearing-related risk management costs are thus difficult to isolate and to assess correctly.

Another indirect cost category whose magnitude is structurally underestimated by clearing members is the cost of capital. As outlined above, calculating, analysing and understanding the true cost of capital related to clearing is difficult for various reasons. When asked to assess the cost of capital, the interviewed clearing members might not have had in mind the full scope of these costs as defined in section 3.2.2.1. Furthermore, the cross-checking of the data revealed that the figure of €128 million for capital costs in 2005 undervalues the magnitude of capital costs in that it mainly accounts for external financing costs. As the empirical research is biased towards the view of collateral-rich clearing members, whose capital base is usually sufficient to cover any clearing-related collateral requirements, most respondents do not need to utilise external financing for clearing. The majority of interviewees consequently cited very low costs of capital for derivatives clearing. However, as the cost of capital also includes the opportunity cost of capital, i.e. the expected return foregone by clearing members due to bypassing other investment alternatives, this cost category is undervalued by the difference of the value of the benchmark portfolio and the value of the executed portfolio (interest payments from the clearing house) as outlined in section 3.2.2.1.

The figure of €579 million for IT costs covers IT systems and their basic clearing-related functions, such as interfacing with clearing houses and integrating the received data with internal systems; the estimate therefore fails to incorporate the IT costs related to enhanced systems that manage complex tasks related to customer and/or NCM relationships and systems development costs. The IT solution needed for this task is much more complex and consequently requires higher expenditures. The figure for IT costs in 2005 is thus underestimated in that it does not include the costs normally incurred from implementing and operating the requisite enhanced and flexible IT solution.

Finally, the estimate of €647 million for derivatives clearing back-office costs in 2005 covers the performance of basic back-office functions related to continuous position management, regular processing and the orderly booking of transactions to (customer/NCM) accounts. However, the figure does not incorporate the costs for functions related to customer/NCM services or customer/NCM relationship management. GCMs in particular incur significant additional costs resulting from the need to manage customer sub-account structures, as this often has to be done manually to some extent. The figure

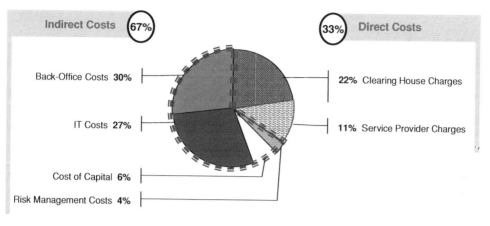

Figure 5.14   Composition of total European derivatives clearing costs in 2005
Source: Author's own.

also does not take into account the average of error account costs, project-related efforts or the full extent of compliance and legal documentation costs. Interviewed clearing members thus underestimated the magnitude of back-office costs; managers generally do not have a complete overview of all of the cost components defined in section 3.2.2.4. This derives from the fact that the defined components of back-office costs are commonly located within several distinct departments and cover various different business segments; no one single manager is likely to have oversight and knowledge of all of these costs. The figure for the magnitude of back-office costs does not incorporate the above-mentioned factors and thus constitutes an underestimate.

To summarise, the estimate of total European derivatives clearing industry costs for 2005 does not reflect all clearing-related indirect costs. It can be assumed that the actual indirect cost figure is higher than suggested. Taking this into account, the finding that indirect costs exceed direct costs remains unchanged, whereas the relative importance of indirect costs increases and the relevance of direct costs decreases. With reference to the available cost estimate, direct costs constituted approximately one-third of total European derivatives clearing costs in 2005, and indirect costs represented roughly two-thirds. Unfortunately, due to a lack of access to more detailed cost data, the magnitude of the difference between the provided figures and the true cost data cannot be quantified; it is therefore not possible to produce an ameliorated cost estimate.

Whereas the results suggest that indirect costs were higher than direct costs in 2005, the relative significance of back-office versus IT costs is more

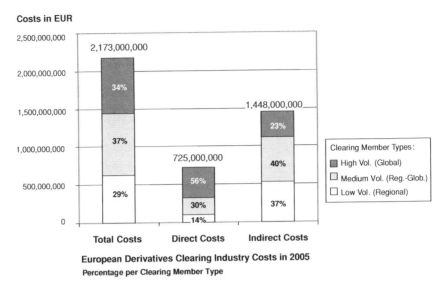

Figure 5.15 Per cent stake of different clearing member types in European derivatives clearing costs in 2005
Source: Author's own.

problematic to determine. The available cost estimate indicates that back-office costs and IT costs constituted 30 and 27 per cent of total industry costs, respectively, revealing that total back-office costs were higher in 2005 than total IT costs.

When analysing back-office versus IT costs, it should be taken into account that the results of the cost estimate are biased towards the information provided by the six benchmark clearing members (refer to Figure 5.5); all but one considered back-office costs more significant. Whereas this is true for the benchmark clearers, it is not necessarily true for any other European clearing member. The twenty-one interviewed clearing members unanimously considered the two categories as the most important sources of indirect costs, but their input did not reveal the dominance of one over the other. It can therefore be concluded that back-office and IT costs constituted the two most significant indirect cost categories, but it cannot be clearly determined which is more so.

Finally, Figure 5.15 outlines the per cent stake held by the different clearing member types in the European costs of derivatives clearing. Whereas total costs are roughly distributed equally across all three clearing member types – i.e. low, medium and high volume clearers must bear 29, 37 and 34 per cent, respectively, of total industry costs – a different picture emerges when direct and indirect costs are compared. The finding that high volume clearing members bear roughly 56 per cent of all direct costs explains their strong lobbying interest in trying to push clearing houses to reduce their fees (which, as outlined above, is particularly relevant from a proprietary perspective).

The figure also illustrates the finding that indirect costs account for the bulk of European derivatives clearing industry costs, of which regionally-to-globally active (medium volume) clearers and regionally active clearers have to bear the largest part (40 and 37 per cent, respectively). These clearing member types consequently have a strong stake in the reduction of indirect clearing costs.

5.2.4 Clearing members' average direct and indirect costs

The fourth step of the cost analysis consists of an assessment of average annual direct and indirect costs of different low, medium and high volume clearing member archetypes. This analysis does not claim to deliver results applicable to any particular clearing member, but it does provide for an archetypical assessment of clearing costs. This in turn offers a deeper understanding of the magnitude of clearing-related costs for different clearing member types and serves to explain the structural particularities of the European Value Provision Network.

The calculation is based on the assumptions underlying the estimate of total European industry costs, as outlined in Appendix 7, as well as on insights from the empirical study and feedback from selected interviewees. This enabled the calculation of the average annual direct and indirect costs for clearing member archetypes, as outlined in Figure 5.16.

For the purpose of this analysis, it was assumed that all of the presented European clearing member archetypes are direct members of all major European clearing houses (Eurex Clearing, LCH.Clearnet, OMX Clearing, MEFF and CC&G). For low and medium volume clearers, this assumption deviates from the definition provided in section 2.3.2. The definition establishes that regionally active (low volume) clearers do not maintain more than a single clearing membership (with their domestic home clearing house). The definition also outlines that while regionally-to-globally active (medium volume) clearers are active (or interested in becoming active) in many markets; they maintain only a single direct clearing relationship with their domestic home clearing house. To clear their transactions in the other (foreign) markets, these members utilise one or several other GCMs as clearing intermediaries.

Market Share	Ø Direct Costs*	Ø Indirect Costs*	Ø TOTAL*	Ø Unit Costs*
HIGH VOLUME CLEARER				
10.00 %	52,509,000	35,006,000	87,515,000	0.20
4.00 %	30,869,000	25,256,000	56,125,000	0.26
3.00 %	24,453,000	21,685,000	46,138,000	0.35
MEDIUM VOLUME CLEARER				
2.00 %	15,145,000	22,718,000	37,863,000	0.43
1.00 %	8,483,000	25,450,000	33,933,000	0.78
0.50 %	4,756,000	21,665,000	26,421,000	1.21
LOW VOLUME CLEARER				
0.30 %	3,093,000	14,092,000	17,185,000	1.32
0.01 %	861,000	4,880,000	5,741,000	13.19
	Costs in EUR			

Figure 5.16   Average annual direct and indirect costs for clearing member archetypes[92]
Note: ø = average.
Source: Author's own.

Figure 5.16 illustrates the dynamics that constitute these structural particularities of the European Value Provision Network concerning the clearing members, as presented in section 2.5.1. The figure shows why it is economical for medium volume clearers to utilise high volume clearers as intermediaries instead of being a direct member of all European CCPs. It also indicates why a relatively small number of European high volume clearers (around seventeen) account for the bulk (roughly 73 per cent) of the total annual European cleared market share (see Figure 2.19).

Generally speaking, service provider charges, risk management, back-office and IT costs are largely fixed costs in the context of this set-up, whereas clearing house charges and cost of capital are partly fixed, but for the most part constitute variable costs. The more clearing house memberships a clearer maintains, the higher the related direct and indirect fixed costs. According to the findings from the empirical study, as outlined in section 5.1, there are economies of scale on the part of the clearing members that enable high volume clearers to economise on their internal structures and processes and consequently leverage their fixed cost base.

Figure 5.16 underlines the existence of economies of scale by illustrating that as cleared volume increases, unit costs decrease. Low and medium volume

[92] The market share refers to the clearer's relative share of the total European exchange-traded derivatives clearing volume, i.e. the sum of cleared volumes at Eurex Clearing, LCH.Clearnet, OMX Clearing, MEFF and CC&G.

clearers therefore have to bear disproportionately high fixed costs, based on the assumption that they are members of all major European clearing houses. The lower a clearing member's market share, the higher its fixed cost burden, and the less economic sense it makes for the clearer to become a member of all European clearing houses. It is simply too expensive to replicate these fixed costs when another firm can provide this service in a more cost-effective manner. In this case, clearing members are better off maintaining a single direct clearing membership and employing the intermediary services of a GCM to connect to any other clearing houses. Low and medium volume clearers in particular will therefore not opt to become members of every major European clearing house. This explains why a very high percentage of the European market share in derivatives clearing is concentrated on a few very high volume clearers; these clearers have cost structures that make it attractive to offer intermediary services, and for low and medium volume clearers, it makes economic sense to utilise these services. Should a low or medium volume clearer nonetheless choose to become a member of many or all major European clearing houses, the driving factors are likely to relate to secrecy, control and reputation, rather than to cost efficiency.

The provided assessment of clearing members' average annual direct and indirect costs is based on theoretical archetypes. In reality, the relationship of cleared volume to cost structure is not so cut and dried; there are cases in which low and high volume clearers operate with cost structures typical for medium volume clearers, and some medium volume clearers have cost structures resembling those typical for low volume clearers, etc. Consequently, the incentive for using a GCM as an intermediary for certain markets instead of maintaining a direct clearing membership can also apply to high volume clearers, depending on their cost structure.

Similar considerations apply to the analysis of the unit costs, which correspond to the number of lots cleared by a clearing member in relation to the sum of total direct and indirect costs. Analysing the unit costs provides insight into the clearing members' costs of production, which are further explored in the following section.

5.2.5 Clearing members' unit costs

Whereas the previous sections provided a detailed explanation and analysis of the magnitude of direct and indirect clearing-related costs that different clearing member types have to bear, this section focuses on putting these costs into context.

As outlined in section 3.2, costs of production imply divergent meanings for different clearing members. For a clearer with a prop. focus, these refer to the costs of doing business, but from the perspective of a clearing member with agency focus, the costs pertain to producing the services it provides to its customers/NCMs. In the latter case, the costs of production form the basis for the commissions charged by a GCM to its NCMs, thus directly impacting the GCM's profit margin.

In addition to the unit cost estimates detailed in Figure 5.16, the expert inquiry revealed that when comparing estimates for unit costs on the basis of fixed costs per lot (i.e. covering service provider charges, risk management, back-office and IT costs), unit costs can be as low as 10 cents for very high volume clearers and as high as €13 for very low volume clearers.

Whereas these unit costs are relevant for clearers with a prop. focus, a different scope of production costs has to be analysed from the perspective of clearing members with an agency focus. Certain costs, such as cost of capital or risk management costs, can only be passed on to customers/NCMs to a limited extent. Depending on which costs a clearing member charges to its customers/NCMs (either directly or as part of commissions), the clearer's production costs can even be significantly lower than 10 cents, i.e. in the range of 2 to 6 cents per lot for very high volume clearers.[93] A thorough comparison of these production costs to the GCMs' commissions exceeds the scope of this study, but the overview of clearing members' costs of production provided here serves to clarify further the structural particularities of the European Value Provision Network.

To summarise, the currently strong position of high volume clearers within the European Value Provision Network is supported by their advantageous cost structure. These clearers have cost structures that make it attractive to offer clearing intermediary services. Due to their scale of business, high volume clearers further benefit from their strong negotiating position towards service providers, which allows them to minimise service provider charges. Clearing houses further strengthen the competitive advantage of European high volume clearers by granting volume discounts.

Network initiatives, which help to reduce indirect costs, can thus have an important impact on the structure of the European VPN. This is true when initiatives entice medium volume clearers to self-clear many markets instead of employing intermediary services, or, more generally, when the attractiveness

---

[93] Cf. interviews.

of becoming a clearer instead of an NCM in many markets increases. Whether certain network initiatives serve to weaken or strengthen the (weak) strong position of (low and medium) high volume clearers in the European VPN is examined in greater detail in the remainder of this study.

5.2.6 Derivatives clearing versus other market infrastructure costs

The previous sections delivered detailed insights on the total costs related to European derivatives clearing; this section benchmarks these costs to other European market infrastructure costs. A first step compares derivatives clearing costs to derivatives trading costs. As derivatives only seldom require settlement of the underlying, and are usually closed out prior to their expiration, a comparison of derivatives clearing costs with settlement costs is not provided. Instead, derivatives clearing costs are compared with the costs of securities trading, clearing and settlement.

The comparison of per-contract fees charged by European and US clearing houses revealed that for all of the analysed benchmark products, trading fees were equal to or significantly exceeded clearing fees. This suggests that, in 2005, variable exchange charges exceeded variable clearing house charges, leaving aside fixed cost charges. These findings are supported by the interviewed clearing members, some of whom explicitly confirmed that exchange charges exceeded clearing house charges in 2005. Due to the interviewees' hesitancy to provide financial details on the questionnaire, it is unfortunately not possible to calculate the exact ratio of total derivatives trading costs to total derivatives clearing costs. A further comparison of total derivatives trading and clearing costs first requires an understanding of the direct and indirect cost categories inherent to derivatives trading. Book (2001) differentiates three cost categories for derivatives trading – information and decision costs, execution costs and fulfilment costs – all of which contain direct and indirect components.[94] Gomber/Schweickert (2002) identify additional indirect trading-related costs, which they classify as timing costs, market impact costs and opportunity costs.[95] Insight provided by market experts suggests that these indirect trading costs are significantly higher than direct trading costs, allowing for the inference that total European derivatives trading costs

[94] Cf. Book (2001), pp. 92–7.
[95] They refer to these costs as 'implicit' costs. Although their research focus is on securities trading, their classification of trading costs is applicable to derivatives trading. Cf. Gomber/Schweickert (2002), p. 486.

exceeded total European derivatives clearing costs in 2005. To the best of this author's knowledge, no detailed analysis or quantitative estimate of total direct or indirect industry-wide derivatives trading costs has yet been conducted, nor are there any publicly available data on the magnitude of direct versus indirect derivatives trading costs. Therefore, the sum of direct and indirect derivatives trading costs is unknown and no comparison to the sum of direct and indirect derivatives clearing costs in 2005 can be conducted. Due to the limited scope of this study, no attempt will be made to calculate these derivatives trading costs to verify the above inference.

In a second step, derivatives clearing costs are benchmarked against the costs of securities trading, clearing and settlement. Direct and indirect securities trading[96] and clearing costs are defined according to the definitions applied to derivatives. Kröpfl (2003) differentiates four direct and indirect cost categories of securities settlement:[97] fees charged by intermediaries (CSDs/ICSDs), liquidity costs, risk costs and back-office costs. Lannoo/Levin (2003) classify fees charged by settlement entities as direct costs and define back-office costs, interface costs, banking and other financial costs, as well as the cost of using intermediaries as the indirect costs of securities settlement.[98] Similar to the findings in derivatives, indirect costs are generally found to exceed direct costs in securities trading, clearing and settlement.[99]

For the purpose of comparing the estimates derived for European derivatives clearing costs in 2005, two studies serve to deliver European benchmarking figures: Morgan Stanley/Mercer Oliver Wyman (eds.) (2003) and Deutsche Börse Group (ed.) (2005a). Despite the shortcomings of the figures derived in these studies,[100] they are currently the only publicly available estimates of European securities trading, clearing and settlement costs.[101] Note that the data presented by the studies merely cover direct charges by exchanges, CCPs and CSDs/ICSDs; they do not account for the service provider charges or indirect costs (as defined in section 3.2). All figures relate to 2002 costs. Whereas the number of transactions in European equity shares grew roughly 26 per cent from 2002 to 2005,[102] any increases or decreases in these costs cannot be

---

[96] See Kaserer/Schiereck (2007) for an analysis of direct and indirect securities trading costs.
[97] Cf. Kröpfl (2003), p. 93.   [98] Cf. Lannoo/Levin (2003), p. 8.
[99] Cf. Giovannini Group (ed.) (2001), p. 66–7; Gomber/Schweickert (2002), pp. 485–9; and Werner (2003), p. 17.
[100] Refer to European Commission (ed.) (2006b), p. 19, for details on the strengths and weaknesses of the studies.
[101] Additional estimates will be available in the near future thanks to a study provided by Oxera (ed.) (2007), which provides for a methodology to derive more precise estimates of the total costs of securities trading, clearing and settlement.
[102] Cf. www.world-exchanges.com.

accounted for due to a lack of reliable data. It is thus assumed that these costs have remained static, i.e. at their 2002 levels.[103]

Based on the findings of the Morgan Stanley/Mercer Oliver Wyman (eds.) (2003) study,[104] Deutsche Börse Group estimates that European investors' expenditures can be broken down as follows, i.e. in terms of direct costs attributable to charges by the respective infrastructure providers:[105] €1.9 billion can be allocated to exchange charges, €100 million to cash equity CCPs and €1.4 billion to CSDs/ICSDs.

These estimates indicate that in terms of absolute costs, European clearing house charges for derivatives clearing were approximately four times higher than charges for cash equities clearing in 2005.[106] Nonetheless, the derivatives market was roughly 6.4 times larger than the cash equities market in terms of size (i.e. number of traded contracts and number of transactions, respectively). Considering that the value-added provided by CCPs can be assumed to be greater in derivatives than in cash equities markets, this finding suggests that customers have benefited from the scale of the derivatives market in terms of comparatively low clearing house charges. Despite the fact that evidence exists suggesting that indirect costs exceed direct costs in securities clearing, there are no publicly available data on the proportion of total direct versus indirect securities clearing costs. This precludes a final conclusion on the magnitude of total European derivatives clearing costs compared to total European securities clearing costs in 2005.

In terms of benchmarking derivatives clearing to securities trading and settlement costs, the estimates indicate that derivatives clearing constitutes the most efficiently organised part of European financial market infrastructure. The comparison shows that the exchange-related charges in the European securities market (€1.9 billion) alone approached the combined direct and indirect clearing-related costs in the European derivatives market (€2.173 billion) in 2005. Taking into account that indirect costs are assumed to exceed direct costs in securities trading, the all-in costs of European securities trading can be expected to significantly exceed the all-in costs of European derivatives clearing.

---

[103] This assumption is not realistic. However, due to the lack of available research on the development of these costs over time, no reliable assumption can be made as to how they evolved from 2002 to 2005.

[104] Cf. Morgan Stanley/Mercer Oliver Wyman (eds.) (2003), p. 19.

[105] Cf. Deutsche Börse Group (ed.) (2005a), pp. 14–15.

[106] Referring to €475 million total clearing house charges for derivatives clearing in 2005, minus approximately €66 million fixed costs, as compared to €100 million in equities clearing in 2005 (assuming that the estimates provided by the Deutsche Börse Group study only account for variable clearing house charges).

Similar findings apply when derivatives clearing costs are benchmarked to securities settlement costs: whereas CSD/ICSD-related charges alone amounted to roughly €1.4 billion in 2005, the need for cross-border settlement necessitates the involvement of additional service providers and intermediaries, resulting in a further increase of direct settlement costs.[107] Given that indirect costs are assumed to exceed direct costs in securities settlement, the all-in costs of European securities settlement are expected to greatly surpass the all-in costs of European derivatives clearing.

To summarise, the benchmarking strongly indicates that derivatives clearing is the most efficient segment within the European market infrastructure. This means that in terms of costs resulting from the interaction between the infrastructure providers (exchanges, clearing houses or CSDs/ICSDs) and their direct customers, the transaction costs related to derivatives clearing are comparatively low. However, this conclusion falls short of actually quantifying the different service levels and value-added functions provided by the different infrastructure providers. Despite the interviewees' suggestion that the value-added function of a clearing house is superior to the value-added function of an exchange,[108] the aforementioned benchmarking of costs fails to incorporate the economic benefit of the services provided by exchanges, clearing houses and CSDs/ICSDs. A final conclusion on which part of the European market infrastructure is most efficient would require quantifying the benefits of these services.

5.2.7 Cost reduction scenarios for clearing members

On the internal side you have things like consolidation of systems, consolidation of teams, outsourcing, lower cost environments, developments in terms of efficiency that is business as usual, as you would expect. We have to keep stripping our costs internally and, if possible, externally.[109]

---

[107] Deutsche Börse Group (ed.) (2005a) estimates the costs allocated to custodians and local settlement agents at €16 billion. Cf. Deutsche Börse Group (ed.) (2005a), p. 15. Whereas this figure indicates significant intermediary costs, it has to be treated with caution, because it includes the costs incurred by the intermediaries themselves for the provision of their services. Cf. European Commission (ed.) (2006b) for a summary of studies that identify a sharp difference among the costs of cross-border versus domestic settlement within Europe. Cross-border settlement charges are found significantly to exceed domestic settlement costs. Deutsche Börse Group (ed.) (2005a).

[108] 'I still believe that the clearing function is better value-added to the global industry than the matching-engine function. Clearing organisations will have the features and the value added pieces that are dramatically harder to build.' Interview with James G. McCormick.

[109] Statement made by interviewed industry participant.

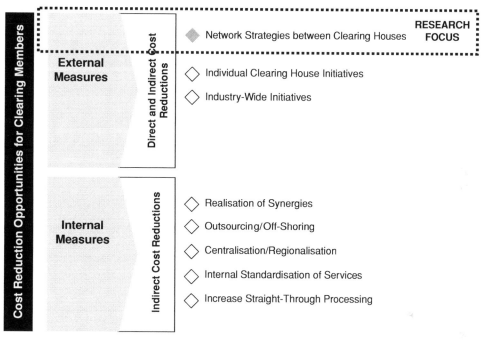

Figure 5.17   Classification of cost reduction opportunities for clearing members
Source: Author's own.

I'm actually thinking away from the large brokerage houses because I think they could be circumvented. Actually, I think that there are costs there that don't need to be there for large users of futures.[110]

Whereas the previous sections analysed the core cost drivers of derivatives clearing as well as the nature, characteristics and magnitude of clearing costs for different clearing member types, this section delivers insights from the expert inquiry on different opportunities for reducing clearing-related costs.

Interviewees identified different opportunities for clearers to reduce transaction costs. These opportunities can be classified as either 'external measures' or 'internal measures'. External measures refer to initiatives that reduce transaction costs that are beyond the clearing members' direct control. External measures can affect direct and/or indirect costs. Internal measures refer to actions launched and controlled by the clearers themselves to cut costs; these initiatives are aimed at reducing indirect costs. Figure 5.17 provides an

---

[110] Interview with Edward F. Condon.

overview of the external and internal measures identified by the interviewed clearers. While the remainder of this study is dedicated to analysing external measures (network strategies in particular) and their impact on transaction costs, other possible cost-reduction scenarios for clearing members are briefly summarised in the following.

Clearing members can only indirectly influence and thus are hardly able to control **external measures**; however, through lobbying efforts, participation in clearing houses' working groups and an involvement in the governance of the clearing house, they can make some headway. Besides network strategies, other external measures to reduce clearing costs include individual clearing houses' initiatives as well as industry-wide initiatives.

Initiatives undertaken by individual clearing houses can reduce direct and/or indirect transaction costs. Interviewees cited the provision of portfolio margining, acceptance of a wider range of collateral, harmonisation and improvement of risk methods, and the introduction of standard processes as examples. Certainly one of the most popular external measures influencing direct costs entails the clearing house reducing its variable or fixed charges. Clearing members with a prop. focus benefit from any kind of reduced rate, including cuts in per-contract fees, volume discounts and rebates or fee caps as well as decreases in fixed clearing house charges.

On the other hand, clearing members with an agency focus stand to gain most from reductions in fixed clearing house charges; these costs cannot be directly passed on to the customers/NCMs and therefore impact the clearer's P&L. NCMs and other customers meanwhile reap the most benefits from a decrease in per-contract fees, because it is difficult for them to monitor whether other forms of reduction – such as diminished fixed clearing house charges, discount schemes or complicated rebates – translate into lower commissions.

Industry-wide initiatives can reduce indirect costs in that they tackle inefficiencies across the board, harmonise processes or introduce standards that require the cooperation and participation of all industry participants, including exchanges, clearing houses, vendors, clearers, customers and other stakeholders. The success of any such initiative depends on a variety of factors, but most importantly on the participation and cooperation of all involved parties; which in turn increases complexity. The adoption of standards can concern mechanical activities, such as give-up processing,[111] the use of standardised application programming interfaces (APIs), standard formatted language,

---

[111] Cf. Berliand (2006), p. 27.

collateral management capabilities, delivery processes,[112] etc. A number of industry-wide initiatives are already underway or being developed to eliminate various inefficiencies.[113]

With regard to **internal measures**, the realisation of synergies refers to a clearer being able to leverage its infrastructure and resources. Increasing the scale and scope of activities allows it to benefit from such synergies, and the enhanced volumes further reduce costs.[114] Synergies can also be realised when clearing members work with strategic partners in joint ventures to share development costs and reduce costs through increased volume.[115] Another way to realise synergies and reduce indirect costs is through the outsourcing or offshoring of certain processes or functions.[116] Outsourcing refers to engaging a third party to execute certain processes and functions that the clearer would have otherwise performed internally. Outsourcing can involve the migration of single functions or processes, or can extend to entire departments.[117] Offshoring refers to taking advantage of lower-cost production factors in remote locations, most importantly labour. Offshored processes or functions can be handed off to a third-party provider or remain in-house. The offshored activity usually fits seamlessly into the overall business of the clearer. Outsourcing and offshoring in clearing usually pertain to non-core back-office and/or IT functions.[118] The objective of outsourcing and offshoring is to improve efficiency, streamline processes and reduce the complexity of the clearer's responsibilities. Of the twenty-one clearing members interviewed for this study, seven claimed to utilise outsourcing or offshoring as a means to reduce

---

[112] Cf. interviews.

[113] See PricewaterhouseCoopers (ed.) (2003) for details. Refer to Bank of New York (ed.) (2004), pp. 13–17, for an overview of different initiatives; and to Nava/Russo (2006), pp. 4–9. Also see Giovannini Group (ed.) (2001); Group of Thirty (ed.) (2003); Giovannini Group (ed.) (2003); Group of Thirty (ed.) (2005); and CESR/European Central Bank (eds.) (2004). Refer to www.cesr-eu.org for more details about the joint work of CESR/ECB on standards for securities clearing and settlement in the EU. Additionally, under the auspices of the European Commission, the Clearing and Settlement Advisory and Monitoring Experts Group (CESAME) was established to advise the Commission on clearing and settlement and has set up two expert groups to work on the removal of tax and legal barriers. For more details on the work of the CESAME Group, refer to www.ec.europa.eu/internal_market/financial-markets/clearing/cesame_en.htm.

[114] Cf. Smith (2001), p. 17.   [115] Cf. Smith (2001), p. 17.

[116] Cf. Smith (2001), p. 17; and Mainelli (2004).

[117] Refer to Fuß (2007) for an analysis of the impact of outsourcing on banking efficiency. With reference to the US banking industry, Fuß (2007) concludes that outsourcing is a strategic necessity. 'Hence, bank management would be ill-advised to merely consider whether or not to outsource. Instead, bank management should contemplate on what to outsource . . . and how to accomplish outsourcing' (Fuß (2007), p. 286).

[118] Non-core functions refer to labour-intensive work not requiring expert knowledge. Important core functions that require expertise and management attention, such as risk management, are usually not outsourced or offshored.

indirect costs, ten said that they currently do not engage in either initiative[119] and four did not specify.

A third internal measure for lowering indirect costs is to pursue a centralisation or regionalisation strategy. Centralisation entails the concentration of all clearing-related mechanical and functional activities in one location, because '[b]anks which process in more than two locations are likely to have a higher overall Cost per Trade'.[120] This can either lead to the creation of a single location or several regional centres, e.g. in Europe, the US and Asia.[121] Regionalisation enables the clearer to benefit from time zone differences by distributing activities around the globe, which allows it to 'follow the sun'.[122] Centralisation and regionalisation cut costs through the consolidation and leveraging of systems, functions and knowledge, but are mainly suitable for high volume clearers active in several markets and geographical locations. Additionally, the internal standardisation of services and processes across the globe permits clearing members to economise on infrastructure. This can either be achieved through proprietary system development or the use of vendor software.[123] Finally, an important internal measure for clearing members is to increase straight-through processing. Increasing STP enhances automation and helps to avoid the duplication of work, i.e. by replacing manual processes with machines, particularly for repetitive and redundant tasks.

Internal measures are critical for clearers, because such initiatives can potentially reap significant savings as well as be fully managed and controlled internally. They are thus the first remedy for reducing clearing-related transaction costs. Nonetheless, cost reductions through internal measures have an important drawback: once internal process optimisation and synergies are exhausted, i.e. the more efficiently a clearer has set up its internal organisation, back-office and IT infrastructure, the higher its dependency on external measures for further cost reductions becomes.

---

[119] Four of these ten participants are in the process of evaluating outsourcing and offshoring as cost reduction opportunities. Note that '[l]eading self-clearing firms, however, value the flexibility and control of retaining those operations in-house and have been loath to go all the way to full-fledged' outsourcing of back-office activities. Hintze (2005), p. 1.

[120] Smith/Wright (2002), p. 9.

[121] For clearers with an agency focus, centralisation does not necessarily imply a centralisation of client relationships. Rather, client relationships are based where the clients are, but clearing management and the functional relationships with the clearing houses, such as back-office, IT and risk management, are concentrated in one or several regional or global locations.

[122] Some clearers 'follow the sun' through offshoring instead of regionalisation.

[123] Cf. interviews.

I cannot control my external direct cost, which means it's a cash outflow that I have to pay to the clearing house and intermediaries. Therefore, I think I have to squeeze efficiencies on my indirect costs. But at some point in time it's the paradigm, that is, beyond a certain transaction volume or risk profile, my indirect cost will jump up to the next level. Because imagine: if I hire one additional risk manager, the cost ratchets up. It's not a clear-cut correlation of one transaction causes an increase of so many percent.[124]

5.2.8 Non-clearing members' perspectives

We always know exactly what our clearer charges us and what those charges are for.[125]

GCM charges are not at all transparent to us.[126]

Whereas the previous sections analysed transaction costs from the viewpoint of clearing members, this section provides a brief overview of relevant NCMs' perspectives. Although the focus of this study is on the first level of the Value Provision Network and the first level of transaction costs, it is important to have a basic understanding of both cost levels to comprehend truly the full impact that network strategies can have on the efficiency of clearing and the structure of the VPN. This section therefore briefly relays the insights gleaned from the expert inquiry regarding the NCMs' level of cost awareness and perception of clearing costs as well as the type of clearing-related costs that NCMs typically incur.

The interviews showed that NCMs are becoming increasingly aware of and interested in understanding clearing-related costs.[127] Of the eight NCMs interviewed, six revealed themselves to be aware of clearing costs, whereas two did not. The latter two respondents made it clear, however, that they wished to understand these costs better in the future. For the most part, NCMs typically incur direct clearing costs in the form of commissions paid to GCMs, but also incur indirect costs if they operate their own risk management and back-office procedures or employ sophisticated IT solutions.[128] In addition, every NCM has to bear the cost of capital resulting from the collateral it has to put up with its GCM.

---

[124] Statement made by interviewed market expert.
[125] Statement made by interviewed non-clearing member representative.
[126] Interview with Aisling O'Reilly.
[127] This finding is underlined by the fact that a comparatively large number of NCMs agreed to participate in the empirical research. Refer to Chapter 4 for details.
[128] Interviewees pointed out that NCMs usually rely on their GCM for most of these functions, and only replicate selected functions and processes. This in turn limits the degree of indirect costs.

Nonetheless, and not surprisingly, the NCMs unanimously regarded direct costs as the core clearing-related cost driver. Commissions are commonly charged on either a per-transaction or fixed cost basis.[129] Interviewees considered the general trend in the market as heading towards a cost-plus pricing scheme. As outlined above, the fees charged by GCMs are typically based on three different components: firstly, the clearer passes on the per-contract fees charged by the clearing house for the cleared contracts; secondly, the clearer allocates a certain percentage of relevant indirect costs to its NCMs; and thirdly comes the profit margin. The second and third components thus constitute the commission charged by the GCMs. The NCMs interviewed for this study revealed that commissions currently range between 10 cents and €1 per contract.

Interviewees were further questioned regarding the perceived transparency of GCM fees. Five out of eight NCMs considered these fees transparent, two did not and one did not specify. Although the majority of NCMs found GCM charges transparent, four of the eight respondents characterised clearing and clearing-related processes as black boxes, i.e. they acknowledged not fully understanding the respective value provision of their clearer. It is therefore doubtful whether they can accurately assess the adequacy of intermediary charges. The remaining four NCMs had a good and detailed understanding of clearing services.

5.2.9 Cost reduction scenarios for non-clearing members

Whereas the previous section provided a brief overview of the clearing-related costs incurred by NCMs, this section delivers insights from the expert inquiry on the various internal measures that NCMs can take to reduce these costs.

NCMs benefit from reductions of indirect costs on the part of the GCM if these savings in fact translate into lower commissions and are not simply absorbed by the clearer. Due to the difficulty of observing potential cost reductions and monitoring their translation into lower commissions, NCMs must pursue other initiatives if they want actively to reduce clearing-related costs. The expert inquiry provided examples of possible internal measures for non-clearing members to undertake. Interviewees identified the following three main cost reduction strategies:

- put pressure on GCM(s);
- unbundle GCM services; and
- become a clearing member.

[129] Cf. interviews.

The first and most obvious measure in attempting to reduce clearing costs is to **put pressure on GCMs** to reduce their fees. Generally, the higher the NCM's number of traded contracts, the greater its leverage for negotiating fees. All of the NCMs interviewed here considered themselves to be in a relatively good negotiating position towards their clearer. Although these respondents expressed their general willingness to change from one clearing intermediary to another, they were hesitant about actually employing this measure. The reluctance to change clearers is based on various reasons. For most respondents, this reluctance stems from the effort and costs that come with such a change; switching clearers involves the renegotiation of contracts, updates of legal documentation, infrastructure adaptations, etc. Furthermore, the service levels they currently receive from their GCM(s) are important to most NCMs; thus, changing clearers solely to obtain lower fees is hardly considered attractive if doing so entails a downgrading of services.

Although we get competitive rates from our clearer, they may not be the most competitive available as it is also a question of service. I do not want to waste time checking the clearer is doing their job properly. It is more efficient to work with a clearer who provides high service levels.[130]

Additionally, many NCMs have a strong relationship with their clearer(s). This relationship might consist of established, smooth operational interaction as well as good personal contacts. However, a strong relationship may also extend to other business areas beyond clearing services, resulting in a somewhat symbiotic relationship between the NCM and GCM(s).[131] Finally, interviewees said that they generally benefited from the high level of competition for their business among GCMs, which further strengthens their negotiating position towards their GCM(s).

Besides putting pressure on their GCM(s), NCMs can also attempt to reduce their clearing costs by **unbundling the services** provided by their clearer. Unbundling services entails breaking up the clearer's value chain by employing other service providers for certain functions or processes currently provided by their GCM. This allows the NCM to create a competitive situation on a per-product or per-process basis. Unbundling services requires a sophisticated understanding of clearing-related processes and functions on the part of the NCM. As outlined above, not all NCMs have such a detailed grasp of the value provision of clearing services. It is therefore not surprising that none of

---

[130] Interview with Aisling O'Reilly.
[131] For a hedge fund, this could, for example, mean that its clearer is also an investor.

them seriously seemed to be considering unbundling GCM services as either a concrete short- or medium-term strategy for cost reduction, despite their avowed interest in the option.

The end-clients who you'd expect to be excited about this, frankly, this type of an innovation is outside of their area of expertise. They're clients, they're traders, you know, this type of efficiency is something that's always been provided to them by a broker. So, they're going to be sheep in terms of 'show me the way and I'll go, but don't expect me to lead'.[132]

Certainly, unbundling is only a viable and attractive strategy if it permits reductions that are not achievable through a simple renegotiation of fees with the clearer.

The third cost reduction opportunity identified by interviewees is for (some) NCMs to **become clearing members**. Of the eight NCMs interviewed for this study, six had considered becoming clearing members; only two had never considered this possibility. Three of the six NCMs who had given this alternative regarded it as a viable future opportunity. The other three do not foresee pursuing this option.[133] As outlined in Chapter 3, becoming a clearing member involves direct and indirect costs; various factors thus have to be taken into account when assessing this opportunity as a cost-reducing measure.

Everyone wants to lower their cost base nowadays, but it comes with a cost as well. The clearing members currently provide us with a service, so in the end a cost-benefit analysis has to be done for this . . . There is a tipping point at which point doing it yourself makes sense.[134]

Firstly, becoming a clearing member only makes sense if the NCM is large-scale enough in terms of the number of contracts cleared at a particular CCP and has sufficient financial resources. Interviewees revealed that whether or not the cost-benefit analysis of becoming a clearing member is positive in the end also depends on additional factors:

- number of markets;
- core business;
- risk perspective;
- effort of setting up clearing membership;
- general interest in involving intermediaries;
- internal cost pressure; and
- GCM rates.

---

[132] Interview with Edward F. Condon.
[133] Also see KPMG (ed.) (2004), p. 21, for a critical evaluation of self-clearing as a means to reduce costs.
[134] Statement made by anonymous referee.

If the NCM is active in many different markets, it will likely not undertake to become a clearing member, because it greatly benefits from the GCM service of providing single access to many markets. Any attempt to replicate this service would involve significant costs.

We trade on most futures exchanges. The majority of our volume is spread over five exchanges. It wouldn't make sense for us to self clear on all of them. If our volume was concentrated on one or two, then on a cost benefit analysis maybe, but again, we're not set up like that.[135]

This leads to the second factor, which pertains to the NCM's core business. Becoming a clearing member can dilute the core business by concentrating resources on extraneous activities. Obtaining clearing membership is therefore not only a cost-benefit consideration, but also a strategic decision for the NCM. The next factor, the risk perspective, is closely related. Whereas for an NCM the risk associated with the clearing house is assumed by the GCM, this risk would transfer to the NCM were it to become a clearing member itself. Whether or not this would constitute a deterrent for pursuing clearing membership depends on the NCM's individual perspective. Even if the cost-benefit analysis proves to be positive, an NCM might balk at the effort involved with setting up the membership, e.g. hiring qualified personnel, introducing processes and establishing infrastructure.

Furthermore, some NCMs have a general interest in involving intermediaries. This can relate to the quality and breadth of services provided by the GCMs:

I am not sure, because it is not just about cost; it is about quality as well. Further, certain intermediary goodies are unavailable internally: like credit lines for example.[136]

It can also relate to other kinds of financial interrelation between NCMs and GCMs:

It's important to maintain a relationship with brokers, because in many ways the majority of assets we manage are introduced through them.[137]

Generally, becoming a clearing member to reduce costs is only relevant to NCMs who are highly sensitive to costs.

If we can prove that becoming a clearing member ourselves can substantially lower our costs, then we'll do that. I don't think that we have come to that point yet

---

[135] Statement made by interviewed non-clearing member representative.
[136] Interview with James G. McCormick.
[137] Statement made by interviewed non-clearing member representative.

though ... I guess historically the results of the investment managers have been pretty good, so the cost side wasn't that important. But nowadays the industry is getting more competitive and we are looking more closely at our cost structure and I believe it is something that will come on the agenda, looking forward.[138]

Finally, NCMs are sceptical about the benefits and cost reduction potential of becoming a clearing member when they consider how dramatically commissions have come down over the past years due to competition between GCMs.

The fact of the matter is that the processing rates are so commoditized, and so low because processing (clearing) is an 'economy of scale' business in the electronic world ... There is little economic justification to clear on a small scale.[139]

Despite these limitations and constraining factors, the expert inquiry nonetheless revealed that several NCMs consider obtaining clearing membership a viable cost-reduction strategy; in the empirical study, this was true for three of the eight interviewees.

As outlined above, the research focus vis-à-vis cost reductions is on the effect that network strategies between clearing houses have on clearing costs. However, network strategies can impact NCMs as well as GCMs. Why this is the case and what the impact could theoretically look like will be detailed further in the remainder of the study.

5.3 Summary of findings

The purpose of Chapter 5 was to examine various aspects of current European derivatives clearing costs, present findings from the empirical study and provide a number of quantitative and qualitative transaction cost analyses. These analyses generated important findings that are crucial for the remainder of the study.

5.3.1 Findings from empirical study

- The expert inquiry revealed that although most clearing members are highly sensitive to clearing costs, few firms apply a structured approach to monitor and manage their total direct and indirect clearing costs (the all-in costs).

---

[138] Statement made by anonymous referee.   [139] Interview with James G. McCormick.

- The analysis also showed that the business focus of the clearer (prop. versus agency) and its market share (low, medium or high) are of particular relevance when assessing the significance of direct versus indirect costs.
- For low and medium volume clearers with a prop. or agency focus, as well as for high volume clearers with an agency focus, indirect costs are of the highest concern. Direct costs are the core cost drivers solely for high volume clearers with a prop. focus.
- This means that for low and medium volume clearers with a prop. or agency focus, as well as high volume clearers with an agency focus, significant P&L effects can only be realised if these clearers overhaul their internal efficiency or benefit from improvements in operational and process efficiency undertaken by their clearing house(s).
- High volume clearing members with a prop. perspective, however, need to engage in lobbying activities and put pressure on clearing houses to reduce fees in order to tackle their largest cost driver.
- Most clearing members engage in both agency and proprietary activity; the difference between the two foci concerns the main revenue-contributing areas within the firm. It should be noted that large investment banks in particular assign significant importance to both areas. This can lead to internal tensions and conflicts between the prop.- and agency-focused businesses.
- Regarding the relevance of the different cost categories, the study revealed that clearing house fees are the core direct cost drivers, whereas back-office and IT expenditures are the biggest source of indirect costs.
- At the same time, clearers tend to underestimate structurally the significance of cost of capital and risk management costs.

5.3.2 Transaction cost analyses – clearing members

- The comparative analysis of per-contract fees charged by the major horizontally and vertically integrated European and US clearing houses produced no clear winner in terms of the most competitive fee levels.
- The cost analyses served to highlight the structural particularities of the European Value Provision Network, such as reasons for the competitive advantages high volume clearers have over medium and low volume clearers.
- Firstly, it was found that clearers enjoy economies of scale. According to the findings from the empirical study and the cost analyses, there exist economies of scale that allow high volume clearers to economise on their internal structures and processes and thus leverage their fixed cost base.

- Due to their scale of business, high volume clearers further benefit from a strong bargaining position towards service providers, which allows them to minimise service provider charges.
- Clearing houses further strengthen the competitive advantage of European high volume clearers by granting them preferential treatment in the form of discounts. Preferential pricing can translate into a competitive advantage for the high volume clearers, as the savings reaped can be substantial.
- Low and medium volume clearers are thus penalised by clearing houses that tailor their discount schemes to high and very high volume clearers.
- This explains the currently dominant position of high volume clearers within the European Value Provision Network, i.e. why a very high percentage of the European market share in derivatives clearing is concentrated on a few very high volume clearers.
- These clearers' cost structures make it attractive for them to offer inter-mediary services. By the same token, it makes economic sense for medium volume clearers to utilise these services. This is the reason why in the current structure of the European VPN, medium volume clearers typically maintain only a single direct clearing relationship (with their domestic home clear-ing house). To clear their transactions in the other (foreign) markets, these members utilise one or more GCMs as clearing intermediaries.
- Network initiatives that help to reduce indirect costs can thus have an important impact on the structure of the European VPN. This is true when initiatives entice medium volume clearers to self-clear many markets instead of employing intermediary services, enabling them to reduce intermediary costs and leverage their internal infrastructure (or, more generally, when the attractiveness of becoming a clearer instead of an NCM in many markets increases).
- The total European costs of derivatives clearing borne by clearing members amounted to roughly €2.173 billion in 2005. At €725 million, direct costs represented 33 per cent of total industry costs, whereas indirect costs of approximately €1.448 billion accounted for 67 per cent of total costs. Due to the shortcomings and limitations inherent to the calculation of the estimate, however, it can be assumed that the true indirect cost figure is higher than suggested.
- Benchmarking these European derivatives clearing costs to other market infrastructure costs strongly indicated that derivatives clearing constitutes the most efficient part of European financial market infrastructure. This means that in terms of costs resulting from the interaction between the infrastructure providers (exchanges, clearing houses or CSDs/ICSDs) and

their direct customers, the transaction costs related to derivatives clearing are comparatively low.

- Additionally, whereas findings from the comparison of per-contract fees charged by various European and US clearing houses suggested that clearing houses do not always translate high volumes into lower fees, the comparison with cash equity clearing costs revealed that customers have benefited from the scale of the derivatives market in terms of comparatively low clearing house charges.

- There are various opportunities for clearing members to reduce clearing costs, which are classified as external or internal measures. The research focus of this study is on the external measures, i.e. initiatives that are beyond the direct control of the clearing members and that potentially affect direct and indirect costs. The external measures analysed for the purpose of this study are network strategies between clearing houses.

- The effect network strategies have on direct and indirect costs, whether certain network initiatives serve to weaken or strengthen the strong position of high volume clearers, and how they impact the unprivileged position of low and medium volume clearers in the Value Provision Network are topics to be examined in the remainder of this study.

5.3.3 Transaction cost analyses – non-clearing members

- Regarding the second level of the VPN and the second level of transaction costs, the analysis revealed that NCMs are becoming increasingly aware of clearing costs and interested in understanding the nature of these costs.

- NCMs were shown to be highly cost sensitive, particularly to the commissions charged by their clearers. However, not all NCMs seem to understand fully the value provision of their clearer, which makes it difficult for them to accurately assess the adequacy of GCM charges.

- NCMs benefit from reductions of the GCMs' indirect costs if the clearers in turn take lower commissions and do not simply absorb the savings. Whether or not NCMs actually benefit is difficult to verify, however, due to the complexity of monitoring how the GCMs allocate these savings internally.

- Due to the difficulty of observing potential cost reductions and monitoring their translation into lower commissions, NCMs must pursue other initiatives if they want actively to reduce clearing-related costs.

- Interviewees identified the following three main cost reduction strategies for NCMs: pressuring their GCM(s) to lower fees, unbundling GCM services or (depending on their scale and other factors) becoming clearing members themselves.

- Meanwhile, any such initiative to reduce clearing costs requires a sophisticated understanding of clearing-related processes and functions; most of the NCMs participating in the study expressed their motivation to hone their understanding of these issues.
- Network initiatives can increase the attractiveness of self-clearing, which could lead to structural changes in the VPN. This aspect is further examined in the remainder of this study.

The findings indicate that the current structure of European derivatives clearing is already very efficient as compared to other parts of the market infrastructure. Does it thus make sense to study ways in which network strategies could increase the efficiency of derivatives clearing, or has this research objective become obsolete? If anything, the importance of researching such efficiency gains has become even more vital. As the analysis has shown, the organisation of derivatives clearing could serve as a role model for other parts of the European market infrastructure.

As outlined above, to evaluate the impact of network strategies on efficiency, it is first necessary to learn more about the transaction costs of clearing; Chapter 5 served to provide this basis. However, it is also essential to have knowledge about the demand- and supply-side scale effects in clearing. To this end, Chapter 6 classifies potential demand- and supply-sided scale effects in clearing and furnishes evidence of their existence.

6 Exploring theoretical basics – scale effects in clearing

While the previous chapter delivered a number of quantitative and qualitative analyses of European derivatives clearing costs, this chapter explores and classifies possible scale effects in clearing. The insights provided by Chapters 5 and 6 serve as a basis for the subsequent analysis of the efficiency impact of different network strategies in Chapters 7, 8 and 9.

The economic literature distinguishes between demand- and supply-side scale effects.[1] Demand-side scale effects are commonly referred to as network effects. Supply-side scale effects include economies of scale and scope.

In the following, these concepts are introduced and applied to clearing. Additionally, evidence for the existence of demand- and supply-side scale effects in clearing is explored. In a first step (section 6.1), demand-side scale effects and their economic implications are analysed. A second step (section 6.2) investigates supply-side effects. This includes insight to clearing houses' cost structures in order to identify the causes and nature of supply-side scale effects. Finally, this chapter's findings are summarised (section 6.3).

6.1 Demand-side scale effects

There exist various industries in which the utility that a user derives from a given product or service increases with the number of other consumers utilising the same product or service.[2] In this case, the users of the product or service constitute a network. The most prominent example of this

---

[1] Cf. Farrell/Saloner (1986), p. 940; Katz/Shapiro (1986a), p. 824; Bessler (1991), p. 275; Besen/Farrell (1994), p. 118; and Junius (1997), p. 7. Alternatively, scale effects can be differentiated as cost- and revenue-sided. Cf. Berger/Humphrey (1997), p. 9. When applying the economic concept of scale effects to clearing, the analysis is based on the separation of the demand and supply sides, because not all clearing houses act according to the principle of profit maximisation.

[2] Cf. Katz/Shapiro (1985), p. 424. See Shy (2001) for a variety of industry examples.

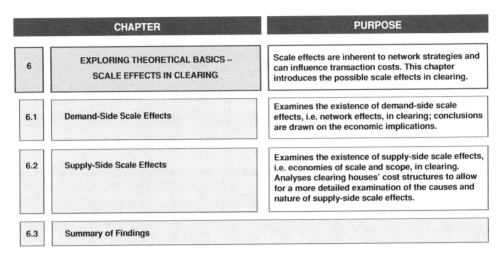

CHAPTER		PURPOSE
6	EXPLORING THEORETICAL BASICS – SCALE EFFECTS IN CLEARING	Scale effects are inherent to network strategies and can influence transaction costs. This chapter introduces the possible scale effects in clearing.
6.1	Demand-Side Scale Effects	Examines the existence of demand-side scale effects, i.e. network effects, in clearing; conclusions are drawn on the economic implications.
6.2	Supply-Side Scale Effects	Examines the existence of supply-side scale effects, i.e. economies of scale and scope, in clearing. Analyses clearing houses' cost structures to allow for a more detailed examination of the causes and nature of supply-side scale effects.
6.3	Summary of Findings	

Figure 6.1   Structure of Chapter 6

effect can be found in communication networks, such as the public telephone network.[3]

Because the value of membership to one user is positively affected when another user joins and enlarges the network,[4] the corresponding markets are said to exhibit network effects[5] or network externalities.[6] Network effects are classified as scale effects on the demand side,[7] because with a linearly

---

[3] For an early analysis of positive network externalities in communications networks, see Rohlfs (1974), p. 16.

[4] As the number of individuals utilising phones increases, so does the number of connection alternatives. In this case, the benefit for individuals is the possibility to communicate with an increased number of other individuals.

[5] The term results from the fact that these effects were first recognised and studied in the context of communication networks, such as those associated with the telephone and telex. However, network effects also exist in many other industries that do not employ physical networks. Cf. Katz/Shapiro (1986b), p. 146. In other words, both physical and virtual networks can exhibit network effects.

[6] Cf. Katz/Shapiro (1994), p. 94. When deciding to join a network, users do not commonly take into account the positive welfare effect associated with their decision. Users thus do not internalise the welfare effect, which results in an externality. Network effects are often externalities, but need not be. While network effects formally apply to a more general concept than network externalities, the two terms are often used interchangeably in the literature on networks, such as in Katz/Shapiro (1994), p. 94. This study also uses the terms interchangeably, but it should be noted that this approach is not without controversy. Liebowitz/Margolis (1998) object to the comingling of these terms, however, especially as concerns indirect network effects. They differentiate network effects from network externalities according to whether the impact of an additional user on other users is somehow internalised. If network effects are not internalised, the equilibrium network size may be smaller than is efficient. They classify network externalities as 'a specific kind of network effect in which the equilibrium exhibits unexploited gains from trade regarding network participation' (Liebowitz/Margolis (1994a), p. 135).

[7] Cf. Farrell/Saloner (1986), p. 940; and Besen/Farrell (1994), p. 118.

increasing network size, the utility that a user derives from consumption increases over-proportionately.

A general distinction can be made between direct and indirect network effects, which can be either positive or negative.[8] Positive direct network effects refer to the benefits a user derives from the consumption of a product that is used by others. The value of some products or services also depends on whether they are offered in isolation or in combination with others.[9] Indirect network effects refer to (positive) externalities that do not result from a direct interconnection with others, but rather through the distribution of complementary goods.[10] Note that networks can also exhibit negative externalities, which result in costs to users from '[c]hanges in the size of an associated network'.[11]

A growing interest in investigating the relevance of network theory for analysing the organisation of financial markets has recently emerged in the economic literature. In the following, the concept of networks is applied to clearing.

6.1.1 Network effects

Networks are common in financial services.[12]

Clearing has very strong network externalities, where the value to a user is greatly increased by the access that is given to a wide range of trading counterparties.[13]

Network theory is applicable to a variety of financial services and to most parts of the transaction value chain. When interaction among consumers is important, markets are likely to exhibit strong network effects.[14] Existing network studies primarily apply to the trading function and exchanges;[15]

---

[8] Cf. Katz/Shapiro (1985), p. 424; Tirole (1988), p. 405; and Economides (1996), p. 679.

[9] Cf. Katz/Shapiro (1994), p. 93.

[10] Indirect network effects resulting from a growing number of network users include an increase in the number of complementary goods offered, learning effects from employing new technologies and less uncertainty about the sustainability of a new technology. Cf. Thum (1995), pp. 8–12. Economides/Salop (1992) provide one of the earliest frameworks and insights into the economics of indirect network effects; studies by Church/Gandal/Krause (2002) show that indirect network effects can give rise to adoption externalities.

[11] Liebowitz/Margolis (1994a), p. 134.   [12] Economides (1993), Abstract.

[13] LCH.Clearnet (ed.) (2006b) p. 5.   [14] Cf. Liebowitz (2002), p. 20.

[15] See, e.g. the contributions of Economides/Siow (1988); Economides (1993); Domowitz (1995); Economides (1996); Domowitz/Steil (1999); Geiger (2000); Book (2001); Di Noia (2001); Claessens et al. (2003); Hasan/Schmiedel (2004b); Hasan/Schmiedel (2004a); Hasan/Schmiedel (2006); and Hasan/Hasenpusch/Schmiedel (2007).

in contrast, little research has been done on post-trading networks.[16] A new stream of recent contributions finds that securities settlement and safekeeping institutions exhibit features of so-called 'two-sided platforms'.[17] Besides that, increasing attention is paid to applying the network economic concepts of 'switching costs' and 'standard setting' to the settlement and safekeeping industry.[18]

Although the clearing function is widely considered to exhibit network effects,[19] the author is not aware of any studies that provide a classification or analysis of clearing-related network effects. Additionally, while some characteristics of 'classic' network industries are applicable to the clearing function, the Value Provision Network has several distinctive features that distinguish it from other network industries; this makes it difficult to apply standard network economic analyses directly.[20] This chapter provides an exploratory attempt to deliver insight into this issue. To accomplish this, it is necessary to:

- elucidate the general idea and basic formation of networks;
- apply the network view to the Value Provision Network; and
- identify and analyse network effects within the VPN (sections 6.1.1.1–6.1.1.4).

Generally, **networks** emerge from links that connect complementary nodes.[21] The structure of a telephone network illustrates the basic organisational principles. Members of this network are connected via a central node (the 'switch node', symbolised by S) that enables all members of the network to interconnect. A phone call from Customer Node A to Customer Node B consists of

---

[16] The studies of Milne (2002); Holthausen/Tapking (2004); Kauko (2005); and Van Cayseele/Wuyts (2005) are among the few contributions to this field. Knieps (2006) provides for a network economic analysis of competition in securities post-trade markets. Although Knieps defines the post-trade functions covered by his analysis to include clearing and settlement, CCP services are left aside. He focuses on the network characteristics of basic clearing services – such as provided by CSDs, ICSDs, custodians or banks.

[17] See Kauko (2002); Rochet (2005); Kauko (2005); Van Cayseele/Voor de Mededinging (2005); and Van Cayseele/Wuyts (2005). In two-sided markets, two or more platforms are needed simultaneously to complete a transaction successfully. Refer to Rochet/Tirole (2001); Parker/Van Alstyne (2005); Armstrong (2006); Rochet/Tirole (2006); and Van Cayseele/Reynaerts (2007) for more details and an analysis of two-sided markets.

[18] See Milne (2005); and Serifsoy/Weiß (2005).

[19] See, e.g. European Central Bank (ed.) (2001b), p. 82; London Stock Exchange (ed.) (2002), p. 5; Russo (2002), p. 237; LCH.Clearnet (ed.) (2003b), p. 3; Heckinger/Lee/McPartland (2003), p. 9; Singapore Exchange (ed.) (2004), p. 8; BNP Paribas Securities Services (ed.) (2005), p. 3; Office of Fair Trading (ed.) (2005), p. 4; Serifsoy/Weiß (2005), p. 8; Corporation of London (ed.) (2005), p. 56; Van Cayseele/Wuyts (2005), p. 3; Schmiedel/Schönenberger (2005), p. 35; Branch/Griffiths (2005), p. 3; LCH.Clearnet (ed.) (2006b), p. 5; LIBA (ed.) (2006), p. 6; Bliss/Papathanassiou (2006), p. 24; and Milne (2007), p. 2945.

[20] Cf. Milne (2007), p. 2947.   [21] Cf. Economides (1996), p. 674.

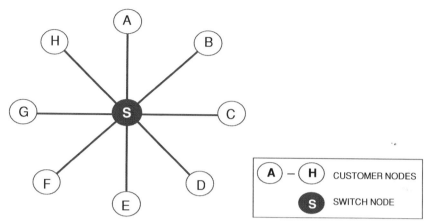

Figure 6.2   Telephone network as a simple star network
Source: Economides (1996), p. 675.

two connections called AS and BS (see Figure 6.2), which represent complementary components. In the case of the telephone network, all components
(AS, BS, etc.) are complementary to each other.[22]

This kind of network exhibits positive network effects: when a network
with n customer nodes is enlarged by one additional customer node (n+1),
2n new ways for interconnection result.[23] An enlargement of the network thus
benefits all members of the network. 'In a typical network, the addition of
a new customer (or network node) increases the willingness to pay for the
network services by all participants.'[24]

Networks can also be classified as horizontal or vertical. Whereas in horizontal networks (such as the telephone network), members are interconnected
to build a network, vertical networks join together complementary goods.[25]
Each good is useless in isolation, as the demand for one good is dependent on
the demand for a complementary good.[26] Network structure varies according
to the characteristics of the relevant industry.

---

[22] Economides/White (1994) differentiate networks in which all components are complementary to each
other, which are referred to as 'two-way networks', and networks in which only some components are
complementary to each other, so-called 'one-way networks'. Cf. Economides/White (1994), pp. 1–5. A
more general distinction differentiates one-way networks as those in which the sensible transactions
can flow in only one direction, whereas the opposite is true in two-way networks.
[23] Cf. Economides (1996), p. 679.
[24] Economides (1993), p. 89.   [25] Cf. Gröhn (1999), p. 25.
[26] Examples of vertical networks include personal computers, operating systems and application software
or video-cassette recorders and video tapes.

When the **network view is applied to the Value Provision Network**, a two-layered and two-level structure results (see Figure 6.3).[27] The first level corresponds to the network structure constituted by a CCP, which acts as the central 'switch node' by becoming the buyer to every seller and the seller to every buyer, and its clearing members.[28] The second level refers to the network structure established by the clearing members acting as GCMs and their respective non-clearing members.

Additionally, the first and second network levels each consist of two layers. A central counterparty constitutes a two-layered network composed of a system layer and a product layer. All of the CCP's clearing members are interconnected through a shared clearing system (system layer). The resulting network corresponds to the physical network, which is the electronic clearing platform provided by the CCP. The clearing system provides the actual clearing services, which include data transfer and processing, bundled network services (e.g. netting and cross-margining)[29] and the guarantee function. Within the clearing system, a subset of clearing members forms horizontal networks in different products. This function is enabled through the network's product layer,[30] which represents the open interest held by a CCP in the respective products. As an example: the network of product A consists of clearing members CM1, CM2, CM6, CM7 and CM8, who demand clearing services for the product, and is represented by the open interest in product A. The networks of (non-fungible) products A and B are not compatible; clearing members cannot close-out open positions in one product by entering into offsetting positions in another product. The two-layered network of the CCP consequently results in a combination of horizontal and vertical networks.[31]

---

[27] The basic idea and set-up of the two-layered structure builds on the principles identified by Book (2001) for derivatives exchanges. Cf. Book (2001), pp. 171–9. The idea of additionally classifying clearing networks as two-level structures is the author's own.

[28] The operations of CCPs constitute a unique combination of one-way network activity (position management) with two-way networks. The latter function involves linking counterparties; this means that, essentially, any clearing member of a CCP can act in two ways, i.e. either as a buyer or a seller to the CCP. The network thus works in both ways. Van Cayseele classifies CSDs/ICSDs in a similar way, i.e. as a unique combination of one-way and two-way activities. Cf. Centre for European Policy Studies (ed.) (2004), p. 1.

[29] Knieps therefore classifies securities clearing services as value-added telecommunications services. Cf. Knieps (2006), p. 54.

[30] A telephone network differs from a clearing network in that the essential relationship between the components is complementary. Within a clearing network, on the other hand, products must possess identical terms in order to be fungible.

[31] Note the differences in terminology: classifying a CCP as a combination of vertical and horizontal networks in the context of network economic terminology has to be differentiated from the use of

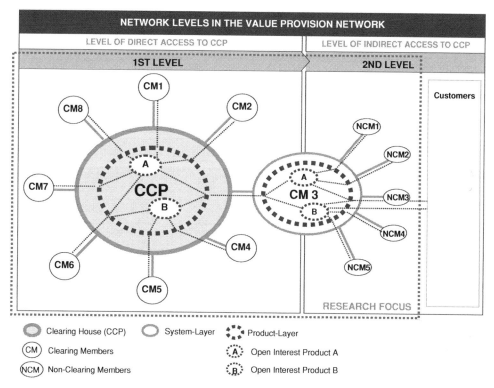

Figure 6.3   Value Provision Network as a two-layered and two-level network
Source: Author's own; idea and structure based on Book (2001), p. 171.[32]

A clearing member acting as a GCM also constitutes a two-layered network that contains a system layer and a product layer. All of the GCM's non-clearing members are interconnected through the GCM's electronic clearing system, which forms the basis for the clearing services provided by the clearing member. Whereas the system layers of the CCP and the GCM require compatibility, they are usually not, and do not have to be, identical. The clearing member will either employ a proprietary or a vendor solution to ensure the compatibility of its in-house system with the CCP system.

Whereas the product layer of the CCP network corresponds to the open interest held by the CCP, the product layer of the GCM network merely mirrors the open positions held by the CCP. The networks of (non-fungible)

---

the term 'vertically integrated clearing house', which refers to the integration of various parts of the transaction chain (such as trading, clearing and settlement).
[32] Book (2001) classifies derivatives exchanges as a two-layered network, consisting of a product layer and a system layer.

products A and B are not compatible on the GCM level either; open positions in one product cannot be closed out by entering into offsetting positions in another product. The two-layered network of the GCM is consequently also a combination of horizontal and vertical networks.

To summarise, the clearing services offered by CCPs and GCMs are network goods. The value-added of these services is impacted by the number of participants in the networks. The following provides a classification of the positive and negative network effects on the first (CCP level) and second (GCM level) network levels that result from changes in the number of participants (sections 6.1.1.1 and 6.1.1.2). In each case, the network effects on the system layer and the network effects on the product layer are differentiated. The way and extent to which network effects on the first and second levels impact one another are also examined (section 6.1.1.3). Additionally, the spill-over of the first and second level network effects on to other parts of the transaction value chain – such as trading and settlement – is investigated (section 6.1.1.4).

6.1.1.1 First level (CCP level) network effects

To begin with, network effects on the first level of the VPN are analysed (see Figure 6.4). The product layer is subject to four different positive network effects: netting, size, cross-margining and open interest effects. A negative effect, in the form of a systemic risk effect, can also emerge. Positive network effects on the system layer include the collateral management, interface, complementary offering, learning and information effects. Negative network effects on the system layer can eventually arise in the form of a performance effect. Finally, the negative monopolistic behaviour effect can arise both on the product and system layers.

6.1.1.1.1 First level network effects: product layer

An important and direct network effect on the product layer resulting from an increasing number of clearing members is referred to as the **netting effect**. Multilateral netting facilities, such as CCPs, strongly economise on the total number of transactions.[33] The more clearers are connected to a CCP, the more transactions can consequently be processed via the clearing house.[34] This increases the utility to each clearing member, as more transactions are available for netting. This accretion of utility results from lower transaction costs through enhanced possibilities for netting. The more transactions

---

[33] Cf. Hills *et al.* (1999), p. 132; Hardy (2004), p. 58; Singapore Exchange (ed.) (2004), p. 8; and Branch/Griffiths (2005), p. 5.

[34] For limitations of this statement, refer to section 6.1.1.3.

		Product Layer	System Layer
1ST LEVEL IN VALUE PROVISION NETWORK	**Positive Network Effects**	**Netting Effect** Enhanced netting opportunities	**Collateral Management Effect** Centralised collateral management
		Size Effect Clearing services for more products	**Interface Effect** Connection to various platforms
		Cross-Margining Effect Increased opportunities for cross-margining	**Complementary Offering Effect** Increased number of complementary clearing services
		Open Interest Effect Certainty regarding sustainability of CCP	**Learning Effect** Greater know-how and expertise
			Information Effect Reduced information asymmetry
	Negative Network Effects	**Systemic Risk Effect** Concentration of risk	**Performance Effect** Overloading of system capacity
		Monopolistic Behaviour Effect Anti-competitive behaviour	

Figure 6.4   First level (CCP level) network effects on the product and system layers
Source: Author's own; idea and structure based on Book (2001), p. 173.

with the same underlying and the same attributes that are available for processing through the CCP, the more netting can occur. Risk management costs can thus be reduced. In addition, the more transactions that are available for the netting of payments across multiple contracts, the less collateral the clearing member has to deposit at the clearing house. In net margining regimes, clearing members profit from reduced capital costs as well as from reduced risk management costs, as less risk monitoring is necessary. The utility to each clearing member is additionally increased through enhanced settlement efficiency.[35] The greater the number of transactions available for the netting of delivery instructions for cash or securities deliveries or the delivery of another underlying, the lower the number of obligations to be settled will be. This in turn results in lower transaction costs through minimising the fees charged by the intermediaries involved in the settlement process as well as in

---

[35] In the clearing of securities, the so-called 'settlement efficiency' is an important indicator for efficiency gains. It is measured by relating the number of executed trades to the number of trades settled. Cf. Devriese/Mitchell (2005), p. 20. Central counterparty clearing commonly results in a settlement efficiency of around 95 to 96 per cent in the cash equity markets and 70 per cent or more in the fixed income markets. Cf. SWX Swiss Exchange (ed.) (2007), p. 10; and LCH.Clearnet (ed.) (2003a), p. 31.

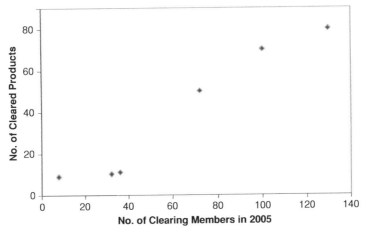

Figure 6.5   Number of cleared derivatives products and clearing members in 2005 (N=6)[36]
Source: Author's own; based on FOW (ed.) (2001); FOW (ed.) (2003); FOW (ed.) (2006); and clearing
houses' websites.

reduced back-office costs resulting from the decrease in back-office errors and
back-office handling.

The **size effect** relates to the number of products cleared through a CCP. The
higher the number of clearing members that route their transactions through
a specific clearing network, the higher the number of cleared products will
likely be. Clearing members of a clearing house with a large network are then
able to clear more products via the respective CCP than members of a smaller
clearing house. This positively impacts transaction costs by allowing clearing
members to leverage their in-house IT systems and back-office. The size effect
is illustrated by Figure 6.5.[37]

The size effect assumes that the number of cleared products is indirectly
determined by the number of clearing members connected to a CCP, as
these connections represent potential demand for the clearing of additional
products. This relationship constitutes an indirect network effect. The number
of cleared products then increases with an accretive network size. In the event
that the size effect leads to a provision of central counterparty clearing services

---

[36] Equity options and single stock futures are each considered one product and are not counted on a
per-stock basis.
[37] Nonetheless, due to the small sample selection of clearing houses, further research is needed to provide
more convincing evidence.

for products that were previously cleared bilaterally, this network effect can help to reduce service provider charges.

The size effect entails another positive indirect network effect, referred to as the **cross-margining effect**. The more clearing members participate in the clearing network, the more products are likely to be cleared through the CCP. As a result, more of the clearing members' transactions are available for cross-margining. The more positions with offsetting risk characteristics that can be margined together as a single portfolio, the higher the utility to clearing members.[38] This scenario positively impacts transaction costs. Enhanced cross-margining opportunities reduce capital costs by reducing the amount of collateral that has to be deposited at the clearing house for risk management purposes. Risk management costs are in turn reduced through minimised risk supervision effort.

The fourth potential positive (and indirect) network effect pertaining to the product layer is referred to as the **open interest effect**. This effect increases the value of the CCP services in several ways. Firstly, the higher the number of clearing members routing their transactions through a specific clearing network, the higher the open interest held by the CCP usually is. Clearing members benefit from an increased centralised holding and management of open interest at a clearing house. Cost reductions can result from more efficient risk management and allocation of risk. The more positions that are regularly marked-to-market, the better the clearing members will be able to manage their collateral, which can in turn positively affect the cost of capital.

Secondly, the standardisation of exchange-traded financial derivatives enables previously established sell or purchase positions to be closed out via appropriate opposite transactions. As new clearing members connect to a particular CCP, they will benefit existing members by giving them additional opportunities to close-out their positions.[39] Settling the legal obligation by close-out instead of actually exercising the contract significantly reduces transaction costs through minimised intermediary fees and lowered back-office costs. The open interest effect is thus closely related to the netting effect. Thirdly, the higher the open interest, the less uncertainty clearing members will have regarding the sustainability of the technical and legal

---

[38] This is supported by the findings of Jackson/Manning (2007), which show 'that margin-pooling benefits exist where multiple assets are cleared through the same clearing arrangement'. Jackson/Manning (2007), p. 30.

[39] Cf. Hills *et al.* (1999), p. 132.

Open Interest (No. of Contracts)   **No. of Participants**

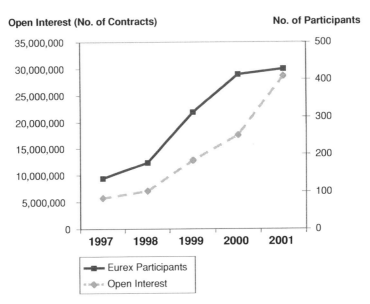

Figure 6.6   Development of open interest and numbers of participants at Eurex from 1997 to 2001
Source: Author's own; based on Eurex (ed.) (2007b), pp. 6–12.

CCP network. The open interest is generally viewed as an indicator of market liquidity and sustainable growth. Figure 6.6 illustrates the open interest effect.[40]

A negative network effect that can arise on the product layer is the **systemic risk effect**. The concentration of risk at the clearing house can potentially lead to a negative network effect.[41] This can result from insufficient or negligent risk management by the CCP in response to a growing number of clearing members. An increase of the systemic risk inherent to a CCP can lead to increased risk management costs and cost of capital. Additionally, the systemic risk effect can lead to a decrease in the clearing members' certainty regarding the sustainability of the CCP network.

---

[40] Note that the number of Eurex participants refers to all trading members (which include clearing members and non-clearing members). The reason why it is necessary to include all trading members into this analysis is explained in section 6.1.1.3. Refer to Eurex (ed.) (2007b), pp. 6–10 for details on the underlying data. In the years subsequent to 2001, an illustration of the open interest effect becomes more difficult. While the number of Eurex participants declined for various reasons (including mergers and acquisitions between existing members), the total number of counterparties active in the market increased. This total number of counterparties active in the market, which includes end-customers, is difficult to observe (even exchanges lack the means to track this number) and it is not publicly available.

[41] Cf. Padoa-Schioppa (2001), p. 4; European Central Bank (ed.) (2002), p. 7; and Chabert/Chanel-Reynaud (2005), p. 2.

6.1.1.1.2 First level network effects: system layer

On the system layer, the physical network of clearing members and their connection to the CCP builds the basis for the following analysis. Positive network effects on the system layer comprise the collateral management, interface, complementary offering, learning and information effects. Negative network effects can eventually arise in the form of the performance effect and the monopolistic behaviour effect.

An indirect positive effect of an increasing number of clearing members is known as the **collateral management effect**.[42] The more counterparties that can be cleared through the CCP network, the greater the potential benefits of optimised and centralised collateral management. The collateral management effect is closely related to the netting effect and the cross-margining effect on the product layer, as well as the interface effect on the system layer. Collateral management is optimised through more netting opportunities and a higher number of transactions available for cross-margining. Clearing members benefit from collateral management optimisation through savings in cost of capital and back-office costs. Additionally, as more collateral is held and managed at a 'secured place', i.e. with a trustworthy and sustainable CCP, the higher the potential savings in risk management costs. Because a less complex infrastructure therefore needs to be maintained for collateral management, reductions in IT costs could be realised. In the event that clearing members had previously employed intermediary solutions to enable centralised collateral management, they may even experience a reduction in service provider charges as a result of this positive network effect.

A second positive network effect on the system layer is referred to as the **interface effect**, which resembles the size effect on the product layer. Clearing members benefit from having several different markets cleared through the same CCP.[43] When clearers clear a high portion of their business through one CCP, they usually wish to conduct their remaining business through the same network to the greatest extent possible, as doing so reduces the required number of interfaces and thus saves money. The number of marketplaces for which the CCP offers clearing services is then indirectly determined by the number of clearing members connected to it; as the clearing members constitute potential demand for the clearing of additional execution venues. This relationship thus constitutes an indirect network effect. An increasing number of clearing members can potentially lead the CCP to connect to a

---

[42] Cf. Heckinger/Lee/McPartland (2003), p. 9; and Branch/Griffiths (2005), p. 5.
[43] Cf. Hardy (2004), p. 58.

greater number of trading locations in order to satisfy this demand. This process can increase the utility for clearers, because costly links to other networks thereby become less necessary[44] and thus reduce service provider charges. Clearing members then profit from reduced transaction costs, which result from lower back-office and IT costs, as well as from improved cross-margining opportunities.[45] Additional cross-margining opportunities can in turn help to reduce costs of capital and risk management costs.

The **complementary offering effect** refers to an indirect positive network effect that increases the number of offered complementary clearing services. These can include automated brokerage solutions for give-up/take-up transactions, enhanced complementary software and technology, and other services outlined in section 2.1.2.3. The supply of a greater number of complementary clearing services is beneficial for clearing members, as it allows them to use the available CCP network for functions and services that might otherwise have required tailor-made (expensive) solutions and/or other service providers' services. Complementary clearing services can thus positively impact (i.e. reduce) IT and back-office costs as well as service provider charges.

The fourth positive network effect on the system layer is the **learning effect**. Technology that requires specific training and knowledge increases in value as it becomes more widely adopted.[46] Specific know-how and supporting technology is more widespread and easily available in a large network than in a small network. Learning effects related to a CCP network occur in the form of integrating the system into the clearing members' in-house technology infrastructure, operating and handling experience, and knowledge about the rule book and regulatory framework. Furthermore, the greater the distribution of the network, the easier it becomes for a clearing member to hire qualified personnel, i.e. back-office staff or risk managers, as more people are likely to be qualified in the system usage with expanding network size. Clearing members also benefit from increased software offerings, which allow clearers to further customise and integrate the clearing system. Learning effects positively impact both back-office and IT costs.

Another positive indirect network effect is the **information effect**. The existence of a single counterparty reduces the level of information asymmetry.[47] Information asymmetry is relevant when market participants hesitate to trade

---

[44] Cf. Serifsoy/Weiß (2005), p. 8.

[45] This reduction of costs through the use of a single system for the clearing of transactions executed in various trading locations can also be classified as demand-side economies of scope.

[46] Cf. Katz/Shapiro (1986a), p. 823.   [47] Cf. Ripatti (2004), p. 22.

with counterparties about whom they have little information. This information asymmetry is particularly important in times of financial crisis, when there is a general suspicion that counterparties may be close to collapse. If there were fears about the solvency of a counterparty that is not a member of the particular CCP network, the whole market might stop trading. Consequently, the more counterparties that connect to a CCP, the more informed the market becomes about the quality of counterparty risk.[48] This effect positively influences market stability, as it minimises the impact of disturbances that the default of even a single participant can have on the equilibrium of capital markets.[49] This in turn positively influences risk management costs.[50]

In addition to the stated positive network effects on the system layer, there is a potential negative network effect to consider. As the network size increases, the danger of overloading the employed system rises. The **performance effect** thus occurs when system capacity is not sufficiently adapted to an increasing network size and increasing system load. The network thereby becomes vulnerable to shocks from major technical failures or physical system disruptions. The loss of clearing functions, even briefly, is costly and disruptive to markets.[51] 'Loss of function over several days, or simply at a critical time in the daily clearing process, can have serious systemic implications, especially if accompanied by other financial disruptions'.[52] The performance effect is technical in origin and can be avoided by effective capacity management.

Finally, the second potential negative (and indirect) network effect pertaining to both the product and system layers is referred to as the **monopolistic behaviour effect**. The higher the number of clearing members routing their transactions through a specific clearing network and the less competitive pressure from other CCP networks exists, the greater the risk that the clearing house will engage in anti-competitive behaviour. Monopolistic behaviour can take the form of charging excessive fees, but also of adhering to inefficient processes and structures, being slow to innovate as well as neglecting to react to market developments and customer demands. The monopolistic behaviour effect can thus counteract positive network effects on the product and system layers, such as the size, cross-margining, interface and

---

[48] This is due to the fact that through novation, the bilateral counterparty risk of variable quality is replaced with a high quality counterparty risk against the CCP.

[49] This is of course only true when there are no doubts about the solvency and competency of the central counterparty in the first place.

[50] Whereas in this case, the reallocation of risk through the CCP serves to reduce systemic risk in the market, the concentration of risk at the clearing house can potentially lead to a negative network effect, as outlined above.

[51] Cf. Group of Thirty (ed.) (2003), p. 3.   [52] Group of Thirty (ed.) (2003), p. 3.

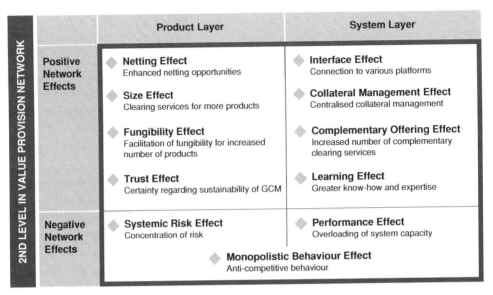

Figure 6.7   Second level (GCM level) network effects on the product and system layers
Source: Author's own; idea and structure based on Book (2001), p. 173.

complementary offering effects. This can result in excessive clearing house charges and translate into increased cost of capital, risk management costs, IT and back-office costs.

6.1.1.2 Second level (GCM level) network effects

In a next step, network effects on the second level of the Value Provision Network are identified (see Figure 6.7). There are four positive network effects on the product layer of the GCM network: netting, size, fungibility and trust effects. The systemic risk effect can arise as a negative effect on the product layer. Positive effects on the system layer include the collateral management, interface, complementary offering and learning effects. Negative network effects on the system layer can occur in the form of the performance effect. Finally, the negative monopolistic behaviour effect can arise both on the product and system layers. Since many of the network effects on the CCP and GCM levels are similar in nature, the second level network effects are briefly summarised in the following.

6.1.1.2.1 Second level network effects: product layer

It outlined in section 2.1.3, the scope of netting services offered by a bank/broker does not include the unique benefits associated with a CCP structure. Nonetheless, the netting services performed by GCMs give rise to a positive network effect: the **netting effect**.

The **size effect** on the GCM level basically follows the same logic as the positive network effect on the CCP's product layer. The higher the number of counterparties routing their transactions through a specific GCM network, the higher the number of products for which clearing services are offered is likely to be. The number of cleared products increases with an accretive network size, because the non-clearing members represent potential demand for the clearing of additional products.

The size effect gives rise to the **fungibility effect**. The more non-clearing members participate in a clearer's network, the higher the number of products will be for which the clearer facilitates fungibility – despite the fact that the products might not be fungible at the respective clearing houses (exchanges).

The **trust effect** constitutes the third positive (indirect) network effect on the product layer. A growing number of network participants results in less uncertainty with regard to a clearer's technical and legal sustainability.

A negative network effect known as the **systemic risk effect** can also occur. Similar to the effect on the CCP layer, the concentration of risk at a particular clearer can potentially increase the systemic risk inherent to a GCM network. Where many market participants rely on the same GCM, counterparty risk and responsibility for risk management may be concentrated to a significant degree in that clearing member.[53] Thus, a risk management failure by such a GCM could have effects similar to a risk management failure by a CCP.[54] The failure can stem from insufficient and negligent risk management on the part of the clearer and can create uncertainty among non-clearing members with regard to the clearer's sustainability.[55]

6.1.1.2.2 Second level network effects: system layer

The positive and negative network effects on the system layer of the GCM resemble those effects at the CCP level. Non-clearing members benefit significantly from having several different markets cleared through the same clearer. The **interface effect** refers to the indirect relationship between the number of execution venues for which the clearer offers services and the number of NCMs connected to a clearer. As the NCMs constitute potential demand for

---

[53] Cf. Bank for International Settlements (ed.) (2004), p. 7.
[54] Cf. Bank for International Settlements (ed.) (2004), p. 7.
[55] In some jurisdictions, such clearers are subject to regulatory capital requirements and other regulations that explicitly address these risks.

the clearing of additional products and markets, a clearer has an incentive to connect to an increasing number of interfaces with an accretive network size.

The interface effect entails another positive indirect network effect, which is the **collateral management effect**. The more non-clearing members that participate in the GCM network and the more products and markets for which the clearer consequently offers its services, the greater the potential benefits of optimised and centralised collateral management are.

Non-clearing members generally strive to leverage their clearing network; therefore, the **complementary offering effect** constitutes an important effect.[56] An increasing network size results in the clearer offering a growing number of complementary clearing services, such as credit intermediation, risk management tools, and other services outlined in section 2.1.2.3.[57]

The fourth positive network effect on the system layer is the **learning effect**. Learning effects related to a GCM network occur in the form of integrating the system into the NCMs' in-house technology infrastructure as well as operating and handling experience.

A negative network effect that can eventuate on the system layer of the GCM is the **performance effect**. With an increasing network size, the employed system can become dangerously overloaded. If system capacity is not sufficiently adapted, the performance effect can arise.

Finally, the second potential negative (and indirect) network effect pertaining to both the product and system layers of the GCM level network is the **monopolistic behaviour effect**. The higher the number of NCMs routing their transactions through a specific GCM network and the less competitive pressure from other GCM networks exists, the greater the risk that the clearer will adopt anti-competitive behaviour. See section 6.1.1.1.2 for a definition of monopolistic behaviour.

6.1.1.3 Interrelation between CCP and GCM level network effects

The analysis of the first and second level network effects shows that many of the network effects on the CCP and GCM levels are similar in nature. It also suggests that the effects from either level can impact one another. The following describes the way and extent to which network effects on the first (CCP) and second (GCM) level networks interrelate.

---

[56] The complementary offering effect on the GCM level is substantial, because the relevant network participants are not only the NCMs utilising the firm as a clearing intermediary, but also some of the intermediary's other customers demanding financial services.

[57] Cf. interviews.

The first important interrelation between the two network levels results from the fact that, strictly speaking, the size of the CCP level network is not determined by the number of clearing members, but rather by the number of counterparties. Counterparties can be clearing members, non-clearing members or other customers. In the extreme, this means that positive or negative network effects on the CCP level can arise despite a downturn in the number of clearing members. If the number of clearing members decreases – for example due to a merger between two GCMs – the network size can nonetheless increase if more NCMs connect to the newly merged entity using the remaining GCMs as intermediaries. Whilst the same is true when a greater number of other customers clear their business through this newly merged entity or through an existing NCM, this scenario will be disregarded for the remainder of this study. In this case, it is not the number of clearing members, but rather the number of counterparties participating in the Value Provision Network that has increased.[58] The size of the CCP network is consequently closely interrelated with the size of the GCM network; the reverse is not true, however.

Taking into account the described interrelation of the two network levels, the question arises: which positive network effects of the GCM level can be replicated on the CCP level and vice versa?

Theoretically, all GCM level network effects could be replicated on the CCP level, but not all CCP level network effects can be replicated on the GCM level. There exist some unique network effects on the CCP level (netting, cross-margining, open interest and information effects) that do not occur on the GCM level and could only be replicated by the GCM if it became the central counterparty itself.

Whereas at first sight it might therefore seem that the value-added function of the GCM level network is minimal (given that it 'simply' intermediates between the CCP network and other counterparties), the opposite is in fact true with reference to today's structure of the Value Provision Network. Today, the value-added function and the network effects on the GCM level are significant, because most clearing intermediaries offer single access to many platforms and markets; the same is not true for CCPs.[59] Therefore, the size,

---

[58] Note that the number of NCMs participating in a clearer's network must not necessarily equal the number of counterparties relevant to the CCP's network. If the GCM offers clearing services for several marketplaces, any new NCM only translates into a new network participant for the CCP networks in which it chooses to be active.

[59] As an example, MF Global Ltd (a leading broker of exchange-listed futures and options) and Fimat Group (one of the world's largest brokerage organisations) are members of more than ten CCPs worldwide,

interface and collateral management effects are significantly greater on the GCM level than they are on the CCP level. The fungibility effect constitutes another network effect that increases the value of the clearing services provided by the GCM level network. The complementary offering effect is greater on the second than on the first network level – again because most clearers offer a wider range of additional products and services to their NCMs.[60] Consequently, it can be assumed that an investor's willingness to pay for clearing services provided by GCM networks is greater than its willingness to pay for the services provided by CCP networks.[61] Nonetheless, these strong and important positive network effects on the GCM level network could be internalised by the CCP level network if CCPs make an effort to engage in network strategies and enlarge their range of complementary clearing services offered.

Engaging in network strategies could theoretically enable the internalisation of the size, interface, collateral management and fungibility effects. Enlarging the range of complementary clearing services offered facilitates the internalisation of the complementary offering effect. Internalising the strong and important GCM level (positive) network effects by the CCP level network is beneficial due to the potential for reducing clearing-related transaction costs, which would in turn increase the industry's efficiency. First level transaction costs can thus be whittled down by means of greater network effects on the CCP level. Additionally, second level transaction costs can be diminished through a disintermediation of the GCM level.

A CCP's engagement in network strategies should thus theoretically be driven by two objectives: firstly, to internalise the second-level network effects; and, secondly, to make their unique CCP-related network effects stronger, thus increasing network participants' willingness to pay for these services. Chapters 7 and 8 provide more detailed insights into this issue.

6.1.1.4 Spill-over effects of CCP and GCM level network effects

In a final step, the following briefly outlines the spill-over effects of CCP and GCM level network effects on other parts of the transaction value chain. Network effects on the CCP level can spill over on to the trading layer and settlement layer. Whereas the settlement layer is positively influenced by the

---

thus offering a single point of access to the world's major marketplaces. For more information, refer to www.mfglobal.com and to www.fimat.com. None of the world's clearing houses offers a comparable breadth of single access to many platforms and markets.

[60] Refer to section 2.1.2.3 for details.

[61] This assumption is supported by the findings from the empirical study that NCMs generally value the services provided by their clearer and that despite an increasing interest in cost reduction, many are reluctant to break off their relationship with their current clearer.

netting effect, the trading layer is positively influenced by a number of network effects. The netting, cross-margining, open interest, collateral management and information effects can positively impact the liquidity and allocation of risk and capital – thus increasing the efficiency of capital markets.[62] Additionally, the information effect positively influences stability by minimising the impact that disturbances arising from the default of a market participant can have on the safe and sound functioning of the market. On the other hand, the repercussions of insufficient risk management, which give rise to the systemic risk effect, can be substantial in that if a CCP were to become fatally wounded, trading could conceivably come to a standstill on the connected trading platforms.[63] In the case of cross-product and cross-currency clearing, risks are concentrated to an even greater extent and may spill over from one market on to another. The performance effect, which results in a loss of clearing functions, can also spill over on to the trading layer and seriously disrupt trading. The monopolistic behaviour effect can possibly disrupt trading activity when excessive clearing fees increase the total transaction costs to a point where trading becomes prohibitively expensive.

In addition to the CCP level network effects, some GCM level network effects can also spill over on to other parts of the transaction value chain. The trust and collateral management effects can positively impact the liquidity and allocation of capital. Negative effects on the trading layer can result from the systemic risk, performance and monopolistic behaviour effects.

To summarise, despite the currently high value-added function of the GCM level network, the most significant positive spill-over effects on to the trading and settlement layers in fact result from CCP level network effects. Additionally, the CCP level boasts unique positive network effects that support market stability and that are not easily replicable on the GCM level network. Nonetheless, although a CCP network is usually larger than a GCM network,[64] and consumers should, by definition (all else being equal), be willing to pay more to join a large network,[65] little indication is found for this being true in the current structure of the Value Provision Network. Whereas the positive network effects on the GCM level translate into cost savings for network

---

[62] Refer to section 2.2 for the impact of CCPs on market efficiency.

[63] Cf. Milne (2002), p. 23. This systemic concern can be dealt with, however, either by ensuring that bilateral trading bypassing the counterparty is still possible in the event of the absence of the CCP or more directly through imposing high and prudent standards for risk management on the CCP.

[64] Insight delivered by Eurex Clearing and the European clearing houses' websites reveals that a very large clearer generally serves between twenty and sixty NCMs, whereas a large CCP serves roughly 100 clearing members (plus the indirect network participants in the form of NCMs).

[65] Cf. Liebowitz (2002), p. 16.

participants that are fairly easy to quantify (such as the savings resulting from the clearer providing a single interface to many markets), the positive network effects on the CCP level are for the most part less apparent, and the associated savings are more difficult to quantify. This further argues for the attractiveness of internalising GCM level network effects on the CCP level network.

6.1.2 Network economic particularities

Network effects in the Value Provision Network entail several economic implications for the organisation of clearing. The question is: which particularities of the first and second level network attributes have to be considered when analysing the impact of network strategies on efficiency and what are their economic implications?

The following paragraph therefore briefly describes the most important economic aspects of networks and applies them to clearing on the CCP and GCM levels.[66] This serves as a basis to subsequently illuminate the network economic particularities inherent to different network strategies and helps to determine their potential for success or failure, which is analysed in section 7.1.2.

The impact of compatibility is analysed first,[67] followed by an examination of the installed base and starting problem; the section concludes with an investigation of the innovative ability of clearing networks.

6.1.2.1 Compatibility

In contrast to the supply-side scale effects, network effects are not necessarily limited to a single institution; they actually affect all compatible goods. In terms of clearing service provision, the employed networks are only rarely compatible initially. As outlined above, clearing member transactions that are routed to a certain clearing house can usually not be netted, cross-margined or closed out with transactions routed to another clearing house.[68] The illustrated network effects are then limited to a single clearing service provider. Clearing service networks employ standards that are proprietary to the respective institution providing the services; these standards exclude other providers

---

[66] This analysis is based on Domowitz's findings regarding the network attributes of exchange services and the respective economic implications for exchange operators. Cf. Domowitz (1995), p. 164.

[67] The concept of network externality has been applied in the literature of standards, in which a primary concern is the best choice of standard to enable compatibility. Cf. Farrell/Saloner (1985); Katz/Shapiro (1985); Liebowitz/Margolis (1994b); and Milne (2005).

[68] This statement is true for clearing houses unless they have signed netting or cross-margining agreements or if fungibility of certain products exists.

from utilisation.[69] The size of the network can therefore only be amplified through the compatibility of clearing systems. If the various provider technologies are compatible, the network size resembles the aggregate number of network members.[70] If they are not compatible, the size of the network remains equivalent to the size of each individual clearing network.

Network theory has generally found compatibility to arise either through the joint adoption of a technological standard, whereby a given group of firms agrees to make its products compatible, or through the construction of an adapter,[71] such as, for example, a clearing link, which interconnects clearing houses.[72] Compatibility between different CCP networks can thus be achieved through different network strategies. The use of proprietary technology that is not compatible with incumbent technology has important implications both for customers and for the market entry of new providers. Customers profit from the standardisation achieved through compatibility in several ways:[73] direct network externalities, market-mediated effects (indirect externalities, as when a complementary good becomes cheaper and more readily available) and enhanced price competition among providers are the chief advantages.[74] These benefits in turn translate into cost savings for network participants.

Similar considerations apply to GCM level networks. These networks are usually proprietary to the respective clearer. GCM networks are by definition compatible with all CCP networks to which the clearer is directly connected. They are commonly also at least somewhat compatible with other clearer networks because they often employ similar or compatible vendor solutions, and because their business model might demand the capability to interact with other GCM networks (i.e. for give-up/take-up services).[75] An important aspect influencing the first and second level network dynamics is that (high volume) clearers have historically striven to produce quasi compatibility between different CCP networks (in keeping with their business model and

---

[69] There is a general distinction between open and proprietary standards. Open standards do not allow the exclusion of certain providers from their utilisation. Cf. Thum (1995), p. 23.

[70] Cf. Katz/Shapiro (1985), p. 424; and Domowitz (1995), p. 168.

[71] Cf. Katz/Shapiro (1985), p. 434; and Katz/Shapiro (1986a), p. 823.

[72] Note that in a financial network, besides the technical aspects of compatibility, there is a need for coordination in time and place. Cf. Economides (1993), p. 92.

[73] Cf. Farrell/Saloner (1985), pp. 70–71.

[74] In the presence of these circumstances, the absence of compatibility means that users bear costs in some fashion – they must either invest in multiple sets of equipment so as to be able to use the alternative technology or incur significant 'translation' costs; otherwise, they will forgo using some of these technologies. Cf. Braunstein/White (1985), p. 340. On the other hand, excessive standardisation may not be beneficial to the markets, as it tends to stifle innovation. Cf. Domowitz (1995), p. 173.

[75] Refer to section 2.1.2.1 for an explanation of give-up/take-up services.

service offerings). In endeavouring to internalise GCM level network effects, CCP level networks enter into direct competition with these clearers. This plays a crucial role in the analysis of the potential success and failure of any network strategy, as it directly impacts the competitive dynamics related to any network initiative. A more detailed analysis is provided in Chapter 7.

6.1.2.2 Installed base

Over time, each network establishes an installed base of physical capital, in the form of previously sold equipment, and human capital, in the form of network participants who are trained to operate that network's products. The installed base influences competition at any point in time due to the positive network externalities that such bases confer on current adopters. With compatible technology, all providers are part of a single network; there is no mechanism by which a firm may establish a lead in terms of an installed base.[76] New providers must establish their own network, as they cannot usually offer services on the basis of existing networks. The new technology is then again likely to be incompatible with the existing networks. In order to establish a new clearing network, either on the CCP or GCM level, newcomers to the market need to overcome two important barriers to entry: firstly, market participants (i.e. clearing members and non-clearing members alike) need to be persuaded that positive network effects will be forthcoming,[77] i.e. assured of an adequate network size in the future; secondly, the utility derived from using the new network needs to outweigh the costs of alternation in the long run.

6.1.2.3 Starting problem

The starting problem concerns the phase of market entry. The initial users of a network have smaller utility due to the relatively small starting size of the network. In markets with significant network effects, the starting problem thus plays a significant role for market entry. To overcome the starting problem, it is crucial to convince an adequate number of users that the network will reach a critical size.[78] A self-strengthening positive participation effect will occur

---

[76] Cf. Katz/Shapiro (1986b), p. 148.

[77] This is important because in the presence of network externalities, a consumer in the market today also cares about the future success of the competing products. Cf. Katz/Shapiro (1986a), p. 824.

[78] Critical mass is defined as the minimal non-zero equilibrium size (market coverage) of a network good or service. For many network goods, the critical mass is of significant size; therefore, for these goods, small market coverage will never be observed – either their market does not exist or it has significant coverage. Cf. Economides/Himmelberg (1994), p. 5. A consumer will thus only be willing to purchase an MP3 player, for example, if he or she is confident that this standard will prevail in the future.

only if users have positive expectations about the new network. Networks are by nature self-reinforcing (meaning that they exhibit positive size externalities); this quality creates switching costs for the existing customers.[79] A similar situation applies to first and second level clearing networks. As argued above, the networks employed for clearing service provision are only rarely compatible initially. Proprietary technology obstructs new market entrants, as they cannot adopt existing standards. They inevitably compete with the incumbents and are thus confronted with a starting problem. The potentially first participants in the new clearing network are likely to hesitate to connect to the new network and route their transactions to be processed there. Their reluctance stems from the expectation that an insufficient number of counterparties will be participating in the network.

6.1.2.4 Innovative ability and lock-in

A related problem concerns the innovative ability related to network products.[80] The question of whether networks impede technological innovation is strongly related to the coordination problem within network industries. If only a few users adopt a new technology, the majority of users can reasonably be expected to prefer the old technology, as positive network effects are more significant there. In this instance, network effects can impede or decelerate technological innovation.[81] It is, therefore, a characteristic of network goods that no one wants to be the first to adopt a new technology or participate in a new network. This can lead to so-called 'lock-in' situations, which perpetuate the survival of inferior technological standards.[82]

---

[79] Cf. Economides (1993), p. 94.

[80] For details on the issue of networks' innovative ability, refer to Farrell/Saloner (1985); and Katz/Shapiro (1994).

[81] Cf. Farrell/Saloner (1985); Farrell/Saloner (1986); Tirole (1988); and Shermata (1997) classify this situation as 'excess inertia'. The opposite case can occur as well, which is referred to as 'excess momentum'. If a significant number of users embrace a new technology, other users might rush to adopt it – even if the new technology is not necessarily superior – for fear of getting stranded. Cf. Farrell/Saloner (1985), pp. 78–9. This situation results in polar equilibriums in which either all or none of the users adopt(s) the new technology.

[82] The concept of technological lock-in is used in the literature to support the reasoning of first-mover-wins. Note that there is considerable debate amongst economists as to whether lock-in actually exists in the form in which users continue to use the inferior product despite the common knowledge that a superior product exists. A commonly cited example for those arguing in favour of the existence of such lock-in situations is the QWERTY keypad (its name resulting from the alignment of the first six letters on the top left-handside), which today is the standard keypad used for computers and typewriters. David (1985) cites this as an example for the survival of an inferior standard, which cannot be overcome due to strong network effects. The QWERTY keypad is classified as an inferior standard, because it is allegedly not the standard that permits the fastest typing speeds. David (1985) substantiates the claim of lock-in with reference to the later developed Dvorak keypad, which is considered to allow for a

The lock-in concept can be applied to the adoption of clearing services on the first and second network levels. On the GCM level, the complementary offering effect in particular could create an installed base and lock-in – especially if the mutual interconnection between the clearer and NCM is very strong and is not only limited to the provision of clearing services, but includes services such as credit intermediation or mutual investments. On the CCP level, lock-in effects could be expected to occur on the product layer, where the open interest establishes an installed base and could lead to a lock-in. Classic lock-in situations can lead to persistence of inefficient and outdated standards. Clearing service networks that have established a de facto standard have little incentive to adopt new technologies and tend to orient their strategies on maintaining the status quo.

The likelihood of lock-in situations arising on the CCP or GCM level in the context of network strategies is further analysed in Chapter 7. Chapter 7 also explores the magnitude of the installed base, starting problem and lock-in effects on the system and product layers and examines how the various network strategies affect innovative ability and compatibility.

6.2 Supply-side scale effects

The industrial structure cannot be explained by focusing on the demand side alone . . . insufficient attention has been paid to the supply side.[83]

Although Domowitz and Steil (1999) argue that it is important to have knowledge about the demand side as well as the supply side when analysing the industrial organisation of marketplaces, supply-side scale effects have long served as the classical concept for explaining industry structures and integration.[84] Supply-side scale effects include economies of scale and scope. In the following, the concepts of these economies are briefly defined and subsequently

---

higher typing rate, but never became a standard. Liebowitz/Margolis (1990) challenge David's (1985) assertion of the Dvorak keypad's superiority by citing counter-studies finding that it did not in fact allow faster typing speeds. Refer to the forum discussion at http://eh.net/forums/QWERTYSu2.html for more details on the debate on this issue. Although doubt was therefore cast on the validity of David's (1985) reasoning, the QWERTY example nonetheless illustrates the basic idea of a lock-in. This study follows the reasoning of Liebowitz (2002), who classifies two forms of lock-in, strong and weak; the weak form of lock-in is not believed to support first-mover-win strategies and strong lock-ins are considered to exist very rarely in the real world. For more details on definitions of lock-in, refer to Liebowitz/Margolis (1995).

[83] Domowitz/Steil (1999), p. 34.

[84] See the contributions of Bain (1956); Stigler (1958); Baumol/Panzar/Willig (1982); and Scherer/Ross (1990).

applied to clearing service provision. Economies of scale at the GCM level are analysed in Chapter 5; this chapter focuses on identifying the areas in which supply-side scale effects occur at the CCP level.

The concepts of economies of scale and scope were originally tailored to fit industrial enterprises. Within the financial services industry, many studies apply these concepts to the banking sector,[85] and an increasing number of studies apply this concept to the exchange industry[86] and to the post-trade processes of settlement and custody.[87] In the following, the concepts are applied to clearing services provided by CCPs. A clearing house is therefore regarded as a producing enterprise that generates a certain output through the use of different input factors. In order to assess the existence of economies of scale and scope, it is necessary to first define how the relevant output of a clearing house can be measured.[88]

A general advantage in researching clearing services for derivatives instead of securities lies in the structure of the relevant output. Whereas for the analysis of securities clearing services it is imperative to analyse a two-dimensional structure of the output, it is adequate to analyse a one-dimensional structure for the provision of derivatives clearing services.[89] Different parameters

---

[85] See, e.g. Benston (1972); Langer (1980); Benston/Hanweck/Humphrey (1982); Benston *et al.* (1983); Murray/White (1983); Clark (1984); Hunter/Timme (1986); Berger/Hanweck/Humphrey (1987); Cebenoyan (1988); Lawrence (1989); Hunter/Timme/Yang (1990); Noulas/Ray/Miller (1990); Gropper (1991); Kolari/Zardkoohi (1991); Bessler (1991); Berger/Hunter/Timme (1993); McAllister/McManus (1993); Pulley/Humphrey (1993); Berger/Humphrey (1994); Clark/Speaker (1994); Berger/Demsetz/Strahan (1999); and Milbourn/Boot/Thakor (1999). Also see Tichy (1990), p. 364, who provides an overview of economies of scale studies prior to 1990.

[86] Malkamäki/Topi (1999) find economies of scale to advance cross-border competition among exchanges. Malkamäki (1999) was the first to empirically research economies of scale in the stock exchange industry. His analysis on the processing of trades at stock exchanges shows large-scale economies for increasing trading volumes. However, he restricts his findings to very large stock exchanges. Book (2001) builds on Malkamäki's research results by empirically analysing the existence of economies of scale in the derivatives exchange industry. Hasan/Malkamäki (2001) research empirically the existence of economies of scale among exchanges in different regions.

[87] Schmiedel/Malkamäki/Tarkka (2002) investigate the existence and extent of economies of scale in depository and settlement systems. Kröpfl (2003) also researches evidence for the existence of economies of scale in securities depository and settlement systems. Van Cayseele/Wuyts (2005) research whether the European settlement and custody institutions operate in an efficient way by estimating a translog cost function and a quadratic cost function. They find that economies of scale and scope clearly exist in this industry. Van Cayseele/Wuyts (2006) examine whether the European settlement institutions are technically efficient by estimating a translog cost function and investigating whether scale economies are fully exploited. The results of their analysis imply that there are economies of scale in this industry. Also refer to Serifsoy/Weiß (2005), who analyse economies of scale and scope in securities clearing and settlement.

[88] Note that what constitutes inputs or outputs for any financial institution is a matter of general controversy. Cf. Schmiedel/Malkamäki/Tarkka (2002), p. 6.

[89] When analysing securities clearing services, two output variables are significant: the total number of positions cleared and the relative number of positions settled. Due to the nature of securities products,

are available for quantifying the output of derivatives clearing houses; their adequacy for an empirical analysis is discussed in the following.

The output of derivatives clearing houses can be quantified through the application of various indicators for its activity of providing clearing services. The most important indicators are the number of contracts cleared[90] and the corresponding value,[91] which can serve as a proxy for determining the risk undertaken by the clearing house. This approach to quantifying the output is based on analysing variables over a specific period.[92] Variables that relate to a certain fixed point in time, such as the open interest, are inadequate for this purpose, as they only reflect a certain date.

To determine the existence of economies of scale and scope in clearing, the number of contracts cleared is used as an output variable.[93] As outlined in section 5.2.1, most clearing houses now charge a per-contract fee, which underscores this variable's suitability for describing a clearing house's output. Furthermore, these data are publicly available. Pitfalls in quantifying the variable can result from inconsistencies in the method of counting contracts, i.e. whether both sides of a transaction (i.e. the buy side and sell side) are counted as two single positions or whether both sides are counted as a single contract.

---

the process of settlement and its efficiency is highly important. Clearing houses can increase the efficiency by employing settlement netting. The respective settlement efficiency is thus an important output variable. The nature of derivatives products meanwhile implies that the measuring of settlement efficiency is negligible in the context of an output analysis, as derivative products are mostly closed out prior to their expiration.

[90] The number of contracts cleared simply results from summarising.

[91] To determine the value of risk taken over by the clearing house, it is first necessary to determine the value of the contracts cleared (CV stands for the contract value). This can be done as follows:

$$CV = \sum_i CS_i \sum_j p_{ij} TC_{ij}$$

CS_i refers to the contract size of product i while p_{ij} stands for the price of a series j of the product i (when referring to options, the exercise price is used; when referring to futures, the settlement price is employed.). TC_{ij} is the number of traded contracts in the series j of product i. The contract size of a product results from multiplying the tick size (ts) with the tick value (tv): $CS = ts \times tv$. Cf. Book (2001), p. 189.

[92] Utilising other indicators for a quantification of the output (e.g. balance sheet variables such as revenue or profit) is not adequate for this analysis, as these indicators generate a biased picture for a number of reasons; the use of P&L-related variables can result in distortions if the clearing houses under analysis do not operate as for-profit companies. In this case, the profit can be influenced by factors that have nothing to do with the actual output, such as the legal structure of a clearing house. Using the revenue figure as an indicator for the output is problematic to the extent that revenues are shaped by the pricing structure and pricing mechanism employed by a clearing house. As profit maximisation cannot be assumed, it could be that a clearing house reduces its fees when revenues augment. In this case, the revenue figure is not adequate for measuring the output of a clearing house.

[93] This applies to findings concerning the CCP level as well as the GCM level.

While the utilisation of the cleared contracts' value as an output variable has the advantage of not being affected by the different contract sizes,[94] there are disadvantages related to product-specific distortions, the complex method of calculation and its limited public availability.

6.2.1 Economies of scale

Economies of scale exist when a proportionate increase of all utilised input variables generates a more than proportionate output increase.[95] When valuating the input in factor prices, existence of economies of scale leads to a declining average cost curve. The concept of economies of scale therefore describes a declining correlation between firm size (measured in potential output per period) and the average costs in the long run.[96] In this case, with a given output, a large firm is capable of producing goods more cheaply than several smaller firms.[97] In contrast, economies of scale signify a degression of fixed costs induced through a long-term variation of a firm's capacity.

The potential sources for economies of scale are manifold.[98] One possible source is the economical use of an enhanced production process that was not available before due to the lack of critical mass necessary for employing this production process.[99] These production processes typically have higher fixed cost components, but decreasing average costs.[100] Another source can lie in the indivisibility of input factors.[101] Economies of scale are also often explained

---

[94] A bisection of the contract size, for example, results in a doubling of the number of contracts traded, but at the same time also to a bisection of the contract value. Therefore, the value of the contracts traded ultimately remains unchanged.

[95] Cf. Grant (1998), p. 201. This study focuses on economies of scale on the firm level, which can also be classified as internal economies of scale. In contrast, external economies of scale emerge on an industry or regional level and cannot be determined by individual firms. External economies of scale provide a framework for analysing the regional agglomeration of firms active within the same industry. Cf. Junius (1997), pp. 1–5.

[96] Cf. Silvestre (1987), p. 80. Also refer to Bohr (1996).

[97] Decreasing average costs related to an ascending output can have several causes. A first explanation concerns the case in which firm size is not variable in the short run, therefore inducing a maximum capacity. Increasing output then allows the allocation of fixed costs across a greater number of output units. This in turn reduces the average costs, as the ratio of used capacity costs and idle time costs is lessened. Cf. Gutenberg (1983), p. 428. These cost savings are also referred to as the degression of fixed costs. Cf. Silberston (1972), p. 374; and Silvestre (1987), p. 80.

[98] Refer to Baumol/Panzar/Willig (1982); Silvestre (1987); Scherer/Ross (1990); Bohr (1996); and Langlois (1999).

[99] Gutenberg (1983), pp. 423–4, characterises this as a 'mutant' increase of capacity – as opposed to a multiple increase in capacity, which only represents a multiplication of capacity and does not allow for cost savings.

[100] Cf. Gaughan (2002), p. 116.

[101] Cf. Robinson (1948), p. 334; Baumol/Panzar/Willig (1982), p. 73; and Junius (1997), p. 3.

in terms of the 'advantages of specialisation' obtained through the division of labour.[102] In addition, economies of scale can be elucidated mathematically.[103] Learning effects can also generate scale economies.[104] Decreasing average costs are then determined by the historic cumulative output rather than by the current output. Learning effects can be modelled using the cost-learning curve.[105]

The realisation of economies of scale can be counteracted by so-called 'diseconomies of scale',[106] which lead to decreasing returns to scale with an increase in output. They can result from an elevated need to coordinate, and in consequence higher levels of bureaucracy or inadequate management capacity.[107] In the first place, economies of scale result in decreasing average costs when capacity is increased.[108]

Economies of scale in clearing service provision consequently exist when an increase of contracts cleared (output) results in decreasing costs per transaction (average costs).

The following analysis assesses the evidence for the existence of economies of scale in clearing. One indicator for the existence of economies of scale in clearing service provision is manifest in the fact that clearing houses commonly discount fees for clearing services according to a volume or revenue discount structure.[109] These discounts reflect the clearing houses' cost structure: given the high fixed costs of providing these types of service, economies of scale associated with high volumes of business can be assumed. At the same time, the discounts also reflect the increased bargaining power available to clearing members conducting high volumes of business.[110]

As outlined above, previous empirical studies of supply-side scale effects in the financial services industry mainly concerned the banking industry. These

---

[102] This effect has first been identified by Smith (1776). Also refer to Chamberlin (1933), pp. 235–6; and Schneider (1977), p. 127.

[103] This is true, e.g. for tanks, ovens and pipes whose capacity depends on their volume, while their material costs largely depend on their surface. Refer to Samuelson/Nordhaus (1989), p. 504; and Baumol/Blinder (1997), p. 168.

[104] Cf. Arrow (1962), pp. 155–73; Baetge (1975), pp. 2495–504; Spence (1981), pp. 49–70; and Corsten (ed.) (2000), p. 206.

[105] Cf. Spence (1981), p. 49. Also refer to Hedley (1976); and Bauer (1986) for details.

[106] Leibenstein (1966) provides for an early analysis of these inefficiencies. Also see Albach (2000), pp. 245–7.

[107] Cf. Scherer/Ross (1990), pp. 102–6; Scheele (1994), pp. 104–7, and Gaughan (2002), p. 117.

[108] The capacity that only results in insignificant scale effects is referred to as the minimum efficient size of the firm. If the firm size increases, the average costs increase as well, due to diseconomies of scale.

[109] Cf. NERA Economic Consulting (ed.) (2004), p. 62. Refer to section 5.2.2 for an analysis of clearing houses' discount schemes.

[110] Cf. NERA Economic Consulting (ed.) (2004), p. 62.

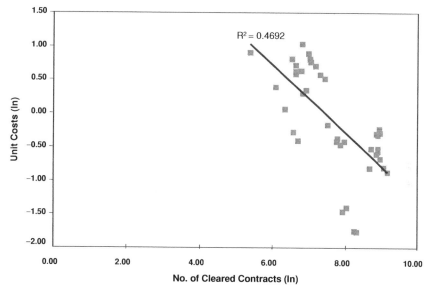

Figure 6.8   Unit costs and number of cleared contracts of selected clearing houses from 1999 to 2005 (N=9)[111]
Source: Author's own; based on FOW (ed.) (2001); FOW (ed.) (2003); FOW (ed.) (2006); and clearing houses' websites.

studies have only recently expanded to include the analysis of the exchange industry as well as the securities depository and settlement industries. The respective research results all conclude that evidence for the existence of supply-side scale effects in these industries is strong.

To the author's knowledge, no attempt has yet been made to empirically analyse the existence of economies of scale in the CCP clearing industry. The following examination seeks empirical evidence for the existence of economies of scale in derivatives clearing services. To this end, a selection of the world's major derivatives clearing houses is analysed.[112] The basis for the examination is the data for the years 1999 to 2005. Figure 6.8 shows the development of unit costs and the number of contracts cleared for selected clearing houses.[113]

---

[111] The sample selection of clearing houses was made based on the availability of data. Only a few clearing houses worldwide publish annual reports. The nine selected clearing houses include entities in China, Greece, Italy, Mexico, Norway, the UK and the USA.

[112] The data used for the analysis comes from a variety of sources, most importantly the annual reports published by clearing houses as well as information collected from the clearing houses' websites covering a seven-year time period (1999–2005). In some cases, additional information was obtained from clearing houses by correspondence.

[113] The total cost variable in this study represents the reported operating expenses of a clearing house, including depreciation. The variables are based on publicly available information, which can be found

The analysis supports that decreasing average costs are related to an increase in the number of contracts cleared. The linear regression of the logarithmised variables 'unit costs' and 'number of cleared contracts' results in a negative gradient of -0.501, with a coefficient of determination of roughly 47 per cent.

Unfortunately, the limited availability of heterogeneous data for the empirical study dilutes the research results in the following way: although the focus of the study lies on derivatives clearing houses, the results are biased due to the fact that a large number of the clearing houses included in the examination provide not only derivatives clearing, but also securities clearing services and do not report the data separately. Furthermore, some of the clearing houses analysed are not independent firms, but part of vertically integrated structures. This fact also distorts the research results, because the calculation of costs is based on the total costs of clearing, whereas the additional output realised by asset classes other than derivatives is not taken into account.[114] A substantiated empirical analysis, i.e. through the estimation of a cost or production function,[115] cannot be properly conducted due to the limitations of the data and the small sample selection. Taking these drawbacks into account, the empirical examination nonetheless provides a convincing indication that there exist potential economies of scale in derivatives clearing services.

6.2.2 Economies of scope

Economies of scope exist when the joint production of two or more products is more cost efficient than their separate production.[116] A diversified firm can thus produce the products A and B more cost efficiently in a joint production

---

in the institutions' financial statements. The information on the number of contracts cleared is derived from FOW (ed.) (2001); FOW (ed.) (2003); and FOW (ed.) (2006).

[114] Malkamäki's (1999) study suffers from similar problems in its analysis of economies of scale at stock exchanges. In his study, Malkamäki includes pure stock exchanges and exchanges offering stock and derivatives trading. His sample selection further includes vertically integrated exchanges and independent exchanges. Cf. Malkamäki (1999), p. 10. Despite this criticism, Malkamäki's research results provide valuable indicators for the existence of economies of scale.

[115] Translog cost functions are increasingly used to determine whether or not economies of scale and scope exist in financial services. Kolari/Zardkoohi (1987) estimate a translog cost function to determine whether financial intermediaries should engage both in balance and off-balance activities. Malkamäki (1999) and Schmiedel/Malkamäki/Tarkka (2002) estimate translog cost functions for their studies, relying on a broader sample of data available for their focus area. Book (2001) on the other hand copes with the problems related to the limited availability of data for his research by providing an analysis of average operating costs in relation to contract turnover for undermining the existence of economies of scale at derivatives exchanges.

[116] Cf. Panzar/Willig (1981), p. 268.

process than two independent firms.[117] Whereas the concept of economies of scale describes the cost trend for a firm producing a single product, the concept of economies of scope refers to multi-product firms.[118] Economies of scope can be explained through the joint usage of production factors for several products.[119] This is feasible if production factors are not sufficiently exploited in a single-product firm and the non-utilised production factors cannot be commercialised in the market.[120] Production factors for joint usage are, for example, technology, management or marketing knowledge. Another cause for economies of scope can lie in the indivisibility of production factors.[121] In this case, it is economical to extend production to further products, if production factors are not being fully exploited.

Economies of scope in clearing thus exist when reductions in average costs can be achieved by means of product level or geographical diversification, the integration of asset classes or an increase in the number of complementary clearing services offered by the CCP.

Diversification at the product level refers to the scope of products for which clearing services are offered. Within the derivatives market, different product types are traded in on- and off-exchange markets and are thus available for clearing – for example, financial derivatives, derivatives on commodities, foreign exchange derivatives, etc. Economies of scope result from a wide product portfolio, which allows better diversification of the risks taken over by the clearing house. This enables the clearing house to economise on its risk management by spreading risks. The clearing house also profits from the diversification of revenue streams resulting from a heterogeneous product portfolio. When clearing houses offer their services for more than one product type, users benefit from a reduction of indirect transaction costs.

Economies of scope can also result from the integration of asset classes, whereby clearing services for different asset classes, i.e. derivatives and securities, are offered through an integrated clearing system. Clearing facilities that process multiple asset classes have additional leeway for scope economies, as they are able to implement innovative risk management procedures, such as cross-collateralising among different asset classes.[122] Generally, the value-added (and the benefits of netting) of a clearing house that offers netting

---

[117] Cf. Willig (1979), p. 346; and Teece (1980). Also refer to Moschandreas (1994), p. 159; and Corsten (ed.) (2000), p. 206.

[118] Cf. Baumol/Panzar/Willig (1982), p. 71. Also see Panzar/Willig (1975); and Panzar/Willig (1977), pp. 481–93.

[119] Cf. Willig (1979), p. 346; and Panzar/Willig (1981), p. 269.   [120] Cf. Teece (1980).

[121] Cf. Panzar/Willig (1981), p. 269.   [122] Cf. Serifsoy/Weiß (2005), p. 9.

functions is measured by the types and number of financial products it clears and the number and activity of its members.[123] Where a clearing house acts as CCP to several markets that are subject to identical or highly correlated risks, the benefit of exposure netting may extend to market risk.[124] This creates the possibility of margin offsets, whereby firms are long in one market and short in another (i.e. margin against a long position in a bond futures contract might be offset against margin against a matching short position in repo.).[125] These benefits increase as the volume and diversity of products included within the clearing house increase.[126] To the extent that regulators recognise these off-sets where a CCP exists and not otherwise, regulatory capital requirements may also be lower.[127] This results in an overall decrease in capital provision requirements for the users and consequently enables them to save on indirect transaction costs. There may thus be economies of scope in CCP clearing for a number of linked markets.[128]

An indication for the existence of economies of scope resulting from the integration of different asset classes can be seen in the recent moves of several clearing houses to integrate derivatives and securities clearing.[129] This trend entails an increase in risk for the central counterparty, while the efficiency gains to – at least large – market participants can be considerable.[130] In addition, if a CCP manages both the cash and derivative sides of a market place, it can take advantage of the clearers having offsetting positions on both sides. In this way, the capital requirement for one clearing house can be lower than the sum of capital requirements for two single clearing houses.[131]

6.2.3 Clearing houses' cost structures

Clearing is a substantially fixed cost business.[132]

The previous section classified and explored possible economies of scale and scope in clearing. Clearing houses' cost structures are analysed in this section in order to shed light on the causes of supply-side scale effects. The analysis is expected to illuminate the potential for economies of scale and scope in clearing and provide the basis for the analysis of the impact of network strategies on clearing houses' costs, to be presented in Chapter 7.

---

[123] Cf. Euronext (ed.) (2004), p. 3.   [124] Cf. Hills *et al.* (1999), p. 125.
[125] Cf. Hills *et al.* (1999), p. 125.   [126] Cf. Euronext (ed.) (2004), p. 3.
[127] Cf. Hills *et al.* (1999), p. 125.   [128] Cf. Hills *et al.* (1999), p. 215.
[129] Cf. Culp (2002).   [130] Cf. Riksbank (ed.) (2002); p. 48, and Ripatti (2004), p. 29.
[131] Cf. Ripatti (2004), p. 29.   [132] LCH.Clearnet (ed.) (2006b), p. 7.

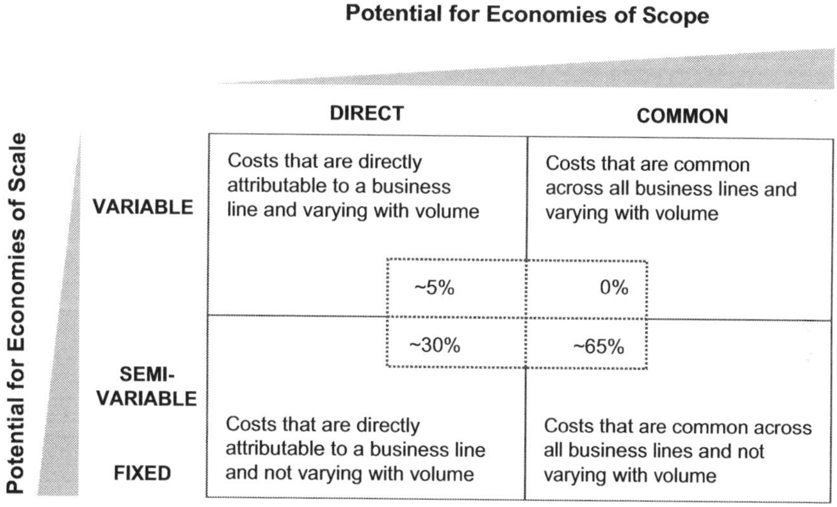

Potential for Economies of Scope

		DIRECT	COMMON
Potential for Economies of Scale	VARIABLE	Costs that are directly attributable to a business line and varying with volume	Costs that are common across all business lines and varying with volume
		~5%	0%
		~30%	~65%
	SEMI-VARIABLE FIXED	Costs that are directly attributable to a business line and not varying with volume	Costs that are common across all business lines and not varying with volume

Figure 6.9   Potential for economies of scale and scope – LCH.Clearnet
Source: LCH.Clearnet (ed.) (2006b), p. 7.

Generally, the potential for scale economies increases with a high percentage of fixed costs that do not vary according to volume, and the potential for scope economies increases when there are costs that are common across business lines. LCH.Clearnet's cost structure serves to exemplify the causes for potential scale and scope effects in clearing. Figure 6.9 shows that roughly 65 per cent of LCH.Clearnet's costs are fixed and common across all business lines – at first sight indicating a high potential for scale and scope economies.

Nonetheless, such a limited example does not warrant a general conclusion. A more detailed examination of clearing houses' cost structures and core cost drivers is thus required to analyse why a large percentage of a clearing house's cost base is fixed[133] as well as to identify the true potential for scale and scope economies.

Clearing houses' costs can generally be differentiated between personnel costs, IT costs (system development and system maintenance costs, including expenses for the data centre, network and hardware costs), depreciation and amortisation, and other costs (such as overhead and general administrative costs). Figure 6.10 compares the cost structures of selected clearing houses in 2005.[134]

---

[133] Cf. Hardy (2006).

[134] The limited availability of clearing houses' cost data resulted in a very small peer group being available for the comparison. Additionally, further limitations result from the appliance of different accounting

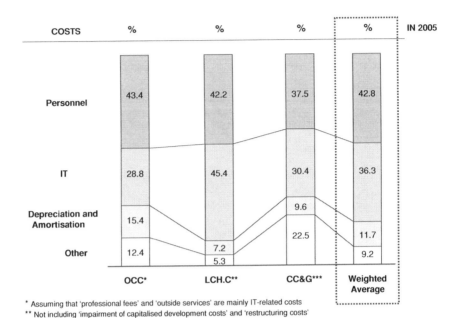

Figure 6.10 Cost structure of selected clearing houses in 2005
Source: Author's own; structure and idea based on Kröpfl (2003), p. 148; data derived from clearing houses' annual reports.

To understand the varying significance of the different cost categories for different clearing houses, it is necessary to recognise the nature and characteristics of each of those categories. Personnel, IT, and depreciation and amortisation costs are naturally interrelated. Usually, the higher the degree of automation, the lower the personnel costs. However, the relative significance of both cost categories as outlined in the clearing houses' annual reports is influenced by a variety of additional factors – most importantly the age of the clearing system and book-keeping-related aspects. Relative to the age of the employed clearing system, IT-related depreciation and amortisation costs decrease. In this case, IT costs mainly consist of system maintenance costs, including expenses for the data centre, network and hardware costs. Depreciation and amortisation costs are relatively low. On the other hand, the older a clearing system, the greater the need for system development will be. New systems or new system components require costly development work.

principles within the peer group and the generally restricted publicly available cost details, which required the partial estimate of costs attributable to the defined categories. Note that for LCH.Clearnet and CC&G, the cost data refers not only to derivatives clearing costs, but to the total of clearing-related costs.

Generally, the more complex the CCPs' services and products, and the more asset classes are cleared, the higher these costs will be. System development costs then lead to an increase in IT costs, or, if they are activated, result in an increase of depreciation and amortisation costs. Book-keeping-related aspects play a significant role in the analysis of clearing houses' cost structures as presented in their annual reports.[135] Isolating true IT costs is difficult if system development or maintenance is executed (fully or partially) by a third-party service provider; the relevant IT costs might then be booked as 'other costs'. Similarly, if system maintenance is performed by in-house staff, costs are likely to be booked as 'personnel costs'.

To summarise, the relative importance of personnel versus IT costs depends on a variety of different factors – not only on the degree of automation – and varies according to the specifics of each CCP. The weighted average as outlined in Figure 6.10 consequently reflects a snapshot of the cost structure of clearing houses with clearing systems that are largely amortised.[136]

6.2.4 Cost implications of scale and scope enlargements

As outlined in section 6.2.1, economies of scale in clearing originate from an increase in the number of contracts cleared, which can result from different scenarios: existing clearing members clear more existing products (market growth), existing clearing members clear new products (possibly new marketplaces), new clearing members clear existing products or new clearing members clear new products.

Section 6.2.2 explains that economies of scope can result from product level or geographical diversification, the integration of asset classes or an increase in the number of complementary clearing services offered by the CCP.

Each of these scenarios has different implications for the respective clearing house's cost structure, which is briefly described in the following. Identifying and understanding these implications is crucial for assessing the true potential for supply-side scale effects in clearing as well as for the later analysis of the impact of different network strategies on clearing houses' cost structures (Chapter 7).

When scale increases are realised through **market growth**, an increase of system capacity will eventually be necessary. Generally, the older the clearing

---

[135] Refer to Kröpfl (2003), pp. 147–8, who identifies similar issues relevant for the analysis of CSDs' and ICSDs' cost structures.

[136] At LCH.Clearnet the development of a new clearing system failed, and the previously capitalised development costs were impaired in 2005. Note that these impairment costs are not included in Figure 6.10.

system, the lower its capacity is likely to be. When an increase in scale results from clearing new products from existing marketplaces, the associated costs highly depend on the complexity and uniqueness of these products' system requirements. If new technology solutions, upgrades or changes to the core architecture of the clearing system are required, significant investments may be involved.

Important factors in determining the costs associated with the connection of **new marketplaces** as a means to increase scale are the level of automation and the use of standard interfaces. The higher the level of automation and the more common the use of standard interfaces, the lower the associated costs will be. Connecting additional execution venues involves interlinking with on- and off-exchange marketplaces. Automation is especially vital with regard to the increase of scale through connecting off-exchange marketplaces. Investments can only be kept to a minimum when transactions are available in an electronic format, which is then usable for further processing, and when the process of transferring transaction information from the execution venue to the clearing house is automated.

The use of standard interfaces is highly relevant for increasing the scale by connecting further on-exchange marketplaces. On-exchange electronic execution can generally result in a higher level of clearing automation and therefore efficiency, as contract standardisation simplifies registration. Investment costs will nonetheless only be kept to a minimum if the format in which the transactions are transferred to the clearing house is based on an industry standard instead of using specific trade capture formats. Otherwise, increasing scale through connecting to various additional execution venues can entail high investment costs, as each interface has to be modelled and built individually.

Additional upgrades or changes to the core architecture of the clearing system are likely to result from integrating new marketplaces that are located in a different regulatory environment. Whereas each clearing system is usually tailored to serve the needs of its original home market(s), regulatory reporting and market functioning particularities may require significant and costly system changes if scale is increased as a result of integrating new regulatory environments.[137]

Economies of scope can be realised if insufficiently exploited production factors are put to use. When analysing the implications of a scope enlargement for a clearing house's cost structure, the extent to which the production factors

---

[137] Although these kinds of integration difficulties can arise in both cash equities and derivatives clearing, the complexities are usually greater in cash equities clearing due to the need for implementing and integrating the complex settlement interfaces.

are not being exploited (and can thus be leveraged) must be considered, as well as to what extent the enlargement of scope requires additional investments into production factors.

When economies of scope are realised through **geographical diversification**, the possible cost implications are similar to those of a scale enlargement through the connection of new marketplaces, meaning that the associated costs highly depend on the level of automation and the use of standard interfaces. On the other hand, the integration of new marketplaces that are located in a different regulatory environment can entail additional upgrades or changes to the core architecture of the clearing system.

The associated costs of enlarging scope through **diversification at the product level** (e.g. derivatives on commodities, foreign exchange derivatives, credit derivatives, etc.) are highly contingent upon the complexity and unique system requirements of these products. If new technology solutions, upgrades or changes to the core architecture of the clearing system are required, substantial investments may be necessary.

When a clearing house decides to enlarge the scope of its clearing services by integrating **new asset classes**, sizable investments can be required for various reasons. First, new asset classes often have different regulatory reporting and market functioning particularities, which might well entail extensive and costly system changes, or even the development of a completely new clearing system. Secondly, some asset classes require greater manual processing and intervention than others, which can translate into increased personnel costs.

Finally, if a clearing house boosts the scope of its services by increasing the number of **complementary clearing services** it offers, major costs may be involved. The further away the service is from the CCP's core clearing services and the more additional knowledge and system solutions the clearing house needs to incorporate, the higher personnel and IT costs are likely to be.

Finally, enlargements in the scale and scope of a clearing house can increase the number of clearing members, the average open interest held by the CCP and the value of transactions cleared. When the **number of connected clearing members** balloons, costs can arise from the technological changes required to accommodate them (i.e. if the clearing system was configured to admit a predefined and restricted number of clearing members and this number is surmounted). More clearing members can also result in increased personnel costs if transactions require a large amount of manual processing[138] or if a

---

[138] This depends on the type of asset class cleared; whereas the clearing of commodity derivatives commonly involves a relatively high amount of manual labour – due to its often relative low degree of electronic processing – the clearing of exchange-traded financial derivatives is largely automated today.

significantly increased error rate necessitates the hiring of additional personnel.[139] Furthermore, the more clearing members are connected, the more complex the administration of the clearing system's account structures becomes, which in turn results in an increased system load – potentially requiring capacity enhancements.

Increases in scale or scope are also likely to result in a **rise of average open interest** held by the CCP. Whether or not such an increase has any cost implications for the clearing house depends on the associated number of clearing members. The more clearing members hold the open interest, the higher the monitoring effort for the CCP will be. A significant open interest increase could require an increase in system capacity, depending on the age and architecture of the clearing system.

An increase in scale boosts the **value of transactions** cleared so long as the scale increase is not achieved via the minimisation of the contract sizes of existing products. Additionally, a scope enlargement through diversification at the product level also leads to an increased value of transactions cleared. Whether or not this increased value has any cost impact depends on the amount of transactions netted and their correlation with other processed positions. An increased value of cleared transactions only results in an increased risk management effort for the clearing house if few positions are netted and correlated.[140]

Generally, increases in a clearing house's scale and scope can both eventually require an **increase in system capacity** or an enhancement of the system's processing power in terms of speed. The older the clearing system, the lower its capacity and processing power is likely to be. Whether or not new technology solutions, upgrades or changes to the core architecture of the clearing system are required also depends on additional factors, such as the complexity of clearing services, products and markets.

6.2.5 Preliminary conclusions

The demand for services offered by a clearing house is subject to high variability in comparison to other industries. This fluctuation results from the direct interdependence of the demand for clearing services and the demand for derivatives products in general. Traded volumes in derivatives markets

---

[139] The more clearing members are involved, the more risk management the CCP may have to perform, and the greater the likelihood of errors in judgements.

[140] Also note that a clearing house employs several risk protection measures related to the value of cleared transactions, such as higher margin requirements, contributions to the default fund, etc.

are erratic;[141] the volume of contracts available for clearing is therefore also erratic. The capacity of the clearing house infrastructure has to be configured to accommodate the greatest expected trading volume available for clearing. This is due to the service character of clearing house offerings. Neither supply nor demand for clearing is storable. On average, the actual utilisation of capacities is therefore relatively low compared to the highest available capacity.[142] The high proportion of non-utilised capacity results in high fixed costs.

The main cause of economies of scale in clearing services therefore lies in the indivisibility of production factors, i.e. the clearing infrastructure. The operation of a clearing house requires a complex infrastructure whose most important component is the clearing system. The related IT costs are to a large degree independent of the number of contracts cleared. The higher the number of contracts cleared through the system, the lower the average costs. An enlargement of the clearing house's scale results in positive effects on the average costs. This implies disadvantages for smaller clearing houses. It is therefore assumed that a minimum optimal clearing house size exists.

Nonetheless, it is important to understand that whether or not any of the outlined costs actually arise when a clearing house increases its scale and/or scope depends on the specific characteristics of the CCP and the initiative pursued. The true potential for supply-side scale economies in network strategies is further analysed in Chapter 7.

6.3 Summary of findings

The purpose of Chapter 6 was to classify and explore possible demand- and supply-side scale effects in clearing. The chapter yielded some crucial insights, which are summarised in the following.

6.3.1 Demand-side scale effects

- The Value Provision Network constitutes a two-layered (product layer and system layer) and two-level (CCP level and GCM level) network structure and exhibits a number of positive and negative network effects.

---

[141] As an example: Book (2001) cites that the peak system load at Eurex on a given trading day was up to 75 per cent higher than the average daily system load in 1999. Cf. Book (2001), p. 191. Variation in demand for derivative products is not only manifest on a day-to-day basis, but intra-day volumes also vary significantly.

[142] The capacity of the Eurex system is, for example, designed to provide headroom of approximately 70 per cent above the peak system load. Cf. Eurex (ed.) (2007a), p. 10.

- Many of the network effects on the CCP and GCM levels are similar in nature and can impact one another.
- An important aspect of the interrelation between the CCP level and GCM level networks is that, strictly speaking, the size of the CCP level network is not determined by the number of clearing members, but rather by the number of counterparties (i.e. clearing members, non-clearing members and other customers). In the extreme, this means that positive and negative network effects on the CCP level can arise despite a downturn in the number of clearing members.
- The size of the CCP level network is consequently closely interrelated to the size of the GCM level network – which is not true the opposite way round.
- Theoretically, all GCM level network effects can be replicated on the CCP level, but not all CCP level network effects can be replicated on the GCM level.
- There exist some unique network effects on the CCP level (netting, cross-margining, open interest and information effects) that do not occur (or are more limited in scope) on the GCM level and could only be replicated by the GCM if it became the central counterparty itself.
- Nonetheless, the value-added function and the network effects on the GCM level are significant in the context of the current structure of the European VPN, because most clearers offer single access to many platforms and markets; the same is not true for CCPs. Therefore, the size, interface and collateral management effects are significantly greater on the GCM level than they are on the CCP level.
- The fungibility effect constitutes another network effect that increases the value of the clearing services provided by GCMs. The complementary offering effect is also greater on the GCM level network than on the CCP level network – again because most clearers offer a wider range of complementary clearing services.
- Additionally, CCP and GCM level network effects exhibit spill-over effects on to other parts of the transaction value chain. Despite the currently high value-added function of the GCM level, the most significant positive spill-over effects on to the trading and settlement layer result from the CCP level network effects. Additionally, the CCP level generates unique positive network effects that support the stability of markets and that are not easily replicable by the GCM level.
- CCPs can internalise the strong and important positive network effects on the GCM level by engaging in network strategies and enlarging the range of the complementary products and services offered.

- A CCP's engagement in network strategies should thus theoretically be driven by two objectives: firstly, to internalise the GCM level network effects; and, secondly, to make their unique CCP level network effects stronger, thus increasing network participants' willingness to pay for these services.
- Internalising the strong and important positive GCM level network effects on the CCP level is beneficial, because doing so may significantly reduce clearing-related transaction costs and thereby increase the efficiency of the industry. First level transaction costs can thus be reduced through greater CCP level network effects. Second level transaction costs can possibly be reduced through a disintermediation of the GCM level.
- The internalisation of GCM level network effects by a CCP through network strategies is further analysed in Chapter 7.
- The economic implications resulting from the network characteristics are articulated in potential barriers to market entry, due to the proprietary character of clearing networks and their general incompatibility. New entrants can only succeed in establishing a network if they achieve a critical size.
- Chapter 7 will also analyse how strong the installed base, starting problem and lock-in effects on the system and product layer can possibly be and how innovative ability and compatibility are affected in the context of different network strategies.

6.3.2 Supply-side scale effects

- A clearing house is regarded as a producing enterprise that generates a certain output through the use of different input factors. To determine the existence of economies of scale and scope in clearing, the number of contracts cleared is used as an output variable.
- Economies of scale in clearing originate from an increase in the number of contracts cleared, which can result from different scenarios: existing clearing members clear more existing products (market growth), existing clearing members clear new products (possibly new marketplaces), new clearing members clear existing products or new clearing members clear new products.
- Economies of scope can result from product level or geographical diversification, the integration of asset classes or an increase in the number of complementary clearing services offered by the CCP.
- Evidence suggests that economies of scale exist in clearing. There are different scenarios for increasing the scale and scope of a clearing house, each

of which has different implications for the respective clearing house's cost structures.

- The analysis of clearing houses' cost structures shows that a high percentage of costs are fixed. Whether or not an increase in scale and scope translates into positive economies is highly dependent on the type of network initiative pursued as well as on the characteristics and cost structure of the involved CCPs.
- The true potential for supply-side scale economies in network strategies is further analysed in Chapter 7.

It is the purpose of this study to determine the efficiency impact of various network strategies. Chapter 6, together with Chapter 5, provides the basis for this analysis. The following Chapter 7 establishes an original framework to finally analyse the impact of network strategies on the efficiency of clearing.

7 What theory reveals – framework for efficiency analysis of network strategies

Interconnection [between competing networks] upsets the normal competitive model in several ways . . . But interconnection also allows competitors to become a source of customers for one another when one provider originates traffic and another eventually delivers it.[1]

The ultimate research objective of this study is to determine the efficiency impact of various network strategies within the European clearing industry. An assessment of this impact serves to identify the most preferable future clearing industry structure.

To this end, Chapter 7 establishes an original framework to explore the impact of network strategies on the efficiency of clearing. The framework builds on the findings of the previous chapters and consists of four matrices that serve to gauge the efficiency impact of the various network strategies. The matrices illustrate the complex relationships between demand- and supply-side scale effects in clearing as well as the impact of these effects on transaction costs and industry efficiency. Additionally, the matrices take other industry-impacting dynamics into account, ultimately revealing that although some scenarios are cost efficient, they are not necessarily profit-maximising for all participants of the Value Provision Network. The analysis conducted in this chapter delivers preliminary findings that are then compared with case study findings in Chapter 8; this allows final conclusions to be drawn regarding the efficiency impact of various network strategies within the European clearing industry.

In the following, four different network strategies are analysed according to the framework introduced in Figure 7.2: cross-margining agreements, clearing links, mergers and acquisitions (M&A) and the creation of a single European CCP. In a first step (section 7.1), the Scale Impact Matrix analyses

---

[1] Coyne/Dye (1998), pp. 100–01.

CHAPTER		PURPOSE
7	WHAT THEORY REVEALS – FRAMEWORK FOR EFFICIENCY ANALYSIS OF NETWORK STRATEGIES	Establishes a framework to analyse the impact of network strategies on the efficiency of clearing.
7.1	Scale Impact Matrix	The Scale Impact Matrix analyses the magnitude of demand- and supply-side scale effects related to a particular network strategy.
7.2	Transaction Cost Impact Matrix and Efficiency Impact Matrix	The Transaction Cost Impact and Efficiency Impact Matrix analyse whether the scale effects translate into proportional efficiency gains or losses.
7.3	Business Model Impact Matrix	The Business Model Impact Matrix illustrates whether the efficiency increase (decrease) translates into a proportional or disproportional profit increase or decrease.
7.4	Preliminary Findings – Impact of Network Strategies on Efficiency	

Figure 7.1   Structure of Chapter 7

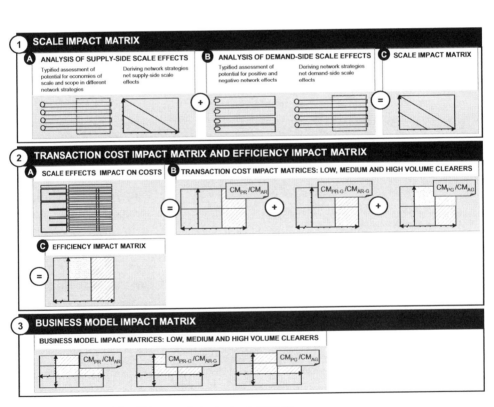

Figure 7.2   Framework for efficiency analysis of network strategies
Source: Author's own.

the magnitude of demand- and supply-side scale effects related to a particular network strategy. The Transaction Cost Impact Matrix and the Efficiency Impact Matrix analyse whether or not these demand- and supply-side scale effects translate into proportional or disproportional efficiency gains or losses for different clearing member types (section 7.2). The Business Model Impact Matrix illustrates whether the efficiency increase (decrease) corresponding to different network strategies translates into a proportional or disproportional profit increase or decrease for different clearing member types (section 7.3). Finally (section 7.4), the preliminary findings obtained from the matrices regarding the efficiency impact of the different network strategies are summarised.

Note that this theoretical assessment of the scale, transaction cost, efficiency and business model impacts is based on archetypes of the various network strategies. Utilising such a simplified and abstract theoretical setting makes it possible to obtain preliminary conclusions on the efficiency impact of these four network strategies. In reality, of course, the network strategies are often more complicated than the archetypes due to the particularities of the individual clearing houses and their members. As outlined in section 3.3, network strategies between clearing houses commonly combine the characteristics of several different archetypical set-ups. The efficiency impact of any real-world network strategy is thus influenced by additional factors that are beyond the scope of this chapter's analysis.[2]

To reflect the complexities associated with each network strategy as accurately as possible, the following analysis utilises the most complex structural set-up of each network strategy as defined in section 3.3.1. More concretely, the cross-margining analysis refers to the one-pot cross-margining approach, and the clearing link analysis assumes the Recognised CCP Model,[3] replicating the size of the Single CCP network. The mergers and acquisitions scenario assumes the full integration of the involved clearing systems, and the Single CCP scenario is modelled by assuming the merger of LCH.Clearnet, Eurex Clearing, CC&G and the clearing houses of OMX and MEFF.

---

[2] Chapter 8 complements the preliminary conclusions presented in this chapter with an assessment of the efficiency impact of different real-world network initiatives.

[3] Although the most complex functional link set-up is the Fully Integrated Systems link, this scenario is not analysed because it is thought to be subsumed by the mergers and acquisitions strategy. McPartland refers to the idea of interlinking various CCPs while each clearing house maintains a reciprocal clearing member status with the others as 'Open Architecture Clearing'. Cf. McPartland (2003a).

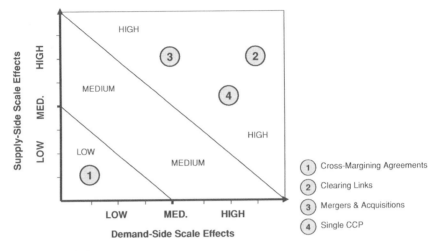

Figure 7.3   Scale Impact Matrix
Source: Author's own.

7.1 Scale Impact Matrix

The first step in the efficiency assessment of network strategies, the Scale Impact Matrix (SIM), serves to classify the demand- and supply-side scale effects of cross-margining agreements, clearing links, mergers and acquisitions, and the single European CCP model (see Figure 7.3). The matrix illustrates the supply-side versus demand-side scale effects inherent to the different network strategies. The vertical axis shows the typified impact of supply-side scale effects; the horizontal axis shows the typified impact of demand-side scale effects.

Identifying the potential magnitude of each network strategy's demand- and supply-side scale effects is important because economies of scale and scope – together with network effects – can impact direct and indirect transaction costs. The higher a network strategy's demand- and supply-side scale effects, the greater the potential to reduce clearing members' transaction costs. The Scale Impact Matrix thus furnishes input for the subsequent analysis of these costs in section 7.2.

The findings of the SIM suggest that clearing links can potentially exert the greatest scale effects. Whereas M&A strategies have higher supply-side and lower demand-side scale effects than the Single CCP scenario, the relative magnitude of their respective 'net' scale effects is comparable. Sections 7.1.1

NETWORK STRATEGY	COST IMPACT	SCALE INCREASE	SCOPE INCREASE	ECONOMIES OF SCALE	ECONOMIES OF SCOPE
(1) Cross-Margining Agreement	Short-Term Amortisation Period	VERY LOW	LOW	VERY LOW	LOW
(2) Clearing Link	Short- to Medium-Term Investment	MEDIUM TO HIGH	HIGH	MEDIUM TO HIGH	HIGH
(3) Mergers & Acquisitions	Long-Term Investment	HIGH	MEDIUM TO HIGH	HIGH	MEDIUM TO HIGH
(4) Single CCP	Very Long-Term Investment	VERY HIGH	HIGH	MEDIUM TO HIGH	MEDIUM TO HIGH

Figure 7.4   Typified assessment of the potential for economies of scale and scope in different network strategies
Source: Author's own.

and 7.1.2 explain how the position of each network strategy on the horizontal and vertical axes is derived.

7.1.1 Analysis of network strategies' supply-side scale effects

For the purpose of assessing the position of the network strategies on the vertical axis, the cost impact associated with each initiative is determined and compared to the potential scale and scope increase, resulting in a typified assessment of the potential for economies of scale and scope (Figure 7.4). Secondly, the 'net supply-side scale effect' of each initiative is derived (Figure 7.5), which is then transferred to the vertical axis of the Scale Impact Matrix (Figure 7.3).

Cross-margining agreements allow the partnering clearing houses jointly to margin certain products. Unless the effort leads to significant growth in the number of traded (and thus cleared) contracts, the clearing houses' scale is unlikely to increase considerably. Instead, cross-margining agreements enlarge the scope of services offered by the partnering clearing houses. Although these agreements can constitute an attractive service to clearing members, their scope impact is limited due to their restriction to a singular service. Cross-margining agreements can involve an increase in personnel costs due to the possible need for manual – and thus cumbersome – processing. On the other

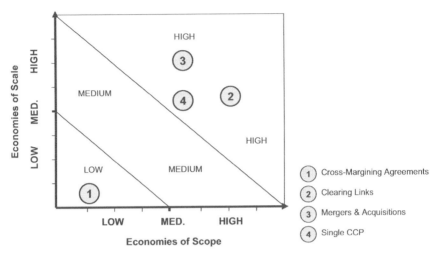

Figure 7.5   Deriving the network strategies' net supply-side scale effects
Source: Author's own.

hand, implementing the required IT solution is unlikely to involve significant long-term investments. Unless the agreement involves complex processing or structures, necessary changes and updates to the IT infrastructure can be expected to have a short-term amortisation period.

Clearing links connect clearing houses and thereby enlarge the scope of offered clearing opportunities. In terms of increasing the partnering clearing houses' scope, links can enable product-level or geographical diversification as well as the integration of new asset classes. In terms of scale enlargement, clearing links can permit existing clearing members to clear new products, new clearing members to clear existing products or new clearing members to clear new products. However, the potential for a true increase in scale is nonetheless limited. It is only when the link structure results in market growth that true scale increases can be realised. Otherwise, despite the fact that clearing members now have the opportunity to utilise their existing relationship to clear products that were previously unavailable at their home CCP, the contractual framework usually ensures that the benefits of the link are shared between the partnering clearing houses. Consequently, as any scale increase de facto occurs on the basis of operating two different clearing systems,[4] further costs incur, which reduces the potential for economies of scale.

---

[4] As outlined above, the scenario of 'Fully Integrated Systems' is subsumed under the M&A-type of network strategy.

To summarise, clearing links can increase the scale and scope of clearing houses, but the potential for scope enlargements is greater. Depending on the particular purpose and structure of the link, the set-up requires medium to strong functional, technical and legal harmonisation and integration. Additionally, as outlined in section 6.2.4, increases in scale and scope can have significant cost implications for the clearing houses. Because clearing links resemble strategic alliances or joint ventures, the necessary adjustments can be expected to entail short- to medium-term investments. This results in an assumed medium to high potential for the realisation of economies of scale (due to a medium to high potential for scale increases with little counteracting forces in terms of necessary investments) as well as an assumed high potential for the realisation of economies of scope (due to a high potential for scope enlargement with little counteracting forces in terms of necessary investments).

In contrast to M&A initiatives, clearing links benefit from the flexibility of their set-up and limited necessity for a strong, and thus complex, integration of structures. It is therefore easier for clearing houses to enlarge their scope of services through links than through **M&A initiatives**, whose counteracting forces in terms of necessary investments to realise scale and scope economies can be expected to be significantly higher. As mergers and acquisitions by definition require the full integration of both entities, high long-term investments are usually required. However, the integration of clearing houses also bears advantages, such as a significant boost in scale. To summarise, M&A initiatives are assumed to have a high potential for the realisation of economies of scale (due to a high potential for a scale increase with counteracting forces in terms of necessary long-term investments) and a medium to high potential for the realisation of economies of scope (due to a medium to high potential for scope enlargement with counteracting forces in terms of necessary long-term investments).

Finally, the strongest form of cooperation, i.e. the creation of a **Single CCP**, offers a high potential for increases in scale and scope, but also involves the most complex and costly integration processes. This initiative allows for significant increases in scale due to the combination of several clearing platforms.[5] Additionally, it offers opportunities for a scope enlargement through product-level and geographical diversification, as well as the possible integration of new asset classes. Whereas possible scale and scope increases can be assumed to be significant, they are counteracted by the significant long-term investments

---

[5] By definition, a Single CCP integrates more markets and clearing members than M&A activity.

necessary for fully integrating the clearing houses' value chains.[6] Additional complexities stemming from integration and coordination processes, possible duplication efforts and slow response times can translate into further costs. To realise scope economies, it is only economical to extend production to additional products if production factors are not already being fully exploited. Making use of unexploited production factors in an integration process this complex requires a very sophisticated allocation and redistribution of resources to minimise investments into technology changes and upgrades. Consequently, the creation of a Single CCP can be expected to have a medium to high potential for the realisation of economies of scale (due to a very high potential for a scale increase with significant counteracting forces in terms of necessary long-term investments and additional complexities in the organisation) and a medium to high potential for the realisation of economies of scope (due to a high potential for scope enlargement with significant counteracting forces in terms of necessary long-term investments).

7.1.2 Analysis of network strategies' demand-side scale effects

To assess the position of the network strategies on the horizontal axis of the Scale Impact Matrix, an analysis of the demand-side scale effects is conducted; this starts with a description of the initiatives' impacts on the CCP and GCM level network sizes (section 7.1.2.1). The second step provides an analysis of the network economic particularities of each network strategy (section 7.1.2.2). Thirdly, a typified assessment of the network strategies' potential for positive and/or negative network effects on the product and system layers is identified (section 7.1.2.3). Thereafter, the potential for the partnering CCPs to internalise GCM level network effects through the respective initiative is analysed. These analyses allow the 'net positive network effects' of the various network strategies to be derived; the results are then transferred to the horizontal axis of the SIM.

7.1.2.1 Impact on CCP and GCM level network sizes

As outlined in section 6.1, network strategies enable clearing houses and GCMs to enlarge the size of their network. When the partnering CCPs are interconnected, the network size resembles the aggregate number of their respective network members.[7]

---

[6] Refer to section 6.2.4 for the cost implications associated with integrating various market places and clearing systems.

[7] Cf. Katz/Shapiro (1985), pp. 424–5.

Apart from cross-margining agreements, the potential for an increase in the size of the **CCP level network** by means of clearing links, M&A and a Single CCP is theoretically equally great; but note that by definition, the aggregate network size of a Single CCP is greater than the network size resulting from M&A initiatives. Clearing links can replicate the size of a Single CCP network if the links are used to interconnect those clearing houses which are otherwise assumed to merge, constituting the Single CCP. Cross-margining agreements are limited in scope by virtue of focusing on a singular service and due to their low degree of technical and legal harmonisation and integration. These agreements therefore do not increase the size of the CCP level network, because they do not establish compatibility between the partners' clearing services. In cross-margining agreements, the size of each partnering CCP level network therefore remains limited to the size of each individual clearing network.

It is important to note that whether or not the network size is truly increased through network strategies depends on the counterparties; even if a particular GCM is a member of both partnering CCPs through its different local legal entities, the network size still increases when each legal entity provides clearing services to different counterparties.

Whereas the clearing link, M&A and Single CCP network strategies thus positively impact the size of the CCP level network, they have the opposite effect on the size of the **GCM level network**. These three strategies actually make it attractive for regionally-to-globally active clearing members to dis-intermediate their away markets' clearers. However, disintermediation might also be tempting for market participants that were previously NCMs at all of the partnering clearing houses, because depending on the type of network strategy, the clearing house network will potentially be able successfully to internalise GCM level network effects. Whereas this makes no difference to the CCP in terms of network size,[8] the clearers' network size can suffer a negative impact.

7.1.2.2 Network economic particularities

Section 6.1.2 briefly described the most important economic aspects of net-works and applied them to clearing on the CCP and GCM levels. The following provides an analysis of these network economic particularities for each net-work strategy. Network economic particularities can ultimately impact the potential success or failure of a certain initiative.

---

[8] There are of course other benefits and drawbacks from the CCP's perspective if an increasing number of counterparties become direct members.

With regard to enlarging the size of the CCP level network, all three strategies were shown to have equal potential. However, more significant differences between the various initiatives emerge when their network economic particularities are factored in.[9] The installed base (section 7.1.2.2.1) and starting problem (section 7.1.2.2.2) are analysed first, followed by an examination of lock-in (section 7.1.2.2.3); the section concludes with an investigation of the growth potential of clearing networks (section 7.1.2.2.4).

7.1.2.2.1 *Installed base*

Every established CCP level network has built an installed base[10] that influences the dynamics of competition and cooperation between clearing houses. When network strategies lead to compatibility between the partnering CCP networks, all providers are part of a single network, and there is no way for a firm to establish a lead in terms of its installed base.[11]

Generally, however, the weaker the network strategy in terms of technical and legal harmonisation and integration, the more leeway exists for clearing houses to establish a lead through benefiting from their installed base. Certain network strategies make all the products and marketplaces processed by the CCPs compatible or include all of the services provided by the clearing houses, but others might affect only particular products, markets or services. It is thus possible for a CCP to establish a lead in terms of its installed base in those products, markets or services that are not subject to the network strategy.

By definition, the Single CCP network model makes all of the products and markets processed by the partnering CCPs compatible and includes all of their services, thus eliminating the opportunity for any of the involved CCPs to establish a lead in the target economic area through its installed base. The same would not be true for an M&A initiative, however, because in this scenario competing clearing house networks still exist. These competing networks provide different services and process different products and marketplaces, and can thus establish a lead over the newly merged entity in terms of installed base.

In contrast to the M&A strategy, in which the newly merged entity faces competition from other clearing houses, the clearing link approach incorporates unique dynamics and fosters competition between the partnering clearing houses. A clearing link set-up usually neither makes all of the products and marketplaces processed by the partnering CCPs compatible nor includes

---

[9] As cross-margining agreements do not serve to enlarge the network size, their network economic implications are negligible and are not further analysed here.

[10] Cf. Dempsey (2006), pp. 163–8.   [11] Cf. Katz/Shapiro (1986b), p. 148.

all of the services provided by the clearing houses. One of the partners can thus establish a lead in terms of its installed base in those products, markets or services that are not subject to the link agreement.

7.1.2.2.2 Starting problem

Creating a lead in terms of installed base can, in turn, translate into a starting problem inherent to the network strategy. As outlined above, the weaker the network strategy is in terms of integration, the more leeway exists for the partnering clearing houses to establish a lead via their installed base, and the greater the associated starting problem. The Single CCP and M&A network strategies consequently do not entail starting problems. On the other hand, clearing links contain an inherent starting problem.

Links offer the following opportunities for different clearing member types: first of all, by permitting regionally-to-globally active clearers to leverage their existing relationship with their domestic home clearing house, links allow these clearers to disintermediate the GCMs they previously employed to clear the products and markets serviced by the away clearing house. Links further benefit regionally-to-globally active clearers that were previously not active in the away clearing house's products and markets. The link enables them to leverage their existing relationship with the home clearing house in terms of obtaining access to a broader range of products and markets.[12] Secondly, links offer opportunities for clearers that were previously members of all of the partnering CCPs. Clearing links could theoretically enable these globally active clearers to give up their multiple clearing relationships by routing all of their transactions through a single clearing house.

The starting problem becomes relevant for these types of clearer in different ways. Clearing members considering the disintermediation of their clearer by leveraging their existing relationship with the home clearing house will be hesitant to utilise the link, because it is unclear whether the utility derived from the link will outweigh the costs of disintermediation in the long run. As links usually do not cover the complete range of services provided or the markets and products cleared by the away clearing house, disintermediating the GCM level has limited appeal when these services, products and markets are important to the regionally-to-globally active clearer.[13]

---

[12] Note that it is assumed, by definition, that this type of clearing member is interested in being active in away markets and products.

[13] On the other hand, M&A initiatives and the creation of a Single CCP – which, by definition, make all of the products and markets processed by the CCPs compatible, and include all services provided by the clearing houses – increase the attractiveness of disintermediation, as the counterparties will not run

The attractiveness of disintermediation is further limited, because the GCM network benefits from its installed base. As outlined above, the value-added function – and thus the installed base – of the GCM level network is significant to its users. To successfully disintermediate the GCM level, the network strategy must thus enable the CCP level network successfully to internalise the GCM level network effects. Otherwise, the benefits stemming from the GCM network's installed base are likely to outweigh any advantages of disintermediation offered by the network strategy. The risk of disintermediation through clearing links is therefore minimal, unless the CCPs are able to convince their clearers to expect positive future network effects – implying that the clearing link will be extended in its scope, and that the clearing houses will compensate for the lost intermediary level by providing these services themselves, thereby successfully internalising second-level network effects. Only then can the utility derived from the CCP level network offset the costs of alternation in the long run, and the starting problem will be overcome.[14]

For regionally-to-globally active clearers that were previously not active in the away clearing house's products and markets, the starting problem stems from the necessity of investing in the link infrastructure[15] and the related dilemma of whether the utility derived from the link will outweigh the associated investments in the long run.

The starting problem also pertains to globally active clearing members that are direct members of all of the partnering clearing houses. Clearing links could theoretically offer them the opportunity to give up their multiple clearing relationships by routing all of their transactions through a single clearing house. In this case, the installed base of the partnering clearing houses plays a substantial role when clearers are deciding which CCP to choose as their sole clearing house. The starting problem will not be overcome unless the CCPs are able to convince their clearers to expect positive future network effects – implying that the clearing link will be extended in its scope, and that the clearing houses will make up for the lost participation in other CCP networks by providing a similar service level and processing all products and markets.

---

the risk of losing out on certain services, products or markets (apart from any additional value-added complementary clearing services provided by the GCM).

[14] Meaning that if disintermediation of the GCM level is attempted through network strategies, then the services offered, markets served and products cleared by the CCPs are to be seen in direct competition with services provided by the GCMs.

[15] As outlined above, clearing members with an agency focus are under greater pressure to adopt any new clearing house initiative (in this case being the link infrastructure) than are clearing members with a proprietary focus.

7.1.2.2.3 Lock-in

The installed base of a CCP or GCM can result in lock-in effects, which can adversely impact the dynamics of a network strategy and potentially stunt the future development of the clearing industry. Lock-in effects can be either weak or strong according to Liebowitz (2002):[16] whereas the weak form can be overcome by competitors introducing sufficiently better products to the market, the strong form implies first-mover-wins and winner-takes-all conditions. Only strong lock-ins lead to potential coordination problems by blocking the adoption of superior products, even though the superiority can overcome any self-compatibility issues for consumers.[17] Weak lock-ins, as outlined in the context of the installed base and starting problem, occur when the utility derived from the network initiative fails to offset the costs of alternation in the long run. The weak form implies that the key to success for providers is thus to create a product whose merits outweigh consumers' switching costs.[18]

It is therefore critical to examine whether any strong lock-in effects exist on the GCM or CCP level that could lead to potential coordination problems, implying first-mover-wins and winner-takes-all conditions. To this end, the following identifies areas on the CCP and GCM network levels that could potentially give rise to strong forms of lock-in. Whether the network effects are truly substantial enough to lead to strong lock-ins is then discussed to assess the likelihood of coordination problems.

On the GCM level, the size, interface, collateral management and complementary offering effects could potentially create an installed base that is substantial enough to result in strong lock-in, especially if the interconnection between the clearer and the NCM is very strong and not limited to provision of clearing services. Lock-in effects on the GCM level can counteract the internalisation of GCM level network effects and thus discourage disintermediation. Despite the fact that the value-added function and GCM level network effects are important to the respective network participants, it can be assumed that scenarios exist in which the CCP network is able to offer services that are sufficiently better from the NCMs' perspective,[19] so that their switching costs

---

[16] Cf. Liebowitz (2002), pp. 31–6. Liebowitz identifies two types of cost associated with lock-ins: the costs of being compatible with one's self (meaning that the new product or solution is largely compatible with the old product or solution) and the costs of possibly losing compatibility with others.

[17] Cf. Liebowitz (2002), p. 32.   [18] Cf. Liebowitz (2002), p. 37.

[19] When clearing houses successfully manage to strengthen their unique CCP level network effects and largely internalise the GCM level network effects, it becomes attractive for regionally-to-globally active clearers to consider disintermediating the GCM level.

can be overcome. To summarise, GCM level network effects appear unlikely to give rise to strong forms of lock-in.

On the CCP level, strong lock-in effects might occur on the product layer due to the open interest effect. Strong lock-ins could impact the competitive dynamics between the partnering clearing houses as well as the dynamics between the network created through the particular initiative and the remaining CCPs active in a defined economic area. Such effects on the clearing house level could influence the success or failure of a network strategy and potentially shape future industry development.

A particular situation resembling strong lock-in arises when products available within a CCP network are not fungible with the products of another – provided that the two clearing house networks hold open interest in identical products. This means that previously established open sell or purchase positions in one network cannot be offset via appropriate opposite transactions in another network. Despite its important repercussion of effectively locking the counterparties into a particular CCP network, the situation should not be confused with the strong lock-in effect. It is not a coordination failure among users that prevents clearers from actually switching, but the legal restrictions established by the exchanges and clearing houses. Additionally, it is important to understand that even despite a lack of fungibility, network participants are only weakly, not strongly, locked into a specific clearing house network. If network participants consider the products of one CCP network to be superior to the corresponding products of another CCP network, they are free to close-out all of their positions in the inferior network and open new positions in the superior network, thereby switching from the inferior to the superior CCP network. It is unlikely, though, that the decision to switch CCP networks is entirely based on clearing-house-related considerations; exchange-related dynamics (such as deeper liquidity, etc.) probably play a larger role.

In this context, the opportunity for a choice of clearing location is a vital factor. If clearing house networks allow users to choose their clearing location by introducing a clearing link initiative,[20] the decision to change networks could in fact be based on purely clearing-house-related considerations. If no choice of clearing location is offered, network participants are locked into a particular clearing network.[21] However, again, this situation should not be confused with strong lock-in. It is not a coordination failure among users

---

[20] By definition, choice of clearing location cannot be offered by M&A or Single CCP initiatives, as these ultimately fully integrate different clearing systems into a single system.

[21] Note that clearing houses alone cannot offer choice of clearing location. Rather, in a first instance, the respective exchanges must give allowance to the use of various clearing houses.

that prevents clearers from actually switching to the superior network, but the legal restrictions established by the exchanges or clearing houses that prohibit the choice of clearing location. Therefore, to eradicate non-network-effect-related coordination problems on the CCP level, the provision of choice of clearing location helps to prevent this particular scenario.

To summarise, provided that opportunities for choice of clearing location exist through clearing links, it appears unlikely that CCP level network effects will lead to strong forms of lock-in. If strong lock-in effects do not exist on the GCM and CCP levels, first-mover-wins and winner-takes-all conditions are consequently also unlikely to exist.

7.1.2.2.4 Growth potential

Finally, if a winner-takes-all scenario is unlikely to exist, the next relevant issue to consider is the growth potential of a clearing network that has resulted from a given network strategy. This also has an impact on the future development of the clearing industry. Whether the new CCP network has arisen from a clearing link, M&A or Single CCP initiative, it can be further enlarged by additional network initiatives.[22] The possibilities for growing the size of the CCP network through additional network initiatives are therefore examined. As outlined above, the services provided as well as the products and markets processed by different clearing houses are not identical, and due to their installed bases, they are not necessarily interchangeable. This is especially true for clearing houses operating in different regulatory environments, as is the case in Europe.

Clearing houses can be assumed to have a natural interest in leveraging their installed base. Although there is no starting problem inherent to clearing networks resulting from M&A and Single CCP initiatives, they are likely to encounter problems when attempting to expand their network to include additional CCPs.[23] In contrast, while clearing links can encounter starting problems, the linked networks are more likely to attract additional CCPs. This is because clearing links offer the partnering clearing houses the opportunity to enlarge the size of their networks, thus strengthening their unique CCP level network effects. Additionally, clearing links give the partnering CCPs leeway

---

[22] Growing the size of a CCP network is of course also achieved through market growth, i.e. counterparties who were previously not at all active in the markets processed by the CCP network can decide to utilise the network. Whether or not a particular network strategy serves to stimulate market growth is not analysed in this context.

[23] Note that, by definition, Single CCP initiatives unify all clearing houses within a defined economic region; consequently, if a Single CCP network were to consider enlarging its size, this would imply partnering with clearing houses outside of the defined economic region.

NETWORK EFFECTS	CROSS-MARGINING AGREEMENTS	CLEARING LINKS	M&A	SINGLE CCP	INFLUENCING FACTORS
Netting Effect	0	+++	++	+++	Depends on potential size of network
Size Effect	0	+++	++	+++	Depends on potential size of network
Cross-Margining Effect	+++	+++	++	+++	Depends on potential size of network
Open Interest Effect	0	+	++	+++	Depends on level of integration
Collateral Management Effect	0	+	++	+++	Depends on level of integration
Interface Effect	0	+++	++	+	Depends on growth potential
Complementary Offering Effect	0	+++	++	+	Depends on integration complexity
Information Effect	0	++	++	++	Depends on equality of trustworthiness
Learning Effect	0	+	++	+++	Depends on level of integration
Systemic Risk Effect	0	0	++	+++	Depends on size of integrated market
Performance Effect	0	0	++	+++	Depends on size of integrated market
Monopolistic Behaviour Effect	0	0	++	+++	Depends on size of integrated market

Figure 7.6   Typified assessment of network strategies' potential for positive and negative CCP level network effects
Source: Author's own.

to benefit from and further leverage their installed bases. For clearing houses with a significant installed base, enlarging the size of their CCP network through clearing links thus appears to be a more attractive strategy when compared to M&A or Single CCP initiatives. This should be particularly true in Europe, where clearing houses' services and processes have been tailored to the specific demands of regional market particularities and different regulatory environments.

7.1.2.3 Potential for network effects

An increasing network size can give rise to positive and negative network effects. The third step in assessing the position of the various network strategies on the horizontal axis of the Scale Impact Matrix is therefore to identify the potential to realise positive and/or negative CCP level network effects on the product and system layers (see Figure 7.6).[24]

---

[24] The assessment provided in Figure 7.6 refers to the theoretical assessment of potential network effects. As outlined above, such an assessment is, in reality, highly dependent on the concrete set-up and structure of a particular network initiative.

Cross-margining agreements translate into a positive network effect on the product layer of the CCP network and do not give rise to any negative network effects. Cross-margining agreements can be stand-alone initiatives or they can be part of other network strategies. The potential to realise cross-margining effects through other network strategies than cross-margining agreements is thus equally great. Because it is possible to replicate the network size of a Single CCP through a link structure, and enter into cross-margining agreements with all clearing houses that would otherwise be part of the Single CCP, these positive network effects can be just as substantial in the context of clearing links and a Single CCP initiative. By definition, the size of a clearing network created through an M&A initiative is smaller than one originating from the Single CCP approach. Size-related network effects are thus greater for clearing link and Single CCP initiatives.

The size and netting effects arising from Single CCP or clearing link initiatives are consequently also stronger than those generated by M&A initiatives. On the other hand, the magnitude of the open interest effect, the collateral management effect and the learning effect depend on the level of technical and legal integration and harmonisation between the partnering clearing houses. These effects are thus expected to be weakest for clearing links and strongest in the case of a Single CCP.

The opposite is true for the interface effect, whose magnitude depends on the growth potential of a CCP network; it is consequently strongest for clearing link initiatives and weakest for a Single CCP network. As the complementary offering effect depends on the complexity of integrating and implementing the network strategy,[25] its potential impact is greatest for weak forms of cooperation (clearing links). Finally, the information effect is assumed to be of equal magnitude for any network initiative, provided that the partnering clearing houses are equally trustworthy.

The stronger the level of technical and legal integration through the network initiatives, the greater the likelihood is that negative network effects will emerge on the product and system layers. Consequently, due to the decentralised structure of a clearing link network, negative network effects counteracting the positive network effect are unlikely to materialise. On the other hand, depending on the size of the combined entities and integrated markets arising from M&A initiatives, the greater the likelihood of negative

---

[25] This is assumed because the higher the complexity of integration and the necessary long-term investments, the less leeway is available for introducing additional complementary clearing services, because doing so would call for additional resources.

network effects. Single CCP initiatives are thus most likely to give rise to negative network effects.

7.1.2.4 Potential to internalise GCM level network effects

As outlined in section 6.1, a CCP's motivation to engage in network strategies should theoretically be driven by two objectives: first, to internalise the GCM level network effects, and second, to strengthen their unique CCP-related network effects. The fourth step in assessing the position of the network strategies on the horizontal axis of the Scale Impact Matrix is therefore to gauge the potential for the partnering CCPs to internalise GCM level network effects through different network strategies.

The potential for internalising the positive GCM level network effects (leaving aside the complementary offering effect) is equally high for clearing link and Single CCP strategies – under the assumption that the link initiative combines all of those CCP networks that would otherwise have been merged into the Single CCP. A clearing link initiative can replicate the size of a Single CCP network, furnish high growth potential, as outlined above, and is unlikely to give rise to negative network effects. In terms of internalising the complementary offering effect of the GCM level, this endeavour is more difficult to realise, because it partially requires clearing houses to provide services that are remote from their core competencies. This would require additional resources, which are less likely to be available when network strategies requiring a high level of technical and legal harmonisation and integration are employed, such as M&A and Single CCP initiatives. Clearing houses engaging in link initiatives will thus have more leeway for utilising resources to enlarge the scope of their complementary clearing services.

Although CCPs could theoretically internalise banking-related services in a cost-efficient manner, such as the provision of credit lines (e.g. by cooperating with financial service providers), clearing houses do not in fact seem bent on replicating the entire scope of complementary clearing services currently provided by GCMs. Replicating the entire scope of the GCMs' complementary clearing services cannot only have an impact on the regulatory status of a CCP (which would then likely be subject to banking supervision), but could also induce potential contagion effects of risk if infrastructure activities are not kept separate from banking services. Consequently, the final scope of complementary clearing services provided by CCP networks ultimately depends on their individual cost-benefit analyses.

Generally, the higher the potential for internalising GCM level network effects, the more incentive regionally-to-globally active clearers have to

NETWORK STRATEGY	NETWORK ECONOMIC PARTICULARITIES	POSITIVE NETWORK EFFECTS	NEGATIVE NETWORK EFFECTS	POTENTIAL TO INTERNALISE 2ND LEVEL NETWORK EFFECTS	NET POSITIVE NETWORK EFFECT
(1) Cross-Margining Agreements	NONE	VERY LOW	NONE	NONE	VERY LOW
(2) Clearing Links	(i) Installed base of CCPs fosters competition between linked CCPs and others (ii) Starting problem inherent to links (iii) High potential to attract additional CCPs to join network	HIGH TO VERY HIGH	NONE	HIGH TO VERY HIGH	HIGH TO VERY HIGH
(3) Mergers & Acquisitions	(i) Installed base of CCPs fosters competition between merged entity and others (ii) No starting problem (iii) Limited potential to attract additional CCPs to join network	MEDIUM TO HIGH	HIGH	MEDIUM	MEDIUM
(4) Single CCP	(i) Within defined economic area, CCPs have no opportunity to establish a lead in terms of their installed base (ii) No starting problem (iii) Limited potential to attract additional CCPs to join network	VERY HIGH	VERY HIGH	HIGH	HIGH

Figure 7.7   Deriving the network strategies' net demand-side scale effect
Source: Author's own.

disintermediate the GCM level. Given that the internalisation of the entire range of GCM level network effects is very difficult to realise, the value-added function of the GCM level will probably endure, despite the disintermediation tendencies spurred by network initiatives. This is because, for some counterparties, it will certainly be more cost efficient to continue to receive a variety of different services from a single clearing intermediary. In the context of clearing link or Single CCP initiatives, disintermediation will therefore make most sense for counterparties that neither rely on a strong mutual (and perhaps symbiotic) relationship with their clearer nor rely on a broad range of complementary clearing services (particularly banking-related services).

7.1.2.5 Net positive network effects

The findings of sections 7.1.2.1 to 7.1.2.4 ultimately allow for an assessment of the 'net positive network effects', as illustrated in Figure 7.7. The net positive network effects are then utilised to determine the position of each network strategy on the horizontal axis of the Scale Impact Matrix (refer to Figure 7.3).

7.2 Transaction Cost Impact Matrix and Efficiency Impact Matrix

Transaction costs can be reduced through network strategies; however, the Scale Impact Matrix revealed that the different network strategies vary in their potential to promote network effects and economies of scale and scope. The Transaction Cost Impact Matrix and the Efficiency Impact Matrix analyse whether or not these demand- and supply-side scale effects translate into proportional efficiency gains or losses for different clearing member types.

The Transaction Cost Impact Matrix (TCIM) serves to analyse the impact that network strategies can have on clearing members' direct and indirect transaction costs. As defined previously, the economic entity relevant for the cost analysis in the context of this study is the clearing member. Consequently, for the purpose of this analysis, six clearing member types as defined in section 2.3.2 are distinguished:

- CM_{PR} (prop. focus, regionally active);
- CM_{AR} (agency focus, regionally active);
- CM_{PR-G} (prop. focus, regionally-to-globally active);
- CM_{AR-G} (agency focus, regionally-to-globally active);
- CM_{PG} (prop. focus, globally active); and
- CM_{AG} (agency focus, globally active).

These six clearing member types are then grouped according to geographical activity, resulting in three customer groups: CM_{PR}/CM_{AR} (regionally active), CM_{PR-G}/CM_{AR-G} (regionally-to-globally active) and CM_{PG}/CM_{AG} (globally active). Whether high demand- and supply-side scale effects can be transformed into an equally positive transaction cost impact for each group is determined in the following. These analyses ultimately reveal the potential of each network strategy to increase efficiency (Efficiency Impact Matrix).

7.2.1 Transaction Cost Impact Matrix (TCIM)

Figure 7.8 summarises the potential impact of demand- and supply-side scale effects on the various transaction cost categories. The findings then serve as input for elaborating a Transaction Cost Impact Matrix for each of the three clearing member groups specified above (sections 7.2.1.1 to 7.2.1.3).

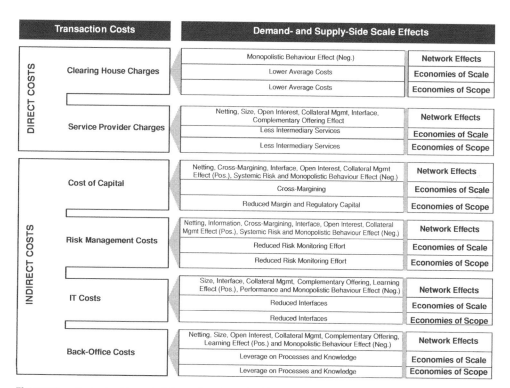

Figure 7.8   Systemised impact of demand- and supply-side scale effects on transaction costs
Source: Author's own.

As outlined in section 6.1.1, **network effects** can impact direct and indirect transaction costs. Positive network effects on the product and system layers serve to reduce transaction costs as follows. The netting effect can reduce charges by intermediaries as well as lower cost of capital, risk management and back-office costs. The size effect entails a possible reduction of charges by intermediaries as well as lowered IT and back-office costs, whereas the cross-margining effect can help to reduce cost of capital and risk management costs. The open interest and collateral management effects can both positively impact intermediary charges, risk management costs, cost of capital and back-office costs. The latter effect can even lead to reduced IT costs.

On the system layer, the interface effect serves to minimise IT costs and intermediary charges, but also creates opportunities for additional cross-margining, thus minimising risk management costs and cost of capital. Risk management costs are further whittled down by the information effect. Complementary clearing service offerings can positively impact IT and back-office costs as well as intermediary charges. Finally, the learning effect serves to trim back-office and IT costs. If negative network effects occur on the product or system layer, transaction costs may climb. The systemic risk effect on the product layer can lead to increased risk-management costs and cost of capital, whereas the performance effect on the system layer eventually boosts IT costs. Finally, the monopolistic behaviour effect can result in excessive clearing house charges and translate into increased cost of capital, risk management costs, IT and back-office costs.

As outlined above, clearing houses can benefit from **economies of scale** by engaging in network strategies. This can lead to a higher number of contracts cleared and thus lower average costs. If the clearing house decides to translate these savings into reduced clearing house charges, clearing members will enjoy lowered transaction costs. However, even if the clearing house does not pass on the savings via a reduction of fees, clearers can nevertheless benefit from the CCP's enlarged scale by requiring fewer intermediary services. Furthermore, if the clearing house allows cross-margining and netting of cleared transactions, cost of capital and risk management costs can be lowered.[26] Depending on the type of network strategy employed, clearers can profit from consolidated interfaces and reduced risk monitoring effort by leveraging their IT infrastructure, back-office processes and knowledge.

Finally, **economies of scope** can positively impact transaction costs. Clearing members benefit from product level as well as geographical diversification, the integration of asset classes or an increase in the number of complementary clearing services offered by the CCP; these measures serve to reduce the intermediary services required, thus lowering the associated costs. Furthermore, economies of scope can help to diminish indirect costs if the clearing house allows cross-margining and netting of all products and asset classes. To the extent that supervisors recognise these offsets, regulatory capital requirements may also be lower. Moreover, reduced risk monitoring efforts cut risk management costs, IT costs can be reduced through streamlining the number of interfaces and clearers can leverage their back-office processes and knowledge.

This systematisation of the impact that demand- and supply-side scale effects can have on transaction costs is utilised to determine the theoretical impact that different network strategies can in turn have on the direct and indirect costs of different clearing member types. For the purpose of this analysis, it is assumed that a clearing member with a prop. focus covers exactly the same markets and products as a clearing member with an agency focus.

---

[26] Cf. Van Cauwenberge (2003), p. 94.

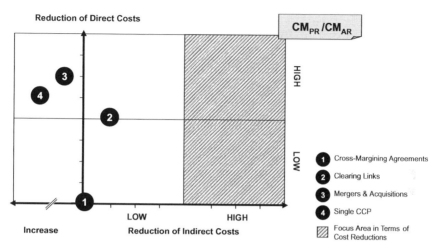

Figure 7.9   Transaction Cost Impact Matrix for regionally active clearing members
Source: Author's own.

Three Transaction Cost Impact Matrices (TCIMs) are thus required for the analysis. One matrix illustrates the potential for cost reductions of regionally active clearing members with a prop. or agency focus (CM_{PR}/CM_{AR}); a second matrix shows this potential for regionally-to-globally active clearers with a prop. or agency focus (CM_{PR-G}/CM_{AR-G}); and a third matrix considers the potential for cost reductions for globally active clearing members with a prop. or agency focus (CM_{PG}/CM_{AG}).

As outlined in Chapter 5, the clearing members' focus area in terms of cost reduction depends on the scale of their business as well as their business perspective. For low and medium volume clearers, the core cost driver is indirect costs. Significant P&L effects can thus only be realised through reductions in indirect costs. The same applies to high volume clearers with an agency perspective; their profit margin can only be raised through reductions in indirect costs. On the other hand, high volume clearers with a prop. perspective strive to reduce direct costs. The hatched area in the Transaction Cost Matrices highlights the focus area of each clearing member type accordingly.

7.2.1.1 TCIM for regionally active clearing members

Figure 7.9 exhibits the Transaction Cost Impact Matrix for regionally active clearing members. It illustrates that for these clearing members, network strategies between their domestic home clearing house and away markets' clearing houses do not have a significantly positive impact in terms of cost reductions.[27] Furthermore, it suggests that high scale effects do not necessarily translate into equally positive savings, as indirect costs can increase through M&A and Single CCP initiatives for this type of clearer.

By definition, a regionally focused clearing member is not active and is assumed to be uninterested in pursuing future activity[28] in the away clearing houses' products and markets. As outlined above, regionally active clearing members benefit most from initiatives that help to reduce indirect costs. However, scale and scope effects positively impact indirect costs only for clearing members that are active in and have a demand for the additional products and markets or for the additional scope offered through a network strategy. As defined, a regionally active clearing member does not have a demand for such a scale or scope enlargement – its indirect costs are therefore not positively impacted.[29]

For similar reasons, regionally active clearing members only benefit from network strategies' demand-side scale effects to the extent that these strengthen the unique CCP-related network effects of their domestic home CCP and they do not involve benefits associated with the away clearing houses' products or markets. In other words, these clearers benefit from network strategies that strengthen the netting, complementary offering, information and learning effects of their home CCP.[30] Whereas clearing links serve this purpose and thus translate into minimal reductions of indirect costs, the equally low positive impact of M&A and Single CCP initiatives is further diminished by negative network effects, which translate into additional costs. M&A and Single CCP initiatives can even cause an increase in indirect costs for regionally active clearers.

These two initiatives give clearing members no choice regarding participation; participation is obligatory. Clearers must thus potentially bear investments that are not outweighed by indirect cost savings. The magnitude of the

---

[27] Clearing members of course benefit from reductions in direct costs, but their positive impact is limited because the core cost driver for this type of clearer is indirect costs.

[28] This analysis does not cover the situation in which the clearing member is actually interested in away markets, but has historically limited itself to regional activity due to the costs associated with becoming and maintaining a clearing membership abroad – and for reasons of confidentiality, has not been willing to employ intermediary services.

[29] Note that, in reality, network strategies between clearing houses can of course involve two regional clearing houses active in different products or markets, with, for example, one clearing house offering clearing services for derivatives and the partnering CCP offering clearing services for equities. A regionally active clearing member could, in this case, be assumed to have an interest in and benefit from such a scope enlargement through a network initiative. However, as the focus of this study is on clearing houses cooperating cross-regionally, this scenario is not covered.

[30] The internalisation of GCM level network effects is, by definition, not of interest for this clearing member type unless doing so would serve to strengthen the named network effects.

increase in indirect costs ultimately depends on the structure and implementation of the network strategy. If the implementation of an M&A initiative results in the survival of the clearing system used by the away clearing house, or if the creation of a Single CCP is realised through the introduction of a completely new clearing system, the regionally active clearer has to bear the costs for implementing and adapting to the new system change, acquisition of knowledge, etc.[31] Apart from the potential improvements in service levels and speed related to a new clearing system, these costs are unlikely to be offset by cost savings.

Clearing links, on the other hand, do not imply additional indirect costs, because participation is optional in this network strategy. In terms of direct cost reductions, clearing links have a limited potential to stimulate reductions in fees charged by the home clearing house for existing products. The clearing members' direct costs are positively impacted only if their domestic home CCP translates the supply-side scale effects realised through a link initiative into reduced clearing house charges. A reduction in clearing house charges for existing products is more likely to eventuate through M&A and Single CCP approaches; in the case of Single CCP initiatives, however, this likelihood is possibly counteracted by the danger of the clearing house implementing monopoly prices.

7.2.1.2 TCIM for regionally-to-globally active clearing members

Regionally-to-globally active clearers are defined to be active (or interested in becoming active) in all of the partnering clearing houses' markets. At the same time, they do not self-clear all of these markets, but instead maintain a single direct clearing relationship, which is with their domestic home clearing house, while acting as NCMs in other (foreign) markets. Regionally-to-globally active clearers thus benefit from network strategies enabling them to clear many markets through their domestic home clearing house, because they can then disintermediate the clearer(s) they employ to access other markets.

The findings of Chapter 5 reveal that the greatest P&L impact for this type of clearing member is delivered by initiatives that help to reduce indirect costs (see Figure 7.10). All scale, scope and network benefits associated with a particular network strategy are thus relevant, as they can translate into

---

[31] In reality, it could be argued that the investment costs related to a Single CCP initiative that clearing members have to bear can be, but do not have to be, greater than the investment costs associated with an M&A initiative. For the purpose of this analysis, they are assumed to be greater, though, because the likelihood that the regionally active clearer loses out is greater in the case of a Single CCP initiative, i.e. in terms of employing the clearing system that is not the surviving system.

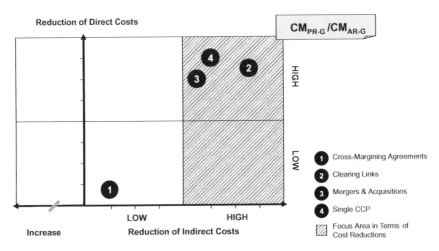

Figure 7.10   Transaction Cost Impact Matrix for regionally-to-globally active clearing members
Source: Author's own.

reduced indirect costs. Whereas cross-margining agreements have very low to low supply-side scale effects, their very low positive network effect might serve to lower cost of capital and risk management costs.

As outlined in section 7.1, clearing links entail medium to high economies of scale, high economies of scope and high to very high network effects. M&A initiatives meanwhile involve high economies of scale, medium to high economies of scope and medium network effects. Finally, a Single CCP initiative implies medium to high economies of scale and scope as well as high network effects. On the other hand, the cost reduction potential of these network strategies is counteracted by investments arising from the potential necessity to implement and adapt to a new system, acquire knowledge, etc. These investments reduce the magnitude of indirect cost reductions depending on the concrete structure of each network strategy. Whereas a link set-up is assumed to necessitate a short-term investment, M&A and Single CCP initiatives are assumed to require medium-term and long-term investments, respectively.[32]

---

[32] This is due to the assumption that clearing members can continue to utilise their established connection to the clearing system of their home clearing house in the case of a clearing link, but most likely need to invest in necessary system upgrades and changes in order to integrate the link set-up into their in-house systems. As outlined above, investment costs related to a Single CCP are assumed to be greater than investments generated by an M&A initiative, because the likelihood that the clearing member will lose out is greater in the case of a Single CCP initiative.

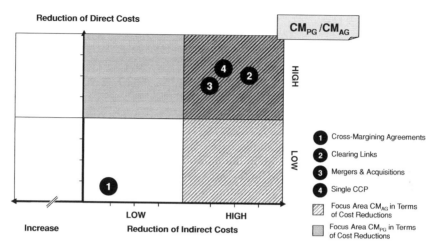

Figure 7.11   Transaction Cost Impact Matrix for globally active clearing members
Source: Author's own.

Although regionally-to-globally active clearers benefit most from indirect cost reductions in terms of P&L, they also benefit from direct cost reductions. With regard to clearing house charges, clearing links have a limited potential to reduce these costs; the Single CCP strategy has a greater potential to do so, but the greatest positive impact can be expected to result from M&A strategies. More significant reductions of direct costs are possible by means of disintermediation. Clearing members benefit from reductions of intermediary charges through economies of scale, scope and network effects. These effects are equally great for clearing links and Single CCP initiatives, but significantly smaller for M&A initiatives.[33] If the impact of demand- and supply-side scale effects on direct costs is taken into account, the Single CCP ends up having the strongest potential for cost reductions, followed by clearing links and then M&A initiatives.

7.2.1.3 TCIM for globally active clearing members

Finally, Figure 7.11 outlines the Transaction Cost Impact Matrix for globally active clearing members. Globally active clearers are defined as being active in all major markets, with direct access to each of the many CCPs. The globally active clearer holds a direct clearing membership with all of the major clearing

---

[33] Also note that the magnitude of these savings is greater for regionally-to-globally active clearing members than for regionally active clearers, due to the larger scope of their business – necessitating the involvement of a greater number of intermediaries.

houses. As these clearers are direct members of all of the partnering clearing houses, their main benefit from network strategies comes from being able to consolidate their various clearing relationships, i.e. centralise these into a single relationship between one legal entity and one clearing house.

Globally active clearing members therefore benefit from all demand- and supply-side scale effects, which can in turn translate into direct and indirect cost reductions. However, business perspective (prop. or agency) also plays a significant role in analysing the cost impact for this clearing member type. Whereas a globally active clearer with an agency focus can realise significant improvements in its profit margin through reducing indirect costs, a globally active clearing member with a prop. perspective benefits most from direct cost reductions.[34]

Cross-margining agreements have a similar impact on the cost reduction potential of globally active clearers and regionally-to-globally active clearing members, but the impact on direct and indirect costs arising from the other network strategies differs as follows. Direct cost reductions can result from economies of scale and scope as well as network effects. Clearing link, M&A and Single CCP initiatives enable clearers to reduce fixed infrastructure fees and thus clearing house charges.[35]

To the extent that clearing houses translate supply-side scale effects into fee reductions, clearing members naturally also benefit from these cost reductions, but the magnitude of potential reductions of intermediary charges is smaller.[36] Therefore, the various network strategies have the same relative degree of impact on direct costs for globally active clearers, but with a slightly smaller magnitude when compared with regionally-to-globally active clearers. This means that the Single CCP initiative possesses the strongest cost-reduction potential, followed by clearing links and M&A initiatives.

On the other hand, in terms of the potential for indirect cost reductions, globally active clearers enjoy a greater magnitude of cost reductions from M&A and Single CCP initiatives than regionally-to-globally active clearing members.[37] The reason for this is that globally active clearers do not have

---

[34] Refer to Chapter 5 for details.

[35] The magnitude of these savings is greater for globally active, i.e. high volume, clearing members, because due to the scale of their business, they require a greater number of communication lines than medium volume clearing members.

[36] The magnitude of these savings is assumed to be smaller for globally active clearing members than for regionally-to-globally active clearers, because they (by definition) do not involve other clearers as intermediaries.

[37] The impact of clearing links on the magnitude of potential cost reductions is similar for both clearing member types, because clearing links are assumed generally to require only short-term investments.

to bear investment costs no matter which clearing house's system survives, because they are already members of all clearing houses by definition. They must only bear investment costs if a network strategy requires the implementation of a completely new clearing system.

7.2.2 Efficiency Impact Matrix

The central criterion for determining the efficiency of clearing is operational efficiency, which is influenced by transaction costs. To increase the efficiency of the clearing industry, it is necessary to minimise clearing members' transaction costs. The efficiency of clearing is thus increased when the transaction costs that clearing members have to bear are reduced (and vice versa). The preceding analyses of the Scale Impact Matrix and Transaction Cost Impact Matrices pave the way for more general conclusions on efficiency.

Whereas the Transaction Cost Impact Matrices serve to illustrate the different network strategies' potential for minimising the transaction costs of different clearing member types, the Efficiency Impact Matrix consolidates the results and allows for conclusions on the overall efficiency impact of cross-margining agreements, clearing links, M&A and Single CCP initiatives.

Figure 7.12 exhibits the Efficiency Impact Matrix, which is derived from consolidating the previously established Transaction Cost Matrices into a single graph. The graph provides an easy-to-understand overview of the overall efficiency impact of different network strategies.

The Efficiency Impact Matrix shows that besides cross-margining agreements, which generally exhibit little or no potential for increasing efficiency, clearing links are the only network strategy that results in efficiency gains for all clearing member types. Whereas regionally active clearers can potentially benefit from medium direct cost reductions and very low indirect cost reductions, regionally-to-globally active clearers with a prop. or an agency focus, as well as globally active clearing members with an agency perspective, can benefit greatly from clearing links. M&A and Single CCP initiatives, on the other hand, do not translate into efficiency gains for all clearing member types. Regionally active clearers potentially suffer from efficiency losses when either of these two initiatives is employed.

Whereas a Single CCP initiative is likely to entail the most significant efficiency losses for regionally active clearers, the opposite is true for globally active clearing members with a prop. focus. Single CCP initiatives have the highest efficiency impact for this latter type of clearer, because they harbour the greatest potential for reducing direct costs (which constitute these clearers'

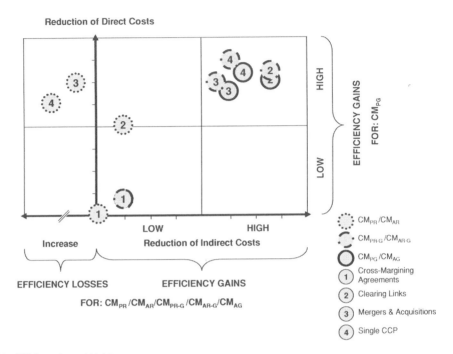

Figure 7.12   Efficiency Impact Matrix
Source: Author's own.

focus area in terms of cost reductions) followed by clearing links and then M&A strategies.

7.3 Business Model Impact Matrix (BMIM)

The previous matrices served to illustrate the complex relationships between demand- and supply-side scale effects in clearing as well as their impact on the transaction costs of different clearing member types and industry efficiency. The Business Model Impact Matrix (BMIM), on the other hand, takes into account additional dynamics impacting the development of the clearing industry.

This matrix illustrates whether the efficiency increase (decrease) corresponding to different network strategies translates into a proportional or disproportional profit increase or decrease for different clearing member types. It thus serves to analyse which network strategies are not only cost efficient, but also profit-maximising for all clearing member types. Consequently, whereas

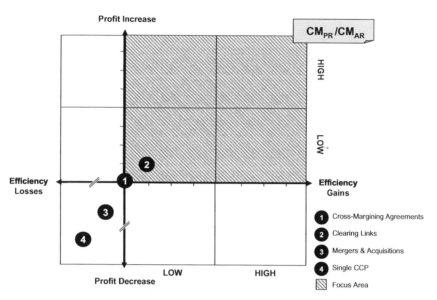

Figure 7.13   Business Model Impact Matrix for regionally active clearing members
Source: Author's own.

the Transaction Cost Impact and Efficiency Impact Matrices delivered insight into the impact of network strategies on clearing members' costs, the Business Model Impact Matrix examines the revenue side and the implications of network strategies on the clearers' respective business models.[38] To achieve this purpose, a matrix is established for each of the three clearing member groups (sections 7.3.1 to 7.3.3).

The horizontal axis replicates the findings from the Efficiency Impact Matrix. Meanwhile, the vertical axis indicates whether a certain network strategy results in a profit increase or decrease for different clearing member types. The hatched area in the BMIM highlights the focus area and indicates a positive impact on the respective clearing member type's business model.

7.3.1 BMIM for regionally active clearing members

Figure 7.13 illustrates the Business Model Impact Matrix for regionally active clearing members. It shows that for prop.- and agency-focused clearers,

---

[38] For clearing members with an agency focus, their business model is to generate profits from clearing their customers' business. The business model of clearing members with a proprietary focus is defined as being efficient to self-clear.

cross-margining initiatives have both a neutral efficiency impact and a neutral profit impact. They consequently neither benefit nor harm the clearer's business model.

Whereas clearing link initiatives lead to slight efficiency gains, and thus enable a low profit increase, the opposite is true for M&A and Single CCP initiatives. Both initiatives actually lead to efficiency losses for regionally active clearers and entail a proportional profit decrease. As the revenues of regionally active clearers remain unaffected by any network strategy,[39] cost decreases or increases translate into proportional profit increases or decreases.

M&A and Single CCP initiatives, with a potentially significantly negative impact on the clearer's business model, could ultimately put this type of clearer out of business. In terms of providing attractive services for agency business, low volume clearers already suffer competitive disadvantages when compared with higher volume clearers,[40] without their domestic home clearing house engaging in network strategies.[41] Regionally active clearers are further disadvantaged when their CCP enters into either an M&A or Single CCP initiative, because while both network strategies enable medium and high volume clearers to increase their efficiency, the internal efficiency of regionally focused clearers is at the same time further decreased. In terms of the clearer's prop. business, self-clearing might become inefficient and too costly for regionally active clearers as a result of an M&A or Single CCP initiative. This could result in the outsourcing of certain clearing-related processes, such as back-office functions, to cut costs, or – depending on the concrete cost structure and size of business – motivate these clearers to become NCMs.

7.3.2 BMIM for regionally-to-globally active clearing members

The Business Model Impact Matrix for regionally-to-globally active clearing members illustrates that all network strategies are beneficial to this type of clearer's business model (see Figure 7.14).

---

[39] The revenues of regionally focused clearers are not affected by network strategies, because this type of clearing member and its respective customers are assumed to have no interest in the away clearing houses' products and markets. Revenues could only increase related to clearing links – if the lowered clearing costs spur trading, in the case of a prop. focus – or, in case of an agency focus, if the clearing house translates its slightly lowered cost base into clearing fee reductions, which in turn stimulate agency trading.

[40] Competitive disadvantages result from their lack of internal economies of scale. Refer to Chapter 5 for details.

[41] However, despite their lack of size, regionally active clearers usually benefit from their perfectly tailored services, which fit the demands and particularities of their regional market precisely.

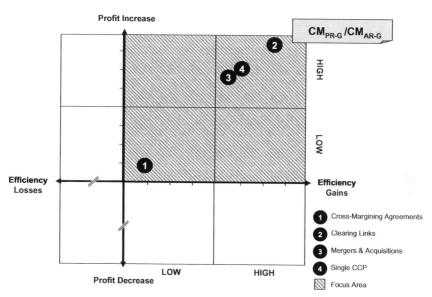

Figure 7.14   Business Model Impact Matrix for regionally-to-globally active clearing members
Source: Author's own.

Cross-margining agreements lead to low efficiency gains and result in a proportional profit increase.[42] In contrast, clearing links, M&A and Single CCP initiatives translate into a disproportionately higher profit increase. This increase results from the positive revenue impact brought about by these network strategies, which, in addition to reducing costs, increase profits. From a prop. perspective, regionally-to-globally focused clearers benefit from the increased scale and scope of services available at a lower cost as well as from positive network effects. Disintermediation and enhanced internal efficiency now increase the attractiveness of self-clearing additional products and markets in-house, which in turn enables the clearer to leverage its infrastructure – thus increasing the theoretical 'revenues' resulting from self-clearing.

Similar considerations apply to regionally-to-globally active clearers with an agency focus. In this case, the disproportionately higher profit increase results from the clearer's enhanced internal efficiency, which positively impacts its profit margin. Additionally, the clearer is able to offer its clients an increased scale and scope of services at lower cost. Finally, clearing links and Single

---

[42] Cross-margining agreements are assumed to have little or no impact on revenues, because a significant increase in revenues would require an increase in the number of cleared contracts spurred by this type of network initiative. Whereas this could occur in reality, such a scenario is not included in this analysis.

CCP initiatives, which enable the CCP to internalise GCM level network effects, further strengthen and enhance the value proposition of regionally-to-globally active clearers. Their revenues are thus increased thanks to a greater profit margin and increased customer traffic.[43]

7.3.3 BMIM for globally active clearing members

Finally, Figure 7.15 illustrates the Business Model Impact Matrix for globally active clearing members. In contrast to the previously outlined matrices, the impact of network strategies on the business model of globally active clearers with a prop. or an agency focus is strikingly different.

For clearers with a prop. focus, the efficiency gains generated by a certain network strategy translate into a proportional profit increase. Network strategies are not assumed to impact revenues, because the scale and scope of services are not broadened. However, clearing services for different products and markets become accessible through a more consolidated infrastructure.[44] This allows clearers to leverage their infrastructure and reduce costs, but in contrast to regionally-to-globally active clearers, globally active clearing members have to overcome additional internal hurdles to realise these internal efficiency gains. Globally active clearers usually employ different legal entities within their company structure to become members of regional CCPs. This set-up can give rise to additional internal and external complexities as well as potential areas of conflict with regard to consolidating the clearing house interfaces.

---

[43] Note that by definition, regionally-to-globally active clearing members and their NCMs and/or customers have an interest in being active in all of the partnering clearing houses' markets and products. It could be argued that due to internal economies of scale, a globally active clearing member can offer the same products and markets at a lower price, so NCMs and/or customers of regionally-to-globally active clearers should in theory consider becoming a member of the higher volume (i.e. globally active) clearer. If the NCMs and/or customers base their decision purely on the basis of commissions charged by the clearers, network strategies do not result in NCMs and/or customers conducting more of their business through their regionally-to-globally active clearer. Instead, these NCMs and/or customers can be expected to switch to a globally active clearer. However, globally active clearers already had a competitive advantage in terms of greater internal economies of scale prior to the network initiative; it would thus have already been attractive for NCMs and/or customers to choose the globally active clearer, had their sole decision criterion been commissions. It is therefore assumed that NCMs and/or customers of regionally-to-globally active clearing members do not base their decision strictly on commission levels, but also take additional factors into account, such as regional proximity, services tailored to the home market, long-term business relationship, etc.

[44] Revenues would only increase to the extent that the enhanced internal efficiency spurs business growth. This scenario, which would lead to a disproportionately higher profit increase, is not covered by this analysis, however.

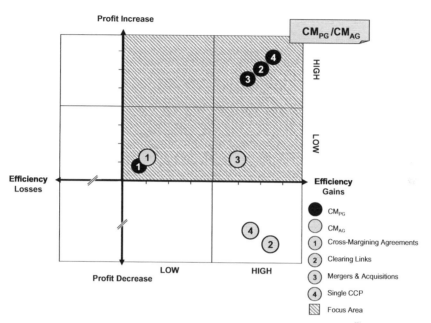

Figure 7.15 Business Model Impact Matrix for globally active clearing members
Source: Author's own.

Internal complexities can emerge by virtue of the different legal entities working under different local budgets and local management. Salaries, bonuses and hierarchies may depend on these budgets, which can make the consolidation of clearing house interfaces a difficult and complex internal undertaking. External difficulties related to consolidating clearing house interfaces can result from NCMs and other customers objecting to such an initiative, i.e. for reasons of demanding local contacts, etc.

For globally active clearers with a prop. focus, all network strategies positively impact their business model. The same is not true for globally active clearers with an agency focus, however. On the one hand, this type of clearing member benefits from high efficiency gains, as outlined in the Efficiency Impact Matrix, but at the same time, they are at risk of being disintermediated.[45] As outlined above, the internalisation of GCM level network effects increases the attractiveness of disintermediation.[46]

[45] Although it is unlikely that a globally active clearer would be put out of business completely, it is also unlikely that the remaining NCMs would do more business (thus making up for the lost NCM business), unless lower internal costs were to be translated into reduced commissions, which would in turn translate into an increase of the number of cleared contracts.

[46] Regionally-to-globally active clearers could, of course, also run the risk of being disintermediated by NCMs that now consider it cost-efficient to self-clear their business. This scenario is not scrutinised here,

Figure 7.7 showed that clearing links have a high to very high potential to internalise GCM level network effects,[47] whereas Single CCP and M&A strategies possess a high and medium potential for internalising GCM level network effects, respectively. It is consequently assumed that in the context of M&A initiatives, efficiency gains are counteracted by a medium strong risk of disintermediation, which results in lost revenues. The overall effect is consequently assumed to be a very low profit increase.

Because clearing link and Single CCP initiatives significantly increase the attractiveness of disintermediation, it is assumed that revenue losses ultimately outweigh the efficiency gains. The only way for globally active clearers with an agency focus to circumvent the risk of disintermediation is to restrict access to the CCP level network.[48]

Influencing the level of access to the CCP network is assumed to be possible when clearing houses are user-owned and/or user-governed. Figure 7.16 illustrates the potential efficiency gains for **globally active clearers with an agency focus** that succeed in restricting access to the CCP network; doing so enables them to circumvent disintermediation and the associated revenue losses. These clearers stand to gain from restricting access to the CCP level network under clearing links, M&A and Single CCP initiatives. However, regionally-to-globally active clearers suffer from restricted access, because they lose their disintermediation benefits and are prevented from leveraging their internal infrastructure. A scenario of restricted access would thus serve to reinforce the structural particularities of the European Value Provision Network by sustaining the competitive advantage held by high volume clearers over lower volume clearers. Globally active clearers would consequently maintain their dominant position within the European VPN, i.e. a very high percentage of the European market share in derivatives clearing would continue to be concentrated in the hands of a few very high volume clearers.

---

as this analysis is concerned with the disintermediation of globally active GCMs by regionally-to-globally active clearers.

[47] Note that the risk of disintermediation through clearing links is minimal, unless the CCPs are able to convince clearing members to expect positive future network effects – i.e. by persuading them that the clearing link will be extended in scope, and that the clearing houses will make up for the lost intermediary level by providing these services themselves, thus successfully internalising GCM level network effects. Only then can the utility derived from the network outweigh the costs of alternation in the long run, and the starting problem will be overcome. For the purpose of this analysis, it is assumed that clearing link initiatives overcome the starting problem. If, in reality, the link initiative fails to convince clearing members to expect positive future network effects, then a Single CCP initiative has by far the greatest potential for successful disintermediation.

[48] Restricted access in this case refers to scenarios in which only globally active clearers are granted full access to a CCP level network resulting from a clearing link, M&A or Single CCP initiative.

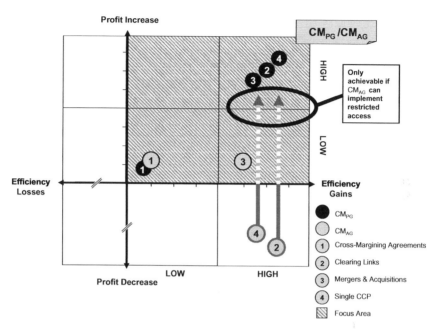

Figure 7.16 Business Model Impact Matrix for globally active clearers that succeed in implementing restricted access to the CCP level network
Source: Author's own.

To summarise, although some network strategies are cost efficient, they are not necessarily profit-maximising for all clearing member types. Regionally active clearers with a prop. or an agency focus suffer from a negative impact on their business model when M&A and Single CCP initiatives are in force. Globally active clearers with an agency focus do not fare well under Single CCP initiatives and clearing links (when these replicate the size of the Single CCP network) that allow unrestricted access to the CCP level network.

7.4 Preliminary findings – impact of network strategies on efficiency

Building on the findings of Chapters 5 and 6, Chapter 7 establishes a framework for analysing the impact of network strategies on the efficiency of European clearing. Four matrices were used to assess the impact of cross-margining agreements, clearing links, M&A and Single CCP initiatives and allowed preliminary conclusions to be drawn about the impact of these network strategies on the efficiency of clearing. The preliminary conclusions drawn from these matrices will be compared to real-world case studies in Chapter 8, which are analysed according to the above-mentioned framework. The findings of the matrices are briefly summarised below, compared to findings of the European Central Bank, and used to further clarify the insights provided by the so-called 'McP Curve' and to evaluate the claim that the clearing industry exhibits 'natural monopoly' characteristics.

7.4.1 Scale Impact Matrix

- The Scale Impact Matrix serves to classify the magnitude of potential demand- and supply-side scale effects related to a particular network strategy.
- The findings from the Scale Impact Matrix suggest that clearing links hold the potential for the greatest 'net' scale economies. Whereas M&A strategies have higher supply-side and lower demand-side scale effects than the Single CCP scenario, the relative magnitude of their respective net scale effects is comparable.

7.4.2 Transaction Cost Impact Matrix

- The Transaction Cost Impact Matrix analysed whether or not the demand- and supply-side scale effects of each network strategy translate into a proportional or disproportional impact on transaction costs for different clearing member types.
- The analysis differentiated the following customer groups: CM_{PR}/CM_{AR} (regionally active clearers with a prop. or an agency focus), CM_{PR-G}/CM_{AR-G} (regionally-to-globally active clearers with a prop. or an agency focus) and CM_{PG}/CM_{AG} (globally active clearers with a prop. or an agency focus).
- For regionally active clearers with a prop. or an agency focus, indirect costs are the core cost driver. Cross-margining agreements have no cost impact for this type of clearer, while M&A and Single CCP initiatives actually increase indirect costs. Clearing links, on the other hand, do not imply additional indirect costs, and could potentially lead to cost reductions. Nonetheless, clearing links are not suited to reduce significantly these clearers' indirect costs.
- For regionally-to-globally active clearers with a prop. or an agency focus, indirect costs are also the core cost driver. These clearers benefit from network strategies enabling them to clear many markets through their domestic home clearing house, thus disintermediating the clearer(s) they

employ as intermediary (ies) to other markets. Cross-margining agreements serve slightly to lower indirect costs, but do not enable disintermediation. While clearing links, M&A and Single CCP initiatives are all suited to reduce significantly these clearers' indirect costs, clearing links (followed by Single CCP and M&A initiatives) turn out to have the greatest positive impact.

- For globally active clearers with a prop. focus, direct costs are the core cost driver. These clearers' main benefit from network strategies comes from the potential to reduce clearing house charges. Cross-margining agreements serve slightly to lower costs, but have no potential significantly to reduce direct costs. Clearing links, M&A and Single CCP initiatives, on the other hand, are all suited to impact significantly these clearers' core cost driver. For globally active clearers with a prop. focus, the Single CCP initiative possesses the strongest cost-reduction potential, followed by clearing links and M&A initiatives.

- For globally active clearers with an agency focus, indirect costs are the core cost driver. These clearers' main benefit from network strategies comes from being able to consolidate their various clearing relationships, i.e. centralise these into a single relationship. Cross-margining agreements serve slightly to lower costs, but do not enable such a consolidation. Clearing links, M&A and Single CCP initiatives are all suited to impact significantly these clearers' core cost driver. For globally active clearers with an agency focus, clearing links (followed by Single CCP and M&A initiatives) turn out to have the greatest positive impact.

7.4.3 Efficiency Impact Matrix

- The Efficiency Impact Matrix consolidated the results of the Transaction Cost Impact Matrices and allowed for conclusions on the overall efficiency impact of the various network strategies to be drawn.
- The Efficiency Impact Matrix shows that besides cross-margining agreements, which generally have little or no impact on efficiency, clearing links are the only network strategy that results in efficiency gains for all clearing member types.
- Regionally active clearers potentially suffer from efficiency losses as a result of M&A and Single CCP initiatives.
- Nonetheless, while clearing links are suited to reduce significantly the core cost driver of globally active clearers with a prop. focus, these clearers enjoy the greatest efficiency gains from a Single CCP initiative.

7.4.4 Business Model Impact Matrix

- The Business Model Impact Matrix illustrated whether the efficiency increase (decrease) corresponding to the different network strategies translates into a proportional or disproportional profit increase or decrease for different clearing member types.
- It illustrated that the efficiency increase (decrease) resulting from different network strategies translates into a proportional profit impact for regionally active clearers; clearing link, M&A and Single CCP initiatives lead to a disproportionately higher profit increase for regionally-to-globally active clearing members.
- For globally active clearers with a prop. focus, the efficiency gains of network strategies translate into a proportional profit increase, whereas for globally active clearers with an agency focus, Single CCP and clearing link initiatives can lead to a disproportional decrease in profits.
- The analysis shows that although some network strategies are cost efficient, they are not necessarily profit-maximising for all clearing member types.
- Regionally focused clearers with a prop. or an agency perspective suffer from efficiency losses and a negative impact on their business model when M&A and Single CCP initiatives are undertaken.
- Although globally active clearers with an agency focus benefit from efficiency gains, they simultaneously suffer from a negative impact on their business model if Single CCP or clearing link initiatives (which replicate the size of the Single CCP network) are set up.
- It was outlined above that particularly large investment banks are active in both proprietary and agency business. The Business Model Impact Matrix illustrated the internal conflict that arises when these firms have to decide whether or not to support a certain network strategy: the only network strategy that has a positive impact on the business model of both the prop. and the agency side relates to M&A initiatives between CCPs. These clearers are thus likely to support M&A initiatives, but unlikely to support a clearing link set-up. For globally active clearers with a prop. focus, a Single CCP initiative is preferable over clearing links, as it has the greatest positive potential impact. For globally active clearers with an agency focus, clearing links actually have a significantly negative impact on their business model, which is why they have an interest in circumventing such a scenario. Whether or not large investment banks support the creation of a Single CCP will probably depend on whether the bank places greater emphasis on proprietary

or agency business. From a prop. perspective, they should absolutely be in favour of a Single CCP; from an agency perspective, however, they can be expected to oppose the implementation of a Single CCP.

7.4.5 Summary of impact

To summarise on the impact that network strategies have on the efficiency of European clearing, the preliminary findings suggest that a clearing link set-up appears to be the most attractive network strategy because it enables all clearing member types to benefit from efficiency gains.

As outlined above, the services provided as well as the products and markets processed by different European clearing houses are not identical, and due to their installed bases, they are not necessarily interchangeable. Enlarging the size of a CCP network through clearing links benefits European clearing houses because it enables them to leverage their significant installed base and helps them to sustain their unique services in cases where these services and processes have been tailored to the specific demands of regional market particularities and different regulatory environments. Additionally, it enables clearing houses to internalise the GCM level network effects and to strengthen their unique CCP level network effects. Clearers can additionally benefit from the high growth potential afforded by links; they may entice other clearing houses outside of the defined European markets to join the network. Links are also not prone to give rise to negative network effects.

The European Central Bank (ECB) finds that '[i]t is clear that, in the short-term, a single infrastructure would maximise network externalities and economies of scale. However, these short-term advantages have to be balanced against the inefficiencies that may be caused in the long run by the absence of competition (e.g. a lack of dynamism and innovation).'[49] In accordance with the doubts expressed by the ECB, the analysis suggests that consolidating the European clearing industry through mergers and acquisitions to form a single monopoly CCP runs the risk of depriving market participants of the competitive forces inherent to a link solution and denies them the benefit of utilising clearing services that have been tailored to best fit regional market particularities. Findings from the Scale Impact Matrix additionally suggest that even in the short term, a single infrastructure created through a Single CCP initiative does not serve to maximise network externalities or economies

---

[49] European Central Bank (ed.) (2001c), p. 3.

of scale. Rather, clearing links incorporate greater potential for economies of scale and scope as well as network effects. The Efficiency Impact Matrix further illustrated that while a Single CCP could potentially lead to efficiency gains for regionally-to-globally and globally active clearers, regionally active clearers suffer efficiency losses. This analysis thus indicated that, even in the short term, a Single CCP is not suited to enhance the efficiency for all European clearing members. However, clearing members benefit from a link solution, because it does not oblige participation and entails lower investments. The link strategy thus translates into efficiency gains for all European clearing members.

Nonetheless, the benefits of a link set-up can only be achieved if the clearing houses endeavour to overcome the link-inherent starting problem.[50] The starting problem will only be overcome and the utility derived from the CCP level network can only offset the individual clearer's costs of alternation in the long run when the partnering CCPs:

- convince their clearers to expect positive future network effects – implying that the clearing link will be extended in its scope;
- compensate for the lost intermediary (GCM) level by providing most of these services themselves – thereby successfully internalising GCM level network effects; and
- make up for the lost participation in other CCP networks by providing a similar service level and processing all products and markets.

Additionally, the benefits of a link set-up can only fully flourish when the partnering clearing houses provide a choice of clearing location. If no choice of clearing location is offered, network participants are locked into a particular clearing network.[51] However, again, this situation does not represent an instance of strong lock-in: it is not a coordination failure among users that prevents clearers from actually switching to the superior network, but the legal restrictions established by the exchanges or clearing houses that prohibit the choice of clearing location. Therefore, to eradicate non-network-effect-related coordination problems on the CCP level, the provision of choice of clearing location helps to prevent this particular scenario. Consequently, provided that opportunities for choice of clearing location exist through clearing links, it appears unlikely that CCP level network effects lead to strong forms of lock-in. If strong lock-in effects do not exist on the GCM and CCP levels, first-mover-wins and winner-takes-all conditions are also unlikely to emerge.

---

[50] Refer to section 7.1.2.2.2 for an explanation of the starting problem.
[51] Note that clearing houses alone cannot offer choice of clearing location. Rather in a first instance, the respective exchanges must give allowance to the use of various clearing houses.

Market participants then benefit from the competitive forces between clearing houses in the context of a clearing link set-up.

The analysis reveals that it is crucial for the success of clearing link initiatives that the partnering CCPs endeavour to compensate for the lost intermediary (GCM) level services by providing most of these services themselves. However, it also showed that it is very difficult for clearing houses to internalise the entire range of GCM level network effects. It can thus be assumed that there will continue to be a justification for the value-added function of the GCM level, despite the attractiveness of disintermediation spurred by such a link initiative. For some counterparties, it will simply remain more cost efficient to retain an intermediary relationship with their GCM(s). Even so, it should be noted that globally active clearers with an agency perspective can still be expected to oppose the implementation of such a clearing link scenario, because their business model is likely to suffer significantly from disintermediation.[52]

The only way for globally active clearers with an agency focus to circumvent the risk of disintermediation is to restrict access to the newly created CCP level network – thus circumventing disintermediation and the associated revenue losses. Influencing the level of access to the CCP network is assumed to be possible only in the case of user ownership or user governance. Despite the finding that a clearing link set-up offers greater efficiency gains for these clearing member types, globally active clearers with an agency focus are likely to prefer the establishment of a Single CCP over the implementation of clearing links. The reason for this is that it is presumably easier to succeed in implementing user ownership or user governance (thus controlling the rules of clearing) for one entity than it is to control the rules of clearing of various entities.

The analysis also revealed that globally active clearers with a prop. focus benefit most, in terms of efficiency gains, from the implementation of a Single CCP. Nonetheless, these clearers will presumably only adopt a Single CCP approach if they have the means to control the rules of clearing, i.e. to ensure that clearing fees are sufficiently reduced and that the consolidated infrastructure does not abuse its monopoly position. Nonetheless, the risk of a user ownership/user governance structure that is dominated by high volume clearers is that these clearing members will succeed in further strengthening their already preferential position within the European VPN and that low and medium clearers will consequently become further disadvantaged.

---

[52] Note that in spite of this negative impact on the business model, the overall efficiency of the industry can still be increased, because disintermediation reduces transaction costs.

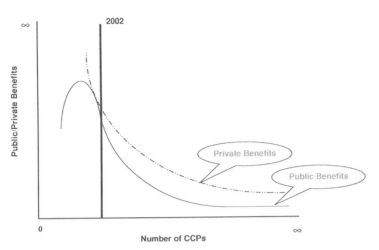

Figure 7.17   McP curve – public versus private benefits in the context of CCP consolidation
Source: McPartland (2002), p. 105.

These conclusions are in accord with and serve to clarify further the insights provided by the **'McP Curve'**.[53] The curve represents the magnitude of private and public benefits (vertical axis)[54] associated with a decreasing number of CCPs, which is indicated on the horizontal axis and decreases from right to left.

The upper line illustrates the financial benefits derived by clearing participants given the number of CCPs. The lower line represents the public benefits associated with the number of Central Counterparties. From right to left, it can be seen that it is in everyone's best interest – including the public interest – to have fewer and fewer CCPs; this was at least the case until approximately 2002. McPartland observes that up to roughly this point in time, there were increasing private financial benefits for clearing participants as well as concurrent public benefits associated with having fewer clearing houses. After 2002, however, the remaining benefits are private; the public benefits begin to become negative at some future point in time. He argues that the real benefit of decreasing the number of clearing houses is that the high volume clearers can greatly simplify their internal operations and achieve significant internal cost

---

[53] Cf. McPartland (2002), pp. 105–6.

[54] Magnitude is represented on the vertical axis. It is primarily a measure of financial magnitude when applicable to private benefits (top line), and intrinsic magnitude when applicable to public benefits (lower line). Many, but not all, public benefits are financial in nature. Nonetheless, the relevant public benefits, given the number of CCPs, are expressed on the vertical axis as though it were a financial measure (relative to the level of private benefits). Cf. McPartland (2002), p. 105.

savings. McPartland (2002) concludes that the greatest cost savings beyond this particular point are consequently private financial benefits, which accrue to the largest clearing members as a result of their significantly streamlined operating efficiencies.

The findings of the analysis in Chapter 7 reinforce the insights provided by the McP Curve, but they also serve to clarify them further. They show that the above conclusions are only true for a reduction in the number of clearing house networks resulting from a Single CCP initiative or a clearing link set-up in which high volume clearing members succeed in restricting access to the CCP level network (and thus in impeding disintermediation). However, if the consolidation of the CCP networks is achieved through a clearing link set-up in which the partnering clearing houses engage to overcome the link-inherent starting problem, choice of clearing location is provided and access to the network is unrestricted, the findings of the McP Curve are unlikely to hold. It is thus only when a Single CCP solution or link set-up that restricts access to the CCP network is employed that the number of clearing house networks becomes reduced beyond the point where high volume clearers (especially clearing members with a prop. focus) benefit most, and public benefits begin to become negative.

Clearing members' ability to control the rules of clearing and influence the structural set-up or level of access to the CCP level network should therefore be minimised. Additionally, it is crucial that clearing houses understand the benefits of engaging in network strategies that enable them to leverage their installed base, strengthen their unique CCP level network effects, internalise GCM level network effects and enlarge the scope of complementary products and services provided by their CCP network.

Finally, when strong network effects and economies of scale exist in an industry, it is often argued that the industry constitutes a **natural monopoly**.[55] Nonetheless, it is disputed whether clearing qualifies as a natural monopoly.[56] The literature both supports and refutes the assertion; some sources advocate classifying the securities clearing and settlement industry as a natural

---

[55] 'A natural monopoly exists if a single supplier can serve the market in question more cost-efficiently than several suppliers, meaning that the cost function in the relevant area of demand is subadditive. Reviews of the cost side of networks focus primarily on the bundling advantages achieved through economies of scale and economies of scope in service provision. These bundling advantages can imply that a single network operator may be able to serve a given market at a lower cost than a number of competing suppliers.' Knieps (2006), p. 49. Also refer to Baumol (1977); and Baumol/Panzar/Willig (1982).

[56] Cf. European Central Bank (ed.) (2001b), p. 84.

monopoly,[57] whereas others oppose this view.[58] Most of these contributions, however, tend to refer to the clearing services provided by CSDs/ICSDs rather than by CCPs.

The preliminary findings of this study provide no evidence supporting the natural monopoly assumption of the European derivatives clearing industry. First of all, the services provided by the different European clearing houses are not necessarily interchangeable. Second, provided that opportunities for choice of clearing location exist through clearing links, it appears unlikely that CCP level network effects lead to strong forms of lock-in. If strong lock-in effects do not exist on the GCM and CCP levels, first-mover-wins and winner-takes-all conditions are consequently also unlikely to exist. Third, despite strong economies of scale and network effects, consolidation in the form of a monopolistic Single CCP was shown potentially to induce highly counteractive forces in the form of necessary investments, costs related to the complexity of integration (possibly giving rise to diseconomies of scale) and negative network effects. Finally, provided that choice of clearing location is guaranteed by clearing houses through links, the European clearing industry can be assumed to be contestable.

The second step of the analysis of the impact of network strategies on the efficiency of clearing comes next: Chapter 8 compares the preliminary findings of this chapter with conclusions from three case studies. This allows final conclusions to be drawn.

---

[57] See Competition Commission South Africa (2001); Cruickshank (2001), p. 325; European Securities Forum (ed.) (2002), p. 6; Lee (2002), p. 12; Russo (2002), p. 237; European Financial Services Round Table (ed.) (2003), p. 2; Heckinger/Lee/McPartland (2003), p. 15; Singapore Exchange (ed.) (2004), p. 8; CONSOB (ed.) (2004), p. 24; Office of Fair Trading (ed.) (2004), pp. 43–4; Branch/Griffiths (2005), pp. 4–5; Rochet (2005), p. 9; Bliss/Papathanassiou (2006), p. 36; LIBA (ed.) (2006), p. 6; and Direction Générale du Trésor et de la Politique Économique (ed.) (2006), p. 5.

[58] See, e.g. Federation of European Securities Exchanges (ed.) (2004), p. 5; and Knieps (2006), p. 59. Milne (2002), pp. 10–13, outlines that certain core functions provided by custodians have the characteristics of a natural monopoly, whereas all other clearing and settlement-related services are competitive in their nature. Also refer to the studies of Van Cayseele/Voor de Mededinging (2005); and Serifsoy/Weiß (2005).

8 Checking theory against reality – case studies of network strategies

The previous chapter delivers preliminary findings regarding the impact of network strategies on the efficiency of clearing; this chapter challenges these conclusions with findings from the empirical study and real-world case studies. In the following, a case study analysis is performed for each of three types of network strategy: clearing links (including cross-margining agreements),[1] mergers and acquisitions, and a Single CCP.

As the centre of the analysis is on the European clearing industry, the selected case studies focus on network strategies that involve European clearing houses. The clearing link study (section 8.1) presents findings from the empirical study concerning cross-margining agreements and clearing links and analyses the link established in 2003 between Eurex Clearing (a Frankfurt-based clearing house) and the Clearing Corporation (a Chicago-based clearing house). The mergers and acquisitions study (section 8.2) examines the merger between the London Clearing House (LCH) and Clearnet (a Paris-based clearing house) in 2003, which produced LCH.Clearnet. In contrast to the other two case studies, the Single CCP study (section 8.3) deals with a hypothetical scenario: the creation of a single clearing house for Europe.

Each case analysis mines the interviewees' perceptions of the respective network strategy in terms of its overall benefits and constraints. Additionally, the interviewees' feedback regarding the suitability of clearing links or a Single CCP to integrate European clearing is presented.[2] Whilst all three case studies are analysed according to the framework established in Chapter 7, the length and detail of the respective studies varies: because the analysis conducted in Chapter 7 identified clearing links as the most suitable network strategy to

---

[1] Note that due to their very low efficiency impact, cross-margining agreements are not analysed separately, but rather as part of the clearing link study.

[2] The suitability of mergers and acquisitions as a means to integrate the European industry is not analysed in the merger study (section 8.2), but in the Single CCP study (section 8.3). The reason for this is that consolidating the European clearing industry through M&A initiatives results in the creation of a Single CCP.

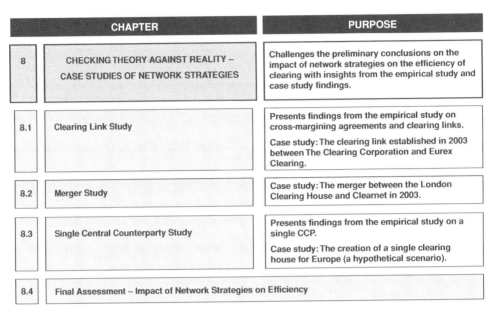

CHAPTER		PURPOSE
8	CHECKING THEORY AGAINST REALITY – CASE STUDIES OF NETWORK STRATEGIES	Challenges the preliminary conclusions on the impact of network strategies on the efficiency of clearing with insights from the empirical study and case study findings.
8.1	Clearing Link Study	Presents findings from the empirical study on cross-margining agreements and clearing links. Case study: The clearing link established in 2003 between The Clearing Corporation and Eurex Clearing.
8.2	Merger Study	Case study: The merger between the London Clearing House and Clearnet in 2003.
8.3	Single Central Counterparty Study	Presents findings from the empirical study on a single CCP. Case study: The creation of a single clearing house for Europe (a hypothetical scenario).
8.4	Final Assessment – Impact of Network Strategies on Efficiency	

Figure 8.1   Structure of Chapter 8

increase the efficiency of the European clearing industry, the clearing link study receives more weight in the subsequent analysis and is conducted in greater detail. Furthermore, due to the limited scope of this study and the lack of detailed data available regarding the merger and Single CCP studies, these two cases are presented in abbreviated form.

In the final assessment (section 8.4), conclusions are drawn regarding the impact of network strategies on the efficiency of European clearing; summarising whether the insights from the case studies support or refute the findings from Chapter 7. This process also reveals the shortcomings of a purely theoretical assessment by outlining the difficulties associated with translating theoretical concepts into reality.

8.1 The clearing link study

This chapter presents insights from the empirical study and a real-world case study, the conclusions of which are compared to the findings from Chapter 7. First, findings from the empirical study regarding cross-margining agreements and clearing links are presented (section 8.1.1). Second, a more detailed analysis of a concrete case study, i.e. the clearing link established between

Eurex Clearing and The Clearing Corporation, is furnished (section 8.1.2). The section concludes by summarising the findings regarding the impact of clearing links on efficiency (section 8.1.3).

8.1.1 Findings from the empirical study

The empirical study furnished insights as to what role the different network strategies play in reality by soliciting feedback from various stakeholders on two critical issues. Interviewees were asked to critique cross-margining agreements (section 8.1.1.1) and clearing links (section 8.1.1.2) in terms of their ability to provide value-added; the interviews produced valuable details about the major benefits and constraints of these initiatives. Furthermore, the stakeholders were asked to comment on the suitability of clearing links as a means to integrate the European clearing industry (section 8.1.1.3).

8.1.1.1 Cross-margining agreements: general benefits and constraints

The industry has hugely benefited [from cross-margining agreements], because the cost of carrying offsetting positions is greatly diminished, and a lot more volume ensues.[3]

The economic benefit given was never sufficient to make it worthwhile . . . I have more money in my pocket now than the industry has ever saved in cross-margining.[4]

Roughly 57 per cent (forty-five out of seventy-nine) of the interviewees issued concrete opinions on cross-margining agreements.[5] At first sight, their over-all assessment appears unambiguous: thirty-two interviewees felt that cross-margining agreements provide value-added and increase the efficiency of clearing, ten respondents saw no value-added and three interviewees were conflicted (see Figure 8.2).

However, the picture becomes fuzzier upon closer analysis. Although the great majority of the interviewed clearing house and exchange representatives, market experts and NCMs acknowledged the value-added provided by such agreements, the clearing members' responses were more divided. Seven clearers asserted that such network strategies provide no value-added; four clearers made the opposite claim. On the other hand, three clearers saw general value in cross-margining agreements, but felt that these initiatives could potentially harm their business model. These clearers are thus classified as 'conflicted'.

---

[3] Interview with William C. Floersch.   [4] Statement made by interviewed market expert.
[5] The remaining interviewees either said that they did not know, had no clear opinion, did not specify their opinion or declined to answer.

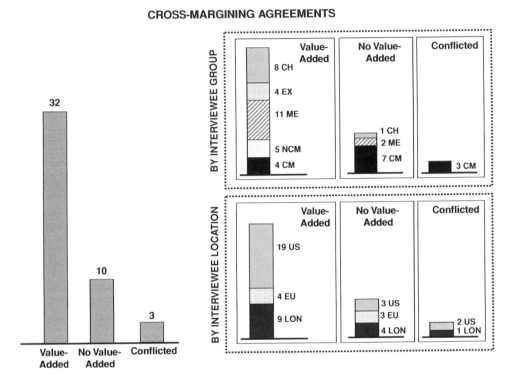

Figure 8.2   Interviewees' assessment of cross-margining agreements[6]
Source: Author's own.

The fact that the US-based interviewees provided the bulk of the concrete assessments[7] is likely due to the significantly greater number of cross-margining initiatives in the US as compared to Europe.[8] To understand the different views expressed with regard to the value-added of cross-margining agreements, the following presents the general benefits and constraints of such initiatives as identified by the interviewees themselves.

Interviewees claimed that in terms of **benefits**, cross-margining agreements generally enable a more efficient use of capital by minimising the costs of carrying offsetting positions. When cross-margining opportunities extend

---

[6] Interviewee groups: CM – clearing member; NCM – non-clearing member; ME – market expert; EX – exchange; and CH – clearing house. Interviewee locations: US – United States; EU – Continental Europe; and LON – London.

[7] 69 per cent of all US-based interviewees provided assessments, whereas only 52 and 41 per cent respectively of all London- and Continental-Europe-based respondents gauged the relevance of this network strategy.

[8] Refer to section 3.3.2 for an overview of European and American cross-margining initiatives.

across different asset classes, clearing members can better leverage the same amount of capital or financial resources, because they can assume a more integrated risk profile. The higher the correlation between the products for which cross-margining is offered, the greater the potential benefits in terms of reduced cost of capital and risk management, as the need for risk monitoring decreases. Reducing the aggregate level of margin that a clearing member is required to post to collateralise the positions held through the participating clearing houses can ultimately lead to higher volumes. This is especially true when counterparties are collateral poor – and thus highly sensitive to the cost of capital – because capital is thereby freed up that can then be allocated for additional trading opportunities. The primary benefit of cross-margining thus lies in its potential to reduce the cost of capital. Consequently, whether or not cross-margining agreements have appeal as stand-alone initiatives greatly depends on individual clearing members' sensitivity to the cost of capital.[9]

In addition to the benefits that cross-margining agreements can provide, the interviewees identified a variety of constraints inherent to the utilisation and implementation of this network strategy. First of all, clearing members will generally consider the trade-off between the potential savings they expect to realise and the back-office and IT development work that will be necessary in order to be able to interact with the cross-margining schema. As outlined in section 3.3.1.1, some initiatives require cumbersome processing. Additionally, as collateral-rich clearing members generally tend to be less interested in cross-margining agreements, the issue of required system changes is not so much about costs, but rather the prioritisation of the multiple demands placed on their IT resources. For globally active clearers with a prop. focus, the implementation of cross-margining agreements is contingent on the internal demand. If a clearer is able to pass on collateral savings to the individual trader level (i.e. has an appropriate internal system in place for this purpose), traders will clearly strive to benefit from such savings, which can affect their bottom-line. The attractiveness of cross-margining agreements is consequently related to whether the charge on capital is computed efficiently within firms.

The enforcement or auditing of those capital charges is still pretty primitive and happens from time to time. It doesn't happen daily, the way I would have thought; it's kind of monthly that people look at these things. I think if regulators require a more regular audit or measurement of how banks or intermediaries in the market are covering the liabilities they have, then they will have to manage them more actively, banks themselves will have to manage them more actively. That means that yesterday

---

[9] Refer to the findings of section 5.1.4.2 for details on the interviewees' assessments of the cost of capital.

they didn't bother to move a position into a clearing system, today they feel they need to, because there will be an economic driver to do it. Banks just don't care enough about it, because they're not under pressure to perform in that way.[10]

High volume clearers with an agency focus are hesitant to support such initiatives, because cross-margining agreements potentially counteract one of the value propositions of their business model.

The job of the broker is to make order out of the chaos of different clearing systems and different methodologies for the customer. To the extent that the exchanges and clearing houses themselves do that, they disintermediate us, the broker. So, you know it is probably good for the clients; it is probably not so good for us.[11]

Additionally, as globally active clearers with an agency focus usually calculate their customers' risk position and the respective margin requirements by taking into account all of their customers' positions at a multitude of clearing houses, the benefit created through a particular cross-margining agreement might not be substantial from the customers' point of view. In this case, the customers of a GCM are unlikely to put pressure on their clearer to participate in a particular cross-margining agreement. Finally, whether or not the collateral offsets induced by a cross-margining initiative are convincingly powerful highly depends on the respective trading strategy:

If you look at the Bund and the Treasury, they are highly correlated; if we are short in Europe, we're generally also short in the US, so we won't get any margin offset. For a trading house like us . . . when we model the collateral offset, it is not as powerful as one might imagine that it could be.[12]

Finally, interviewees also identified several constraints in terms of implementing cross-margining agreements on the clearing house level. On the one hand, most clearing processes are electronic, so it is easier to quantify the risk as well as the opportunities associated with correlated products. On the other hand, it is difficult to find highly correlated products cleared at different CCPs in the first place. This is particularly true for cross-margining in products across different currencies.[13] When considering whether or not to engage in

---

[10] Statement made by interviewed exchange representative.   [11] Interview with Gary Alan DeWaal.

[12] Statement made by interviewed clearing member representative.

[13] Cf. interviews. This was also the reason that one of the interviewed clearing houses attributed no value-added to cross-margining agreements: 'Because you do not have total, full correlation between products in different currencies, you would have to set the parameters so far away from each other that I don't think you would get much benefit from it.' Statement made by interviewed clearing house representative.

cross-margining agreements, clearing houses have to weigh up the benefits versus the expected competitive impact.

8.1.1.2 Clearing links: general benefits and constraints

Now, is a clearing link going to be bad for the market? It is going to be bad for some people in the market; is it going to be bad for the end-users that use those markets? Well, it is probably going to be very good for them, because it will increase the amount of competition, lower costs, and this will lead to an increase in volumes. So it will be good for the market as a whole.[14]

Links are largely irrelevant for us because we pretty much have established operations in all the places we want to be, and as we go to new places, we expand that presence.[15]

As for clearing links, roughly 71 per cent (fifty-six out of seventy-nine) of all interviewees gave a concrete assessment (see Figure 8.3).[16] Again, akin to the cross-margining analysis, the assessments were not monolithic.

The majority of interviewees assessed clearing link initiatives as providing value-added, but (as compared to cross-margining agreements) more respondents denied the potential value-added or were conflicted. The assessment provided by clearing members was again diverse. Ten clearers felt that clearing link strategies provide no value-added, while six clearers held the opposite view. Four clearing members were conflicted; on the one hand, they noted benefits associated with link solutions, but also cited the potential harm these initiatives could inflict on their business model. To elaborate on the different views vis-à-vis the value-added of clearing links, the general benefits and constraints of such initiatives (as identified by the interviewees themselves) are presented next.

The interviewees emphasised a number of benefits. First of all, clearing links can reduce transaction costs by providing a single point of entry to various markets. This reduces interface and system maintenance and hardware costs, and leads to more streamlined management of open positions. Link solutions can also generate collateral savings[17] and potentially enhance liquidity. In addition, clearing links can potentially improve upon stand-alone cross-margining agreements: links are mechanically usually more efficient and allow for greater STP than plain cross-margining arrangements. The latter are more cumbersome by nature, because the cooperation between the clearing

---

[14] Interview with Michael G. McErlean.   [15] Interview with Paul J. Brody.

[16] The remaining participants either felt that they did not know, had no clear opinion, did not specify their opinion or declined to answer.

[17] Provided the link agreement includes cross-margining arrangements between the partnering clearing houses. Cf. interviews.

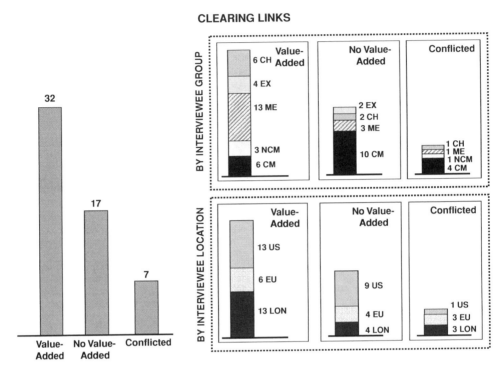

Figure 8.3   Interviewees' assessment of clearing links[18]
Source: Author's own.

houses is limited to a singular service. Due to the restricted scope of pure cross-margining agreements, the partnering clearing houses have to limit the risk sharing among them. These limits tend to present operational burdens or incur additional technology costs to clearing members.

The unique character of links enables clearers to gain local access to foreign markets, thus permitting a choice of jurisdiction. Note that the interviewees' opinions differed on the utility of this supposed benefit:

Jurisdiction is important! We would never clear, as an example, a Eurodollar in Singapore, because we don't understand the jurisdiction the way we do in the US. But when you look at Europe and the US, I don't think that it matters that much. I don't think that we wouldn't clear in the US because of jurisdiction. As long as you are in an OECD regulated capital market I think that it doesn't matter.[19]

---

[18] Interviewee groups: CM – clearing member; NCM – non-clearing member; ME – market expert; EX – exchange; and CH – clearing house. Interviewee locations: US – United States; EU – Continental Europe; and LON – London.

[19] Interview with Steve G. Martin.

I do not think that it is relevant anymore. I think once upon a time, when the regulatory world was uneven, there was advantage to that. I do not see a material difference in the level of regulation around the world anymore. This is the big difference of the last 10 years. I think everyone is sort of at a common playing field.[20]

Whereas the ultimate benefit of jurisdictional choice within Europe and the US offered through clearing links is debatable, interviewees acknowledged the advantage that clearing links can give to smaller, less developed and possibly niche markets and their local users. Links can provide these markets with an opportunity to be part of bigger pools of liquidity. Regionally-to-globally active clearers in particular can thus benefit from direct access to the away market:

Many of the Asian brokerage firms tend to be smaller; they don't have the capital of a Morgan Stanley or a Goldman Sachs, so the Asian clearing houses can play a role in representing the financial standing and credit standing of their smaller brokerage firms. Just to give you an example, the Eurex clearing house would not take a lot of Asian-based brokers as their clearing members, but they might take the Singapore clearing house or someone with a stronger capital base. So, yes, I think these clearing links are going to be very, very important in the future.[21]

Accessing smaller and less developed markets through a clearer's trusted and well-established CCP relationship can spur the development of these markets, particularly when market participants trust that the CCP's level of expertise can be transferred to the partnering clearing house, thus increasing the attractiveness of interacting with this CCP.

Besides these general benefits, interviewees identified a number of constraints regarding the utilisation and implementation of clearing link initiatives. As is the case with cross-margining initiatives, whether or not a link set-up delivers benefits to clearers depends on individual cost-benefit analyses as well as on the particular clearing houses' requirements. In line with the findings of the theoretical analysis, interviewees pointed out the limited attractiveness and benefits of clearing links for globally active clearers. Not only have most of them already implemented a relatively efficient global infrastructure, but for clearers with an agency focus, links also expose them to the threat of disintermediation.

I don't think clearing links add much value. I really do believe that there is a limited amount of value that a clearing link is able to bring to the table. I think that the value a clearing link brings is largely geared to local players in the market and it essentially

---

[20] Interview with Gary Alan DeWaal.   [21] Interview with Fred Grede.

disintermediates the global intermediaries who have provided that service; and I'm not too bothered by it, to be perfectly honest, but some of my competitors get very worried.[22]

I am slightly conflicted in that part of what we have as a competitive advantage is that we can actually offer all these exchange accesses anyway. People will come to us, because we can do it. If you narrow that down, then what I think will happen is that you end up with the big institutions, the big hedge funds just becoming members themselves, which gets rid of our competitive advantage. We are always a bit conflicted about this one, I think![23]

Whereas interviewees observed that links can theoretically help to enhance the efficiency of globally active clearers' in-house operations, they also noted that the final link set-up must provide great benefits and involve low costs of implementation in order for it to be considered attractive.

But essentially, again, the brokers have found a way around this inefficiency and that's why . . . you have to really question who is going to pay for any further links, and I think the incentive to pay is low.[24]

The potential for cost savings for globally active clearers is taken down another notch if an additional fee is charged for the utilisation of the link. Regionally-to-globally active clearers will benchmark the link fee charged for the clearing of positions at the away CCP with the commissions charged by their respective GCM. However, globally active clearers only end up better off if their internal efficiency gains exceed the link fee, or if the fee is lower than the internal costs of utilising their global infrastructure. However, respondents stressed that the efficiency gain must be fairly substantial in order to make a link solution attractive to globally active clearers.

Even if they [the clearing house] were to charge a tenth of a cent for this facility, it is going to exceed the IT and back-office savings. So, you can see our sensitivity to any increase in fees is very high.[25]

Interviewees also confirmed this study's previous findings regarding the starting problem inherent to clearing links. Unless their customers pressure them to utilise the initiative, clearers with an agency focus are unlikely to adopt a link initiative.[26] Globally active clearing members with a prop. perspective also

---

[22] Statement made by interviewed clearing member representative.
[23] Ibid.   [24] Ibid.   [25] Ibid.
[26] Retail investors, for example, focus on investing in their home countries' securities, and are unlikely to put great pressure on the clearer to adopt this strategy. Cf. interviews. For details on investors' market choices, refer to Schiereck (1995); Schiereck (1996a); and Schiereck (1996b).

have little incentive to participate, unless the initiative translates into significant cost savings that can be passed on to the individual traders. Whereas the regionally focused clearers interviewed did not express much interest in link initiatives, the regionally-to-globally active clearers confirmed their general interest in this network strategy.

In addition to these limitations concerning the adoption of links on the clearing members' part, interviewees identified several other obstacles that might discourage clearing houses from voluntarily engaging in clearing link arrangements.

> I think the clearing houses, the providers in this space, are more likely to merge or buy one another than they are to have this nice world where everybody allows systems to be interlinked and cross-margin one another.[27]

Implementing clearing links can be cumbersome for clearing houses, especially on the regulatory side. They have to establish default proceedings and obtain regulatory approval. The process becomes even more unwieldy when links involve clearing houses that are subject to different regulatory regimes.[28] Cross-border linkages can also be hampered by potential political hurdles if a link is perceived as a threat to local businesses and markets. Additionally, the implementation of links can generate overhead and additional costs at the partnering clearing houses. On the one hand, clearing links benefit the partnering clearing houses by enabling them to provide clearing services for a broader range of products and markets. At the same time, clearing houses might be worried that the implementation of a particular clearing link could limit their business development responsiveness by requiring all of the partnering clearing houses to develop clearing facilities for that product. When clearing houses expect to either lose business to the partnering CCP or suspect that they are essentially being locked out of the other clearing houses' markets (which could also stifle business development) through a link, they will be reluctant to enter into such an agreement. Finally, one of the most important complicating factors in implementing clearing link agreements is rooted in the underlying motivation of the link set-up. Interviewees explained that, to date, no clearing link initiative exists that was created to enhance the efficiency of clearing and thus positively impact the efficiency of capital markets. Developments have usually been driven by the exchange side rather than the clearing side. Therefore, the value of links generally depends on the objective being pursued by the initiator of the link.

---

[27] Statement made by anonymous referee.   [28] Cf. interviews.

8.1.1.3 Suitability of clearing links to integrate European clearing

> Whether clearing links are a viable way to consolidate Europe, is a very hard question to answer, because there is no real precedent I can think of in the industry where links work particularly well.[29]

The empirical study also explored whether market participants perceive clearing links as a suitable approach to integrating the European clearing industry and thus increasing its efficiency. Whereas merely 14 per cent of the US-based respondents delivered an assessment, 65 per cent of the interviewees located in Continental Europe and 78 per cent of all London-based respondents expressed an opinion on this issue (see Figure 8.4).

Fourteen interviewees deemed clearing links as a viable scenario for European integration, thirteen respondents expressed the opposite opinion and ten interviewees were indifferent.[30] Note that four of the fourteen participants in favour of links as a viable integration strategy believed that a merger creating a Single European CCP would be preferable to a clearing link scenario. One interviewee from the group opposed to the clearing link solution felt that European derivatives clearing is sufficiently efficient and not necessarily in need of integration initiatives. Most of the indifferent respondents argued similarly, i.e. stating that although they are in favour of any initiative that results in a reduction of transaction costs, the European industry does not necessarily need to consolidate further its derivatives clearing houses to improve efficiency. The remaining indifferent interviewees expressed the view that market forces will ultimately dictate the proper future course of European clearing and did not explicitly advocate a particular structure. The interviewees cited the pros and cons of a link solution as well as potential success factors for consolidating Europe in this way. Their comments are summarised in the following.

On the **plus side**, clearing links were perceived as beneficial because they keep up and enforce competition between the European clearing houses.

> So there would be a huge incentive for a CCP with great technology...The CCP that has the best technology is going to attract the greatest number of clearing firms.[31]

---

[29] Statement made by interviewed industry participant.
[30] Analysing solely the European respondents' answers results in a slightly more articulate assessment, with thirteen interviewees negating, ten endorsing the suitability of clearing links and nine expressing indifference.
[31] Interview with John McPartland.

ARE CLEARING LINKS SUITED TO INTEGRATE THE EUROPEAN CLEARING INDUSTRY?

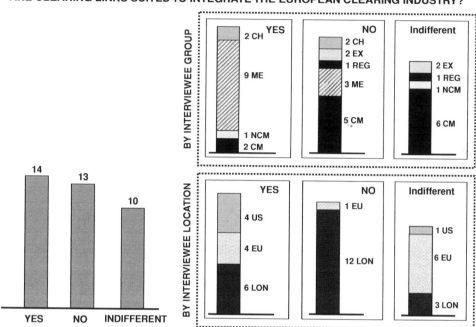

Figure 8.4   Interviewees' assessment of the suitability of clearing links to integrate the European clearing industry[32]
Source: Author's own.

Additionally, the implementation of clearing links allows for the existence and development of specialised clearing houses within smaller European or niche markets.

> Because those contracts would die out if you didn't have the closeness to the market as well as closeness to the member, bank, etc.[33]

Some interviewees observed that compared to stronger forms of integration, such as M&A or Single CCP initiatives, clearing links are a comparatively cheap way to increase quickly the efficiency of European clearing.

> Clearing links generally are a fantastic model because they give everyone what they want and they are rather cheap and efficient.[34]

---

[32] Interviewee groups: CM – clearing member; NCM – non-clearing member; ME – market expert; EX – exchange; CH – clearing house; and REG – regulator. Interviewee locations: US – United States; EU – Continental Europe; and LON – London.
[33] Statement made by interviewed clearing house representative.   [34] Interview with Philip Simons.

Finally, links were considered to be a way to potentially spur regulatory har-monisation within Europe, which would facilitate further consolidation.

As for the **drawbacks** of integrating Europe through a link solution, some interviewees contended that clearing links are likely to provide fewer benefits – in terms of economies of scale – than a Single CCP strategy. They went on to explain that clearing links encourage CCPs to maintain their proprietary clearing systems. Therefore, this approach fails to reduce the actual number of clearing systems within Europe, and the market in turn does not reap the savings that would result from a true consolidation of the systems.

The interviewees also identified potential **success factors** for consolidating Europe through a link solution. They emphasised that the partnering Euro-pean clearing houses must somehow be convinced of the attractiveness of participating in the link structure, which not only involves a positive business case, but also concerns competitive aspects.

That is always the problem with links – there is usually an advantage to one side, not necessarily an advantage to the other side, and there is a cost involved. So links are difficult things; unless you can persuade both parties that there is an advantage to each of them there is always a different advantage to the parties. It is tough to persuade the party that is opening up its market that the market is going to grow and that their slice of the business will continue to grow, despite opening it up. The basic problem with free market economics is how you persuade people that it is better than protectionism.[35]

The use of standard interfaces and similar technology generally minimises the costs of interlinking for the partnering CCPs and also translates into cost savings for clearing members. To minimise the costs of implementing the link solution, three market experts suggested that clearing houses should first engage in harmonisation and establishing standards in operation. Two market experts and one clearing house representative took the opposite tack, suggesting that the implementation of European clearing links would spur technical and regulatory harmonisation, and that this would be achieved more efficiently and rapidly once the links were set up. They reasoned that harmonising the European clearing industry through clearing links would ultimately entail shifting the burden of connecting different marketplaces from the clearing intermediaries to the clearing houses.

What is going to happen is that the CCPs then are going to start, they will have to start uniformly automating their process over time, so that the protocols will become more

---

[35] Interview with Peter Cox.

uniform, the time deadlines more uniform, the haircuts more uniform, because the CCPs themselves now are assuming the operational burdens that used to be assumed by the trade intermediaries. Eventually the CCPs will then become more efficient.[36]

Additionally, three clearing house representatives felt that the decision of which European clearing houses ought to be part of the initial link solution and which CCPs ought to join at a later stage should be carefully evaluated, including a detailed assessment of the cross-border demand for each partnering clearing house's markets and its participation in the network.

But you have to look at demand first, because the initial costs of setting up can be quite expensive, and that has to be taken on by the exchanges and the clearing houses, because you can't force your members to go through that.[37]

Finally, six interviewees supported the theoretical finding that in order to implement successfully a clearing link solution, clearing houses must be prepared to enlarge the scope of their value proposition to accommodate those clearing members that had previously utilised an intermediary to clear the away markets. This ultimately implies that the scope of services offered by each of the involved CCPs must enable clearing members to centralise all of their clearing-related processes at their home clearing house of choice. This is the only way potentially to provide benefits to globally active clearers, make disintermediation attractive for regionally-to-globally active clearers and encourage former NCMs to become direct clearing members. The problem here is that most clearing houses are, for various reasons, ill-prepared for dealing with a growing number of NCMs becoming clearing members:

There are two reasons why we are not well suited to do that: one is that . . . all of our systems and all of our thinking is oriented to dealing with very few, well-capitalised companies. We are not well suited to dealing with a lot of counterparties, even if they are all hedge funds; retail gets a whole new mess . . . but we are not well suited for that. We don't have the people for it, we don't have the systems for it, and we frankly don't have the mentality for it . . . The second part of the equation is, as long as [clearing houses] are owned by the intermediaries, it is a very difficult management path to announce that you are entering that market space.[38]

This implies that the partnering clearing houses would likely need to build up expertise in a range of products and services in which they were previously not active, which commonly also involves an expansion of the CCPs' capacity.[39]

---

[36] Interview with John McPartland.   [37] Statement made by interviewed clearing house representative.
[38] Interview with Richard Jaycobs.   [39] Cf. interview.

Clearing houses that are not dedicated to coping with these issues might thus lose out on the opportunities offered by the link set-up and ultimately also inhibit its success.

8.1.2 Case study: Eurex Clearing and the Clearing Corporation

Well, I think that history speaks for itself there. I would be surprised if anyone other than the consultants derived any value-added from [the clearing link]. It was an unmitigated disaster![40]

The business case for this clearing link continues to stand in the economic world, because it permits certain efficiencies . . . if you look at it in terms of economic benefits to the end-user, there are economic benefits! Therefore, it is something that's worthwhile. However, the people who actually do not gain from it are the intermediaries, because their business of clearing or acting as intermediary has been taken away.[41]

This case study analyses the clearing link, known as the Global Clearing Link (GCL), established in 2003 between the German-Swiss clearing house Eurex Clearing AG (ECAG) and the US-American clearing house The Clearing Corporation (CCorp). Although only one of the partnering CCPs is based in Europe, this network initiative still qualifies as a valuable case study analysis for various reasons: first and foremost, the link involves one of Europe's largest derivatives clearing houses, ECAG. The structure of the GCL involves a sufficiently complex set-up, extending across several regulatory regimes and various products as well as covering a variety of the partnering clearing houses' functions. It thus serves to showcase ECAG's strengths and weaknesses for engaging in future European network initiatives. Additionally, the initiative was undertaken long enough ago to provide a fairly substantial period for analysis. On the other hand, the GCL is recent enough to constitute an adequate concept for the analysis of current and future clearing links. Finally, it also allows European clearing to be analysed in a global context, as the link extends across different time zones. The main drawback of this case study is the limited publicly available data on both clearing houses.

The following analysis commences with an introduction to the case study (Part I), consisting of profiles of the partnering clearing houses (section 8.1.2.1). A synopsis of the Global Clearing Link initiative itself, including its background and objectives, is provided in the next section (section 8.1.2.2). The concept and structure of the GCL are then outlined (section 8.1.2.3),

---

[40] Interview with Steve G. Martin.   [41] Statement made by interviewed market expert.

followed by a description of its current status (section 8.1.2.4). The case study analysis (Part II) presents the interviewees' assessment of the Global Clearing Link initiative (section 8.1.2.5) and furnishes a separate analysis according to the framework established in Chapter 7: in a first step, the Scale Impact Matrix is used to analyse the magnitude of the scale effects related to the clearing link (section 8.1.2.6); in a second step, the Transaction Cost Impact Matrix and the Efficiency Impact Matrix determine whether these scale effects translate into an equally positive transaction cost impact, i.e. efficiency gain, for different clearing member types (section 8.1.2.7). Finally, the Business Model Impact Matrix illustrates whether the efficiency increase (decrease) translates into a proportional or disproportional profit increase or decrease for different clearing member types (section 8.1.2.8).

Part I: Introduction

8.1.2.1 Profiles of the partnering clearing houses

8.1.2.1.1 Eurex Clearing

Eurex Clearing AG was established in 1998 as a result of a merger between the two derivatives exchanges DTB (Deutsche Terminbörse) and SOFFEX (Swiss Options and Financial Futures Exchange).[42] The merger resulted in the creation of Eurex, a German-Swiss joint venture engaged in derivatives trading and clearing. Eurex is a public company and is owned in equal parts by Deutsche Börse AG (DBAG) and SWX Swiss Exchange (SWX).

Under this joint venture structure, Eurex today not only operates the Eurex exchanges, but also the central counterparty Eurex Clearing and the Electronic Communication Networks Eurex Bonds and Eurex Repo. Eurex's corporate structure involves several legal entities (see Figure 8.5) – Eurex Zürich AG, half of which is owned by DBAG and half by SWX, wholly owns Eurex Frankfurt AG. Eurex Frankfurt AG in turn is the holding company for Eurex Deutschland, Eurex Clearing AG,[43] Eurex Bonds GmbH, Eurex Repo GmbH and US Exchange Holdings, Inc.

---

[42] For the following overview of ECAG's history, corporate structure, clearing activities and clearing access, refer to Eurex (ed.) (2006); and www.eurexchange.com.

[43] In contrast to Eurex Frankfurt AG and Eurex Clearing AG, Eurex Deutschland is a self-regulatory organisation under German public law and functions as the German-regulated exchange (formerly DTB). Under Swiss law, Eurex Zürich AG assumes a similar function. Cf. Geiger (2000), pp. 133–40.

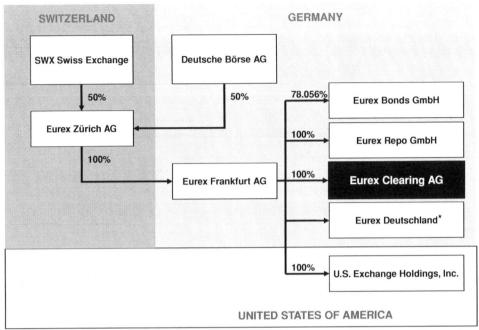

Figure 8.5   Organisational and corporate structure Eurex Clearing AG[44]
Source: Eurex (ed.) (2006), p. 2.

Prior to the merger in 1998, both exchanges were already vertically integrated, i.e. operating trading *and* clearing systems. Eurex Clearing AG was subsequently established to provide a standardised clearing system, acting as a central counterparty for all trades executed on Eurex Zürich and Eurex Deutschland, and supervised by German authorities. In the years that followed, ECAG expanded its services from derivatives clearing to include central counterparty services for other products and asset classes, such as bonds traded on Eurex Bonds GmbH, repos traded on Eurex Repo GmbH, for the majority of all cash equities traded on the FWB Frankfurter Wertpapierbörse (the Frankfurt Stock Exchange, part of Deutsche Börse AG) and for cash equities and exchange traded funds (ETFs) traded electronically on the Irish Stock Exchange.

Since its creation, ECAG has continuously increased in scale. Whereas in December 1998, Eurex Clearing closed the year as the world's fourth largest

---

[44] Minority shareholdings are not included.

derivatives clearing house, clearing 248,222,487 contracts, it then went on to become the world's second largest clearing house from 1999 to 2001. In December 2002, ECAG closed the year as the world's largest derivatives clearing house, with 801,200,873 cleared contracts; it was able to maintain this position in 2003. Since then, it has continued to be among the world's three premier clearing houses (the OCC, the CME and ECAG) and has maintained its status as Europe's largest exchange-traded derivatives CCP.[45]

Market participants can apply for admission as either a General Clearing Member (GCM) or a Direct Clearing Member (DCM) to become a direct counterparty to ECAG. The difference between these memberships is that GCMs can clear their own and their clients' transactions as well as those of exchange participants that do not hold a clearing licence (NCMs), while DCMs can clear their own transactions, their clients' transactions and the transactions of their 100 per cent company-affiliated NCMs. Clearing members must comply with the minimum capital requirements of ECAG,[46] contribute to the clearing fund[47] and maintain appropriate clearing and settlement accounts and adequate back-office installations.[48]

8.1.2.1.2 The Clearing Corporation

In 1925, The Clearing Corporation (CCorp), then named The Board of Trade Clearing Corporation (BOTCC), was founded by the Chicago Board of Trade (CBOT) membership. Its incorporation as an independent clearing house for futures markets in the US resulted from a petition submitted by representatives of the CBOT membership:[49] in 1883, the CBOT, a Chicago-based futures exchange, opened its own internal clearing house. As a wholly owned division of the CBOT, the clearing house initially acted as a common fund, taking payments of member debits and paying out member credits. In 1903, a preliminary petition calling for a clearing house with total independence

---

[45] Refer to section 2.5 for details of ECAG's market share and a graphical overview of the world's largest clearing houses. All data is derived from FOW (ed.) (2001); FOW (ed.) (2003); and FOW (ed.) (2006).

[46] The minimum liable equity capital required (which is calculated on a quarterly basis) was €125 million for GCMs and €12.5 million for DCMs, as of March 2007. Irrespective of these requirements, the actual amount of liable equity capital to be maintained by the clearing members must not be lower than 10 per cent of the 30 days' average or 250 days' average of the total margin requirements. The highest amount determined applies.

[47] As of March 2007, the minimum contribution to the clearing fund stood at €5 million for GCMs and €1 million for DCMs or at 2 per cent of the 30 days' average or 250 days' average of the total margin requirements. The highest amount determined applies.

[48] For more details on ECAG's membership requirements, refer to www.eurexchange.com.

[49] For the following overview of CCorp's history, corporate structure, clearing activities and clearing access, refer to The Clearing Corporation (ed.) (2003); and www.clearingcorp.com.

from the exchange was submitted by the exchange membership. There were five votes from that time until the incorporation of an independent entity, operating under clearing member oversight, was approved in 1925. BOTCC was established as a Chicago-based, stockholder-owned Delaware corporation; and has operated under the supervision of the Commodities Futures Trading Commission (CFTC) since 1974. In order to become a clearing member, a firm or an individual had to own stock in BOTCC, resulting in the clearing member stockholders owning the clearing house.[50]

In November 2003, following the 23 October endorsement by its stockholders, BOTCC implemented a corporate and capital realignment. Besides agreeing on changing the name from BOTCC to CCorp,[51] the new corporate structure most importantly allowed non-stockholder participants to clear trades through CCorp without owning stock.[52] The capital realignment resulted in previous shareholders of CCorp holding approximately 85 per cent of the company and in Eurex acquiring an approximately 15 per cent equity participation in CCorp.[53]

In addition to clearing the CBOT's futures contracts, the firm began clearing cash equities, bonds and government securities traded at the CBOT in the early 1930s. From the late 1980s to the late 1990s, the clearing house also processed trades for the New York Cotton Exchange. In 2000, CCorp expanded its clearing activities to perform clearing functions for an exchange outside of its existing relationship with the CBOT – the Merchants' Exchange. In 2001, CCorp further broadened its services and began processing futures contracts traded through the BrokerTec Futures Exchange. A year later, in 2002, CCorp established a wholly owned subsidiary, the Guarantee Clearing Corporation (GCC), providing clearing services to the Intercontinental Exchange (ICE), the Commodities Management Exchange (CMXchange) and ChemConnect.[54]

---

[50] In 2003, CCorp was owned by eighty-seven clearing member shareholders, a sampling of which included: ABN AMRO, Bear Stearns, Carr Futures, Citigroup, Credit Swiss, Deutsche Bank, Fimat, Fortis Clearing, Goldenberg Hehmeyer, Goldman Sachs, JPMorgan, Lehman Brothers, Marquette Partners, Merrill Lynch, Morgan Stanley, Prudential Securities, Refco, UBS Warburg and others. Cf. Eurex/The Clearing Corporation (eds.) (04.09.2003a), p. 8.

[51] For consistency's sake, the clearing house will be referred to as 'CCorp' throughout the remainder of this study.

[52] The corporate and capital realignment also provided for stockholders to buy and sell shares without the previous restrictions related to firm trading activity, and treated each share equally in voting on corporate issues. Cf. FOW (ed.) (2006).

[53] Further details of the corporate and capital realignment are outlined in section 8.1.2.2, as this was closely related to the partnership deal signed between Eurex and CCorp to create the clearing link subject to this analysis.

[54] Cf. The Clearing Corporation (ed.) (2003), p. 9; and FOW (ed.) (2003).

From its inception in 1925 until 2004, CCorp managed to increase continuously in scale. In 1929, CCorp cleared more than 9 million contracts. After volumes had dramatically decreased to just 1.9 million in 1942 and 1943, volumes climbed back up, reaching as high as 11 million per year in the 1950s, and topping 17 million in 1961. CCorp purchased its first computer in 1963 to increase successfully the efficiency of its clearing process; by 1985, CCorp had facilitated the development of a paperless clearing process. By 1998, it had grown to become the world's second largest derivatives clearing house, with a record 281,189,436 contracts cleared. Until the year 2000, CCorp continued to be the largest clearing house for futures in the US. From 2000 to 2004, it maintained a strong position among the world's five premier clearing houses (the CME, the OCC, ECAG, LCH.Clearnet and CCorp) and was the second largest clearing house for futures in the US. From the end of 2003 to the end of 2004, volumes cleared by CCorp fell sharply, by almost 99 per cent, and continued to fall in the following years. Today, CCorp merely clears approximately 0.1 per cent of the volumes currently processed by its former peers, now the world's premier CCPs.

The reason for the precipitous decline in the number of cleared contracts was the result of two developments: in January 2004, the CBOT and the Chicago Mercantile Exchange (CME) implemented their Common Clearing Link, which entailed the transfer of all CBOT clearing activities from CCorp to the CME's own clearing house. In February of the same year, Eurex launched its US exchange (Eurex US, today under new ownership, and now called the US Futures Exchange) for which CCorp provides clearing services. However, the clearing business provided by this new agreement did not make up for the lost volumes previously cleared for the CBOT. Today, CCorp continues to provide a full range of clearing services for contracts listed by US Futures Exchange (USFE) and furnishes a variety of clearing services for other exchanges and marketplaces.

Market participants can apply to become an Individual Clearing Member or a Clearing Member. The difference between these clearing memberships is that whereas ICMs are only allowed to clear their own transactions, Clearing Members can clear their own transactions, their clients' transactions and those of affiliated exchange participants that do not have a clearing licence (NCMs). Clearing members must comply with the minimum capital requirements of CCorp,[55] contribute to the clearing fund, maintain appropriate clearing

---

[55] As of July 2006, minimum capital requirements related to the number of open positions and business activity. The minimum capital requirement for all clearing members stood at $5 million. Cf. FOW (ed.) (2006).

and settlement accounts, and satisfy CCorp's requirements on operational capabilities and efficiencies.[56]

8.1.2.2 Background and objectives of the initiative

In May 2003, CCorp and Eurex announced that they would enter into a long-term agreement to create a global clearing solution; the initiative was referred to as the Global Clearing Link (GCL).[57] One-and-a-half years later, on 28 October 2004, the clearing houses launched the roll-out. As the objectives of this clearing link initiative were highly correlated with the dynamics of the US exchange landscape in the new millennium, particularly in the years 2002 to 2004, the background that gave rise to these developments is briefly summarised in the following.[58]

In 1994, the CBOT introduced Project A, its after-hours electronic trading system.[59] While Project A allowed the CBOT to reap some regional market benefits, it eventually became clear that the exchange would need an enhanced electronic trading platform to expand into overseas markets.[60] In 2000, the CBOT and Eurex created a joint venture company called a/c/e (alliance/CBOT/Eurex) to operate a single global electronic trading platform. The a/c/e platform, which was based on that of Eurex, provided for enhanced electronic trading at the CBOT.[61] The a/c/e platform thus allowed the CBOT and Eurex to share the same technology and distribution capabilities. The CBOT subsequently migrated all of its business from Project A to a/c/e. CCorp reacted by developing an interface that accepted the position transaction record from a/c/e and converted it to a format recognisable by the clearing house and its members.[62]

Whereas initially scheduled for a five-year term,[63] Eurex and the CBOT agreed in mid-2002 to shorten the remaining term of the a/c/e alliance to January 2004, and to eliminate, by the same date, all product and cooperation restrictions previously in place until 2008.[64] This essentially liberated Eurex to

---

[56] For more details on CCorp's membership requirements, refer to www.clearingcorp.com.

[57] Cf. Eurex/The Clearing Corporation (eds.) (27.05.2003).

[58] The described dynamics largely pertain to the competitive situation of the involved exchanges, rather than those of the partnering clearing houses. Nonetheless, these dynamics ultimately shaped the benefits and drawbacks of the clearing link; they thus play a crucial role for the analysis of the network initiative.

[59] Refer to www.cbot.com for more details.

[60] Cf. The Clearing Corporation (ed.) (2003), p. 7.

[61] Cf. Chicago Board of Trade/Eurex (eds.) (24.07.2000).

[62] Cf. The Clearing Corporation (ed.) (2003), p. 7. For more details on the success and difficulties related to a/c/e, refer to Book (2001), pp. 266–83.

[63] Cf. Book (2001), p. 281.   [64] Cf. Eurex (ed.) (10.01.2003).

compete fully in the US market in all products and to establish new partnerships. Only six months later, in January 2003, the CBOT decided to completely abandon the a/c/e system and replace it with the Liffe-Connect system as soon as the renegotiated terms of the alliance ran out in early 2004.[65] Eurex countered this move by announcing plans to create its own exchange under US regulation, continuing the use of the a/c/e infrastructure and launching a range of US dollar-denominated products – most importantly, US treasury futures – in direct competition with the CBOT's most successful product suite. The launch of this new US exchange was scheduled to coincide with the CBOT's transfer of business from the a/c/e system to the new Liffe-Connect system. As this process required CBOT's traders to undergo a complicated change in technology,[66] Eurex encountered a unique window of opportunity to challenge CBOT's dominant position in the market for treasury derivatives, particularly since these products had increasingly been traded electronically through the a/c/e system rather than being executed on the CBOT's floor. As the world's largest derivatives exchange, Eurex had become renowned for providing very efficient electronic trading. Given that one of Eurex's parent organisations, Deutsche Börse, was the owner of the a/c/e system,[67] the use of the a/c/e infrastructure for its new US exchange gave Eurex immediate distribution to key traders.

Shortly after the CBOT announced its new technology strategy and Eurex heralded the creation of its new exchange, the seventy-five-year working relationship between the CBOT and CCorp came to an abrupt end. This relationship had weathered strife in previous years, when CCorp attempted to expand its business beyond its exclusive arrangement with the CBOT. In particular, CCorp's decision to perform some clearing functions for BrokerTec, a direct competitor with the CBOT in interest rate futures, created tension between the two long-time partners.[68] This manoeuvre led the CBOT to demand the formalisation of an exclusive clearing agreement between the CBOT and CCorp.[69] Additional tensions arose when rumours emerged that the CBOT was considering outsourcing its clearing operation to the CME's in-house clearing house (and thus away from CCorp) and when CCorp signalled its willingness to negotiate with Eurex to provide clearing services for its forthcoming US venture.[70]

---

[65] Cf. Kalbhenn (2003), p. 8.   [66] Cf. Falvey/Kleit (2006), p. 18.
[67] Cf. Falvey/Kleit (2006), p. 18.   [68] Cf. Collins (2003).
[69] In their seventy-five-year working relationship, the CBOT and CCorp had surprisingly never formalised their cooperation through a contract. Cf. Collins (2003).
[70] Cf. Collins (2003).

These dynamics finally culminated in the CBOT and the CME announcing plans to create the Common Clearing Link in April 2003, whereby it was agreed that the CME would perform all of the CBOT's clearing operations instead of CCorp. It was after this announcement was made, and despite the fact that the CBOT/CME agreement was definite, that the CBOT submitted its first purchase offer to CCorp[71] in an attempt to complicate Eurex's launch into the US futures market.[72] A second offer was submitted later in 2003; CCorp refused both purchase offers.[73] At this stage, CCorp began tying together other strategic alternatives,[74] ending in the signing of a letter of intent with Eurex to develop a clearing connection in May 2003. In September 2003, the two companies sealed the final partnership deal.

The primary objectives pursued by this network initiative at the time of its creation were thus compelling to both partners: Eurex, wanting to set up its own US exchange within the relatively short time frame of one year, was in need of a US-regulated clearing house (called 'Designated Clearing Organisation', DCO) to provide clearing services to this entity. Being confronted with the task of not only setting up a new exchange, but also a new clearing house under US regulation from scratch, made the option of entering into an agreement with an incumbent clearing house very attractive. Building a US clearing house infrastructure from the bottom up would likely have required substantially greater investments in terms of both time to market and costs. Not only was CCorp a well-trusted and reputable central counterparty with strong roots in the local Chicago futures community, but it had also developed solutions, experience and know-how in dealing with the a/c/e platform – the system that Eurex continued to use for its new US exchange. Additionally, partnering with CCorp created another unique window of opportunity for Eurex's US venture, potentially enabling it to compete directly for treasury products.

CBOT had signed an agreement with the CME and thus planned to move its business from CCorp to the CME clearing house. This decision had the following implications. Whereas all new positions opened on the CBOT were automatically transferred to the CME clearing house for processing, it was unclear what would happen to the 'old' open interest (i.e. positions that had been opened prior to the introduction of the new trading and clearing

---

[71] Cf. Kentouris (2003a), p. 5.

[72] Besides the strategic move of trying to acquire CCorp, CBOT and CME launched other measures to thwart the market entry of the new competitor. Eurex asserts that CME and CBOT engaged in illegal anti-competitive activity, and has filed an antitrust lawsuit. For details on the lawsuit, refer to Falvey/Kleit (2006), pp. 46–7.

[73] Cf. Rosenberg (2004).   [74] Cf. Rosenberg (2004).

system) that CCorp held on behalf of its clearing members. Eurex's window of opportunity thus resulted from the open question of who actually 'owned' the open interest and from the possibility that the 'old' open interest in CBOT's treasury products would remain at CCorp until the expiration of the contracts in March 2004. With the launch of Eurex US in February 2004, the holding of open interest in US treasury contracts from the CBOT and Eurex US at a single clearing house was envisaged to create attractive opportunities for traders and unique dynamics for Eurex US. It was unclear whether CBOT would succeed in claiming the legal ownership of the open interest and thus in transferring the open interest in treasury products from CCorp to the CME prior to the launch of Eurex US; particularly as such a move required the cooperation and execution on the part of a number of parties, including the CFTC to authorise the transfer of the open interest from CCorp to the CME.[75] CCorp was thus the ideal partner for Eurex.

Although counting on the success of Eurex's new US exchange was risky, CCorp's strategic options at that time were either to accept the CBOT's purchase offer (and thereby be put out of business)[76] or to try to expand its business by pursuing independent growth opportunities.[77] Once CCorp had made the choice to expand its business – independent of any exclusive arrangements and without the almighty CBOT – the cooperation agreement with Eurex represented a tempting opportunity. Eurex, at that time twice the size of CCorp in terms of cleared volume, the world's largest derivatives exchange and raring to grow its business, was an attractive partner for CCorp.

The partnership deal signed between Eurex and CCorp consequently generated a number of compelling benefits:[78]

- all market participants in US treasury futures were already connected to the a/c/e trading platform and CCorp's clearing infrastructure;
- market participants could thus benefit from continuity through the use of existing trading and clearing infrastructure;
- enhanced value for market participants could potentially be created through additional trading and clearing opportunities in US and European products;

---

[75] Cf. Falvey/Kleit (2006), p. 18. The CBOT ultimately succeeded, with the approval of the CFTC, in transferring the open interest from the CCorp to the CME prior to the launch of Eurex US. Whilst in this case the CBOT effectively claimed the legal ownership of the open interest that CCorp held on behalf of its clearing members, the general question of who legally owns the open interest still sparks debate. For an example of a more recent debate, refer to de Téran (2007), p. 33.

[76] It was agreed that the CME would perform all of the CBOT's clearing operations, regardless of whether or not CCorp accepted the CBOT's offer. From the CBOT's perspective, the benefits from the acquisition lay in the assumption of CCorp's registration as a DCO and the subsequent ease of transitioning the open interest from CCorp to the CME.

[77] Cf. Kentouris (2003b), p. 16.   [78] Cf. Eurex/The Clearing Corporation (eds.) (04.09.2003a), pp. 9–10.

- of the top twenty Eurex exchange customers, eighteen were shareholders as well as clearing members of CCorp; and
- additional synergy potential was offered in that ECAG provided 98 per cent of the risk transfer in euro-denominated fixed income futures and CCorp cleared over 98 per cent of all USD-denominated treasury futures.

8.1.2.3 Concept and structure of the initiative

In September 2003, when the two companies signed their non-exclusive long-term partnership deal,[79] they agreed that CCorp would clear for Eurex's new US exchange and that their link would give members of both clearing houses direct access to US and European products. Additionally, it was agreed that subject to shareholder approval, CCorp would change its corporate and capital structure, allowing Eurex to take a 15 per cent equity stake in CCorp[80] through its 100 per cent subsidiary US Exchange Holdings, Inc. Nonetheless, CCorp would remain independent and continue to provide services to multiple marketplaces. Eurex and CCorp further agreed to make joint decisions concerning core areas of the partnership.[81] The initial term of the partnership was seven years, with subsequent automatic three-year renewals.

In October 2003, the shareholders of CCorp approved the corporate and capital restructuring plan, allowing Eurex to build up the equity partnership in CCorp,[82] and resulting in the following additional changes.[83] Eurex was given one seat on the Board of Directors of CCorp; the existing shareholders elected the remaining eight board members. Eurex was granted the option to increase its stake to 51 per cent in the event that an outside bidder attempted to wrest control of CCorp. Finally, the guarantee function previously performed through the company capital would now be performed through a separate clearing fund. It would thus no longer be necessary to hold a stake in the clearing house to clear at CCorp.

---

[79] The sole exclusivity related to Eurex agreeing that the US clearing of interest rate products denominated in euros or USD could only be performed through CCorp.

[80] Cf. Eurex/The Clearing Corporation (eds.) (04.09.2003b).

[81] This included, for example, the cross-margining of additional products with Eurex's US products, building additional clearing links for interest rate products, changing the rules regarding the clearing of Eurex products, CCorp offering clearing services for US interest rate products for other market operators and CCorp entering into strategic alliances, joint ventures, mergers or acquisitions with competing market operators. Cf. Eurex/The Clearing Corporation (eds.) (04.09.2003a), p. 14.

[82] It was agreed that the existing shareholders of CCorp would hold equity of $85 million, and thus 85 per cent of the capital base, and that Eurex would contribute $15 million. CCorp offered a share buy-back programme to allow shareholders to monetarise a certain amount of their equity interest while continuing to use CCorp's clearing services.

[83] Cf. Eurex/The Clearing Corporation (eds.) (04.09.2003a), pp. 13–14; and Eurex/The Clearing Corporation (eds.) (04.09.2003b).

Phase I 'EU Link'	Phase II 'US Link'	Phase III 'Cross Link'
- CCorp clearing members will be able to clear CFTC-approved EU products traded at Eurex - CCorp clearing participants will be able to utilise portfolio margining between EU and US products and one common collateral pool	- Clearing members of Eurex Clearing will be able to clear US products traded at Eurex US - Clearing members of Eurex Clearing will be able to utilise portfolio margining between EU and US products and one common collateral pool	- Allow 21 hours' trading of CFTC-approved European benchmark derivatives through listing on Eurex US - CCorp clearing participants and clearing members of Eurex Clearing will be able to clear EU products traded on Eurex US

Figure 8.6   Three-phased implementation approach of the Global Clearing Link
Source: Based on Eurex/The Clearing Corporation (eds.) (2004b), p. 7.

Two months later, in December 2003, CCorp and Eurex announced plans to launch the Global Clearing Link (GCL) on 28 March 2004, subject to the fulfilment of applicable US and European regulatory requirements and the finalisation of all regulatory actions. As the project evolved, the following details of the clearing link initiative emerged:[84] the GCL would be introduced in a three-phased implementation following the planned launch of Eurex US (Eurex's new US exchange) in February 2004 in order to reduce the regulatory complexity of the roll-out. CCorp would then provide clearing services for products traded on Eurex US, and the GCL would be implemented to provide additional functionality and benefits.

With regard to the business purpose, Phases I and II of the GCL can be classified as a 'Single Exchange Support' type of link; Phase III was intended to be a 'Cross-Listing Support' type of link. In terms of the functional set-up, the GCL was constructed as a 'Recognised CCP Model', with the partnering clearing houses participating in each other's systems as equals. The link set-up therefore required a medium level of functional, technical and legal harmonisation and integration.

Phase I (the so-called 'EU Link') of the GCL was designed to enable clearing members of CCorp to clear European derivatives traded on Eurex.[85] CCorp

---

[84] Cf. Eurex/The Clearing Corporation (eds.) (16.12.2003); Eurex/The Clearing Corporation (eds.) (04.05.2004); Eurex/The Clearing Corporation (eds.) (2004a); and Eurex/The Clearing Corporation (eds.) (2004b).

[85] Note that this included only those euro-denominated European products traded on Eurex approved by the CFTC, i.e. products permitted to be traded on Eurex trading terminals in the US pursuant to a so-called CFTC 'no action letter'. Cf. Eurex/The Clearing Corporation (eds.) (2004b), p. 7.

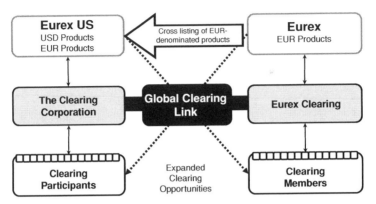

Figure 8.7   The Global Clearing Link concept (Phases I to III implemented)
Source: Based on Eurex (ed.) (2004), p. 21.

clearing participants would thus be able to leverage their infrastructure and utilise portfolio margining between EU and US products as well as one common collateral pool. Phase II (the so-called 'US Link') of the GCL would then enable ECAG's clearing members to clear USD-denominated products traded at Eurex US. These same members would then be able to utilise portfolio margining between EU and US products and one common collateral pool. Finally, in Phase III (the so-called 'Cross Link'), euro-denominated benchmark derivatives previously traded exclusively on Eurex would be cross-listed on Eurex US. This would then allow for twenty-one hours of trading and assure the full fungibility of these products. CCorp's and ECAG's clearing members would then be able to clear these European products traded on Eurex and Eurex US. The GCL, when fully implemented, was configured to allow customers of Eurex and Eurex US to choose their clearing house, provide fungibility of certain products between the two exchanges, and leverage existing processes and infrastructures, while at the same time preserving established clearing member relationships.[86]

8.1.2.4 Status of the initiative

Whereas Phase I had initially been scheduled to be implemented on 28 March, the launch did not in fact take place until the end of October 2004.[87] As US authorities were busy for a long time with the approval of Eurex US and because certain aspects of the GCL required approval from regulatory authorities in the US and Europe, the regulatory complexities translated into a far

---

[86] Cf. Eurex/The Clearing Corporation (eds.) (04.05.2004).
[87] Cf. Eurex/The Clearing Corporation (eds.) (28.10.2004).

lengthier approval process than initially anticipated. The CFTC's announcement on 9 July 2004 of the resignation of its acting Chairman (effective 23 July that year)[88] did not simplify matters.

The implementation of Phases II and III of the GCL required CFTC action beyond what CCorp had originally requested for the first phase of the link.[89] Although the clearing houses started to seek approval for Phase II in March 2005, this process has not been completed to date. The main reason for the delay is that by the time the US regulators had given approval for Phase I of the GCL, Eurex US had started to suffer from decreasing volumes. By mid-2005, as volumes traded on Eurex US continued to decline, Eurex came under increasing pressure from its parental companies to achieve a turnaround of its US business.[90] This finally resulted in Eurex selling 70 per cent of its shares in Eurex US to Man Group plc, one of the world's largest futures brokers, in July 2006.[91]

However, the implementation of Phase II lost traction not only due to Eurex US's lack of volumes; additional US regulatory requirements – asking, for example, ECAG to apply for a DCO licence – also served to slow down the approval process. To this day, Phase II has not regained momentum. Although the application process is formally still pending – ECAG has yet to submit its DCO application to the CFTC – this project is currently unlikely to be high up on ECAG's priority list. The volume of contracts cleared through CCorp is currently far too low to provide significant value-added for ECAG's clearing members, even if they were given the opportunity directly to clear these contracts.[92]

Part II: Analysis

8.1.2.5 Interviewees' assessment of the case study

We were very anti. And certainly most people in the London market were not in favour of it.[93]

I think that is a wonderful cross-regional initiative.[94]

---

[88] Cf. CFTC (ed.) (09.07.2004).   [89] Cf. Eurex/The Clearing Corporation (eds.) (04.05.2004).
[90] Cf. Rettberg (2005), p. 24; and Handelsblatt (ed.) (05.12.2005), p. 33.
[91] Cf. Eurex/Man Group (eds.) (27.07.2006).
[92] This statement was made by the author as of April 2007.
[93] Statement made by interviewed clearing member representative.
[94] Interview with Edward F. Condon.

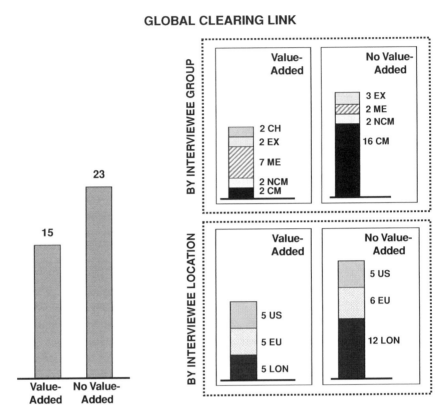

Figure 8.8   Interviewees' assessment of the Global Clearing Link[95]
Source: Author's own.

Whereas section 8.1.1 presented the findings from the empirical study on cross-margining agreements and clearing links in general, including their suitability to integrate European clearing, this section furnishes a concrete evaluation of the GCL initiative.[96] Figure 8.8 illustrates whether or not different stakeholders in clearing believe that the GCL provides value-added. As compared to the request for a more general assessment of clearing links, significantly fewer interviewees were knowledgeable enough about the GCL

[95] Interviewee groups: CM – clearing member; NCM – non-clearing member; ME – market expert; EX – exchange; and CH – clearing house. Interviewee locations: US – United States; EU – Continental Europe; and LON – London.
[96] Note that interviewees' judgement related to the overall success, benefits and limitations of the GCL and not to any particular phase of the GCL.

to provide detailed feedback: roughly 48 per cent (thirty-eight out of seventy-nine) were able to give a concrete assessment.[97]

A majority of twenty-three interviewees felt that the GCL initiative did not provide value-added, whereas fifteen interviewees endorsed the initiative. With regard to the response rate, the group of clearing members was the best informed about the GCL; 86 per cent of all interviewed clearing members were able to provide an informed assessment of it. The NCMs and exchanges interviewed also proved to have a good understanding of this network initiative – in each case, 50 per cent of the respondents shared their view of the GCL. On the other hand, only 32 per cent of the interviewed market experts knew enough about the GCL to issue an assessment. Surprisingly, the interviewees who turned out to be the least informed about the GCL were the clearing house representatives; only two out of nine felt that they had a good enough grasp of the initiative to assess whether or not it provides value-added.

Among the respective interviewee groups, the majority of clearing members and exchanges took a negative view of the GCL. Market experts and clearing houses, on the other hand, looked upon the initiative favourably. Finally, the NCMs were evenly split on the issue. With regard to location, a mere 29 per cent of the US-based respondents delivered an assessment, while 65 and 63 per cent of the interviewees located in Continental Europe and London (respectively) expressed an opinion on the GCL. Figure 8.8 shows that whereas a solid majority of the London-based respondents did not endorse the GCL, the responses from the Continental-Europe- and US-based interviewees were more mixed. The interviewees' reasons for or against the GCL are analysed in detail according to the established framework in the following sections (sections 8.1.2.6 to 8.1.2.8) in order to identify the major benefits and drawbacks of this network initiative.

8.1.2.6 Scale Impact Matrix

In accordance with the framework developed in Chapter 7, the first step in the efficiency assessment of the Global Clearing Link (GCL) consists of establishing the Scale Impact Matrix (SIM). For this purpose, the magnitude of supply-side (section 8.1.2.6.1) as well as demand-side (section 8.1.2.6.2) scale effects is analysed. This enables the derivation of the SIM for the GCL (section 8.1.2.6.3), whose results will be compared to the conclusions of the analysis in section 7.1.

---

[97] The remaining either felt that they had insufficient knowledge about the GCL, had no clear opinion or did not specify their opinion.

NETWORK STRATEGY	COST IMPACT	SCALE INCREASE	SCOPE INCREASE	ECONOMIES OF SCALE	ECONOMIES OF SCOPE
The Global Clearing Link - ECAG -	Medium-Term Investment	LOW TO MEDIUM	LOW	LOW TO MEDIUM	LOW
The Global Clearing Link - CCorp -	Medium-Term Investment	LOW TO MEDIUM	LOW TO MEDIUM	LOW	LOW TO MEDIUM

Figure 8.9   Assessment of economies of scale and scope in the Global Clearing Link
Source: Author's own.

8.1.2.6.1 Analysis of supply-side scale effects

Analysing the supply-side scale effects related to the GCL initiative entails the assessment of both the cost impact for the partnering clearing houses[98] and the realised increase in scale and scope. Doing so allows conclusions on the economies of scale and scope for both CCPs, which in turn enables the derivation of the GCL's net supply-side scale effects for the two clearing houses.

For ECAG, the implementation of Phase I of the GCL gave rise to low to medium economies of scale and low economies of scope. This assessment is due to the combined factors of the medium-term investment required to implement the EU Link, a low to medium scale increase and a low scope increase. For CCorp, however, the implementation of Phase I of the GCL resulted in low economies of scale and low to medium economies of scope. This assessment is attributed to the medium-term investment required from CCorp to implement the EU Link and a low to medium scale and scope increase, respectively.

Phase I of the GCL allows members of CCorp to clear a range of European products traded on Eurex through their existing relationship with CCorp. Whereas this resulted in a greater number of technical, operational and legal

---

[98] Due to the lack of publicly available cost data on either clearing house, no detailed cost or unit cost development analyses can be performed. The following classification is utilised for this purpose: short-term investments entail a one- to two-year amortisation period, medium-term investments a three- to six-year amortisation period and long-term investments an amortisation period equal to or greater than seven years.

adaptations and expenses for CCorp than for ECAG,[99] the particularities of this clearing link initiative included the reimbursement of software development costs from Eurex Frankfurt AG to CCorp.[100] In terms of investments, this clearing link initiative benefited from the fact that CCorp had already established an interface to the a/c/e system and that the CCPs cooperated on the basis of an outsourcing agreement that served to minimise the impact of link-related software development costs.[101] It is thus assumed that the average development costs that both clearing houses had to bear in the context of the GCL initiative are roughly comparable and can be classified as medium-term investments.[102] Note that besides investments in the clearing system itself, the implementation of Phase I and the preparatory work for Phase II gave rise to additional costs, mainly legal expenses; the fact that the partnering clearing houses were subject to different regulatory regimes created a number of hurdles and complexities. This translated into legal costs to solve regulatory hurdles associated with the clearing link initiative. Nonetheless, these

---

[99] The opposite is true for Phase II of the GCL, as this would have enabled ECAG's members to clear USD products traded on Eurex US through their existing clearing relationship with ECAG. The implementation of Phase II would have thus required ECAG to deal with a greater number of technical, operational and legal adaptations than CCorp. Although Phase II has not been implemented to date, both clearing houses had already started to engage in the development of necessary changes by the end of 2004 and in 2005. In 2005, ECAG wrote these costs off as extraordinary depreciation. Due to the unavailability of detailed cost data, it is impossible to isolate concrete figures, but DBAG's annual report suggests that these development costs ranged between €0.5 million and €8 million. Cf. Deutsche Börse Group (ed.) (2006a), pp. 150–51.

[100] Whereas DBAG's annual report reveals that in 2004, Eurex Frankfurt AG reimbursed CCorp with €2.3 million for software development costs, it falls short of specifying whether these costs related solely to Phase I or also included expenses incurred from Phase II of the GCL. It is also unclear what percentage of CCorp's total GCL-related costs this amount compensates for. Cf. Deutsche Börse Group (ed.) (2005b), p. 194.

[101] Generally, clearing links can, but do not necessarily have to, operate on the basis of outsourcing agreements. Outsourcing agreements enable the away clearing house to act legally as central counterparty to its clearing members' transactions in the home clearing houses' contracts, which are available for clearing through a link, without actually technically performing these services. In the context of outsourcing agreements, the home clearing house thus continues to perform technically all or most of the clearing services.

[102] DBAG's annual report of 2004 specifies that changes for the Global Clearing Link were introduced with Eurex Release 7.0 in 2004. Cf. Deutsche Börse Group (ed.) (2005b), p. 56. GCL-related costs are classified as medium-term investments, because DBAG's annual reports of 2004 to 2006 reveal that average costs for a software release are roughly between €5 and €10 million, with an average depreciation over four to five years. Cf. Deutsche Börse Group (ed.) (2005b), p. 156; Deutsche Börse Group (ed.) (2006a), p. 150; and Deutsche Börse Group (ed.) (2007a), p. 156. As Eurex operates an integrated trading and clearing platform, every new software release is thus composed of trading- and clearing-related system changes. It is consequently assumed that the GCL-related software development costs were lower than €10 million and depreciated over a shorter period.

project-related costs did not impair the realisation of economies of scale and scope.

The **scale increase** realised by **ECAG** during Phase I is classified as low to medium for the following reasons. Prior to the launch of the EU Link in October 2004, Eurex asserted that more than 10 per cent of its total volume was generated by US users; this figure was expected to grow to almost 20 per cent over the years following the introduction of the GCL.[103] This means that in 2004, prior to the launch of Phase I, roughly 107 million contracts were generated by US-based users.[104] An increase in scale as expected would have translated into approximately 125 (153) million contracts cleared through the link in 2005 (2006) – which would have been classified as a high to very high scale increase. According to CCorp, it processed and cleared a much lower number of contracts through Phase I of the GCL, i.e. roughly 10 (13) million contracts in 2005 (2006),[105] which is classified as a low to medium scale increase.[106] Note that Eurex's initial estimate of an increase in European products generated by US-based users as a result of the GCL was predicated not only on volume increases potentially realised through Phase I, but also on increases expected to be generated from cross-listing in Phase III, which was never realised. Additionally, Eurex did not specify the time frame for the expected growth rates.

Although **CCorp** also benefited from a low to medium increase in the number of cleared contracts through Phase I of the GCL, this scale increase did not translate into an equally great magnitude of economies of scale – which is due to CCorp's particular position. At the time of the EU Link's introduction, CCorp suffered from a continuously shrinking scale, mainly resulting from the CBOT's move to the CME clearing house and the stagnating development of Eurex US. By the end of 2004, annually cleared volumes were only roughly 1.4 per cent of the volumes processed the previous year. In 2005, one year after the launch of the EU Link, volumes continued to decline, reaching only 0.5 per cent of the volumes processed in 2003. Whereas the European contracts processed through Phase I of the GCL benefited CCorp, as every contract

---

[103]   Cf. Morgan Stanley (ed.) (2004), p. 4.

[104]   For regulatory reasons, US-based entities cannot become clearing members of ECAG. Prior to the introduction of Phase I of the GCL, they therefore had to employ a clearing intermediary that was a member of ECAG to clear their trades executed on Eurex. The EU Link has since enabled US-based entities to clear their trades executed on Eurex without necessarily having to employ an intermediary by clearing through CCorp.

[105]   Cf. The Clearing Corporation (ed.) (19.12.2006).

[106]   This means that in 2005 (2006), only roughly 0.8 (0.9) per cent of ECAG's cleared volume originated from the use of Phase I of the GCL.

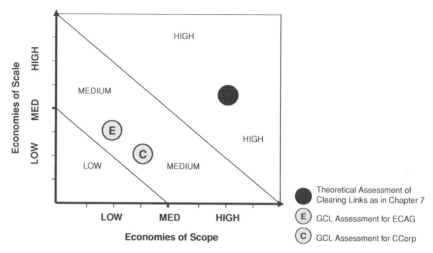

Figure 8.10 Deriving the Global Clearing Link's net supply-side scale effects
Source: Author's own.

cleared through the link generates revenues, these contracts did not translate into equally great economies of scale. Due to the outsourcing agreement, CCorp only provided a limited number of original clearing services for Eurex's European products, and was thus unable to leverage its fixed cost base to the same degree as ECAG through Phase I of the GCL.

Regarding the **increase in scope** realised by the partnering CCPs through the EU Link, ECAG and CCorp were able to benefit from a low and low to medium scope increase, respectively. For **ECAG**, Phase I of the GCL enabled a geographical diversification of its customer base by providing US-based counterparties with the opportunity to clear their transactions in European products without having to employ an intermediary. As this scope increase is limited in its extent, it is classified as a low scope increase.

CCorp, on the other hand, benefited from a greater increase in scope through the EU Link than ECAG, because the link helped it to achieve product as well as geographical diversification. The scope increase for CCorp is therefore classified as low to medium. These classifications allow the Global Clearing Link's net supply-side scale effects to be derived, as outlined in Figure 8.10.

8.1.2.6.2 Analysis of demand-side scale effects

The analysis of demand-side scale effects consists of the following steps: firstly, the GCL's impact on the network sizes is described (section 8.1.2.6.2.1); secondly, the network economic particularities of the GCL are analysed (section 8.1.2.6.2.2); thirdly, the positive and negative network effects on the product and system layers are identified (section 8.1.2.6.2.3); and fourthly, the extent to which the partnering CCPs internalised GCM level network effects through the GCL are scrutinised (section 8.1.2.6.2.4). This allows deriving the associated net demand-side scale effects in a final step (section 8.1.2.6.2.5).

8.1.2.6.2.1 Impact on network sizes. The GCL had an asymmetric impact on each of the partnering CCPs' network size. The implementation of Phase I of the link increased the size of ECAG's network, which then resembled the aggregate number of network members of ECAG and CCorp (but only those of CCorp's clearers that utilised Phase I). In contrast, Phase I had no impact on CCorp's network size. Phase II would have enabled CCorp to increase its network size, but this second phase has yet to come into effect. Although Phase I increased the size of ECAG's network, the usage of this new interconnection has thus far been moderate. Currently, five participants use the EU Link to clear their European transactions on Eurex,[107] having disintermediated their clearer(s). All five of these participants can be classified as regionally-to-globally active clearing members. The empirical study served to identify potential reasons for the low usage of the EU Link to date; these reasons are summarised in the following.

Globally active clearing members confirmed the findings from Chapter 7, affirming that they have very little interest in utilising clearing links with a limited functionality and scope, such as the EU Link. These types of clearer have already established a global presence that enables them to clear internally all of the most important marketplaces worldwide.

The global clearers already had the efficiencies in-house, within their global organisation, which enables them to process their volumes at the respectively ideal places. They do not depend on structures such as the GCL to do that, because they have already established a global presence.[108]

The only potential benefit offered by the EU Link for globally active clearers with an agency focus relates to the difference in the way that US clearing houses and German clearing houses treat customer assets[109] – i.e. the segregation of customer collateral.[110] Whereas under US law, clearing houses are obliged to perform segregation, German law does not permit clearing

---

[107] This statement is based on information provided by Eurex, as of April 2007.
[108] Interview with Jürg Spillmann.   [109] Cf. interviews.
[110] Refer to section 3.2.2.1 for details on segregation and its potential impact on the clearing members' cost of capital.

houses to accept anything other than the clearing members' own collateral (i.e. German clearing houses cannot support segregation). As outlined above, non-segregated customer accounts can translate into increased cost of capital for clearers. The EU Link introduced an opportunity for clearers to process their Eurex transactions in a segregated environment by allowing a range of Eurex's euro-denominated products to be cleared through CCorp's segregated clearing environment, thus theoretically enabling clearers to reduce their cost of capital.

Nonetheless, this solution has in reality failed to provide great value-added for globally active clearers with an agency focus – to date, none of these clearers has chosen to participate in the EU Link. For one thing, these clearers do not expect such a scenario to yield significant cost advantages;[111] on the other hand, most globally active clearers with an agency focus have already established a well-functioning internal workaround to compensate for the fact that ECAG does not support segregation.[112] Additionally, the EU Link did not allow Eurex's complete product suite to be cleared through CCorp; only the euro-denominated products that had been approved by the CFTC were eligible. The attractiveness of participating in Phase I of the GCL to achieve operation in a segregated environment was therefore further tarnished. Finally, clearers expressed their reluctance to transfer customer relationships from Europe to the US, which would have been necessary in order to clear Eurex transactions through the EU Link.[113] To summarise, from the viewpoint of globally active clearers, participation in Phase I of the GCL offered few – if any – benefits over existing arrangements.[114] As the empirical study was biased towards the view of globally active clearers, this also explains why the majority of interviewed clearing members felt that the GCL initiative did not provide value-added.

As outlined in Chapter 7, clearing links usually afford regionally-to-globally active clearers the opportunity to disintermediate their clearing intermediaries for the away market(s). Clearing intermediaries understandably felt threatened by the EU Link, which provides clearing members of CCorp with the opportunity to clear directly their transactions in European products traded on Eurex through their established clearing membership with CCorp. When Phase I was launched, some of these clearers even publicly pronounced their

---

[111] The transaction cost impact for clearers participating in Phase I of the GCL will be further examined in section 8.1.2.7.
[112] Cf. interviews.   [113] Cf. interviews.   [114] Cf. Interviews.

fear of being disintermediated[115] and of thereby suffering from a decreasing network size and lower revenues.

Since the advent of the EU Link, disintermediation has continued to provide a value proposition for an increasing number of CCorp's regionally-to-globally active clearers. Disintermediation can benefit these clearing members by potentially freeing up financial resources,[116] giving them more control[117] and allowing them to process their Eurex business in their home regulatory environment.[118] Nonetheless, with a total of five clearers currently using the EU Link, the participation of regionally-to-globally active clearers has remained low. Because only Eurex's CFTC-approved euro-denominated products can be cleared through CCorp, GCM disintermediation is merely appealing for members whose European activity is limited to this product suite.[119] The EU Link is therefore only likely to spur disintermediation among medium volume clearers in the US that lack a global distribution network and are active in a limited number of European products and markets.[120] However, the EU Link has additional drawbacks for medium volume clearers in terms of disintermediation. For one thing, the link gives US customers access to only one European marketplace (i.e. the Eurex markets). Activity in any market other than that of Eurex thus requires the deployment of a European clearing intermediary.[121]

All it is is a cheaper way of offering GCM services, at the end of the day. And the reason that the link doesn't have more customers is because the link is only with Eurex, but a customer who trades multiple exchanges needs to have a link with everybody, the same way a GCM would. If you go to a GCM they have a link with Eurex, Liffe, etc. So there is not very much value offered through that link, even though it is offered cheap.[122]

CCorp also did not make up for all of the back-office and regulatory reporting services that are commonly provided by the European GCMs for their US-based customers.[123] Disintermediation through the EU Link therefore either meant retaining an intermediary relationship with a third party to provide these services or providing these functions in-house; both options naturally

---

[115] Cf. Larsen/Grant (2005); and interviews.   [116] Cf. interviews.
[117] Cf. interviews.   [118] Cf. interviews.
[119] Medium volume US clearing members can potentially benefit from not disintermediating their European clearer if they are active in a number of European markets and their clearer prices are based on a sliding scale. Any reduction in the volumes processed through the clearing intermediary can, in this case, translate into increasing costs charged for the remaining European volume.
[120] Cf. interviews.   [121] Cf. interviews.
[122] Interview with Richard Jaycobs.   [123] Cf. interviews.

entail additional costs. Medium-sized US clearers might have additional reasons for being reluctant to disintermediate their European GCM, such as a strong mutual relationship with their clearer.

Some US-based market participants actually succeeded in employing the EU Link to put pressure on their European clearing intermediary to cut its commissions or otherwise risk being disintermediated and losing business,[124] and thereby managed to obtain lower fees without actually having to self-clear their Eurex business. Finally, some of the interviewees favourably disposed to the initiative suggested that many market participants simply do not understand the value proposition of the EU Link and that the clearing houses have at the same time failed to promote the link sufficiently.[125]

8.1.2.6.2.2 Network economic particularities. Now that the GCL's impact on the network sizes has been discussed, its network economic particularities will be analysed next. The case study supports the findings from Chapter 7 as follows:

- Because the EU Link did not make all of the products and services offered by ECAG compatible, ECAG was able to benefit from its installed base. Had they been implemented, Phases II and III would have enabled CCorp potentially significantly to benefit from its installed base, too. CCorp's installed base was in fact significantly weakened as a result of a mandatory open interest transfer[126] from the CBOT's open positions to the CME clearing house prior to the launch of Eurex US[127] as well as the low volumes later provided for clearing by Eurex US.

- The installed bases created a starting problem inherent to the EU Link, which affected the following clearing member types of CCorp with potential interest in the initiative: regionally-to-globally active clearing members of CCorp that had previously employed a GCM as intermediary to clear Eurex's European products, regionally-to-globally active clearing members of CCorp that had previously not been active at Eurex, and globally active clearing members of CCorp that had previously also been a member of ECAG (through one of their European subsidiaries).

- For regionally-to-globally active clearing members of CCorp that had previously employed a GCM as an intermediary to clear Eurex's European

---

[124] Cf. Larsen/Grant (2005).   [125] Cf. interviews.

[126] Details on the circumstances of this open interest transfer are outlined in the following analysis of lock-in effects.

[127] Also see Sal. Oppenheim (ed.) (2006), pp. 15–16, on the launch of Eurex US.

products, the EU Link offered them the opportunity to disintermediate their European clearer. The issues constituting a starting problem are outlined above and boil down to whether the utility derived from the link outweighs the costs of disintermediation in the long run.

- For regionally-to-globally active clearing members of CCorp that had previously not been active at Eurex, the starting problem arose from having to invest in the link functionality. Additionally, these clearers faced the costs of having to either establish an intermediary relationship with a third party to provide the back-office and regulatory reporting services that are required to support Eurex's European products or set up these functions in-house. This type of clearer thus had to decide whether the utility derived from the EU Link and the pursued business opportunities would make up for the associated investments in the long run.
- Finally, for globally active clearing members of CCorp that were already members of ECAG, the EU Link enabled them to centralise their clearing at CCorp. The starting problem in this case resulted from several factors, including ECAG's strong installed base, coupled with the erosion of CCorp's installed base. The fact that the link did not cover Eurex's complete product suite constituted yet another drawback. Last but not least, the link fee charged by CCorp as well as the low internal prioritisation of implementing the GCL (due to a lack of external customer and internal pressure/demand for utilisation of the link) further exacerbated the starting problem.[128]
- The installed bases and the starting problem inherent to the EU Link constituted weak forms of lock-in. As outlined in sections 6.1.2.4 and 7.1.2.2.2, the key to success in overcoming weak forms of lock-in is to create a product that is strong enough to offset the consumers' switching costs. The relatively low level of utilisation of and interest in the EU Link suggests that for most clearing members of CCorp with potential interest in the initiative, the value-added provided by this initiative was too weak to overcome switching costs.[129] Note that switching costs in this case refer not only to the costs associated with the initiative, but also include the intangible factors that aggravated the starting problem, such as the widespread failure of relevant clearing members to recognise the true value proposition of the EU Link, the low internal prioritisation of implementing the link,[130] the negative impact of insignificant volumes on Eurex US,[131] the erosion of CCorp's installed

---

[128] Cf. interviews.   [129] Cf. interviews.   [130] Cf. interviews.   [131] Cf. interviews.

base[132] and regulatory and political issues creating further uncertainty about the future development of the initiative.[133]

- Regarding evidence of whether strong forms of lock-in exist on the GCM level, the fact that five of CCorp's clearing members chose to disintermediate their European clearer supports the conclusions of the previous chapter: GCM level network effects do not constitute strong forms of lock-in.

- This case study also illustrates non-network-effect-related coordination problems on the CCP level, even though these are not directly related to the introduction of the GCL. These problems were instead rooted in the competitive dynamics within the US exchange and clearing industry at the time of the clearing link's implementation, and as such constitute an interesting example.[134] In this case, the problems stemmed from product non-fungibility and the absence of choice of clearing location between CCorp and the CME as well as from the mandatory open interest transfer from CCorp to the CME clearing house.[135]

8.1.2.6.2.3 Network effects. The third step in the analysis of demand-side scale effects of the GCL comprises the typified assessment of positive and negative network effects on the product and system layers (see Figure 8.11). This assessment shows that, overall, members of ECAG's clearing network benefited from more and greater positive network effects on the product layer as compared to members of CCorp's clearing network. This is largely due to the competitive situation of the partnering clearing houses at the time of the implementation of the GCL, but the specifics of the initiative also play a role, in particular that only the first phase has been implemented.

---

[132] Cf. interviews.   [133] Cf. interviews.

[134] As outlined in section 8.1.2.2, Eurex US was launched with the objective of taking advantage of a very particular window of opportunity in the US futures industry. When the CBOT decided to transfer its trading from the a/c/e to the Liffe-Connect system, its prime products were US fixed income futures. These had historically been traded on the CBOT's floor, but electronic trading had surged on the a/c/e platform, which had been introduced in cooperation with Eurex. The transfer of electronic trading from the a/c/e platform to the CBOT's new system created a unique opportunity for Eurex. Additionally, when the CBOT migrated its business to the new trading system in January 2004, it also launched its Common Clearing Link with the CME. With the launch of Eurex US in February 2004, the holding of open interest in US treasury contracts from the CBOT and Eurex US at a single clearing house would have created attractive opportunities for traders and unique dynamics for Eurex US. However, when the CBOT succeeded, with the approval of the CFTC, in transferring its open interest from the CCorp to the CME prior to the launch of Eurex US, these competitive dynamics were prevented from coming into play. Cf. Falvey/Kleit (2006), p. 18.

[135] Cf. interviews.

NETWORK EFFECTS	GLOBAL CLEARING LINK - ECAG -	GLOBAL CLEARING LINK - CCorp -	INFLUENCING FACTORS
Netting Effect	+	0	Depends on potential size of network
Size Effect	++	0	Depends on potential size of network
Cross-Margining Effect	+	0	Depends on potential size of network
Open Interest Effect	++	0	Depends on level of integration
Collateral Management Effect	0	+	Depends on level of integration
Interface Effect	0	0	Depends on growth potential
Complementary Offering Effect	0	+	Depends on integration complexity
Information Effect	0	0	Depends on equality of trustworthiness
Learning Effect	0	+	Depends on level of integration
Systemic Risk Effect	0	0	Depends on size of integrated market
Performance Effect	0	0	Depends on size of integrated market
Monopolistic Behaviour Effect	0	0	Depends on size of integrated market

Figure 8.11   Typified assessment of the Global Clearing Link's positive and negative network effects
Source: Author's own.

As outlined above, Phase I of the clearing link had no impact on CCorp's network size. In other words, because no additional clearing members joined CCorp's network, the netting effect was zero.[136] The ECAG clearing network, on the other hand, saw a slight rise in the number of participants, which in turn led to somewhat enhanced netting opportunities. Similar considerations apply to the size and open interest effect. Since the launch of the EU Link, members of the ECAG network have benefited from the growing number of products cleared through the CCP; for some of these, cross-margining opportunities were subsequently granted,[137] culminating in an increase in the open interest held by ECAG.[138]

---

[136] Note that the netting effect would have become relevant for CCorp's clearing network with Phase II.
[137] CCorp would generally be willing to enable cross-margining between Eurex's European products and other products cleared through CCorp to benefit its clearing members. However, as no significant correlation currently exists between Eurex's product suite and other products cleared through CCorp, no such cross-margining can be offered. Cf. interviews.
[138] It is certainly disputable whether or not the five clearing members of CCorp that served to enlarge the size of ECAG's network truly constituted potential demand for these additional products. More case study research is needed to support the existence of the size effect in reality.

This case study illustrates that within a clearing link set-up, the members of a clearing house can benefit from positive network effects on the product and system layers even if their CCP's network size remains unchanged. In the context of the EU Link, members of CCorp can profit from the collateral management,[139] complementary offering[140] and learning effects.[141] Even though the size of CCorp's clearing network was not affected by this link, clearing members still benefit from the utilisation of CCorp's system. Finally, there is no evidence that the EU Link has given or will give rise to any negative network effects.

8.1.2.6.2.4 Internalisation of GCM level network effects. In the fourth step of the analysis of demand-side scale effects emanating from the GCL, the extent to which the partnering clearing houses were able to internalise GCM level network effects is gauged. As only Phase I of the GCL was implemented, only CCorp was in a position to internalise GCM level network effects. ECAG would have had the opportunity to internalise GCM level network effects in Phase II of the GCL through offering direct access to products cleared through CCorp.

The findings of the case analysis and the empirical study suggest that CCorp was only able to internalise GCM level network effects to a minor extent through the EU Link for the following reasons:

- The link interconnects only two clearing house networks and does not cover the complete ECAG product suite.
- The number of complementary services offered by CCorp to compensate for the lost intermediary level is very limited.
- CCorp therefore only succeeds in internalising the size, interface and collateral management effects provided by the GCM level network to a very low degree, because GCMs continue to furnish access to a much broader range of markets and products as well as offer a greater number of services.
- Consequently, the value-added provided by the EU Link is only sufficient to overcome switching costs for limited clearing numbers with a very particular profile.
- Due to CCorp's limited ability to internalise GCM level network effects, the incentive for most of its clearing members to disintermediate the GCM level

---

[139] Clearing members of CCorp benefit from the more centralised holding and management of collateral enabled through the EU Link.

[140] CCorp offers its clearing members a certain number of complementary services to facilitate the utilisation of the EU Link, such as automatic payment and delivery instructions, etc.

[141] The learning effect benefits clearing members of CCorp in that their home clearing house's technology is potentially more widely adopted through the EU Link.

NETWORK STRATEGY	NETWORK ECONOMIC PARTICULARITIES	POSITIVE NETWORK EFFECTS	NEGATIVE NETWORK EFFECTS	POTENTIAL TO INTERNALISE 2ND LEVEL NETWORK EFFECTS	NET POSITIVE NETWORK EFFECT
The Global Clearing Link - ECAG -	(i) Benefits from its installed base through the EU Link (ii) Has starting problem inherent to Link	LOW	NONE	NONE	LOW
The Global Clearing Link - CCorp -	(i) Unable to benefit from its installed base through Phases II and III, as they have not been implemented. Installed base further weakened through mandatory open interest transfer from CCorp to CME (ii) Has starting problem inherent to Link (iii) Clearing members are weakly locked in	VERY LOW	NONE	VERY LOW	VERY LOW

Figure 8.12   The Global Clearing Link's net demand-side scale effects
Source: Author's own.

network was thus minimal; for most of its clearing members, it was in fact more cost efficient to continue to receive a variety of different services from a single clearing intermediary, i.e. their European GCM.

8.1.2.6.2.5 Net positive network effects. The findings vis-à-vis the demand-side scale effects finally allow deriving the associated 'net' demand-side scale effects as outlined in Figure 8.12.

8.1.2.6.3 Overview Scale Impact Matrix

In a final step, the Scale Impact Matrix for the Global Clearing Link (GCL) is derived. The net demand- and supply-side scale effects identified in sections 8.1.2.6.1 and 8.1.2.6.2 serve to determine the respective matrix. Figure 8.13 illustrates this impact and also allows for a comparison with the assessment of clearing links as detailed in section 7.1.

The Scale Impact Matrix shows that the magnitude of scale effects realised through the GCL (Phase I) is significantly below the theoretical potential assigned to clearing link initiatives. These case study findings support the theoretical conclusions outlined in Chapter 7 by demonstrating that these significant clearing link benefits can only be achieved if the partnering clearing houses replicate the size of a Single European CCP network and endeavour to overcome the link-inherent starting problem. To overcome the starting

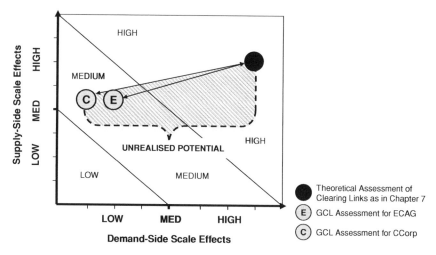

Figure 8.13   The Global Clearing Link's Scale Impact Matrix
Source: Author's own.

problem and to ensure that the utility derived from the CCP level network will offset the costs of alternation in the long run, the partnering CCPs must:

- convince their clearers to expect positive future network effects – implying that the clearing link will be extended in its scope;
- compensate for the lost intermediary (GCM) level services by providing most of these services themselves – thereby successfully internalising GCM level network effects; and
- make up for their clearers' lost participation in other CCP networks by providing a similar service level and processing all products and markets.

The case study analysis showed that in the context of the GCL, ECAG and CCorp did not deliver on these crucial issues. It demonstrated that the clearing houses did not sufficiently strive to overcome the starting problem:

- the link connected only two clearing networks;
- in the context of the EU Link, CCorp did not sufficiently make up for the lost intermediary level – CCorp was only able to internalise GCM level network effects to a minor extent through the EU Link; and
- the EU Link did not make Eurex's complete product suite available to CCorp's clearing members.

The widespread failure of relevant clearing members to recognise the potential value proposition of the EU Link, the low internal prioritisation of implementing the link, the negative impact of insignificant volumes on Eurex US, the erosion of CCorp's installed base, the mandatory open interest transfer from

CCorp to the CME clearing house, regulatory and political issues as well as competitive dynamics created further uncertainty about the future development of the initiative and inhibited CCorp's members from expecting positive future network effects and thus aggravated the starting problem. All of these elements resulted in a significant amount of unrealised potential, as outlined in Figure 8.13.

8.1.2.7 Transaction Cost Impact Matrix and Efficiency Impact Matrix

The Scale Impact Matrix revealed that different network strategies have varying potential for the realisation of network effects and economies of scale and scope. The Transaction Cost Impact Matrix and the Efficiency Impact Matrix analyse whether or not these demand- and supply-side scale effects translate into proportional efficiency gains or losses for different clearing member types.

Whereas the Scale Impact Matrix served to identify the magnitude of demand- and supply-side scale effects related to the Global Clearing Link (GCL), the Transaction Cost Impact Matrix (TCIM) analyses whether or not these scale effects translate into equally great reductions of transaction costs for different clearing member types. In the following, three TCIMs are established to analyse the impact of the GCL on the clearing members' direct and indirect transaction costs. The TCIMs are derived from the empirical study (i.e. the information relayed in the questionnaires and the interviews conducted with various clearing member representatives). Despite the low rate of return of the questionnaires (refer to Chapter 4 for details), one globally active clearing member with an agency focus,[142] a regionally-to-globally active clearing member with a prop. focus[143] and a regionally active clearing member with an agency focus provided responses.[144] Due to the fact that the interviewees provided only a qualitative assessment of the impact of the GCL on their costs, it is not possible to assign any detailed figures or percentages to the magnitude of cost reductions. Therefore, the classifications 'low', 'medium' and 'high' continue to be used throughout the following analysis. The Efficiency Impact Matrix (EIM) finally consolidates the results of the TCIMs, allowing for conclusions on the overall efficiency impact of the GCL initiative.

---

[142] Cf. interviews.   [143] Cf. interviews.

[144] Cf. interviews. Note that the relevant criteria for the classification are not the profit contribution of the customer versus proprietary business, but rather the interviewees' feedback and professional backgrounds.

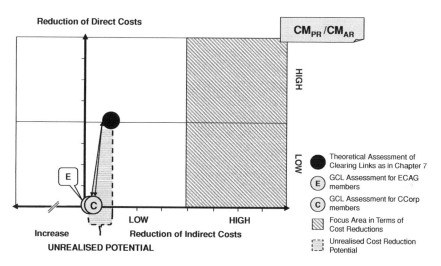

Figure 8.14   Transaction Cost Impact Matrix for regionally active clearing members
Source: Author's own.

8.1.2.7.1 TCIM for regionally active clearing members

Figure 8.14 exhibits the TCIM for Phase I of the GCL for regionally active clearing members of ECAG and CCorp, respectively. It illustrates that the following findings from Chapter 7 are supported by this case study:

- clearing links do not result in a negative transaction cost impact for regionally active clearing members, but rather incorporate potential for cost reductions; and
- nonetheless, clearing links are not suited to reduce significantly these clearers' core cost driver, either.

Regionally active clearing members only benefit from positive network effects that strengthen the unique CCP-related network effects, i.e. the netting, complementary offering, information and learning effects of their domestic home CCP. The analysis of demand-side scale effects showed that ECAG's clearing members benefit from limited netting effects, but do not realise any complementary offering, information or learning effects. This in turn translates into zero to minimal reductions in indirect costs. Clearing members of CCorp benefit from a limited magnitude of complementary offering and learning effects, but do not realise any netting or information effects. This translates into very minor reductions of indirect costs.

In terms of direct cost reductions, the analysis in Chapter 7 suggested that clearing links generally have a limited capacity to reduce fees charged by

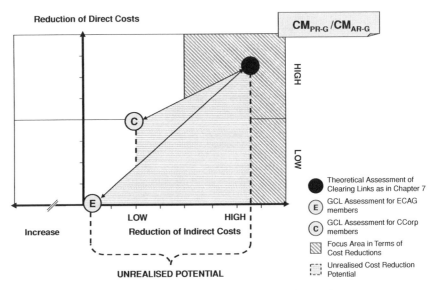

Figure 8.15   Transaction Cost Impact Matrix for regionally-to-globally active clearing members
Source: Author's own.

the home CCP for existing products. Findings from the case study support this, given that neither of the partnering clearing houses reduced fees for existing products as a result of the GCL initiative. This is not surprising, though, because any fee reduction is only likely to occur if the CCP benefits from significant economies of scale that can then be translated into reduced clearing house charges. The analysis of the supply-side scale effects showed that the magnitude of economies of scale was low to medium for ECAG and low for CCorp.

For regionally active clearers with a prop. or an agency focus, indirect costs are the core cost driver. The unrealised potential for reducing these clearers' indirect costs is a direct result of the limitations and drawbacks of the GCL initiative (as outlined in section 8.1.2.6).

8.1.2.7.2 TCIM for regionally-to-globally active clearing members

Figure 8.15 exhibits the TCIM for Phase I of the GCL for regionally-to-globally active clearing members of ECAG and CCorp, respectively. It illustrates that the following findings from Chapter 7 are supported by this case study:

- Regionally-to-globally active clearing members benefit from the opportunity to clear many markets through their domestic home clearing house, which allows them to disintermediate the clearer(s) they employ as intermediaries to other markets.

- Clearing links can serve this purpose, but their attractiveness highly depends on the size of the clearing network (i.e. the number of interconnected clearing houses) as well as on the partnering CCPs' engagement in overcoming the link-inherent starting problem.
- A significant P&L impact can only be realised for these clearers and the utility derived from the link can only offset the costs of alternation in the long run when the link is extended in its scope and the clearing houses compensate for the lost intermediary (GCM) level services by providing most of these services themselves – thereby successfully internalising GCM level network effects.

As outlined above, Phase I of the GCL did not give clearing members of ECAG the opportunity for disintermediation. Regionally-to-globally active clearing members of ECAG wishing to clear products for which CCorp constitutes the home CCP must continue to employ a US-based intermediary. Phase II of the GCL, which has not yet been introduced, would have provided them with the opportunity to disintermediate. In terms of direct cost reductions, ECAG's clearing members therefore failed to benefit from either reduced clearing house or service provider charges. Whereas the low to medium scale economies and the low scope economies did not translate into indirect cost reductions for these clearers, clearing members nonetheless realised minimal cost benefits from the positive network effects outlined in Figure 8.11.

For regionally-to-globally active clearers with a prop. or an agency focus, indirect costs are the core cost driver. Overall, this adds up to a significant degree of unrealised potential for indirect transaction cost reductions for ECAG's regionally-to-globally active clearing members.

Clearing members of CCorp that chose to disintermediate their European clearer and take advantage of the EU Link were able to realise direct cost reductions. For these clearing members, it is cheaper to utilise CCorp, which charges a fee for the utilisation of the link to clear Eurex's European products, than it is to continue to use their European clearing intermediary. The low economies of scale, low to medium economies of scope, very low net positive network effects and the benefits of disintermediation all translate into low reductions of indirect costs. Indirect cost reductions result from clearing members having more control over their positions, collateral pooling, reduced haircuts and more centralised risk management. Consequently, although regionally-to-globally active clearing members of CCorp realised certain direct and indirect cost reductions, the EU Link did not yield significantly positive P&L effects.

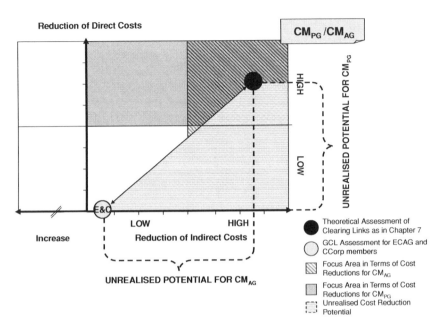

Figure 8.16   Transaction Cost Impact Matrix for globally active clearing members
Source: Author's own.

The unrealised potential for a significant reduction of indirect transaction costs of CCorp's regionally-to-globally active clearing members is a direct result of the limitations and drawbacks of the GCL initiative (as outlined in section 8.1.2.6).

8.1.2.7.3 TCIM for globally active clearing members

Figure 8.16 exhibits the TCIM for Phase I of the GCL for globally active clearing members of ECAG and CCorp, respectively. It illustrates that the following findings from Chapter 7 are supported by this case study:[145]

- Globally active clearers with a prop. focus mainly benefit from network strategies that serve to reduce clearing house charges.
- The main benefit from network initiatives for globally active clearers with an agency focus comes from being able to centralise various clearing relationships into a single relationship with one clearing house.

---

[145] By definition, globally active clearing members are members of each of the partnering clearing houses. This assumption was supported by the case study findings, as those clearers that were classified as high volume and globally active clearers were indeed members of both CCPs. For this reason, there is no need to differentiate the transaction cost impact for clearing members of ECAG versus members of CCorp (see Figure 8.16).

- The starting problem for these clearers will only be overcome and the utility derived from the link can only offset the costs of alternation in the long run when the partnering CCPs are able to convince their clearers to expect positive future network effects – implying that the clearing link will be extended in its scope – and make up for their clearers' lost participation in other CCP networks by providing a similar service level and processing all of the other CCP's products and markets.

For globally active clearers with a prop. focus, direct costs are the core cost driver. From these clearers' perspective, the GCL did not offer any value-added. Due to the limited magnitude of supply-side scale effects, the GCL did not bring down clearing house charges, and thus failed to reduce these clearers' core cost driver. The unrealised potential for a significant reduction of direct transaction costs of globally active clearing members is a direct result of the limitations and drawbacks of the GCL initiative (as outlined in section 8.1.2.6).

For globally active clearers with an agency focus, indirect costs are the core cost driver. These clearers' main benefit from network strategies comes from being able to consolidate their various clearing relationships, i.e. centralise these into a single relationship. The findings of the Scale Impact Matrix showed that the EU Link does not constitute a sufficiently attractive scenario for these clearers, because it only interconnects two clearing houses and does not make Eurex's complete product suite available to CCorp's clearing members. The benefits of using CCorp instead of ECAG as a clearing house are consequently not compelling for these clearers. The unrealised potential for a significant reduction of indirect transaction costs of globally active clearing members is a direct result of the limitations and drawbacks of the GCL initiative (as outlined in section 8.1.2.6).

Consequently, not a single globally active clearer opted to utilise the EU Link to convert its joint clearing relationship with ECAG and CCorp into a single relationship with CCorp. One interviewed clearing member pointed out that he and his firm had actually been able to realise minimal indirect cost reductions through back-office cost savings and via the utilisation of segregated accounts at CCorp enabled by the EU Link.[146] Because this was not found to be true for the remaining interviewed globally active clearers, the magnitude of indirect cost reductions was classified as zero to very low.

This case study provides a prime example of a clearing link that, due to its structure, has basically no appeal to globally active clearers. The significantly

---

[146] Cf. interviews.

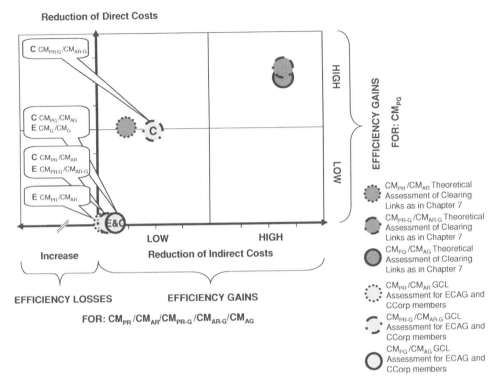

Figure 8.17   The Global Clearing Link's Efficiency Impact Matrix
Source: Author's own.

unrealised potential, as outlined in Figure 8.16, illustrates why globally active clearing members will usually abstain from utilising clearing links with a very limited functionality and scope, such as the EU Link.

8.1.2.7.4 *Efficiency Impact Matrix*

The Efficiency Impact Matrix (EIM), as outlined in Figure 8.17, consolidates the previously established TCIMs into a single graph to summarise the overall efficiency impact of the GCL initiative. The EIM illustrates that the following finding from Chapter 7 is supported by this case study: clearing links result in efficiency gains for all clearing member types.

Phase I of the GCL did not generate efficiency losses for any clearing member type, but it did not result in any significant efficiency gains, either. Regionally-to-globally active clearing members of CCorp with a prop. or agency focus can benefit most from this clearing link initiative if their particular situation allows them to disintermediate their European clearer(s).

8.1.2.8 Business Model Impact Matrix

The final step in the case study analysis consists of establishing a Business Model Impact Matrix (BMIM) for each of the different clearing member types. The BMIM illustrates whether the efficiency increase resulting from the GCL (Phase I) translates into a proportional or disproportional profit increase or decrease for different clearing member types. The BMIMs thus serve to analyse the revenue side and the implications of the GCL on the clearing members' respective business models.

The horizontal axis replicates the findings from the Efficiency Impact Matrix; the vertical axis indicates whether a certain network strategy results in a profit increase or decrease for different clearing member types. The hatched area in the BMIM highlights the focus area and indicates a positive impact on the respective clearing member type's business model. The BMIMs thus illustrate whether the GCL impacted the clearing members' cost or revenue side (or both). As no concrete figures on revenue impacts were relayed over the course of the empirical study, the assessment is based on an estimate from more general information provided by the interviewees.

Due to the fact that interviewees provided only a qualitative assessment of the GCL's impact on their revenues, it is impossible to assign any detailed figures or percentages either to the magnitude of revenue increases or decreases, or to the resulting profit increase or decrease. Therefore, the classifications 'low', 'medium' and 'high' continue to be used throughout the analysis.

8.1.2.8.1 BMIM for regionally active clearing members

Figure 8.18 exhibits the BMIM for the GCL (Phase I) for regionally active clearing members of ECAG and CCorp, respectively. It illustrates that the following findings from Chapter 7 are supported by this case study:

- revenues for this clearing member type remain largely unaffected by a clearing link set-up;
- as transaction costs can be slightly reduced, the respective efficiency gains convert into a proportional profit increase; and
- clearing links consequently have a neutral or a slightly positive impact on the business model of regionally active clearers.

The TCIMs showed that the cost impact of the EU Link for ECAG's clearing members was zero to very low. As the EU Link has no revenue impact for

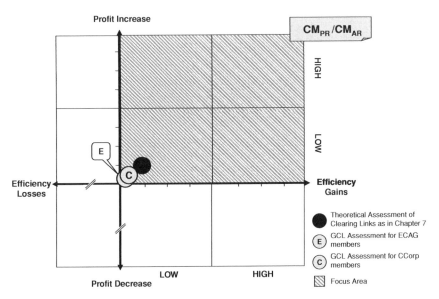

Figure 8.18 Business Model Impact Matrix for regionally active clearing members
Source: Author's own.

these clearing members,[147] the zero to very low efficiency gain converts into a proportional, and thus equally insignificant, profit increase. The same is true for regionally active clearing members of CCorp. Their revenues are also not affected, and their very low efficiency gain translates into an equally minimal profit increase.

8.1.2.8.2 BMIM for regionally-to-globally active clearing members

Figure 8.19 exhibits the BMIM for the GCL (Phase I) for regionally-to-globally active clearing members of ECAG and CCorp, respectively. It illustrates that the following findings from Chapter 7 are supported by this case study:

- revenues for this clearing member type can (significantly) increase through a clearing link set-up;
- as transaction costs can also be (significantly) reduced through clearing links, the respective efficiency gains convert into a disproportionately higher profit increase;
- clearing links consequently have a positive (possibly a significantly positive) impact on the business model of regionally-to-globally active clearing members;

---

[147] The associated efficiency gains are too minimal and are unlikely to impact the level of prop. or agency trading and thus clearing.

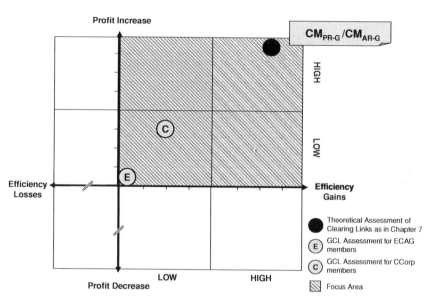

Figure 8.19   Business Model Impact Matrix for regionally-to-globally active clearing members
Source: Author's own.

- whether or not regionally-to-globally active clearers are able to benefit from the significantly positive potential of a clearing link initiative depends on the following factors:
  - (i) the concrete structure, scope and particularities of the clearing link initiative; and
  - (ii) the clearer's internal set-up and structure, the level of complementary (banking) services they receive from their clearing intermediary and the resulting business case to assess the attractiveness of disintermediating their GCM.

The analysis of the TCIM showed that the cost impact of the EU Link for ECAG's clearing members is zero to very low. As the EU Link has no revenue impact for these clearing members,[148] the zero to very low efficiency gain converts into a proportional, and thus equally insignificant, profit increase.

The same is not true for regionally-to-globally focused clearing members of CCorp, however. Because their revenues experience a slight increase, their low efficiency gain translates into a low to medium profit increase. Clearing

---

[148] The associated efficiency gains are too minimal and are unlikely to impact the level of prop. or agency trading and thus clearing. Phase I of the GCL also failed to provide regionally-to-globally active clearing members of ECAG with the opportunity to disintermediate their clearer in other markets to leverage their infrastructure.

members of CCorp utilising the EU Link thus benefit from a disproportionately higher profit increase. For clearing members with a prop. focus, this profit increase results from the disintermediation of their European clearer and from enhanced internal efficiency. Greater control, reduced haircuts, and the fact that they can leverage their back-office and systems infrastructure all help to free up financial resources that can be used to trade – and thus clear – more contracts.

Clearing members of CCorp with an agency perspective also benefit from a disproportionately higher profit increase. This gain stems from their increased internal efficiency and the ability to offer a broader range of products and markets to their NCMs/customers, which in turn increases their attractiveness. These clearers are thus able to offer their customers an increased scale and scope of services at lower costs. Revenues are in turn increased due to a greater profit margin and by virtue of existing or new NCMs/customers conducting more of their business through this clearing member of CCorp. The low efficiency gains realised through the utilisation of the EU Link thus translate into a disproportionately higher profit increase for clearing members of CCorp.

8.1.2.8.3 BMIM for globally active clearing members

Figure 8.20 exhibits the BMIM for the GCL (Phase I) for globally active clearing members of ECAG and CCorp, respectively. It illustrates that the following findings from Chapter 7 are supported by this case study:

- Clearing links affect globally active clearing members with different business focuses (i.e. prop. versus agency) differently.
- For clearers with a **prop. focus**, the efficiency gains generated by a certain network strategy translate into a proportional profit increase. Clearing links are unlikely to impact revenues, however, because the scale and scope of services are not broadened.
- Clearing links can consequently have a positive or significantly positive impact on the business model of globally active clearing members with a prop. focus.
- Whether or not globally active clearing members with a prop. focus are able to benefit from the significantly positive potential of a clearing link initiative depends on the following factors:
  (i) the concrete structure, scope and particularities of the clearing link; and
  (ii) the clearer's ability to overcome internal hurdles to realise these efficiency gains.

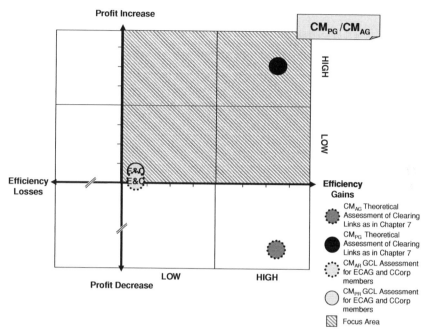

Figure 8.20 Business Model Impact Matrix for globally active clearing members
Source: Author's own.

- Whereas transaction costs for clearing members with an **agency focus** can be (significantly) reduced through clearing links, these efficiency gains are counteracted by (significant) revenue losses through disintermediation.
- For this type of clearing member, the efficiency gains through a clearing link initiative can convert into a proportional or disproportional profit decrease.
- Clearing links can consequently have a negative (possibly a significantly negative) impact on the business model of globally active clearers with an agency focus.
- Whether or not globally active clearing members with an agency focus suffer from a negative business model impact through a clearing link initiative depends on the following factors:
    - (i) the concrete structure, scope and particularities of the clearing link;
    - (ii) the resulting attractiveness of disintermediation through the clearing link; and
    - (iii) whether decreases in revenues outweigh the efficiency gains.

The analysis of the TCIMs showed that the cost impact of the EU Link for globally active clearing members is zero to very low. Clearing members with a prop. focus could benefit from a profit increase if enhanced internal efficiency frees up financial resources that are then used to trade – and thus clear – more contracts. In this case, their revenues increase slightly and their zero to very low efficiency gain translates into a disproportionately higher profit increase. However, the associated efficiency gains are too minimal and are unlikely to impact the level of prop. trading or clearing. As the EU Link therefore had no revenue impact for these clearing members, the zero to very low efficiency gain converts into a proportional, and thus equally insignificant, profit increase.

The same is not true for globally active clearing members with an agency focus. Whereas they benefit from minimal efficiency gains through the EU Link, they simultaneously suffer from disintermediation. When CCPs succeed in internalising GCM level network effects through a clearing link initiative, disintermediation becomes increasingly attractive. The findings of the Scale Impact Matrix outlined that the internalisation of GCM level network effects is achieved only to a very low degree in the context of the GCL (Phase I). Nonetheless, globally active clearers lost NCMs as a result of disintermediation through the EU Link, which negatively impacted their revenues. However, as only five regionally-to-globally active clearing members have so far chosen to participate in the EU Link and disintermediate their European clearer(s), the resulting revenue impact for the globally active clearers is assumed to be minimal. It is therefore further assumed that the equally minimal efficiency increase through Phase I made up for the minimal decrease in revenues. The resulting profit impact is therefore zero.

Although the globally active clearers with an agency focus did not suffer from significant profit decreases or experience a negative impact on their business model as a consequence of the GCL, the case study does indicate that this is a possible scenario. In fact, in the pre-launch phase of the EU Link, clearers with this particular profile publicly accused ECAG of harming their business model,[149] which lends support to the negative impact theory. In the end, the disintermediation option was of such limited appeal to regionally-to-globally active clearing members that the business model of globally active clearers with an agency focus was not negatively impacted.

8.1.3 Summary of findings – impact of clearing links on efficiency

The purpose of this chapter is to challenge the findings from Chapter 7 with insight provided by the empirical study and a case study. This allows drawing final conclusions regarding the impact of clearing links on the efficiency of

---

[149] Cf. Larsen/Grant (2005).

European clearing. The findings obtained from both the empirical study and the GCL case study support and clarify the preliminary conclusions. The findings are summarised in the following.

8.1.3.1 Scale Impact Matrix

- The Scale Impact Matrix showed that the magnitude of demand- and supply-side scale effects realised through the Global Clearing Link (GCL) (Phase I) falls significantly below the theoretical potential assigned to clearing link initiatives.
- The case study findings support the conclusions generated in Chapter 7 by clarifying that in order to achieve the potentially significant benefits of a clearing link set-up, the partnering clearing houses must endeavour to replicate the size of a Single European CCP network and surmount the link-inherent starting problem.
- To overcome the starting problem and ensure that the utility derived from the CCP level network will offset the costs of alternation (that clearing members have to bear) in the long run, the partnering CCPs must:
    (i) convince their clearers to expect positive future network effects – implying that the clearing link will be extended in its scope;
    (ii) compensate for the lost intermediary (GCM) level services by providing most of these services themselves – thereby successfully internalising GCM level network effects; and
    (iii) make up for their clearers' lost participation in other CCP networks by providing a similar service level and processing all products and markets.
- The case study analysis revealed that the GCL initiative left a significant amount of unrealised potential in its wake because:
    (i) the link connected only two clearing networks;
    (ii) in the context of the EU Link, CCorp did not sufficiently compensate for the lost intermediary level; it was only able to internalise GCM level network effects to a minor extent through the EU Link; and
    (iii) the EU Link did not make Eurex's complete product suite available to CCorp's clearing members.
- The clearing houses thus did not adequately attempt to overcome the starting problem.
- Additionally, the widespread failure of relevant clearing members to recognise the potential value proposition of the EU Link, the low internal prioritisation of implementing the link, the negative impact of insignificant volumes on Eurex US, the erosion of CCorp's installed base, the mandatory open interest transfer from CCorp to the CME clearing house, regulatory

and political issues as well as competitive dynamics created further uncertainty about the future development of the initiative and inhibited CCorp's members from expecting positive future network effects and thus aggravated the starting problem.

8.1.3.2 Transaction Cost Impact Matrix

- For regionally active clearing members (CM_{PR}/CM_{AR}), the findings described in section 7.2.1.1 were supported. The unrealised potential for a reduction of indirect transaction costs is a direct result of the limitations and drawbacks related to the GCL initiative; these shortcomings were identified in the discussion of the Scale Impact Matrix.
- The theoretical findings from section 7.2.1.2 with respect to regionally-to-globally active clearing members (CM_{PR-G}/CM_{AR-G}) were also buoyed by the case study results. Again, the unrealised potential for a reduction of indirect transaction costs for clearing members of CCorp is a direct result of the limitations and drawbacks related to the GCL initiative identified in the discussion of the Scale Impact Matrix. ECAG's clearing members were also deprived of the full potential for indirect transaction cost reductions, mainly due to the fact that Phase II of the GCL has not been implemented.
- Finally, for globally active clearing members (CM_{PG}/CM_{AG}), the findings described in section 7.2.1.3 were also supported. For these clearers, the significant unrealised potential of the GCL stems from the limited magnitude of supply-side scale effects (which impeded any reduction of clearing house charges), the fact that the GCL only interconnected two clearing houses and that it failed to cover the complete ECAG product suite; furthermore, the benefits of using CCorp instead of ECAG as a clearing house turned out to be under-whelming. These factors explain why globally active clearing members will usually abstain from utilising clearing links with a very limited functionality and scope, such as the EU Link.

8.1.3.3 Efficiency Impact Matrix

- Clearing links result in efficiency gains for all clearing members.

8.1.3.4 Business Model Impact Matrix

- Clearing links have a neutral or a slightly positive impact on the business model of regionally active clearers (CM_{PR}/CM_{AR}).
- Clearing links can benefit regionally-to-globally active clearing members (CM_{PR-G}/CM_{AR-G}) through a positive (possibly a significantly positive) impact on their business model. Whether or not regionally-to-globally active

clearing members are able to benefit from the significantly positive potential of a clearing link initiative depends on the following factors:

(i) the concrete structure, scope and particularities of the clearing link; and

(ii) the clearer's internal set-up and structure, the level of complementary (banking) services they receive from their clearing intermediary, and the resulting business case to assess the attractiveness of disintermediating their GCM.

• Clearing links can have a positive or even significantly positive impact on the business model of globally active clearing members with a prop. focus (CM_{PG}). Whether or not these clearers are able to benefit from the significantly positive potential of a clearing link initiative depends on the following factors:

(i) the concrete structure, scope and particularities of the clearing link; and

(ii) the clearer's ability to overcome internal hurdles to realise these efficiency gains.

• Clearing links can have a negative (possibly a significantly negative) impact on the business model of globally active clearing members with an agency focus (CM_{AG}). Whether or not these clearers suffer from a negative business model impact through a clearing link initiative depends on the following factors:

(i) the concrete structure, scope and particularities of the clearing link;

(ii) the resulting attractiveness of disintermediation through the clearing link; and

(iii) whether decreases in revenues outweigh the efficiency gains.

To summarise, this case study yielded some crucial findings regarding clearing link initiatives as a means to increase the efficiency of the European clearing industry. The study demonstrated that clearing link initiatives increase the efficiency for all clearing member types and also identified the crucial success factors necessary to exploit the full potential of clearing link initiatives.

8.2 The merger study

This section presents insights from the empirical study and a real-world case study regarding the efficiency impact of mergers and acquisitions, the conclusions of which are compared to the findings from Chapter 7. First, an analysis of a concrete case study, i.e. the merger between the London Clearing House and Clearnet, is furnished (section 8.2.1). The section concludes by summarising the findings regarding the impact of mergers and acquisitions on efficiency (section 8.2.2).

As opposed to the clearing link study presented in section 8.1, the findings from the empirical study regarding M&A initiatives are not presented separately; they are instead described as part of the specific merger case study. Additionally, the question of whether M&A activities are suited to integrate European clearing is addressed in the Single CCP study in section 8.3.[150]

8.2.1 Case study: the London Clearing House and Clearnet

They could have delivered the same things three years ago, had they never merged. It was never worth it. It was a ridiculous merger! Any way you look at it – it is difficult to come up with anything positive from it. I can't see any value-added at all.[151]

I think the merger between LCH and Clearnet makes and made very good sense indeed.[152]

This case study analyses the merger implemented in 2003 between the London Clearing House Ltd (LCH) and the Paris-based clearing house Clearnet SA. This network initiative provides valuable material for a case study analysis for various reasons. The transaction constitutes one of Europe's most recent and important cross-border M&A deals between CCPs. The merger combined two of Europe's major derivatives clearing houses to create the LCH.Clearnet Group Ltd – now Europe's second largest derivatives CCP. As the transaction involved two clearing houses being subject to different regulatory regimes, careful scrutiny of the complexities involved in such a cross-border merger reveals important findings relevant for future M&A deals between European CCPs. Additionally, the initiative was undertaken long enough ago to furnish a fairly substantial period for analysis. On the other hand, the merger is recent enough to constitute an adequate concept for the analysis of current and future M&A deals. Finally, the case study serves to showcase LCH.Clearnet's strengths and weaknesses with an eye to engaging in future European network initiatives.

The introductory part (Part I) of the following analysis profiles the partnering clearing houses (section 8.2.1.1), the background and objectives of the initiative (section 8.2.1.2), its concept and structure (section 8.2.1.3) and its

---

[150] The Single CCP study also provides insight into whether interviewees generally prefer competition and an oligopolistic market structure over consolidation of the European clearing industry via M&A initiatives to create a single market infrastructure.

[151] Statement made by interviewed clearing member representative.   [152] Ibid.

current status (section 8.2.1.4). The second part (Part II) analyses the case study, the results of which are derived from the interviewees' assessment of the merger (section 8.2.1.5).

Part I: Introduction

8.2.1.1 Profile of the partnering clearing houses
8.2.1.1.1 The London Clearing House

The London Clearing House Ltd (LCH) was established in 1888 as the London Produce Clearing House to clear contracts for commodities such as coffee and sugar traded in London.[153] In 1973, the company became the International Commodities Clearing House Ltd (ICCH) to reflect the overseas activities it was pursuing at that time. A decade later, in the 1980s, the company and its focus changed radically, when ownership passed from United Dominions Trust to a consortium of six British clearing banks. At this time, the clearing house expanded its business to provide clearing services to the then International Petroleum Exchange (IPE, in 1981), London International Financial Futures Exchange (Liffe, in 1982) and London Metal Exchange (LME, in 1987). In the early 1990s, as overseas clearing activities were discontinued, the company was re-named the London Clearing House (LCH) to reflect its primary centre of activity, the London markets. For a time, it operated as an unlisted, not-for-profit private limited company under English law. In October 1996, majority ownership of LCH transferred to the whole clearing membership. The three exchanges (Liffe, LME and IPE) whose contracts it cleared acquired minority ownership. This resulted in clearing members holding 75 per cent, Liffe maintaining a 17.7 per cent stake, and LME and IPE holding a combined stake of 7.3 per cent in the CCP.

Throughout the years, LCH has expanded its services. It began clearing cash equities in 1995. During the late 1990s and the early years of the new century, LCH expanded to introduce clearing for cash bonds, repos, inter-bank interest rate swaps and energy (gas and power). By 2003, LCH was acting as the central counterparty to its members in the following markets and products:
- futures and options on Euronext.liffe, IPE and LME;
- cash equities on the London Stock Exchange (LSE), virt-x and EDX;

---

[153] For the following overview of LCH's history, corporate structure and clearing activities, refer to www.lchclearnet.com; FOW (ed.) (2001); and FOW (ed.) (2003).

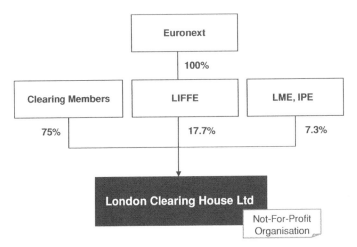

Figure 8.21   Pre-merger ownership structure London Clearing House
Source: Based on Euronext (ed.) (2003), p. 9.

- repos and cash bonds;
- inter-bank interest rate swaps; and
- OTC energy swaps transacted on ICE (IntercontinentalExchange Inc.) and Endex (European Energy Derivatives Exchange).

In 1998, LCH closed the year as the world's third largest and Europe's largest derivatives clearing house, with 266,889,517 contracts cleared.[154] In the following year, LCH was ousted by Eurex Clearing and Clearnet, which both had stronger growth in volumes. From 1999 to 2002, LCH alternated between being the world's fifth or sixth largest derivatives clearing house and maintained its status as Europe's third largest derivatives clearing house.

Market participants could apply to become a General Clearing Member (GCM) or an Individual Clearing Member (ICM) of LCH. The difference between these membership categories is that GCMs can clear their own transactions and their clients' transactions as well as those of exchange participants that do not hold a clearing licence (NCMs), while ICMs are only able to clear their own transactions. All clearing members were required to purchase an LCH 'A' share at a price set by the Board,[155] comply with the clearing house's minimum capital requirements, contribute to the clearing fund and fulfil

---

[154] Refer to section 2.5 for details on LCH's market share and a graphical overview of the world's major derivatives clearing houses. All data is derived from FOW (ed.) (2001); FOW (ed.) (2003); and FOW (ed.) (2006).

[155] As an example, in April 2003, the price for such a share was £297,615. Cf. FOW (ed.) (2003).

additional operational requirements.[156] The requirement of holding shares in the clearing house was later abandoned and dropped as a prerequisite for becoming a clearing member of LCH.

8.2.1.1.2 Clearnet

Clearnet SA (Clearnet) was established in 1888 as a French bank, the Banque Centrale de Compensation SA, to clear contracts traded in Paris commodity markets.[157] In 1990, it became a subsidiary of MATIF,[158] and then an indirect subsidiary of SBF – Bourse de Paris, when that body took over MATIF in 1998. In 1999, all of the regulated markets in Paris were brought together and subsequently run by a single body – the Société des Bourses Françaises (SBF). In March 2000, the SBF, the Amsterdam Exchanges and the Brussels Exchanges agreed to merge into an entity called Euronext. Following the Euronext merger, Clearnet merged with the clearing houses of the Brussels and Amsterdam exchanges, thus assuming the clearing activities previously undertaken by AEX-OptieClearing BV in Amsterdam and BXS Clearing in Brussels.[159]

The integration of the CCPs was intended to provide central clearing within the Euronext Group and resulted in Clearnet, as a recognised bank under French law, becoming the clearing house for all transactions traded on the Euronext markets.[160] Clearnet operates through branch offices in Paris, Amsterdam and Brussels, which were formed from the clearing units used by the Euronext constituent exchanges prior to the merger. As a subsidiary of Euronext Paris, Clearnet operated as a for-profit French credit institution and had to abide by the banking regulations under the supervision of the Banque de France. The French banking authorities regularly monitored Clearnet's procedures and accounts.

---

[156] For further details on the membership requirements, refer to www.lchclearnet.com.

[157] For the following overview of Clearnet's history, corporate structure and clearing activities, refer to www.lchclearnet.com; FOW (ed.) (2001); and FOW (ed.) (2003).

[158] MATIF (Marché à Terme d'Instruments Financiers) was formed in 1986 with its own clearing house, La Chambre de Compensation des Instruments Financiers, which later became MATIF SA. In 1988, MATIF commenced trading commodities, having merged with the local commodity exchanges in Paris, Lille and Le Havre. It then took over the Banque Centrale de Compensation, which assumed the clearing function for commodities contracts. Cf. www.clearnetsa.com/about/history.asp.

[159] Additional mergers in 2001 involved Liffe in London and BVLP in Portugal. Note that following the merger of Euronext and Liffe, LCH continued to provide clearing services for the London derivatives market.

[160] The integration extended to the implementation of unified market rules and harmonised admission criteria, such as the implementation of standard capital adequacy and risk management procedures. French, Belgian and Dutch regulators reached an agreement to work in tandem to establish a homogenous legal framework and provide joint supervision.

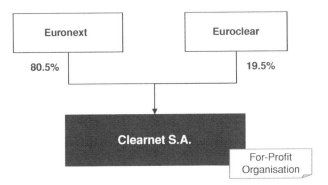

Figure 8.22   Pre-merger ownership structure Clearnet
Source: Based on Euronext (ed.) (2003), p. 9.

Prior to the merger with LCH, Clearnet was 80.5 per cent owned by the Euronext Group and 19.5 per cent owned by Euroclear. Euronext is a 100 per cent publicly quoted company on the SBF. Euroclear Bank is 100 per cent member-owned (i.e. by banks) and for-profit.

By 2003, as part of the Euronext Group, Clearnet was responsible for the clearing of all cash equities, bonds and derivatives traded on the Euronext exchanges. It additionally provided central counterparty and netting services to OTC bond and repo. markets. Transactions flowed to Clearnet for this purpose through a number of automated systems and gateways: EuroMTS, MTS France, MTS Italy, BrokerTec, eSpeed, SLAB, ETCMS and Viel & Cie Prominnofi.

In 1999, Clearnet closed the year as the world's fourth largest and Europe's second largest derivatives clearing house, with 240,140,823 contracts cleared.[161] One year later, in 2000, with rising volumes, Clearnet climbed to become the world's third largest derivatives clearing house. In the years prior to the merger with LCH, Clearnet had maintained its position as the world's fourth largest and Europe's second largest derivatives clearing house.

Market participants were able to apply to become a General Clearing Member (GCM) or Individual Clearing Member (ICM). Both categories of clearing member were required to satisfy Clearnet's rules on operational procedures during regular audits and to maintain a minimum level of net assets.

---

[161] Refer to section 2.5 for a graphical overview of the world's major derivatives clearing houses. Market shares based on data provided by FOW (ed.) (2001); FOW (ed.) (2003); and FOW (ed.) (2006).

8.2.1.2 Background and objectives of the initiative

In April 2000, LCH and Clearnet announced plans to form an alliance that would ultimately result in a merger of both clearing houses.[162] In December 2003, after initial negotiations had been abandoned and then re-launched, the merger was finally implemented. The underlying dynamics and background to these developments are briefly outlined in the following.

When both clearing houses announced their initial plans to create a consolidated European clearing house in April 2000, a joint venture was scheduled to be implemented by early 2001, with a full merger to follow.[163] Although integration plans were relatively substantial and detailed at this point in time, merger talks stagnated over the course of the year. Whereas Clearnet and its parent company, Euronext, were tied up with the integration of the exchange merger that had formed Euronext,[164] additional industry developments hampered the cooperation between Clearnet and LCH.

As a reaction to the Euronext merger, Deutsche Börse and the London Stock Exchange (LSE) at the same time negotiated their so-called 'iX' venture.[165] The combination of the German and British exchanges tempted the major players to consider an alliance between the respective clearing houses, LCH and Eurex Clearing.[166] Over the course of the year, the likelihood of successfully implementing a joint venture or merger between LCH and Clearnet dimmed, and in October 2000, LCH affirmed that it had put negotiations with Clearnet on hold and had instead launched talks with ECAG.[167] LCH subsequently concentrated on a possible merger with its German counterpart, but these negotiations ultimately went nowhere. When the iX venture fell through, the appeal of negotiating a partnership between LCH and Eurex Clearing waned.

In the midst of these developments in 2001, the European Securities Forum (ESF) published its blueprint for a single pan-European CCP, identifying a preference on the part of the major market participants (investment banks and brokers) for a clearing house outside exchange control and operating on a not-for-profit basis.[168] Most of the largest market participants supported the initiative led by the ESF on behalf of its twenty-eight international investment bank members to create an independent pan-European clearing system. The group was pushing for a horizontal clearing house for all markets.[169] This backdrop of public pressure and lobbying activities from market participants

---

[162] Cf. Handelsblatt (ed.) (05.04.2000), p. 35; and Jones (2003).
[163] Cf. Bank for International Settlements (ed.) (2000b), p. 42.   [164] Cf. Kentouris (2000a), p. 11.
[165] Cf. Schönauer (2002), p. 27.   [166] Cf. Kentouris (2000b), p. 1.
[167] Cf. Handelsblatt (ed.) (13.10.2000), p. 44; and LCH.Clearnet (ed.) (2004c), pp. 4–5.
[168] Cf. FOW (ed.) (2001).   [169] Cf. Kharouf (2001).

complicated further negotiations between LCH/Clearnet and LCH/ECAG, respectively. Based on the constellation at that time, Euronext would have controlled almost 50 per cent of the merged entity – a scenario that was not welcomed by market participants, many of whom publicly opposed vertical integration. LCH's not-for-profit structure as opposed to ECAG's and Clearnet's for-profit orientation thus constituted a stumbling block to merger activity: as recipients of profit-sharing benefits via annual rebates and as holders of a 75 per cent stake in the clearing house, LCH's members certainly wanted a say in any merger proceedings to make sure that any M&A initiative would be realised in their best interest. Cooperation with for-profit clearing houses such as Clearnet and Eurex Clearing, both part of a recently publicly listed group, thus proved to be difficult.

It was only by the end of 2001 that merger talks between Clearnet and LCH regained traction. At this point in time, investment banks were continuing to put pressure on clearing houses to reduce fees as well as lobbying against the vertical integration of clearing houses and for the creation of a user-controlled single European CCP based on a horizontal model. In the exchange arena, the fate of European exchange consolidation was at the centre of debate and the ownership of Liffe and LSE, both of which were acquisitions targets at that time, was considered key in this arena. When Euronext succeeded in acquiring the London derivatives market Liffe – one of LCH's most important customers – in November 2001, it suddenly held significant stakes in both clearing houses. A basis for renewed Anglo-French merger talks was thus created.[170] Negotiations were subsequently resurrected and this time culminated in a successful merger agreement that was implemented in December 2003: LCH and Clearnet merged under a UK holding company named LCH.Clearnet Group Ltd.

After lengthy negotiations, the initial difficulties relating to the ownership structure of LCH were solved,[171] and the shareholding members of LCH finally agreed to the merger once Euronext, despite remaining the largest single shareholder of the merged entity, agreed to reduce its shareholding and limit its voting rights.[172] This helped to assuage the fears of the investment banks and brokers, whose primary objective continued to be the impediment of the vertical integration of clearing house structures in Europe.

---

[170] Cf. Hellmann (2003), p. 3.

[171] LCH's users had to be persuaded to accept the end of their previous arrangement, in which they had majority-governed and owned their clearing house. For their part, Euronext's shareholders had to be persuaded to give up full control over and ownership of a profitable subsidiary.

[172] Further details on the concept and structure of the initiative are outlined in section 8.2.1.3.

The primary objectives pursued by this network initiative at the time of its implementation were thus compelling to both partners: for LCH, being majority-owned and controlled by its clearing members, the merger with Clearnet constituted an opportunity towards the creation of a more centralised European CCP and the further integration of Europe's financial markets.[173] By combining two of Europe's largest clearing houses, banks and brokers hoped to reduce clearing-related costs by avoiding duplication of clearing technology in Europe,[174] benefit from economies of scale on the part of the merging CCPs and move towards a more seamless securities market.[175] Backing for the merger consequently also came from the ESF.[176] With Euronext's agreement to limit its voting rights and reduce its shareholding, Clearnet was thus an ideal partner for LCH and its owners.

Euronext's rationale for agreeing to the deal with LCH was driven by other motives, however:[177] Clearnet had limited growth prospects at that time, and its fees were expected to come under attack from market participants; LCH, on the other hand, had more promising prospects for growth. Through continued participation in the merged entity, Euronext hoped to benefit not only from significant financial returns, but also from considerably enhanced commercial opportunities.[178] Financial gains resulted from liquidating parts of Euronext's shareholding in Clearnet, and were also expected to come from the clearing house's proclaimed dividend policy of distributing at least 50 per cent of annual distributable profits.[179] Furthermore, it was hoped that the merger would translate into commercial opportunities for Euronext: Euronext believed that the merged entity could serve as a catalyst for further CCP consolidation in Europe. Plus, as the expected 'future partner of choice for CCPs and international markets', LCH.Clearnet's broad international client base could thus support Euronext's growth, diversification and globalisation strategies.[180] Additionally, there was a chance that the deal could further Euronext's ambition to merge with the LSE,[181] and by serving to align Euronext with the demands of the ESF and the major market participants,

---

[173] Even if this move would ultimately fail to lead to the creation of a single European CCP, from the viewpoint of LCH and its owners it was a means of creating a viable competitor to Eurex Clearing, the vertically integrated clearing house of DBAG, which had risen to become the world's largest derivatives clearing house in 2002 and 2003. Supporting the merger of LCH and Clearnet thus had the benefit of creating a counterweight in Europe that would at least be partially controlled and owned by clearing members.

[174] Cf. Jones (2003).   [175] Cf. Ascarelli (2003), p. M1.   [176] Cf. Skorecki (2003a), p. 29.

[177] Cf. Dickson (2003), p. 22.   [178] Cf. Euronext (ed.) (2003), p. 6.

[179] Cf. Euronext (ed.) (2003), p. 20.   [180] Cf. Euronext (ed.) (2003), p. 6.

[181] LCH had started to clear the most liquid equities at the LSE in the first quarter of 2001.

the merger was also considered to be helpful in isolating Deutsche Börse with its vertical silo strategy. Finally, cost savings generated by LCH.Clearnet for Euronext's clients were expected to enhance volumes and liquidity on the Euronext markets.

The merger agreement signed between LCH and Clearnet consequently offered a number of compelling benefits:

- The clearing houses brought complementary products to the venture.[182] LCH's core products were fixed income, whereas Clearnet was more focused on cash equities clearing.
- Further commercial opportunities for the newly created entity and enhanced value for market participants could therefore arise through extension to a larger geographic zone and a broader range of products.[183]
- The merged entity would be able to take trades from a wide variety of trading platforms, which was considered a major step towards the further integration of the European capital market infrastructure.[184] The deal thus satisfied market participants' demands for the continued consolidation of European clearing houses.[185]
- Potential IT-related and non-IT-related merger synergies were envisaged to translate into substantial savings in clearing members' own businesses,[186] which market participants had also long demanded.
- Efficiency improvements, including these substantial cost reductions, could lead to value creation for both clients and shareholders of the new CCP.[187]

8.2.1.3 Concept and structure of the initiative

In May 2002, Euronext Chief Executive Officer (CEO) Jean-Francois Théodore confirmed that talks had taken place between Clearnet and LCH, but did not provide specifics on the nature of the potential cooperation. Due to regulatory complexities and problems concerning the ownership and corporate structures of both clearing houses,[188] it was not until one year later – in June 2003 – that the merger was officially announced. The main debates among the parties concerned the corporate structure (for-profit versus not-for-profit) of the CCP, the distribution of shareholding and voting rights between the exchanges and clearing members, and under which regulatory regime the merged entity should operate, i.e. which European body ought to be given ultimate regulatory authority over the multi-national clearing house.[189]

---

[182] Cf. Gidel (2000).   [183] Cf. Euronext (ed.) (2003), p. 16.
[184] Cf. Neue Züricher Zeitung (ed.) (26.06.2003), p. 23.   [185] Cf. Grass/Davis (2003), p. 19.
[186] Cf. Euronext (ed.) (2003), p. 15.   [187] Cf. Euronext (ed.) (2003), p. 5.
[188] Cf. Schönauer (2003a), p. 23.   [189] Cf. Handelsblatt (ed.) (26.06.2003), p. 19.

In addition to myriad finalisation details and the satisfaction of various conditions – including obtaining the necessary regulatory approvals[190] – the parties to the deal would face several more hurdles in the months following the merger announcement. The LSE, confronted with the prospect of Euronext's future influence in the LCH.Clearnet Group and fearful that Euronext would not only fortify its growing influence in London,[191] but also use its share-holding in the clearing house to exact preferential treatment from the merged entity, was visibly discontent with the merger.[192] It subsequently threatened to put an end to its established clearing relationship with LCH and proceeded to launch negotiations with Eurex Clearing and the European arm of DTCC regarding the future provision of clearing services.[193] These manoeuvres obviously posed a threat to the successful realisation of the merger agreement.[194] It was only when the dispute was finally settled – LCH accommodated the LSE with a reduction in fees, and the LSE decided in November 2003 to maintain its existing relationship with LCH – that the merger negotiations could resume. The merger was completed in late 2003, with the establishment of the LCH.Clearnet Group Ltd (LCH.C Group) on 19 December and the subsequent acquisition of Clearnet on 22 December 2003.[195]

The final terms of the merger were designed to strike a balance between the shareholders of Euronext and LCH's users in order to garner their support for the deal. A brief summary of the terms of the merger follows.[196] LCH and Clearnet became wholly owned subsidiaries of the new holding company LCH.C Group, which would operate as an unlisted, for-profit, private limited company incorporated in England. The operating subsidiaries based in London and Paris, LCH and Clearnet, were re-branded as LCH.Clearnet Ltd (LCH.C Ltd) and LCH.Clearnet SA (LCH.C SA), respectively. Central counterparty clearing services thus continued to be provided through these operating companies.[197] Consequently, LCH.C Ltd continued to be supervised by the

---

[190] Cf. LCH.Clearnet (ed.) (2003b), p. 3.
[191] Cf. Jones (2003).   [192] Cf. Handelsblatt (ed.) (15.10.2003), p. 20.
[193] Cf. Schönauer (2003b), p. 21; and FAZ (ed.) (02.07.2003), p. 22.
[194] Cf. Schönauer (2003c), p. 23. Despite the fact that volumes provided by the LSE merely amounted to 6.5 per cent of LCH's cleared volumes, the question of whether LCH or Eurex would provide future clearing services to the London exchange was expected to give direction to the issue of European exchange consolidation. Were the LSE to select ECAG as its future clearing house, the likelihood of a potential merger between DBAG and the LSE would probably increase. In this case, the incentive for Euronext to agree to a merger of Clearnet and LCH would ultimately have to be reconsidered.
[195] Cf. LCH.Clearnet (ed.) (2004b), p. 4.
[196] For the following overview of the merger details, refer to LCH.Clearnet (ed.) (2003a); Euronext (ed.) (2003); and LCH.Clearnet (ed.) (2003b).
[197] Clearnet's existing proximity service representation in Brussels and Amsterdam was thus also maintained.

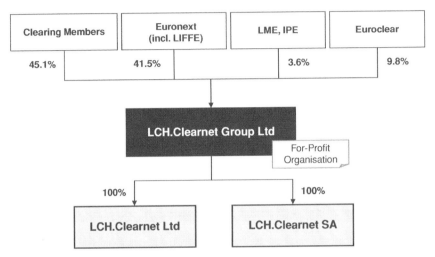

Figure 8.23   Post-merger ownership structure LCH.Clearnet Group, as of January 2004
Source: Based on Euronext (ed.) (2003), p. 9.

UK Financial Services Authority (FSA) and LCH.C SA remained under the watch of French banking authorities working with other relevant European regulatory authorities. Although the holding company is incorporated in the UK, as the financial holding company of a group in which Clearnet is the only credit institution, LCH.C Group is supervised on a consolidated basis by the French banking regulatory authorities.

The deal valued the merged entity at €1.2 billion, with Clearnet and LCH each valued at €600 million. To ensure the group's independence from Euronext (LCH.C Group's largest single shareholder), the exchange sold 7.6 per cent of LCH.Clearnet to current clearing members of LCH for approximately €91 million, bringing its total share to 41.5 per cent. In addition, Euronext's voting rights were capped at 24.9 per cent. The final shareholding structure therefore resulted in the exchanges and clearing members both holding 45.1 per cent of the group; the remaining 9.8 per cent are held by Euroclear.[198] Given the different shareholding structures of LCH and Clearnet prior to the merger – one user-dominated, the other exchange-dominated – the post-merger ownership structure struck a balance between both parties and avoided the dominance of one over the another.[199]

---

[198] To benefit its shareholders, LCH.C Group opted to pursue a dividend policy of distributing at least 50 per cent of annual distributable profits. From the financial year 2006 onwards, the group has sought to achieve an EBIT target of €150 million. Once this target is achieved in any given year, 70 per cent of the excess will be made available for the benefit of users.

[199] Cf. LCH.Clearnet (ed.) (2004c), p. 2.

Since then, the shareholding and voting rights of Euronext in the LCH.C Group have nonetheless been reconsidered several times. In 2005, Euronext offered to reduce its voting stake in the group in an attempt to win the bid for the LSE.[200] This offer conformed to the UK's Competition Commission's previously established rule that Euronext had to reduce its stake in the LCH.C Group to less than 15 per cent as part of the acquisition process.[201] In the wake of unsuccessful merger negotiations, however, Euronext's voting stake remained unchanged. In March 2007, LCH.C Group and Euronext announced the repurchase of Euronext's shares.[202] Under the agreement, Euronext will retain a 5 per cent holding in the group's outstanding shares after the buy-back programme is completed. Users will then hold 73.3 per cent of the shares.[203] This restructuring was unanimously approved by LCH.C Group's shareholders on 15 June 2007.[204]

The post-merger holding company is run by a board of directors drawn from the main stakeholders and includes three independent directors, one of whom is the Chairman.[205] The operating subsidiaries LCH.C Ltd and LCH.C SA are run by boards of their own. Whereas the two operating companies remain separate for legal and regulatory purposes, the group management is to ensure that they are managed as a single entity wherever practical and beneficial. As LCH.C Ltd and LCH.C SA continued to be distinct legal entities subsequent to the merger, they maintained their own rule-books and processes applicable to clearing members and clearing member applicants.

The implementation of the merger was structured to proceed in three phases (see Figure 8.24):[206] Phase I was dedicated to harmonising operating procedures and was aimed at conveying immediate benefits to users that were

---

[200] Cf. Wall Street Journal (ed.) (09.07.2005).

[201] Cf. LCH.Clearnet (ed.) (2006a), p. 27.   [202] Cf. LCH.Clearnet/Euronext (eds.) (12.03.2007).

[203] Cf. LCH.Clearnet/Euronext (eds.) (12.03.2007).

[204] Cf. LCH.Clearnet (ed.) (15.06.2007). The proclaimed background and rationale for the repurchase is outlined as follows: 'The LCH.Clearnet board considers that this repurchase is an opportunity for LCH.Clearnet's customer and shareholder interests to be more closely aligned and LCH.Clearnet will, as a result, be better positioned to respond to ongoing challenges and developments in the clearing sector.' LCH.Clearnet/Euronext (eds.) (12.03.2007). It is therefore obvious that the shareholding structure implemented at the time of the merger ultimately did not succeed in soothing the initial tensions between the two shareholding groups of the LCH.Clearnet Group. 'In order to implement considerably lower tariffs and promote the longer term success of the company, the LCH.Clearnet Board considers that it is necessary to reduce the shareholding of its largest "returns-focused" shareholder, Euronext.' LCH.Clearnet/Euronext (eds.) (12.03.2007).

[205] The Group Chief Executive and his deputy have executive authority.

[206] For the following overview of the merger integration, refer to LCH.Clearnet (ed.) (2003a); LCH.Clearnet (ed.) (2003b); and Euronext (ed.) (2003).

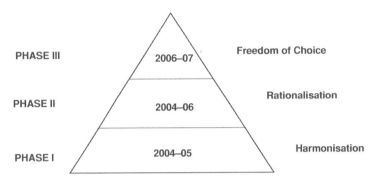

Figure 8.24 Integration phasing of the LCH/Clearnet merger
Source: Based on LCH.Clearnet (ed.) (2003a), p. 18.

not depending on major system changes.[207] The rationalisation of operating systems was scheduled to be realised in Phase II, including the major IT work of migrating to a common technical platform.[208] Finally, Phase III was designed to bring freedom of choice to clear, i.e. enable users to hold positions at either CCP.[209] Each phase requires approval by the relevant regulatory authorities.

Due to the complexities of integrating the diverse and multinational structures of both CCPs, it was clear at the time of the merger that the creation of a fully integrated LCH.C Group would have to be realised incrementally. Furthermore, due to regulatory, legal and other complexities, it was obvious that even the successful realisation of Phases I to III would not lead to the creation of a single CCP, in the sense of a single, consolidated clearing house entity with a single membership and a single legal framework.

---

[207] The product base of LCH and Clearnet is not altered during this phase. Instead, priority is given to the harmonisation of systems and procedures and to the identification of best practices for risk management between the two operational centres. Although legal membership remains separate, requirements are harmonised together with the default fund contribution basis in each centre.

[208] By the end of Phase II, both CCPs are scheduled to use the same technology platform. Although the two CCPs will continue to operate as distinct CCPs, the technological standardisation will create savings for the clearing houses and their users. Integrating the IT platform also lays the foundation for the third phase of the integration process.

[209] Upon completion of this integration phase, each clearing house will be able to provide full clearing services for the entire LCH.Clearnet Group product range. This gives users free choice over the legal entity through which they wish to clear their business. Although LCH.Clearnet announced plans possibly to introduce cross-margining for some offsetting positions held by users of both CCPs as early as in Phase I, positions continue to be divided between the two CCPs on the basis of their existing activities at this stage. This division is to be eliminated in Phase III. The final implementation of the last phase, which will supposedly give clearing members the choice to clear all of their business through either CCP, is dependent upon the successful integration of risk management and reporting techniques in Phase I as well as upon the rationalisation of systems in Phases I and II.

Consequently, instead of aiming to create a single, fully integrated clearing house, it was foreseen to maintain a group structure with separate linked CCPs that would provide choice of clearing location. Clearing members will then be able to clear all of their business through either CCP using a common set of legal and operating procedures through the same technological platform. In the years following the merger, LCH and Clearnet were designated to continue to operate as separately regulated CCPs with their own membership, financial resources and default funds. Operational integration of the two CCPs was expected to proceed over three to four years and to be completed by 2007.

8.2.1.4 Status of the initiative

The time-line for the integration phasing of the merger implementation was announced in December 2003; however, one year later, by the end of 2004, it had already become clear that the publicised time-lines could not be met. In its 2004 annual report, LCH.C Group was forced to acknowledge the following:

At the time of the merger, LCH.Clearnet expected to generate various potential cost savings, which had been identified in the merger prospectus, by 2007. The process of integrating the two businesses has not been as rapid as expected with a consequent impact on the delivery of synergy benefits. Post-merger, a fuller picture of the underlying state of the two business' infrastructures was understood together with the impact on the expected benefits. As a result, we do not expect to realise all cost savings over the same timeframe as identified at the time of the merger.[210]

Problems in implementing the phased integration as scheduled resulted from difficulties in the internal management of processes and working practices – which ultimately led to the remoulding of the management team – and from unexpected complexities related to the cross-border nature of the group.[211] Significant challenges also arose from the integration of the IT infrastructure, which proved to be a lot more complex than the management had initially expected; the phased integration thus suffered additional lengthy delays.

The progressive migration to a common systems architecture by 2007, which was intended to streamline processes into a single platform and bring about significant cost savings, was initially pursued through the so-called

---

[210] LCH.Clearnet (ed.) (2005), p. 5.   [211] Cf. LCH.Clearnet (ed.) (2005), p. 6.

Generic Clearing System (GCS) project.[212] The systems strategy was based on using the best of the system components available from the merged entities[213] and was designed to establish a collective systems architecture for LCH.C Ltd and LCH.C SA while continuing to operate two core clearing platforms.[214] By May 2005, sixteen months into the project, LCH.C Group had already missed one public go-live date;[215] by the end of 2005, the group had reneged on delivering an important new software program necessary for process integration between the merged CCPs in the context of the GCS project. This failure resulted in an impairment charge of €20.1 million when it became obvious that some of the previously capitalised development costs could not be brought into economic use.[216]

It thus became apparent in the second post-merger year, 2005, that the crucial integration of the clearing systems would require a lot more time and resources than initially envisaged. The original time-line became further forestalled due to persistent difficulties in the internal management of processes and working practices. Regulatory complexities related to the group's cross-border nature as well as dissimilar regulatory regimes and bankruptcy laws made the harmonisation of operating procedures a difficult task. In its 2005 annual report, LCH.C Group stated:

The Board is organised to reflect the peculiar nature of the Company; its size and composition may sometimes have undermined the efficiency of its work, despite the capacity and good willingness of the individuals. For that reason we initiated a review of governance in order to identify ways of improvement and to seek sound interaction with the management.[217]

Despite the group's efforts to deal with these integration issues and respective changes within the management structure to cope better with the targets of the merger,[218] the above-mentioned problems continued to persist throughout 2006. Further restructuring of the group's management thus followed in 2006. In May, Gérard de la Martinière stepped down as Chairman and in July, David Hardy resigned as CEO of the holding company.[219] Shortly after Hardy's departure, the clearing house announced that, because the GCS project had proven to be neither economically nor technically viable, it had decided to close down the project and to discontinue the use of its assets

---

[212] Cf. LCH.Clearnet (ed.) (2003b), p. 8.
[213] Cf. LCH.Clearnet (ed.) (2005), p. 7.
[214] Cf. LCH.Clearnet (ed.) (2003b), p. 8.
[215] Cf. Annesley (2006), p. 12.
[216] Cf. LCH.Clearnet (ed.) (2006a), p. 23.
[217] LCH.Clearnet (ed.) (2006a), p. 11.
[218] Cf. LCH.Clearnet (ed.) (2006a), p. 9.
[219] Cf. LCH.Clearnet (ed.) (05.07.2006).

in the group's future technology strategy.[220] By 2006, it had thus become evident that the migration to a common system architecture through the GCS constituted one of the group's major spending projects[221] and was simply not economically or technically feasible. In its 2006 annual report, LCH.C Group explained:

Our analysis of the integration requirements indicated higher potential costs than those anticipated at the start of the project. The growing scope of the project, caused in large part by additional requirements associated with plans to provide optionality in the post trade process, brought the cost benefit ratio into some question. We therefore decided to halt the work on the project until a revised business case can be supported, and before entering into software development expenditure.[222]

The newly appointed CEO, Roger Liddell, was subsequently asked to take on the responsibility for the preparation of a new long-term IT strategy for the group,[223] with a short- to medium-term focus on optimising the use of existing technology.[224] Other unforeseen complexities of the merger integration related to the fact that the services, products and markets covered by the two CCPs were not identical and thus not easy to harmonise, which became evident in attempts to coordinate their fee grids:

To those involved from the beginning, the realisation soon set in that it was going to be a long and painful process with total and complete fee standardisation being an impossibility, at least in the short- to medium-term. Certain aspects of the fee grid were so ingrained at a local level that to change them dramatically could affect the structure of the market and pose a threat to volume.[225]

As a result of all of the difficulties related to the post-merger integration, LCH.C Group continues to be far behind its originally envisaged integration time-line and has yet to realise the projected associated IT and non-IT savings. To what extent the final integration of the two clearing houses will resemble the plans initially announced in 2003 remains to be seen, however.

---

[220] Cf. LCH.Clearnet (ed.) (21.07.2006). This resulted in an impairment charge of €47.8 million, which substantially related to the GCS assets. The total cost of GCS was €121.3 million, of which a large portion was expensed directly to the Income Statement as occurred. The GCS project was thus fully written off by mid-2006. Cf. LCH.Clearnet (ed.) (2006d), p. 2.

[221] Cf. LCH.Clearnet (ed.) (2007), p. 7.

[222] LCH.Clearnet (ed.) (2007), p. 11.   [223] Cf. LCH.Clearnet (ed.) (21.07.2006).

[224] Cf. LCH.Clearnet (ed.) (2007), p. 15.   [225] LCH.Clearnet (ed.) (2006c), p. 3.

Part II: Analysis

8.2.1.5 Interviewees' assessment of the case study

> The merger has brought no benefits at all. It was a nightmare! It was very costly, wasted enormous capital and resources. The benefits might be realised long-term, but so far it hasn't paid off.[226]

> Conceptually it is where we should be going, but there is a long way from the PowerPoint to the delivery.[227]

This section presents the interviewees' assessment of the merger of LCH and Clearnet. Their insights serve as input for the comparison of the case study findings with the conclusions from Chapter 7 regarding the impact of M&A initiatives on the efficiency of the European clearing industry.

In a first step, interviewees were asked whether the merger initiative had made sense to them in 2003 (Figure 8.25). Roughly 37 per cent (twenty-nine out of seventy-nine) of the interviewees gave concrete feedback.[228] In terms of the response rate, the group of European-based clearing members was the best informed about the merger; all of the London-based clearing members gave an assessment and roughly 86 per cent of the clearers based in Continental Europe were able to contribute an opinion.[229]

In terms of their answers, a small majority of the interviewees (sixteen versus thirteen) stated that they thought that the merger had made sense in 2003. However, the breakdown of these figures according to interviewee groups delivers interesting insights. Of the group of interviewed clearing members, a small majority (nine versus seven) stated that at the time of the merger, they did not believe that the initiative had made sense. This assessment is rather surprising at first sight, because as owners of LCH at the time of the merger, Europe's major clearing members had supported the deal in 2003 by buying out parts of Euronext's shares in the merged entity.

Closer scrutiny of the clearers' answers reveals that three of the nine London-based clearing members and six of the seven clearers based in Continental

---

[226] Statement made by interviewed clearing member representative.

[227] Interview with Steve G. Martin.

[228] The remaining either felt that they had insufficient knowledge of the merger, had no clear opinion or did not specify their opinion.

[229] US-based clearing members knew less about the merger initiative – only one out of five provided an assessment. Whereas a reasonable number of interviewed exchanges provided feedback (40 per cent), the response rate within the group of market experts, NCMs and clearing houses was a lot lower (25, 13 and 11 per cent respectively).

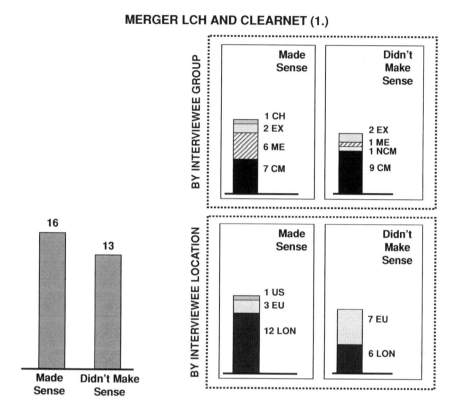

Figure 8.25 Interviewees' assessment of whether or not the merger of LCH and Clearnet had made sense in 2003[230]
Source: Author's own.

Europe reported that they did not believe that the initiative had made sense at the time. Thus, although to all outward appearances, the members of LCH supported the initiative in 2003, there are indications that their private evaluation was more critical.[231]

---

[230] Interviewee groups: CM – clearing member; NCM – non-clearing member; ME – market expert; EX – exchange; and CH – clearing house. Interviewee locations: US – United States; EU – Continental Europe; and LON – London.

[231] Note that clearing members of LCH that voted on the deal only correspond to the group of London-based respondents. Additionally, it has to be taken into account that the interviewed individuals representing this group of clearing members were not necessarily the decision-makers in 2003, i.e. those actually voting on the merger between LCH and Clearnet. The majority of interviewed clearing members based in Continental Europe were also not in a position to vote on the merger directly in 2003.

No one in the investment banking community really believed in the benefits promoted by LCH at the time of the merger, i.e. all the benefits announced in the merger statement.[232]

This critical evaluation can be explained in terms of the underlying dynamics and objectives pursued by the owners of LCH at the time of the merger. Although many of the banks and brokerages voting on the merger were far from certain if they would truly benefit from any cost savings by 2007 and also had difficulty assessing the magnitude of their potential savings,[233] they nonetheless had political reasons for supporting the initiative.[234]

Although these findings indicate that many clearing members affected by the transaction were in fact aware at the time of the merger that the realisation of integration benefits would take time and that the ultimate magnitude of cost savings was uncertain, the majority of stakeholders naturally expected to see some kind of tangible integration benefits in the post-merger years.

As outlined in section 8.2.1.4, due to all of the stumbling blocks to the successful realisation of the merger integration, the LCH.C Group continued to trail far behind its original time-line (and the associated IT and non-IT savings) at the time the interviews were conducted (February to May 2006). To no surprise, the vast majority of respondents who were asked to assess whether the merger has so far (as of the date of the interview) provided value-added in the sense of efficiency gains, i.e. cost savings, gave negative feedback (see Figure 8.26).

The merger has been a disaster. They promised a number of things to people. They promised to reduce transaction costs and it hasn't happened. They promised technological harmonisation, and it hasn't happened . . . It was a waste of time in retrospect. We spent a lot of time evaluating it and the strategy was that we would have a platform by now, by 2005 I believe, and it is still not there and it gets put off in terms of two years. So, no, it hasn't worked out.[235]

---

[232] Statement made by interviewed clearing member representative.
[233] Cf. Skorecki (2003b), p. 29; and interviews.
[234] The merger was perceived as an initiative that would in the best case scenario help Europe to move towards a more consolidated infrastructure, but in the medium term would yield little savings and would possibly even necessitate additional spending on technology. Cf. Skorecki (2003b), p. 29.
[235] Statement made by interviewed clearing member representative.

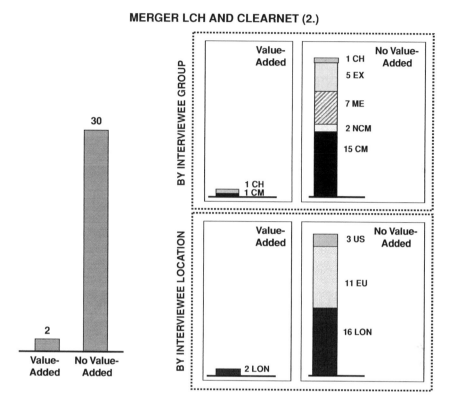

Figure 8.26   Interviewees' assessment of whether or not the merger of LCH and Clearnet has so far provided value-added (answers provided in May 2006)[236]
Source: Author's own.

Roughly 41 per cent (thirty-two out of seventy-nine) of all interviewees provided concrete feedback on this question.[237] Concerning the response rate, the group of European-based clearing members again proved to be the best informed about the merger; all of the London-based clearing members gave an assessment and roughly 86 per cent of the clearers based in Continental Europe were able to contribute feedback.[238]

---

[236] Interviewee groups: CM – clearing member; NCM – non-clearing member; ME – market expert; EX – exchange; and CH – clearing house. Interviewee locations: US – United States; EU – Continental Europe; and LON – London.

[237] The remaining either felt that they had insufficient knowledge of the merger, had no clear opinion or did not specify their opinion.

[238] US-based clearing members knew considerably less about the merger initiative – only one out of five provided an assessment. Whereas a reasonable number of interviewed exchanges gave feedback

The reasons for interviewees' negative assessment of the merger initiative are briefly summarised in the following. Respondents criticised the merger as being poorly planned in the first place, and then badly executed and managed. They were particularly critical of the lack of systems integration and failure of the system development project, which had been designed to bring significant savings for clearers that maintain interfaces to both clearing houses. Additionally, interviewees characterised the group as fragmented and lacking integration, adding that it has failed to harmonise processes and has not yet implemented a common default fund or coordinated rules and processes.

The two platforms are completely separate, you cannot choose one versus the other – and it's as if there were two different clearing houses; the default funds are not harmonised, the rules are not harmonised, so there is no immediate financial tangible benefit.[239]

Respondents acknowledged, however, that the integration of both clearing houses is further complicated by the highly complex regulatory environment in which the LCH.C Group finds itself; having to deal with eleven European regulators significantly slows the harmonisation and integration process. The interviewees also cited political and protectionist issues as impediments to effective integration.

Some interviewees felt that the complexity of the integration process and the lack of tangible benefits had actually translated into costs for LCH.C Group and some of its users.[240]

I think the cost of harmonisation has been very high and very little has been achieved so far in terms of single systems and integration . . . You could say that they actually failed to deliver anything of any significance at all, and they spent a lot of money doing it . . . it is a big fear that what we end up doing is paying twice, because we ultimately pay for the developments to be done in terms of integrating systems and things at the clearing house, but then we'll end up paying again because we have to redevelop our own systems and infrastructure to cope with those changes. And that is a concern.[241]

Other interviewees stated that although they were hoping and waiting for the merger to pay off in terms of cost reductions, they had so far not incurred

---

(50 per cent), the response rate within the group of market experts, NCMs and clearing houses was lower (25, 25 and 22 per cent, respectively).

[239] Statement made by interviewed clearing member representative.

[240] The integration of the two clearing houses entails administrative costs, mostly due to operating duplicate production environments, while incurring the costs for the development of an integrated system. Cf. Aykroyd (2005), p. 7.

[241] Statement made by interviewed clearing member representative.

significant merger-related investments. Nonetheless, LCH.C Group is finding that customers will likely have to bear an investment, possibly substantial, into existing processes and technology.[242] Depending on the clearing member's concrete structure and business focus, overly rapid change may even work against some of the clearing members' interests.[243] This is particularly true for regionally (CM_{PR}/CM_{AR}) or regionally-to-globally (CM_{PR-G}/CM_{AR-G}) focused clearing members.[244]

We are a member of both [CCPs], so for us to eliminate one would save hundreds of thousands of dollars. It is very clear, however, that if you are a domestic retail stockbroker based in Paris, it is of no benefit; in fact, quite the opposite, it's actually a cost, because most mergers will look for some form of overhaul of the systems, which will mean they'll have to invest in technology in order to continue to operate with the new system.[245]

Whereas on the one hand, globally active clearers generally hope to realise benefits from consolidating their dual interfaces they maintain to LCH.C Ltd and LCH.C SA, other considerations can also come into play: in particular, globally active clearers with an agency focus (CM_{AG}) increasingly face the risk of disintermediation as the merger integration process proceeds.

In addition to citing the merger's unsuccessful attempts at integration, some interviewees also complained that the resulting entity is not the magnet for future European CCP consolidation that it was envisaged as, but has instead proven to be an inefficiently functioning clearing house that is slow to innovate.[246] Overall, many interviewees regarded the LCH and Clearnet merger as a showcase for the difficulties related to consolidating the European clearing industry through M&A initiatives.

One interviewee among those recognising value-added in the merger emphasised some of its positive effects and intangible strategic benefits. The clearing member representative pointed out that the combined company constitutes a large and viable competitor to Eurex Clearing, and thus fosters much stronger competition between clearing houses within Europe. Another respondent suggested that the merger had already triggered a number of fee reductions.

Taking into account the status of the merger integration at the time the interviews were conducted, the predominance of rather negative feedback is not surprising. Given the significant delay in the group's integration efforts,

---

[242] Cf. Hardy (2004), p. 59.   [243] Cf. Hardy (2004), p. 59.
[244] Cf. interviews.   [245] Statement made by interviewed clearing member representative.
[246] Regarding the capacity bottlenecks and difficulties related to assigning resources of LCH.C Group to projects other than the integration process, see also LCH.Clearnet (ed.) (2004c), p. 5; and Craig (2005).

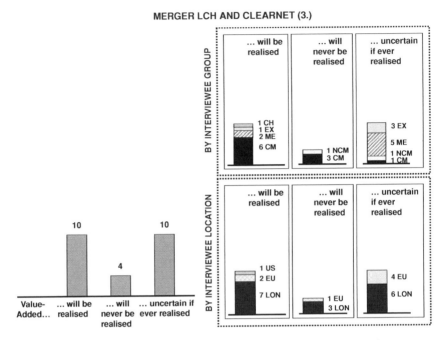

Figure 8.27 Interviewees' assessment of whether or not the expected value-added of the LCH and Clearnet merger will be realised in the future (answers provided in May 2006)[247]
Source: Author's own.

stakeholders understandably found it difficult to lavish praise on the merger. The clearing members' growing impatience for tangible merger benefits[248] was partly addressed by the LCH.C Group's strategy – launched later in 2006 – of reducing fee levels in an attempt finally to accommodate users' demands for post-merger cost reductions.[249] Whether or not these fee reductions truly reflect an increase in internal efficiency on LCH.C Group's part or merely represent a quick fix to appease disgruntled clearing members (many of which are users and shareholders of the CCP at the same time) and protect the group's competitive position remains unclear, however.[250]

In a final step, interviewees were asked whether they believe that the value-added expected at the time of merger will be realised in the future (Figure 8.27). Only 30 per cent (twenty-four out of seventy-nine) of the interviewees

---

[247] Interviewee groups: CM – clearing member; NCM – non-clearing member; ME – market expert; EX – exchange; and CH – clearing house. Interviewee locations: US – United States; EU – Continental Europe; and LON – London.

[248] Cf. LCH.Clearnet (ed.) (2005), p. 2.   [249] Cf. LCH.Clearnet (ed.) (27.09.2006).

[250] LCH.C Group argues that its main motive for cutting fee levels for various product groups in 2006 and 2007 was effectively to confront the competitive challenges threatening the group with the potential loss of future clearing revenues to competing CCPs. Cf. LCH.Clearnet (ed.) (2007), pp. 6–7.

provided concrete feedback.[251] In terms of the response rate, the group of London-based clearing members proved to be the most knowledgeable about the merger; 78 per cent of all London-based clearing members gave an assessment.[252] Whereas ten respondents trusted that the value-added will be realised in the future, an equally great number of interviewees expressed uncertainty as to whether the value-added will ever be realised. Four individuals were of the opinion that the value-added will never be realised.

For the group of clearing members, this means the following: of the seven clearing members who believed that the merger made sense in 2003 (Figure 8.25), six still believed that the promised value-added will be realised in the future; only one felt uncertain as to whether the merger will ever pay off. Of the nine clearing members who had been sceptical about the merger in 2003, three now believed that the value-added would never be realised.[253] This shows that the clearing members who were initially convinced of the merger's validity continued to believe in its potential for long-term success, despite their frustration about the unrealised integration benefits at the time the interviews were conducted in 2006.

Clearing members may or may not still harbour these opinions today. In April 2007, a number of LCH.C Group's shareholding clearing member firms engaged in setting up the so-called Project Turquoise[254] announced that they had chosen the European subsidiary of the US-based DTCC for trade clearing instead of LCH.Clearnet.[255] This would seem to raise doubt about these clearers' continued commitment towards LCH.C Group. On the other hand, ongoing support for the merged entity was shown by the LCH.C Group's clearing members' approval for the repurchase of Euronext's shares. This could be interpreted as evidence of their belief in and continued long-term commitment to making the LCH.Clearnet merger a success.

As for the other stakeholders in the group, Figure 8.27 indicates that some have become sceptical about the group's ability successfully to implement the

---

[251] The remaining either felt that they had insufficient knowledge, had no clear opinion or did not specify their opinion.

[252] Roughly 29 per cent of the clearers based in Continental Europe were able to contribute. US-based clearing members exhibited less knowledge about the merger initiative – only one out of five provided an assessment. Whereas a reasonable number of interviewed exchanges issued feedback (40 per cent), the response rate within the group of market experts, NCMs and clearing houses was a lot lower (25, 25 and 11 per cent, respectively).

[253] The remaining respondents had no clear opinion or did not clearly specify their opinion.

[254] Project Turquoise consists of seven large investment banks and was launched in 2006 with the objective of trading the shares of the 300 largest European companies by 1 November 2007 and thereby disintermediating, among others, Deutsche Börse, the LSE and Euronext exchanges. Cf. LCH.Clearnet (ed.) (2007), p. 6; and Pratley (2007), p. 25.

[255] Cf. Cohen (2007), p. 21.

merger or realise value-added. The group tacitly acknowledges this scepticism (and thus supports the finding of the empirical study) by voicing its intention to pursue a strategy designed 'to repair commercial relationships with the Group's clients and exchange partners so as to restore confidence in the Group's ability to deliver'.[256]

8.2.2 Summary of findings – impact of mergers and acquisitions on efficiency

Going back to the difficulty LCH.Clearnet has had in delivering the benefits of that merger – it's not that the people at LCH.Clearnet are incompetent, it's because the challenges to be overcome are so great.[257]

The purpose of this case study was to challenge the findings of Chapter 7 regarding the impact of mergers and acquisitions on the efficiency of European clearing. The findings obtained from the analysis of the merger between LCH and Clearnet underscore and clarify the preliminary conclusions. The findings thus allow final conclusions to be drawn and are summarised in the following.

8.2.2.1 Scale Impact Matrix – supply-side scale effects
- The implementation of M&A initiatives between clearing houses involves a high degree of value chain, technical and legal harmonisation and integration efforts. The implementation of such network initiatives is thus complex, time-consuming and involves high long-term investments.
- Whereas M&A initiatives have a strong potential to increase scale, the ultimate magnitude of realised economies of scale is diminished by necessary long-term investments.
- When an M&A between CCPs leads to a scope enlargement, the implementation becomes even more complex and time-consuming and involves higher long-term investments than deals that merely lead to an increase in scale.
- Consequently, whereas M&A initiatives have a medium to strong potential for an increase in scope, the ultimate magnitude of realised economies of scope is again impacted by necessary long-term investments.
- The case study also showed that the ultimate magnitude of economies of scale and scope realised through M&A initiatives between European CCPs is not only impacted by counteracting forces in terms of necessary long-term investments, but also by regulatory and political complexities as well as the difficulties associated with governing a multinational entity.

---

[256] LCH.Clearnet (ed.) (2007), p. 7.   [257] Interview with Philip Bruce.

- These complexities can potentially even translate into diseconomies of scale due to increased communication costs, duplication of efforts, management-heavy organisations, slow response times to customer needs, inertia, etc.

8.2.2.2 Scale Impact Matrix – demand-side scale effects

- M&A initiatives enable clearing houses to enlarge the size of their network. Whereas such network strategies positively impact the size of the CCP level network, the opposite is true for the GCM level network. The full integration of the partnering CCPs can make it attractive for some market participants to disintermediate their clearer(s).
- With regard to the network economic particularities inherent to M&A initiatives between CCPs, a third clearing house network can theoretically establish a lead in terms of installed base. The newly merged entity can thus face competition from other CCPs.
- The case study also suggests that in the event that an M&A initiative does not result in the full integration of the partnering CCPs, but rather functions like a clearing link agreement in which the clearing houses continue to operate as separate legal and technical entities united under a common holding company, each of the partnering clearing houses is given the opportunity to establish a lead by benefiting from their installed base. In this case, the M&A initiative is likely to exhibit starting problems similar to those inherent to clearing links, which could constitute weak forms of lock-in.
- The case studies demonstrated that it is particularly true for European CCPs that the services provided as well as the products and markets processed by different clearing houses are not identical, and due to their installed bases, they are not necessarily interchangeable.
- The growth potential of a CCP network, itself the result of an M&A initiative, is likely to be very limited.[258] The appeal of joining such a CCP network is limited for other clearing members, because potential partners usually do not have the leeway to benefit from and further leverage their installed base.[259]

---

[258] At the time of the merger, LCH.C Group announced that their objective was to act as catalyst for further CCP consolidation in Europe and internationally in becoming 'the partner of choice for CCPs and international markets around the world'. LCH.Clearnet (ed.) (2003a), Foreword. This vision has not been realised to date, and no further growth of the network (through engaging in additional network initiatives) has been achieved.

[259] Additional considerations can certainly come into play, such as the general willingness of a clearing house to engage in network strategies or issues concerning the compatibility of governance structures, etc.

- M&A initiatives between CCPs suffer from the drawback that the majority of resources must be devoted to the integration of the partnering clearing houses; this type of network initiative is thus unlikely to leave sufficient resources for engaging in additional projects or spurring innovation. The lack of adequate resources also hampers the potential for the internalisation of GCM level network effects (and consequently diminishes the attractiveness for regionally-to-globally active clearers to disintermediate the GCM(s) they utilise outside of their domestic home market).

8.2.2.3 Transaction Cost Impact Matrix

- For regionally active clearing members (CM_{PR}/CM_{AR}), indirect transaction costs can increase if their home clearing house engages in M&A initiatives. The nature of these initiatives gives clearing members no choice of participation; participation is obligatory. The magnitude of the increase of indirect costs depends on the structure of the M&A initiative and the characteristics of the clearing member firm itself.
- Regionally-to-globally active clearing members (CM_{PR-G}/CM_{AR-G}) benefit from the opportunity to clear many markets through their home clearing house, because they are thereby able to disintermediate the GCM(s) they utilise outside of their domestic home market. M&A initiatives between two CCPs serve this purpose to only a minor extent due to the restricted number of interconnected marketplaces and limited availability of clearing house resources to internalise GCM level network effects successfully. If the M&A initiative does not result in the full integration of the partnering CCPs, but rather functions like a clearing link agreement (in which the clearing houses continue to operate as separate legal and technical entities, united under a common holding company) – the attractiveness of disintermediation is further diminished depending on the partnering CCPs' efforts to overcome the link-inherent starting problem.
- Globally active clearing members with an agency focus (CM_{AG}) mainly benefit from M&A initiatives by virtue of being able to centralise their various clearing relationships into a single relationship with one clearing house, which reduces their indirect costs. Due to the restricted number of interconnected marketplaces, M&A initiatives between two CCPs serve this purpose to only a minor extent. If the M&A initiative does not result in the full integration of the partnering CCPs, but rather functions like a clearing link agreement (in which the clearing houses continue to operate as separate legal and technical entities, united under a common holding company), the attractiveness of centralising the clearer's various clearing

relationships into a single relationship with one clearing house is further diminished depending on the partnering CCPs' efforts to overcome the link-inherent starting problem.

- Globally active clearing members with a prop. focus (CM_{PG}), on the other hand, mainly strive to benefit from the reductions in clearing house fees that can result from M&A initiatives. Depending on the extent of this type of clearers' control over the merged CCP's governance, M&A initiatives are more likely (at least in the medium term) to result in a cut of clearing house fees rather than enable a reduction of indirect costs. Whether or not such fee reductions truly reflect an increase in internal efficiency of the merged entity or merely represent a quick fix to appease the clearing members that exert control over the CCP is subject to further research.
- When M&A initiatives fail to translate into indirect cost savings and merely accommodate clearing members by means of fee cuts, globally active clearers with a prop. focus benefit significantly, whilst all other clearing member types remain unable to reduce their core cost driver (i.e. indirect costs).

8.2.2.4 Efficiency Impact Matrix

- M&A initiatives do not translate into efficiency gains for all clearing member types. Regionally focused clearers (CM_{PR}/CM_{AR}) actually suffer from efficiency losses as a result of M&A initiatives.

8.2.2.5 Business Model Impact Matrix

- Whereas M&A initiatives between two CCPs can benefit globally active clearing members with an agency focus (CM_{AG}) in terms of efficiency gains, they are unlikely to result in significant profit decreases through disintermediation. Globally active clearing members (CM_{PG}/CM_{AG}) are thus likely to support M&A initiatives that lead to an oligopolistic industry structure.

To summarise, this case study delivers several crucial findings regarding cross-border mergers and acquisitions between CCPs as a means to increase the efficiency of the European clearing industry. It importantly demonstrates that M&A initiatives do not increase efficiency for all clearing member types. Regionally focused clearers (CM_{PR}/CM_{AR}) suffer from efficiency losses as a result of M&A initiatives, which can ultimately even negatively impact their business model. Regionally-to-globally active clearing members (CM_{PR-G}/CM_{AR-G}) and globally active clearers (CM_{PG}/CM_{AG}) can benefit from M&A initiatives in terms of efficiency gains and a positive impact on their business model.[260]

The case study also illustrates the inherent complexity of such initiatives. For one thing, it shows that every established national CCP has built an installed base, which influences the dynamics of competition and cooperation between clearing houses. Particularly with regard to the harmonisation of the European clearing industry, the study reveals the great difficulties of employing a merger initiative for this purpose; when consolidation is achieved through a merger, the process of bringing together two major European CCPs is very time-consuming and resource-intensive. Combining two businesses with very different historical experiences, profiles and legal environments is an extraordinarily complicated undertaking.

The case study effectively shows that, within Europe, the full integration and harmonisation of the value chain of multinational partnering CCPs is currently likely to stumble over regulatory and political hurdles. In addition to the technical and legal dimensions associated with merging, an immense effort is necessary to overcome ingrained local market practices. In the case of the LCH.Clearnet merger, it was thus clear from the start that even a successful realisation of the merger would not result in a Single CCP structure; the two multinational CCPs were simply too incongruent. Despite this knowledge, additional and unexpected difficulties surfaced during the final implementation phase. The merger finally turned out to be more complex, time-consuming and resource-depleting than initially expected.

The case study also shows that M&A initiatives between two major European CCPs are not necessarily a means to spur the further harmonisation or integration of the European clearing industry – LCH.Clearnet has hardly succeeded in becoming the partner of choice for European CCPs and international markets around the world. The clearing houses' services and processes

---

[260] Note that in the context of the LCH.Clearnet merger, regionally-to-globally active clearing members with either a prop. or an agency focus (CM_{PR-G}/CM_{AR-G}) have thus far been unable to realise the maximum potential P&L impact from the merger initiative, because the structure of the merger does not enable clearing members to choose between the two clearing houses for processing all markets and products served by the group. In fact, the merger has translated into costs that are not balanced by equally great internal savings for some clearing members. On the other hand, the CM_{PR-G}/CM_{AR-G} groups have realised some benefits from the reduction of clearing house fees. Globally active clearing members with a prop. focus (CM_{PG}) have significantly benefited from the positive P&L impact of the reduction of clearing house fees, whereas clearers with an agency focus (CM_{AG}) have not managed to benefit from a positive P&L impact through the reduction of indirect transaction costs. On the other hand, and on a positive note for this latter type of clearing member, the merger has posed no threat to its business model because it only interlinks two European CCPs: due to the lack of integration between the two clearing houses, counterparties have thus far not been tempted to disintermediate their clearer.

have generally been tailored to the specific demands of regional markets and different regulatory environments. These services, products and processes are thus not identical, and due to the clearing houses' installed bases, they are not necessarily interchangeable. In order for CCP networks to attract additional clearing houses and thus serve as catalysts for the further harmonisation and integration of the clearing industry, a network initiative that enables the potential partner CCPs to leverage their installed base must be chosen. Local market conventions and structures can thereby be improved and the complexity of cross-border harmonisation can be mitigated.

8.3 The single central counterparty study

Part I: Introduction

This section presents insights from the empirical study regarding the efficiency impact of establishing a Single CCP for Europe; the conclusions are compared to the findings from Chapter 7. In a first step, the background and objectives of this kind of network strategy are outlined (section 8.3.1), followed by the presentation of the findings from the empirical study (section 8.3.2). The section concludes by summarising the findings regarding the impact of a Single CCP on the efficiency of European clearing (section 8.3.3).

8.3.1 Background and objectives of the initiative

A number of market participants have actively called for the creation of a single European CCP.[261]

As outlined in section 3.3.2, the idea to create a Single CCP solution for a certain economic area is not new. Since 2000, when the ESF launched its blueprint for the creation of a single pan-European CCP, the implementation of such an initiative within Europe has continued to find support among different stakeholders in clearing.[262] In the centre of those advocating a single European CCP are a group of 'major global investment banks, which have expressed support

---

[261] European Commission (ed.) (2006c), p. 8.
[262] For an overview of the dynamics at play in Europe in the years 2000/2001, refer to section 8.2.1.2.

for the idea of a single European CCP, which would be multi-currency and multi-product (i.e. equities, bonds, derivatives and commodities)'.[263]

As outlined in section 8.2.1.2, the major global investment banks' support of the merger between LCH and Clearnet eclipsed the ESF's initial plan to launch a single European CCP. However, in the post-merger years, it soon became clear that the initiative was not working out as envisaged by those demanding a single market infrastructure; it had failed to serve as a catalyst for continued consolidation or to spur the creation of a more centralised European CCP. Since then, and since the European Commission officially launched its consultation with regard to clearing,[264] some stakeholders (again, most importantly, a group of major global investment banks) have stepped up their lobbying efforts to promote the creation of a single European CCP.

Although there are a multitude of industry associations, some major global investment banks have been vociferously advocating their position via the London Investment Banking Association (LIBA).[265] Despite LIBA's unequivocal lobbying efforts, some of the banks it represents remain divided on certain issues;[266] the reasons for this are identified in section 8.3.2. Besides LIBA, LCH.Clearnet has been an important proponent for the full integration of European CCPs (serving all European markets and asset classes into a single entity), especially since 2006.[267] Despite assurances from Deutsche Börse's CEO, Reto Francioni, that the organisation was 'in a discussion on different formats of a single European equity clearinghouse'[268] in 2006, no serious attempt to launch a single European CCP within Europe has been made to date.

In spite of the continued relevance of the Single CCP scenario and ongoing discussions on the topic, no concrete proposals have yet been put forth for creating a 'single European clearing house'. Consequently, there is some confusion among stakeholders as to how to go about establishing a single European CCP. Some stakeholders think it entails forging a merger between Eurex Clearing and LCH.Clearnet,[269] while others advocate the creation of a

---

[263] Hart/Russo/Schönenberger (2002), p. 7.
[264] For details on the European Commission's consultation with the market, refer to European Commission (ed.) (2002b) and to Chapter 1 of this study.
[265] LIBA is the principal trade association for investment banks with operations in London. For more details on LIBA, refer to www.liba.org.uk.
[266] Cf. interviews.   [267] Refer to LCH.Clearnet (ed.) (2006b); and Hardy (2006).
[268] Deutsche Börse Group (ed.) (2006b), p. 17.
[269] Whereas such a merger would create a unified clearing solution for large parts of the European market in terms of cleared volumes (refer to section 2.5.1 for current market share distributions), it would certainly fall short of creating a truly unified clearing solution for the whole of Europe. Smaller or niche markets, smaller issuers and intermediaries, and less sophisticated investors might find themselves on the fringes.

completely new CCP rather than merging existing clearing houses. Still others are convinced that the best way to go about things is to combine all European clearing houses under a common holding company. The scope of this elusive Single CCP remains unclear: whereas the initial idea originated in the area of cash equities clearing, most proponents have since made it clear that they ultimately favour a multi-asset class solution.[270]

Although there is currently no consensus on how best to erect a single European CCP, proponents share the belief that it would deliver significant economies of scale and scope as well as important positive network effects. This network strategy is thus thought by many stakeholders to be the most suited to increase the efficiency of European clearing and to enhance the integration of European markets.[271]

As outlined above, for the purpose of this study, the scenario of creating a Single CCP refers to the full integration (by means of M&A initiatives) of Europe's five major clearing houses: Eurex Clearing, LCH.Clearnet, OMX Clearing, CC&G and MEFF. It is further supposed that this Single CCP would cover securities and derivatives, because it is in Europe's best interest to build up a more integrated clearing structure, in contrast to the US's more fragmented arrangement, and leverage the advantages of doing so.

Part II: Analysis

8.3.2 Findings from the empirical study

Many insights into a Single CCP initiative for Europe were gathered during extensive interviews with stakeholders; the findings are summarised in the following. Interviewees were first asked to detail their expectations of a single European CCP in terms of major benefits and constraints (section 8.3.2.1). Their feedback clarified their positions for or against the initiative and enabled the author to assess whether or not the various stakeholders in clearing believe that the creation of a Single CCP is truly suited to integrate European clearing (section 8.3.2.2).

---

[270] 'The industry requirement is for a cross-product European central counterparty. We believe that the largest immediate benefits and impact to the industry would be generated from a solution that prioritises equities. The initial scope of this plan will accordingly be European equities, but the intention is that the model will be extended across both fixed income and listed and OTC derivatives either immediately or at a later stage.' European Securities Forum (ed.) (2000), p. 9.

[271] See, e.g. LCH.Clearnet (ed.) (2006b), pp. 3–5.

8.3.2.1 Single European CCP: potential benefits and constraints

It is not necessarily the case that a single, not-for-profit, monopolistic entity is the best result. My experience has shown that whenever you can introduce competition and whenever you can introduce a for-profit motivation, you tend to get better service ultimately. Creating monopolies even for not-for-profit organisations is usually something that one has to do or should do as a last resort . . . you get less innovation and you get less efficiency when you are not required to look over your shoulder and see somebody competing.[272]

For an Anglo-Saxon investment bank, for us to say that we are not in favour of competition is quite a hard thing to say and we wouldn't normally expect to say that, but for clearing services, we believe that as a consequence of the economies of scale and network effects – it makes a logical sense to us that clearing is centralised. If you forego competition as a lever to reduce costs, we believe that user governance is the right answer to control costs.[273]

The interviewed stakeholders had various reasons for supporting or opposing the creation of a single European CCP.[274] The benefits and drawbacks, as identified by the interviewees, are summarised in the following; some of these affect all stakeholders in clearing, whereas others only pertain to particular market participants.

Those interviewees **supporting** the creation of a single European CCP argued that due to the economies of scale and scope, as well as network effects in clearing, a Single CCP is in their opinion most likely to lead to cost reductions and thus ultimately to increase the efficiency of the European clearing industry as a whole. Many of them are also convinced that the provision of clearing services constitutes a natural monopoly.

By creating a 'one-stop-shopping' solution, a Single CCP could potentially benefit globally active clearing members by reducing interfaces and furnishing a single set of rules, thus bringing about standardisation and harmonisation of processes, rules and regulations.[275] A Single CCP is further expected to reduce transaction costs by leading to a reduction in clearing house fees, cost of capital and back-office costs by eradicating the cost of duplication for globally active clearing members and enabling regionally-to-globally active clearers to

---

[272] Interview with Harvey Pitt.   [273] Statement made by interviewed clearing member representative.

[274] Refer to section 8.3.2.2 for details on the number of interviewees supporting or opposing the creation of a single European CCP.

[275] Note that for regionally focused or regionally-to-globally active clearing members, cost reduction through a reduction of interfaces is not applicable, because they never maintained multiple CCP interfaces. However, regionally-to-globally active clearing members benefit from the one-stop-shopping aspect, which enables them to disintermediate the GCM they previously employed for clearing markets other than that served by their home CCP.

leverage their internal infrastructure. Regarding the impact a fully consolidated single European CCP would have on risk management, respondents had varying opinions. Whereas twelve interviewees were convinced that such a structure would increase systemic risk, five respondents felt that a monopoly CCP would instead reduce systemic risk due to portfolio effects. Respondents were also divided as to whether or not they believed that a Single CCP would serve to increase the competition between European exchanges.

Finally, it is important to note that none of the interviewees supporting the creation of a single European CCP did so unconditionally. For clearing members, the issue of governance was chief among their concerns: whereas the high volume clearers stated that they want to be granted a significant stake in the governance of the clearing house, medium and low volume clearers emphasised their demand for equal access to the CCP. The latter groups do not want to see the creation of a closed club or be controlled by the major investment banks; as smaller clearers, they fear being locked out.

Well, I wouldn't be supportive of a Single CCP if it resulted in a closed club, limiting access. We would like to have one clearing house where we could do one-stop-shopping and have competitive rates. That would be great. I would be worried about a situation where too few banks are the only ones that have the plugging-in ability. This would obviously limit competition on the level of the intermediaries and risk overly high prices.[276]

The aversion to the creation of a closed club was in fact shared by a number of different stakeholders. Besides the issue of governance, respondents who generally supported the creation of a single European CCP had additional prerequisites, such as reconciling the regulatory and technical environment, including operational procedures, prior to the creation of the Single CCP. Two clearing member representatives, a market expert and a regulator cited the need for a single European regulator. Finally, some respondents pointed out that before European clearing can be consolidated into a single infrastructure, LCH and Clearnet must be properly integrated.

Those **opposed** to the creation of a Single CCP for Europe voiced their convictions that monopolies create inefficiencies stemming from a lack of competitive pressure and warned of the potential power of the monopolistic structure to set inflated prices. Nine interviewees also cited the expected lack of innovation as an additional drawback of an inefficient monopolistic structure. Interviewees were also concerned about the complexities inherent to creating a Single CCP for Europe not only in terms of the time and resources required

---

[276] Statement made by interviewed non-clearing member representative.

for successful integration, but also with regard to the political and regulatory issues raised. In their view, the costs and complexities related to the set-up of a single European CCP on the part of the clearing houses as well as their clearing members dwarf the benefits of aggregation.

To me it is really as much a question of the cost of changing as it is a question of the efficiency at a particular point.[277]

Another drawback of a Single CCP in Europe was said to be its limited ability to deal with and accommodate national market dynamics and characteristics. A monopolistic CCP is believed to be unable to react efficiently to market demands. Consequently, unless the single European CCP is established as a statutory monopoly, the inefficiencies of such a set-up are considered likely to motivate the entrance of new competitors.

I think the problem is . . . that there is a demand for a clearing house to be very flexible and be able to provide services quickly – but by creating an enormous, huge, single CCP, it is very difficult to see that they would be able to fulfil specific requests from a small market. Will they need to? So how will this be handled? Will there pop up new clearing houses, new service providers? Yes, there will! That is why I think it is impossible to say that there should be one single CCP that should provide all the services needed and to be innovative.[278]

Twenty-four interviewees therefore regarded competition as a superior way to ensure the efficiency of the European clearing industry. The preference of respondents opposing the creation of a monopolistic CCP is consequently to have at least two competing European CCPs.[279] The benefits of a more competitive environment are considered to include greater striving for excellence, workflow efficiencies, competitive pressure on fee levels and increased innovation.

Thirteen interviewees were on the fence with regard to the creation of a single European CCP, however. Particularly clearing members, but also three NCMs, two exchanges and one clearing house were **undecided** for the following reasons: whereas these individuals acknowledged the expected benefits of reduced costs, they were hesitant about the operational complexities, investments, time and costs involved in successfully implementing this sort of

---

[277] Interview with Susan M. Phillips.

[278] Statement made by interviewed clearing house representative.

[279] Many of the US-based interviewees who argued against a Single CCP were of the opinion 'that in some respects the CME is perceived as more nimble and efficient than the OCC, and one has to wonder whether that is because the OCC has been enshrined as a monopoly and there is no existing competition.' Statement made by interviewed market expert.

initiative. For ten interviewees, these concerns intensified as the LCH.Clearnet merger proved to be plagued with difficulties and failed to deliver the expected benefits.

I think what we are seeing today with LCH.Clearnet is another classic example of their inability to mix oil and water and we are just not seeing the sort of consolidation benefits that you would expect to gain from the integration of two CCPs, partly because you've just got two very different environments that they are trying to shoehorn together.[280]

As for the globally active clearers, those who were conflicted in some respects were nonetheless looking forward to the potential cost reductions afforded by avoiding duplication costs in Europe and by cuts in clearing house fees. At the same time, these clearers expressed concern about being disintermediated.

Of all of the interviewees who commented on the concept of a single European CCP, twelve said that although the initiative is theoretically appealing, it is simply not possible to implement such a scenario in Europe successfully.

The reason for different types of clearers supporting, opposing or being conflicted towards the creation of a single European CCP is summarised in the following: regionally and regionally-to-globally active clearers were most concerned about the potentially disproportionate distribution of costs and benefits among clearers.[281]

How should something like that function in reality? Should all German clearers then get rid of their clearing infrastructure and migrate their back-offices to support the LCH.Clearnet system, or should clearers in London and France replace their clearing infrastructure and migrate their back-offices to support the Eurex system? And who is going to pay for that? Are the French banks then going to compensate German clearers for this migration or vice versa? I have no solution as to how these different interests and the related extra costs for migration that would be imposed on the industry should be balanced. That's why I can't see the feasibility of creating such a European single CCP.[282]

As outlined above, the regionally-to-globally active clearers interviewed for this study were especially concerned about having equal and free access to the

---

[280] Statement made by interviewed industry participant.
[281] A disproportionate distribution of benefits can result if the Single CCP mainly passes on the benefits of scale to high volume clearers, or passes them on disproportionately, by using a sliding scale based on size. In this case, the playing field would be less level for low and medium volume clearers in Europe. Low volume clearers are also concerned about which clearing system will survive and the resulting investments that will have to be made. Cf. interviews.
[282] Statement made by interviewed exchange representative.

centralised market infrastructure, because this parameter directly affects their ability to successfully disintermediate their away markets' GCM(s).

Because the issue of governance is of such great importance, particularly to globally active clearers, some more insights from the empirical study are provided in the following to reveal the most crucial issues:

- Globally active clearers demanded that a single European CCP be user-governed and/or user-owned.
- Whereas some regionally and regionally-to-globally active clearers were in favour of a for-profit (possibly even listed) Single CCP, globally active clearers were found generally to prefer the idea of a not-for-profit Single CCP operating as a utility. Such a structure is most likely to enable the high volume clearers to attain maximum pricing power and reduce (or at least keep in check) the risk of being disintermediated.
- Similarly, control over the consolidated infrastructure through holding significant stakes in the governance can also serve to diminish and limit the Single CCP's ability to enlarge the scope of its complementary clearing service offerings. This form of control can also impede the internalisation of GCM level network effects, thus inhibiting the Single CCP from becoming a viable competitor to globally active clearers.
- 'A single central counterparty not owned by a single interest group may put as much competitive pressure on sell-side banks as it does on the exchanges.'[283]
- These findings suggest that at the centre of the discussion on the governance of clearing houses is the question of who sets the rules for clearing and what his or her agenda is.[284]

Finally, findings from the empirical study also served to support the conclusion drawn in section 7.4, which is that European clearing does not constitute a natural monopoly. Some interviewees representing high volume clearers indicated that if a monopolistic CCP were to be created, they would use it until it became slow and inefficient, at which point they would either create their own CCP or use another competing clearing house.[285] Other interviewees saw a high likelihood that new and competing clearing houses would continue to be launched even if a single European CCP was implemented.

---

[283] Interview with Philip Bruce.   [284] Cf. interviews.

[285] Another example illustrating the contestability of the European clearing industry is that, in 2007, the global investment banks involved in the creation of Project Turquoise selected the European subsidiary of US-based DTCC as their clearer instead of utilising LCH.Clearnet. Additional evidence that the European clearing industry does not constitute a natural monopoly is provided by LCH.Clearnet, which stated in 2006 that '[t]he threat of volume moving elsewhere or rival exchanges launching identical products with cheaper fees was real'. LCH.Clearnet (ed.) (2006c), p. 3. For further evidence on the contestability of the European clearing industry, also refer to virt-x Exchange (ed.) (2005), pp. 1–3.

8.3.2.2 Suitability of a single CCP to integrate European clearing

> I think that conceptually, as a concept, you have to support it. But you have to temper that support with some realism; Europe is not one market, Europe is not one country, Europe is not one currency . . . and even if we had one today, it wouldn't work because of the political and regulatory regime in Europe.[286]

> You have to look at it from the different perspectives. If I was a client, I would want as few clearing houses as possible. But that wouldn't suit us as there'd be no competitive advantage and it would effectively mean that people would just become members of the clearing house and disintermediate firms like us [global investment banks]. From a proprietary point of view, I think I'd want a similar perspective with a bit more competition in it, so that it keeps the costs down. From our point of view, I think it is pretty good as it is, because it gives us a competitive advantage.[287]

The empirical study revealed whether or not stakeholders support the creation of a Single CCP as a viable way to integrate the European clearing industry and thus increase its efficiency. Roughly 86 per cent (sixty-eight out of seventy-nine) of all interviewees provided concrete feedback.[288] Regarding the response rate, all of the interviewees based in London and Continental Europe were able to respond to this question, whereas 69 per cent of the US-based interviewees expressed an opinion on the issue.

Figure 8.28 illustrates that the majority of interviewees opposed the creation of a single European CCP. In total, thirty-five respondents were against and twenty in support of such an initiative; thirteen interviewees were reluctant to provide a concrete assessment. The figure also shows that the group of clearing members has no unequivocal structural preference. As outlined above, clearing members are a heterogeneous group with divergent interests; their individual viewpoints are shaped by the scale of their cleared volumes and whether their focus is on prop. or agency business.[289] Whereas five clearing members advocated the creation of a single European CCP, six opposed this scenario and seven were conflicted. The divergent interests held by these respondents were detailed in the previous section.

With regard to geographical location, a clear majority of respondents based in Continental Europe and the US proved to be against the creation of a single European CCP. The answers provided by the group of

---

[286] Interview with Steve G. Martin.

[287] Statement made by interviewed clearing member representative.

[288] The remaining interviewees were either not asked to provide an assessment, felt that they had insufficient knowledge, had no clear opinion or did not specify their opinion.

[289] When analysing Figure 8.28, it should also be taken into account that the group of clearing members interviewed in the context of the empirical study is biased towards the viewpoint of globally active clearers. Refer to Chapter 4 for details.

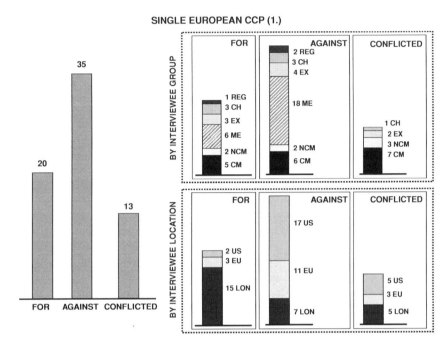

Figure 8.28 Interviewees' assessment of whether or not they support the creation of a single European CCP to integrate the European clearing industry[290]
Source: Author's own.

London-based interviewees were more diverse, however: whereas several of these respondents advocated the creation of a Single CCP for Europe, an equally great number was against the concept or conflicted about it. The reason for the different response patterns according to interviewee location lies in historical particularities related to marketplace dynamics and structures as well as in the interviewees' individual backgrounds.

As detailed in section 2.5.1, Continental Europe has seen the development of horizontal and vertical structures with varying degrees of user ownership and/or user governance. Under the influence of DBAG, particularly the German marketplace has become familiar in past decades with the benefits offered by vertically integrated structures. Given that many of the respondents based in Continental Europe were German, their reluctance to support a Single CCP scenario for Europe comes as little surprise. Whereas the London marketplace has historically been at the forefront of advocating and supporting the creation of horizontal structures and has regarded clearing houses as

[290] Interviewee groups: CM – clearing member; NCM – non-clearing member; ME – market expert; EX – exchange; CH – clearing house; and REG – regulator. Interviewee locations: US – United States; EU – Continental Europe; and LON – London.

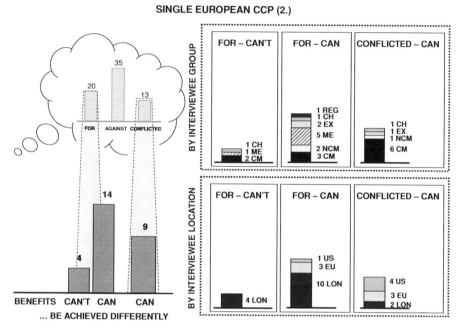

Figure 8.29 Assessment of how many interviewees who were *for* or *conflicted* about the creation of a single European CCP believed that the potential benefits of the initiative can/cannot be achieved differently[291]
Source: Author's own.

utility-like entities that should preferably be user-owned and/or user-governed, the empirical study indicates that this strong sentiment is slowly fading, at least in the derivatives arena. Finally, the US marketplace has also witnessed the development of both horizontal (securities and options) and vertical (futures) structures, with varying degrees of user ownership and/or user governance. The fact that most US-based respondents had a futures background explains their reluctance to support Single CCP structures (and indicates that they are content with the less centralised structure of the American futures clearing industry).

Whereas Figure 8.28 suggests that the majority of interviewees opposed the creation of a single European CCP, a significant number nonetheless advocated the initiative or felt conflicted about it. The next figure (Figure 8.29) therefore assesses how many of the interviewees who were either

[291] Interviewee groups: CM – clearing member; NCM – non-clearing member; ME – market expert; EX – exchange; CH – clearing house; and REG – regulator. Interviewee locations: US – United States; EU – Continental Europe; and LON – London.

for or *conflicted* about the creation of a single European CCP believed that the initiative's potential benefits can or cannot be achieved by different means.

Figure 8.29 illustrates that of the twenty interviewees advocating a single European CCP, the vast majority (fourteen out of twenty) believed that the benefits of a Single CCP can generally be achieved via other means. Most of these individuals thought that a Single CCP is theoretically the best solution, but that it is simply not feasible to implement this kind of structure in Europe. Four of these interviewees suggested a clearing link initiative as an alternative, and three argued in support of a more harmonised environment without further specification.

Only four of the twenty interviewees advocating a single European CCP were of the opinion that the benefits of a single European CCP cannot be achieved by different means.[292] Finally, of the thirteen interviewees who were conflicted, the majority (nine out of thirteen) believed that the benefits of a Single CCP can generally also be achieved through a different initiative.

8.3.3 Summary of findings – impact of a single CCP on efficiency

Now, the honest truth is that the small guys do not benefit from major levels of consolidation. And all attempts to bring cross-border differences down generally hurt niche players that are geographically constrained.[293]

The purpose of this case study was to challenge the findings of Chapter 7 regarding the impact of a Single CCP on the efficiency of European clearing. The findings obtained from this study underscore and clarify the preliminary conclusions. This allows drawing final conclusions. The findings are summarised in the following.

8.3.3.1 Scale Impact Matrix – supply-side scale effects
- The implementation of a Single CCP involves a very high degree of value chain, technical and legal harmonisation and integration efforts. The implementation of such a network strategy is thus very complex and time-consuming, and likely to involve very high long-term investments.
- Whereas the creation of a Single CCP offers high potential for increases in scale and scope, the extremely complex and thus costly integration process can be assumed to involve significant investments. The ultimate magnitude

---

[292] Two respondents did not make clear whether or not they believed that the benefits of a Single CCP structure can or cannot be achieved differently.

[293] Statement made by interviewed clearing member representative.

of economies of scale and scope is therefore diminished by these counter-acting forces.

- Additional complexities (including regulatory and political hurdles) related to integration and coordination, together with possible duplicated efforts, increased communication costs and slow response times can translate into further costs, possibly even to diseconomies of scale.

8.3.3.2 Scale Impact Matrix – demand-side scale effects

- A Single CCP positively impacts the size of the CCP level network; the opposite is true for the GCM level network. The full integration of the partnering clearing houses makes it attractive for a number of market participants to disintermediate their clearer(s).
- Whereas a single European CCP (when fully integrated) eliminates the opportunity for any of the involved clearing houses to establish a lead in Europe through their installed base, it cannot be assumed that the creation of a Single CCP would inhibit the emergence of new, competing clearing houses within Europe. The consolidated infrastructure could thus face competition from new market entrants.
- This similarly suggests that the growth potential of a Single CCP network is likely to be limited. The appeal for other clearing houses to join such a CCP network is limited, because potential partners usually do not have the leeway to benefit from and further leverage their installed base.
- Single CCP initiatives (as a particular form of M&A initiatives) have the drawback that the majority of resources must be committed to the integration of the partnering clearing houses; this type of network initiative is thus unlikely to leave sufficient resources for additional projects or to spur innovation. The drain on resources also hampers the potential for the internalisation of GCM level network effects (and consequently diminishes the attractiveness for counterparties to disintermediate their clearer(s)).

8.3.3.3 Transaction Cost Impact Matrix

- For regionally active clearing members (CM_{PR}/CM_{AR}), indirect transaction costs are likely to increase if their home clearing house engages in M&A initiatives leading towards the creation of a Single CCP. The nature of these initiatives gives clearers no choice of participation; participation is obligatory. The magnitude of the increase of indirect costs depends on the structure of the initiative and the characteristics of the clearing member.[294]

---

[294] One of the most crucial issues in this context is which clearing system will 'survive'.

Clearers must thus potentially bear investments that will not be outweighed by cost savings or increased revenues.

- Regionally-to-globally active clearing members (CM_{PR-G}/CM_{AR-G}) benefit significantly from the opportunity to clear many markets through their home clearing house, thus disintermediating their away market(s) clearer(s). The magnitude of such a cost reduction depends on the structure of the initiative and the characteristics of the clearing member. Cost reductions can be counteracted by investments resulting from the need to implement and adapt to a new system, acquire knowledge, etc.
- For globally active clearers with an agency focus (CM_{AG}), the main benefit of a Single CCP rests in the ability to centralise their various clearing relationships into a single relationship with one clearing house, which significantly reduces their indirect costs. For these clearers, cost reductions are unlikely to be counteracted by investments resulting from the need to implement and adapt to a new system, because they are already members of all European CCPs.
- Globally active clearing members with a prop. focus (CM_{PG}), on the other hand, strive to benefit from reductions in clearing house fees as a result of a Single CCP.

8.3.3.4 Efficiency Impact Matrix

- A single European CCP does not translate into efficiency gains for all clearing member types. Regionally active clearers (CM_{PR}/CM_{AR}) in fact suffer from efficiency losses as a result of a Single CCP.

8.3.3.5 Business Model Impact Matrix

- Whereas a single European CCP benefits globally active clearing members with a prop. focus (CM_{PG}) or an agency focus (CM_{AG}) in terms of efficiency gains, clearers with an agency focus are likely to suffer from revenue decreases due to disintermediation. It is thus doubtful that globally active clearing members with an agency focus would support the creation of a Single CCP, unless they were somehow able to retain a significant stake in the CCPs' governance and/or ownership.
- User governance and/or user ownership is the only means for clearers with an agency focus (CM_{AG}) to exercise control over the rules of European clearing and restrict access to the CCP network – and thus the only way to circumvent disintermediation and the associated revenue losses.

8.4 Final assessment – impact of network strategies on efficiency

The purpose of Chapter 8 is to challenge the conclusions of Chapter 7 with case study findings and insights from the empirical study. For this purpose, three case studies were performed analysing clearing links, mergers and acquisitions, and a Single CCP initiative. The results of the analyses support the preliminary findings: the network strategy best suited to enhance the efficiency of European derivatives clearing is a clearing link set-up, because it is the only network strategy that facilitates efficiency gains for all clearing member types.

Besides supporting the findings of Chapter 7, the case studies also serve to provide more detailed insights into the complexities inherent to the implementation of different network strategies in Europe.

8.4.1 Clearing links

- Many interviewees found it difficult to assess the suitability of a clearing link solution for European clearing. One of the obstacles to judging clearing links is that no link set-up actually exists that could serve as an adequate role model for Europe. Clearing links have so far been implemented with the primary objective of serving trading purposes – a fact that was also found to apply to the case study of the link between Eurex Clearing and The Clearing Corporation.
- The GCL (Phase I) is a prime example of a clearing link initiative whose dedicated purpose was not necessarily to enhance the efficiency of the clearing industry, and it thus consequently failed to deliver significant benefits and to overcome the starting problem. It showed that whereas such a clearing link can serve to increase slightly the efficiency of clearing for some market participants, there remains a huge unrealised potential for efficiency gains.[295]
- The case study thus illustrates that if a link interconnects too few clearing networks, does not compensate for the lost intermediary (GCM) level by providing most of these services themselves (thereby successfully internalising GCM level network effects) and neglects to offer a full choice of clearing location (including all products), it will ultimately fail to gain traction. Consequently, if the partnering clearing houses do not adequately attempt

---

[295] The unrealised potential for efficiency gains is a direct result of the limitations of the GCL initiative, which have been identified in the context of the section 8.1.2.6.

to overcome the link-inherent starting problem, a significant amount of potential for efficiency gains will go unrealised. Such a link initiative is not designed to increase significantly the efficiency of the European clearing industry.

- Additionally, the failure of relevant clearing members to recognise the potential value proposition of a clearing link set-up, low internal prioritisation of implementing the link, mandatory open interest transfers, regulatory and political issues can create further uncertainty about the future development of a clearing link initiative and inhibit clearing members from expecting positive future network effects and thus aggravate the starting problem.
- The case study also suggested that not all stakeholders have a comprehensive grasp of the concept and value proposition of clearing links in general. Surprisingly, clearing houses in particular proved to know little about the Global Clearing Link. Although the GCL was never a concept intended to invite other CCPs to participate, for a European clearing link initiative to be successful, it is important that all European CCPs understand the value of interconnecting. A link initiative can only flourish if clearing houses truly understand the value of leveraging their installed base, internalising the GCM level network effects and using the initiative to strengthen their unique CCP level network effects.

8.4.2 Mergers and acquisitions

- The case study of the merger between the London Clearing House and Clearnet revealed that the complexities of successfully implementing M&A initiatives between European clearing houses are even greater than assumed in Chapter 7. In reality, the counteracting forces, such as necessary long-term investments as well as additional regulatory and political hurdles, significantly impede mergers. Within Europe, the full integration of the partnering CCPs, which is necessary to achieve the maximum efficiency gains, has proved to be next to impossible.
- The very high complexity of integration inherent to M&A initiatives also decelerates the CCPs' ability to innovate and increases costs. If M&A strategies are employed to increase the efficiency of European clearing, it is thus likely that many potential efficiency gains will remain unrealised.
- Additionally, the insights generated by the case study underscored the finding that M&A initiatives do not benefit all clearing members, as they potentially have a detrimental impact on low volume clearers with a regional business focus.

- The LCH.Clearnet merger is a prime example of an M&A initiative between CCPs that has so far failed to deliver on precisely those issues critical for realising high efficiency gains for medium and high volume clearers.
- The case study also suggests that M&A initiatives between two major European CCPs by no means necessarily spur the further harmonisation or integration of the European clearing industry.

8.4.3 Single CCP

- The insights from the empirical study and the M&A and Single CCP case studies supported the preliminary findings of Chapter 7 regarding the complexities of combining European clearing houses with different historical backgrounds, profiles and legal environments as well as the near impossibility of consolidating European CCPs into a single group.
- Additionally, the case study insights underlined the findings regarding the unequal distribution of benefits and costs inherent to this type of network strategy. A single European CCP initiative does not benefit all clearing members; it can in fact exert a detrimental impact on low volume clearers with a regional business focus.
- High volume clearers with an agency focus prefer the establishment of a Single CCP over clearing links, because clearing links can have a significantly negative impact on their business model and it is generally easier to succeed in lobbying for user ownership/governance (thus controlling the rules of clearing) of one single entity than it is for various entities. High volume clearers with an agency focus are therefore likely to oppose a Single CCP unless they have a substantial say in the governance of the clearing house and can influence the rules of clearing. This is the only way for them to circumvent the risk of disintermediation and the associated revenue losses.
- The analysis also supported the finding that globally active clearers with a prop. focus are likely to benefit most, in terms of efficiency gains, from the implementation of a Single CCP. Nonetheless, this group of clearers will only support a Single CCP if it can secure the means to control the rules of clearing, i.e. make sure that clearing fees (i.e. their core cost driver) are sufficiently reduced and that the consolidated infrastructure does not abuse its dominant position. Whether or not such fee reductions truly reflect an increase in internal efficiency of the merged entity or merely represent a quick fix to appease the clearing members that exert control over the Single CCP would require further research.

- When Single CCP initiatives fail to translate into indirect cost savings and merely accommodate clearing members by offering fee cuts, globally active clearers with a prop. focus benefit significantly, whilst all other clearing member types remain unable to reduce their core cost driver (i.e. indirect costs).
- Regarding the issue of governance, the M&A and the Single CCP case studies revealed that ceding partial control over a clearing house in the context of a merger as a trade-off for efficiency gains makes sense from the perspective of high volume clearers with an agency perspective, as long as the resulting structure is not a monopoly. If the CCP is a monopoly, the risk of disintermediation is likely to exceed the potential benefits for these clearers.

Finally, the case studies also lent support to the preliminary finding that European derivatives clearing does not constitute a natural monopoly. Despite the widespread belief that clearing generally qualifies as a natural monopoly, no evidence of this was found in multinational markets, such as the European clearing industry, in which '[n]ew clearing arrangements are emerging all the time'.[296]

To summarise, whereas different network strategies have varying potential to increase the efficiency of the European clearing industry, clearing links were found to be the only initiative that generates efficiency gains for all clearing members. Particular attention must also be given to the impact of harmonisation and integration initiatives on smaller regional or niche markets and on clearing members with less negotiating and lobbying power than Europe's high volume clearers. Although a clearing link strategy is best suited to benefit all clearers, the implementation of such an initiative will also be cumbersome and demand a lot from the different stakeholders. Furthermore, there are many kinds of clearing link initiative, and not all of them can serve to increase the efficiency of European clearing. Therefore, the parameters and prerequisites identified in this study as necessary for enhancing the efficiency of the European clearing industry through a link set-up will be summarised and further detailed in Chapter 10. Prior to that and based on the findings of Chapters 7 and 8, Chapter 9 provides a quantitative assessment of the efficiency impact of European network strategies.

---

[296] Moskow (2006).

9 Quantifying the efficiency impact – European network strategies

Analysing the impact of network strategies on the efficiency of European clearing consists of a three-step approach: the findings derived in Chapters 7 and 8 (step 1 and 2) serve as the basis for a quantification of the efficiency impact of European network strategies, which is presented in this chapter (step 3).

First, the quantified efficiency impacts of a European clearing link set-up and a single European CCP are presented in terms of total costs borne by European clearing members (section 9.1). The next section (section 9.2) breaks these costs down into the members' average direct and indirect costs. The calculation of the respective efficiency impact is based on the findings of sections 5.2.3 and 5.2.4, as well as the conclusions derived in Chapters 7 and 8. Finally, a summary of the insights derived in this chapter is provided (section 9.3).

9.1 Total European industry costs

Whereas section 5.2.3 introduced an estimate of the total European clearing industry costs in 2005, this section presents the recalculated estimate under the assumption of implemented European clearing links (section 9.1.1) and a single European CCP (section 9.1.2), i.e. quantifies the potential efficiency impact of each network strategy. As the calculation of costs is based on the results presented in section 5.2.3, the same caveats apply to the figures presented in the following.[1] For details on the quantitative analysis and the underlying assumptions, refer to Appendix 8.

---

[1] An additional caveat applies to the estimated efficiency impact: the implementation of European clearing links or a single European CCP is likely to impact the composition of all-in clearing costs for different clearing member types (see Figure 5.5). When a certain network strategy enables a disproportionately higher/lower reduction of indirect costs as compared to direct costs (or vice versa) for certain clearing member types, then this affects the ratio of direct to indirect costs. This kind of development is not

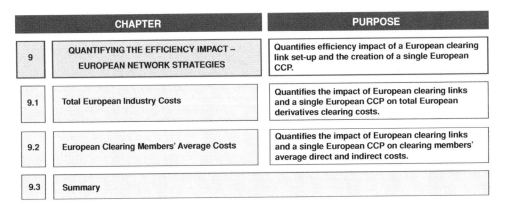

CHAPTER		PURPOSE
9	QUANTIFYING THE EFFICIENCY IMPACT – EUROPEAN NETWORK STRATEGIES	Quantifies efficiency impact of a European clearing link set-up and the creation of a single European CCP.
9.1	Total European Industry Costs	Quantifies the impact of European clearing links and a single European CCP on total European derivatives clearing costs.
9.2	European Clearing Members' Average Costs	Quantifies the impact of European clearing links and a single European CCP on clearing members' average direct and indirect costs.
9.3	Summary	

Figure 9.1   Structure of Chapter 9

9.1.1 Efficiency impact of clearing links

This section furnishes a recalculation of the 2005 total costs borne by European clearing members according to the assumption of implemented clearing links between Eurex Clearing, LCH.Clearnet, OMX Clearing, MEFF and CC&G.

Figure 9.2 outlines the quantitative results of the analysis.[2] Under the assumption of implemented European clearing links, total European costs of derivatives clearing would have amounted to roughly €1.503 billion in 2005, representing a reduction of 31 per cent when compared with the original estimate. Although this figure pertains to the first level of transaction costs, i.e. all of the direct and indirect costs borne by clearing members, any such cost reduction also benefits market participants with indirect access to the market infrastructure. NCMs and other customers, for example, benefit from cost reductions when the savings are redistributed within the VPN and are ultimately passed on (either directly or indirectly as part of commissions) by the clearers to their respective NCMs and/or other customers. Under a clearing link scenario, direct costs would have come to about €523 million, or been trimmed by roughly 28 per cent. Indirect costs would have weighed in at €980 million, representing a 32 per cent decrease compared to the original 2005 estimate.

Figure 9.3 outlines the per cent stake the different clearing members would have held in the costs of European derivatives clearing in 2005 under the

accounted for in this quantitative analysis. This is due to the lack of a basis for providing well-founded assumptions as to how different network strategies affect the composition of all-in clearing costs for the different clearing member types.

[2] Figures are rounded to millions of euros; €100,000 to €499,000 are rounded down, whereas €500,000 to €999,000 are rounded up.

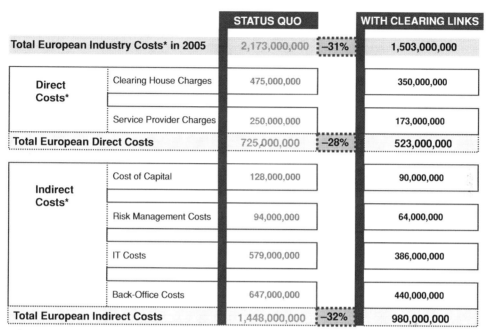

		STATUS QUO		WITH CLEARING LINKS
Total European Industry Costs* in 2005		2,173,000,000	–31%	1,503,000,000
Direct Costs*	Clearing House Charges	475,000,000		350,000,000
	Service Provider Charges	250,000,000		173,000,000
Total European Direct Costs		725,000,000	–28%	523,000,000
Indirect Costs*	Cost of Capital	128,000,000		90,000,000
	Risk Management Costs	94,000,000		64,000,000
	IT Costs	579,000,000		386,000,000
	Back-Office Costs	647,000,000		440,000,000
Total European Indirect Costs		1,448,000,000	–32%	980,000,000

* Costs in EUR

Figure 9.2   Total European derivatives clearing costs in 2005 – efficiency impact of clearing links
Source: Author's own.

assumption of implemented European clearing links. Although the results have to be interpreted cautiously for the reasons described in the introductory part of section 9.1, the findings suggest that high volume clearers with a prop. focus can be expected to continue to have a strong lobbying interest in pushing clearing houses to reduce their fees if clearing links are introduced in the future. As for cutting indirect costs further, the other clearing member types would likely have an interest in advocating additional external as well as pursuing internal measures (as identified in section 5.2.7).

9.1.2 Efficiency impact of a single CCP

The following presents the efficiency impact of a Single CCP on the total costs of European derivatives clearing in 2005. This section thus furnishes a recalculation of the 2005 total costs borne by European clearing members according to the assumption of an implemented Single CCP created through a merger between Eurex Clearing, LCH.Clearnet, OMX Clearing, MEFF and CC&G.

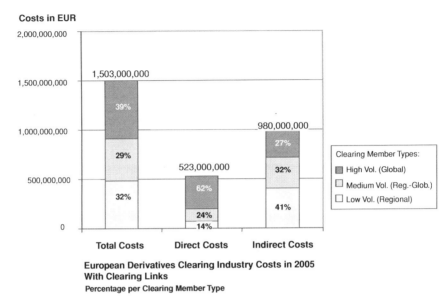

European Derivatives Clearing Industry Costs in 2005
With Clearing Links
Percentage per Clearing Member Type

Figure 9.3   Per cent stake of different clearing member types in European derivatives clearing costs in 2005 –
under the assumption of implemented European clearing links
Source: Author's own.

Figure 9.4 outlines the quantitative results of the analysis.[3] Under the
assumption of an implemented single European CCP, total European costs of
derivatives clearing would have amounted to roughly €1.958 billion in 2005.
As compared to the status quo ante, the implementation of a Single CCP
would have reduced total costs by roughly 10 per cent. Direct costs would
have come to approximately €629 million, or roughly 13 per cent less than
the original 2005 estimate of €725 million. Meanwhile, indirect costs could
have been reduced by roughly 8 per cent, for a total of €1.329 billion, under
the same schema.

When comparing the effect of clearing links and a Single CCP on total costs
(Figures 9.2 and 9.4), it has to be kept in mind that the figures being compared
represent the aggregate of individual cost impacts for each of the 219 European
clearing members.[4] This means that a particular clearing member might have
experienced more substantial reductions in, say, the cost of capital under a

---

[3] Figures are rounded to millions of euros; €100,000 to €499,000 are rounded down, whereas €500,000
to €999,000 are rounded up.
[4] Refer to section 2.5.1 for details on the structure of the European VPN and the total number of clearing
members.

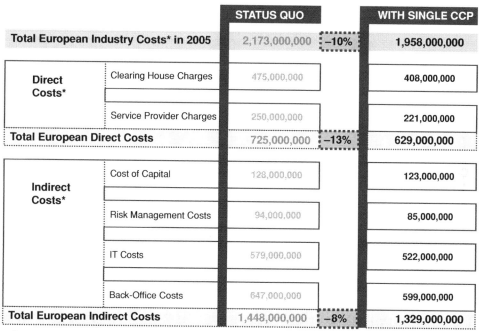

		STATUS QUO		WITH SINGLE CCP
Total European Industry Costs* in 2005		2,173,000,000	–10%	1,958,000,000
Direct Costs*	Clearing House Charges	475,000,000		408,000,000
	Service Provider Charges	250,000,000		221,000,000
Total European Direct Costs		725,000,000	–13%	629,000,000
Indirect Costs*	Cost of Capital	128,000,000		123,000,000
	Risk Management Costs	94,000,000		85,000,000
	IT Costs	579,000,000		522,000,000
	Back-Office Costs	647,000,000		599,000,000
Total European Indirect Costs		1,448,000,000	–8%	1,329,000,000

* Costs in EUR

Figure 9.4   Total European derivatives clearing costs in 2005 – efficiency impact of a single European CCP
Source: Author's own.

Single CCP initiative, whereas another clearer might have reaped better gains from clearing links.

Figure 9.5 outlines the per cent stake that the different clearing members would have held in the European costs of derivatives clearing in 2005 under the assumption of an implemented Single European CCP. Again, even though certain caveats have to be kept in mind (see the introductory part of section 9.1), the results nevertheless suggest that high volume clearers with a prop. focus can be expected to continue to pressure clearing houses to reduce their fees if a Single CCP is introduced in the future. To reduce indirect costs further, on the other hand, other clearing member types would likely advocate additional external and internal measures (as identified in section 5.2.7). Figure 9.5 also illustrates that under the Single CCP scenario, low volume clearers would likely suffer from significant efficiency losses.

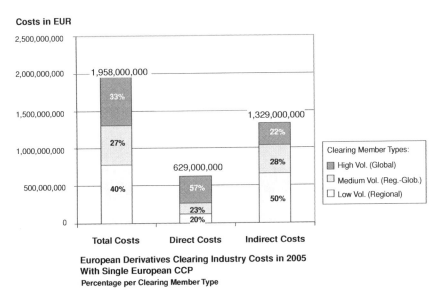

Figure 9.5 Per cent stake of different clearing member types in European derivatives clearing costs in 2005 – under the assumption of an implemented single European CCP
Source: Author's own.

9.2 European clearing members' average costs

Section 5.2.4 presented an estimate of European clearing members' average direct and indirect costs. This section assesses the average costs for different clearing member types assuming the implementation of either European clearing links (section 9.2.1) or a single European CCP (section 9.2.2). Again, this analysis does not claim to deliver results applicable to any particular clearing member, but instead provides an archetypical assessment of clearing costs.

The estimated costs enable a better understanding of the efficiency impact that European clearing links or a Single CCP can have on different clearing member types' average costs and also serves to illuminate the possible effect that certain network strategies could thus have on the structure of the European VPN.[5] The calculation of these costs is based on the results presented in section 5.2.4 and the findings of Chapters 7 and 8.[6]

---

[5] A detailed interpretation of these results and their possible effect on the structure of the European VPN are discussed in more detail in section 10.1.

[6] The calculation of European clearing members' average costs under the assumption of implemented European clearing links and a Single CCP are based on the results of the calculation as outlined in

Market Share	Ø Direct Costs		Ø Indirect Costs		Ø TOTAL Costs	
	STATUS QUO	CLEARING LINKS	STATUS QUO	CLEARING LINKS	STATUS QUO	CLEARING LINKS
HIGH VOLUME CLEARER						
10.00%	52,509,000	42,288,000	35,006,000	27,673,000	87,515,000	69,961,000
4.00%	30,869,000	24,860,000	25,256,000	19,966,000	56,125,000	44,826,000
3.00%	24,453,000	19,694,000	21,685,000	17,142,000	46,138,000	36,836,000
MEDIUM VOLUME CLEARER						
2.00%	15,145,000	8,288,000	22,718,000	12,195,000	37,863,000	20,483,000
1.00%	8,483,000	4,643,000	25,450,000	13,661,000	33,933,000	18,304,000
0.50%	4,756,000	2,603,000	21,665,000	11,629,000	26,421,000	14,232,000
LOW VOLUME CLEARER						
0.30%	3,093,000	2,358,000	14,092,000	10,738,000	17,185,000	13,096,000
0.01%	861,000	656,000	4,880,000	3,718,000	5,741,000	4,374,000
	Costs in EUR					

Figure 9.6   Average annual direct and indirect costs for clearing member archetypes – under the assumption of implemented European clearing links
Note: Ø = average.
Source: Author's own.

9.2.1 Efficiency impact of clearing links

This section presents an estimate of the average annual direct and indirect costs European clearing member archetypes would incur under the assumption of implemented European clearing links (Figure 9.6). From these figures, the clearing members' average unit costs can be derived, and the efficiency impact of clearing links for these clearing member archetypes can be gauged (Figure 9.7).

Figures 9.6 and 9.7 show that increasing volumes continue to lead to economies of scale on the part of the clearers; unit costs thus decrease with an increase of the number of contracts cleared. The figures reinforce the previous findings of Chapters 7 and 8 with quantitative cost data, showing that all clearing member types benefit from European clearing links in the form of efficiency gains.

Appendix 8. These results enable the identification of the efficiency impact of the network initiatives on the direct and indirect costs of different clearing member types and finally lead to the results outlined in Figures 9.6, 9.7, 9.8 and 9.9.

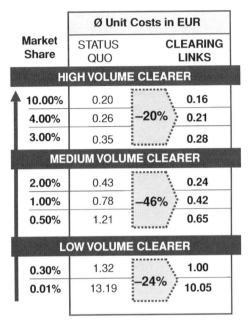

Figure 9.7   Average unit costs for clearing member archetypes – under the assumption of implemented European clearing links
Note: Ø = average.
Source: Author's own.

In particular, medium volume clearers benefit from reduced unit costs. If European clearing links were implemented, some of these clearers would enjoy unit cost levels comparable to those currently exhibited by high volume clearers. This illustrates the finding that under a European clearing link scenario, it would make sense for medium volume clearers to self-clear all European markets in which they are active. It would thus be logical for a number of medium volume clearers to consider disintermediating their away markets' GCM(s).

Section 5.2.4 described unit costs as the central decision criterion for clearing members when assessing the economic prudence of becoming a direct member of one or more clearing houses in relevant markets. Network initiatives were also identified as possibly having an important impact on the structure of the European VPN, in particular when initiatives result in increased economic attractiveness for regionally-to-globally active clearers of self-clearing many markets instead of employing intermediary services. Figure 9.7 therefore suggests that the currently strong position of high volume

Market Share	Ø Direct Costs		Ø Indirect Costs		Ø TOTAL Costs	
	STATUS QUO	SINGLE CCP	STATUS QUO	SINGLE CCP	STATUS QUO	SINGLE CCP
HIGH VOLUME CLEARER						
10.00%	52,509,000	46,517,000	35,006,000	30,620,000	87,515,000	77,137,000
4.00%	30,869,000	27,346,000	25,256,000	22,092,000	56,125,000	49,438,000
3.00%	24,453,000	21,663,000	21,685,000	18,968,000	46,138,000	40,631,000
MEDIUM VOLUME CLEARER						
2.00%	15,145,000	10,034,000	22,718,000	14,673,000	37,863,000	24,707,000
1.00%	8,483,000	5,620,000	25,450,000	16,438,000	33,933,000	22,058,000
0.50%	4,756,000	3,150,000	21,665,000	13,993,000	26,421,000	17,143,000
LOW VOLUME CLEARER						
0.30%	3,093,000	3,863,000	14,092,000	17,586,000	17,185,000	21,449,000
0.01%	861,000	1,075,000	4,880,000	6,090,000	5,741,000	7,165,000
	Costs in EUR					

Figure 9.8   Average annual direct and indirect costs for clearing member archetypes – under the assumption of an implemented single European CCP

Note: Ø = average.

Source: Author's own.

clearers within the European VPN could be diluted if a clearing link set-up were to be implemented.[7]

9.2.2 Efficiency impact of a single CCP

This section presents an estimate of the average annual direct and indirect costs European clearing member archetypes would have to bear under the assumption of an implemented single European CCP (Figure 9.8). From these figures, the clearing members' average unit costs can be derived, and the efficiency impact of a Single CCP for these clearing member archetypes can be identified (Figure 9.9).

Figures 9.8 and 9.9 show that increasing volumes continue to lead to economies of scale for the clearers; unit costs thus decrease with an increase of the number of contracts cleared. The figures also illustrate the findings from Chapters 7 and 8 with quantitative cost data: they show that medium and

---

[7] A detailed interpretation of these results and their possible effect on the structure of the VPN are discussed in more detail in section 10.1.

⌀ Unit Costs in EUR		
Market Share	STATUS QUO	SINGLE CCP
HIGH VOLUME CLEARER		
10.00%	0.20	0.18
4.00%	0.26	−12%	0.23
3.00%	0.35	0.31
MEDIUM VOLUME CLEARER		
2.00%	0.43	0.28
1.00%	0.78	−35%	0.51
0.50%	1.21	0.79
LOW VOLUME CLEARER		
0.30%	1.32	1.64
0.01%	13.19	+25%	16.46

Figure 9.9   Average unit costs for clearing member archetypes – under the assumption of an implemented single European CCP
Note: ø = average.
Source: Author's own.

high volume clearers benefit from a Single CCP, but that the efficiency gains are not as great as those produced by European clearing links.

In particular, medium volume clearers benefit from reduced unit costs. Figure 9.9 shows that when a single European CCP is implemented, some of these clearers enjoy unit cost levels comparable to those currently exhibited by high volume clearers. This lends credibility to the finding that it makes sense for a number of medium volume clearers to self-clear all European markets in which they are active – thus disintermediating their away markets' GCM(s) – if a single European CCP is in place.

Last but not least, the figures illustrate that not all clearing member types stand to benefit from the implementation of a single European CCP – low volume clearers are negatively affected by significant efficiency losses, i.e. cost increases. For low volume clearers, the Single CCP scenario diminishes the economic appeal of self-clearing, because their costs of production increase.[8]

---

[8] A detailed interpretation of these results and their possible effect on the structure of the VPN are discussed in more detail in section 10.1.

9.3 Summary

This chapter constitutes the final phase of a three-step approach to analyse the impact of network strategies on the efficiency of European clearing. Based on the findings derived in Chapters 7 and 8, this chapter presents a quantification of the potential efficiency impact of a European clearing link set-up and a single European CCP, the results of which are briefly summarised in the following.

9.3.1 Total European industry costs

- Under the assumption of implemented European clearing links, total European costs of derivatives clearing would have amounted to roughly €1.503 billion in 2005, representing a reduction of 31 per cent. Direct costs would have come to about €523 million, and thus reduced by roughly 28 per cent. Indirect costs would have weighed in at €980 million, representing a 32 per cent decrease.
- Under the assumption of an implemented single European CCP, total European costs of derivatives clearing would have amounted to roughly €1.958 billion in 2005. The implementation of a Single CCP would thus have reduced total costs by roughly 10 per cent. Direct costs would have come to approximately €629 million, i.e. reduced by roughly 13 per cent. Indirect costs would have been reduced by roughly 8 per cent, for a total of €1.329 billion.
- Figure 9.10 summarises these findings by giving an overview of the estimated potential savings under the assumption of implemented European clearing links or an implemented Single CCP for Europe. It reveals that while clearing links could result in annual total cost savings of approximately €670 million, a Single CCP would merely save European clearing members around €215 million in total costs. Annual direct costs savings could amount to roughly €202 million in the case of implemented European clearing links. A Single CCP would bring about fewer annual direct cost savings of only approximately €96 million. Total indirect costs would be reduced annually by €468 million through clearing links, but only by €119 million in the case of a single European CCP.
- The finding that a Single CCP provides less overall benefits to the market as compared to clearing links, results from the fact that some clearing member types are negatively affected by the implementation of a Single CCP.

POTENTIAL SAVINGS THROUGH:		CLEARING LINKS	SINGLE CCP
Total European Industry Costs in 2005		–670,000,000 EUR	–215,000,000 EUR
Direct Costs	Clearing House Charges	–125,000,000 EUR	–67,000,000 EUR
	Service Provider Charges	–77,000,000 EUR	–29,000,000 EUR
Total European Direct Costs		**–202,000,000 EUR**	**–96,000,000 EUR**
Indirect Costs	Cost of Capital	–38,000,000 EUR	–5,000,000 EUR
	Risk Management Costs	–30,000,000 EUR	–9,000,000 EUR
	IT Costs	–193,000,000 EUR	–57,000,000 EUR
	Back-Office Costs	–207,000,000 EUR	–48,000,000 EUR
Total European Indirect Costs		**–468,000,000 EUR**	**–119,000,000 EUR**

Figure 9.10   Total European derivatives clearing costs in 2005 – overview of estimated potential savings under the assumption of implemented European clearing links or an implemented single European CCP
Source: Author's own.

9.3.2 European clearing members' average costs

- Under the assumption of implemented European clearing links, all clearing member types benefit from efficiency gains: high volume clearers can potentially reduce their unit costs by 20 per cent. Medium volume clearers enjoy significantly reduced costs; they can benefit from unit cost savings of roughly 46 per cent. This means that some of these clearers would enjoy unit cost levels comparable to those currently exhibited by high volume clearers. It would thus make sense for medium volume clearers to self-clear all European markets in which they are active and consider disintermediating their away markets' GCM(s). Finally, also low volume clearers can potentially benefit from efficiency gains and pocket a lowering of unit costs by roughly 24 per cent.
- Under the assumption of an implemented single European CCP, however, not all clearing member types benefit from efficiency gains: low volume clearers are negatively affected by significant efficiency losses; their unit costs can increase by up to 25 per cent. For some low volume clearers, the

Single CCP scenario can thus diminish the economic appeal of self-clearing. Medium and high volume clearers, on the other hand, benefit from a Single CCP, but the efficiency gains are not as great as those produced by a European clearing link scenario. High volume clearers can potentially reduce their unit costs by approximately 12 per cent. Medium volume clearers enjoy greater efficiency gains than high volume clearing members; their unit costs can be reduced by roughly 35 per cent. This means that it would also make sense for medium volume clearers to self-clear all European markets in which they are active and consider disintermediating their away markets' GCM(s) in the case of a Single CCP.

Based on the findings of Chapters 7, 8 and 9 on the efficiency impact of various network strategies within the European clearing industry, Chapter 10 proceeds to determine the most preferable future European industry structure and delivers recommendations for its development. Additionally, the research results are applied to European exchange-traded cash equities clearing as well as to Europe with respect to its global positioning.

10 Introducing the future network economy – development of the clearing industry

The previous chapters served to provide conclusions on the efficiency impact of various network strategies within the European clearing industry. Based on these findings, this chapter identifies the most preferable future clearing industry structure and delivers recommendations for the industry's future development.

The following sections summarise and build on the insights obtained from the previous chapters to create an outlook on the future development of the European clearing industry (section 10.1), followed by an application of the research results to European clearing with regard to its global context (section 10.2). The chapter closes by summarising these findings (section 10.3).

10.1 Future development of the European clearing industry

We want dynamic, integrated capital markets in the EU – not segmented ones. And we are determined to achieve them. For all our customers, investors and companies. And to strengthen the European economy.[1]

This study's objective was to identify the network strategy best suited to increase the efficiency of European clearing. In line with the above-quoted claim by Commissioner Charlie McCreevy (European Commission), it is considered to be a prerequisite that such an efficiency increase benefit all clearing members. Therefore, network strategies that favour some while penalising others (such as the Single CCP) are not regarded as viable scenarios.

In keeping with the Commission's vision to further European market integration, a recommendation for the future development of European derivatives clearing is formulated (section 10.1.1). The findings on derivatives

---

[1] McCreevy (2006a), p. 5.

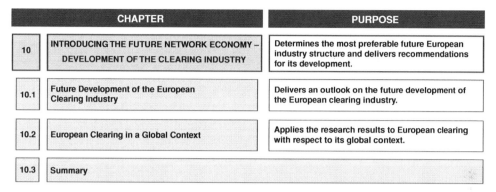

Figure 10.1   Structure of Chapter 10

clearing are then applied to European cash equities clearing (section 10.1.2). A third step serves to gauge whether Europe's major clearing houses are sufficiently well-positioned, prepared and flexible to reap the benefits of a clearing link structure (section 10.1.3). This assessment serves as a basis to consider the reconcilability of this study's conclusions with the European Commission's decision to call upon the industry to establish a Code of Conduct (section 10.1.4). At this juncture, the critical question is which European clearing houses actually ought to be linked. A fifth step (section 10.1.5) therefore provides a basic framework designed to serve as a starting point for European CCP managers to determine their European clearing link strategy. Finally, the structural changes that clearing links are likely to spur in the European Value Provision Network are described (section 10.1.6).

10.1.1 Recommendation for European derivatives clearing

Competition is important in achieving the overall objective of creating a safe, efficient and integrated EU clearing and settlement infrastructure. The basic conditions for this goal are transparency and open access. To avoid discrimination against classes of participants and competitive distortions, participation requirements should be fair and open within the scope of services offered by the CCP. However, these rules and requirements for fair and open access should be balanced against and aimed at controlling and limiting risks.[2]

The research objective of this study was to determine the efficiency impact of different network strategies within the European clearing industry. This

---

[2] Tumpel-Gugerell (2006).

in turn served to identify the European industry structure best suited to increase the efficiency of clearing for all clearing members. The study revealed that particular attention must be given to the impact of harmonisation and integration initiatives on smaller regional or niche markets and on clearing members with less negotiating and lobbying power than Europe's high volume clearers.[3]

Given these criteria, clearing links emerged as the sole network strategy suited to integrate the European clearing industry and generate efficiency gains for all clearing members. To summarise, the implementation of clearing links between European CCPs was found to hold the following potential benefits for stakeholders in clearing:

- All clearing member types stand to benefit from a decrease of direct and indirect costs, resulting in a substantial reduction of unit costs.
- Low volume clearers would not risk being put out of business through European clearing links and would potentially also benefit from reduced unit costs.
- Medium volume clearers would be given the opportunity to disintermediate their away markets' clearing intermediaries, which would in turn lead to a significant unit cost reduction. Disintermediation becomes even more attractive when clearing houses succeed in internalising GCM level network effects.
- Clearing links would stimulate the internalisation of GCM level network effects by the CCP level. This internalisation process is ultimately beneficial, because it increases the industry's overall efficiency.
- High volume clearers could reduce their unit costs, as they would be given the option to select the CCP that will serve as their gateway to other European markets.
- European clearing houses would benefit because they could leverage their installed base, internalise GCM level network effects, strengthen their unique CCP level network effects and continue to offer services tailored to the specific demands of regional market particularities to an increased number of network participants.
- Market participants and clearing houses alike would benefit from the competitive forces,[4] enhanced flexibility and adaptability, innovation opportunities and high growth potential inherent to link set-ups.

---

[3] Also refer to European Commission (ed.) (2002a), p. 2.
[4] Certainly, it has to be ensured that competition between clearing houses does not lead to competition in the area of risk management, i.e. in charging insufficient levels of margin.

Besides increasing the efficiency of the European clearing industry, a clearing link set-up could also be expected to have the following positive effects on European markets as a whole:

- Smaller regional and European niche markets could be strengthened.
- Competition between Europe's regional markets would be spurred, which could also lead to the further integration and harmonisation of European capital markets.
- Clearing links do not lead to a concentration of risk at a single market infrastructure and are unlikely to give rise to negative network effects. The spreading of risk over various European CCPs could serve to increase the market's stability.
- Ultimately, all market participants (including those with indirect access to the market infrastructure) stand to benefit from such an efficiency increase.

Whereas this study identified clearing links as the network strategy best suited to increase the efficiency of European clearing, it also revealed that the mere implementation of links between European CCPs does not automatically increase the efficiency of the clearing industry. If certain prerequisites are not fulfilled, a significant amount of unrealised potential for efficiency gains will be left unexploited. Therefore, the parameters and prerequisites identified in this study as necessary for enhancing the efficiency of the European clearing industry through a link set-up are summarised and further detailed in the following.

Clearing links' full potential for efficiency gains can only be exhausted if the partnering clearing houses adequately attempt to overcome the link-inherent starting problem. In addition, clearing members should not be forced to participate in the link. The costs of alternation and the link-inherent starting problem can only be successfully surmounted if the partnering CCPs take the following steps:

- Convince clearing members to expect positive future network effects. Although this means that the partnering CCPs must strive to replicate the size of a Single CCP network, it does not necessarily mean that all European CCPs must be interlinked right from the start. Rather, clearing members must trust the clearing houses that the scope of the clearing link set-up will gradually be extended over time to cover all major European markets.[5]

---

[5] A more detailed framework for determining which European clearing houses actually ought to be linked is presented in section 10.1.5.

- Make up for the lost intermediation services formerly furnished by GCM(s) by providing (most) of these services themselves, thereby successfully internalising GCM level network effects.
- Compensate for the lost participation in other CCP networks by providing a similar service level and processing all products and markets of the linked clearing houses. CCPs must thus provide for a full choice of clearing location.
- Make sure that they sufficiently educate market participants about the benefits of such a link set-up. The failure of relevant clearing members to recognise the potential value proposition of a clearing link set-up and low internal prioritisation of implementing the link can potentially aggravate the starting problem.
- Engage to educate other clearing houses and stakeholders about the benefits of such a link set-up. As such a European clearing link scenario must be a concept intended to invite other CCPs to participate, it is important that all European clearing houses appreciate the value of interconnecting. A link initiative can only flourish if clearing houses truly understand the value of leveraging their installed base, internalising the GCM level network effects and making their unique CCP level network effects stronger through it. Mandatory open interest transfers, and regulatory and political issues can create further uncertainty about the future development of a clearing link initiative and inhibit clearing members from expecting positive future network effects and thus inhibit the starting problem to be overcome.

If the partnering clearing houses fail to overcome the link-inherent starting problem, a significant amount of potential for efficiency gains will go unrealised. Under these circumstances, a link initiative will not exert a positive impact on the efficiency of the European clearing industry. It is therefore absolutely vital that the above-mentioned prerequisites be met if a link set-up is to succeed. Implementing European clearing links without careful planning and a dedicated strategy for tackling the starting problem will only waste time and resources and do very little to enhance the efficiency of the European clearing industry.

Given that European derivatives clearing (in its current form) has been found to be very efficient, some European CCPs will hesitate to adopt a clearing link strategy. They should generally only implement the link strategy if they are willing to address the identified issues necessary to overcome the starting problem.[6] However, despite the effort involved, the benefits for clearing houses

---

[6] Certainly, as outlined in section 3.3.1.2, European CCPs can consider engaging in the implementation of clearing links for various other reasons. However, as long as the partnering clearing houses fall short

of engaging in such a network strategy are manifold: as outlined above, a link set-up enables the partnering clearing houses to leverage their installed base, internalise GCM level network effects, strengthen their unique CCP level network effects and continue to offer services tailored to the specific demands of regional market particularities to an increased number of network participants. These advantages need to be recognised by industry decision-makers. However, unless the partnering clearing houses are truly prepared – and have the leeway in terms of their ownership and governance structure – to fulfil the necessary conditions, the strategy of increasing the efficiency of European clearing through links will fail.

Determining the most adequate ownership and governance structure of clearing houses to fulfil these necessary conditions requires dedicated research. Nonetheless, a number of findings support the assumption that fully fledged corporations, rather than profit-seeking CCPs beholden to their members, can meet the necessary conditions with greater ease. The reasons supporting this assumption are briefly summarised in the following:

- It was outlined in Chapter 7 that although globally active clearers with an agency focus benefit from efficiency gains under a link set-up, they simultaneously suffer from a negative impact on their business model. Clearing links were found to increase significantly the attractiveness of disintermediation, which inputs these clearers adversely. In this case, the only way for these clearers to circumvent the risk of disintermediation and the associated revenue losses is to somehow restrict access to the CCP level network. However, they can only accomplish this if clearing houses are user-owned and/or user-controlled; otherwise, there is no way for them to influence the rules of clearing to restrict the level of access to the CCP network. In the context of clearing link initiatives, restricting access to the CCP level network is obviously attractive for globally active clearers with an agency focus. However, regionally-to-globally active clearers are harmed by restricted access, because they lose their disintermediation benefits and cannot leverage their internal infrastructure. Restricting access to the CCP level network would thus serve to reinforce the current competitive advantage high volume clearers have over lower volume clearers. This suggests that clearing members' ability to influence the level of access to the CCP network should be minimised.
- User ownership and/or user control are likely to impede the fulfilment of the prerequisites identified as necessary for overcoming the link-inherent

of tackling the identified prerequisites, the respective clearing link(s) will exhibit significant unrealised potential for efficiency gains.

starting problem, because these measures essentially turn each of the part-nering European CCPs into direct competitors of the European high vol-ume clearers with an agency focus.[7] It is thus questionable whether a user-controlled clearing house would have the leeway to follow this route.[8] 'A single intermediary-owned/controlled CCP can and likely will establish policies and practices that promote the interest of large intermediaries with little or no regard for the best interests of smaller intermediaries or true end-users.'[9] Demutualisation and public ownership promote a strong gov-ernance framework that is better able to represent the full spectrum of clearing member types.

- It was previously explained that overcoming the link-inherent starting prob-lem requires clearing houses to create additional value that will outweigh the clearing members' costs of alternation. This means that clearing houses must be innovative and actively pursue growth opportunities. 'Intermediary-owned/controlled utilities are generally rewarded for cost minimisation rather than growth and value creation for shareholders. In consequence, in the long run they neither minimise costs nor create value.'[10] In contrast, the safety and efficiency record of demutualised, publicly owned clearing houses can be directly measured in terms of shareholder returns.[11]

- Additional drawbacks of user-owned/user-governed structures have been identified by the Direction Générale du Trésor et de la Politique Économique:[12] conflicts of interest can arise between users according to their activities and their customers (i.e. the pricing schedule may favour certain types of user). User-controlled structures also potentially offer lower incentives for innovation as they do not generally tend to maximise opera-tional efficiency. Finally, these structures may be more prone to systemic risk issues: when owners are primarily concerned about reducing the fee levels

---

[7] With regard to the issue of clearing house governance, the M&A and Single CCP case studies revealed that giving up partial control over a clearing house in the context of a merger as a trade-off for efficiency gains makes sense from the perspective of high volume clearers with an agency perspective, as long as the resulting structure is not a monopoly. It is only in the context of a monopoly CCP and clearing links that replicate the size of the Single CCP network that the risk of disintermediation is likely to exceed the potential benefits. This finding is coherent with the decision of the clearing members that were owners of LCH at the time of the merger with Clearnet to support the establishment of a governance structure in which they did not have full control over the clearing house.

[8] Also refer to European Central Bank (ed.) (2001b), p. 85, for examples of a potential conflict of interest when users of a CCP also control the governance of the clearing house. However, little research has so far been provided on the governance of CCPs. Hart *et al.* (2004) provide a comprehensive analysis on conflicts of interest typically arising in securities clearing and settlement infrastructures and consider actions that authorities can take to ensure that CCPs adopt adequate corporate governance mechanisms.

[9] Donohue (2006), p. 18.   [10] Donohue (2006), p. 23.   [11] Cf. Donohue (2006), pp. 19–20.

[12] Cf. Direction Générale du Trésor et de la Politique Économique (ed.) (2006), p. 6.

they have to pay, they may be apt to under-invest in the infrastructure's (operational) security requirements.[13]

While more research is needed on this issue, a number of arguments nonetheless suggest that if European clearing houses were to become fully fledged corporations, they could be expected to have greater motivation and incentives to implement measures to overcome the link-inherent starting problem.

10.1.2 Application of findings to cash equities clearing

A number of respondents underlined the need to avoid damaging the efficiency of existing national structures, and to ensure that the needs of smaller issuers and intermediaries and of less sophisticated investors [are] not forgotten.[14]

Before it can be determined which of this study's findings on derivatives clearing are applicable to cash equities clearing, it is first necessary to recall the different particularities and dynamics of derivatives versus cash equities markets (see section 2.2.3).

For one thing, due to the immediacy of the trade life cycle, the process of cash equities clearing is generally less complex. In addition, there is a greater level of product and process standardisation in European cash equities clearing;[15] proprietary systems play a more prominent role in derivatives clearing.[16] Furthermore, a greater number of smaller counterparties are active in cash equities markets, which comes with a greater home bias of the investors.[17] Finally, European cash equities markets have more clearing members with a regional focus relative to European derivatives markets.

This study revealed that regionally active clearers in particular suffer from efficiency losses when any network initiative other than clearing links is

---

[13] Also refer to Köppl/Monnet (2006), who show that profit-oriented CCPs (as opposed to user-oriented CCPs) can avoid certain hold-up problems and that this governance structure can be better for users of the clearing house by implementing the efficient trade-off between the volume of trade and overall default risk.

[14] European Commission (ed.) (2002a), p. 2.

[15] Whereas a greater level of product and process standardisation could ultimately translate into lower integration complexities and lower necessary investments were a single European CCP (rather than a European clearing link initiative) to be installed for cash equities clearing, additional complexities related to the issue of settlement location would be likely to arise. Therefore, the assumption that the implementation of a Single CCP requires greater investments from the involved CCPs and clearing members (as compared to a clearing link structure) is considered applicable to cash equities clearing.

[16] Cf. interviews.

[17] For details on investors' home bias, refer to Schiereck (1995); Schiereck (1996a); and Schiereck (1996b).

implemented.[18] Given the abundance of regionally active clearers in European cash equities markets, it thus seems more important than ever to avoid the implementation of a single European CCP. This network strategy would be especially detrimental to smaller regional players, niche markets and their specialised clearers in the cash equities arena.

This underscores the fact that particular attention must be given to the impact of harmonisation and integration initiatives on smaller regional or niche markets and on clearing members with less negotiating and lobbying power than Europe's high volume clearers. Fortifying smaller regional cash equities markets thus seems imperative and this study revealed that only clearing links can serve this purpose and increase the efficiency of clearing for all clearing member types.

10.1.3 Competitive dynamics in the European clearing industry

Current ownership structures and financial models are a potential obstacle to consolidation (David Hardy, CEO, LCH.Clearnet Group).[19]

It has been shown that in order to implement clearing links that truly serve to enhance the efficiency of European clearing, the involved clearing houses must succeed in overcoming the link-inherent starting problem. It is therefore necessary to gauge whether Europe's major clearing houses are sufficiently well-positioned, prepared and have the leeway in terms of their ownership and governance structure to reap the benefits of such a clearing link structure. ECAG and LCH.Clearnet, Europe's top two CCPs, face different challenges in this regard.

ECAG faces the challenge of having to balance the needs and interests of its two parent companies; one is a publicly quoted company and the other is owned by numerous Swiss banks. Additional challenges arise, because a European clearing link strategy would transform ECAG into a direct competitor to its high volume clearers with an agency focus.[20] Pursuing such a network strategy is therefore likely to upset some of the clearing house's major customers. Finally, ECAG's clearing strategy has thus far lacked a clear stand-alone value proposition; it has tended to go along with the exchanges' strategies.

---

[18] Cross-margining agreements result in a very low positive efficiency impact.

[19] LCH.Clearnet (ed.) (2006b), p. 14.

[20] Also see Scott (2003), p. 6, for a detailed discussion on the clearing houses' dilemma of balancing the interests of their most profitable customers, whose volume enables them to provide opportunities for netting, against the interest of the CCPs' owners, other customers and future customer base.

This suggests that even if ECAG is able to recognise the associated benefits of a European clearing link, the implementation as well as the fulfilment of the identified prerequisites will likely prove cumbersome and require great determination on the part of its parent companies and management. Nonetheless, with regard to their governance structure, European CCPs like ECAG, which are part of a quoted company structure, are generally in a good starting position. As outlined in section 10.1.1, these CCPs have greater motivation and incentives as well as more leeway to leverage their installed base, strengthen their unique CCP-related network effects, internalise GCM level network effects and enlarge the scope of complementary products and services provided by their CCP network. The biggest challenge for vertically integrated CCPs will likely be the establishment of a clearing house strategy with a clear stand-alone value proposition, and to give their clearing house managers enough freedom to implement a strategy that is not dictated by the exchanges' strategies.

In contrast, due to its governance and ownership structure, LCH.Clearnet is likely to have very limited leeway to engage in fulfilling the prerequisites for implementing successful European clearing links, i.e. to attempt adequately to overcome the link-inherent starting problem. **LCH.Clearnet** operates under the influence of a subset of its clearing members. Depending on what type of clearing member they are (i.e. low, medium or high volume), the members in this subset may have divergent interests. The study showed that whereas low and medium volume clearers should theoretically have an interest in the implementation of European clearing links regardless of whether or not they are able to control the rules of the interlinked clearing network, high volume clearers are unlikely to support this sort of network strategy. As outlined above, high volume clearing members will prefer a single European CCP or any other structure that ensures them the means to control the rules of clearing. Consequently, with regard to having enough leeway to implement measures to overcome the link-inherent starting problem, European CCPs that are part of a user-owned or user-controlled structure – like LCH.Clearnet – certainly find themselves in a very difficult starting position.

To summarise, this study found that whereas Europe's vertically integrated clearing houses have traditionally lacked a clear stand-alone value proposition and their managers will face hurdles in implementing such a strategy, these firms nonetheless have the greatest incentive to implement structures that ultimately serve to increase the efficiency for all European clearing members. The same is not true for CCPs operating under the ownership or control of a subset of their clearing members.

10.1.4 Reconcilability of findings with the Code of Conduct

This study's conclusions support the European Commission's decision to call upon the industry to establish a Code of Conduct (Code) and are in line with the measures detailed in the Code for cash equities clearing.

With or without a Code, European clearing houses operating as (part of) fully fledged corporations should have a natural interest in engaging in the establishment of European clearing links and fulfilling the identified prerequisites. However, not all of Europe's clearing houses are sufficiently well-positioned, prepared and flexible to reap the benefits of a clearing link structure. Considering the different incentives for Europe's major clearing houses to engage in increasing the efficiency of European clearing as well as their divergent starting positions, the Code seems like a good catalyst to spur talks between the European clearing houses on establishing clearing links. The positive effect of the Code is thus that it forces European CCPs to think about granting access to their network and engaging in interoperability with other CCPs.

European CCP managers should therefore regard the Code as an opportunity to reposition and realign their strategy to best cope with future challenges, and to best serve all of their customers. ECAG should thus use this opportunity to establish a clearing strategy that is not only driven by its exchange strategy, but has a stand-alone value proposition. For LCH.Clearnet, the Code offers an opportunity to balance the wants and needs of its major owners (and users), and reposition and realign its strategy to confront future challenges effectively and ultimately best serve all of its customers.

When considering the further implementation of the Code's measures regarding access and interoperability,[21] stakeholders in clearing should be aware that although the implementation of links was found to be the best way to truly enhance the efficiency of European clearing, the mere implementation of a quasi 'random' clearing link set-up between European CCPs will not automatically increase the efficiency of the clearing industry. It is vital to the success of a European clearing link initiative that its implementation be both economical for the partnering clearing houses and serve customer demand. Only then can demand- and supply-side scale economies fully blossom and the link-inherent starting problem be overcome. The European Commission should thus refrain from forcing any particular link on to the market. This leads to the next crucial question of which European clearing houses actually ought to be linked: who should link to whom?

---

[21] For details, refer to FESE/EACH/ECSDA (eds.) (2006), pp. 6–8.

10.1.5 Who should link to whom

> [Managers] first need to realize that different customers can use the same network in a variety of ways. Individuals may be using a network in every conceivable way, but if managers look at usage in the aggregate, they will see patterns emerge. And that's important because for each major usage pattern that managers identify in their network, they need to develop a different strategy.[22]

The results of this study revealed that to exhaust clearing links' full potential for efficiency gains, the partnering clearing houses must convince clearing members to expect positive future network effects. Although this means that the partnering CCPs must strive to replicate the size of a Single CCP network, it does not necessarily mean that all European CCPs must be interlinked right from the start. It is neither necessary nor economical to establish clearing links between virtually *all* European CCPs from the very start in order to increase the efficiency of European clearing successfully. Merely establishing random clearing links between Europe's clearing houses would not necessarily increase the efficiency of clearing. Rather, clearing members must trust that the scope of the clearing link set-up will gradually be extended over time to cover all major European markets.

For the purpose of this study, it was assumed that the Single CCP network connected Europe's five major derivatives CCPs (ECAG, LCH.Clearnet, OMX Clearing, MEFF and CC&G); it remains unclear, however, whether clearing links must in reality truly interconnect all of these clearing houses or whether links between a subset of these or other European CCPs could constitute the optimum network size.[23] The crucial question for European stakeholders in clearing is therefore: who should link to whom? Or, more precisely: which European clearing houses should establish clearing links between one another?

It is beyond the scope of this study to specify which European clearing houses ought to engage in the clearing link initiative or the type of link they ought to establish. This section instead provides a basic framework designed to serve as a starting point for European CCP managers to shape their European clearing link strategy. At this juncture, it must be emphasised that European clearing members cannot be assumed to value all potential clearing links equally; in other words, some clearing links are better suited than others to increase truly the efficiency of European clearing. To assess the economic value

---

[22] Coyne/Dye (1998), p. 101.
[23] The optimum network size in this case refers to what has been equated with the 'size of the single CCP network' throughout this study. This refers to the optimum network size from the viewpoint of medium and high volume clearers, i.e. a network size that serves to overcome the link-inherent starting problem.

of any particular clearing link and its respective potential to increase efficiency, CCPs must understand how their various customers value particular links. This will require European CCPs to analyse their customers' usage patterns in detail. The clearing link strategy for Europe should be formulated on the basis of these findings.

For the purpose of identifying the value of any particular clearing link between European CCPs, it is necessary to regard the European clearing industry (including all European clearing houses) as one large network. Today, information technology and mapping software can generally serve to identify how customers actually use networks as well as how they value each of a network's links.[24] For clearing house managers, the greatest problem actually lies in the current structure of the European clearing network.

Identifying usage patterns is challenging because this network is currently not interconnected by links between CCPs, but rather through high volume GCMs offering one-stop-shopping solutions. CCP managers can thus only partially rely on their proprietary data to track and identify individual usage patterns. There are consequently two ways for clearing houses to create a workaround to identify usage patterns of the European clearing network: (i) they must either find a way of cooperating to provide a consolidated data analysis; or (ii) every European CCP must engage in extensive market research, most importantly including in-depth talks with their current and potential clearing members.

The following basic framework, which could serve as a starting point for CCP managers in identifying their European clearing link strategy, builds on a concept established by Coyne/Dye (1998) for network-based businesses.[25]

Different types of clearer can use the European clearing network in a variety of different ways. At one extreme, clearers (mostly low volume) will use and value only one CCP (their home clearing house) within the European clearing network. At the other extreme, other clearers (mostly high volume) that travel throughout the network will value whatever CCP is most convenient for processing a particular transaction. Between these extremes, most European clearing members are likely to concentrate on a subset of all European CCPs. Individual clearers may be using the European clearing network in every conceivable way, but looking at aggregate usage will reveal patterns. According to Coyne/Dye (1998), three distinct usage patterns can generally emerge: zero concentration, zone concentration and lane concentration. For clearing house managers, it is important to identify and understand the major usage patterns

---

[24] Cf. Coyne/Dye (1998), p. 100.   [25] Cf. Coyne/Dye (1998), pp. 101–9.

of their CCP network, because '[e]ach of these three patterns requires a different strategy'.[26]

10.1.5.1 Zero concentration

The zero concentration pattern refers to a situation in which European clearers, in aggregate, use the European clearing network at random. This means that whereas a particular clearing member utilises only one (hypothetical) clearing link, other clearers make use of other links to roughly the same degree. Coyne/Dye (1998) explain that in some networks, even if customers do not actually use most of the links in the system, what they really value is the general connectivity to the entire network. The number of links plays an important role in zero concentration patterns: at first, adding one clearing link will only slightly enhance the value of the network, but when the number of links increases beyond a certain point, the clearing network will be highly valued and the link-inherent starting problem will be overcome.

10.1.5.2 Zone concentration

A different usage pattern emerges when large numbers of clearing members concentrate their usage in some portion(s) of the clearing network. When a CCP's clearing members show zero concentration patterns, it makes strategic sense for the managers of the clearing house to think of the network as separate zones of concentrated use. It is then logical to focus the establishment of links on these zones. Managers must be careful not to include links that are not valuable to most customers within a particular zone, but the number of clearing links has to again be sufficient to overcome the link-inherent starting problem. Managers of CCPs with zone and zero concentration patterns need to remember the importance of the perception of ubiquity (but to be perceived by its clearing members as being ubiquitous, a particular European CCP does not necessarily need to establish a link with all other European CCPs). The most important challenge is to know when to stop expanding the CCP network. When clearing members place a high value on general connectivity, the perception of ubiquity can matter more than the actual number of clearing links.

10.1.5.3 Lane concentration

In a lane concentration pattern, clearing members heavily use or heavily value individual clearing links. When a CCP's clearing members show lane

---

[26] Coyne/Dye (1998), p. 100.

concentration patterns, it makes strategic sense for managers to focus on these particular lanes. Lane concentration can be beneficial for clearing houses in that it allows CCPs to concentrate on the most profitable links, so that they do not need to subsidise less profitable links.

In reality, different clearing member types can show divergent concentration patterns. Recognising the underlying usage patterns that ought to dictate a CCP's clearing link strategy is a challenging task, requiring that clearing house managers closely monitor and truly understand their customers. Once they have made this effort, clearing house managers then need to develop a coherent strategy that combines the divergent needs of their various clearing members. Whereas some clearing links will mostly service existing clearing members, others are potentially suited to attract new ones.

For CCPs, the key to formulating a successful European clearing link strategy is in knowing and understanding the needs and wants of their current and potential clearing members. A European clearing link strategy must build on this knowledge to overcome the link-inherent starting problem and effectively increase the efficiency of European clearing.

The most significant challenge for all European clearing houses in this respect is that they have not traditionally been especially service- or customer-oriented. These aspects of the business have instead historically been taken on by the banks and brokers serving as clearing intermediaries. European clearing houses would therefore do well to rethink their relationship with the outside world.

10.1.6 Structural changes in the Value Provision Network

This study revealed that in order to increase the efficiency of European clearing, clearing links between European CCPs should be established according to the identified principles and in accordance with the necessary prerequisites. These links can potentially stimulate cost reductions for all clearing member types, opportunities for disintermediation, enhanced CCP level network effects and the internalisation of GCM level network effects; these benefits are all likely to spur structural changes in the European Value Provision Network (refer to section 2.5.1 for details on the current structure of the European VPN). The following therefore summarises the structural changes that can be expected to occur in the VPN if European clearing links are properly implemented.

One of the central features of a properly implemented European clearing link set-up is that it would empower clearing members with less negotiating and lobbying power than Europe's high volume clearers. Such an initiative could enable some of these members to self-clear markets instead of employing intermediary services. This could cause some of the European market share to shift from high volume clearers to medium and low volume clearers. The currently strong position of high volume clearers within the European VPN could thus be diluted if a clearing link set-up were to be implemented. However, high volume clearers would still benefit from dramatic reductions in both direct and indirect costs.

As outlined above, under a link set-up, medium volume clearers would benefit from the opportunity of disintermediation. The position of smaller low volume clearers with a regional focus and medium volume clearers would also be strengthened because they would be able to leverage their local market knowledge by providing tailor-made services for domestic markets. The market share within the European VPN would likely be further redistributed as the attractiveness of self-clearing increases for a greater number of current NCMs. Current NCMs might also be tempted to self-clear because the overall efficiency of the industry would be increased, CCPs could start to provide one-stop-shopping solutions and competition between European CCPs would further stimulate competitive fee levels. Particularly for hedge funds, which process large volumes and care about secrecy[27] – but have in the past relied on the services of the large investment banks (which serve as their prime brokers) – self-clearing could become very attractive. Under a link set-up, clearing houses would consequently face the issue of taking in a greater number of market participants as clearing members.

Structural changes in the European VPN could also result from the competitive dynamics between European CCPs and high volume GCMs. Chapter 6 explained that the value-added function and the network effects on the GCM level are significant in today's VPN, because most globally active clearers offer single access to many platforms and markets (one-stop-shopping), whereas the same is not true for European CCPs. The size effect, interface effect, fungibility effect, collateral management effect and complementary offering effect were thus found to be significantly greater on the GCM level than they are on the CCP level.

With an implementation of European clearing links, these dynamics would likely be altered. As clearing houses strengthen their unique CCP level network effects and internalise GCM level network effects, investors' willingness to pay for these clearing services can be expected to increase. Strengthening the unique CCP level network effects benefits the market as a whole, because the

---

[27] Refer to Maisch (2007) for more details on hedge funds' considerations regarding secrecy and self-clearing.

most significant positive spill-over effects to the trading and settlement layer result from CCP level network effects. Internalising the strong and important positive GCM level network effects by the CCP level network is beneficial for the market as a whole because it increases the efficiency of the clearing industry.

Competitive dynamics between European CCPs and high volume GCMs will particularly hinge on the complementary offering effect. It was outlined earlier in the study that internalising the full scope of GCMs' complementary service offerings is a complex and difficult endeavour for clearing houses, because it partially requires CCPs to engage in the provision of services that are far removed from their core competencies. This particularly concerns banking services. Although there are scenarios in which CCPs could theoretically internalise banking-related services in a cost-efficient manner by cooperating with financial service providers, it is generally assumed not to be economical for clearing houses to try to replicate the entire scope of complementary clearing services currently provided by high volume GCMs; many of these services are simply too distant from the CCPs' core competencies. Additionally, replicating the entire scope of the GCMs' complementary clearing services would not only have an impact on the regulatory status of a CCP (which would then likely be subject to banking supervision), but could also induce potential contagion effects of risk if infrastructure activities are not kept separate from banking services. Consequently, the final scope of complementary clearing services provided by CCP networks will ultimately depend on their individual cost-benefit analyses.

Given that the internalisation of the entire range of GCM level network effects is very difficult to realise, the value-added function of the GCM level will probably endure, despite the disintermediation tendencies spurred by clearing link initiatives. This is because for some counterparties, it will be more cost efficient to continue to receive a variety of different services from the banks/brokers acting as their clearing intermediary. Counterparties that greatly depend on banking-related services rely on a strong mutual (and perhaps symbiotic) relationship with their clearer or have other reasons for close cooperation with their clearing intermediary, and will probably continue to maintain these relationships (and thus be disinclined to disintermediate).

European CCPs and high volume GCMs will therefore face great challenges and opportunities if a European clearing link scenario is implemented. Most importantly, clearing houses and GCMs alike will be required to refocus and rethink their strategies. Both groups will need to acquire a better and more detailed understanding of their customers in order ultimately to develop and define their respective market niches. Once they have done so, they can continue to leverage their installed base and specific competitive advantage to provide unique value-added and tailor-made services to their customers. Implementing a customer-focused strategy will require innovation, creativity and determination. Ultimately, these dynamics might possibly even give rise to new forms of cooperation between CCPs, banks/brokers and other financial service providers, which will lead to further structural changes in the European Value Provision Network.

10.2 European clearing in a global context

We emphasise the need to recognise that Europe is part of the global economy. It attracts capital from the rest of the world and European investors also invest outside the EU. EU financial market integration efforts should not hinder or obstruct these activities.[28]

The rapid growth of cross-border trading, which spans many clearing systems and increases global interdependence, underscores the fact that the clearing industry is ultimately global in coverage.[29] Therefore, any network strategy employed to increase the efficiency of European clearing must also be evaluated in a global context.

The introduction of clearing links would not only increase the efficiency of the European clearing industry, but the strategy also appears unlikely to hinder or obstruct global transaction flow and processing for the following reasons:

- Clearing networks established through links (provided that these have been implemented properly) have a high growth potential. They make it attractive for other clearing houses to join the network.
- Joining this kind of clearing network enables the partnering clearing houses to leverage their installed base, strengthen their unique CCP level network effects, internalise GCM level network effects and continue to offer services tailored to the specific demands of regional market particularities to an increased number of network participants.
- Market participants and clearing houses alike would benefit from the competitive forces, enhanced flexibility and adaptability, innovation opportunities and high growth potential inherent to the link set-up.

---

[28] LIBA (ed.) (2004), p. 1.   [29] Also refer to Congress of the United States (ed.) (1990), p. 56.

The identified prerequisites for the successful implementation of clearing links also apply to any clearing house outside of Europe wishing to join the network. As in the case of Europe, clearing links' full potential for efficiency gains can only be exhausted if the partnering clearing houses adequately attempt to overcome the link-inherent starting problem and if clearing members are not forced to participate in the link.

Global clearing links could serve to generate a broad scale of additional opportunities for the involved CCP and their clearing members. Certainly, the considerations outlined in section 10.1.5 regarding who should link to whom also apply on a global scale. It is vital to the success of any clearing link that its implementation be both economical for the partnering clearing houses and serve customer demand. Prior to the implementation of any particular clearing link, it is thus crucial for clearing house managers to gain an understanding of the true wants and needs of all their current and potential clearing members.

To summarise, integrating the European clearing industry through a clearing link set-up appears to be suited to support global growth strategies.

10.3 Summary

This chapter served to identify the most preferable future clearing industry structure and delivered recommendations on the industry's future development. Additionally, the research results were applied to European exchange-traded cash equities clearing as well as to Europe with regard to its global positioning. The conclusions derived in this chapter are summarised in the following.

10.3.1 Future development of the European clearing industry

- Particular attention must be given to the impact of harmonisation and integration initiatives on smaller regional or niche markets and on clearing members with less negotiating and lobbying power than Europe's high volume clearers. Network strategies that favour some but penalise others are thus not regarded as viable solutions to further European market integration.
- Given these criteria, clearing links emerged as the sole network strategy that generates efficiency gains for all clearing members. Links are suited

to integrate the European derivatives and cash equities clearing industry, respectively.

- Although clearing links are the network strategy best suited to increase the efficiency of European clearing, the mere implementation of 'random' links between European CCPs will not automatically increase the efficiency of the clearing industry. Links require careful preparation and are not 'quick fixes'.
- Should the partnering clearing houses fail to overcome the link-inherent starting problem, a significant amount of potential for efficiency gains will go unrealised. In this instance, a link initiative would have a negligible impact on the efficiency of the European clearing industry.
- Unless the partnering clearing houses have – or are given – the leeway in terms of their ownership and governance structure to fulfil the necessary conditions, however, the strategy of increasing the efficiency of European clearing through links will fail.
- A number of arguments suggest that if European clearing houses were to operate as fully fledged corporations rather than profit-seeking CCPs beholden to their members, they could be expected to have greater motivation and incentives to implement measures to overcome the link-inherent starting problem.
- Consequently, whereas Europe's vertically integrated clearing houses have traditionally lacked a clear stand-alone value proposition and their managers will face hurdles in implementing such a strategy, these firms nonetheless have the greatest incentive to implement structures that will ultimately serve to increase the efficiency for all European clearing members. The same is not true for CCPs operating under the ownership or control of a subset of their clearing members.
- This study's conclusions support the European Commission's decision to call upon the industry to establish a Code of Conduct (the Code) and are in line with the measures detailed in the Code for cash equities clearing.
- It is vital to the success of a European clearing link initiative that its implementation be both economical for the partnering clearing houses and serve customer demand. The European Commission should thus refrain from forcing any particular link on to the market.
- Although the results of this study revealed that to exhaust clearing links' full potential for efficiency gains, the partnering clearing houses must strive to replicate the size of a Single CCP network, it does not necessarily mean that all European CCPs must be interlinked right from the start.

- It is neither necessary nor economical to establish clearing links between virtually *all* European CCPs from the very start in order to increase successfully the efficiency of European clearing. Rather, clearing members must trust that the scope of the clearing link set-up will gradually be extended over time to cover all major European markets.
- A basic framework was provided that can serve as a starting point for European CCP managers to determine which European clearing houses actually ought to be linked and to thus derive their European clearing link strategy:
  - (i) To assess the economic value of any particular clearing link and its respective potential to increase efficiency, CCPs must understand how their various customers value particular links. This will require European CCPs to analyse their customers' usage patterns in detail. The clearing link strategy for Europe should be formulated on the basis of these findings.
  - (ii) According to Coyne/Dye (1998), three distinct usage patterns can generally emerge: zero concentration, zone concentration and lane concentration. Each of these three patterns requires a different strategy.
  - (iii) For CCPs, the key to formulating a successful European clearing link strategy is in knowing and understanding the needs and wants of their current and potential clearing members. A European clearing link strategy must build on this knowledge to serve to overcome the link-inherent starting problem and effectively increase the efficiency of European clearing.
- Clearing links could spur structural changes in the European VPN by increasing the economic attractiveness for counterparties to self-clear (many) markets instead of employing intermediary services. This could cause the majority of the European market share to shift from high volume clearers to medium and low volume clearers. The currently strong position of high volume clearers within the European VPN could thus be diluted if a clearing link set-up were to be implemented. However, high volume clearers would still benefit from substantial cost reductions.
- Structural changes in the European VPN could also result from the competitive dynamics between European CCPs and high volume GCMs. European CCPs and high volume GCMs will face great challenges and opportunities in the event that such a European clearing link scenario is implemented. Most importantly, clearing houses and GCMs alike will be required to refocus and rethink their strategies. Both groups will need to acquire a better

and more detailed understanding of their customers in order ultimately to develop and define their respective market niche.

10.3.2 European clearing in a global context

- The introduction of clearing links would not only increase the efficiency of the European clearing industry, but the strategy also appears to be suited to support global transaction flow and processing as well as global growth strategies.

In a final step, Chapter 11 recapitulates the most important findings of this study, provides a critical discussion of the research results and concludes with suggestions for further areas of research.

11   Summary, discussion and recommendations for future research

This study examined both the efficiency and structure of the clearing industry. Clear-cut definitions together with a concise characterisation and descriptive analysis of the current state of the clearing industry set the stage for the following analytical objectives. Besides defining the efficiency of clearing and identifying ways to measure it, this study aimed to determine the efficiency impact of various integration and harmonisation initiatives within the clearing industry. The ultimate research objective was to identify the network strategy best suited to increase the efficiency of clearing, benefiting all clearing members. Based on these findings, the most preferable future clearing industry structure was identified and recommendations on the industry's future development were delivered. Although the focal point of the research was the European exchange-traded derivatives clearing industry, the results of the analysis were eventually applied to European exchange-traded cash equities clearing and to European clearing in a global context.

This final chapter summarises the study's most important findings (section 11.1). A critical discussion of the research results leads to recommendations for future research (section 11.2).

11.1 Summary of research results

This section summarises the study's most important findings, chapter by chapter.

11.1.1 Chapter 2 – Setting the stage – definitions and industry setting

Depending on the type of service provider, the process of clearing encompasses a number of services. Most clearing houses today act as a so-called central counterparty (CCP). Central counterparty clearing has become an integral part of clearing services and can even be said to constitute the core of modern financial market infrastructure. These clearing services not only benefit individual market participants, but markets as a whole, by increasing the efficiency of capital markets. While market participants benefit significantly from the CCP services and additional value-added clearing services provided by these clearing houses, there is another important category to consider: complementary clearing services. These services are not required to maintain the life cycle of a trade, but market participants benefit enormously from them. Nonetheless, today's CCPs rarely provide a full range of complementary clearing services. These clearing services are usually delivered by the banks/brokers acting as clearing members of various CCPs.

A starting point for the study was provided by identifying and characterising the tiered structure in which the provision of clearing services usually takes place: the so-called Value Provision Network (VPN). The VPN consists of two levels of access to the clearing house, direct and indirect. This study concerned the first level of direct access, and to this end, six different clearing member types were differentiated according to their focus of activity and average European cleared market share: regionally active (low volume) clearers with a prop. or an agency focus, regionally-to-globally active (medium volume) clearers with a prop. or an agency focus, and globally active (high volume) clearers with a prop. or an agency focus.

The study also had to consider the particularities of the current structure of the European VPN. First, while there are a number of CCPs, two of them dominate the European market: Eurex Clearing and LCH.Clearnet. Second, a relatively small number of European high volume clearers account for the bulk of the total annual European cleared market share (i.e. approximately seventeen clearing members account for over 70 per cent of the market share).

11.1.2 Chapter 3 – Defining the core issues – efficiency and network strategies

The two core research issues were industry efficiency and industry structure. The central criterion for determining the efficiency of clearing was operational efficiency, which is influenced by transaction costs. To increase the (operational) efficiency of clearing, it is necessary to minimise clearing members' transaction costs. The efficiency of the clearing industry is thus increased when the transaction costs that clearing members have to bear are reduced (and vice versa).

The total transaction costs of clearing are composed of direct and indirect costs, and can be impacted by integration and harmonisation initiatives between clearing houses, referred to as network strategies. For the purpose of this study, four different types of network strategy were distinguished: cross-margining agreements, clearing links, mergers and acquisitions (M&A), and the creation of a Single CCP (within a defined asset class and economic area).

11.1.3 Chapter 4 – Collecting empirical insights – introduction to the empirical study

Due to a lack of existing research on the issues of efficiency of clearing and industry structure, which could have served as a basis for this study, the author conducted a comprehensive original empirical study. This empirical study consisted of seventy-nine one-to-one interviews with different stakeholders in clearing and the distribution of a questionnaire. Although the attempts to collect quantitative data ultimately proved unsuccessful, the interviews provided extensive qualitative data that was used as the basis for the analyses of Chapters 5 and 8.

11.1.4 Chapter 5 – Analysing costs of derivatives clearing – transaction cost studies

To determine the efficiency impact of the different network strategies within the clearing industry, it was first necessary to research the transaction costs of European derivatives clearing. With regard to the relevance of clearing costs to different clearing member types, the analysis revealed the following. For low and medium volume clearers with a prop. or an agency focus, as well as for high volume clearers with an agency focus, indirect costs are the core cost drivers. For high volume clearers with a prop. focus, however, direct costs constitute the core cost drivers.

The cost analysis also brought to light reasons for the structural particularities of the European VPN and for the competitive advantage that high volume clearers have over medium and low volume clearers. First, the analysis revealed the existence of economies of scale that allow high volume clearers to leverage their fixed cost base. Due to their scale of business, high volume clearers further benefit from a strong negotiating position. Additionally, clearing houses tend to grant high volume clearers preferential treatment in the form of discounts. These factors explain the dominant position of high volume clearers in the European VPN, i.e. why a very high percentage of the average annual European cleared market share in derivatives is concentrated on a few high volume clearers. These clearers' cost structures allow them to offer intermediary services, and for low and medium volume clearers, it makes economic sense to utilise these services.

According to the analyses, network strategies that encourage low and medium volume clearers to self-clear their own markets instead of employing intermediary services could have a significant impact on the structure of the European VPN. Self-clearing enables these market participants to reduce intermediary costs and leverage their internal infrastructure. The research also revealed that NCMs are becoming increasingly aware of clearing costs; many of them view obtaining clearing membership as a viable cost-cutting strategy.

The cost analysis also provided the critical step of generating a quantitative estimate of the total European costs of derivatives clearing borne by clearing members, which amounted to roughly €2.173 billion in 2005. At €725 million, direct costs represented 33 per cent of total industry costs, whereas indirect costs of roughly €1.448 billion accounted for 67 per cent of total costs.[1] A benchmarking of the European costs of derivatives clearing to other market infrastructure costs suggested that European derivatives clearing constitutes the most efficient part of the European financial market infrastructure.

11.1.5 Chapter 6 – Exploring theoretical basics – scale effects in clearing

Network strategies can give rise to demand- and supply-side scale effects, which can in turn influence the costs of clearing. To establish a basis for analysing the efficiency impact of different network strategies, both demand- and supply-side scale effects in clearing were first classified and explored.

The network structure of the VPN was found to consist of two layers (product layer and system layer) and two levels (CCP level and GCM level) and to exhibit a number of positive and negative network effects. Although many of the network effects on the CCP and GCM level are similar, the CCP level gives rise to unique positive network effects that are difficult for GCMs to replicate. Furthermore, by engaging in network strategies and enlarging their range of complementary clearing services, CCPs can internalise network effects that occur on the GCM level. Internalising the strong and important GCM level network effects by the CCP level network is beneficial due to the associated potential for reducing clearing-related transaction costs, thus increasing the industry's efficiency.

Evidence further suggested that economies of scale and scope are likely to exist in clearing, but whether or not increases in either one translate into positive economies for CCPs is highly dependent on the type of network

---

[1] Due to the shortcomings and limitations inherent to the calculation of the estimate, however, it can be assumed that the true indirect cost figure is higher than suggested.

strategy pursued and the characteristics and cost structure of the partnering clearing houses.

11.1.6 Chapter 7 – What theory reveals – framework for efficiency analysis of network strategies

The ultimate research objective of this study was to determine the efficiency impact of various network strategies within the European clearing industry. To this end, an original framework was established that built on the insight of the previous chapters. The analysis based on this framework provided the following preliminary conclusions. Besides cross-margining agreements, which generally have little or no potential to increase efficiency, clearing links are the only network strategy that results in efficiency gains for all clearing member types. Whereas the efficiency impact of cross-margining agreements is neutral or minimal for all clearing members, regionally active clearers potentially suffer from efficiency losses as a result of M&A and Single CCP initiatives. The analysis further showed that although some network strategies are cost efficient, they are not necessarily profit-maximising for all clearing member types. Single CCP and clearing link initiatives, for example, can exert a negative impact on the business model of globally active clearers with an agency focus. The only way for these clearers to circumvent this negative impact is to succeed in restricting access to the CCP level network. However, restricting access to the CCP level network has a detrimental impact on other clearing member types. It would serve to reinforce the current structural particularities of the European VPN, by strengthening the competitive advantage high volume clearers have over lower volume clearers; globally active clearers would thus continue to dominate within the European clearing industry.

Clearing houses could profit immensely from the implementation of a clearing link initiative. A link set-up would enable them to internalise GCM level network effects, strengthen their unique CCP level network effects, leverage their installed base and continue to offer services tailored to the specific demands of regional markets and different regulatory environments to an increased number of network participants.

Nonetheless, the benefits of a European clearing link set-up can only be achieved if the clearing houses endeavour to overcome the link-inherent starting problem. Links offer various opportunities for different clearing member types. The starting problem becomes relevant for these clearers in different ways, but it essentially concerns the question of whether the utility derived from making use of the link set-up will outweigh the individual clearer's costs of alternation in the long run.

11.1.7 Chapter 8 – Checking theory against reality – case studies of network strategies

The purpose of Chapter 8 was to check the preliminary conclusions of Chapter 7 with case study findings and insights from the empirical study. For this purpose, three case studies were performed to analyse clearing links, mergers and acquisitions, and a Single CCP initiative. The results of the studies supported the preliminary findings and provided a more detailed insight into the complexities of implementing these network strategies in Europe.

The network strategy best suited to enhance the efficiency of European derivatives clearing is a clearing link set-up, because it is the only model that enables all clearing member types to benefit from efficiency gains. However, certain caveats apply: should the partnering clearing houses not adequately attempt to overcome the link-inherent starting problem, a significant amount of potential for efficiency gains will go unrealised. Such a link initiative is then not designed to increase significantly the efficiency of the European clearing industry. The link-inherent starting problem can only be successfully surmounted if the partnering CCPs:

- are able to convince clearing members to expect positive future network effects (clearers must trust the clearing houses that the scope of the clearing link set-up will gradually be extended over time to cover all relevant major European markets);
- make up for the lost intermediary services formerly furnished by GCM(s) by providing (most of) these services themselves, thereby successfully internalising GCM level network effects;
- compensate for the lost participation in other CCP networks by providing a similar service level and processing all products and markets of the linked clearing houses; thus providing for a full choice of clearing location; and
- engage to educate market participants, other clearing houses and stakeholders sufficiently about the benefits of such a link set-up.

The failure of relevant clearing houses and clearing members to recognise the potential value proposition of a clearing link set-up, low internal prioritisation of implementing the link, mandatory open interest transfers, regulatory and political issues can create further uncertainty about the future development of a clearing link initiative and can thus potentially aggravate the starting problem.

Meanwhile, the mergers and acquisition study revealed that the complexities of successfully implementing M&A initiatives between European clearing houses are even greater in reality than previously assumed theoretically.

The Single CCP case study supported the preliminary findings regarding the inherent complexities of combining European clearing houses and underscored the unequal distribution of costs and benefits (on the part of Europe's clearing members) inherent to this network strategy. The study also revealed that high volume clearers with an agency focus are likely to prefer a Single CCP to clearing links, because it tends to be easier to control the rules of clearing when a Single CCP network is in place. However, the Single CCP loses its appeal for high volume clearers with an agency focus if they find themselves unable to exert such control; they will then presumably not succeed in circumventing disintermediation and the associated revenue losses. The analysis also supported the finding that globally active clearers with a prop. focus stand to benefit most from the implementation of a Single CCP in terms of efficiency gains. Nonetheless, this group of clearers will only support a Single CCP if it can secure the means to control the rules of clearing, i.e. make sure that clearing fees are sufficiently reduced and that the consolidated CCP infrastructure does not abuse its dominant position.

11.1.8 Chapter 9 – Quantifying the efficiency impact – European network strategies

The findings derived in Chapters 7 and 8 served as the basis for a quantification of the efficiency impact of a European clearing link set-up and a single European CCP. The results showed that under the assumption of implemented European clearing links:

- Total European costs of derivatives clearing would have been reduced by 31 per cent to roughly €1.503 billion in 2005.
- Direct costs would have come to about €523 million; thus reduced by roughly 28 per cent.
- Indirect costs would have weighed in at €980 million, representing a 32 per cent decrease.

Under the assumption of an implemented single European CCP, on the other hand:

- Total European costs of derivatives clearing would have amounted to roughly €1.958 billion in 2005 (which equals a reduction of roughly 10 per cent).

- Direct costs would have come to approximately €629 million, representing a 13 per cent reduction.
- Indirect costs could have been reduced by roughly 8 per cent, for a total of €1.329 billion.

The conclusion that the industry-wide cost reduction potential of a clearing link initiative is approximately three times greater than that of a Single CCP is rooted in the findings of Chapters 7 and 8, which showed that low volume clearers suffer from efficiency decreases when a Single CCP is implemented, but can benefit from efficiency gains through clearing links. Medium and high volume clearers, on the other hand, benefit from a Single CCP, but efficiency gains are not as great as those produced by a European clearing link set-up. A clearing link scenario was further found to reduce the unit costs of high, medium and low volume clearers by roughly 20, 46 and 24 per cent, respectively. A Single CCP, on the other hand, was found to reduce the unit costs of high and medium volume clearers by about 12 and 35 per cent, respectively, but to actually increase the unit costs of low volume clearers by approximately 25 per cent. For some low volume clearers, the Single CCP scenario can thus diminish the economic appeal of self-clearing.

11.1.9 Chapter 10 – Introducing the future network economy – development of the clearing industry

The findings of this study led to conclusions on the future clearing industry structure and delivered recommendations on the industry's development.

Clearing links emerged as the sole network strategy that succeeds in generating efficiency gains for all clearing members and is thus best suited to integrate the European clearing industry. This finding is applicable to European derivatives and cash equities clearing alike. Furthermore, the creation of clearing links has the potential to support European clearing with regard to its global context and growth.

Successfully implemented European clearing links can be expected to lead to positive structural changes in the European VPN, such as the empowerment of customers. The majority market share is likely to shift from high volume clearers to medium and low volume clearers. The VPN could also be invigorated by the competitive dynamics between the clearing houses and high volume GCMs.

Nonetheless, the mere implementation of 'random' links between virtually all European CCPs would not automatically increase the efficiency of the clearing industry. If the partnering clearing houses do not adequately attempt to overcome the link-inherent starting problem or if clearing members are forced to participate in the link, a significant amount of potential efficiency gains will go unrealised. Such a link initiative is then not designed to have a noteworthy positive impact on the efficiency of the European clearing industry.

Europe's major clearing houses were found to have different starting positions and varying degrees of leeway – in terms of their ownership and governance structure – to reap the benefits of a clearing link initiative. A number of arguments suggested that if European clearing houses were to operate as (part of) fully fledged corporations, rather than profit-seeking CCPs beholden to their members, they could be expected to have greater motivation and incentives to implement measures to overcome the link-inherent starting problem.

This study's conclusions support the European Commission's decision to call upon the industry to establish a Code of Conduct and are in line with the measures detailed in the Code for cash equities clearing. Furthermore, it was found to be vital to the success of a European clearing link initiative that its implementation be both economical for the partnering clearing houses and serve customer demand. The European Commission should thus refrain from forcing any particular link on to the market. For CCPs, the key to formulating a successful European clearing link strategy is in knowing and understanding the needs and wants of their current and potential clearing members. Implementing European clearing links without careful planning and a dedicated strategy for tackling the starting problem will waste time and resources and do very little to enhance the efficiency of the European clearing industry.

11.2 Discussion and recommendations for future research

In a final step, this study closes by providing a critical discussion of the research results, which leads to recommendations for areas of future research. This study went beyond a simple emulation of analyses designed for other industries and developed new insights into the specific features of clearing and the particularities of the clearing industry. Due to the current dearth of research on clearing, it was not possible to address succinctly and accurately all relevant issues. Many areas for future studies thus exist in this field. The following suggestions are predicated upon the research conducted in this study:

- This research focused on the transaction costs that clearing members have to bear (first level transaction costs). Although the study touched upon second level transaction costs, additional research analysing the costs of clearing faced by NCMs and other customers should be conducted. This research should address whether cost reductions on the clearing member level are truly passed on to NCMs and other customers.

- The extensive qualitative data obtained from the interviews served as vital input and formed the basis for the cost analyses and case studies. Nonetheless, more research based on quantitative data is needed on the different cost categories and total costs of clearing. This should particularly strive to address the shortcomings and limitations inherent to the calculation of the indirect cost estimates presented in this study.

- The analyses conducted throughout this study concerned the costs of derivatives clearing, but these costs are merely a subset of the transaction costs that an investor faces when carrying out a trade. Future research is required to provide an integrated analysis of the complete range of costs faced by investors.

- While this research served to identify and characterise different network effects in clearing, further research on the magnitude of these positive and negative effects could shed light on their significance and characteristics. Theoretical studies would be useful in this context.

- It was also observed that CCP and GCM level network effects can have spillover effects on to the trading and settlement layers. Future studies could be devoted to a more detailed investigation of these effects.

- Another important interrelation concerns the CCP and the GCM network levels and the associated positive and negative network effects. While this study centred on the issue of internalising GCM level network effects by the CCP level network, other dynamics were left aside. To analyse the interrelation of the network effects on both levels, it would be revealing to adopt the network economic two-sided markets' view.

- It was found that every established CCP network has built an installed base that influences the dynamics of competition and cooperation between clearing houses. GCM networks also benefit from their installed base. Clearing houses and GCMs alike should strive to leverage their installed base. An in-depth analysis of the dynamics of CCP versus GCM level network effects in the context of European clearing links will regard more details of the future structure of the European VPN.

- More network economic research is also needed with regard to standard setting in the clearing industry.

- The analysis suggested an inverse relationship between average costs and the number of contracts cleared, but empirical research is needed to examine and substantiate the existence of economies of scale in clearing, including an estimate of a translog cost function.

- More empirical research is also needed to underscore the existence of economies of scope in clearing.
- This study identified the complexities of combining European clearing houses due to their disparate historical backgrounds, profiles and legal environments. The ongoing harmonisation and integration of European clearing processes and alignment of legal and regulatory environments will have an impact on the potential to realise economies of scale and scope through network initiatives. Future research is required to evaluate this impact.
- If at any point in the future, European rules and regulations are harmonised, and processes are standardised, a reviewed analysis of the dynamics of the clearing industry should take place to reassess the issues of network effects as well as economies of scale and scope.
- It was concluded that qualitative evidence suggests that European derivatives clearing does not constitute a natural monopoly. However, more empirical research is needed to examine this aspect.
- Clearing links were identified as the network strategy best suited to increase the efficiency of European clearing. A basic framework was provided that could serve as a preliminary guide for European CCP managers to identify the most appropriate clearing link strategy. Additional research is nonetheless required to determine which European CCPs should ultimately establish clearing links.
- Additional econometric analyses measuring the efficiency of clearing and the efficiency impact of network strategies would be useful to complement the insights and conclusions derived in this study.
- This study showed that the final success of a European clearing link set-up depends on the extent to which the partnering CCPs comply with certain prerequisites. However, the ultimate success of a European clearing link set-up will also depend on the resolution of the political, legal and technical issues surrounding the requirements for interoperability. More research addressing these details is therefore required.
- The case study analysis suggested that mandatory open interest transfers can potentially aggravate the link-inherent starting problem. More research is needed on the issue of who actually owns the open interest that CCPs hold on behalf of their clearing members. Such research should also provide a more detailed analysis of the economic impact of mandatory open interest transfers.

- This study found that European clearing houses should be interested in pursuing clearing link initiatives because they can then leverage their installed base, internalise GCM level network effects, strengthen their unique CCP level network effects and continue to offer services tailored to the specific demands of regional market particularities to an increased number of network participants. Nonetheless, the motivation and driving factors encouraging or impeding CCPs to engage in particular network strategies should be studied in greater detail. Such a study should also take into account an analysis of the potential revenue impact of different network strategies on the partnering clearing houses.
- A number of findings supported the assumption that becoming fully fledged corporations, rather than profit-seeking CCPs beholden to their members, would be most suitable, creating incentives for clearing houses to engage in European clearing links. However, more detailed research is needed in the area of clearing houses' governance, taking into account the micro- and macroeconomic role of CCPs as well as the private and public stakeholders' interests.
- This study concluded that Europe's vertically integrated clearing houses, which are part of a quoted company structure, ought to have great incentives to implement structures that ultimately serve to increase the efficiency for all European clearing members. The same was not found to be true for CCPs operating under the ownership or control of a subset of their clearing members. Nonetheless, it remains questionable whether the managers of vertically integrated clearing houses will in reality succeed in implementing a clearing strategy that has a clear stand-alone value proposition; up until now, they have had very limited room for manoeuvre and have largely gone along with the exchange's strategy. More research on the issue of vertically versus horizontally integrated clearing would be useful in this context.
- The focus of this research was on analysing integration and harmonisation initiatives in the clearing industry. It was briefly outlined that the dynamics in the clearing industry are closely linked with dynamics in the trading arena. More research is needed on these interrelationships.
- The application of the findings of this study to cash equities clearing did not take into account the efficiency impact resulting from network strategies on the ICSD/CSD level. Particularly for cash equities clearing, it seems necessary to consider the dynamics between network strategies on the CCP and the ICSD/CSD levels. Further research is thus required to analyse the competitive forces and dynamics that are at play in this respect.

- The results of this research concerned derivatives clearing and were subsequently applied to cash equities clearing. Whether or not it is economically sound to strive towards clearing cash equities and derivatives through the same clearing system and clearing links requires further analysis.
- Broadening the scope of complementary clearing services offered by the partnering CCPs was identified as one of the critical issues with regard to successfully implementing clearing links and overcoming the starting problem. While it was suggested that scenarios exist in which it could make economic sense for CCPs to offer banking-related services, further research is necessary to identify the opportunities and risks inherent to such endeavours. The focus should be on analysing the potential contagion effects of risk that could arise if infrastructure activities are not kept separate from banking services.
- Risk management is a central aspect of derivatives clearing. It was outlined in this study that network strategies can potentially increase systemic risk and that it is therefore crucial that a network initiative encourage (or at least not impede) cautious risk management practices. It must also be ensured that competition does not take place with regard to margin levels. Nonetheless, this study did not explicitly integrate and analyse risk management issues. Further research should thus be conducted on this topic.
- This study concluded with a brief outlook on European clearing in a global context. This outlook should be complemented by additional studies on the structure of the VPN in other regions in order to evaluate and identify whether dynamics similar to those revealed for Europe exist on a global scale.
- The research of this study focused on analysing current transaction costs and the efficiency impact of known network strategies. Future studies could take a more innovative view by identifying new forms of technology-enabled cooperation between clearing houses that might have an even greater efficiency impact than clearing links. Strongly linked to this issue is the question of innovation in clearing: what is the future role of clearing houses? Will initiatives emerge that successfully compete with CCPs, particularly in the OTC market? Who are the potential competitors of clearing houses? What impact will this have on the structure of the VPN and the efficiency of clearing?

Appendices

Matrix overview of clearing-related transaction costs (part I)

	DIRECT COSTS		INDIRECT COSTS			
	Clearing House Charges	Service Provider Charges	Cost of Capital	Risk Management Costs	IT Costs	Back-Office Costs
Costs of initiating contracts	• One-off admission fee • Fixed annual/monthly fee • Communication charges • Minimum transaction charges • Membership fees	• Initial one-off payments • Fixed fees • Communication charges	• Contribution to default fund • Funding effort for minimum capital requirements • Funding effort for regulatory capital requirements	• Adaptation of risk management structures and architecture	• Integration of new interface • Integration of software and hardware	• Initial costs, i.e. employment of dedicated back-office personnel, set-up of specific account structures, etc. • Replication of processes and structures of a CCP
Cost of completing contracts	• Per-contract fees • Fees for additional services	• Per-contract fees • Fees for additional services	• Collateral/cash deposited at clearing house for initial margin	• Continuous risk management processes	• Continuous management of IT	• Position management • Continuous management of back-office processes
Cost of executing contracts	• Option exercise fees • Future settlement fees • Fees for additional services	• Option exercise fees • Future settlement fees • Fees for additional services	• Amount of liquidity at customer tied to ensure funding of intra-day margin calls	• Continuous risk management processes	• Continuous management of IT	• Position management • Option exercises • Continuous management of back-office processes
Cost of controlling contracts	• Event-driven charges • Fees for additional services	• Event-driven charges • Fees for additional services	• Collateral/cash deposited at clearing house for variation margin • Amount of liquidity at customer tied to ensure funding of intra-day margin calls	• Continuous risk management processes	• Continuous management of IT	• Continuous management of back-office processes • Error account • Replication of processes and structures of a CCP
Cost of adapting contracts	• Fees charged for additional services • Penalties • Charges for service level upgrades	• Upgrade of bandwidth or other non gratuitous changes to infrastructure, service levels or fee structure	• (Intra-day) margin calls	• Changes to risk management systems, i.e. changes in margin calculation method	• Management of adaptations, e.g. connection to a new platform, new release management, testing, etc.	• Costs related to adaptations affecting back-office structures and knowledge through extension of services or integration of new platforms

Source: Author's own.

Matrix overview of clearing-related transaction costs (part II)

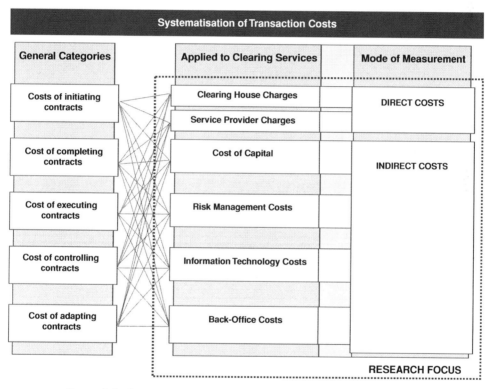

Source: Author's own.

Appendix 3

List of interviewees

Disclaimer

The views expressed by research participants in interviews are their own and do not necessarily represent the official stance of their organisation. The interviewees are not associated with the final conclusions of this study. The findings of this study thus do not necessarily reflect the views of the individuals interviewed in the context of this study. Any proposition that is forwarded is arrived at through a rigorous, independent academic methodology.

Organisation*	Name of Interviewee(s) and Position at Time of Interview	Type of Interview	Interviewee Location
ABN AMRO	Simons, Philip: Head of Exchange-Traded Derivatives Clearing Operations and Sales (ABN AMRO), former Head of European Brokerage/Global Execution/E-Business (Cargill)	In person	London
Arnold & Porter	Born, Brooksley: Retired Partner (Arnold & Porter), former Chairperson (CFTC)	In person	US
Bank of New York (BoNY)	Bodart Paul: Executive Vice President (BoNY), Board Member (Euroclear)	By telephone	Continental Europe
Bear Stearns	Sapato, Bernard: Managing Director	In person	US
BNP Paribas	Lloyd, Jonathan: Head of Clearing, Settlement and Custody	By telephone	Continental Europe
Bourse Consult	Cox, Peter: Partner (Bourse Consult), former CEO (OM London Exchange (OMLX)), former Director (LSE)	In person	London
Caxton Associates	Ostlund, Tomas: Principal	By telephone	US
Chicago Board of Trade (CBOT)	Dan, Bernard W.: President and CEO	In person	US

Organisation*	Name of Interviewee(s) and Position at Time of Interview	Type of Interview	Interviewee Location
Chicago Mercantile Exchange (CME)	Davidson III, John P.: Managing Director and Chief Corporate Development Officer (CME), former Member Board of Directors (OCC), former Managing Director and Co-Head Global Equity Operation (Morgan Stanley & Co.)	In person	US
Citigroup	Kirchmann, Alfred: Vice President Corporate and Investment Banking, Global Transaction Services	In person	Continental Europe
The Clearing Corporation (CCorp)	Jaycobs, Richard: CEO (CCorp), former CEO onExchange, founder (Acknowledge Systems), former Director (Computer Trading Corporation), former Chief Technology Officer (Tudor Investment Corporation)	In person	US
Commerzbank	Gründer, Gabriele: Manager Operations	In person	Continental Europe
Commodity Futures Trading Commission (CFTC)	Lawton, John C.: Deputy Director and Chief Counsel, Division of Clearing and Intermediary Oversight; and Markman, Natalie A.: Senior Special Counsel to the Director, Division of Clearing and Intermediary Oversight; and Radhakrishnan, Ananda K.: Director, Division of Clearing and Intermediary Oversight	In person	US
The Depository Trust & Clearing Corporation (DTCC)	Callahan, Mary Ann: Managing Director International; Henderson, Neil: Managing Director; and Till, Bernard M.: Vice President	In person; except Bernie Till via telephone	US
Deutsche Börse Group	Riess, Rainer: Managing Director, Head of Stock Market Business Development; Röthig, Jürgen: Managing Director, Head of Trading/Clearing/Information Operations; and Heckinger, Richard: Head of US Representative Office (Deutsche Börse), former COO (Stock	In person In person In person	Continental Europe Continental Europe US

(*cont.*)

Organisation*	Name of Interviewee(s) and Position at Time of Interview	Type of Interview	Interviewee Location
	Exchange of Hong Kong), former Chief Executive (Hong Kong Securities Clearing Corp.)		
Dresdner Bank	Vetter, Joachim: Head of Operations	In person	Continental Europe
Dresdner Kleinwort (DrK)	Yarrow, Alan: Vice Chairman (DrK), Chairman (DrK Ltd, DrK Sec. Ltd, DrK Asia), Chairman (London Investment Banking Association), Vice President (British Bankers' Association), Member (UK Take-Over Panel), Board Member (Securities Institute), Member (FSA Practitioners Panel), Chairman (Complinet)	In person	London
Dwpbank (Deutsche Wertpapier Service Bank AG)	Scheer, Sascha: Head of Derivative Services (ETD & OTC)	In person	Continental Europe
DZ BANK AG	Schnee, Claus: Manager Operations and Services, Operations Derivatives Exchanges	In person	Continental Europe
Eurex	Arbuckle, Manuela: Director, Eurex Business Development, formerly Operations Manager (Deutsche Bank)	In person	London
Eurex	Chiesa, Orlando: Head of Clearing Strategy (Eurex), former Secretary General (European Association of Central Counterparty Clearing Houses (EACH)), Member (Giovannini Group on Clearing)	In person	Continental Europe
Eurex	Gisler, Daniel: Member (Executive Board Eurex Clearing), Supervisory Board Member (EEX European Energy Exchange), Executive Director (SWX Group), former Chairman (EACH), Member (CCP12 and the CESAME Group)	In person	Continental Europe
Eurex US	McErlean, Michael G.: Board Member (Eurex US), Director of Sales and Marketing (Eurex US), former Global	In person	US

Organisation*	Name of Interviewee(s) and Position at Time of Interview	Type of Interview	Interviewee Location
	Co-Head of Futures Services (Goldman Sachs)		
Euronext.liffe	Bruce, Philip: Senior Strategy Advisor (Euronext.liffe), former Head of Corporate Strategy (London Stock Exchange), former Managing Director of Strategy and Development (London Clearing House)	In person	London
The Evolution Group	Fong, Yew-Meng: Company Secretary, former Managing Director (Deutsche Bank), former Director (FOA), former Executive Director (Goldman Sachs)	In person	London
Federal Reserve Bank (FED) Washington	Parkinson, Patrick M.: Associate Director Division of Research and Statistics	In person	US
Federal Reserve Bank of Chicago	McPartland, John: Financial Markets Advisor to the Federal Reserve Bank of Chicago, International Clearing and Settlement Consultant, former President and CEO (CME Depository Trust Co.), former Deputy Manager (CME Clearing House), former CME Member, current Member (CFTC Technology Advisory Committee)	In person	US
FIMAT	Cirier, Patrick: COO Europe, European Chapter Deputy Chairman (FIA)	In person	London
FIMAT	DeWaal, Gary Alan: FIMAT Group's Global General Counsel and Director of Legal and Compliance, Senior Executive Vice President and General Counsel (FIMAT USA, LLC), Group Chief Ethics Officer and Member of the Global Executive Committee of the FIMAT Group, Professor of Law at Brooklyn Law School, Member (and past President) (Law and Compliance Executive Committee of the FIA), Member (New York Mercantile Exchange's Business Conduct Committee)	In person	US

(*cont.*)

Organisation*	Name of Interviewee(s) and Position at Time of Interview	Type of Interview	Interviewee Location
Financial Services Authority (FSA)	Foster, Andrew: Manager Clearing and Settlement Markets Division	In person	London
FMI Consulting	Yuill, John: Director	In person	London
Fortis	Peters, Martin: Head of Operations, Client Support Frankfurt	In person	Continental Europe
Fortis Clearing Chicago (O'Connor & Company)	Floersch, William C.: CEO (Fortis Clearing Chicago), President and CEO (O'Connor & Company), Vice Chairman (OCC), former Chairman (The Clearing Corporation), former Vice Chairman (Board of Directors) and Chairman (Executive Committee, CBOE)	In person	US
The Futures and Options Association (FOA)	Jenkins, Hugo: Managing Director	In person	London
Futures Industry Association (FIA)	Damgard, John: President; and Wierzynski, Barbara: General Counsel and Executive Vice President	In person	US
Gartmore	O'Reilly, Aisling: Head of Derivatives	In person	London
The George Washington University	Phillips, Susan M.: Dean and Professor of Finance, Public Representative (NFA), former Chairperson (CFTC)	In person	US
Getco LLC	Spanbroek, Mark: Partner	In person	London
Global Strategies Ltd	Wilkinson, Alex: Managing Director	In person	London
GlobeOp	Condon, Edward F.: Director, former Managing Director (Credit Suisse)	In person	London
Goldenberg, Hehmeyer & Co. (GHCO)	Hehmeyer, Christopher K.: Co-Chairman and Founding Partner (GHCO), Director (NFA), former Director (CBOT)	In person	US
Goldman Sachs	Dawley, Michael C.: Managing Director and Futures Product Leader (Goldman Sachs), Chairman (The Clearing Corporation), Member (and past Chairman) (Board of Directors and Executive Committee, FIA),	In person	US

Organisation*	Name of Interviewee(s) and Position at Time of Interview	Type of Interview	Interviewee Location
	Member (CME's Clearing House Risk Committee), Member (CFTC's Global Markets Advisory Committee), Voting Delegate (SFOA), Advisory Board Member (Kent State University's Masters of Financial Engineering Program), Member (CME and CBOT), former Vice Chairman (BrokerTec Futures Exchange)		
HDM Consulting	Mlynarski, Hank: Director (HDM Consulting), former Head of Corporate Development (Eurex US), former President (BrokerTec Futures), former Senior Vice President (Instinet Corp.), former CEO (Chicago Board Brokerage), former Senior Vice President Strategic Planning (CBOT)	In person	US
HSBC	Glover, Linda J.: Manager Global Clearing Services; and Worlledge, James P.: Manager Global Clearing Services	In person	London
HVB (Bayerische Hypo- und Vereinsbank)	van den Brink, Evert: Managing Director Sales and Risk Management, Brokerage, Clearing and Custody, Business Corporates and Markets	In person	Continental Europe
ICAP	Corrigan, Danny: Director, International Business Development (ICAP), former Advisor (LCH)	In person	London
Illinois Institute of Technology, IIT Stuart Graduate School of Business	Gorham, Michael: Director and Industry Professor (IIT Centre for Financial Markets), former Director of Market Oversight (CFTC)	In person	US
Interactive Brokers Group/ Timber Hill	Brody, Paul J.: Chief Financial Officer (Interactive Brokers Group LLC and Timber Hill LLC), Board Member (OCC)	In person	US
International Securities Exchange (ISE)	Krell, David: President and CEO, Co-Founder of ISE	In person	US

(cont.)

Organisation*	Name of Interviewee(s) and Position at Time of Interview	Type of Interview	Interviewee Location
Independent Consultant	Dutterer, Dennis: former President and CEO (CCorp), former Interim President (Chicago Board of Trade) and former General Counsel (Commodity Futures Trading Commission)	In person	US
JPMorgan	Berliand, Richard: Managing Director, Head of Global Cash Equities, Futures & Options and Prime Brokerage (JPMorgan), Member (Supervisory Board of Deutsche Börse AG), Chairman (Futures Industry Association)	In person	London
Kalorama Partners, LLC	Pitt, Harvey L.: CEO (Kalorama Partners), former Chairman (Securities and Exchange Commission (SEC))	In person	US
Katten Muchin Rosenman LLP	Rosenzweig, Kenneth M.: Partner (Katten Muchin Rosenman LLP), Member (Executive Committee of the Law and Compliance Division of the FIA)	In person	US
Kirkland & Ellis LLP	Young, Mark D.: Partner	In person	US
LCH.Clearnet Group	Hardy, David: CEO (LCH.Clearnet Group), Member (Board of FOA and the Futures Industry Institute), Member (FSA's Financial Services Practitioner Panel), Member (Institute for Financial Markets (IFM)), former CEO (London Clearing House Ltd), former Board Member (IPE), former Board Member (London Commodity Exchange)	In person	London
London Stock Exchange (LSE)	Tanner, John: Head of Post-Trade Services	By e-mail	London
MAKO	Preuss, Andreas: COO and Board Member	In person	London
Merchants' Exchange	Hurst, Stephen D.: Founder	In person	US

Organisation*	Name of Interviewee(s) and Position at Time of Interview	Type of Interview	Interviewee Location
Merrill Lynch	Mathias, John: Director of Financial Futures and Options, Global Markets and Investment Banking, Director of Debt Markets, Member of the Board of Directors (Merrill Lynch), Director Merrill Lynch (Futures Asia), Global Manager Listed Derivatives Markets Relations (Merrill Lynch), Director and Board Member (FOA), Member of the Exchange Council (Eurex Deutschland), Voting Delegate (SFOA), former Chairman (European Chapter of the FIA)	In person	London
Ministry for Economics, Transportation and State Development for the State of Hessen/ Exchange Supervisory Authority	Hiestermann, Karsten: Ministerialrat (Engl. 'Head of Department'); and Winterhoff, Armin: Regierungsdirektor (Engl. 'Senior Expert')	In person	Continental Europe
Morgan Stanley	Farnham, Adrian: Executive Director, Market Infrastructure Group (Morgan Stanley), Member (London Member Group of SWX Swiss Exchange and virt-x), Member (virt-x Advisory Committee), Representative (LIBA)	In person	London
National Futures Association (NFA)	Roth, Daniel J.: President and CEO	In person	US
New York Clearing Corporation (NYCC)	Haase, Jr., George F.: President	In person	US

(cont.)

Organisation*	Name of Interviewee(s) and Position at Time of Interview	Type of Interview	Interviewee Location
New York Stock Exchange Group (NYSE)	McNulty, James J.: Director (NYSE), Non-Executive Director (ICAP), former President and CEO (CME), former Managing Director (UBS Warburg), former Partner (O'Connor and Associates)	In person	US
OCC (The Options Clearing Corporation)	Hender, George S.: Vice Chairman; and Luthringshausen, Wayne: Chairman and CEO	In person In person	US US
OEN Consulting	Nägeli, Otto E.: Managing Partner, former CEO (RüdBlass Privatbank), former Deputy CEO (Eurex) and Member (Executive Board of SWX)	In person	Continental Europe
OMX Group	Flodström, Ann: Senior Vice President Derivatives Operations (OMX Group), Chairman (EACH)	In person	Continental Europe
Schneider Trading	Brown, Richard: Senior Manager	In person	London
SEB	Martin, Steve G.: Clearing Manager, SEB Futures	In person	London
Sullivan & Cromwell LLP	Raisler, Kenneth M.: Partner, Head of Commodities, Futures and Derivatives Group (Sullivan & Cromwell LLP), Member (Board of Directors, FIA), former General Counsel (CFTC), former Chairman (Association of the Bar of the City of New York's Committee on Futures Regulation), former Member (The Group of Thirty Derivatives Project)	In person	US
Sungard GMI	Meens, Christopher: Managing Director	In person	London
SWX Swiss Exchange	Spillmann, Jürg: Head of the Executive Committee (SWX Group), Deputy CEO (Eurex)	In person	Continental Europe

Organisation*	Name of Interviewee(s) and Position at Time of Interview	Type of Interview	Interviewee Location
TransMarket Group	McCormick, James G.: President and CEO (TransMarket Group), Member (CBOT and CME), registered Principal (National Association of Securities Dealers), Vice Chairman (The Clearing Corporation)	In person	US
UBS	Templer, Bill: Managing Director, Co-Global Head of Exchange-Traded Derivatives	In person	London
Vega Financial Engineering	Grede, Fred: Chairman (Vega Financial Engineering), Consultant (FIA), former COO (Hong Kong Exchanges and Clearing Corporation), former CEO (Hong Kong Futures Exchange), former Executive Vice President (CBOT)	By telephone	US
Winton Capital	Settle, Kurt: Head of Trading Operations	In person	London

* Name of organisation at time of interview.

Appendix 4

Questionnaire

Questionnaire "clearing services for global markets"

Research objective

The focus of this study lies on the identification of the most cost-efficient organisation of clearing service provision in the light of globalised capital markets, and the question of which structures best match the demands of global markets.

Structure of questionnaire

The following questionnaire is composed of five different parts, which replicate the structure of the study. Part 1 is composed of general questions concerning the relevance of CCP clearing; Part 2 concerns the transaction cost analysis of derivatives clearing; Part 3 relates to analysing economies of scale; Part 4 studies different industry initiatives; and Part 5 asks for basic respondent information.

Confidentiality and anonymity

Please be aware that you must not be worried about the confidentiality of the information you provide, as all information will be made anonymous and will otherwise not be disclosed to third parties. For details regarding the anonymity and non-disclosure, please refer to the non-disclosure confirmation.

Please, do not hesitate to contact me in case you need further explanation or clarification regarding this questionnaire and any of the herein asked questions. Please return this questionnaire either via e-mail (scanned), by sending it through the post to my home address, or by handing it to me in person at the occasion of our interview.

Kind regards,

Tina Hasenpusch

Thank you very much for supporting this research!

Part 1 Relevance of CCP clearing

1. It is often said that the utilisation of CCPs enhances the efficiency of capital markets. On a scale from 1 (very low) to 5 (very high), how do you rate the relevance of CCPs for enhancing...

	Not Relevant 0	Very Low 1	Low 2	Medium 3	High 4	Very High 5
... the allocation of risk?	☐	☐	☐	☐	☐	☐
... the allocation of capital?	☐	☐	☐	☐	☐	☐
... market liquidity?	☐	☐	☐	☐	☐	☐
... cross-border capital flows?	☐	☐	☐	☐	☐	☐
... transaction cost efficiency?	☐	☐	☐	☐	☐	☐
... innovation (new products and services)?	☐	☐	☐	☐	☐	☐
Other:	☐	☐	☐	☐	☐	☐

Comments:.......................

2. Besides bringing benefits to capital markets on the whole, CCPs also create benefits for individual market participants; some of these benefits are listed below. On a scale from 1 (very low importance) to 5 (very high importance), how important are the following value propositions offered by CCPs to your business?

	Not Important 0	Very Low 1	Low 2	Medium 3	High 4	Very High 5
Ensured anonymity after trade execution	☐	☐	☐	☐	☐	☐
Safety of execution	☐	☐	☐	☐	☐	☐
Reduction of credit and operational risk	☐	☐	☐	☐	☐	☐
Reduction of margin through netting	☐	☐	☐	☐	☐	☐
Increased straight-through processing	☐	☐	☐	☐	☐	☐
Facilitation of settlement (through netting)	☐	☐	☐	☐	☐	☐
Other:	☐	☐	☐	☐	☐	☐

Comments:.......................

3. CCPs provide various services to their clearing members. On a scale from 1 (very low) to 5 (very high), please assess the importance of the following CCP services in terms of the value-added they provide to your business.

	Not Important	Very Low	Low	Medium	High	Very High
	0	1	2	3	4	5
Trade matching/confirmation	☐	☐	☐	☐	☐	☐
Collateral management services	☐	☐	☐	☐	☐	☐
Cash management services	☐	☐	☐	☐	☐	☐
Delivery management services	☐	☐	☐	☐	☐	☐
Centralised risk management (margining and default fund)	☐	☐	☐	☐	☐	☐
Exposure netting (reduce the total credit risk exposure)	☐	☐	☐	☐	☐	☐
Position netting (offsetting positions into one single net obligation)	☐	☐	☐	☐	☐	☐
Settlement netting	☐	☐	☐	☐	☐	☐
Cross-margining	☐	☐	☐	☐	☐	☐
Mark-to-market discipline	☐	☐	☐	☐	☐	☐
Transaction management services (i.e. option exercises, expiry of futures, corporate actions, etc.)	☐	☐	☐	☐	☐	☐
Give-up/take-up services	☐	☐	☐	☐	☐	☐
Position transfer services	☐	☐	☐	☐	☐	☐
Brokerage system	☐	☐	☐	☐	☐	☐
Other:	☐	☐	☐	☐	☐	☐

Comments: . . . .

Part 2 Transaction cost analysis – derivatives clearing

For handling the subsequent questions, please take into account the following guidelines and definitions:

Guidelines

A. In the following, please calculate the daily average figures as follows:

$$\text{daily average} = \frac{\text{Sum of estimated monthly figures (Jan. } - \text{Dec.)}}{\text{No. of trading days in respective year}}$$

B. Please specify if the figures you provide are not euro denominated.
C. If questions are not applicable to your business, please indicate "N.A.".

Glossary

Transaction costs: For the purpose of this study, the transaction costs of derivatives clearing services are defined as the total costs a customer (i.e. clearing member) has to bear for using a certain clearing

	house for clearing derivatives transactions. Transaction costs can be either direct or indirect.
Direct (transaction) costs:	Direct clearing-related transaction costs are monetarily quantifiable and can be measured directly, such as fees charged by clearing houses and intermediaries. Intermediaries include back-office vendors, GCMs, CSDs/ICSDs, custodians, (correspondence) banks, central banks and telecommunications companies.
Indirect (transaction) costs:	Indirect clearing-related transaction costs are difficult to isolate and can only be estimated or measured indirectly with the help of auxiliary variables. In this study, indirect transaction costs comprise the following four cost categories:

Cost of capital	Capital costs arising from default fund contributions, margin bound at the clearing house, liquidity tied to intra-day margin calls, or any kind of funding effort related to the utilisation of the respective clearing house.
Risk management costs	Internal costs borne by the clearing member arising from the risk management effort related to the utilisation of a certain clearing house. This category involves mainly personnel costs.
IT costs	IT costs related to connectivity charges to clearing houses borne by the clearing member. These costs mainly comprise personnel costs and system maintenance costs.
Back-office costs	Internal costs borne by the clearing member arising from the back-office processes necessary for the utilisation of a certain clearing house. Back-office costs include volume-driven costs (such as transaction and event management, i.e. corporate actions, expiries/deliveries, settlement processing, etc.) and connectivity-driven costs (application of specific accounting principles, management of accounts at correspondence banks, costs for continuous reconciliation of data, etc.).

CCG = Cassa di Compensazione e Garanzia, Italy

MEFF = Mercado Español de Futuros Financieros, Barcelona and Madrid

4. Please tick the appropriate box for each of the following statements.

	NO	YES
Does your business use a cost management system to estimate, record and monitor clearing-related costs?	☐	☐
If not, do you regularly monitor clearing-related costs by some other means?	☐	☐
Do you include the calculation/monitoring of indirect costs?	☐	☐

5. Please estimate the relationship of your direct and indirect clearing-related costs (and cross out the incorrect alternative):

higher by a rough factor of . . . .

Direct costs are   than indirect costs.

lower by a rough factor of . . . .

6. The total of your clearing-related transaction costs equals 100 per cent. Please provide a rough estimate of the percentages for each of the following transaction cost categories:

%

Direct costs	Fees charged by clearing houses:	
	Fees charged by intermediaries:	
	Other:	
Indirect costs	Cost of capital:	
	Risk management costs:	
	IT costs:	
	Back-office costs:	
	Other:	
		SUM = 100%

7. Please specify the average monthly clearing fees charged to your firm by the following clearing houses in 2005:

	Eurex Clearing	LCH.Clearnet	OMX	MEFF	CCG	Others
Average fixed monthly fees in 2005	............EUR	............EUR	............EUR	............EUR	............EUR	............EUR
Average monthly infrastructure/ line/connectivity fees in 2005*	............EUR	............EUR	............EUR	............EUR	............EUR	............EUR
Average monthly transaction-driven fees in 2005 (before rebates)**	............EUR	............EUR	............EUR	............EUR	............EUR	............EUR
Average monthly event-driven fees in 2005***	............EUR	............EUR	............EUR	............EUR	............EUR	............EUR
Average monthly fees charged for additional services in 2005****	............EUR	............EUR	............EUR	............EUR	............EUR	............EUR

* Infrastructure/line or connectivity fees are charged by clearing houses for connecting a specific customer location to the clearing house – either through the internet or via dedicated lines. These lines are commonly leased to the customer for the time he holds his specific clearing member status. The line fee then covers the usage and initial installation of the line(s). Some clearing houses outsource this service to dedicated telecommunications companies, which in turn directly charge clearing members.

** Transaction-driven fees refer to the per-transaction fees charged by clearing houses. Please specify the average of total transaction fees charged, excluding rebates or differences of fees charged for product or product groups (e.g. stock indexes, currencies, etc.), but including minimum fees per month. **If clearing fees are not itemised separately, please specify the all-in fee.**

*** Event-driven fees result from any "event" affecting a derivatives transaction. Such event-driven fees may thus be charged for option exercises, assignments and adjustments, futures contracts tendered, assigned, cash settled, etc.

**** Additional services can include the service provision for give-up executions, allocations, claims, EFPs, APS executions, transfers, specialised account structures, reports, etc.

8. Please specify the monthly average of other clearing-related charges and depreciation in 2005:

	Eurex Clearing	LCH.Clearnet	OMX	MEFF	CCG	Others
Monthly average of other charges and depreciation in 2005*	............EUR	............EUR	............EUR	............EUR	............EUR	............EUR

* Other clearing-related charges can include penalty payments, e.g. for delayed payments or deliveries, as well as possible charges for service level upgrades, such as non-gratuitous network or bandwidth upgrades (insofar as this service is not outsourced to another service provider), etc. Clearing-related depreciation can result from investments to clearing-house-specific hardware and software requirements (i.e. servers, routers and operating software).

9. What kind of rebates did you receive on the fees charged by the following clearing houses and how high were these in 2005? Please specify:

	Eurex Clearing	LCH.Clearnet	OMX	MEFF	CCG	Others
Kind of rebate (transaction fee, infrastructure fee, etc.)						
Average monthly fee rebate (either in percentages or absolute figures)	.... % of .... fee ....EUR	.... % of .... fee ....EUR	.... % of .... fee ....EUR	.... % of .... fee ....EUR	.... % of .... fee ....EUR	.... % of .... fee ....EUR

10. Which of the following intermediaries do you employ for the internal organisation of derivatives clearing services and how many of each?

	No	Yes	If yes – how many firms?
Back-office vendors	☐	☐	....
CSDs/ICSDs	☐	☐	....
Custodians	☐	☐	....
(Correspondence) banks	☐	☐	....
Central banks	☐	☐	....
Telecommunications companies	☐	☐	....
Others (i.e. consultants, etc.)	☐	☐	....

Comments: ....

11. Please specify your average monthly fees paid to the following intermediaries in 2005:

Average Monthly Fee in 2005

Back-office vendors	EUR
CSDs/ICSDs	EUR
Custodians	EUR
(Correspondence) banks	EUR
Central banks	EUR
Telecommunication companies	EUR
Others	EUR

Comments: ....

12. Please specify your cash/collateral tied to the respective clearing houses in 2005:

	Eurex Clearing	LCH.Clearnet	OMX	MEFF	CCG	Others
Contribution to default fund in 2005	.... EUR	.... EUR	.... EUR	.... EUR	.... EUR	.... EUR
Average daily cash margin at clearing house in 2005	.... EUR	.... EUR	.... EUR	.... EUR	.... EUR	.... EUR
Average daily collateral margin at clearing house in 2005	.... EUR	.... EUR	.... EUR	.... EUR	.... EUR	.... EUR
Average daily credit lines/capital tied to ensure funding of intra-day margin calls in 2005	.... EUR	.... EUR	.... EUR	.... EUR	.... EUR	.... EUR
Funding effort for minimum capital requirements in 2005	.... EUR	.... EUR	.... EUR	.... EUR	.... EUR	.... EUR
GCMs: funding effort for non-segregated business in 2005	.... EUR	.... EUR	.... EUR	.... EUR	.... EUR	.... EUR

Comments: ....
....

13. Do you maintain excess collateral at the following clearing houses to reduce the number of margin calls? If yes, please specify:

	NO	YES
Eurex Clearing	☐	☐
If yes, how high was this on a daily average in 2005?		. . . . .EUR
LCH.Clearnet	☐	☐
If yes, how high was this on a daily average in 2005?		. . . . .EUR
OMX	☐	☐
If yes, how high was this on a daily average in 2005?		. . . . .EUR
MEFF	☐	☐
If yes, how high was this on a daily average in 2005?		. . . . .EUR
CCG	☐	☐
If yes, how high was this on a daily average in 2005?		. . . . .EUR
Others	☐	☐
If yes, how high was this on a daily average in 2005?		. . . . .EUR

Comments: . . . .

14. When you initially became a clearing member of the respective clearing house....

	...did you have any funding effort for regulatory capital requirements?		...did you have to hire additional qualified back-office personnel?		...did you have to adapt your operational/back-office procedures?		...did you have to adapt your risk management structures and architecture?	
	No	Yes	No	Yes	No	Yes	No	Yes
Eurex Clearing	☐	☐	☐	☐	☐	☐	☐	☐
	If yes, how high were these? .... EUR		If yes, how many additional headcounts? ....(no. of headcounts)		If yes, pls. estimate the effort in man-days ....(no. of man-days)		If yes, pls. estimate the effort in man-days ....(no. of man-days)	
LCH.Clearnet	☐	☐	☐	☐	☐	☐	☐	☐
	.... EUR		............(no. of headcounts)		............(no. of man-days)		............(no. of man-days)	
OMX	☐	☐	☐	☐	☐	☐	☐	☐
	.... EUR		............(no. of headcounts)		............(no. of man-days)		............(no. of man-days)	
MEFF	☐	☐	☐	☐	☐	☐	☐	☐
	.... EUR		............(no. of headcounts)		............(no. of man-days)		............(no. of man-days)	
CCG	☐	☐	☐	☐	☐	☐	☐	☐
	.... EUR		............(no. of headcounts)		............(no. of man-days)		............(no. of man-days)	

Comments: ....

15. Please specify your risk-management-related costs for the respective clearing houses in 2005:

	Eurex Clearing	LCH.Clearnet	OMX	MEFF	CCG	Others
How many headcounts did you employ for the risk management of the respective clearing house business in 2005?						
GRAND TOTAL:						
How high were your average monthly customer losses (i.e. compensation or default) in 2005?	............EUR	............EUR	............EUR	............EUR	............EUR	............EUR
Did you outsource parts of your clearing-related risk management to a third party in 2005? If yes, pls. specify which parts and the average monthly costs involved.	PARTS: ....EUR	PARTS: ....EUR	PARTS: ....EUR	PARTS: ....EUR	PARTS: ....EUR	PARTS: ....EUR

16. Please specify your IT costs for the respective clearing houses in 2005:

	Eurex Clearing	LCH.Clearnet	OMX	MEFF	CCG	Others
How many headcounts did you employ for maintaining technical interfaces to the clearing house in 2005?						
Did you outsource parts of your derivatives-clearing-related IT to a third party in 2005? If yes, pls. specify which parts and the average monthly costs involved.	PARTS: ....EUR	PARTS: ....EUR	PARTS: ....EUR	PARTS: ....EUR	PARTS: ....EUR	PARTS: ....EUR

17. How high were your clearing-related back-office costs in 2005? Please provide figures per clearing house or indicate the grand total:

	Eurex Clearing	LCH.Clearnet	OMX	MEFF	CCG	Others
How many headcounts did you employ in the derivatives clearing back-office in 2005?						
GRAND TOTAL:						
Did you outsource parts of your derivatives clearing back-office to a third party in 2005? If yes, pls. specify which parts and the average monthly costs involved.	PARTS: ....EUR	PARTS: ....EUR	PARTS: ....EUR	PARTS: ....EUR	PARTS: ....EUR	PARTS: ....EUR
Average monthly error account in 2005	...........EUR	...........EUR	...........EUR	...........EUR	...........EUR	...........EUR
GRAND TOTAL:						

Comments: ....
....
....

18. In this section, you are asked to compare total clearing costs with total trading and settlement costs. Please consider that the 'total' should include both direct and indirect transaction costs. *

	STEP 1	STEP 2
Clearing costs vs. trading costs	☐ Total trading costs are higher than total clearing costs OR ☐ Total trading costs are lower than total clearing costs	Total trading costs are higher by a factor of roughly................ OR Total trading costs are lower by a factor of roughly................
Clearing costs vs. settlement costs	☐ Total settlement costs are higher than total clearing costs OR ☐ Total settlement costs are lower than total clearing costs	Total settlement costs are higher by a factor of roughly .... OR Total settlement costs are lower by a factor of roughly................

*Total trading/settlement costs therefore also comprise indirect costs such as maintenance of IT infrastructure and other operational costs.

NO   YES

Do you regularly compare total trading costs to total clearing costs?   ☐   ☐

If yes, how often (monthly, quarterly, yearly, etc.)? ....

Do you regularly compare total settlement costs to total clearing costs?   ☐   ☐

If yes, how often (monthly, quarterly, yearly, etc.)? ....

Do you regularly compare total settlement costs to total trading costs?   ☐   ☐

If yes, how often (monthly, quarterly, yearly, etc.)? ....

Part 3 Scale effect analysis

19. Various network initiatives (mergers/alliances/partnerships, etc.) could be implemented to harmonise/consolidate the clearing service industry in the future. Some of the potential benefits of harmonisation/consolidation are listed below. On a scale from 1 (very low importance) to 5 (very high importance), please rate their importance.

	Not Important 0	Very Low 1	Low 2	Medium 3	High 4	Very High 5
Clearing fee reductions	☐	☐	☐	☐	☐	☐
Reduction of no. of involved intermediaries	☐	☐	☐	☐	☐	☐
Increased scope for cross-margining	☐	☐	☐	☐	☐	☐
Harmonised collateral arrangements	☐	☐	☐	☐	☐	☐
Single margin approach per product	☐	☐	☐	☐	☐	☐
Optimised default fund contributions	☐	☐	☐	☐	☐	☐
Lower capital costs	☐	☐	☐	☐	☐	☐
Enhanced netting opportunities	☐	☐	☐	☐	☐	☐
Enhancements to risk mgmt. best practices	☐	☐	☐	☐	☐	☐
Reductions of risk mgmt. costs	☐	☐	☐	☐	☐	☐
Simplification and rationalisation of back-office processes	☐	☐	☐	☐	☐	☐
Increased choice of trading location	☐	☐	☐	☐	☐	☐
Increased choice of settlement location	☐	☐	☐	☐	☐	☐
Increased speed of innovation	☐	☐	☐	☐	☐	☐
Single interface to multiple markets	☐	☐	☐	☐	☐	☐
Single membership gateway	☐	☐	☐	☐	☐	☐
Choice of jurisdiction in which to clear	☐	☐	☐	☐	☐	☐
Reduction of the no. of technical interfaces	☐	☐	☐	☐	☐	☐
Harmonisation of systems and procedures	☐	☐	☐	☐	☐	☐
Enhanced straight-through processing	☐	☐	☐	☐	☐	☐

Increased scope for one-stop-shopping	☐	☐	☐	☐	☐	☐
Round-the-clock processing	☐	☐	☐	☐	☐	☐
Independence from trading platforms	☐	☐	☐	☐	☐	☐
Independence from settlement platforms	☐	☐	☐	☐	☐	☐
User participation in governance	☐	☐	☐	☐	☐	☐
Commercial set-up of clearing house (i.e. for-profit or not-for-profit)	☐	☐	☐	☐	☐	☐
Other:	☐	☐	☐	☐	☐	☐

Comments: . . . .

20. If a clearing house decided to offer clearing services for various derivatives product types (i.e. financial derivatives, derivatives on commodities, foreign exchange derivatives, etc.) via a fully integrated clearing system, what impact would you expect this to have on the following transaction cost categories? Please rate the impact on a scale from –3 (significant decrease) to +3 (significant increase):

	Decrease				Increase		
	Significant	Medium	Small		Small	Medium	Significant
	–3	–2	–1	0	+1	+2	+3
Fees charged by clearing house	☐	☐	☐	☐	☐	☐	☐
Fees charged by intermediaries	☐	☐	☐	☐	☐	☐	☐
Number of intermediaries needed	☐	☐	☐	☐	☐	☐	☐
Your average cash/collateral (margin) bound at clearing house	☐	☐	☐	☐	☐	☐	☐
Your contribution to default fund	☐	☐	☐	☐	☐	☐	☐
Your regulatory capital requirements	☐	☐	☐	☐	☐	☐	☐
Your total cost of capital	☐	☐	☐	☐	☐	☐	☐
Your internal risk management costs	☐	☐	☐	☐	☐	☐	☐
Your IT costs	☐	☐	☐	☐	☐	☐	☐
Your back-office costs	☐	☐	☐	☐	☐	☐	☐

	Decrease				Increase		
	Significant	Medium	Small		Small	Medium	Significant
	−3	−2	−1	0	+1	+2	+3
Your total transaction costs related to clearing at the respective clearing house	☐	☐	☐	☐	☐	☐	☐
Other:	☐	☐	☐	☐	☐	☐	☐

Comments: . . . .

21. If a clearing house decided to offer clearing services for financial derivatives and equities (representing the full spectrum of underlyings to the respective equity and equity index derivatives) via a fully integrated clearing system, what impact would you expect this to have on the following transaction cost categories? Please rate the impact on a scale from −3 (significant decrease) to +3 (significant increase):

	Decrease				Increase		
	Significant	Medium	Small		Small	Medium	Significant
	−3	−2	−1	0	+1	+2	+3
Fees charged by clearing house	☐	☐	☐	☐	☐	☐	☐
Fees charged by intermediaries	☐	☐	☐	☐	☐	☐	☐
Number of intermediaries needed	☐	☐	☐	☐	☐	☐	☐
Your average cash/collateral (margin) bound at clearing house	☐	☐	☐	☐	☐	☐	☐
Your contribution to default fund	☐	☐	☐	☐	☐	☐	☐
Your regulatory capital requirements	☐	☐	☐	☐	☐	☐	☐
Your total cost of capital	☐	☐	☐	☐	☐	☐	☐
Your internal risk management costs	☐	☐	☐	☐	☐	☐	☐
Your IT costs	☐	☐	☐	☐	☐	☐	☐
Your back-office costs	☐	☐	☐	☐	☐	☐	☐
Your total transaction costs related to clearing at the respective clearing house	☐	☐	☐	☐	☐	☐	☐
Other:	☐	☐	☐	☐	☐	☐	☐

Comments: . . . .

22. If a clearing house decided to enlarge its scale by connecting further on- and off-exchange marketplaces, thus increasing the volume cleared in existing products, what impact would you expect this to have on the following transaction cost categories? Please rate the impact on a scale from −3 (significant decrease) to +3 (significant increase):

	Decrease				Increase		
	Significant	Medium	Small		Small	Medium	Significant
	−3	−2	−1	0	+1	+2	+3
Fees charged by clearing house	☐	☐	☐	☐	☐	☐	☐
Fees charged by intermediaries	☐	☐	☐	☐	☐	☐	☐
Number of intermediaries needed	☐	☐	☐	☐	☐	☐	☐
Your average cash/collateral (margin) bound at clearing house	☐	☐	☐	☐	☐	☐	☐
Your contribution to default fund	☐	☐	☐	☐	☐	☐	☐
Your regulatory capital requirements	☐	☐	☐	☐	☐	☐	☐
Your total cost of capital	☐	☐	☐	☐	☐	☐	☐
Your internal risk management costs	☐	☐	☐	☐	☐	☐	☐
Your IT costs	☐	☐	☐	☐	☐	☐	☐
Your back-office costs	☐	☐	☐	☐	☐	☐	☐
Your total transaction costs related to clearing at the respective clearing house	☐	☐	☐	☐	☐	☐	☐
Other:	☐	☐	☐	☐	☐	☐	☐

Comments: . . . .

Part 4 Case study analysis

For handling the subsequent questions, please take into account the following guidelines and definitions:

Guidelines

On the following pages you will be asked to evaluate the following actual and hypothetical initiatives according to the impact you (would) expect these initiatives to have on your clearing-related transaction costs:
- the Eurex/CCorp Global Clearing Link (GCL), Phase I and Phase II;
- a fictitious clearing link between Eurex Clearing and CME (see Glossary);
- the merger of LCH and Clearnet from two viewpoints (see Glossary);
- a fictitious merger of LCH.Clearnet and Eurex Clearing.

Even if a certain initiative has not affected or would not affect your business, please evaluate the impact you would expect it to have on your transaction costs!

Glossary

Global Clearing Link (GCL) Phase I (EU Link):	The so-called 'Phase I' of the GCL enables clearing members of The Clearing Corporation (CCorp) to clear CFTC-approved EUR-denominated products traded on Eurex through their existing clearing membership. This gives CCorp's customers direct access to the European product range of Eurex. Phase I is therefore often also referred to as the 'EU Link'. Phase I came into effect in October 2004.
Global Clearing Link (GCL) Phase II:	'Phase II' of the GCL will supposedly allow clearing members of Eurex Clearing to clear USD-denominated products traded on Eurex US through their existing clearing membership. Phase II is therefore also referred to as the 'US Link'. Phase II is still pending regulatory approval.
Merger of LCH and Clearnet:	LCH.Clearnet has been employing a phased approach to the integration process. Full integration will entail migration to a common technical platform and will give clearing members the opportunity to clear their business through either CCP; both will use a common set of legal and operating procedures. Due to regulatory, legal and other complexities, however, these integration phases will not result in a single consolidated clearing house entity with a common membership and legal framework. When evaluating the merger, you will first be asked to describe the impact the merger has had on your business so far. Secondly, you will be asked for the impact you expect the merger to have after full integration has been realised.
Fictitious merger of LCH. Clearnet and Eurex Clearing:	When evaluating this hypothetical initiative, please assume that both entities are fully integrated, including the utilisation of a common technical platform,

which would enable clearing members to clear their business through a single consolidated clearing house entity with a single membership and single legal framework. The full spectrum of cross-margining and netting opportunities would be available to clearing members. This case study is intended to simulate the impact of the creation of a single European CCP.

Fictitious Clearing Link between Eurex Clearing and CME: When evaluating this hypothetical initiative, please assume that the clearing link would enable clearing members of Eurex Clearing to clear USD Fixed Income derivatives traded on the CBOT through their existing clearing membership and that clearing members of CME would be able to clear EUR Fixed Income derivatives traded on Eurex through their existing clearing membership. Cross-margining is assumed to be provided between the EUR and USD Fixed Income derivatives for the clearing members of both entities.

23. Please indicate whether the following initiatives have affected (would affect) your business:

	NO	YES
We were affected by the Global Clearing Link, Phase I.	☐	☐
We would participate in the Global Clearing Link, Phase II.	☐	☐
We would utilise a clearing link between Eurex Clearing and CME (as defined in the Glossary).	☐	☐
We were affected by the merger of LCH and Clearnet.	☐	☐
We would be affected by a merger of LCH.Clearnet and Eurex Clearing (as defined in the Glossary).	☐	☐

Comments: . . . .

24. Do you believe that the proposed fictitious merger of LCH.Clearnet and Eurex Clearing adequately simulates the benefits and hurdles involved in the creation of a single European CCP?

	NO	YES
	☐	☐

Comments: . . . .

25. Please assess whether the following initiatives (would) provide value-added to your business.

	NO	YES
The Global Clearing Link, Phase I	☐	☐
The Global Clearing Link, Phase II	☐	☐
A clearing link between Eurex Clearing and CME	☐	☐
The merger of LCH and Clearnet	☐	☐
A merger of LCH.Clearnet and Eurex Clearing	☐	☐

Comments: . . . .

26. How do/would you estimate the impact of the Global Clearing Link, Phase I on the following transaction cost categories? Please tick the appropriate box:

Transaction Costs

	Decreased by . . . % −					0	Increased by . . . % +				
	71–100	51–70	31–50	11–30	1–10	0	1–10	11–30	31–50	51–70	71–100
Fees charged by clearing houses											
Fees charged by intermediaries											
Your cash/collateral (margin) bound at clearing house											
Your contribution to default fund											
Your regulatory capital requirements											
Your total cost of capital											
Your internal risk management costs											
Your average error account											
Your IT costs											
Your back-office costs											
Utilisation of segregated accounts at CCorp											
Your total transaction costs related to clearing											
Other											

Comments:..
....
....

27. How would you estimate the impact of the Global Clearing Link, Phase II on the following transaction cost categories? Please tick the appropriate box:

Transaction Costs

	Decreased by . . . % −					0	Increased by . . . % +				
	71–100	51–70	31–50	11–30	1–10		1–10	11–30	31–50	51–70	71–100
Fees charged by clearing houses											
Fees charged by intermediaries											
Your cash/collateral (margin) bound at clearing house											
Your contribution to default fund											
Your regulatory capital requirements											
Your total cost of capital											
Your internal risk management costs											
Your average error account											
Your IT costs											
Your back-office costs											
Utilisation of segregated accounts at CCorp											
Your total transaction costs related to clearing											
Other											

Comments: ....
....

28. How would you estimate the impact of a (fictitious) clearing link between Eurex Clearing and CME (as defined in Glossary) on the following transaction cost categories? Please tick the appropriate box:

Transaction Costs

	− Decreased by . . . %					0	+ Increased by . . . %				
	71–100	51–70	31–50	11–30	1–10	0	1–10	11–30	31–50	51–70	71–100
Fees charged by clearing houses											
Fees charged by intermediaries											
Your cash/collateral (margin) bound at clearing house											
Your contribution to default fund											
Your regulatory capital requirements											
Your total cost of capital											
Your internal risk management costs											
Your average error account											
Your IT costs											
Your back-office costs											
Utilisation of segregated accounts at CME											
Your total transaction costs related to clearing											
Other											

Comments:...
....
....

29. How do/would you estimate the impact of the merger of LCH and Clearnet on the following transaction cost categories to date? Please tick the appropriate box:

Transaction Costs

	Decreased by . . . % −					0	Increased by . . . % +				
	71–100	51–70	31–50	11–30	1–10		1–10	11–30	31–50	51–70	71–100
Fees charged by clearing houses											
Fees charged by intermediaries											
Your cash/collateral (margin) bound at clearing house											
Your contribution to default fund											
Your regulatory capital requirements											
Your total cost of capital											
Your internal risk management costs											
Your average error account											
Your IT costs											
Your back-office costs											
Your total transaction costs related to clearing											
Other											

Comments:..
....
....

30. How do/would you estimate the impact of the merger of LCH and Clearnet on the following transaction cost categories after full integration has been realised (see Glossary)? Please tick the appropriate box:

	Transaction Costs										
	Decreased by . . . %							**Increased by . . . %**			
	−						+				
	71–100	51–70	31–50	11–30	1–10	0	1–10	11–30	31–50	51–70	71–100
Fees charged by clearing houses											
Fees charged by intermediaries											
Your cash/collateral (margin) bound at clearing house											
Your contribution to default fund											
Your regulatory capital requirements											
Your total cost of capital											
Your internal risk management costs											
Your average error account											
Your IT costs											
Your back-office costs											
Your total transaction costs related to clearing											
Other											

Comments: ....
....
....

31. How would you estimate the impact of the (fictitious) merger of LCH.Clearnet and Eurex Clearing (as defined in Glossary) on the following transaction cost categories after full integration has been realised? Please tick the appropriate box:

	Decreased by . . . % (−)					0	Increased by . . . % (+)				
	71–100	51–70	31–50	11–30	1–10	0	1–10	11–30	31–50	51–70	71–100
Fees charged by clearing houses											
Fees charged by intermediaries											
Your cash/collateral (margin) bound at clearing house											
Your contribution to default fund											
Your regulatory capital requirements											
Your total cost of capital											
Your internal risk management costs											
Your average error account											
Your IT costs											
Your back-office costs											
Your total transaction costs related to clearing											
Other											

Comments:...
....
....

32. How high have your investment costs for the following initiatives been to date?

INVESTMENT COSTS

Global Clearing Link Phase I .... EUR
Global Clearing Link Phase II .... EUR
Merger of LCH and Clearnet .... EUR
Comments: ....

33. Please provide a rough estimate of the following investment costs. How high...

INVESTMENT COSTS

... do you expect your additional investment .... EUR
costs to be by the time the full integration of the
merger of LCH and Clearnet has been achieved?
... would you expect your investment costs to .... EUR
be for adjusting to a full merger integration of
LCH.Clearnet and Eurex Clearing?
... would you expect your investment costs to .... EUR
be for adjusting to a clearing link between Eurex
Clearing and CME?
Comments: ....

34. After how many years do you think the benefits of the following initiatives will (would) have outweighed the related investment costs?

NO. OF YEARS

Global Clearing Link Phase 1 (EUR Link)
Global Clearing Link Phase 2 (USD Link)
Merger of LCH and Clearnet
(fictitious) Merger of LCH.Clearnet and Eurex Clearing
(fictitious) Clearing Link Eurex Clearing and CME
Comments: ....

Part 5 Basic respondent information

35. What is your clearing member status at the following clearing houses – and in which year did you acquire the respective status? Please specify if more than one entity within your group is a clearing member at the respective clearing house:

	STATUS	NO. OF ENTITIES	YEAR
Eurex Clearing			
LCH.Clearnet			
OMX			
MEFF			
CCG			
Others			

36. What were your reasons for choosing your company's clearing member status?

	False	True
We believe the clearing member status positively impacts our market reputation.	☐	☐
Clearing services are a (small or large) part of our business model.	☐	☐
We don't want to leave the clearing of our traded volume to a third party.	☐	☐
We would have preferred a different clearing status, but don't fulfil the minimum capital requirements.	☐	☐
We would have preferred a different clearing status, but we consider this status too costly.	☐	☐

Comments and further explanation: . . . .

37. What was your average daily transaction volume per clearing house in 2005 in derivatives and equities?

	Eurex Clearing	LCH. Clearnet	OMX	MEFF	CCG	Others
Derivatives no. of contracts						
Equities no. of transactions						

	NO	YES
38. Do you operate an integrated risk management for equities and derivatives?	☐	☐
Comments:	☐	☐
39. Do you operate an integrated back-office for equities and derivatives?	☐	☐
Comments:	☐	☐
40. Do you operate integrated IT operations for equities and derivatives?	☐	☐
Comments:	☐	☐

41. How would you classify your business focus?

Domestic	☐
Global	☐

Comments: . . . .

42. How would you classify your organisational structure?

Domestic	☐
Global	☐

Comments: . . . .

43. How do you organise clearing in your firm?

Cost centre	☐
Profit centre	☐

Comments: . . . .

44. How would you classify your organisational structure (i.e. functional organisation or organisation according to business areas/asset classes)?

Functional organisation   ☐

Organisation according to business areas/asset classes   ☐

Comments: ....

45. How high is your average equity capital (of the entity you employ as a clearing member)?

.... EUR

Comments: ....

46. In how many different asset classes do you conduct business and which are these (equities, derivatives, commodities, etc.)?

....

47. How many trading locations/platforms are you connected to and which are these?

....

48. What is the type and structure of your customer base?

....

49. Name of your company

....

(The name of your company is only requested to facilitate the tracking of the questionnaires. The questionnaire will be made anonymous for the statistical analysis and the publication. For details regarding the anonymity and non-disclosure, please refer to the non-disclosure confirmation.)

Thank you very much for your contribution!

Appendix 5

Sample interview guide clearing members

1. Introductory questions

- Your company is a GCM/ICM/NCM of some/all of the following clearing houses: Eurex Clearing, LCH.Clearnet, OMX, MEFF and CCG. What was your motivation for choosing the respective clearing status?
- In your opinion, what is the most important service/value-added provided by a CCP?
- Given that different clearing houses provided clearing services for the same exchanges/products, what were your reasons for switching your clearing membership from one clearing house to another?

2. Transaction cost analysis

- Are you cost sensitive in your choice of clearing location?
- I have identified the following cost components related to clearing services; is this list complete? Direct costs – clearing house charges, service provider charges; indirect costs – cost of capital, risk management costs, information technology costs, back-office costs.
- Would you say that clearing-related costs generally matter to you?
- Do you use a cost management system to monitor clearing costs? If not, do you monitor clearing costs by some other means? Do you monitor direct and indirect costs, or only direct costs?
- Which are higher in your company – direct costs or indirect costs? Can you provide a rough estimate of their relative magnitude, i.e. the ratio of direct costs to indirect costs?
- The total of your clearing-related costs equals 100 per cent. Please estimate the percentages for each of the following six transaction cost categories: clearing house charges, service provider charges, cost of capital, risk management costs, information technology costs and back-office costs.
- In what respect do you think your clearing cost drivers are different from those of other ICMs/GCMs?
- Can you provide an estimate (in EUR or USD) of your direct and indirect clearing costs in 2005?
- Do you see any correlation between clearing-related transaction costs and different structures for clearing service provision (i.e. for-profit vs. not-for-profit clearing houses, user-governed vs. non-user-governed, vertical vs. horizontal integration)?

- The practice of outsourcing clearing-related functions (either to a third party or within company structures) enables firms to 'follow the sun'. Outsourcing is also viewed as a cost-saving mechanism. Do you agree? Are you planning to outsource certain clearing-related functions? If yes, in which areas do you expect to see cost savings? How high do you expect these savings to be?
- Which costs are higher, your total clearing-related costs or your total trading/settlement costs, and what is their approximate ratio?
- Are the cost drivers related to derivatives clearing different from the cost drivers related to securities clearing?

3. Network strategies

- Do you think the (European) clearing industry should be further integrated and harmonised? Why or why not?
- Do you think that cross-margining agreements/clearing links/a Single CCP provide value-added? Please specify.
- What are the benefits and drawbacks of these initiatives?
- Generally speaking, what do you think is the best way to further the integration of the (European) clearing industry: clearing links, M&A or a Single CCP?
- GCMs: Do you replicate certain CCP processes for your clients by providing additional value-added clearing services? Would you welcome the provision of broader services by CCPs? In other words, are there any clearing services currently offered by GCMs that you would like to see offered by CCPs?

4. Efficiency impact of network strategies

- What impact would you expect clearing links, M&A or a Single CCP to have on your clearing costs?
- Can you estimate the impact these initiatives might have on particular costs (i.e. a 50 per cent reduction of capital costs, etc.)?
- GCMs: Would you pass on the benefits of CCP consolidation to your clients?

5. Case studies of network strategies

Eurex and CCorp – Global Clearing Link:
- Were you supportive of the Global Clearing Link (GCL) between Eurex and CCorp?
- Has the GCL created any value-added?
- How has Phase I impacted your clearing-related transaction costs to date?
- How do you estimate the (potential) impact of the Global Clearing Link Phase I and Phase II on your clearing-related transaction costs?

- Did you consider utilising Phase 1 to take advantage of segregation by clearing Eurex's CFTC-approved European contracts through CCorp?

LCH and Clearnet – Merger:

- Were you in support of the merger of LCH and Clearnet?
- Has the merger created any value-added? If not, do you think any value-added will be realised in the future?
- How has the merger of LCH and Clearnet impacted your clearing-related transaction costs to date? What impact do you foresee on these costs after full integration has been realised?
- How important is the successful completion of the following initiatives for reducing your transaction costs: integration of risk management, integration of IT (clearing platform) and the replacement of multiple (back-office) technologies, interfaces, membership criteria and operating procedures with a single, harmonised operating infrastructure?

Single European CCP:

- Are you in support of the creation of a single European CCP?
- In which areas would you expect the most significant savings for your business under a Single CCP?
- Is your internal structure conducive to the realisation of the potential savings related to a Single CCP? If it is not, would you be willing to invest in the reorganisation/adaptation of your internal structures and processes to achieve these savings?
- Could the same benefits be realised by different means?
- How do you think your direct and indirect clearing costs would be affected by a Single CCP as compared to an oligopoly market?
- Do you expect these savings to be significantly different from the potential savings offered by other integration and harmonisation initiatives?
- How many years do you think it would take for the benefits of a Single CCP initiative to supersede the related investment costs?

6. Future development of clearing and global outlook

- How do you think clearing houses can best meet the demands of global markets? What do you think the future role of clearing houses in a global market setting should be?
- Will harmonisation and integration occur on a global scale as well?
- Which kinds of network initiatives would facilitate global harmonisation and integration?
- Regarding the domestic constituency: Does everything have to be global? What should stay local?
- If you could simply snap your fingers and create your personal 'global clearing services dreamland', what would this dreamland be like? Please describe the ideal scenario, including its most important characteristics.

  Thank you very much for your time!

Appendix 6

Clearing house fees

The clearing house fee comparison is based on the following assumptions and caveats:

- Fees charged in currencies other than the euro were converted to euros according to the exchange rate on 29 September 2006.
- Clearing houses usually charge per-contract fees, but the number of contracts necessary to enable a €500,000 hedge depends on the value of a contract on a given day. As these values fluctuate for equity options/futures and index options/futures, it should be kept in mind that the fees in the chart represent a snapshot of that particular date.
- Particularly in the case of equity options/futures, the number of necessary contracts varies depending on the value of the underlying. For the purpose of the equity options clearing fee comparison, only equity options with a contract size of 100 shares were taken into account.
- An additional caveat applies to the equity options fees charged by OMX, because OMX calculates these as a per cent of the premium; these fees represent a snapshot of fees at a particular point in time.
- The equity option clearing fees charged by LCH.Clearnet and the respective trading fees relate to French equity options. The new clearing fees (as of January 2007) were included for comparative purposes.
- The equity futures clearing fees charged by LCH.Clearnet and the respective trading fees relate to Universal Stock Futures.
- Equity futures traded on OneChicago can be cleared through the CME or the OCC. The fee split between trading and clearing fees is artificial and based on estimates obtained from the expert interviews. OneChicago charges an all-in fee.
- For the purpose of this comparison, the all-in fees charged by OneChicago for equity futures relate to its eligible member rate.
- The fees charged by the CME relate to its equity/clearing member fees.
- The fees charged by the CBOT (T-Bond) relate to its fees for equity members (registered clearing FCMs).
- No rebates or (annual) discounts were taken into account in the fee comparison.

Hedged amount: €500,000 / Reference date: 29 September 2006 / Fees in EUR

Product	Fee	EUREX	LCH.Clearnet	OMX	MEFF	CC&G	CME	OCC
Equity Options	**Clearing**	**4.08**	**24.00 (6.00)***		**9.00**	**12.00**	N.A.	**3.36**
	Trading	19.92	66.00	91.20	9.00	62.40	N.A.	22.68 (CBOE) 14.16 (ISE)
	All-In	24.00	90.00 (72.00)*	91.20	18.00	74.40	N.A.	26.04 (CBOE) 17.52 (ISE)
Equity Futures	**Clearing**	**6.12**	**6.00**		**9.00**	**13.20**	**5.64****	
	Trading	29.88	42.00	200.00	9.00	60.00	8.52***	
	All-In	36.00	48.00	200.00	18.00	73.20	14.16	N.A.
Index Options	Product	Euro STOXX 50	FTSE 100	OMXS-30	N.A.	S&P/MIB	N.A.	S&P 500
	Clearing	**0.65**	**0.25**		N.A.	**1.56**	N.A.	**0.13**
	Trading	3.19	2.08	17.27	N.A.	4.27	N.A.	0.89
	All-In	3.84	2.33	17.27	N.A.	5.83	N.A.	1.02
Index Futures	Product	Euro STOXX 50	FTSE 100	OMXS-30	IBEX35	S&P/MIB	S&P 500	N.A.
	Clearing	**0.65**	**0.25**		**2.50**	**0.65**	**0.30**	N.A.
	Trading	3.19	2.08	17.27	2.50	2.60	0.74	N.A.
	All-In	3.84	2.33	17.27	5.00	3.25	1.04	N.A.
Interest Rate (physical delivery)	Product	Bund Future	N.A.	R2 Future	Bono 10	N.A.	T-Bond Future	N.A.
	Clearing	**0.17**	N.A.		**0.75**	N.A.	**0.30**	N.A.
	Trading	0.83	N.A.	9.82	1.50	N.A.	0.30	N.A.
	All-In	1.00	N.A.	9.82	2.25	N.A.	0.60	N.A.
Interest Rate (cash settled)	Product	3-month Euribor Future	Euribor Future	Stibor FRA	N.A.	N.A.	Eurodollar Future	N.A.
	Clearing	**0.02**	**0.02**		N.A.	N.A.	**0.04**	N.A.
	Trading	0.10	0.19	1.45	N.A.	N.A.	0.05	N.A.
	All-In	0.12	0.21	1.45	N.A.	N.A.	0.09	N.A.

* As of January 2007

** Cleared through the CME or the OCC

*** Traded on OneChicago (fee split is artificial; based on estimates from expert interviews)

Appendix 7

Total European derivatives clearing costs in 2005

The calculation of the total European derivatives clearing costs in 2005 was based on the assumptions regarding the Value Provision Network (section 2.3), the structure of the European clearing industry as outlined in section 2.5.1 and the findings from the empirical study and transaction cost analysis, as presented in Chapter 5. The calculation consisted of three steps, which are detailed in the following:

1. Calculation of total costs for the six benchmark clearing members;
2. Calculation of total costs for the remaining 213 European clearing members.
3. Calculation of total European derivatives clearing costs.

Step 1: Calculation of total clearing costs for each of the six benchmark clearing members;[1]

Step 1.1: Calculation of fixed costs per clearing house and clearing member:

- The fixed clearing house charges borne by these six clearing members included membership fees and connectivity/technical fees (such as line fees, charges for clearing working stations and other IT equipment where applicable).
- Eurex Clearing provided information on the number of lines, working stations, sites, etc. used by these six clearing members.
- Combined with information published by Eurex Clearing, MEFF and CC&G on what they charge for the above services, the benchmark clearing members' fixed costs were calculated.
- No comparable information on LCH.Clearnet's or OMX's fees was publicly available. For the purpose of this study, it was thus assumed that fixed costs of a clearing membership at LCH.Clearnet roughly equal the fixed charges incurred by a clearing member through its membership at Eurex Clearing. OMX clearing house charges are accounted for at a later stage of the calculation of total clearing house charges (step 1.3).
- Of the six benchmark clearers, four were high volume clearing members, one was a low volume clearer and one was a medium volume clearer. In this study, low volume clearers were assumed to be a member only at their home country CCP. In contrast, medium and high volume clearers were defined as being active at all of the European clearing houses, i.e. assumed to be direct members of Eurex Clearing, LCH.Clearnet, OMX, MEFF and CC&G.
- Based on the outlined information, the fixed costs per clearing house and benchmark clearing member were calculated.

Step 1.2: Calculation of variable clearing house charges per clearing house and clearing member:

- Based on information provided by Eurex Clearing, which was extended and adapted with the help of the interviewees, the European market share for each of the six benchmark clearers was estimated. Their combined European market share was estimated to be 22.8 per cent.

---

[1] For details on the benchmark clearing members and their respective cost structures, refer to Figure 5.5.

- For each of the five European clearing houses, benchmark products were selected. These benchmark products correspond to the products identified for the comparison of clearing house fees in Appendix 6 (except for OMX's clearing house charges, which are accounted for at a later stage of the calculation of total clearing house charges; refer to step 1.3).
- Based on the publicly available information on the number of cleared contracts in the selected benchmark products in 2005, the benchmark clearing member's market share and the respective clearing fees charged by the clearing house,[2] the total clearing fees charged per benchmark product were calculated. This sum represents the variable clearing house charges for the benchmark products per clearing house and clearing member.
- Most of the Eurex Clearing, LCH.Clearnet, MEFF and CC&G products selected as benchmarks were among the highest volume products in 2005. To account for the remaining clearing house products, the 'rest volume' charges per clearing house and clearing member were calculated.
- To determine the 'rest volume' charges, the 'rest volume' per clearing house and clearing member (rest volume = total number of cleared contracts per clearing house multiplied by the benchmark clearing member's market share minus total number of benchmark products cleared by benchmark clearing member per clearing house) was multiplied by the total clearing fees charged for the benchmark products per clearing house and clearing member divided by the total number of cleared benchmark products per clearing house and clearing member.
- The fact that clearing fees charged for other exchange-traded derivatives products may in reality vary from those fees charged for the selected benchmark products is thus neglected for the purpose of this calculation.
- The final step in the calculation of variable costs per clearing house and clearing member consisted of estimating the option exercise and future settlement charges.
- Based on estimates provided by a market expert, the average rate of equity and index options exercises was assumed to be 6 per cent, the average rate of equity futures and fixed income futures settlements was assumed to be 3 per cent, and the average rate of index futures settlements was assumed to be 7 per cent.
- Together with publicly available data on the average open interest at Eurex Clearing, LCH.Clearnet, MEFF and CC&G, the market share of the benchmark clearers and the respective fees charged by the clearing house, the option exercise and future settlement charges per clearing member and clearing house were calculated.
- Summarising the variable clearing house charges for the benchmark products, the 'rest volume' charges, and the option exercise and future settlement charges resulted in the total variable clearing house charges per clearing house and clearing member.

Step 1.3: Calculation of total clearing house charges per clearing member:

- Summarising the fixed charges and the variable clearing house charges resulted in the total clearing house charges per benchmark clearing member. No rebates or (annual) discounts were taken into account.
- To account for discrepancies resulting from: (i) having had to leave out OMX clearing house charges (due to unavailability); (ii) the artificial fee split between trading and clearing fees at Eurex; and (iii) setting fixed costs of a clearing membership at LCH.Clearnet to equal fixed

---

[2] Clearing fees charged by Eurex Clearing are based on an artificial fee split, as outlined.

charges of a membership at Eurex Clearing, the total clearing house charges per benchmark clearing member were assumed to represent merely 70 or 80 per cent of the actual charges and were adjusted accordingly.

- This adjustment and the resulting figure of total clearing house charges per benchmark clearing member were cross-checked with interviewees from three of the relevant benchmark clearing member firms.

Step 1.4: Calculation of service provider charges, cost of capital, risk management costs, IT costs and back-office costs per clearing member:

- Based on the findings regarding the composition of the all-in clearing costs for the six benchmark clearers (refer to Figure 5.5) and the amount of the total clearing house charges per benchmark clearing member as derived in steps 1.1 to 1.3, estimates for the remaining cost categories were calculated.

Step 2: Calculation of total costs for the remaining 213 European clearing members:

The basis for the following calculation is presented in Figure 2.19, i.e. the assumptions regarding the average market share distribution of low, medium and high volume European clearing member types.[3] Based on the insight provided by the analysis of the benchmark clearing members and publicly available lists of clearing members of the different European clearing houses, the residual 213 European clearing members (i.e. the total of 219 European clearing members minus the six benchmark clearing members) and the composition of their all-in clearing costs were subdivided as follows:[4]

European clearers (213)	Low Volume		Medium Volume			High Volume		
No. of clearers per category	137		63			13		
Type	LOW1	LOW2	MED1	MED2	MED3	HIGH1	HIGH2	HIGH3
No. of clearers per subdivision	113	24	19	22	22	7	3	3
DIRECT COSTS	15%	18%	18%	25%	40%	50%	50%	60%
Clearing house charges	5%	10%	10%	15%	25%	30%	40%	50%
Service provider charges	10%	8%	8%	10%	15%	20%	10%	10%
INDIRECT COSTS	85%	82%	82%	75%	60%	50%	50%	40%
Cost of capital	10%	5%	5%	5%	5%	5%	3%	5%
Risk mgmt. costs	5%	5%	5%	5%	5%	2%	2%	5%
IT costs	30%	36%	34%	32%	30%	18%	20%	15%
Back-office costs	40%	36%	38%	33%	20%	25%	25%	15%

Step 2.1: Calculation of fixed costs per clearing member type:

- Low volume clearers were assumed to be a member of only a single European clearing house, their domestic home CCP. Medium and high volume clearers were defined as being active

[3] The total number of European clearing members is based on publicly available information on clearing members of Eurex Clearing, LCH.Clearnet, OMX, MEFF and CC&G. Note that institutions are counted and not legal entities. Refer to section 2.5.1 for details.

[4] With regard to the archetypical cost structure of different clearing member types in Europe, it should be noted that the underlying insight on the cost structure of European benchmark clearing members is biased towards high volume clearers (Figure 5.5). Of the six benchmark clearers, four were high volume clearing members, one was a low volume clearer and one was a medium volume clearer.

at all of the European clearing houses and thus assumed to be direct members of Eurex Clearing, LCH.Clearnet, OMX, MEFF and CC&G.

- Note that in section 2.3, regionally-to-globally active clearers were defined as being active (or interested in becoming active) in many markets. They were assumed to maintain a single direct clearing relationship, which is with their domestic clearing house. To clear their transactions in the other (foreign) markets, these members were defined as utilising one or several other GCMs as clearing intermediaries. Due to the lack of publicly available data and the complexities of including the costs associated with these intermediary relationships, the medium volume clearers were assumed to be direct members of Eurex Clearing, LCH.Clearnet, OMX, MEFF and CC&G. This approach was also helpful in exploring the dynamics that gave rise to the structural particularities (see section 2.5.1) of the European Value Provision Network.

- Based on the results of the fixed cost calculation for the six benchmark clearing members, and with reference to the archetypes of European clearing members outlined above, the fixed costs per clearing member type (LOW1, LOW2, MED1, MED2, MED3, HIGH1, HIGH2, HIGH3) were calculated.

Step 2.2: Calculation of variable clearing house charges per clearing member type:

- Drawing upon the results of the variable cost calculation for the six benchmark clearing members, and with reference to the archetypes of European clearing members outlined above, the fixed costs per clearing member type (LOW1, LOW2, MED1, MED2, MED3, HIGH1, HIGH2 and HIGH3) were calculated.

Step 2.3: Calculation of total clearing house charges per clearing member type:

- Summarising the fixed charges and the variable clearing house charges resulted (prior to adjustment) in the total clearing house charges per clearing member type.

- To account for discrepancies resulting from: (i) having had to leave out OMX clearing house charges (due to unavailability); (ii) the artificial fee split between trading and clearing fees at Eurex; and (iii) setting fixed costs of a clearing membership at LCH.Clearnet roughly equal to the fixed charges incurred by a clearing member at Eurex Clearing, the total clearing house charges per relevant benchmark clearing member were assumed to represent merely 70 or 80 per cent of the actual charges and were adjusted accordingly.

Step 2.4: Calculation of service provider charges, cost of capital, risk management costs, IT costs and back-office costs per clearing member type:

- Based on the assumptions regarding the composition of the all-in clearing costs for the remaining 213 European clearers and the amount of the total clearing house charges per clearing member type (as derived in the previous steps), the amounts for the remaining cost categories per clearing member type were calculated.

Step 3: Calculation of total European derivatives clearing costs

- Combining the sums derived in steps 1 and 2 provided the total European derivatives clearing costs in 2005, as shown in Figure 5.13.

- The resulting sum was compared to the aggregate of the revenues of Eurex Clearing, LCH.Clearnet, OMX, MEFF and CC&G in 2005. The two figures seem to be in line, although the comparison is hampered by the limited availability of 'true' revenue figures from the clearing houses. Accounting differences, bookings within a group company structure and other discrepancies impede comparison.[5] In addition, the clearing house charges for connectivity/technical fees do not necessarily represent revenues for the CCPs if they themselves have to rent or lease the lines and connectivity services.

To summarise, the calculation of the total European derivatives clearing costs in 2005 was based on a number of sensitive assumptions:

- The cost structure assessment was based on the information provided by the six benchmark clearing members. This information is biased towards the data provided by the four high volume clearers. Consequently, the assessment of the archetypical cost structure for various low and medium volume clearing members in Europe is highly sensitive.
- In order to determine the 'rest volume' charges, the fact that in reality clearing fees charged for other exchange-traded derivatives products may vary from those charged for the selected benchmark products was neglected here.
- To account for discrepancies resulting from: (i) having had to leave out OMX clearing house charges (due to unavailability); (ii) the artificial fee split between trading and clearing fees at Eurex; and (iii) setting fixed costs of a clearing membership at LCH.Clearnet roughly equal to the fixed charges incurred by a clearing member at Eurex Clearing, the total clearing house charges per benchmark clearing member were assumed to represent merely 70 or 80 per cent of the actual charges and were adjusted accordingly.
- Clearing house fees charged in currencies other than the euro were converted according to exchange rates valid in December 2005.

---

[5] Lannoo/Levin (2001) encounter similar difficulties in measuring operating costs of settlement institutions. Refer to Lannoo/Levin (2001), p. 17 for details.

Appendix 8

Efficiency impact of clearing links and a Single CCP

The calculation of the efficiency impact of European clearing links and a single European CCP was based on the results and method of calculation outlined in Appendix 7, including the respective assumptions regarding the Value Provision Network, the structure of the European clearing industry and the composition of all-in costs of the six benchmark clearing members and the remaining 213 European clearers. The main caveat concerning the calculation relates to the following sensitive assumptions:

- The calculation of the efficiency impact was based on assumptions regarding the impact of network strategies on fixed clearing house charges. These assumptions were in turn based on the conclusions derived in Chapters 7 and 8.
- The calculation was built on the status quo of the cost structures for the benchmark clearing members and the remaining 213 European clearers, as classified in Appendix 7. This assumption was due to a lack of data that would have allowed for an accurate assessment regarding the changes in the composition of the all-in clearing costs due to these network strategies.

European clearing links:

Low volume clearers:

- The total fixed clearing house charges for European low volume clearers, as derived in Appendix 7, were used as a basis for this calculation.
- Low volume clearers were assumed to be a member of only one European clearing house, their domestic home CCP. For the purpose of this analysis, they were thus assumed to be direct members of either Eurex Clearing, LCH.Clearnet, OMX, MEFF or CC&G. This assumption was based on publicly available information regarding the list of clearing members of the different European clearing houses.
- It was further assumed that European clearing links foster competition between European CCPs. Fixed clearing house charges, including membership fees and connectivity/technical fees (such as line fees, charges for clearing working stations and other IT equipment where applicable), would therefore be subject to competitive forces. Low volume clearers would benefit from the competition, as the fixed clearing house fees charged by their home country CCP would be reduced.
- These competitive forces were assumed to be most likely to affect Europe's two major clearing houses, Eurex Clearing and LCH.Clearnet.

- Fixed clearing house charges for Eurex Clearing and LCH.Clearnet (under the assumption of implemented European clearing links) were therefore assumed to be the average of current fixed clearing house charges at Eurex Clearing, LCH.Clearnet, OMX, MEFF and CC&G.
- Reductions of variable clearing house charges were not accounted for.
- Based on the resulting figure of total clearing house charges per clearing member type, figures for the remaining cost categories per low volume clearing member type were calculated.

Medium volume clearers:

- The total fixed clearing house charges for European medium volume clearers, as derived in Appendix 7, were used as a basis for this calculation.
- In this study, medium volume clearers were defined as being active at all of the European clearing houses, i.e. assumed to be direct members of Eurex Clearing, LCH.Clearnet, OMX, MEFF and CC&G.
- Medium volume clearers were nonetheless assumed to have a preference for utilising their original domestic home clearing house as their central gateway for access to the markets cleared by Eurex Clearing, LCH.Clearnet, OMX, MEFF and CC&G. The assumption of which clearing member would consequently choose which clearing house was based on publicly available information regarding the list of clearing members of the different European clearing houses.
- It was further assumed that European clearing links foster competition between European CCPs. Fixed clearing house charges, including membership fees and connectivity/technical fees (such as line fees, charges for clearing working stations and other IT equipment where applicable), were therefore assumed to be subject to competitive forces. Medium volume clearers would benefit from the competition, as the fixed clearing house fees charged by their home country CCP would be reduced.
- These competitive forces were assumed to be most likely to affect (in the first place) Europe's two major clearing houses, Eurex Clearing and LCH.Clearnet.
- Fixed clearing house charges for Eurex Clearing and LCH.Clearnet (under the assumption of implemented European clearing links) were therefore assumed to be the average of current fixed clearing house charges at Eurex Clearing, LCH.Clearnet, OMX, MEFF and CC&G.
- Reductions of variable clearing house charges were not accounted for.
- Based on the resulting figure of total clearing house charges per clearing member type, figures for the remaining cost categories per medium volume clearing member type were calculated.

High volume clearers:

- The total fixed clearing house charges for European high volume clearers, as derived in Appendix 7, were used as a basis for this calculation.
- In this study, high volume clearers were defined as being active at all of the European clearing houses, i.e. assumed to be direct members of Eurex Clearing, LCH.Clearnet, OMX, MEFF and CC&G.
- In contrast to medium volume clearers, high volume clearers were not necessarily assumed to have a preference for utilising their original home country clearing house as their central clearing house for access to the markets cleared by Eurex Clearing, LCH.Clearnet, OMX, MEFF and CC&G.

- For the purpose of this calculation, these clearers were instead assumed to have based their decision on various factors, including the clearing houses' fixed costs, service levels, technical and risk management standards, etc. It was thus not assumed that high volume clearers would automatically select the European CCP with the lowest fixed charges as their central clearing provider.
- It was further assumed that European clearing links foster competition between European CCPs. Fixed clearing house charges, including membership fees and connectivity/technical fees (such as line fees, charges for clearing working stations and other IT equipment where applicable), were therefore considered subject to competitive forces. High volume clearers would benefit from the competition, as the fixed clearing house fees charged by their home country CCP would be reduced.
- Fixed clearing house charges for high volume clearers (under the assumption of implemented European clearing links) were therefore assumed to be the average of current fixed clearing house charges at Eurex Clearing, LCH.Clearnet, OMX, MEFF and CC&G.
- Reductions of variable clearing house charges were not accounted for.
- Based on the resulting figure of total clearing house charges per clearing member type, figures for the remaining cost categories per high volume clearing member type were calculated.

Calculation of total European derivatives clearing costs:

- The total costs for low, medium and high volume clearers were combined to produce the results outlined in Figures 9.2 and 9.3, which present the total European derivatives clearing costs in 2005 under the assumption of implemented European clearing links.

Single European CCP:

Low volume clearers:

- The total fixed clearing house charges for European low volume clearers, as derived in Appendix 7, were used as a basis for this calculation.
- For the purpose of this study, participation in the Single CCP was assumed to be obligatory and only one clearing system was assumed to have 'survived'.
- Given that LCH.Clearnet and Eurex Clearing are Europe's two largest clearing houses, it seemed reasonable to assume that one of their clearing systems would prevail in case of creating a Single European CCP through M&A initiatives between Eurex Clearing, LCH.Clearnet, OMX, MEFF and CC&G.
- The hypothetical Single CCP's fixed clearing house fees (including membership fees and connectivity/technical fees, e.g. line fees, charges for clearing working stations and other IT equipment) for the various clearing member types were set equal to those charged by Eurex Clearing/LCH.Clearnet prior to the establishment of the Single CCP network. Due to the monopolistic nature of this initiative, these fixed charges were not assumed to be subject to competitive forces.
- For the purpose of this study, it was assumed that fixed costs related to a clearing membership at LCH.Clearnet were roughly equal to those charged by Eurex Clearing.
- All European low volume clearers were thus assumed to incur the fixed clearing house charges related to a membership at Eurex Clearing/LCH.Clearnet, which implied a cost increase for a number of clearers.
- Reductions of variable clearing house charges were not accounted for.
- Based on the resulting figure of total clearing house charges per clearing member type, figures for the remaining cost categories per low volume clearing member type were calculated.

Medium volume clearers:

- The total fixed clearing house charges for European medium volume clearers, as derived in Appendix 7, were used as a basis for this calculation.
- For the purpose of this study, participation in the Single CCP was assumed to be obligatory and only one clearing system was assumed to have 'survived'.
- Given that LCH.Clearnet and Eurex Clearing are Europe's two largest clearing houses, it seemed reasonable to assume that one of their clearing systems would prevail.
- The hypothetical Single CCP's fixed clearing house fees (including membership fees and connectivity/technical fees, e.g. line fees, charges for clearing working stations and other IT equipment) for the various clearing member types were set equal to those charged by Eurex Clearing/LCH.Clearnet prior to the establishment of the Single CCP network. Due to the monopolistic nature of this initiative, these fixed charges were not assumed to be subject to competitive forces.
- For the purpose of this study, it was assumed that fixed costs related to a clearing membership at LCH.Clearnet were roughly equal to those charged by Eurex Clearing.
- In this study, medium volume clearers were defined as being active at all of the European clearing houses, i.e. assumed to be direct members of Eurex Clearing, LCH.Clearnet, OMX, MEFF and CC&G.
- Medium volume clearers were nonetheless assumed to have a preference for utilising their original domestic home clearing house as their gateway to access the markets cleared by Eurex Clearing, LCH.Clearnet, OMX, MEFF and CC&G. Under the assumed scenario of a Single CCP, clearing members would have no choice of clearing house.
- All European medium volume clearers were thus assumed to incur the fixed clearing house charges related to a membership at Eurex Clearing/LCH.Clearnet, which could imply a suboptimal solution for a number of medium volume clearers.
- Reductions of variable clearing house charges were not accounted for.
- Based on the resulting figure of total clearing house charges per clearing member type, figures for the remaining cost categories per medium volume clearing member type were calculated.

High volume clearers:

- The total fixed clearing house charges for European high volume clearers, as derived in Appendix 7, were used as a basis for this calculation.
- For the purpose of this study, participation in the Single CCP was assumed to be obligatory and only one clearing system was assumed to have 'survived'.
- Given that LCH.Clearnet and Eurex Clearing are Europe's two largest clearing houses, it seemed reasonable to assume that one of their clearing systems would prevail.
- The hypothetical Single CCP's fixed clearing house fees (including membership fees and connectivity/technical fees, e.g. line fees, charges for clearing working stations and other IT equipment) for the various clearing member types were set equal to those charged by Eurex Clearing/LCH.Clearnet prior to the establishment of the Single CCP network. Due to the monopolistic nature of this initiative, these fixed charges were not assumed to be subject to competitive forces.
- For the purpose of this study, it was assumed that fixed costs related to a clearing membership at LCH.Clearnet were roughly equal to those charged by Eurex Clearing.

- In this study, high volume clearers were defined as being active at all of the European clearing houses, i.e. assumed to be direct members of Eurex Clearing, LCH.Clearnet, OMX, MEFF and CC&G.
- High volume clearers were assumed not to have a preference for utilising their original home country clearing house as their central clearing house for access to the markets cleared by Eurex Clearing, LCH.Clearnet, OMX, MEFF and CC&G.
- For the purpose of this calculation, these clearers were instead assumed to have based their decision on various factors, including the clearing houses' fixed costs, service levels, technical and risk management standards, etc. It was thus not assumed that high volume clearers would automatically select the European CCP with the lowest fixed charges as their central clearing provider.
- All European high volume clearers were thus assumed to incur the fixed clearing house charges related to a membership at Eurex Clearing/LCH.Clearnet, which could imply a suboptimal solution for a number of high volume clearers.
- Reductions of variable clearing house charges were not accounted for.
- Based on the resulting figure of total clearing house charges per clearing member type, figures for the remaining cost categories per high volume clearing member type were calculated.

Calculation of total European derivatives clearing costs:

- The total costs for low, medium and high volume clearers are shown in Figures 9.4 and 9.5, which present the total European derivatives clearing costs in 2005 that would have occurred under the assumption of an implemented European Single CCP.

In summary, the calculation of the efficiency impact of European clearing links and a single European CCP falls short of reflecting the full scope of changes in the composition of the all-in clearing costs that could be expected to occur under a European clearing link or a single European CCP initiative. Taking all of these potential changes into account would certainly affect the magnitude of the resulting efficiency impact. Furthermore, although the calculation of the overall efficiency impact is based on the identified changes in fixed clearing house charges, both network initiatives could in reality also lead to reductions of variable clearing house charges, which would translate into an even greater impact on efficiency.

Bibliography

Accenture (ed.) (2001): 'Leaving Safe Havens: The Accelerating Evolution of the European Exchange Landscape', White Paper, Sulzbach/Frankfurt a.M. 2001.

Achleitner, Ann-Kristin (2001): *Handbuch investment banking*, 2nd edition, Wiesbaden 2001.

Adrangi, Bahram/Chatrath, Arjun (1999): 'Margin Requirements and Futures Activity: Evidence from the Soybean and Corn Markets', in: *Journal of Futures Markets*, Vol. 19, No. 4, pp. 433–55.

AFEI *et al.* (eds.) (2006): 'Post-Trading in Europe: Calls for Consolidation', Position Paper, Paris and London, 2006.

AFTI/Eurogroup (eds.) (2002): *Analyse Comparative du Coût des Opérations Titres en Europe et aux USA, et Perspectives d'Évolution*, Paris 2002.

Albach, Horst (2000): *Allgemeine betriebswirtschaftslehre: einführung*, 2nd edition, Wiesbaden 2000.

Allen, Douglas W. (2000): 'Transaction Costs', in: Bouckaert, Boudewijn/De Geest, Gerrit (eds.): *Encyclopedia of Law and Economics*, Vol. I. *The History and Methodology of Law and Economics*, Cheltenham 2000, pp. 893–926.

Annesley, Christian (2006): 'Did Lack of IT Involvement at Outset Doom LCH.Clearnet's Grand Vision?', in: *Computer Weekly*, 18.07.2006, p. 12.

Armstrong, Mark (2006): 'Competition in Two-Sided Markets', in: *Rand Journal of Economics*, Vol. 37, No. 3, pp. 668–91.

Arrow, Kenneth J. (1962): 'The Economics of Learning by Doing', in: *Review of Economic Studies*, Vol. 29, No. 3, pp. 155–73.

Ascarelli, Silvia (2003): 'London Clearing, Clearnet Agree to Merge', in: *Wall Street Journal*, 26.06.2003, p. M1.

Averdiek-Bolwin, Christoph (1998): *Die Effizienz von Aktienbörsen*, Munich 1998.

Aykroyd, Elliott (2005): 'Derivatives Still Driving LCH-C Business', in: *Futures and Options Week*, 21.03.2005, p. 7.

Baetge, Jörg (1975): 'Betriebliche lernprozesse', in: Wittmann, Waldemar/Grochla, Erwin (eds.): *Handwörterbuch der Betriebswirtschaft: Enzyklopädie der Betriebswirtschaftslehre*, No. 1, 4th edn, Stuttgart 1975, pp. 2495–504.

Bain, Joe S. (1956): *Barriers to New Competition: Their Character and Consequences in Manufacturing Industries*, Cambridge 1956.

Bank for International Settlements (ed.) (1989): 'Report on Netting Schemes', Report by the Group of Experts on Payment Systems of the Central Banks of the Group of Ten Countries, Basel 1989.

(1997a): 'Clearing Arrangements for Exchange-Traded Derivatives', Report by the Committee on Payment and Settlement Systems of the Central Banks of the Group of Ten Countries, Basel 1997.

(1997b): 'International Banking and Financial Market Development', Report by the Monetary and Economic Department, Basel 1997.

(1998): 'OTC Derivatives: Settlement Procedures and Counterparty Risk Management', Report by the Committee on Payment and Settlement Systems and the Euro-Currency Standing Committee of the Central Banks of the Group of Ten Countries, Basel 1998.

(2000a): 'Clearing and Settlement Arrangements for Retail Payments in Selected Countries', Report by the Working Group on Retail Payment Systems on behalf of the Committee on Payment and Settlement Systems, Basel 2000.

(2000b): 'Structural and Regulatory Developments', in: *BIS Quarterly Review*, August, pp. 40–45.

(2001): 'Recommendations for Securities Settlement Systems', Report in Cooperation with the Committee on Payment and Settlement Systems and the Technical Committee of the International Organization of Securities Commissions, Basel 2001.

(2004): 'Recommendations for Central Counterparties', Consultative Report by the Committee on Payment and Settlement Systems and the Technical Committee of the International Organization of Securities Commissions, Basel 2004.

(2006): 'International Convergence of Capital Measurement and Capital Standards: A Revised Framework, Comprehensive Version', Report by the Basel Committee on Banking Supervision, Basel 2006.

Bank of New York (ed.) (2004): *The Changing World of Securities Processing in Europe: A Review of the Current Industry Initiatives*, Brussels 2004.

Barnes, Dan (2005): 'A Different Kind of European Union', in: *The Banker*, No. 3, p. 51.

Bates, David S./Craine, Roger (1999): 'Valuing the Futures Market Clearinghouse's Default Exposure During the 1987 Crash', in: *Journal of Money, Credit and Banking*, Vol. 31, No. 2, pp. 248–72.

Bauer, Hans H. (1986): 'Das Erfahrungskurvenkonzept', in: *WiSt, Wirtschaftswissenschaftliches Studium*, Vol. 15, No. 1, pp. 1–10.

Baumol, William J. (1977): 'On the Proper Cost Test for Natural Monopolies in a Multiproduct Industry', in: *American Economic Review*, Vol. 67, pp. 809–22.

Baumol, William J./Blinder, Alan S. (1997): *Microeconomics*, 7th edn, San Diego 1997.

Baumol, William J./Panzar, John C./Willig, Robert D. (1982): *Contestable Markets and the Theory of Industry Structure*, New York 1982.

Baums, Theodor/Cahn, Andreas (eds.) (2006): *Die Zukunft des Clearing und Settlement*, Berlin 2006.

Baur, Dirk (2006): 'Integration and Competition in Securities Trading, Clearing and Settlement', IIIS, University of Dublin, Trinity College and Joint Research Centre European Commission, Research Paper, Dublin/Ispra 2006.

Benston, George J. (1972): 'Economies of Scale in Financial Institutions', in: *Journal of Money, Credit and Banking*, Vol. 4, No. 2, pp. 312–41.

Benston, George J. *et al.* (1983): 'Economies of Scale and Scope in Banking', Board of Governors of the Federal Reserve System, Research Paper, No. 64, Washington D.C. 1983.

Benston, George J./Hanweck, Gerald A./Humphrey, David B. (1982): 'Scale Economies in Banking: A Restructuring and Reassessment', in: *Journal of Money, Credit and Banking*, Vol. 14, No. 4, pp. 435–56.

Berger, Allen N./Demsetz, Rebecca S./Strahan, Philip E. (1999): 'The Consolidation of the Financial Services Industry: Causes, Consequences, and Implications for the Future', in: *Journal of Banking and Finance*, Vol. 23, pp. 135–94.

Berger, Allen N./Hanweck, Gerald A./Humphrey, David B. (1987): 'Competitive Viability in Banking: Scale, Scope, and Product Mix Economies', in: *Journal of Monetary Economics*, Vol. 20, No. 3, pp. 501–20.

Berger, Allen N./Humphrey, David B. (1994): 'Bank Scale Economies, Mergers, Concentration and Efficiency: The US Experience', Wharton Financial Research Institute, Working Paper, No. 25, Philadelphia 1994.

  (1997): 'Efficiency of Financial Institutions: International Survey and Directions for Future Research', Wharton Financial Research Institute, Working Paper, No. 5, Philadelphia 1997.

Berger, Allen N./Hunter, W. C./Timme, S. G. (1993): 'The Efficiency of Financial Institutions: A Review and Preview of Research Past, Present, and Future', in: *Journal of Banking and Finance*, Vol. 17, pp. 221–49.

Berliand, Richard (2006): 'Working Together', in: Eurex (ed.): *Derivatives Outlook 2007*, Frankfurt a.M./Zurich 2006, pp. 26–7.

Bernanke, Ben S. (1990): 'Clearing and Settlement During the Crash', in: *Review of Financial Studies*, Vol. 3, No. 1, pp. 133–51.

Besen, Stanley M./Farrell, Joseph (1994): 'Choosing how to Compete: Strategies and Tactics in Standardization', in: *Journal of Economic Perspectives*, Vol. 8, No. 2, pp. 117–31.

Bessler, Wolfgang (1989): *Zinsrisikomanagement in Kreditinstituten*, Wiesbaden 1989.

  (1991): 'Financial Conglomerates in the United States', in: Krümmel, Hans-Jacob/Rehm, Hannes/Simmert, Diethard B. (eds.): *Allfinanz: Strukturwandel an den Märkten für Finanzdienstleistungen, Beihefte zu Kredit und Kapital*, No. 11, Berlin 1991, pp. 265–98.

Blattner, Niklaus (2003): 'The Financial System and the Regulatory Challenges in Securities Clearing and Settlement Systems', Swiss National Bank, Speech at the 7th Conference of Central Securities Depositories, 12 June, Lucerne 2003.

Bliss, Robert R./Kaufman, George G. (2005): 'Derivatives and Systemic Risk: Netting, Collateral, and Closeout', Federal Reserve Bank of Chicago, Working Paper, No. 3, Chicago 2005.

Bliss, Robert R./Papathanassiou, Chryssa (2006): 'Derivatives Clearing, Central Counterparties and Novation: The Economic Implications', Working Paper, Winston-Salem/Frankfurt a.M. 2006.

Bliss, Robert R./Steigerwald, Robert S. (2006): 'Derivatives Clearing and Settlement: A Comparison of Central Counterparties and Alternative Structures', in: *Economic Perspectives*, Federal Reserve Bank of Chicago, 4Q/06, pp. 22–9.

BNP Paribas Securities Services (ed.) (2005): Response to Directorate General Competition's Invitation to Comment on 'Overview of EU25 Securities Trading, Clearing Central Counterparties and Securities Settlement: An Overview of Current Arrangements', Paris 2005.

Bohr, Kurt (1996): 'Economies of Scale and Scope', in: Kern, Werner/Schröder, Hans-Horst/Weber, Jürgen (eds.): *Handwörterbuch der Produktionswirtschaft: Enzyklopädie der Betriebswirtschaftslehre*, No. 7, 2nd edn, Stuttgart 1996, pp. 375–86.

Book, Thomas (2001): *Elektronischer Börsenhandel und globale Märkte: eine ökonomische Analyse der Veränderungen an Terminbörsen*, Wiesbaden 2001.

Bortenlänger, Christine (1996): *Börsenautomatisierung: Effizienzpotentiale und Durchsetzbarkeit*, Munich 1996.

Bortz, Jürgen/Döring, Nicola (2002): *Forschungsmethoden und Evaluation: für Human- und Sozialwissenschaftler*, 3rd edn, Berlin/Heidelberg/New York 2002.

Bössmann, Eva (1981): 'Weshalb gibt es Unternehmungen?: der Erklärungsansatz von Ronald H. Coase', in: *Zeitschrift für die gesamte Staatswissenschaft*, Vol. 137, No. 4, pp. 667–74.

Bourse Consult (ed.) (2006): The US Exchange World, Online Publication, date of publication: 16.11.2006, retrieved: 16.06.2007, available at: www.bourse-consult.com/Commentaries/5E25CCFA-266C-4796-95C0-5B6295A8D900.html.

Branch, Sonya/Griffiths, Mark (2005): 'Competition Aspects of Clearing and Settlement: Learning the Lessons from the Regulated Industries', Clifford Chance, Commentary, London 2005.

Braunstein, Yale M./White, Lawrence J. (1985): 'Setting Technical Compatibility Standards: An Economic Analysis', in: *The Antitrust Bulletin*, Vol. 30, No. 2, pp. 337–55.

Brealey, Richard A./Myers, Stewart C. (2000): *Principles of Corporate Finance*, 6th edn, Boston *et al.* 2000.

Bressand, Albert/Distler, Catherine (2001): 'When Clearing Matters: CCPs and the Modern Securities Industry's Value Chain', in: Promethee (ed.): *The Central Counterparties Dialogue*, Paris 2001, pp. 4–6.

Bufka, Jürgen/Schiereck, Dirk (1999): 'Risikoadjustierung der Kapitalkosten über die BCG-methode: Überlegungen zur weiterentwicklung pragmatischer Ansätze', in: *ZfB, Zeitschrift für Betriebswirtschaft*, Vol. 69, pp. 1455–61.

Bufka, Jürgen/Schiereck, Dirk/Zinn, Kai (1999): 'Kapitalkostenbestimmung für diversifizierte Unternehmen: ein empirischer Methodenvergleich', in: *ZfB, Zeitschrift für Betriebswirtschaft*, Vol. 69, pp. 115–31.

Burns, Joseph M. (1983): 'Futures Markets and Market Efficiency', in: Streit, Manfred E. (ed.): *Futures Markets: Modelling, Managing and Monitoring Futures Trading*, Oxford 1983, pp. 46–74.

Burns, Mary Ann (2005): 'The FCM Infrastructure Play', in: *Futures Industry Magazine*, November/December, online Publication, retrieved: 04.03.2007, available at: www.futuresindustry.org/fi-magazine-home.asp?a=1079&iss=163.

Burns, Mary Ann/Acworth, Will (2006): 'The FCM Strategy Play', in: *Futures Industry Magazine*, March/April, online Publication, retrieved: 03.01.2007, available at: www.futuresindustry.org/fi-magazine-home.asp?a=1101.

Casey, Jean-Pierre/Lannoo, Karel (2006a): 'The MiFID Implementing Measures: Excessive Detail or Level Playing Field', European Capital Markets Institute, ECMI Policy Brief, No. 1, Brussels 2006.

(2006b): 'The MiFID Revolution', European Capital Markets Institute, ECMI Policy Brief, No. 3, Brussels 2006.

Cebenoyan, A. Sinan (1988): 'Multiproduct Cost Functions and Scale Economies in Banking', in: *Financial Review*, Vol. 23, No. 4, pp. 499–512.

Centre for European Policy Studies (ed.) (2004): 'Regulating Clearing and Settlement in the EU: A CEPS Roundtable', Minutes of the Roundtable Discussion, 24 November, Brussels 2004.

CESAME Group (ed.) (2004): *Mandate for the Advisory and Monitoring Group on EU Clearing and Settlement*, Brussels 2004.

(2006): 'Synthesis Report of the Meeting Held on 12 June', Brussels 2006.

CESR/European Central Bank (eds.) (2004): 'Standards for Securities Clearing and Settlement in the European Union', September Report, Brussels/Frankfurt a.M. 2004.

CFTC (ed.) (09.07.2004): 'CFTC announces Resignation of Chairman James E. Newsome', Press Release, No. 4950–04, Washington D.C. 2004.

Chabert, Dominique/Chanel-Reynaud, Gisèle (2005): 'The Organisation of Securities Clearing and Settlement Infrastructures in Europe', Working Paper, Lyon 2005.

Chabert, Dominique/El Idrissi, Lalla-Sanaâ (2005): 'Competition and Integration of Securities Settlement Infrastructures in Europe: An Approach in Terms of Composite Goods', Working Paper, Lyon 2005.

Chamberlin, Edward H. (1933): *The Theory of Monopolistic Competition*, Cambridge 1933.

Chicago Board of Trade/Eurex (eds.) (24.07.2000): 'CBOT and Eurex Announce Alliance Launch Date', Press Release, Chicago/Frankfurt a.M. 2000.

Chicago Mercantile Exchange (ed.) (2003): 'Annual Report 2002', Chicago 2003.

Church, Jeffrey/Gandal, Neil/Krause, David (2002): 'Indirect Network Effects and Adoption Externalities', Foerder Institute for Economic Research, Working Paper, No. 30, Tel Aviv 2002.

Citigroup (ed.) (2003): 'Creating a Safe and Level Playing Field: White Paper on Issues Relating to Settlement of Securities in Europe', Frankfurt a.M./London 2003.

(2006): 'CCPs: A User's Perspective', Discussion Paper for the Joint Conference of the European Central Bank and the Federal Reserve Bank of Chicago on Issues related to Central Counterparty Clearing, 3–4 April, Frankfurt a.M. 2006.

Claessens, Stijn *et al.* (2003): 'The Growing Importance of Networks in Finance and its Effects on Competition', Working Paper, Amsterdam/Toulouse/Washington D.C. 2003.

Clark, Jeffrey A. (1984): 'Estimation of Economies of Scale in Banking Using a Generalized Functional Form', in: *Journal of Money, Credit and Banking*, Vol. 16, No. 1, pp. 53–68.

Clark, Jeffrey A./Speaker, Paul J. (1994): 'Economies of Scale and Scope in Banking: Evidence from a Generalized Translog Cost Function', in: *Quarterly Journal of Business and Economics*, Vol. 33, pp. 3–25.

Clarke, Michael C./Naumowicz, Dean (1999): *An Introduction to the Legal Aspects of Collateralization*, London/New York 1999.

Coase, Ronald H. (1937): 'The Nature of the Firm', in: *Economia*, Vol. 4, pp. 386–405.

Cohen, Norma (2005): 'Speciality Finance: Deutsche Börse's Bid Highlighted Competition', in: *Financial Times*, 29.03.2005, p. 20.

(2007): 'Turquoise Reality Being Fleshed Out', in: *Financial Times*, 19.04.2007, p. 21.

Collins, Bruce M./Fabozzi, Frank J. (1991): 'A Methodology for Measuring Transaction Costs', in: *Financial Analysts Journal*, Vol. 47, No. 2, pp. 27–44.

Collins, Daniel P. (2003): 'Clearing Brouhaha fuels CBOT/CME Rumours', in: *AllBusiness*, May, online publication, retrieved: 03.04.2007, available at: www.allbusiness.com/human-resources/544852-1.html.

Competition Commission (ed.) (2005): 'Working Paper on Exchanges and Post-Trade Services: An Overview', June, London 2005.

Competition Commission South Africa (ed.) (2001): 'The Competition Commission Approve JSE/SAFEX Merger', Media Release, 30.07.2001, No. 16, Sunnyside 2001.

Congress of the United States, Office of Technology Assessment (ed.) (1990): 'Trading Around the Clock: Global Securities Markets and Information Technology', Background Paper, OTA-BP-CIT-66, Washington D.C. 1990.

CONSOB (ed.) (2004): Annual Meeting with the Financial Market, Speech by Chairman Lamberto Cardia, 7 June, Milan 2004.

Contractor, Farok J./Lorange, Peter (1988): 'Competition vs. Cooperation: A Benefit/Cost Framework for Choosing Between Fully-Owned Investments and Cooperative Relationships', in: *Management International Review*, Special Issue, Vol. 28, pp. 5–18.

Copeland, Thomas E./Weston, John Fred (1998): *Financial Theory and Corporate Policy*, 3rd edn, New York *et al.* 1998.

Corporation of London (ed.) (2005): 'The Future of Clearing and Settlement in Europe', Report by Bourse Consult, City Research Series, No. 7, London 2005.

Corrigan, Gerald E. (1996): 'Payments, Clearance and Settlement Systems: The Systemic Risk Connection', in: Goldman Sachs (ed.): *Symposium on Risk Reduction in Payments, Clearance and Settlement Systems*, 25–26 January, New York 1996, pp. 13–18.

Corsten, Hans (ed.) (2000): *Lexikon der Betriebswirtschaftslehre*, 4th edn, Munich/Vienna 2000.

Cotter, John (2001): 'Margin Exceedences for European Stock Index Futures Using Extreme Value Theory', in: *Journal of Banking and Finance*, Vol. 25, pp. 1475–1502.

Cotter, John/Dowd, Kevin (2005): 'Extreme Spectral Risk Measures: An Application to Futures Clearinghouse Margin Requirements', Working Paper, Dublin/Nottingham 2005.

Coyne, Kevin P./Dye, Renée (1998): 'The Competitive Dynamics of Network-Based Businesses', in: *Harvard Business Review*, January/February, pp. 99–109.

Craig, Philip (2005): 'A Tale of Two Exchanges', in: *Waters Magazine*, online publication, date of publication: 01.11.05, retrieved: 14.05.07, available at: http://db.riskwaters.com/public/showPage.html?page=302798.

Cruickshank, Don (2001): 'Clearing and Settlement: The Barrier to a Pan-European Capital Market, Commentary', in: *International Finance*, Vol. 4, No. 2, pp. 321–333.

Culp, Christopher L. (2002): 'Clearing: A Risk Assessment', in: *Futures Industry Magazine*, July/August, online publication, retrieved: 13.06.2005, available at: www.futuresindustry.org/fi-magazine-home.asp?a=782.

Dale, Richard (1998a): 'Risk Management in US Derivative Clearing Houses', The London Institute of International Banking, Finance and Development Law, Essays in International Financial and Economic Law, No. 14, London 1998.

(1998b): 'Derivatives Clearing Houses: The Regulatory Challenge', in: Ferrarini, Guido A. (ed.): *European Securities Markets: The Investment Services Directive and Beyond*, London/The Hague/Boston 1998, pp. 295–313.

(1998c): 'Risk Management and Public Policy in Payment, Clearing and Settlement Systems', in: *International Finance*, Vol. 1, No. 2, pp. 229–59.

David, Paul A. (1985): 'Clio and the Economics of QWERTY', in: *American Economic Review*, Vol. 75, No. 2, pp. 332–7.

Davidson III, John P. (1996): 'Common Clearing Revisited', in: *Futures Industry Magazine*, April/May, online publication, retrieved: 07.08.2006, available at: www.futuresindustry.org/fi-magazine-home.asp?a=516.

Davison, Laurence (2005): 'Muddy Clearing Waters for Eurex', in: *Futures and Options Week*, 18.04.2005, pp. 10–11.

Day, Theodore E./Lewis, Craig M. (2004): 'Margin Adequacy and Standards: An Analysis of the Crude Oil Futures Market', in: *Journal of Business*, Vol. 77, No. 1, pp. 101–35.

Dempsey, Chip (2006): 'Clearing: How Has it Evolved? What Will the Future Bring?', in: United Nations Conference on Trade and Development/SFOA (eds.): *The World's Commodity Exchanges: Past – Present – Future*, Chêne-Bourg/Geneva 2006, pp. 163–8.

De Téran, Natasha (2007): 'Carbon Sparks Debate on Open Interest: LCH, ICE and European Climate Exchange Row Erupts over Clearing Services', in: *Financial News*, 10.12.2007, p. 33.

Deutsche Börse Group (ed.) (2002): 'Cross-Border Equity Trading, Clearing and Settlement in Europe', White Paper, Frankfurt a.M. 2002.

(10.02.2003): 'Zentraler Kontrahent für Aktien startet am 27. März', Press Release, Frankfurt a.M. 2003.

(2005a): 'The European Post-Trade Market: An Introduction', White Paper, Frankfurt a.M. 2005.

(2005b): 'Annual Report 2004', Frankfurt a.M. 2005.

(2006a): 'Annual Report 2005', Frankfurt a.M. 2006.

(2006b): 'Annual Press Briefing 2006', Frankfurt a.M. 2006.

(2007a): 'Annual Report 2006', Frankfurt a.M. 2007.

(2007b): *MiFID: Best Execution and Market Transparency – Information for Investment Firms*, Frankfurt a.M. 2007.

Devriese, Johan/Mitchell, Janet (2005): 'Liquidity Risk in Securities Settlement', National Bank of Belgium, Working Paper, No. 72, Brussels 2005.

DeWaal, Gary A. (2005a): 'America Must Create a Single Financial Regulator', in: *Financial Times*, online publication, date of publication: 19.05.2005, retrieved: 01.10.2006, available at: www.ft.com/cms/s/0/72edfde0-c804-11d9-9765-00000e2511c8.html.

(2005b): 'Streamlining Regulation', in: *The Washington Times*, online publication, date of publication: 02.08.2005, retrieved: 01.10.2006, available at: www.washingtontimes.com/op-ed/20050801-094053-4581r.htm.

Di Noia, Carmine (2001): 'Competition and Integration Among Stock Exchanges in Europe: Network Effects, Implicit Mergers and Remote Access', in: *European Financial Management*, Vol. 7, pp. 39–72.

Diamond, Douglas W. (1984): 'Financial Intermediation and Delegated Monitoring', in: *Review of Economic Studies*, Vol. 51, No. 3, pp. 393–414.

Dickson, Martin (2003): 'A Long and Winding Road but a Fruitful End', in: *Financial Times*, 26.03.2003, p. 22.

Direction Générale du Trésor et de la Politique Économique (ed.) (2006): 'Economic Challenges in the Integration of Clearing and Settlement Industries in Europe', Diagnostics Prévisions et Analyses Économiques, No. 106, Paris 2006.

Domowitz, Ian (1995): 'Electronic Derivatives Exchanges: Implicit Mergers, Network Externalities and Standardization', in: *Quarterly Review of Economics and Finance*, Vol. 35, No. 2, pp. 163–75.

Domowitz, Ian/Steil, Benn (1999): 'Automation, Trading Costs, and the Structure of the Securities Trading Industry', in: Litan, Robert E./Santomero, Anthony M. (eds.): *Brookings-Wharton Papers on Financial Services*, Washington D.C. 1999, pp. 33–81.

Donald, David C. (2007): *Der Einfluss der Wertpapierabwicklung auf die Ausübung von Aktionärsrechten*, Frankfurt a.M. 2007.

Donohue, Craig S. (2006): 'Efficient Clearing and Settlement Systems: A Case for Market-Driven Solutions', Speech at the 10th European Financial Markets Convention, 8 June, Zurich 2006.

DTCC (ed.) (2000a): 'A White Paper to the Industry on T + 1', New York 2000.

(2000b): 'Central Counterparties: Development, Cooperation and Consolidation, A White Paper to the Industry on the Future of CCPs', London/New York 2000.

(2002): 'GSCC goes live with three Cross-Margining Agreements in 2002', online publication, retrieved: 29.11.2006, available at: www. dtcc.com.

Dyer, Jeffrey H. (1997): 'Effective Interfirm Collaboration: How Firms Minimize Transaction Costs and Maximize Transaction Value', in: *Strategic Management Journal*, Vol. 18, No. 7, pp. 535–56.

EACH (ed.) (2004a): 'Comments of EACH on the CPSS-IOSCO Recommendations for Central Counterparties', Public Letter sent to CPSS-IOSCO Task Force on Securities Settlements Systems, 9 June, Zurich 2004.

(2004b): 'Comments of EACH on Communication from the Commission to the Council and the European Parliament "Clearing and Settlement in the European Union"', COM(2004)312, Public Letter sent to European Commission, 30 July, Zurich 2004.

(2004c): 'Functional Definition of a Central Counterparty Clearing House', Position Paper, Zurich 2004.

Economides, Nicholas (1993): 'Network Economics with Application to Finance', in: *Financial Markets, Institutions and Instruments*, Vol. 2, No. 5, pp. 89–97.

(1996): 'The Economics of Networks', in: *International Journal of Industrial Organisation*, Vol. 14, No. 2, pp. 673–99.

Economides, Nicholas/Himmelberg, Charles (1994): 'Critical Mass and Network Evolution in Telecommunications', Working Paper, New York 1994.

Economides, Nicholas/Salop, Steven C. (1992): 'Competition and Integration Among Complements, and Network Market Structure', in: *Journal of Industrial Economics*, Vol. XL, No. 1, pp. 105–23.

Economides, Nicholas/Siow, Aloysius (1988): 'The Division of Markets is Limited by the Extent of Liquidity', in: *American Economic Review*, Vol. 78, No. 1, pp. 108–21.

Economides, Nicholas/White, Lawrence J. (1994): 'One-Way Networks, Two-Way Networks, Compatibility, and Public Policy', Working Paper, New York 1994.

Edwards, Franklin R. (1981): 'The Regulation of Futures Markets: A Conceptual Framework', in: *Journal of Futures Markets*, Vol. 1, Supplement, pp. 417–40.

(1983): 'The Clearing Association in Futures Markets: Guarantor and Regulator', in: *Journal of Futures Markets*, Vol. 3, No. 4, pp. 369–92.

Edwards, Franklin R./Neftci, Salih N. (1988): 'Extreme Price Movements and Margin Levels in Futures Markets', in: *Journal of Futures Markets*, Vol. 8, No. 6, pp. 639–55.

Eisenbeis, Robert A. (1997): 'International Settlements: A New Source of Systemic Risk?', in: *Economic Review*, Federal Reserve Bank of Atlanta, Second Quarter, pp. 44–50.

Eurex (ed.) (10.01.2003): 'Eurex to Launch US Exchange', Frankfurt a.M./Zurich 2003.

(2003a): *Quick Reference Guide Clearing*, Frankfurt a.M./Zurich 2003.

(2003b): *Clearing: Risk Based Margining*, Frankfurt a.M./Zurich 2003.

(2004): 'The Launch of Eurex US: A Vital Step in Building the Global Liquidity Network', Press Conference, 9 February, Chicago/Frankfurt a.M./Zurich 2004.

(2006): *Many Markets: One Clearing House*, Frankfurt a.M./Zurich 2006.

(2007a): 'Eurex Technology Roadmap', Presentation, Frankfurt a.M./ Zurich 2007.

(2007b): *Eurex Monthly Statistics: Derivatives Market October 2007*, Frankfurt a.M./Zurich 2007.

Eurex/Man Group (eds.) (27.07.2006): Media Release of Man Group plc and Eurex, Frankfurt a.M./Zurich/London 2006.

Eurex/The Clearing Corporation (eds.) (27.05.2003): 'Eurex and Board of Trade Clearing Corporation to Create Global Clearing Solution', Press Release, Frankfurt a.M./Zurich/Chicago 2003.

(04.09.2003a): 'The Clearing Corporation and Eurex Form First Global Clearing Partnership', Presentation at the Joint Press Conference, Buergenstock *et al.* 2003.

(04.09.2003b): 'Partnership Deal Signed between The Clearing Corporation and Eurex', Press Release, Frankfurt a.M./Zurich/Chicago 2003.

(16.12.2003): 'The Clearing Corporation and Eurex Clearing Finalize Details of Global Clearing Link', Press Release, Frankfurt a.M./Zurich/Chicago 2003.

(04.05.2004): 'CCorp and Eurex Clearing Finalize Terms of Global Clearing Link', Press Release, Frankfurt a.M./Zurich/ Chicago 2004.

(28.10.2004): 'Eurex and CCorp to Immediately Roll Out Phase I of the Global Clearing Link', Press Release, Frankfurt a.M./Zurich/Chicago 2004.

(2004a): *Global Clearing Link: Conceptual Overview*, Frankfurt a.M./Zurich/Chicago 2004.

(2004b): 'Global Clearing Link Overview Presentation: Concepts and Benefits', Delivered to Operations Task Force, 26 March, Frankfurt a.M./Zurich/Chicago 2004.

Euroclear (ed.) (2003): *Delivering Low-Cost Cross-Border Settlement*, Brussels 2003.

Euronext (ed.) (2003): 'LCH.Clearnet: Europe's Leading Independent Group of Central Counterparty Clearing Houses', Analyst Presentation, 25 June, London/Paris 2003.

(2004): 'Response to the European Commission Invitation to Comment on the "Overview of EU25 Securities Trading, Clearing Central Counterparties and Securities Settlement: An Overview of Current Arrangements"', Paris 2004.

(2005): 'Comments on the Further Remedy Option Regarding Interoperability of Central Counterparties', London/Paris 2005.

European Banking Federation (ed.) (2004): 'Response to the Commission's Communication on the London Economics Paper', Enclosure to Letter No. 0809, Brussels 2004.

European Central Bank (ed.) (2001a): *Payment and Securities Settlement Systems in the European Union*, Blue Book, Frankfurt a.M. 2001.

(2001b): 'Die Rolle Zentraler Kontrahenten bei der Konsolidierung der Wertpapierabwicklung', in: *ECB Monthly Report*, August, Frankfurt a.M. 2001, pp. 77–87.

(2001c): 'The Eurosystem's Policy Line with Regard to Consolidation in Central Counterparty Clearing', Position Paper, Frankfurt a.M. 2001.

(2002): 'Consolidation in the European Securities Infrastructure: What is Needed?', Speech of Sirkka Hämäläinen, Member of the ECB's Executive Board, Launch of the ECB-CFS Research Network Workshop on Capital Markets and Financial Integration in Europe, 30 April, Frankfurt a.M. 2002.

European Commission (ed.) (2002a): 'Commission Communication on Clearing and Settlement: Summary of Responses', Brussels 2002.

(2002b): 'Clearing and Settlement in the European Union: Main Policy Issues and Future Challenges, Commission Consults on Clearing and Settlement', Consultation Document, 28 May, Brussels 2002.

(28.04.2004): 'Securities Trading: Commission Sets Out its Strategy and Priorities for Clearing and Settlement', Press Release, Brussels 2004.

(2004): 'Clearing and Settlement in the European Union: The Way Forward', COM(2004)312, Brussels 2004.

(2005): 'Report on Definitions', CESAME Group Meeting, 24 October, Brussels 2005.

(02.11.2006): 'Clearing and Settlement: Commissioner McCreevy Welcomes Industry's New Code of Conduct', Press Release, Brussels 2006.

(07.11.2006): 'Note on the Forthcoming Study on the Development of a Methodology to Monitor the Evolution of Prices, Costs and Volumes', Brussels 2006.

(2006a): 'Draft Working Document on Post-Trading', Brussels 2006.

(2006b): 'Annex 1 to Draft Working Document on Post-Trading: Analysis of Studies Examining European Post-Trading Costs', Working Document, Brussels 2006.

(2006c): 'Competition in EU Securities Trading and Post-Trading: Issues Paper', Working Document, Brussels 2006.

(2006d): 'Update on Definitions', CESAME Group Meeting, 12 June, Brussels 2006.

(2006e): 'Monitoring the Evolution of Prices, Costs and Volumes of Post-Trading Activities, Note on the Forthcoming Study on the Development of a Methodology to Monitor the Evolution of Prices, Costs and Volumes', Brussels 2006.

(02.08.2007): 'Cover Note on the Publication of a Methodology for Monitoring the Evolution of Trading and Post-Trading Prices, Costs and Volumes', Brussels 2007.

(2007): 'Fourth Meeting of the Monitoring Group, Code of Conduct on Clearing and Settlement, Report of the Meeting on 10 October', MOG/4/2007, Brussels 2007.

European Financial Services Round Table (ed.) (2003): 'Securities Clearing and Settlement in Europe', Position Paper, Brussels 2003.

European Parliamentary Financial Services Forum (ed.) (2006): 'Unblocking the Plumbing: Clearing and Settlement', Briefing Notes Prepared by the Industry Advisory Committee to the European Parliamentary Financial Services Forum, Brussels 2006.

European Securities Forum (ed.) (2000): *EuroCCP: ESF's Blueprint for a Single Pan-European Central Counterparty*, Frankfurt a.M./London 2000.

(2002): 'Contribution to the Joint CESR/ECB Consultation on Clearing and Settlement', Position Paper, London 2002.

Falvey, James M./Kleit, Andrew N. (2006): 'Commodity Exchanges and Antitrust', Working Paper, Berkeley 2006.

Fama, Eugene F. (1970): 'Efficient Capital Markets: A Review of Theory and Empirical Work', in: *Journal of Finance*, Vol. 25, No. 2, pp. 383–417.

(1976): *Foundations of Finance: Portfolio Decisions and Securities Prices*, New York 1976.

(1991): 'Efficient Capital Markets II', in: *Journal of Finance*, Vol. 46, No. 5, pp. 1575–617.

Farrell, Joseph/Saloner, Garth (1985): 'Standardization, Compatibility, and Innovation', in: *Rand Journal of Economics*, Vol. 16, No. 1, pp. 70–83.

(1986): 'Installed Base and Compatibility: Innovation, Product Preannouncements, and Predation', in: *American Economic Review*, Vol. 76, no. 5, pp. 940–55.

FAZ (ed.) (02.07.2003): 'London kämpft um Clearing-Lösung', in: *Frankfurter Allgemeine Zeitung*, p. 22.

Federation of European Securities Exchanges (ed.) (2004): 'Comments on the Commission Communication on Clearing and Settlement in the European Union', COM(2004)0312, Brussels 2004.

Fenn, George W./Kupiec, Paul H. (1993): 'Prudential Margin Policy in a Futures-Style Settlement System', in: *Journal of Futures Markets*, Vol. 13, No. 4, pp. 389–408.

Ferscha, Rudolf W./Potthoff, Volker (2002): 'Aufbruch in eine neue Industriekultur: im ersten Quartal 2003 startet der zentrale Kontrahent für den Kassamarkt', in: *Börsen-Zeitung*, 26.06.2002, No. 120, p. 5.

FESE/EACH/ECSDA (eds.) (2006): *European Code of Conduct for Clearing and Settlement*, Brussels *et al.* 2006.

Figlewski, Stephen (1984): 'Margins and Market Integrity: Margin Setting for Stock Index Futures and Options', in: *Journal of Futures Markets*, Vol. 4, No. 3, pp. 385–416.

Financial Services Authority (ed.) (2006): *Assessment of LCH.Clearnet Limited Against the CPSS-IOSCO Recommendations for Central Counterparties*, London 2006.

Fischer, Marc (1992): 'Der Transaktionskostenansatz und vertikale Integration', University of Frankfurt, Working Paper, No. 4, Frankfurt a.M. 1992.

Fishe, Raymond P. H./Goldberg, Lawrence G. (1986): 'The Effects of Margins on Trading in Futures Markets', in: *Journal of Futures Markets*, Vol. 6, No. 2, pp. 261–71.

FOW (ed.) (2001): *World Clearing Houses for Exchange Traded and OTC Products*, London 2001.

(2003): *World Clearing Houses for Exchange Traded and OTC Products*, London 2003.

(2006): *The World's Central Counterparty Organisations for Securities and Derivatives Clearing*, London 2006.

Francis, Jack C. (1976): *Investments: Analysis and Management*, 2nd edn, New York 1976.

Friedrichs, Jürgen (1990): *Methoden empirischer Sozialforschung*, 14th edn, Opladen 1990.

Friend, Irwin (1966): 'Broad Implications of the SEC Special Study', in: *Journal of Finance*, Vol. 21, No. 2, pp. 324–32.

(1972): 'The Economic Consequences of the Stock Market', in: *American Economic Review*, Vol. 62, No. 1/2, pp. 212–19.

Fuß, Carolin (2007): *The Impact of Outsourcing on Banking Efficiency: Empirical Evidence from the US Banking Industry*, Hamburg 2007.

García, Alejandro/Gençay, Ramo (2006): 'Valuation of Collateral in Securities Settlement Systems for Extreme Market Events', Discussion Paper, Ottawa/Burnaby 2006.

Gaughan, Patrick A. (2002): *Mergers, Acquisitions and Corporate Restructurings*, 3rd edn, New York 2002.

Gay, Gerald D./Hunter, William C./Kolb, Robert W. (1986): 'A Comparative Analysis of Futures Contract Margins', in: *Journal of Futures Markets*, Vol. 6, No. 2, pp. 307–24.

Geiger, Albert M. (2000): *Konsolidierung der europäischen Börsenlandschaft am Beispiel der Eurex*, Oestrich-Winkel 2000.

Gemmill, Gordon (1994): 'Margins and the Safety of Clearing Houses', in: *Journal of Banking and Finance*, Vol. 18, No. 5, pp. 979–96.

Gerke, Wolfgang/Rapp, Heinz-Werner (1994): 'Strukturveränderungen im internationalen Börsenwesen', in: *Die Betriebswirtschaft*, Vol. 54, No. 1, pp. 5–23.

Giddy, Ian/Saunders, Anthony/Walter, Ingo (1996): 'Alternative Models for Clearance and Settlement: The Case of the Single European Market', in: *Journal of Money, Credit and Banking*, Vol. 28, No. 4, pp. 986–1000.

Gidel, Susan A. (2000): 'Clearing the Deck', in: *Futures Industry Magazine*, June/July, online publication, retrieved: 07.05.2007, available at: www.futuresindustry.org/fi-magazine-home.asp?v=p&a=646.

Giordano, Francesco (2002): 'Cross-Border Trading in Financial Securities in Europe: The Role of Central Counterparty', ECMI Short Paper, No. 3, Brussels 2002.

Giovannini Group (ed.) (2001): *Cross-Border Clearing and Settlement Arrangements in the European Union*, Brussels 2001.

   (2003): *Second Report on EU Clearing and Settlement Arrangements*, Brussels 2003.

Gizycki, Marianne/Gray, Brian (1994): 'Default Risk and Derivatives: An Empirical Analysis of Bilateral Netting', Bank Supervision Department, Reserve Bank of Australia, Discussion Paper, No. 9409, Sydney 1994.

Goldberg, Linda *et al.* (2002): *Securities Trading and Settlement in Europe: Issues and Outlook*, Current Issues in Economics and Finance, Federal Reserve Bank of New York, New York 2002.

Gomber, Peter (2000): *Elektronische handelssysteme: innovative konzepte und technologien im wertpapierhandel*, Heidelberg 2000.

Gomber, Peter/Schweickert, Uwe (2002): 'Der Market Impact: Liquiditätsmaß im elektronischen Wertpapierhandel', in: *Die Bank*, No. 7, pp. 485–9.

Grant, Jeremy (2005): 'Futures Brokers Seek to Slash Clearing Costs', in: *Financial Times*, 28.03.2005, p. 16.

Grant, Robert M. (1998): *Contemporary Strategy Analysis: Concepts, Techniques, Applications*, 3rd edn, Cambridge 1998.

Grass, Doris/Davis, Paul (2003): 'Europäische Clearinghäuser fusionieren', in: *Financial Times Deutschland*, 26.06.2003, p. 19.

Green, Edward J. (1997): 'Money and Debt in the Structure of Payments', in: *Bank of Japan Monetary and Economic Studies*, Vol. 15, No. 1, pp. 63–87.

   (2000): 'Clearing and Settling Financial Transactions, Circa 2000', Paper presented at The Federal Reserve Bank of Atlanta '2000 Financial Markets Conference', 15–17 October, Chicago 2000.

Gröhn, Andreas (1999): *Netzwerkeffekte und Wettbewerbspolitik: eine ökonomische Analyse des Softwaremarktes*, Tübingen 1999.

Gropper, Daniel M. (1991): 'An Empirical Investigation of Changes in Scale Economies for the Commercial Banking Firm, 1979–1986', in: *Journal of Money, Credit and Banking*, Vol. 23, No. 4, pp. 718–27.

Group of Thirty (ed.) (2003): *Clearing and Settlement: A Plan of Action*, Washington D.C. 2003.

(2005): *Global Clearing and Settlement: A Plan of Action – Interim Report of Progress*, April, Washington D.C. 2005.

Guadamillas, Mario/Keppler, Robert (2001): 'Securities Clearance and Settlement Systems', World Bank, Policy Research Working Paper, No. 2581, Washington D.C. 2001.

Gutenberg, Erich (1983): *Grundlagen der Betriebswirtschaftslehre – erster Band: die Produktion*, 24th edn, Berlin/Heidelberg/New York 1983.

Hachmeister, Alexandra/Schiereck, Dirk (2006): 'The Impact of Post-Trade Anonymity on Liquidity and Informed Trading: Evidence from the Introduction of the Xetra Central Counterparty', European Business School, Working Paper, No. 11, Frankfurt a.M. 2006.

Hagermann, Robert L. (1973): 'The Efficiency of the Market for Bank Stocks: An Empirical Test: Comment', in: *Journal of Money, Credit and Banking*, Vol. 5, No. 3, pp. 846–55.

Handelsblatt (ed.) (05.04.2000): 'Position von Clearstream weiter geschwächt: Wettbewerb verschärft sich weiter, Fusion von London Clearing House und Clearnet', in: *Handelsblatt*, No. 68, p. 35.

(13.10.2000): 'Wertpapierabwicklung – Eurex spricht mit London', in: *Handelsblatt*, No. 198, p. 44.

(26.06.2003): 'LCH und Clearnet schaffen die Fusion', in: *Handelsblatt*, No. 120, p. 19.

(15.10.2003): 'Nervenkrieg um die Londoner Börse', in: *Handelsblatt*, No. 198, p. 20.

(05.12.2005): 'Börse berät über Zukunft der Eurex US', in: *Handelsblatt*, No. 235, p. 33.

Hanley, William J./McCann, Karen/Moser, James T. (1996): 'Improving Regulatory Standards for Clearing Facilities', Chicago Fed Letter from the Federal Reserve Bank of Chicago, No. 101, Chicago 1996.

Hardouvelis, Gikas A./Kim, Dongcheol (1995): 'Margin Requirements, Price Fluctuations, and Market Participation in Metal Futures', in: *Journal of Money, Credit and Banking*, Vol. 27, No. 3, pp. 659–71.

Hardy, David (2004): 'The Future of Clearing', in: Young, Patrick L. (ed.): *An Intangible Commodity*, Petts Wood 2004, pp. 56–62.

(2006): 'The Case for a Single European Clearing House', in: *Financial Times*, online publication, date of publication: 08.06.2006, retrieved: 30.07.2007, available at: www.ft.com/cms/s/4ba947fc-f5c2-11da-bcae-0000779e2340.html.

Harris, Larry (2003): *Trading and Exchanges: Market Microstructure for Practitioners*, Oxford et al. 2003.

Hart, Terry L. et al. (2004): 'Governance of Securities Clearing and Settlement Systems', European Central Bank, Occasional Paper Series, No. 21, Frankfurt a.M. 2004.

Hart, Terry L./Russo, Daniela/Schönenberger, Andreas (2002): 'The Evolution of Clearing and Central Counterparty Services for Exchange-Traded Derivatives in the United States and in Europe: A Comparison', European Central Bank, Occasional Paper Series, No. 5, Frankfurt a.M. 2002.

Hartzmark, Michael L. (1986): 'The Effects of Changing Margin Levels on Futures Market Activity, the Composition of the Traders in the Market, and Price Performance', in: *Journal of Business*, Vol. 59, No. 2, pp. 147–80.

Harvard Research Group (ed.) (2003): *Clearing and Settlement: Making Financial Information Flow*, Boxborough 2003.

Hasan, Iftekhar/Hasenpusch, Tina/Schmiedel, Heiko (2007): 'Cross-Border Mergers and Alliances between Exchanges: A Global Perspective', in: Shojai, Shahin (ed.): *World of Exchanges: Adapting to a New Environment*, London 2007, pp. 27–41.

Hasan, Iftekhar/Malkamäki, Markku (2001): 'Are Expansions Cost Effective for Stock Exchanges?: A Global Perspective', in: *Journal of Banking and Finance*, Vol. 25, pp. 2339–66.

Hasan, Iftekhar/Malkamäki, Markku/Schmiedel, Heiko (2002): 'Technology, Automation, and Productivity of Stock Exchanges: International Evidence', Bank of Finland, Discussion Papers, No. 4, Helsinki 2002.

Hasan, Iftekhar/Schmiedel, Heiko (2004a): 'Networks and Equity Market Integration: European Evidence', in: *International Review of Financial Analysis*, Vol. 13, No. 5, pp. 601–19.

(2004b): 'Do Networks in the Stock Exchange Industry Pay Off?: European Evidence', in: Schmiedel, Heiko/Bank of Finland (eds.): *Performance of International Securities Markets*, Bank of Finland Studies, No. E:28, Helsinki 2004, pp. 177–220.

(2006): 'Networks and Stock Market Integration: Empirical Evidence', in: Bagella, Michele/Becchetti, Leonardo/Hasan, Iftekhar (eds.): *Transparency, Governance, and Markets*, Amsterdam/Kidlington 2006, pp. 395–417.

Hax, Herbert (1991): 'Theorie der Unternehmung: Information, Anreize und Vertragsgestaltung', in: Ordelheide, Dieter/Rudolph, Bernd/Büsselmann, Elke (eds.): *Betriebswirtschaftslehre und ökonomische Theorie*, Stuttgart 1991, pp. 51–72.

Heckinger, Richard/Lee, Ruben/McPartland, John W. (2003): 'CCPs: How Many Are Too Many? How Few Are Too Few?', Presentation at the London School of Economics, 9 June, London 2003.

Hedley, Barry (1976): 'A Fundamental Approach to Strategy Development', in: *Long Range Planning*, Vol. 9, pp. 2–21.

Hellmann, Norbert (2003): 'Europäische Clearer im gemeinsamen Bett', in: *Börsen-Zeitung*, 26.06.2003, p. 3.

Hicks, John R. (1935): 'A Suggestion for Simplifying the Theory of Money', in: *Economica*, Vol. 2, No. 5, pp. 1–19.

Hills, Bob *et al.* (1999): 'Central Counterparty Clearing Houses and Financial Stability', in: *Financial Stability Review*, Bank of England, No. 6, pp. 122–34.

Hills, Bob/Young, Chris (1998): 'Competition and Cooperation: Developments in Cross-Border Securities Settlement and Derivatives Clearing', in: *Bank of England Quarterly Bulletin*, Vol. 38, No. 2, pp. 158–65.

Hintze, John (2005): 'Regulators are Cautious as Clearers Outsource', in: *Securities Industry News*, 19.09.2005, pp. 1 and 16.

Hirata de Carvalho, Cynthia (2004): 'Cross-Border Securities Clearing and Settlement Infrastructure in the European Union as a Prerequisite to Financial Markets Integration: Challenges and Perspectives', Hamburg Institute of International Economics, Discussion Paper, No. 287, Hamburg 2004.

Holthausen, Cornelia/Tapking, Jens (2004): 'Raising Rival's Costs in the Securities Settlement Industry', European Central Bank, Working Paper Series, No. 376, Frankfurt a.M. 2004.

Horn, Norbert (2002): 'Die Erfüllung von Wertpapiergeschäften unter Einbeziehung eines zentralen Kontrahenten an der Börse: sachenrechtliche Aspekte', in: *Zeitschrift für Wirtschafts- und Bankrecht*, Special Enclosure, No. 2, pp. 3–23.

Huang, Jiabin (2006): *Legal Aspects of the Role and Functions of Central Counterparties*, London 2006.

Hull, John C. (2001): *Einführung in Futures- und Optionsmärkte*, 3rd edn, Munich/Vienna/Oldenbourg 2001.

Hunter, William C./Timme, Stephen G. (1986): 'Technical Change, Organizational Form, and the Structure of Bank Production', in: *Journal of Money, Credit and Banking*, Vol. 18, No. 2, pp. 152–66.

Hunter, William C./Timme, Stephen G./Yang,Won K. (1990): 'An Examination of Cost Subadditivity and Multiproduct Production in Large US Banks', in: *Journal of Money, Credit and Banking*, Vol. 22, No. 4, pp. 504–25.

Instinet (ed.) (2007): 'Alternative Execution Venues: What are they and Does Asia Need them?', Presentation by John Fildes, Managing Director, at the 5th Asia Pacific Trading Summit, 10 May, Singapore 2007.

Iori, Giulia (2004): 'An Analysis of Systemic Risk in Alternative Securities Settlement Architectures', European Central Bank, Working Paper Series, No. 404, Frankfurt a.M. 2004.

Jackson, John P./Manning, Mark J. (2007): 'Comparing the Pre-Settlement Risk Implications of Alternative Clearing Arrangements', Bank of England, Working Paper, No. 321, London 2007.

Jones, Huw (2003): 'Wrap up: London Clearing House, Clearnet to Merge', in: *Reuters*, online publication, date of publication: 25.06.2003, retrieved: 30.06.2003, available at: www.reuters.com.

JPMorgan (ed.) (2005): 'European Parliament Exchange of Views on Clearing and Settlement in the EU', Remarks by Diana Dijmarescu, Vice President JPMorgan, 2 February, Brussels 2005.

Junius, Karsten (1997): 'Economies of Scale: A Survey of the Empirical Literature', Kiel Institute of World Economics, Working Paper, No. 813, Kiel 1997.

Kahl, Kandice H./Rutz, Roger D./Sinquefield, Jeanne C. (1985): 'The Economics of Performance Margins in Futures Markets', in: *Journal of Futures Markets*, Vol. 5, No. 1, pp. 103–12.

Kahn, Charles M./McAndrews, James/Roberds, William (1999): 'Settlement Risk Under Gross and Net Settlement', Federal Reserve Bank of Atlanta, Working Paper, No. 10a, Atlanta 1999.

Kalavathi, L./Shanker, Latha (1991): 'Margin Requirements and the Demand for Futures Contracts', in: *Journal of Futures Markets*, Vol. 11, No. 2, pp. 213–37.

Kalbhenn, Christopher (2003): 'Eurex geht in die Offensive', in: *Börsen-Zeitung*, 11.01.2003, No. 7, p. 8.

Kaserer, Christoph/Schiereck, Dirk (2007): 'Die Kosten der Eigenkapitalbeschaffung: ein Vergleich der Emissions- und Handelskosten in Frankfurt und London', in: *GoingPublic Magazin*, No. 1, pp. 8–10.

Katz, Michael L./Shapiro, Carl (1985): 'Network Externalities, Competition, and Compatibility', in: *American Economic Review*, Vol. 75, no. 3, pp. 424–40.

(1986a): 'Technology Adoption in the Presence of Network Externalities', in: *Journal of Political Economy*, Vol. 94, no. 4, pp. 822–41.

(1986b): 'Product Compatibility Choice in a Market with Technological Progress', in: *Oxford Economic Papers*, Vol. 38, November Supplement, pp. 146–65.

(1994): 'Systems Competition and Network Effects', in: *Journal of Economic Perspectives*, Vol. 8, no. 2, pp. 93–115.

Kauko, Karlo (2002): 'Links between Securities Settlement Systems: An Oligopoly Theoretical Approach', Bank of Finland, Discussion Paper, No. 27, Helsinki 2002.

(2005): 'Interlinking Securities Settlement Systems: A Strategic Commitment?', Bank of Finland, Discussion Paper, No. 26, Helsinki 2005.

Keim, Donald B./Madhavan, Ananth (1998): 'The Cost of Institutional Equity Trades', in: *Financial Analysts Journal*, Vol. 54, No. 4, pp. 50–69.

KELER (ed.) (1998): *Disclosure Framework for Securities Settlement Systems*, Budapest 1998.

Kentouris, Chris (2000a): 'LCH, Clearnet Postpone their Merger Plans', in: *Securities Industry News*, Vol. 12, No. 39, p. 11.

(2000b): 'No Clear Path: LCH, Eurex Central Counterparty Talks Derailed', in: *Securities Industry News*, Vol. 12, No. 47, p. 1.

(2003a): 'BOTCC Pursues Deals in Wake of CBOT's Departure', in: *Securities Industry News*, Vol. 15, No. 18, p. 5.

(2003b): 'BOTCC-Eurex Link Cuts Down Cross-Border Barriers', in: *Securities Industry News*, Vol. 15, No. 22, p. 16.

Kharouf, Jim (2001): 'New Map for European Clearing', in: *Futures Industry Magazine*, June/July, online publication, retrieved: 07.05.2007, available at: www.futuresindustry.org/fi-magazine-home.asp?v=p&a=707.

King, Mervyn J. (2000): *Bank and Brokerage: Back Office Procedures and Settlements*, Chicago/London/New Dehli 2000.

Knieps, Günter (2006): 'Competition in the Post-Trade Markets: A Network Economic Analysis of the Securities Business', in: *Journal of Industry, Competition and Trade*, Vol. 6, No. 1, pp. 45–60.

Knoppe, Marc (1997): *Strategische Allianzen in der Kreditwirtschaft*, Munich/Vienna 1997.

Knott, Raymond/Mills, Alastair (2002): 'Modelling Risk in Central Counterparty Clearing Houses: A Review', in: *Financial Stability Review*, Bank of England, No. 12, pp. 162–73.

Kohl, Helmut *et al.* (1974): 'Abschreibungsgesellschaften, Kapitalmarkteffizienz und Publizitätszwang: Plädoyer für Vermögensanlagegesetz', in: *Zeitschrift für das gesamte Handels- und Wirtschaftsrecht*, Vol. 138, pp. 1–49.

Kolari, James W./Zardkoohi, Asghar (1987): *Bank Costs, Structure and Performance*, Lexington 1987.

(1991): 'Further Evidence on Economies of Scale and Scope in Commercial Banking', in: *Quarterly Journal of Business and Economics*, Vol. 30, No. 4, pp. 82–107.

Köppl, Thorsten V./Monnet, Cyril (2006): 'Central Counterparties', Working Paper, Kingston/Frankfurt a.M. 2006.

(2007): 'Guess What: It's the Settlements! Vertical Integration as a Barrier to Efficient Exchange Consolidation', in: *Journal of Banking and Finance*, Vol. 31, pp. 3013–33.

KPMG (ed.) (2004): *State of the Investment Management Industry in Europe*, London *et al.* 2004.

Kress, Sabine L. (1996): *Effizienzorientierte Kapitalmarktregulierung: eine Analyse aus institutionenökonomischer Perspektive*, Wiesbaden 1996.

Kröpfl, Stefan (2003): *Effizienz in der Abwicklung von Wertpapiergeschäften: Transaktionskosten und Wettbewerb in Europa*, Berlin 2003.

Kroszner, Randall S. (1999): 'Can Financial Markets privately regulate Risk?: The Development of Derivatives Clearing Houses and Recent Over-the-Counter Innovations', Working Paper, Chicago 1999.

— (2000): 'The Supply and Demand for Financial Regulation: Public and Private Competition Around the Globe', Paper presented at the Federal Reserve Bank of Kansas City Symposium on 'A Global Economic Integration: Opportunities and Challenges', 25 August, Chicago/Jackson Hole 2000.

— (2006): 'Central Counterparty Clearing: History, Innovation, and Regulation', Speech at the Joint Conference of the European Central Bank and the Federal Reserve Bank of Chicago on Issues related to Central Counterparty Clearing, 3–4 April, Frankfurt a.M. 2006.

Kupiec, Paul H. (1997): 'Margin Requirements, Volatility, and Market Integrity: What Have we Learned Since the Crash?', Board of Governors of the Federal Reserve System Finance and Economics Discussion Series, No. 22, Washington D.C. 1997.

Kupiec, Paul H./White, Patricia (1996): 'Regulatory Competition and the Efficiency of Alternative Derivative Product Margining Systems', Board of Governors of the Federal Reserve System Finance and Economics Discussion Series, No. 11, Washington D.C. 1996.

Labrecque, Thomas G. (1996): 'Payments, Clearance and Settlement Systems: The Systemic Risk Connection', in: Goldman Sachs (ed.): *Symposium on Risk Reduction in Payments, Clearance and Settlement Systems*, 25–26 January, New York 1996, pp. 19–22.

Lambe, Geraldine (2005): 'One Hit Wonder', in: *The Banker*, No. 3, 2005, p. 18.

Lamnek, Siegfried (1995): *Qualitative Sozialforschung, vol. 1: Methodologie*, Weinheim 1995.

Langer, Martha J. (1980): 'Economies of Scale in Commercial Banking', Banking Studies Department, Working Paper, New York 1980.

Langlois, Richard (1999): 'Scale, Scope and the Reuse of Knowledge', in: Dow, Sheila C./Earl, Peter E. (eds.): *Economic Organization and Economic Knowledge: Essays in Honour of Brian J. Loasby*, Aldershot 1999, pp. 239–54.

Lannoo, Karel/Levin, Matthias (2001): 'The Securities Settlement Industry in the EU: Structure, Costs and the Way Forward', CEPS Research Report, Brussels 2001.

— (2003): 'Clearing and Settlement in the EU', in: Deutsche Bank (ed.): *Frankfurt Voice – EU Financial Market Special*, Frankfurt a.M. 2003, pp. 2–16.

Larsen, Peter T./Grant, Jeremy (2005): 'Man Group Apologises to Eurex Chief After Insults in E-Mail Over Price Cutting', in: *Financial Times*, online publication, date of publication: 09.02.2005, retrieved: 18.04.2007, available at: www.ft.com/cms/s/ f4cbee9e-7a3e-11d9-ba2a-00000e2511c8.html.

Lattemann, Christoph /Neumann, Dirk (2002): *Clearing und Settlement im Wandel: eine Perspektive für den europäischen Wertpapierhandel*, Karlsruhe 2002.

Lawrence, Colin (1989): 'Bank Costs, Generalized Functional Forms, and Estimation of Economies of Scale and Scope', in: *Journal of Money, Credit and Banking*, Vol. 21, No. 3, pp. 368–79.

LCH.Clearnet (ed.) (2003a): *Creating the Central Counterparty of Choice*, Amsterdam/Brussels/London/Paris 2003.

(2003b): *Merger Announcement: Clearnet and LCH to Merge to Form the LCH.Clearnet Group*, London/Paris 2003.

(2004a): 'Further Comments of LCH.Clearnet on the Study "Overview of EU25 Securities Trading, Clearing Central Counterparties and Securities Settlement: An Overview of Current Arrangements" ', Public Letter, London/Paris 2004.

(2004b): *Report and Consolidated Financial Statements 2003*, London/Paris 2004.

(2004c): 'Roadmap to the Future', ISSA Symposium, 17 June, Presentation by Andrew Lamb, Chief Executive LCH.Clearnet Ltd, London/Paris 2004.

(2005): *Report and Consolidated Financial Statements 2004*, London/Paris 2005.

(05.07.2006): 'Board Changes', Press Release, London/Paris 2006.

(21.07.2006): 'LCH.Clearnet Rationalises IT Strategy', Press Release, London/Paris 2006.

(27.09.2006): 'LCH.Clearnet revises Fee Structure to Deliver Members Over 15 per cent Savings in Financial and Equity Derivatives Markets', Press Release, London/Paris 2006.

(2006a): *Annual Report 2005*, London/Paris 2006.

(2006b): 'The Need to Remove Structural Barriers to Consolidation of CCP Clearing', Discussion Paper, CESAME Meeting, 20 February, London/Paris 2006.

(2006c): 'ECO: The LCH.Clearnet Newsletter', No. 5, November, London/Paris/ Brussels/Amsterdam/Lisbon 2006.

(2006d): *Interim Report, Half Year to 30 June 2006*, London/Paris 2006.

(15.06.2007): 'LCH.Clearnet Restructures to Deliver Low-Tariff Strategy', Press Release, London/Paris 2007.

(2007): *Annual Report 2006*, London/Paris 2007.

LCH.Clearnet/Euronext (eds.) (12.03.2007): 'LCH.Clearnet and Euronext Announce Repurchase by LCH.Clearnet of Shares Held by Euronext to More Closely Align Customer and Shareholder Interests', Press Release, London/Paris 2007.

Lee, Ruben (1998): *What is an Exchange?: The Automation, Management, and Regulation of Financial Markets*, Oxford *et al.* 1998.

(2000): 'Promoting Regional Capital Market Integration', Paper prepared for the Inter American Development Bank, No. 1, Oxford 2000.

(2002): 'The Future of Securities Exchanges', Wharton Financial Institutions Centre, No. 14, Philadelphia 2002.

Leibenstein, Harvey (1966): 'Allocative Efficiency vs. "X-Efficiency" ', in: *American Economic Review*, Vol. 56, No. 3, pp. 392–415.

LIBA (ed.) (2004): 'Guiding Principles for the Development of EU Clearing and Settlement Policy, Response to the EU Commission's Communication on Clearing and Settlement', COM(2004)312, London 2004.

(2006): 'Response to the DG Competition Issues Paper dated 24 May 2006: Competition in EU Securities Trading and Post-Trading', Public Letter, 7 July, London 2006.

Liebowitz, Stan J. (2002): *Re-thinking the Network Economy: The True Forces that Drive the Digital Marketplace*, New York 2002.

Liebowitz, Stan J./Margolis, Stephen E. (1990): 'The Fable of the Keys', in: *Journal of Law and Economics*, Vol. 33, No. 1, pp. 1–25.

(1994a): 'Network Externality: An Uncommon Tragedy', in: *Journal of Economic Perspectives*, Vol. 8, No. 2, pp. 133–50.

(1994b): 'Market Processes and the Selection of Standards', Working Paper, Dallas 1994.

(1995): 'Path Dependency, Lock-In and History', in: *Journal of Law, Economics and Organization*, Vol. 11, No. 1, pp. 205–26.

(1998): 'Network Externalities (Effects)', online publication, retrieved: 20.10.2005, available at: www.utdallas.edu/~liebowit/palgrave/network.html.

Linciano, Nadia/Siciliano, Giovanni/Trovatore, Gianfranco (2005): 'The Clearing and Settlement Industry: Structure, Competition and Regulatory Issues', CONSOB, Quaderni di Finanza, Discussion Paper, No. 58, Rome 2005.

Loader, David (2004): *Clearing, Settlement and Custody*, 2nd edn, Oxford/Burlington 2004.

(2005): *Clearing and Settlement of Derivatives*, Oxford/Burlington 2005.

Löber, Klaus M. (2006): 'The Developing EU Legal Framework for Clearing and Settlement of Financial Instruments', European Central Bank, Legal Working Paper Series, No. 1, Frankfurt a.M. 2006.

London Economics (ed.) (2005): 'Securities Trading, Clearing, Central Counterparties and Settlement in EU 25: An Overview of Current Arrangements', Report commissioned by the Competition Directorate General of the European Commission, London 2005.

London Stock Exchange (ed.) (2002): 'Response to the European Commission Communication on Clearing and Settlement', Public Letter, 28 May, London 2002.

London Stock Exchange/Oxera (eds.) (2002): 'Clearing and Settlement in Europe: Response to the First Report of the Giovannini Group', London 2002.

Longin, Francois M. (1999): 'Optimal Margin Level in Futures Markets: Extreme Price Movements', in: *Journal of Futures Markets*, Vol. 19, No. 2, pp. 127–52.

Mainelli, Michael (2004): 'Bracing for Zero Marginal Competitive Cost: Investment Banking Restructures', Online Publication, Z/Yen Limited, retrieved: 05.09.2007, available at: www.zyen.com/Knowledge/Articles/zero_marginal_competitive_cost.htm.

Maisch, Michael (2007): 'Hedgefonds kritisieren Verhalten der Banken', in: *Handelsblatt*, 15.06.2007, p. 23.

Malkamäki, Markku (1999): 'Are there Economies of Scale in Stock Exchange Activities?', Bank of Finland, Discussion Paper, No. 4, Helsinki 1999.

Malkamäki, Markku/Topi, Jukka (1999): 'Strategic Challenges for Exchanges and Securities Settlement', Bank of Finland, Discussion Paper, No. 21, Helsinki 1999.

Mayring, Philipp (2007): *Qualitative Inhaltsanalyse: Grundlagen und Techniken*, 9th edn, Weinheim 2007.

McAllister, Patrick H./McManus, Douglas A. (1993): 'Resolving the Scale Efficiency Puzzle in Banking', in: *Journal of Banking and Finance*, Vol. 17, pp. 389–405.

McCreevy, Charlie (2006a): 'Clearing and Settlement: The Way Forward', Speech before the Economic and Monetary Affairs Committee of the European Parliament, No. 450, 11 July, Brussels 2006.

(2006b): 'Clearing and Settlement Code of Conduct', Speech at the Press Conference, No. 659, 7 November, Brussels 2006.

McPartland, John W. (2002): 'Select Clearing Issues', Presentation at the London School of Economics, 21 June, London 2002.

(2003a): 'Open Architecture Clearing', in: *Futures Industry Magazine*, Outlook 2003, online publication, retrieved: 01.01.2006, available at: www.futuresindustry.org/fi-magazine-home.asp?a=989.

(2003b): 'Understanding the Mutual Offset System', in: *Futures Industry Magazine*, Outlook 2003, online publication, retrieved: 06.04.2006, available at: www.futuresindustry.org/fi-magazine-home.asp?a=990.

(2005): 'Clearing and Settlement Demystified', Federal Reserve Bank of Chicago, Chicago Fed Letter, January, No. 210, Chicago 2005.

Merrill Lynch (ed.) (2006): 'A User Perspective on European Clearing and Settlement', Presentation of Bob Wigley, Chairman Merrill Lynch EMEA at the CESAME Meeting, 20 February, Brussels 2006.

Milbourn, Todd T./Boot, Arnould W. A./Thakor, Anjan V. (1999): 'Megamergers and Expanded Scope: Theories of Bank Size and Activity Diversity', in: *Journal of Banking and Finance*, Vol. 23, pp. 195–214.

Milne, Alistair (2002): 'Competition and the Rationalisation of European Securities Clearing and Settlement', Working Paper, London 2002.

(2005): 'Standard Setting and Competition in Securities Settlement', Bank of Finland, Discussion Paper, No. 23, Helsinki 2005.

(2007): 'The Industrial Organization of Post-Trade Clearing and Settlement', in: *Journal of Banking and Finance*, Vol. 31, pp. 2945–61.

Moerschen, Tobias/Schiereck, Dirk (2005): 'Momentum and Contrarian Investing Beyond CRSP and TAQ', in: *Journal of Business and Economic Perspectives*, Vol. 31, pp. 123–30.

Mogford, Anuszka (2005): 'The Road Ahead', in: *Futures and OTC World*, No. 4, pp. 34–7.

Morgan Stanley (ed.) (2004): *Decelerating Trading; Inexpensive but Awaiting Catalyst, Equity Research Europe: Deutsche Börse*, London 2004.

Morgan Stanley/Mercer Oliver Wyman (eds.) (2003): 'Structural Shifts in Securities Trading: Outlook for European Exchanges', Research Paper, London 2003.

Moschandreas, Maria (1994): *Business Economics*, New York 1994.

Moser, James T. (1998): 'Contracting Innovations and the Evolution of Clearing and Settlement Methods at Futures Exchanges', Federal Reserve Bank of Chicago, Working Paper Series, No. 26, Chicago 1998.

Moskow, Michael H. (2006): 'Public Policy and Central Counterparty Clearing', Speech at the Joint Conference of the European Central Bank and the Federal Reserve Bank of Chicago on Issues related to Central Counterparty Clearing, 3–4 April, Frankfurt a.M. 2006.

Mühlfeld, Claus *et al.* (1981): 'Auswertungsprobleme offener Interviews', in: *Soziale Welt*, Vol. 32, pp. 325–52.

Murawski, Carsten (2002): 'The Impact of Clearing on the Credit Risk of a Derivatives Portfolio', Working Paper, Zurich 2002.

Murray, John D./White, Robert W. (1983): 'Economies of Scale and Economies of Scope in Multiproduct Financial Institutions: A Study of British Columbia Credit Unions', in: *Journal of Finance*, Vol. 38, No. 3, pp. 887–902.

NASDAQ (ed.) (02.10.2007): 'NASDAQ to Acquire Boston Stock Exchange and Key Exchange Assets', Press Release, New York 2007.

National Futures Association (ed.) (2006): 'Glossary', online publication, retrieved: 16.11.2006, available at: www.nfa.futures.org/BASICnet/glossary.aspx?term=C.

Nava, Mario/Russo, Daniela (2006): 'Post Post-Trading Infrastructure: How to Foster Integration?', Presentation to the CESAME Group, 23 October, Brussels 2006.

NERA Economic Consulting (ed.) (2004): 'The Direct Costs of Clearing and Settlement: An EU-US Comparison', City Research Series, No. 1, London 2004.

Neue Züricher Zeitung (ed.) (26.06.2003): 'Fusion von Clearnet und London Clearing House: ein Schritt zur Integration der Finanzmärkte Europas', in: *Neue Züricher Zeitung*, p. 23.

Neus, Werner (1998): *Einführung in die Betriebswirtschaftslehre aus institutionen-ökonomischer Sicht*, Tübingen 1998.

New York Foreign Exchange Committee (ed.) (1997): *Guidelines for Foreign Exchange Settlement Netting*, New York 1997.

Niels, Gunnar/Barnes, Fod/van Dijk, Reinder (2003): 'Unclear and Unsettled: The Debate on Competition in the Clearing and Settlement of Securities Trades', in: *European Competition Law Review*, Vol. 24, No. 12, pp. 634–9.

Noulas, Athanasios G./Ray, Subhash C./Miller, Stephen M. (1990): 'Returns to Scale and Input Substitution for Large Banks', in: *Journal of Money, Credit and Banking*, Vol. 22, No. 1, pp. 94–108.

Office of Fair Trading (ed.) (2004): 'Competition Review of the Financial Services and Markets Act 2000', Report prepared for the OFT by Oxera, London 2004.

     (2005): 'Anticipated Acquisition by Deutsche Börse AG of the London Stock Exchange plc', Decision Paper, London 2005.

OM Group (ed.) (2002): 'Electricity Market Settlement Solutions to Meet Rapidly Changing Market Requirements with Lower Risk', White Paper, Stockholm 2002.

Oxera (ed.) (2007): 'Methodology for Monitoring Prices, Costs and Volumes of Trading and Post-Trading Activities', Study prepared for European Commission, Directorate General Internal Market and Services (MARKT/2006/14/G), Oxford/Brussels 2007.

Padoa-Schioppa, Tommaso (2001): 'Clearing and Settlement of Securities: A European Perspective', Speech at Symposium of the Deutsche Bundesbank Payment and Securities Settlement Systems in Germany against the Background of European and International Developments, 5 September, Frankfurt a.M. 2001.

Panzar, John C./Willig, Robert D. (1975): 'Economies of Scale and Economies of Scope in Multi-Output Production', Bell Laboratories, Discussion Paper, Murray Hill 1975.

     (1977): 'Economies of Scale in Multi-Output Production', in: *Quarterly Journal of Economics*, Vol. 91, No. 3, pp. 481–93.

     (1981): 'Economies of Scope', in: *American Economic Review*, Vol. 71, No. 2, pp. 268–72.

Parker, Geoffrey C./Van Alstyne, Marshall W. (2005): 'Two-Sided Network Effects: A Theory of Information Product Design', in: *Management Science*, Vol. 51, No. 10, pp. 1494–504.

Parkinson, Patrick M. (2001): 'Achieving Regulatory Coherence, in: PROMETHEE (ed.): *The Central Counterparties Dialogue*, April, Paris 2001, pp. 28–9.

Parkinson, Patrick M. *et al.* (1992): 'Clearance and Settlement in US Securities Markets', in: *Federal Reserve Bulletin*, March 1992, pp. 182–4.

Phillips, Susan M./Tosini, Paula A. (1982): 'A Comparison of Margin Requirements for Options and Futures', in: *Financial Analysts Journal*, Vol. 38, No. 6, pp. 54–8.

Picot, Arnold (1982): 'Transaktionskostenansatz in der Organisationstheorie: Stand der Diskussion', in: *Die Betriebswirtschaft*, Vol. 42, pp. 267–84.

(1985): 'Transaktionskosten', in: *Die Betriebswirtschaft*, Vol. 45, pp. 224–5.

(1991a): 'Ein neuer Ansatz zur Gestaltung der Leistungstiefe', in: *Zeitschrift für betriebswirtschaftliche Forschung*, Vol. 43, pp. 336–57.

(1991b): Ökonomische Theorien der Organisation: ein Überblick über neuere Ansätze und deren betriebswirtschaftliches Anwendungspotential', in: Ordelheide, Dieter/Rudolph, Bernd/Büsselmann, Elke (eds.): *Betriebswirtschaftslehre und ökonomische Theorie*, Stuttgart 1991, pp. 143–70.

Picot, Arnold/Dietl, Helmut (1990): 'Transaktionskostentheorie', in: *WiSt, Wirtschaftswissenschaftliches Studium*, Vol. 19, pp. 178–84.

Picot, Arnold/Reichwald, Ralf/Wigand, Rolf (1996): *Die grenzenlose Unternehmung*, Wiesbaden 1996.

Pratley, Nils (2007): 'Green for Turquoise', in: *The Guardian*, 19.04.2007, p. 25.

PricewaterhouseCoopers (ed.) (2003): *Global Clearing and Settlement: A Plan of Action: Improving Safety and Efficiency of International Securities Markets*, London 2003.

Pulley, Lawrence B./Humphrey, David B. (1993): 'The Role of Fixed Costs and Cost Complementarities in Determining Scope Economies and the Cost of Narrow Banking Proposals', in: *Journal of Business*, Vol. 66, No. 3, pp. 437–62.

Rettberg, Udo (2005): 'Eurex stößt in den USA auf große Probleme', in: *Handelsblatt*, 12.09.2005, No. 176, p. 24.

Rettberg, Udo/Zwätz, Dietrich (1995): *Das kleine Terminhandelslexikon – Derivate: Optionen, Futures, Swaps und Futures-funds*, Düsseldorf 1995.

Richter, Rudolf (1990): 'Sichtweise und Fragestellung der neuen Institutionenökonomik', in: *Zeitschrift für Wirtschafts- und Sozialwissenschaften*, Vol. 110, pp. 571–91.

(1994): *Institutionen ökonomisch analysiert: zur jüngeren Entwicklung auf dem Gebiet der Wirtschaftstheorie*, Tübingen 1994.

Riksbank (ed.) (2002): 'Central Counterparty Clearing for the Securities Market', in: *Financial Stability Report*, Central Bank of Sweden, No. 2, pp. 47–58.

Ripatti, Kirsi (2004): 'Central Counterparty Clearing: Constructing a Framework for Evaluation of Risks and Benefits', Bank of Finland, Discussion Paper, No. 1, Helsinki 2004.

Robinson, Joan (1948): *The Economics of Imperfect Competition*, London 1948.

Rochet, Jean-Charles (2005): 'The Welfare Effects of Vertical Integration in the Securities Clearing and Settlement Industry', Working Paper, Toulouse 2005.

Rochet, Jean-Charles/Tirole, Jean (2001): 'Platform Competition in Two-Sided Markets', Working Paper, Toulouse 2001.

(2006): 'Two-Sided Markets: A Progress Report', in: *Rand Journal of Economics*, Vol. 37, No. 3, pp. 645–67.

Rohlfs, Jeff (1974): 'A Theory of Interdependent Demand for a Communications Service', in: *Bell Journal of Economics*, Vol. 5, pp. 16–37.

Rosati, Simonetta/Russo, Daniela (2007): 'Market Integration in the Post-Trading: Lessons from Europe', Presentation at the Capco Institute Breakfast 'World of Exchanges', 23 May, Frankfurt a.M. 2007.

Rosenberg, Janice (2004): 'Drama in the Windy City: Chicago Rivals Team Up as Eurex Enters Game', in: *Financial Engineering News*, pp. 10–11, March/April, online publication, retrieved: 12.08.2006, available at: www.fenews.com.

Russo, Daniela/Terol, Ignacio R. (2000): 'The Euro Area Securities Clearing and Settlement Infrastructure: Recent Changes and Issues for Debate', Paper presented at the Conference on 'The Operational Framework of the Eurosystem and Financial Markets', 5–6 May, Frankfurt a.M. 2000.

Russo, Filippo (2002): 'The Evolving Role of Central Counterparty Clearing Houses', in: *Economia, Società, Istituzioni*, Vol. 2, pp. 223–59.

Sabatini, Giovanni (2003): 'Internalisation and Consolidation of the Settlement of Payments and Securities Transactions', Speech at the Global Conference on Private and Public Sector Challenges in the Payment System, 12–13 June, Frankfurt 2003.

Sal. Oppenheim (ed.) (2006): 'International Stock Exchanges: The New Exchange World', Research Report, Cologne/Frankfurt a.M. 2006.

Samuelson, Paul A./Nordhaus, William D. (1989): *Economics*, 13th edn, New York 1989.

Scheele, Martin (1994): *Zusammenschluß von Banken und Versicherungen: Analyse des Privatkundengeschäfts anhand industrieökonomischer Modelle, neue betriebswirtschaftliche Forschung*, Wiesbaden 1994.

Scherer, Frederic M./Ross, David (1990): *Industrial Market Structure and Economic Performance*, 3rd edn, Boston 1990.

Schiereck, Dirk (1995): *Internationale Börsenplatzentscheidungen institutioneller Investoren*, Wiesbaden 1995.

(1996a): 'Die Ziele des Anlegers bei der Wahl des Börsenplatzes', in: *Zeitschrift für Bankrecht und Bankwirtschaft*, Vol. 8, pp. 185–96.

(1996b): 'Börsenplatzentscheidungen institutioneller Investoren', in: *Zeitschrift für Betriebswirtschaft*, Vol. 66, pp. 1057–79.

Schmidt, Christiane (1997): 'Am Material: Auswertungstechniken für Leitfadeninterviews', in: Friebertshäuser, Barbara/Prengel, Annedore (eds.): *Handbuch qualitative Forschungsmethoden in der Erziehungswissenschaft*, Weinheim/Munich 1997, pp. 544–68.

Schmidt, Hartmut (1977): 'Vorteile und Nachteile eines integrierten Zirkulationsmarktes für Wertpapiere gegenüber einem gespaltenem Effektenmarkt', Kommission der Europäischen Gemeinschaften (ed.), *Reihe Wettbewerb: Rechtsangleichung*, No. 30, Brussels/Luxembourg 1977.

Schmidt, Hartmut (1983): 'Marktorganisationsbestimmte Kosten und Transaktionskosten als börsenpolitische Kategorien', in: *Kredit und Kapital*, Vol. 16, pp. 184–204.

(1988): *Wertpapierbörsen: Strukturprinzip, Organisation, Kassa- und Terminmärkte*, Munich 1988.

Schmidt, Reinhard (1992): 'Transaktionskostenorientierte Organisationstheorie', in: Freese, Erich (ed.) *Handbuch der Organisation*, 3rd edn, Stuttgart 1992.

Schmiedel, Heiko/Malkamäki, Markku/Tarkka, Juha (2002): 'Economies of Scale and Technological Development in Securities Depository and Settlement Systems', Bank of Finland, Discussion Paper, No. 26, Helsinki 2002.

Schmiedel, Heiko/Schönenberger, Andreas (2005): 'Integration of Securities Market Infrastructures in the Euro Area, European Central Bank', Occasional Paper Series, No. 33, Frankfurt a.M. 2005.

Schneider, Helmut (1977): *Mikroökonomie*, 3rd edn, Munich 1977.

Schnell, Rainer/Hill, Paul B./Esser, Elke (2005): *Methoden der empirischen Sozialforschung*, 7th edn, Munich/Vienna 2005.

Schönauer, Felix (2002): 'Euronext-chef bestätigt Kontakte mit tochter Clearnet: das London Clearing House flirtet heftig mit früheren Wunschpartnern', in: *Handelsblatt*, 29.05.2002, No. 101, p. 27.

Schönauer, Felix (2003a): 'Warum London Clearing House und Clearnet so lange für eine Einigung brauchen', in: *Handelsblatt*, 20.01.2003, No. 13, p. 23.

(2003b): 'Chancen der Eurex in London sinken', in: *Handelsblatt*, 31.10.2003, No. 210, p. 21.

(2003c): 'Londoner Börse kann Fusion zerstören', in: *Handelsblatt*, 17.11.2003, No. 221, p. 23.

Schulte, Stefan (1992): *Internationaler Aktienemmissionsmarkt: eine Beurteilung der operationalen und institutionellen Effizienz*, Frankfurt a.M. 1992.

Schulze, Niels/Baur, Dirk (2006): 'Economic Impact Study on Clearing and Settlement', Annex II, European Commission's Draft Working Document on Post-Trading, Brussels 2006.

Schwartz, Robert A./Francioni, Reto (2004): *Equity Markets in Action: The Fundamentals of Liquidity, Market Structure and Trading*, New Jersey 2004.

Scott, Susan V. (2003): 'Moving Markets: Strategic Developments in the Clearing and Settlement Industry', Working Paper, London 2003.

SEC (ed.) (1998): 'Regulation of Exchanges and Alternative Trading Systems: Final Rule Release No. 34-40760', online publication, date of publication: 08.12.1998, retrieved: 08.06.2007, available at: www.sec.gov/rules/final/34-40760.txt.

Securities Industry Association (ed.) (2005): 'Background Note on the Organisation in the US Market for Clearing and Settlement', Prepared by the Cross-Border Subcommittee of the Securities Industry Association for the European Commission, London *et al.* 2005.

Serifsoy, Baris (2007): 'Stock Exchange Business Models and their Operative Performance', in: *Journal of Banking and Finance*, Vol. 31, pp. 2978–3012.

Serifsoy, Baris/Weiß, Marco (2005): 'Settling for Efficiency: A Framework for the European Securities Transaction Industry', Working Paper, Frankfurt a.M. 2005.

Shermata, Willow A. (1997): 'Barriers to Innovation: A Monopoly, Network Externalities, and the Speed of Innovation', in: *The Antitrust Bulletin*, Vol. 42, pp. 937–72.

Shy, Oz (2001): *The Economics of Network Industries*, Cambridge and New York 2001.

Silberston, Aubrey (1972): 'Economies of Scale in Theory and Practice', in: *Economic Journal*, Vol. 82, No. 325, pp. 369–91.

Silvestre, Joaquim (1987): 'Economies and Diseconomies of Scale', in: Eatwell, John/Milgate, Murray/Newman, Peter K. (eds.): *The New Palgrave: A Dictionary of Economics*, No. 2, London/Basingstoke 1987, pp. 80–83.

Simmons, Michael (2002): *Securities Operations: A Guide to Trade and Position Management*, Toronto *et al.* 2002.

Singapore Exchange (ed.) (2004): 'Public Consultation of the Draft Competition Bill', Public Letter, Singapore 2004.

Skorecki, Alex (2003a): 'London Explores Alternatives', in: *Financial Times*, 26.06.2003, p. 29.

(2003b): 'All-clear from "Good Europeans"', in: *Financial Times*, 26.06.2003, p. 29.

Smith, Adam (1776): *An Inquiry into the Nature and Causes of the Wealth of Nations*, London 1776.

Smith, Jeremy (2001): 'Driving Down the Cost of Investment Banking: Can Banks Really Reduce their Processing Costs?', Z/Yen Limited, Presentation at the Centre for the Study of Financial Innovation, 24 September, London 2001.

Smith, Jeremy/Wright, Giles (2002): 'Competitive Cost Benchmarking Survey: Equity and Debt Products 2002', Z/Yen Limited, Presentation, London 2002.

Société Générale/Calyon (eds.) (08.01.2007): 'Société Générale and Calyon Plan to Merge their Brokerage Activities Currently Carried out by Fimat and Calyon Financial', Press Release, Paris 2007.

Spence, A. Michael (1981): 'The Learning Curve and Competition', in: *Bell Journal of Economics*, Vol. 12, No. 1, pp. 49–70.

Steele, Tim (2005): 'Imperfect Harmony', in: *STP Magazine*, No. 4, 27.04.2005, p. 26.

Stigler, George J. (1958): 'The Economies of Scale', in: *Journal of Law and Economics*, Vol. 1, pp. 54–71.

Stiglitz, Joseph (1981): 'The Allocation Role of the Stock Market: Pareto Optimality and Competition', in: *Journal of Finance*, Vol. 36, No. 2, pp. 235–51.

SWX Swiss Exchange (ed.) (03.03.2006): 'SWX Swiss Exchange Introduces a Central Counterparty Service', Press Release, Zurich 2006.

(2007): 'Frequently Asked Questions', Zurich 2007.

Tapking, Jens/Yang, Jing (2004): 'Horizontal and Vertical Integration in Securities Trading and Settlement', Bank of England, Working Paper, No. 245, London 2004.

Teece, David J. (1980): 'Economies of Scope and the Scope of the Enterprise', in: *Journal of Economic Behaviour and Organisation*, Vol. 1, No. 3, pp. 223–47.

Telser, Lester G. (1981): 'Margins and Futures Contracts', in: *Journal of Futures Markets*, Vol. 1, No. 2, pp. 225–53.

Thackray, John (1997): 'Crossed Wires', in: *Derivatives Strategy*, April, online publication, retrieved: 20.11.2006, available at: www.derivativesstrategy.com/magazine/archive/supp/0497fea1.asp.

The Clearing Corporation (ed.) (2003): *Stockholders Record: A History Trusting, Growing, Leading Clearing*, Chicago 2003.

(2004): 'Global Clearing Link: Concepts and Benefits', Presentation delivered to Operations Task Force, Chicago 2004.

(19.12.2006): 'The Clearing Corporation Clears More than 23 Million Derivatives Contracts on the Global Clearing Link', Press Release, Chicago 2006.

Thommen, Jean-Paul/Achleitner, Ann-Kristin (2006): *Allgemeine Betriebswirtschaftslehre: umfassende Einführung aus managementorientierter Sicht*, 5th edn, Wiesbaden 2006.

Thum, Marcel (1995): *Netzwerkeffekte, Standardisierung und staatlicher Regulierungsbedarf*, Tübingen/Munich 1995.

Tichy, Gunther (1990): 'Bankengröße und Effizienz', in: *Kredit und Kapital*, No. 3, pp. 358–87.

Tirole, Jean (1988): *The Theory of Industrial Organization*, Cambridge, MA, 1988.

Trichet, Jean-Claude (2006): 'Issues Related to Central Counterparty Clearing', Speech at the Joint Conference of the European Central Bank and the Federal Reserve Bank of Chicago on Issues related to Central Counterparty Clearing, 3–4 April, Frankfurt a.M. 2006.

Tsetsekos, George/Varangis, Panos (1997): 'The Structure of Derivatives Exchanges: Lessons from Developed and Emerging Markets', Working Paper, Drexel/Washington D.C. 1997.

Tumpel-Gugerell, Gertrude (2006): 'Issues Related to Central Counterparty Clearing', Opening Speech at the Joint Conference of the European Central Bank and the Federal Reserve

Bank of Chicago on Issues related to Central Counterparty Clearing, 3–4 April, Frankfurt a.M. 2006.

UBS (ed.) (25.05.2006): 'UBS übernimmt globales Futures- und Optionsgeschäft von ABN AMRO', Investor Release, New York 2006.

Uhlir, Helmut (1990): 'Organisierte Terminmärkte: eine notwendige Ergänzung der Kassamärkte', in: *Österreichisches Bank-Archiv*, No. 10, pp. 746–51.

Van Cauwenberge, Steven (2003): 'New Structure for Clearing and Settlement Systems in the EU', in: *Financial Stability Review*, National Bank of Belgium, pp. 83–103.

Van Cayseele, Patrick (2005): 'Complementary Platforms: The Provision of Custody for Internationally Diversified Investors', Discussion Paper, Leuven 2005.

Van Cayseele, Patrick/Reynaerts, Jo (2007): 'Complementary Platforms', Working Paper, Amsterdam/Leuven 2007.

Van Cayseele, Patrick/Voor de Mededinging, Raad (2005): 'Competition and the Organisation of the Clearing and Settlement Industry', Working Paper, Leuven/Amsterdam 2005.

Van Cayseele, Patrick/Wuyts, Christophe (2005): 'Cost Efficiency in the European Securities Settlement and Safekeeping Industry', Discussion Paper, Leuven/Amsterdam 2005.

(2006): 'Measuring Scale Economies in a Heterogeneous Industry: The Case of European Settlement Institutions', SUERF Studies, No. 3, Vienna 2006.

virt-x Exchange (ed.) (2005): 'LSE Merger Inquiry – New Remedy Option – Interoperable Central Counterparties', Public Letter to UK's Competition Commission, 13 September, London 2005.

Wall Street Journal (ed.) (09.07.2005): 'Euronext Offers to Reduce Stake', in: *Wall Street Journal – Eastern Edition*, Vol. 246, No. 47, p. C4.

Warshawsky, Mark J. (1989): 'The Adequacy and Consistency of Margin Requirements in the Markets for Stocks and Derivative Products', Board of Governors of the Federal Reserve System, Staff Study, Washington D.C. 1989.

Weiss, David M. (1993): *After the Trade Is Made: Processing Securities Transactions*, 2nd edn, New York 1993.

Wendt, Froukelien (2006): 'Intraday Margining of Central Counterparties: EU Practice and a Theoretical Evaluation of Benefits and Costs', Oversight Department, Payments Policy Division De Nederlandsche Bank, Discussion Paper, Amsterdam 2006.

Werner, Swen (2003): 'Interoperability and Interlinking: The Way Forward for the C&S Industry', in: Deutsche Bank (ed.): *Frankfurt Voice: EU Financial Market Special*, Frankfurt 2003, pp. 17–27.

West, Richard R. (1975): 'On the Difference between Internal and External Market Efficiency', in: *Financial Analysts Journal*, Vol. 31, No. 6, pp. 30–34.

(1986): 'The Efficiency of Securities Markets', in: Fabozzi, Frank J./Zarb, Frank G. (eds.): *Handbook of Financial Markets: Securities, Options and Futures*, 2nd edn, Homewood 1986, pp. 21–33.

West, Richard R./Tiniç, Seha M. (1974): 'Corporate Finance and the Changing Stock Market', in: *Financial Management*, Vol. 3, No. 3, pp. 14–23.

(1979): *Investing in Securities: An Efficient Market Approach*, Reading 1979.

Williamson, Oliver E. (1979): 'Transaction Cost Economics: The Governance of Contractual Relations', in: *Journal of Law and Economics*, Vol. 22, No. 2, pp. 233–61.

(1981): 'The Economics of Organization: The Transaction Cost Approach', in: *American Journal of Sociology*, Vol. 87, No. 3, pp. 548–77.

(1985): *The Economic Institutions of Capitalism: Firms, Markets, Relational Contracting*, New York 1985.

Willig, Robert D. (1979): 'Multiproduct Technology and Market Structure', in: *American Economic Review*, Vol. 69, No. 2, pp. 346–51.

Wöhe, Günter (1996): *Einführung in die allgemeine Betriebswirtschaftslehre*, 19th edn, Munich 1996.

Wright, Ben (2005): 'London Stock Exchange: LSE Takeover Saga Turns Up a New Chapter', in: *The Business*, 03.04.2005, p. 9.

Wright, Chris (2003): 'Developments in Market Clearing and Settlement Arrangements: Some Balance Sheet Recognition and Measurement Issues', Paper for the 16th Meeting of the IMF Committee on Balance of Payments Statistics, 1–5 December, Washington D.C. 2003.

(2004): 'Central Counterparty Clearing and Settlement: Implications for Financial Statistics and the Balance of Payments, Bank of England', Paper for the 17th Meeting of the IMF Committee on Balance of Payments Statistics, 26–29 October, Pretoria 2004.

Young, Patrick L. (2007): *The Exchange Manifesto*, London 2007.

Zentraler Kreditausschuss (ed.) (2004): 'Communication from the Commission to the Council and the European Parliament "Clearing & Settlement in the European Union: The Way Forward" ', Public Letter to the European Commission, 21 July, Berlin 2004.

Index

Made in the USA
Lexington, KY
05 February 2013